WESTERN LIVES

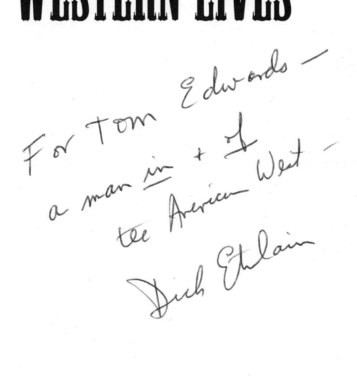

For Tom Edwards —
a man in + of
the American West —

Dick Etulain

The American West. From Michael P. Malone and Richard W. Etulain, *The American West: A Twentieth-Century History* (Lincoln: University of Nebraska Press, 1989). Courtesy of the University of Nebraska Press.

WESTERN LIVES

A Biographical History of the American West

Edited by

RICHARD W. ETULAIN

Published in cooperation with the
University of New Mexico Center for the Southwest

UNIVERSITY OF NEW MEXICO PRESS
ALBUQUERQUE

Library of Congress Cataloging-in-Publication Data

Western lives : a biographical history of the American West /
edited by Richard W. Etulain.
p. cm.
"Published in cooperation with the University of New Mexico
Center for the Southwest."
Includes bibliographical references and index.
ISBN 0-8263-3472-5 (pbk. : alk. paper)
1. West (U.S.)—Biography. 2. West (U.S.)—History.
I. Etulain, Richard W.
II. University of New Mexico. Center for the Southwest.
F590.5.W47 2004
978'.009'9—dc22
2004009061

Design and composition by Maya Allen-Gallegos
Typeset in Granjon 11.5 / 13
Display type set in Mesquite, Birch, and Granjon Family

To Frank and Margaret Szasz
engaging scholars
superb colleagues
warm, encouraging friends

Also by Richard W. Etulain

Author
Owen Wister

Ernest Haycox

Religion in the Twentieth-Century West: A Bibliography

Re-imagining the Modern American West:
A Century of Fiction, History, and Art

The American West—Comparative Perspectives: A Bibliography

Telling Western Stories: From Buffalo Bill to Larry McMurtry

Coauthor
Conversations with Wallace Stegner on Western History and Literature

The American West: A Twentieth-Century History

Editor
Jack London on the Road: The Tramp Diary and Other Hobo Writings

The American Literary West

Western Films: A Short History

Writing Western History: Essays on Major Western Historians

Basques of the Pacific Northwest: A Collection of Essays

Contemporary New Mexico 1940–1990

Myths and the American West

Does the Frontier Experience Make America Exceptional?

César Chávez: A Brief Biography with Documents

Coeditor

Interpretive Approaches to Western American Literature

The Popular Western: Essays Toward a Definition

The Idaho Heritage

Idaho History: A Bibliography

The Frontier and American West

Anglo-American Contributions to Basque Studies

Basque Americans

Fifty Western Writers: A Bio-Bibliographical Guide

A Bibliographical Guide to the Study of Western American Literature

Faith and Imagination: Essays on Evangelicals and Literature

The Twentieth-Century West: Historical Interpretations

Religion and Culture

The American West in the Twentieth Century: A Bibliography

Researching Western History: Topics in the Twentieth Century

Religion in Modern New Mexico

By Grit and Grace: Eleven Women Who Shaped the American West

Portraits of Basques in the New World

With Badges and Bullets: Lawmen and Outlaws in the Old West

The Hollywood West

The American West in 2000: Essays in Honor of Gerald D. Nash

Wild Women of the Old West

Chiefs and Generals

Contents

Introduction

A mericans enjoy biography. Although changing fashions of historical writing cycle in and out, stirring life stories of leaders as well as
common folk continue to intrigue our nation's readers. Through the
centuries, beginning with the earliest Native American Creation
Stories to our most recent histories, we have narrated and interpreted
the lives of thousands of significant men and women.

This persistent interest in biography proves that, quite simply, we
are drawn to tales about other humans. We look to their courageous
and triumphal actions as models for our lives, and we also learn lessons
from the tragedies and failures that beset other people. Century after
century, the lives of historical figures, if clearly and invitingly portrayed
in compelling biographies, overflow with a vicarious power that continues to draw readers.

Not surprisingly, westerners follow other Americans in their
strong interest in biography. Our histories, too, are alive with dramatic figures. The historical stories of the American West, commencing with contacts between Native Americans and incoming
Europeans and ending with more recent multicultural activities, are
replete with intriguing men and women. Since the sixteenth century,
historians of the American West have marched thousands of human
figures across their pages, like so many high-stepping performers in
a never-ending parade.

This history of the American West builds on that long, clear interest in biography. We, too, are convinced that stories of the past speak
helpfully to the present. Individual lives, as well as the memorable
events and ideas in which those individuals participated, have shaped
and continue to mold the history of the American West. This volume,
then, is a history of the region as seen through the illuminative lives of
several emblematic men and women.

In planning this book, the volume editor asked contributors to
accomplish two overlapping goals. They were to deal with the lives of
notable westerners, but they were also to demonstrate how each of these
lives illustrated or broke from the main currents of the region's history.
These revealing links between important westerners and their times
are featured ingredients of all these essays.

A few words of introduction are necessary to make explicit the
connections between these subjects and their times. In the first five

essays, roughly one third of the volume, the authors cover the period from initial contacts between Indians and Europeans to the mid-nineteenth century. In the first essay, Gary Clayton Anderson, a noted specialist in Indian history, uses two Indian leaders—Wakantapi and Juan Sabeata—to help "define how Indians and Europeans interacted in the early West." Then well-known Borderlands specialist John L. Kessell provides a smoothly written essay on two Spanish Basque men, Juan Bautista de Anza, father and son, and their illuminating leadership roles in the eighteenth-century Southwest. In the third essay, Cheryl J. Foote, a scholar of Borderlands and frontier history, selects Texan Stephen F. Austin and the intriguing doña Tules of New Mexico to explicate the Mexican period of southwestern history. In the next chapter, William L. Lang, a recognized editor and scholar, utilizes George Vancouver, Lewis and Clark, and David Thompson to illuminate imperial rivalries in the late-eighteenth and early-nineteenth centuries in the Pacific Northwest. Then Barton H. Barbour, a widely published specialist in fur trade history, uses Jedediah S. Smith and Marcus and Narcissa Whitman to demonstrate the central roles of mountain men and missionaries in the first half of the nineteenth century.

The next five essays treat the period from roughly 1850 to 1900. In the opening piece in this quintet, Anne F. Hyde, known for her work in nineteenth-century western history, utilizes Mormon Sam Brannan and mining-town pioneer Elizabeth Byers to discuss the shaping significance of the Latter-day Saints and mining rushes and camps on the frontier West. Then leading Chicano scholar Richard Griswold del Castillo adds much to our understanding of cultural conflicts and compromises in the mid-nineteenth-century Far West through his treatment of two Hispanics, Mariano Vallejo and María Amparo Ruiz de Burton. In the next chapter, Elliott West, building on his several award-winning publications, explains how the life stories of Native Americans Sarah Winnemucca and Chief Joseph cast light on the difficult dilemmas Indians faced in the late-nineteenth-century American West. One of the country's leading agriculture historians, R. Douglas Hurt, utilizes biographical vignettes of two men, Henry Miller and Charles Lux, and two women, Rachel Calof and Nannie Alderson, to discuss ranching and farming in the second half of the nineteenth century. In the concluding section on the nineteenth century, noted western historian Glenda Riley employs the careers of Buffalo Bill Cody and Annie Oakley to show how these two people became emblematic and illuminative figures of an American Wild West.

The final five essays focus on the twentieth-century American West. In the first of these, Mark W. T. Harvey, drawing upon his considerable backgrounds in environmental and early-twentieth-century American history, uses the lives of James J. Hill, Jeannette Rankin, and John Muir to treat major themes in the period from 1890 to 1920. For the interwar 1920s to 1940, Katherine G. Aiken, author of several essays and a valuable book on western social history, employs the vibrant life of Sister Aimee Semple McPherson to help us understand transformations in these dramatic decades. Jon Hunner, drawing on his own illuminative research on World War II and the Cold War, utilizes the mythical figure of Rosie the Riveter and the career of noted scientist and administrator J. Robert Oppenheimer to demonstrate how World War II transformed the American West. In the penultimate essay, Mark S. Foster, a well-published specialist in modern American and western history, uses the lives of Walt Disney, César Chávez, and Barbara Jordan to elucidate the West's evolving identity in the 1950s, 1960s, and 1970s. In the final chapter, Carl Abbott, a leading urban and western scholar, shows how the life of computer whiz and investor Paul Allen helps clarify the historical trends in a recent, diverse, high-tech West.

Each writer concludes his or her essay with an appended section of the most useful sources for that topic. In the closing section, the volume editor provides a selective, evaluative guide to some of the most useful books and essays dealing with the American West.

This collection of essays is intended primarily for students and general readers. Still, the contributors were also urged to base their chapters on the best scholarship available on their subjects. We think specialists in the region's history, as well as other American historians, will also find the collection appropriate for their research and for their classrooms.

The editor wishes to thank those who helped in the preparation of this volume. First of all, he wants to express appreciation to the fifteen scholars and teachers who prepared these essays. Thanks also to Michael Fischer, dean of Arts and Sciences at the University of New Mexico, and Richard Robbins, chair of the University of New Mexico History Department, for their support of the Center for the American West, through which this book was planned and begun. Cindy Tyson and David Key, staff members at the center, also helped in the preparation of this volume. Virginia Scharff, the new center director (now the Center for the Southwest), has likewise been supportive. As so often in the past, my immense gratitude goes to editor and good friend David Holtby, who encouraged, supported, and guided this project from beginning to end. I'm also indebted to Karen Taschek and Evelyn Schlatter for their highly competent work with the manuscript. Finally, the page of dedication expresses my large thanks to two extraordinary people daily important to me during twenty-two years of co-labors at the University of New Mexico.

CHAPTER I

Wakantapi and Juan Sabeata

Indian Leadership and Early European Invasion in the New West

GARY CLAYTON ANDERSON

The year was 1683. That fall a young, illegal fur trader, a *coureur de bois,* as the French called them, named Pierre Charles Le Sueur quietly ascended the Mississippi River in search of people whom he called the Sioux. Somewhere near the falls named St. Anthony's, or modern Minneapolis, Le Sueur met Wakantapi, the undisputed leader of the Dakota, or Eastern Sioux people. Wakantapi embraced this young Frenchman, eyeing all the time the marvelous parcels of trade goods that he carried with him. The two men, one Indian and one European, would forge a twenty-year relationship, one that helped define how Indians and Europeans interacted in the early West.

In the same year, far to the south, New Mexican governor Domingo Jironza Petrís de Cruzate settled in for the coming winter at El Paso del Norte. To his surprise, a large delegation of Indians from the Great Plains suddenly interrupted his quiet. They were led by Juan Sabeata, a Mexican Indian by birth, who came seeking the Christian God, or so he said. Sabeata, his supposed Indian name, begged the governor to send missionaries and military troops to his people. In return, the Spaniards could save many souls in the villages that Sabeata informed the governor existed all across the southern plains.

Contemporaries, Sabeata and Wakantapi never met. They came from different parts of the continent, representing as leaders very different Indians. But they had much in common, especially in regard to leadership. They rose to power during a time when Indian communities were stretched to their limits. In the Southwest, Sabeata witnessed early invasion from Spain, and in the lands bordering the upper Mississippi River, Wakantapi had met French traders who first penetrated the region in 1650. With the arrival of the first Spanish conquerors, Native populations entered a period of decline. The appearance of Frenchmen along the upper Mississippi River led to the same result. Sabeata and Wakantapi had a difficult charge: they needed to help their people adjust to the changing conditions European invasion suddenly thrust upon them.

Those changes included especially the introduction of new diseases. Hernando Cortés's expedition into Mexico in 1519 carried smallpox. American Indians had not had biological contact with Europe for thousands of years—the thawing of the iced-over land bridge that had once connected Siberia and Alaska had isolated Native Americans—and they had not developed immunity to a whole series of pathogens, including smallpox. The impact of the early epidemics in central Mexico reduced the population by fully 95 percent—from roughly 20 million people to 1 million by 1600—and evidence suggests diseases reached the Rio Grande Valley shortly thereafter.

The lower part of the Rio Grande and much of east Texas were likely the first regions to be infected. The expedition of Hernando de Soto reintroduced smallpox. It had actually entered Florida, but de Soto spent his last days along the Mississippi River and in east Texas. Somewhere along the river, de Soto died of the disease in 1541. Considerable loss of life occurred among the Caddo Indians, who had built many large agricultural communities. Archaeologists have long since pointed to the massive numbers of abandoned mounds and villages that can be found throughout east Texas and western Louisiana. The villages were mostly unoccupied by Caddos when Europeans arrived. Caddo populations, which must have been very large, had fallen to 10,000 to 15,000 by 1700.

A similar story is plausible for the Pueblo Indians of New Mexico. While scholars have found about 140 sites for major Pueblo towns, some of these were already abandoned when the first Spanish settlement at San Juan was constructed along the upper Rio Grande in 1598. "Smallpox and the sickness which the Mexicans call *Cocolitzli* [epidemic fever]" killed thousands of Pueblo Indians in the 1630s and 1640s, according to one missionary account. Populations just in the central Rio Grande communities fell from 60,000 to 30,000 during the seventeenth century. The number of Pueblo communities continued to decline throughout the eighteenth century. A mere fourteen communities were occupied by 1800, suggesting a decline in communities that reached 90 percent.

Perhaps the best evidence of decline and change in Native populations is found on the Plains, a region explored by Francisco Vázquez de Coronado in 1541 and again in 1601 by Juan de Oñate. The journals of Oñate are particularly useful in speculating on Indian populations of the plains. Along the upper Arkansas River, probably near

Gary Clayton Anderson

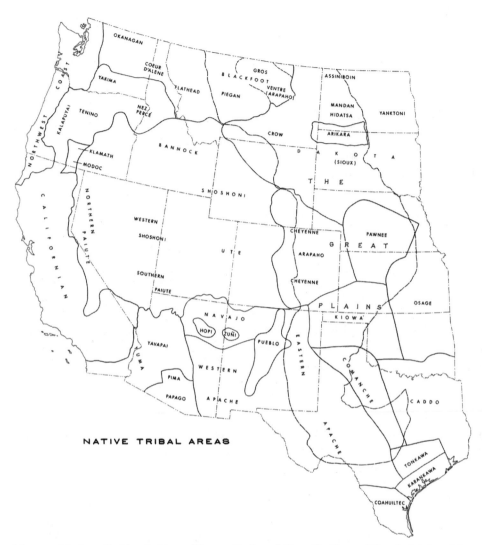

Map 1.1: Native tribal lands. From Warren Beck and Ynez D. Haase, *Historical Atlas of the American West* (Norman: University of Oklahoma Press, 1989), 8. © 1989 by the University of Oklahoma Press. Reprinted by permission.

present-day Wichita, the Spanish explorer found a complex of river villages that he never fully explored. He noted, though, that the Wichita towns extended down the Arkansas some thirty miles at least; their southernmost community likely was in the vicinity of Tulsa, Oklahoma. These Wichita, part of the Caddoan complex of people, also show up along the Canadian and Red Rivers, where large populations existed in 1500. Other people related to the Wichita in language and culture, later called Pawnees and Arikaras, inhabited valleys to the north, beyond the eyes of Oñate. They too had dozens of villages, along the Platte, Republican, and Missouri rivers.

Just to the north and east of the Caddo speakers, along the Mississippi and the central Missouri rivers, other farmer Indians existed who belonged to the Siouan language stock. Along the banks of the Missouri River itself were the powerful Osage Indians, as well as the Iowa, Ponca, Omaha, Oto, and Kansas. The French reached these towns by the 1680s. Some Siouans—generally called Mandans, Hidatsas, and Crows—had pushed on up the Missouri River into what would become North and South Dakota. These people all lived in sedentary villages and farmed, making them vulnerable to disease.

Just to the east of the farmer Indians were the most powerful of the Siouan group, the Lakota/Nakota/Dakota, or Sioux of Sitting Bull, Red Cloud, and Little Crow. The first two men would later lead the western, or Lakota, branch of Sioux, and Little Crow, an Eastern Dakota Sioux Indian, was likely a direct descendent of Wakantapi. Living on the fringe of agriculture, their women prepared a field or two for corn each spring, but these communities survived mostly by hunting and fishing. Such a lifestyle would be an advantage when it came to surviving the many epidemics that hit the plains. One epidemic in particular, reported by the French in 1751, carried off many Wichita and Osage Indians but failed to reach the Sioux, who were more migratory and often away from the avenues that carried disease—the river systems of the West.

Smallpox reappeared in a massive epidemic that moved back and forth across the plains between 1777 and 1881. It spread up the Missouri, depleting the populations of the farmer groups. An even more debilitating pathogen seems to have been malaria, which French Jesuits found up and down the Illinois River in 1700. Very likely the "fever and ague," so frequently reported, was in fact the Cocolitzli reportedly killing large numbers of Pueblo Indians. But such fevers are very difficult to identify since even the Europeans were often mystified as to what they were.

Chronicling the changes that occurred to the various western Native people that resulted from these epidemics has become one of the more perplexing issues in modern western history. That such epidemics moved westward and northward, into the Rocky Mountains and onward to California and the Pacific Northwest, seems certainly plausible—or that they were introduced as well along the Pacific Ocean from ship traffic. But to the modern historian, it is really more important to look beyond the existence of the changes and determine the impact of epidemics on Native societies. They certainly had one major effect—they left fragmented tribes and bands wherever they appeared.

The farmer societies, which included most of the Indians on the plains, were highly vulnerable to invasions of smallpox, measles, mumps, and especially malaria, since they generally lived along slow-moving rivers. Caddos, Wichitas, Pawnees, and Osage Indians likely perished at nearly the same rate as the Pueblos. As they abandoned towns, survivors were forced to turn more to hunting, leading to a decline in matrilineal social organization and the rise in patrilocalism. Such a shift had an impact on the status of women and men and likely led to more aggressive societies, with male organizations that promoted warfare.

Demographic change, migration as well as warfare, then, constituted just a few of the major challenges Indian leaders faced in the sixteenth and seventeenth centuries as Europeans came among them, offering trade but at times bringing disease and war. How could such leaders maintain their communities or, when disaster struck, how could they remold them with the survivors? And to what extent would compromise be necessary with the newly arriving Europeans? Clearly, after the Spanish and French entered the Rio Grande and the Mississippi rivers, band reorganization and perhaps even cultural collapse were real problems for all the American Indians in that part of the American West.

The efforts of Sabeata and Wakantapi to maintain their communities during this period of change have escaped most accounts of western history. They did not command legions of warriors like Sitting Bull. Worse, they made only fleeting comments to the Europeans whom they met, words that often provide little clear evidence as to their motives. Yet both men developed strategies for dealing with Europeans, and their efforts tell us much about the changing world of the American Indian in the late-seventeenth-century West as Europeans arrived, reordered political and economic relationships, and sought to conquer the land and its resources.

What is more, both Wakantapi and Sabeata, through their words, reveal the obligations that they had to the people who followed them. They were tribal leaders working in tribal settings. They quickly recognized that their success or failure at manipulating the Europeans who ventured into their lands often determined their future as leaders as well as the future of their people.

Still, so much is wanting in our knowledge of both men. Juan Sabeata likely came of age in the 1640s or 1650s in the Parral mission district of central Nueva Vizcaya. He would be recognized by Spanish authorities as the premier leader of his people three decades later, well after he fled from his mission. Wakantapi, or Sacred Born, was born near Mille Lac Lake in current north-central Minnesota, the Dakota stronghold in 1650. He emerged as the main leader of the Dakota, or Eastern Sioux, people in the decade of the 1680s.

These men quickly recognized the threat as well as the positive aspects of the European advance. Wakantapi discovered that his world was threatened by the French manipulation of the fur trade. French traders came sporadically, and they often gave weapons to the enemies of the Dakota. In a similar fashion, Juan Sabeata witnessed the incredible turmoil that followed Spanish invasion. The Spanish settlers of north Mexico often sought Indian slaves to work in their mines. To survive during such a period of flux, Sabeata had to use all of the manipulative charm he could muster to preserve the independence of his people and at the same time utilize the power and presence of the Spanish invaders, who increasingly controlled access to trading networks, which included metal arms and horses.

Sabeata's early world was truly chaotic, much more so than that of Wakantapi. Sabeata was a Conchos River Indian, the group of people belonging to several dozen tribes that included the linguistically related Tobosos, Julimes, and Chizos. The Spanish later called these tribes *Jumanos,* a generic term meaning roughly "humans," which reflected their extensive agricultural efforts along the Rio Grande and their successful political organization. The rationale is somewhat obscure, but some Spanish officials came to use the word *Jumano* as a synonym for people with tattoos and later applied the name to the Wichita Indians as well as those living southeast of Santa Fe, New Mexico. The Jumanos dominated the southern plains of Texas in 1600 as well as much of the mountain region of north Mexico, acquiring horses very early. Part of the reason for Spanish admiration of these people was their considerable military power and the fact that Spain never really conquered them.

The Spanish recognized early on that the Jumano stronghold existed along the Rio Grande south of El Paso as well as on the Concho River, which joined the Rio Grande at La Junta de los Rios. La Junta, a large Jumano town, became a major trading center well before the arrival of Spanish explorers. From La Junta, Jumano trading brigades moved eastward into the lands of the Coahuiltecan Indians of southeast Texas and northward into the Caddo and Wichita towns of east Texas and southern Oklahoma. Much of the early information that the Spanish obtained about the Jumano people came also from the Jumanos' exchange brigades, which often entered Pueblo communities. They carried goods of every sort to Pueblo exchange fairs, supplying the Pueblos especially with dried buffalo meat.

The Conchos River was a major tributary of the Rio Grande, flowing northward from central Nueva Vizcaya for nearly two hundred miles before joining the Rio Grande at La Junta de los Rios. When

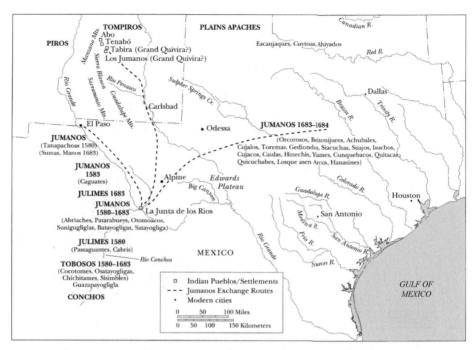

Map 1.2: The Jumano world. From Gary Clayton Anderson, *The Indian Southwest 1580–1830: Ethnogenesis and Reinvention* (Norman: University of Oklahoma Press, 1999), 18. © 1999 by the University of Oklahoma Press. Reprinted by permission.

the Spanish first entered Nueva Vizcaya in the late sixteenth century, they settled at Durango but soon explored the regions beyond. Franciscan missionaries made the initial leaps into the Conchos valley, building a series of mission stations just after the turn of the century. By 1625, some eight missions existed in the north, the most prominent San Francisco de los Conchos on the headwaters of the river.

Unfortunately for Sabeata's people, who lived nearby, the Spanish soon discovered silver in considerable quantities in Parral, also in the headwaters region. A rush into the Conchos valley commenced in 1631. The Spanish miners needed labor and turned to the Indians, some of whom were quickly subdued. Drawing on the ancient *encomienda* system, which gave grants of labor to Spanish hidalgos, or elites, thousands of Indians were forced into the mines, leaving their villages for extended periods. Even though the Spanish brought in cattle herds to feed the surrounding populations, apparently much of the Indian economy was negatively affected. Farmland was abandoned, and most of the Indians remaining on the lower Conchos who lived outside Spanish towns or missions turned to hunting, gathering, and pilfering. While Spanish settlers made efforts to irrigate the lands closest to the river, drought cycles hit in the 1620s, 1640s, 1650s, and especially in the 1660s.

These events brought suffering to Spanish ranches and farms; along with various diseases, they had a catastrophic impact on the southern Conchos River Indians.

The changing conditions soon led to starvation in Indian camps and even some missions. Indians fled, taking as many relatives as possible. So many left, particularly from the missions, where there were fewer restraints, that irrigated fields had to be abandoned. The Spaniards called the fleeing Indians "apostates," or neophytes who had turned their backs on the Catholic faith. Their leaders, often intelligent, capable men, were dubbed *ladinos,* or Indians who possessed knowledge of the Spanish lifestyle. They were also often viewed as cunning and sagacious. Ladinos knew both the Spanish language and other Indian languages; they also had tended livestock, particularly horses, for Spanish settlers, and learned the arts of breeding such animals while at missions or working on Spanish ranches.

The number of ladinos accelerated dramatically after the people along the entire central and southern Conchos River erupted in war in 1648. For more than four years, Tarahumares, Tobosos, and Conchos Indians fought their Spanish captors. Though a brief respite then ensued, allowing missionaries to consolidate their efforts, in the 1660s, more conflict broke out, and all-out war persisted throughout the 1680s and 1690s, spurred by continued Spanish slave raiding as well as the Pueblo Revolt in 1680 far to the northwest. The worst fighting probably occurred in the 1690s, when the entire Spanish population of northern Nueva Vizcaya was threatened. The most dominant band leading the rebellion was the "Jumanos Tabosos," as the governor of Nueva Vizcaya noted, "because the bravest of them are Tobosos."

These Toboso Jumanos found many other allies to the north near La Junta de los Rios. Early Spanish expeditions into La Junta in the 1590s had found a settlement of ten thousand sedentary farmers—probably the largest on the Rio Grande—living in well-built houses with granaries nearby, stuffed with corn, beans, and dried squash. The La Junta people irrigated lands along the river, planting some crops on islands in the river. Once moving above the Rio Grande, their communities could be found all the way into El Paso to the north. As the wars broke out in the south, ladino refugees found the community at La Junta an ideal sanctuary. Indeed, Spanish officials had long known of the existence of the La Junta community and of its general hostility to Spaniards. Corrals had been built to house the Spanish horses and cattle that had been stolen from the ranches below on the Conchos River during the fighting.

The wars produced a new economy in the vicinity of La Junta, one dramatically affected by the Spanish despite their lack of control over its development. Jumanos grew an excess of food, which they exchanged for other items. They often used Spanish goods, including clothing and even leather shoes. Using horses, which had appeared at La Junta in large numbers probably just after 1630, the La Junta Jumanos entered the plains to hunt buffalo, finding massive herds in the middle Pecos, Brazos, Colorado, and Nueces rivers of Texas. With meat, hides, manufactured goods, food, and horses, they organized an extensive exchange system that ran from the Caddo and Coahuiltecan Indian towns in eastern Texas westward into the Pueblo communities, especially those that were concentrated in the saline district of southeast New Mexico.

Socially, the Jumano refugees who fled the upper Conchos also used La Junta as a place to rebuild their many fragmented bands. Literally dozens of small groups, or fractured bands, appeared in the region, receiving assistance from the permanent residents of La Junta. A process of ethnogenesis resulted as new leaders emerged who brought order and control to the fragmented collections of people. This ethnogenesis often involved the creation of new social, political, and economic orders and even hybrid folklore and religious beliefs. Reformed Indian bands turned for leadership to ladinos such as Sabeata because these men possessed the knowledge and capabilities to direct diverse groups, bands that likely possessed different languages and customs. Ladinos had seen such a process of band reconfiguration in the missions of Mexico, where ethnogenesis often occurred in the molding of a community.

Most of the upper, or southern, Concho River Indians had their villages disrupted very early by the Spanish, and it is impossible to determine just how they lived before the arrival of the Spaniards. Accounts of the early, unconquered Jumanos suggest a matrilineal social organization. Women controlled the farming and the household, and men from another clan married into this female-dominant world. Husbands generally owned very little and sought companionship in various male societies that promoted hunting and, later, livestock raising. But the settled nature of early Jumano societies suggests that they were more prone to look inward to community development, and the rich religious and social life that it promoted, than to engaging in extensive war.

Spanish invasion severely disrupted this settled existence, especially for Sabeata's people, who lived closest to the Spanish. As Sabeata and his people fled villages, or missions, to become apostates, they joined bands that were more migratory in nature. The acquisition of horses had much to do with this new lifestyle. Housing also became more temporary: Sabeata's people lived in brush shelters rather than stable, earthen houses. Even at La Junta, Spanish raiding had an effect. The housing at La Junta demonstrates this change: it became less permanent as the seventeenth century progressed, showing a decline in stability. Stress from the droughts and disease likely also contributed to change: populations declined from 10,000 people at La Junta in 1590 to 2,500 by 1680.

Accordingly, by the 1680s, two separate types of people, often closely related linguistically and culturally, emerged at La Junta and beyond. While the Jumanos living in the vicinity of the town seemingly tried to maintain their matrilineal organizations, the people who fled out onto the plains to follow men like Sabeata were forced to abandon most of their matrilineal past. Indeed, much more flexible social rules became the norm on the plains, with patrilocal marriage becoming more typical. Patrilocal marriage also allowed for polygamy and especially provided for the incorporation of outsiders, even people from different ethnic backgrounds. Sabeata's band clearly faced extreme social and economic pressures, much more so than Wakantapi's Dakota, who at first seemed quite secure in their northern Minnesota homeland.

Nevertheless, these Dakota had also witnessed considerable change to their upper Mississippi River homeland, starting in AD 1450. The river had once been the locale of a vibrant sedentary, agricultural community that stretched literally to its source in current northern Minnesota. But climactic change soon affected farming, particularly in the sixteenth century, with the mini–ice ages producing decades in which crops could not be grown north of Iowa. Agricultural collapse occurred to some degree, perhaps even the evacuation of north-central Minnesota by Indian farmers closely related to the Dakota, leaving behind Wakantapi's people, who had to become more dependent on hunting for survival.

Despite the collapse, vestiges of agriculture remained. When the early French arrived, women of a few Dakota bands had planted and tended cornfields. Pierre Charles Le Sueur brought seed (wheat, perhaps) with him in 1700 on his final visit to the region, with the hope of convincing Dakota women to produce crops and feed his men. But the weather remained cold, and the French/Dakota agricultural experimentation waned. The years of 1685 and 1700 were some of the coldest of the period for North America, so cold that lakes froze over near Robert de Cavalier de la Salle's small settlement on La Vaca Bay in south Texas as well as near Biloxi, where Le Sueur cut ice from a nearby lake in 1700. Even so, Dakota women harvested wild rice in considerable quantities, a crop that the climate had not severely affected. Rice often sustained the Dakota society during the harsh winter months, when it was so cold that hunting became impossible.

Despite agricultural decline, some evidence suggests that matrilineal clan order still existed amongst Wakantapi's people, with the harvesting of wild rice supporting a more settled existence. For the most part, when

Le Sueur first arrived in 1683, the Dakota lived in well-developed, large bark houses along the south shores of Mille Lacs Lake—suggesting a strongly sedentary life—with nearly a dozen communities in the region. But these populations were certainly in a state of decline, as malaria and possibly smallpox had visited the region. Indeed, at least a thousand Huron Indians had fled into the upper Mississippi Valley in 1649 after their villages had been devastated by smallpox and Iroquois raids. They probably spread the disease throughout the region.

Even though the Dakota towns seemed to be quite well organized and sedentary, Wakantapi was described as a "Big Chief," suggestive of a rising patrilocal order. What is more, some Sioux Indians, described as Tetons and Yanktons, well before 1700 had crossed the Mississippi River into the plains of western Minnesota, where they hunted buffalo. These people, for sure, became patrilocal and gradually lost clan designations. They acquired horses probably as early as the 1720s. When French fur traders reached their land, encouraging more hunting, the transition became complete: all vestiges of matrilineal organization disappeared.

Wakantapi and Sabeata, then, faced common problems. Climate change, disease, and European invasion had so altered their homelands that they were forced to adapt to a new way of life, one that was much more mobile and tied to hunting than to sedentary villages. More importantly, exchange was a crucial part of their lives, and Europeans had introduced new weapons, clothing, and horses. For those communities that turned more and more to hunting, exchange became crucial, since hunters brought mostly protein into the village; with diets generally lacking carbohydrates, it was necessary to forge relationships with other people who were still producing crops.

In these societies, success as a leader hinged upon organizing alliances and exchanges with other societies, some Indian and some European. Indeed, a society like the Sioux probably spent more time exchanging for produce in other Indian towns than negotiating relationships with Europeans. For such exchanges to work, these leaders tried to incorporate partners into their networks, often through the process of kinship adoption or through the development of alliance. It is almost impossible to separate these two elements so crucial to Indian leadership: adopting an individual, or a number of individuals, for the sake of trade or alliance.

Indians who exchanged items sought out other groups of people who had useful foods or goods that would complement their diet or economy. Obviously European-manufactured goods became sought-after items, but such goods were so novel that exchange was difficult, since a sense of value equivalent did not exist. But such a problem might also surface when Indians exchanged hides for corn. For the Sioux people, who increasingly lacked agricultural products, extensive exchange relationships with the Iowa, Omaha, and Otoe Indian farmers in northern Iowa and along the Missouri River offered them the opportunity for a diverse diet. But again, who was to say how much corn was to be given for one buffalo hide?

Indians all along the Mississippi River, as well as those in the Southwest, had solved the problem many centuries before European arrival with the creation of the "calumet." Le Sueur, on his way up the Mississippi River in 1700, gave an excellent description of this celebration when he reached the Arkansas towns. He described the calumet as a ceremony designed to "mark an alliance" or to honor an important visiting dignitary, even to note the "adoption" of such an individual. The honored person first smoked a long, catlinite pipe "adorned with feathers painted in different colors." As the pipe was passed, the smoke came to represent the joining of the men as brothers, as kinsmen. For several nights to follow, the villagers then danced with the pipe held in hand, moving "to the cadence of the sound of their voices and the sound of several pails covered with skin formed like drums."

The calumet came to a conclusion on the third afternoon. The honored person—in this case, Le Sueur—was carried into the center of the village on a skin and showered with presents, usually consisting of food. At times, the food was placed in the mouths of the honored visitors, further confirming their position as members of the tribe. While the presents were being showered upon the guests, the Arkansas Indian leaders recounted the many brave deeds they had done, affirming their position of importance in the society and the alliance that then existed between them and the visitors. At the conclusion, the new relatives were expected to repay the presents with gifts of their own. The degree of respect and the value of the alliance hinged upon "the presents that are given in return [italics mine]."

Indians, then, across the West, saw exchange as a familial/economic/political act, one that made relatives, allowed mechanisms for the exchange of goods, and cemented military alliances. Once created, the alliance/exchange could exist for many years. Tribal societies generally looked inward, trusting only their relatives, and Indians simply did not exchange gifts with strangers. Gift giving was crucial in their societies, and stinginess was a sin. Moreover, it was after the formation of such "fictive," or created, kinship relationships that trust emerged. Naturally, senior leaders, or chiefs, negotiated the dancing of the calumet, had possession of the "sacred" pipe that made it possible, and decided which groups to approach. Customarily, when encountering a group on the plains or even on the Mississippi River, the raising of the pipe high in the air signaled a willingness to dance and give gifts or make relatives and alliances and exchange goods.

Le Sueur first smoked the calumet with Wakantapi and other Dakota people in 1683, when he reached the regions above Lake Pepin, near St. Anthony Falls. Here he constructed a trading post that he seems to have occupied, off and on, until 1690. Hunting for beaver and otter in these lands was unbelievably productive during those early years, and the French traders received significant returns for the small outlay of presents that they gave the Sioux. Although Le Sueur never admitted it in his correspondence, he also no doubt married a Dakota woman during this period, as he became very closely attached to Wakantapi's family. It would have been almost impossible for him to avoid such a marriage, as once a relative, and a very important one at that, Wakantapi would have insisted that he marry a Dakota woman, most likely his daughter.

French coureurs de bois had been taking Indian wives for many years. The custom became so prevalent, and so necessary for successful trade, that a term even came to represent it—*la façon du pays*. The custom of the country, or the need to fulfill familial obligations in an Indian town, required marrying an Indian woman. While compiling his journal of adventure on the upper Mississippi in 1700, Le Sueur made reference to the custom only briefly: "Several of our French like the life of libertinage of the savages and retired among them, leaving their wives and children." But the custom did not require that coureurs de bois remain forever among the Indians. Many came in the fall for the winter hunt, stayed into spring, and returned east in early summer. In tribal societies, men were expected to leave for long periods, hunting or exchanging, and uncles usually played major roles in rearing children. These relationships, then, could be permanent, but familial obligations did not require the constant attention to children on the part of the biological father that was common among Europeans.

Under orders from the governor-general of Canada, Le Sueur built a second trading post on the northern end of Lake Pepin in 1695 and stayed the winter, renewing his close relationship with Wakantapi's people. The following spring, he convinced a young Dakota chief, likely Wakantapi's son, to accompany him to Montreal, where this man, Tioscate, met the governor. Tioscate's meeting went well, but unfortunately, he soon took sick from smallpox and died. This freed Le Sueur to pursue a mining project in the Far West. Previously, while in the Sioux lands, he had discovered copper ore.

After traveling to France, Le Sueur received a commission from the king to open his copper mines in 1699. He made his final trip into Wakantapi's homeland in the summer of 1700. But as he reached the Falls of St. Anthony, rather than staying in that locale, as he always had done, he proceeded west, up the Minnesota River, into the land of the Western Sioux, bypassing his old ally, Wakantapi.

Le Sueur's actions produced a crisis for Wakantapi's leadership and for the Dakota, or Eastern Sioux, people. These Frenchmen had become the source for much-needed muskets and ammunition, knives, and kettles. And as in the past, when Le Sueur moved up the Mississippi River, he heard of continued intertribal war. The river, an artery of trade, was literally being fought over by dozens of tribes from both its eastern and western banks. The Sioux and their allies, the Iowas and Osages, had recently struck the Illinois and Piankashaws. The Fox, Kickapoos, Potawatomies, and others were coming to the aid of the Illinois. The struggles were tied to the growing pressures on hunting grounds, often the product of increased French trade.

Le Sueur realized that his movement into the west beyond the confines of the Mississippi River greatly disturbed the Eastern Sioux, his relatives. As his party of two dozen men moved up the Minnesota River, nine Dakotas from Wakantapi's people caught up with him and begged him to return to the Falls of St. Anthony. They noted that the lands of the Minnesota River were those of the Iowa, Otoes, and Western Sioux. Having made their speech, they then "[wept] over Mr. Le Sueur's head, saying . . . Take pity on us." More importantly, in departing, the Eastern Sioux noted that the Western Sioux "do not use canoes, cultivate the earth, or gather wild rice." In other words, they could not maintain the exchange relationship, offering rice and corn, to the same degree as Wakantapi's people.

As these nine men scurried back to tell Wakantapi the news, Le Sueur proceeded westward. He noted in his diary that above the banks of the Minnesota, large prairies soon revealed themselves, where buffalo roamed in numbers. He soon entered the small Blue Earth River and built a log fort on a hill some four miles from its mouth. Within days of its completion, a dour Wakantapi arrived and camped outside the walls.

Almost simultaneously, two Frenchmen arrived who informed Le Sueur that the Eastern Sioux had pillaged them, taking their guns and goods in retaliation for Le Sueur's abandonment of them. Wakantapi did not go to see Le Sueur himself but sent representatives, who explained that men from other towns had pillaged the French, not Wakantapi's people. An incensed Le Sueur told them to take back the beaver pelts they had brought—that "we shall no longer be good friends." A tense situation soon developed as Le Sueur tried to get rid of the Eastern Sioux. His efforts, however, became more problematic when he learned that the Iowas, Otoes, and Osage Indians, tribes who Le Sueur had hoped would come and plant crops nearby, had failed to leave their towns near Spirit Lake, Iowa, and on the Missouri River.

Finally, on November 26, 1700, a large delegation of Dakota people joined the ones living below Le Sueur's new establishment. They pitched tepees in the woods and watched as Wakantapi approached the fort and asked that Le Sueur visit him. Agreeing, Le Sueur entered a large council house, filled with sixteen men and many women and children. Le Sueur must have noted that the women and children were out of place, not generally found in such a council. All had their faces blackened, and they wept after Le Sueur sat down. Wakantapi, sitting next to Le Sueur, then put three spoonfuls of wild rice into the Frenchman's mouth, noting that all the people in the room were related to Tioscate, the unfortunate man who had accompanied Le Sueur to Montreal. At his name, everyone wept, some over the shoulders of Le Sueur.

Wakantapi, in a dramatic fashion, then rose and invoked again the name Tioscate. He begged Le Sueur to have pity on his people, "to give life to his wives and children who were wasting with hunger." Pointing to the women and children in the room, Wakantapi made his final plea: "Behold thy children, thy brethren, thy sisters; it is for thee to see whether thou wishes them to live or die. They will live if thou givest them powder and ball."

Le Sueur, the hardened French coureur de bois, crumbled. Despite his hopes of pushing into the West and making new relationships with the Western Sioux, the Iowa, and the Otoes, he realized that he must recognize these old obligations. He promptly invited the delegation to the fort, where they walked around the walls three times. As they proceeded, the elders and the women and children continued to cry, "My father, take pity on us."

Four days later, after many other Dakotas had joined Wakantapi, a large council took place in which Frenchmen and Indians smoked the sacred calumet. The Indians offered a massive collection of beaver pelts, and Le Sueur reciprocated by distributing presents. Wakantapi insisted that Le Sueur should "no longer regard us as Sioux, but as Frenchmen," a considerable concession. Chiefs in positions of power always stressed the need to join their tribal family. Le Sueur then asked the Dakotas to abandon their villages on Mille Lac Lake and move to his new fort, where he would provide seed for planting. Many did thereafter, beginning an exodus out of the woodlands of eastern Minnesota into the prairie land of the West that continued into the early decades of the eighteenth century. Le Sueur would depart his fort that spring, however, leaving a dozen or so Frenchmen behind. Wakantapi would never see him again but would remain an active leader of his people, greeting French traders who came into the upper Mississippi River and dancing the calumet with them well into the 1720s.

Wakantapi initially had defined the relationship that existed with Le Sueur, then saw it change and was forced to use all his manipulative skills to reshape it. Sabeata, on the other hand, had a much different reaction to the Spanish invasion. Rather than beaver skins, Spanish settlers in the Southwest needed labor, in particular Indian labor. This need was especially true for Spanish miners, who depended on Indians, and for Spanish missionaries, who built their churches and fields with neophyte workers. Just in the vicinity of Parral, Nueva Vizcaya, some thirty large irrigated fields had been constructed by the 1680s. But because of the fighting that had erupted and the exodus of Indians, only four of them were producing crops.

Once free from Spanish labor systems, Sabeata, and the many refugees who followed him, wanted little to do with Spanish soldiers and missionaries. The exchange network they had developed on the plains actually avoided towns that had Spaniards in them, including the pueblos along the upper Rio Grande. Instead, Sabeata's Jumanos had developed extensive ties with the Tompiro-speaking desert pueblos of southeastern New Mexico, those generally identified as Abó, Tenabó, Tabira, and "el pueblo de los Humanos," the last a community that likely housed a few Jumano people. They had no Spanish occupants.

How many Indians constituted this Jumano exchange system is difficult to determine. Sabeata apparently indicated to the Spanish governor at El Paso in 1683 that some 10,000 Indians participated. Since the La Junta population was somewhere between 2,000 and 3,000 by this time, those riding with Sabeata on the plains likely numbered 7,000 people. Sabeata also listed more than two dozen bands by their names, many of them headed by ladinos like himself. He gave the Christian, baptized names of many chiefs—Don Juan, Alonso, Bartolomé, Luis, Don Francisco, and José. Each band likely averaged nearly 300 people. Such a number seems consistent with the type of economy that emerged, one where considerable amounts of labor was necessary to process hundreds of buffalo hides and dressed meat each year.

Strong leadership, usually coming from a "Big Man," was necessary to orchestrate such an economic process. Spanish expeditions into the Colorado and Guadalupe river valleys of Texas in the 1690s confirm this, as on one occasion, Domingo Terán de los Rios watched as the men of each Jumano band performed a cavalry parade, Sabeata and his people leading the affair. The Cibola Jumanos came second, the chief carrying a likeness of the Lady of Guadalupe like a flag (further demonstrating a connection to missions). Some of the chiefs even made rather bold demands on the Spanish visitors, such as arguing against their proceeding on into Caddo lands, an obvious attempt to control the trade goods Terán had brought with him.

Gary Clayton Anderson

Figure 1.1: *Karankawa Indians of the Gulf Coast,* Lino Sánchez y Tapia.
Watercolor. People of the Southwest exchange network. Courtesy of the
Gilcrease Museum, Tulsa, Oklahoma.

These people, a mix of refugees, some of whom still maintained vestiges of the Christian faith acquired in Mexican missions, were quite successful at reinventing themselves. They had gone through ethnogenesis, even merging Christianity with more prevailing religious practices associated with plains buffalo hunting. The men gave considerable attention to their dress, utilizing both Spanish manufactured clothing and skins.

But why, given Jumano success, did their leaders enter El Paso and speak with the Spanish governor after avoiding these people for so many years? The trip for Sabeata, much like the one Wakantapi made to see Le Sueur, was not one of curiosity. Sabeata knew much of what had happened in the Southwest over the course of the previous two decades, and he went to the Spanish governor with a purpose—he had invented a ruse, one seemingly designed to get assistance from Spaniard soldiers, whom, while once his enemy, he now needed.

The Jumano world was facing many difficulties. The droughts that had affected the Conchos River also hurt the Indian towns along the Rio Grande. During the 1650s, 1660s and 1670s, several pueblos in the

Jaranames

Figure 1.2: *Aranama Indians Near Goliad, Texas,* Lino Sánchez y Tapia. Watercolor. People of the Southwest exchange network. Courtesy of the Gilcrease Museum, Tulsa, Oklahoma.

Saline district of New Mexico had been abandoned. In one pueblo, 450 Indians starved to death. La Junta itself had lost three quarters of its population. The droughts also hurt the very resource that had promoted the Jumano exchange network as buffalo herds declined. These animals could no longer be found in the southern extremities of the Pecos River or much below the Colorado River in Texas by the 1680s. Buffalo herds were also severely affected by the cold weather that had descended upon the plains in the decades after 1680. As Sabeata put it, the herds were some three days' travel by horse, north from La Junta, and these hunting grounds had become contested by a variety of people.

Then disease returned. Smallpox devastated Indians in Coahuila in 1673, destroying entire towns. Spanish missionaries watched as hundreds of people died, so many that burial became impossible. It is unclear to what extent the epidemic reached La Junta, but the Indian exchange networks provided a ready avenue for spreading viruses, and

Spanish reports reveal that north Mexico and very likely the Great Plains itself where the Jumanos worked were infested with smallpox between 1675 and 1691. La Salle's small conclave at La Vaca experienced a bout with smallpox in 1687.

The Indians of the Rio Grande had certainly faced European pathogens prior to this period. But the epidemics came at such a difficult time. Droughts had destroyed markets, and entire bands of people disappeared. Even worse, others were invading Jumano lands. These were Wichitas and Apaches, the latter in particular taking over the best hunting grounds along the upper Colorado River.

The Apache threat had been building since 1600. A fight over control of access to exchange with the Tompiro Pueblos of southeastern New Mexico seems to have surfaced in the 1650s. Apaches and Jumanos did virtually the same thing economically. They hunted buffalo for meat and hides and used these commodities to get access to the Pueblo towns, where carbohydrates and other goods could be acquired. The Apaches added yet another commodity to the mix—Indian slaves taken on the plains. Spanish sources tell us much about the Jumano exchange network, but they also suggest these Indians either disdained slavery or had little access to slaves. Increasingly, the combination of Apache raids, lost markets in New Mexico, and drought and disease were driving the Jumanos off the plains and back into La Junta.

It was with a heavy heart that Sabeata turned to the Spanish for help. He first entered El Paso in 1682 but was told to come back the next year to see Governor Petrís. When he finally met this man, he knew exactly what the governor wanted to hear. He first told the governor of a battle with Apaches and that during the fighting, a miracle had occurred in which a cross and the image of a virgin nun had saved the victory. Out of reverence for these events, Sabeata concluded, the Jumanos now wanted the help of missionaries and Spanish soldiers, and Sabeata carefully outlined the many bands and numbers of people who would readily accept baptism. Although they wanted "ministers," Sabeata did not disguise the fact that Spanish soldiers would also be useful in dealing with their enemies, the Apaches.

The Spanish governor agreed to help. He ordered Juan Domínguez de Mendoza and twenty men to journey with Sabeata and his people into the buffalo killing grounds on an expedition that left just after New Year's Day, 1684. Mendoza's journal suggests that much of what Sabeata said was true. La Junta had a large population, and missionaries soon entered the town and baptized more than five hundred Indians, mostly Julime Jumanos, who were "versed in the Mexican Language," or Nahuatl. When Mendoza's party reached other Jumano villages, all the women and children kissed the habits of the fathers, welcoming them. Clearly Sabeata and other leaders had hailed the Spanish as saviors well before they even arrived.

But Mendoza also came to see the agenda that Sabeata had planned. As Mendoza entered village after village, the chiefs entertained him royally; women built huts of reed for the Spanish soldiers and then tried to entice them in. "But I did not consent to it, because of the evil results which might follow," Mendoza claimed in his report to the governor. He wished to avoid the familial responsibilities that such actions warranted. Although failing to entice the Spanish soldiers—if Mendoza's word is accurate—with the offer of wives, Sabeata was more successful at embroiling Mendoza and his men in an all-out war with the Apaches. After several clashes with the Apaches, however, the Spanish captain finally called Sabeata into his tent and ordered him to leave the group. The Spanish soldiers would protect Jumano hunters to some extent but not initiate war on Apaches.

Sabeata's exchange network worked in the Southwest much like it did along the upper Mississippi River. Sabeata and his people came bearing gifts and established alliances with either the Pueblos in the west or the Caddos and Coahuiltecans in the east. These ties were undoubtedly based on relationships that took the form of alliances and often involved intermarriage. The willingness of Sabeata and his people to embrace Spanish Christianity once more—after it had been used to repress them—demonstrated the extent to which exchange and alliances were based on cultural conformity. Indians in the Southwest simply could not exchange goods or work as allies with people who were their enemies.

Thereafter, Sabeata worked tirelessly to maintain the Jumano presence on the southern plains. But after the Spanish soldiers withdrew, missionaries at La Junta soon found it impossible to sustain their stations. They departed the region in 1685. In that same year, La Salle found several Jumano bands living just south of the Caddo, people with whom the Jumanos had a strong alliance. Once at the Caddo towns, Jumanos and Caddos convinced their "new" allies, the French, to go against the Apaches; several Frenchmen joined an expedition in which an entire Apache camp was overrun. Many Indians were killed and captured, some to face horrible execution in the Caddo towns.

Ironically, at the same time the Jumanos were using their new French allies to drive off Apaches, Sabeata and several Jumano leaders had sent messages to the Spanish in Parral, announcing the existence of these new Europeans in Texas. Undoubtedly, Sabeata realized that these new "Spaniards," as they called them, would be viewed with suspicion by Spanish officials. By giving clear, detailed reports on the number of French explorers and displaying the goods they gave in

Lipanes.

Figure 1.3: *Lipan Apache Indians North of the Rio Grande,* Lino Sánchez y Tapia. Watercolor. People of the Southwest exchange network. Courtesy of the Gilcrease Museum, Tulsa, Oklahoma.

exchange to the Jumanos, Sabeata once again convinced Spanish authorities to send soldiers into Texas.

The Spanish sent a number of expeditions into Texas between 1685 and 1691, all of them guided, for the most part, by Jumano Indians. But it took Spanish soldiers several years to find the abandoned fort La Salle had built near La Vaca Bay; Jumano guides apparently took their time finding it, as they wanted to use the Spaniards, much as they had Mendoza, to protect them against the invading Apaches. At times, Jumano leaders even tried to threaten Spanish leaders, hoping to keep them in their temporary villages erected along the Colorado and Guadalupe rivers rather than let them explore to the north and east.

Sabeata, however, failed in his efforts to stem the Apache menace, and by 1691 both the Spanish and the French retired from La Junta and Texas. When they did return in 1715, Apaches had reached the outskirts of La Junta and were living in small towns in tepeelike dwellings. They had forced the Jumanos to leave their communities on the Colorado and Guadalupe rivers, and Spanish soldiers found only the remains of these once-thriving exchange communities when they sent expeditions into the area after 1709. Apaches now provided the buffalo meat and hides that Jumano farmers in La Junta still needed; they exchanged these commodities for horses, corn, clothing, and jewelry. Not surprisingly, many former Jumanos now lived in those thriving southern plains Apache camps, people who likely still remembered Sabeata and who still spoke some Nahuatl. The Cibola Jumanos, on the other hand, a band closely related to Sabeata's, built at least one permanent village at La Junta and turned to farming once again.

The transformations that occurred in the Southwest, or on the plains west of the upper Mississippi River, put stresses on Indian leadership. Wakantapi's people survived, despite the chief's near failure with Le Sueur, and while Sabeata succeeded in getting Spanish soldiers into Texas, his people were likely forced to become Apaches. Whether failing or succeeding, Indian leaders had certain advantages. They came from tribal societies that were not static, something historians have been slow to recognize. They were able to change social and political structures as well as economies rather quickly. And after being disrupted or losing populations from war, disease, and drought, they incorporated people, some being taken in war and others simply joining them.

The process of incorporation could occur on many different levels. Wakantapi "incorporated" Le Sueur and his men into his Eastern Sioux society by making them relatives and providing them with wives, the latter no doubt quite willing to marry a Frenchman, given the many bounties that Europeans could provide. This relationship lasted for more than a decade. But the marriages and alliances meant that these same Frenchmen had obligations to the tribal society that they had joined. When Le Sueur avoided those obligations in 1700, Wakantapi was quick to point out his social indiscretion: that the French must care for their wives and children as well as their brothers and fathers-in-law. To fail to do so was to invite pillage or even war. But when pillaging failed to bring Le Sueur back to the Mississippi River, Wakantapi "became" a Frenchman. Relationships, alliances, and exchange made his world.

Sabeata employed a similar tactic in dealing with Spaniards in the Southwest. He used the vestiges of the Catholic religion that still existed among his people to convince Spanish leaders to help defend the new society he helped create. Of course, this meant convincing his people they must embrace that religion, to some degree, when Spanish missionaries and soldiers came to their rescue. This decision must have been difficult, given the mistreatment of these same Indians while they lived in Spanish missions or, worse, worked in mines. But like the Sioux to the north, Sabeata's people were adaptable. They had moved to the plains and developed a buffalo-hunting society in a few decades, no easy task in itself. Kissing the robes of Franciscan fathers was a modest concession compared to the benefits offered by Spanish arms.

Successful Indian leaders understood how to deal with Europeans. They instructed them in ceremonies, making sure they understood the obligations that came with such institutions. They often convinced Europeans to take on familial responsibilities, creating both fictive, or ceremonial, and affine, or blood, kinship bonds that required support, something that benefited the entire society. They worked tirelessly to maintain alliances with Europeans, recognizing the sorts of compromises that were necessary to maintain them. And when faced with few other choices, they convinced their people, as in the case of Wakantapi, to try farming or, as in the case of Sabeata, Catholicism. Indian leadership involved presentation, manipulation, and compromise, qualities readily identifiable in these two men, Sabeata and Wakantapi, and very likely found among Indian chiefs all across the new West.

Essay on Sources

The ideas for this article draw on my two books, *Kinsmen of Another Kind: Dakota-White Relations in the Upper Mississippi River, 1650–1862* (Lincoln: University of Nebraska Press, 1984), and *The Indian Southwest, 1580–1830: Ethnogenesis and Reinvention* (Norman: University of Oklahoma Press, 1999). Both volumes are indebted to the early "structural" anthropology of Marshall Sahlins and Elman Service and even more so to the "structural Marxism" of the French school (which Sahlins briefly converted to in the 1970s), ideas developed by Maurice Godelier, Claude Meillassoux, Maurice Bloch, and Emmanuel Terray. I believe that early American Indians had a very firm idea of how their economies should work and how Europeans should work within them. The roles of the two Indian leaders discussed in this essay, Wakantapi and Sabeata, help make this point.

The primary sources for Le Sueur's contact with the upper Mississippi River Sioux include the various journals the French explorer kept. Several of the journals are contained in *Mémoires de Mr le Sueur,* Archives Nationales, Paris, France. While most entries are in Le Sueur's hand, some sections of this 115-folio manuscript are in Claude Delisle's hand. These journals, nevertheless, cover the entire period of Le Sueur's last voyage up the Mississippi River, from 1699, when he landed at Biloxi, until 1702. Much of the earlier information on Le Sueur's life in the upper Mississippi River is also contained in this journal.

Several other parts of his journal were copied and published in Pierre Margry, *Découvertes et établissements des Français dans l'Ouest et dans le Suc l'Amérique Septrionale (1614–1754),* 6 vols. (Paris: Maisonneuve Preres et Ch. LeClerc, Editeurs, 1876–88), vol. 5, and again in the

Wisconsin Historical Society Collections, 31 vols. (Madison: Wisconsin Historical Society, 1855–1931), vol. 17. Mildred Mott Wedel has an excellent discussion of the provenance of the various journals in "Le Sueur and the Dakota Sioux," in *Aspects of Upper Great Lakes Anthropology: Papers in Honor of Lloyd A. Winford,* ed. Elden Johnson (St. Paul: Minnesota Historical Society Press, 1974).

The primary sources that directly relate to the life of Juan Sabeata include several collections of edited documents. See in particular Herbert Eugene Bolton, ed., *Spanish Exploration in the Southwest, 1542–1706* (New York: Scribner, 1908), for information on Mendoza's expedition, as well as Charles Wilson Hackett, ed., *Historical Documents Relating to New Mexico, Nueva Vizcaya, and Approaches Thereto, in 1773,* 3 vols. (Washington, D.C.: Carnegie Institution, 1923–27), and Pichardo's Treatise on the *Limits of Louisiana and Texas,* 4 vols. (Austin: University of Texas Press, 1931). The French landing along the Texas coast in 1685 is best followed in Abbé Jean Cavelier, *The Journal of Jean Cavelier: The Account of a Survivor of La Salle's Texas Expedition,* ed. and trans. Jean Delanglez (Chicago: Institute of Jesuit History, 1938), and Henri Joutel, *A Journal of La Salle's Last Voyage* (New York: Corinth Books, 1962).

Several secondary sources are helpful in following Sabeata's life. See in particular J. Charles Kelley, "Juan Sabeata and Diffusion in Aboriginal Texas," *American Anthropologist* 57 (October 1955): 981–95, as well as Kelley's dissertation titled "Jumano and Patarabueye: Relations at La Junta de los Rios" (Harvard University, 1947). The best discussion of early Spanish activity in Nueva Vizcaya is Oakah L. Jones, Jr., *Nueva Vizcaya: Heartland of the Spanish Frontier* (Albuquerque: University of New Mexico Press, 1988). Several other articles are useful: see J. W. Williams, "New Conclusions on the Route of Mendoza, 1683–1684," *West Texas Historical Association Yearbook* 38 (October 1958): 111–34, and Alonso de Posada, "The Report of Fray Alonso de Posada in Relation to Quivira and Teguayo," ed. S. Lyman Tyler and H. Darrel Taylor, *New Mexico Historical Review* 33 (October 1958): 285–314.

CHAPTER 2

Juan Bautista de Anza
Father and Son—Pillars of New Spain's Far North

JOHN L. KESSELL

The news stung. Shouted from horseback, blurted in cantinas, whispered at mass, it fell on disbelieving ears. For as long as most could remember, Juan Bautista de Anza, captain for life of the garrison at Fronteras, had been their protector. Yet on May 9, 1740, Anza lay dead, victim of an Apache ambush.

The event seemed so improbable. The captain was much too savvy a campaigner. Had he not recently lectured Sonora's governor about just such ambushes? Still, according to a Jesuit visitor who heard the story over a decade later, our only source today, Anza was concluding a routine patrol through Pima mission villages in the Santa Cruz River Valley of present-day southern Arizona. For whatever reasons, he rode out ahead of his men. Apaches, bows drawn, had sprung from cover, loosing their arrows and felling the forty-six-year-old Spaniard from his horse. Apparently they tore off the crown of his scalp as a trophy and were gone. Respected veteran Juan Mateo Manje, whom Captain Anza had known well, likened the practice of scalp taking among Sonora's Indians to the European seizure of enemy battle flags. The swiftness of Spanish retaliation—three days after Anza's death, thirteen killed and fourteen captives—implied that punishment might have been inflicted on a nearby camp of friendly Apaches.

In the captain's quarters at Fronteras, thirty miles south of today's Douglas, Arizona, his mourning widow gathered about her the two girls from her late husband's previous union along with their own four children: Francisco Antonio, fifteen; María Margarita, thirteen; Josefa Gregoria, eight; and Juan Bautista the younger, not yet four, who was most like his father. To be certain—from the year 1718, when the elder Anza, a Basque from Spain, first appeared in the records of Sonora, for seven decades thereafter, until 1788, with the burial of his American-born namesake—the sequential careers of this venturous father and son amply illustrate the vitality of colonial New Spain's far northwestern frontier, today's American Southwest.

For two centuries before the Anzas, realities and mirages commingled north of the city of Mexico, beckoning the restless. Eyewitness reports by Álvar Núñez Cabeza de Vaca and fray Marcos de Niza, embellished in a climate of wonder, had set in motion one of North America's great false starts. The grandly medieval exploration carried out between 1540 and 1542 by the several units under Francisco Vázquez de Coronado had begun with banners waving and ended in disgrace. More than three hundred European horsemen and footmen, heirs of the Spanish *Reconquista* yet carrying among them Native wooden and obsidian weapons, led forth a thousand imposing Mexican Indian fighters. They had lost no battle. Defeated instead by an endless topography that offered no hope of immediate return, they had at least experienced the vastness of the continent. And they had met face-to-face a medley of its scattered Native peoples, from the Yumas of the Colorado River in the west to the Wichitas of present-day central Kansas. Then they withdrew, and colonization stalled.

Not for the next 185 years did another notable Spaniard travel as broadly as Coronado in the far north. A military bureaucrat, Inspector General Pedro de Rivera, and his staff went out from Mexico City in 1724 and came back in 1728, neither with much fanfare. Rivera rode eight thousand miles, reviewed two dozen garrisons, installed Juan Bautista de Anza the elder at Fronteras, proposed cutting defense costs by more than one third, and drew up a needed code of reforms that were largely ignored. Colonization, meanwhile, given time and chance, had streamed northward.

The biggest incentive at first was silver. An especially bountiful strike in the late 1540s at Zacatecas, 350 miles northwest of Mexico City, set off a series of bonanzas financed in large part by Basque venture capitalists. Humanity, hybrid in race and estate, swarmed the camps. Free and slave laborers, mining engineers, bakers, whores, blacksmiths, homeless vagrants, jugglers, and children jostled for space. Storekeepers stocked a surprisingly wide array of hardware, dry goods, and confections. The insatiable demand for meat, hides and tallow, wool, wheat, and eggs brought stockmen and farmers. Such frantic intrusion also brought war.

Spaniards called them *Chichimecas.* A generic term of deep derision, it served to reduce the various culturally distinct seminomadic Native groups of the high desert simply to enemies. The European invaders thought first to stamp them out, hunting them on search-and-destroy missions, placing bounties on male heads, and selling their families into

John L. Kessell

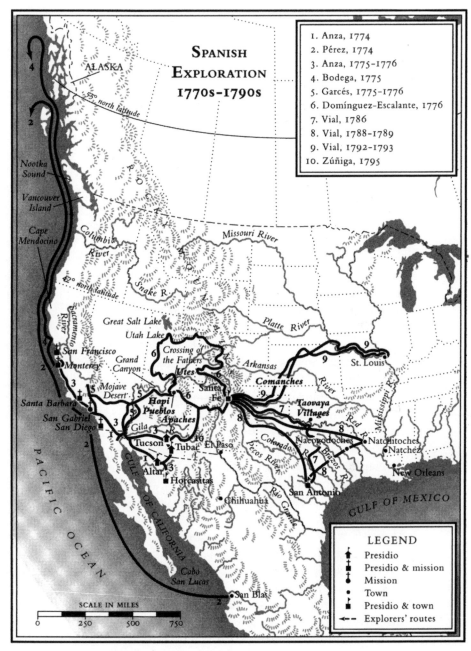

Map 2.1: Spanish Exploration, 1770s to 1790s. From John L. Kessell, *Spain in the Southwest: A Narrative History of Colonial New Mexico, Arizona, Texas, and California* (Norman: University of Oklahoma Press, 2002), 284. Copyright 2002 by the University of Oklahoma Press. Reprinted by permission.

slavery. But the Chichimecas fought back, forming confederations, learning to ride, and becoming ever more nomadic. Exasperated, the Spaniards set out salaried frontier garrisons, or presidios, and fortified nearly all their built spaces, even to experimental wagons meant for protection of supplies to the mines and silver to Mexico City. Nothing seemed to work. By the 1580s and 1590s, astute captains, taking advantage of a prolonged drought and the slow attrition of Chichimeca fighting men, had evolved a welfare program. In exchange for peace, the Spanish government agreed to provide foodstuffs, clothing, axes, copper kettles, bolts of cloth, and other assistance and ban slaving. Delegations of Chichimeca headmen, escorted to Mexico City, gawked at what Spaniards had wrought. In the long run, peace by purchase proved cheaper than war.

Given the profusion of mines fanning northward across Nueva Vizcaya, roughly the modern Mexican states of Durango and Chihuahua, prospectors counted on the progression to continue at higher latitudes. Yet they were wrong. Studying the U.S.-Mexican border on a map today, starting at the Pacific shore and trending more east than south, the surveyors' dead-straight line is inconvenienced slightly at the Colorado River, then proceeds with only three corrections until it is swept along with the current and big bends of the Rio Grande all the way to the Gulf of Mexico. No Spanish colonial miner could have known that beyond that line, in New Spain's far north, mining would count for practically nothing. Even the modest mines operated in the latter-day Mexican state of Sonora during the 1720s and 1730s by the first Juan Bautista de Anza lay below that line.

Juan de Oñate had to see for himself. Affluent son of a major Basque developer of the Zacatecas district, don Juan got together a consortium in the 1590s to invest in pacification of the town-dwelling and clothed peoples inhabiting a northern land optimists had already begun calling the new Mexico. By terms of a contract negotiated with the viceroy in Mexico City, Oñate was exalted as proprietor and first governor of New Mexico in turn for outfitting, transporting, and settling there its first two hundred soldier-colonists and their families. When in the summer of 1598 they came among the Pueblo Indians with all their baggage, dependents, and hungry animals, this motley train of settlers contrasted sharply with the martial cavalcade of Coronado. Yet Oñate met every challenge, among them fierce battles with Pueblo Indians and desertion of most of his colonists, while prospecting at every turn. Assay results, however, belied the vast mineral potential he kept reporting to Mexico City. Finally after a decade, lamenting his expenditure of 600,000 pesos, Juan de Oñate resigned.

Wise counselors urged that New Mexico be abandoned. In reply, the colony's Franciscan missionaries swore abruptly to having administered

Christian baptism to upward of seven thousand Pueblo Indians. Surely a gross exaggeration, it served. The Spanish government straightaway converted the kingdom and provinces of New Mexico from proprietary to crown colony, assuming costs, appointing a salaried governor, and subsidizing a continued Franciscan ministry to seemingly tolerant Pueblo Indians. Because of New Mexico's unusual status as a missionary project, the friars wielded uncommon authority. Exercising a spiritual monopoly as the colony's only Roman Catholic priests, they also controlled the triennial supply caravans. Their dozens of missions, taken together, occupied the best arable lands, employed most Pueblo Indians, and ran more sheep than anybody else. Santa Fe, the colony's only chartered municipality, never amounted to more than a few hundred residents. Others lived in valleys as far north as Taos and especially downriver on several large properties, or *estancias*. While periodic epidemics and Apache raiding steadily dragged down Pueblo Indian numbers, the small Hispanic community of cousins procreated.

All alone in the far north, the friars' city of God on the Rio Grande, contested from within by governors and colonists who coveted Indian land and labor, endured for three generations until mission Indians tore it down. Driven to desperation by drought and colonial persecution, they rose in the monumental Pueblo Revolt of 1680, putting to death twenty-one Franciscans and hundreds of colonists. The surviving two thousand Hispanic men, women, and children, still greatly outnumbered, fled down the Rio Grande to El Paso. Exactly one hundred years later, the second Juan Bautista de Anza governed New Mexico.

During the 1690s, while Spaniard Diego de Vargas fought grimly to restore upriver New Mexico, other colonies crossed the line into the far north. Like New Mexico, each spread up from the south over well-worn migration routes resembling the widespread fingers of a hand with its forearm at Mexico City. Into these fingers flowed culturally Hispanic families, provisions, and the mail, always south to north and back, with virtually no east-west contact among them. Although every one of these frontier colonies sustained the familiar reciprocal triad of Indian mission, presidio, and town and depended on limited farming and extensive herding, each had its origin in a different year and purpose: New Mexico (1598, 1609), mining, Franciscan missions; southern Arizona (1691), Jesuit expansion; Texas (1690, 1716), countering French Louisiana; and Baja-Alta California (1697, 1769), securing the Pacific coast. And while the younger Anza bid heroically in the later eighteenth century to string webs of intercourse from one to another, colonial Santa Fe, Tucson, San Antonio, and Monterey remained firmly tied to the south, never to each other.

French colonial design, meanwhile, extending westward from the Mississippi Valley toward Texas and across the Great Plains in the direction of New Mexico, had goaded Spanish imperial strategists in Madrid and Mexico City to imagine New Spain's far north as a single, defensible outer frontier. The end of the European dynastic War of the Spanish Succession by treaty in 1714 assured efficiency-minded Bourbon Felipe V his throne and his empire. A half century later, when Great Britain replaced France as Spain's major rival for western North America, the enlightened Carlos III redoubled attention to the far north. And so it was during this eighteenth-century era of overarching imperial rivalry and everyday warfare with highly mobile Native groups that the Anzas, father and son, made their marks.

Inspector General Rivera liked young Anza. The resourceful Basque immigrant hailed from Hernani, a close-built cluster of three- and four-story stone houses half a dozen miles inland from Spain's animated north-coast port of San Sebastián. From there, Juan had likely sailed around 1712, toward the close of the War of the Spanish Succession. His father, Antonio, a pharmacist, businessman, and local officeholder, had lived his entire life in the same house. Juan's birth in that secure place on June 29, 1693, presented his parents a second child and, as time would tell, the eldest of four boys. As he grew, the lad took an interest in town affairs, learning at his father's side about property law and the court system and witnessing legal documents by age sixteen. Yet he sensed a wider world. Wandering about San Sebastián with a younger cousin, he visualized the marvels of the Spanish Indies. At the age of nineteen or twenty, Juan had emigrated. Within a decade, adhering to a centuries-old pattern, the cousin, Pedro Felipe de Anza, followed, joining Juan in the far north, where he oversaw the latter's mining and ranching interests.

Juan Bautista de Anza must have landed at humid Veracruz and made the ascent to New Spain's stunning viceregal capital, set in a bowl-like valley and lake and surrounded by perennially snow-clad volcanos. Passing through Guadalajara and on up the Pacific slope, a further land journey of seven hundred miles seems to have brought him to Culiacán in Sinaloa, where his mother had relatives. He cannot have stayed long. By 1718, he was fully invested with other old-country Basques four hundred miles farther north at a remote mining camp in the dry, gray-brown, mesquite-covered hinterland of Sonora.

The *real de minas* of Nuestra Señora de Guadalupe de Aguaje, a clutter of squat adobe structures, pole-and-mud huts, and tents, sat in a dusty depression between slopes punctured by hand-dug shafts. In January 1718, this restless camp was under inspection. Captain

Antonio Bezerra Nieto and his attendants examined, however diligently, account books and scales in Aguaje's ten stores or stacks of supplies, the shoring and condition of its seven mines, and payroll records. Most everything conformed to royal regulations, including the store and San Antonio Mine, owned by Juan Bautista de Anza. Another inventory of goods, also in compliance, belonged to a woman, Rosa de Sierra.

Captain Bezerra's parting decree, witnessed and signed by the literate Anza, required at least four workers continuously at each mine, threatened livestock thieves with forced service at the presidio of Fronteras, and forbade residents of all classes to carry knives and machetes. Fines went toward completing the Aguaje jail. Bezerra may also have turned recruiter, discussing with the promising, twenty-four-year-old Anza a career in the frontier officer corps. The rare peninsular Spaniard, energetic and of proven nobility and blood purity, made an ideal candidate. Don Antonio may also have foreseen the young Basque as a son-in-law.

Four years later, Ensign Juan Bautista de Anza wed María Rosa Bezerra Nieto. "Well-built, light-complected, with full beard and straight hazel hair," Anza had enlisted and now lived at his father-in-law's well-fortified, fifty-man garrison of Janos in Nueva Vizcaya, thirty miles due south of New Mexico's present-day boot heel. Above the presidio and farming community of Janos, the road divided, one branch leading north and east to El Paso and the other west into the province of Sonora via the unkempt presidio of Fronteras. Already Anza, deeply involved in Sonoran affairs, had enemies, none more tenacious than don Gregorio Álvarez Tuñón y Quirós, the mostly absentee captain for life of Fronteras.

Few groups of European compatriots hung together more tightly in foreign parts than Basques and their descendants. Natural allies of the equally enterprising Society of Jesus, or Jesuits, whose founders were Basque, they formed an imposing economic and political ring in Sonora. To ambitious non-Basques, these unholy associates seemed bent on monopolizing the province and controlling access to Indian laborers for mines and ranches. Álvarez hated them, vowing that he would, in the words of a Jesuit superior, not rest until all of them were burden bearers in his mine. During near civil war in the early 1720s, Anza, labeled by the opposition a notorious troublemaker, traveled to Mexico City as spokesman for the pro-Basque party. Previous complaints of malfeasance, meanwhile, had led to the arrest of Álvarez, then his acquittal. Recoiling, he turned up in 1723 with orders from the governor of Nueva Vizcaya to inspect the presidio at Janos, to which Anza had recently returned.

However smug the captain of Fronteras felt watching the mounted and fully armed troopers of Janos pass in review before him, he could find no ready fault with them, their commander, or Anza. They were a tough, efficient, battle-tested cavalry unit. Few presidios could measure up. The viceroy in Mexico City, in fact, had heard so many damning reports about the corruption and ill success of the frontier military that he requested permission from the crown for a general inspection. Royal authorization had come in 1724. As a result, in October 1726, Brigadier General Pedro de Rivera reined up at Janos. Except for the high price of goods deducted from the soldiers' salaries, he lauded the operation. If the inspector general was looking for an unfit officer of whom to make an example, he had to wait. He asked that Juan Bautista de Anza, now lieutenant of Janos, escort him and his party on to the presidio at Fronteras, still under nominal command of Gregorio Álvarez Tuñón y Quirós.

Fronteras lay in near ruin. Its captain had never lived on-site, choosing instead to reside far to the south at the headquarters of his mining hacienda. In effect debt peons, his demoralized troops rotated in service to him personally. Worse, Álvarez had been pocketing for years the salaries of phantom soldiers. The others rarely ventured out of their run-down adobe complex. Apache raiding parties, relying on the garrison's unpreparedness, entered with impunity through nearby passes, causing frightened colonists and Jesuit missionaries to complain loudly. Rivera listened. Formulating fifteen charges against Álvarez, the inspector general sacked him on the spot. Then—after composing a set of specific regulations that ranged from dress code, personal cleanliness, and attendance at mass to an order that troopers learn to use lances as the Apaches did—Rivera put Juan Bautista de Anza in command. Soon after lawyers in Mexico City lost Álvarez's case for a second acquittal, Sonora's deadly plague of 1728 struck down the Basque-Jesuit ring's most outspoken critic. At that, the crown imposed a posthumous indignity, appointing Anza to attach the multifarious Álvarez estate and ensure payment of a huge fine into the royal treasury before other creditors had their day.

While the thirty-three-year-old Captain Anza put his shoulder to revitalizing Fronteras, the defensive, rapid-strike-and-retaliate warfare with Western Apaches never let up. Efforts to attract certain bands to peace with food and gifts, much as captains had done on the Chichimeca frontier a century and a half earlier, proved transient. As if Apaches were not enough, authorities informed Anza that pacification of the fiercely defiant Seri Indians also devolved upon him. Nonagricultural fishing and foraging inhabitants of the Gulf of California's seared Sonoran coast, two hundred miles southwest of Fronteras, Seris interfered with pearl fishing and killed trespassers. Hence in 1729, Captain

Anza and thirty of his men joined the district officers of Sinaloa and Sonora, militia units, and Yaqui Indian auxiliaries in a campaign in which Anza commanded launches to invade the Seri refuge of Tiburón Island. A bold stroke, it hardly inconvenienced the Seris.

Besides warfare, the other constant in the captain's professional life was his special relationship with the Jesuits and his defense of their sprawling northwestern missionary enterprise. He knew the history. Beginning in 1591, stouthearted Jesuit missionaries had crossed the western Sierra Madre north of Culiacán. With their appealing material goods, faith, and charisma, they had proceeded relentlessly from one river valley to the next up the Pacific slope, converting to nominal Christianity a succession of Indian nations. The renowned Jesuit pied piper, explorer, and cartographer, Eusebio Francisco Kino, had reached today's southern Arizona exactly a hundred years later, in 1691.

Over the next two decades, Father Kino mounted dozens of expeditions, often escorted by Lieutenant Juan Mateo Manje, crisscrossing along Native trails a desert-and-jagged-mountain expanse called the Pimería Alta, land of the Upper Pima Indians. He ventured north as far as the valley of the Gila River and west to the Colorado, which with the aid of Native swimmers he crossed in a big basket balanced on a raft. Watching the sunrise over the head of the Gulf of California, Kino certified that Baja California was a peninsula, not an island after all. He envisioned a Spanish town where modern Yuma, Arizona, sprawls today. He urged that Jesuits advance northeastward to the Hopi Pueblo Indians, apostates from Franciscan Catholicism since the Pueblo Revolt of 1680. And he yearned to explore farther and cross on land to the Pacific coast of California.

Although Kino died in 1711, halting Jesuit expansion beyond the Pimería Alta, his protégé, testy old Father Agustín de Campos, imparted the vision to Juan Bautista de Anza. When Jesuits sought to reoccupy three mission stations that had been without resident priests since Kino's day, Anza smoothed the way, installing them in the spring of 1732: one at Soamca, just south of the Mexican-U.S. boundary; another at Guevavi, a few miles north; and the last at San Xavier del Bac, near present-day Tucson. Two years later, when mission Indians fled to the hills, Anza talked them back. He made the captain's quarters at Fronteras a hospice for sick Jesuits, where doña María Rosa attended them. She was pregnant with Juan Bautista the younger in 1736 when her husband took in distraught, sixty-seven-year-old Father Campos. The venerable priest had suffered a nervous breakdown, armed the Pimas of his mission, and vowed to fight to the death any superior who tried to force his retirement. Scandalously, he had also spoken ill of fellow Jesuits. Anza mediated a settlement, and Campos retired.

Figure 2.1: Eusebio Francisco Kino's culminating 1710 map showing the land passage to California. Bibliothèque Nationale, Paris. From John L. Kessell, *Friars, Soldiers, and Reformers: Hispanic Arizona and the Sonora Mission Frontier, 1767-1856* (Tucson: University of Arizona Press, 1976).

The two of them had talked long about Baja California, unique among provinces in the far north. Because the Society of Jesus had financed its occupation in 1697 and since then maintained it through a special Pious Fund, California belonged to the Jesuits. Inspector General Rivera had bypassed the presidio of Loreto since its captain and soldiers were Jesuit employees. All the same, the crown was pressuring the Jesuits to extend their sphere to the north and settle the bays of San Diego and Monterey as ports of haven for returning, Acapulco-bound Manila galleons. Kino and Campos had discussed how opening a supply route overland from Sonora could advance the project. Anza wanted that honor. When in 1734 desperate Pericú Indians at the southern tip of the peninsula rose and martyred two missionaries, the Jesuits were forced to look in the opposite direction. They requested that Captain Anza be put in command of a punitive expeditionary force. Sinaloa-Sonora's ambitious first governor, however, anxious to see what the Jesuits might be hiding in California, eventually crossed

John L. Kessell

the gulf himself. Anza, meanwhile, hoped that the overland way to California might be paved with silver from a freak bonanza in 1736.

In October of that year, a startled Yaqui Indian prospector, Antonio Siraumea, combing rough hill country southwest of modern-day Nogales, came upon large, partially buried chunks of silver. Word got around the mining camp of Agua Caliente, about a dozen miles away, and others swarmed to the site, laying hands on more slabs, one weighing in excess of a ton. Eager to maintain order, the local deputy magistrate, who lived next to Agua Caliente at a place he called Arizona, notified his district superior, who at the time was Anza.

How to explain this rare phenomenon? Were these irregular pieces of silver someone's previously hidden treasure? Did they result from illegal smelting? Or were they ore from natural veins? The answer would determine the king's share. When Captain Anza and a column of soldiers arrived, he ordered as many of the lucky miners as had not yet slipped away to appear, make declarations, and turn over the silver to him until Mexico City rendered a decision. Although he entertained pleas that the precious metal be returned, as presiding royal official he impounded it all and posted guards at the source. The resulting array of documents, executed in the home of Anza's deputy, bore Arizona as the point of origin. And because later officials mistakenly transposed the phenomenal discovery to that place, not only did the Basque word *Arizona* (the good oak) become synonymous with bountiful mineral wealth, but also subsequently the name of the Grand Canyon state.

From Fronteras, Captain Anza forwarded to the viceroy samples of the silver *planchas* or *bolas,* the documentary record, and a petition. He asked that he be granted license to explore north and west toward California, which he still believed could be an island. While he awaited answers, Anza found himself drawn as protagonist into the bizarre revelation of a self-proclaimed Native prophet of the god Montezuma.

The episode had begun with a major disruption in central Sonora as Native workers deserted missions, mines, and ranches seeking the blessings of this supposed holy man and healer. Spies reported that the Indian Agustín Aschuhuli was preaching a new order. Indians and Spaniards would exchange roles, the former being raised to owners and the latter reduced to workers. Aschuhuli demanded of his worshipers gifts and food for him and for his six pretty young female attendants, and a black-shrouded idol rigged to appear as if it were smoking cigars. The accompanying wild mix of ritual had perverted certain Roman Catholic practices. Hastening halfway across Sonora to the port of Guaymas, Anza apprehended Agustín, who confessed, blaming the devil. Absolved, executed, and hung from a tall palm tree, Aschuhuli served as an example. Finally, at the center of the affected region, Anza and a Jesuit priest, proclaiming the folly of adherence to the false god Montezuma, ceremonially burned the idol.

Ordered back to the site of the mysterious silver trove with mining experts, Captain Anza renewed the inquiry, concluding that the slabs were in fact ore from several veins, not treasure. That limited the king's share to the standard fifth, which Anza dutifully collected before returning the impounded metal. He supervised as well the registration of mining claims, first to the Yaqui discoverer and then to others. In Mexico City, the viceroy's chief adviser took exception. He had assumed previously that the find was ancient Aztec treasure and as such should be shipped straightaway to Spain. Juan Bautista de Anza and his alleged experts were obviously incompetents. The case demanded further investigation. But by then, the discovery had played out. As late as May 1740, the viceregal bureaucracy still had under advisement Anza's California project and a possible royal commendation for his decisive action against the false prophet. But during that month, Apaches closed Anza's career.

His legacy was secure, for about twenty years, until his son and namesake undeliberately began to eclipse it. Young Anza rose to command a presidio, then to govern a province. He fought dozens of battles with Apaches, Seris, and other Native adversaries and made peace with some. He led colonists overland to California. Both father and son, devout Spanish Catholics, benefited the Jesuits, underwrote presidial chapels at their posts, and administered tithe collection in Sonora and New Mexico. And like his father, the younger Anza carried out most orders of his superiors with dispatch. One royal decree, however, conveyed in strictest secrecy and concerning the Jesuits, caused him unspeakable agony. The elder Anza might rather have died.

The second Juan Bautista de Anza had grown up in the financially and socially safe world of his father's making. The boy's godfather and first cousin once removed, Pedro Felipe de Anza, possessed the Midas touch. Wherever Pedro Felipe ventured, into mines, merchandise, ranch land, or cattle, whether alone or as partner of any of a dozen intermarried Basques, he made money. He and Agustín de Vildósola, godfather of young Juan's sister Josefa Gregoria, shared in lucrative joint ventures in western Sonora, with small respect for indigenous peoples. When the elder Captain Anza died, Vildósola, the overall commander of provincial militia, found himself largely responsible in 1740 as Yaquis and allied Native peoples in southern Sonora conspired in a prolonged and sometimes violent protest against the Jesuit missionary regime. Upon Vildósola's final negotiated settlement, a grateful viceroy made him governor of Sonora, a post he occupied until 1748. Anza's widow, María Rosa, with her younger children, other kin, and servants, meanwhile, seems to have resided alternately at the mining town of Basochuca north of Arizpe and on one of the family's ranch properties along the present-day Arizona-Sonora border.

This next generation was no less closely interlinked. When Juan was ten, his sister Josefa Gregoria married a Vildósola at Basochuca. Another home-country Basque, Gabriel Antonio de Vildósola, took a father's interest in Juan. The boy was confident and quick. Someone taught him an elegant, studied penmanship. Also to shoot. In his mid-teens, with an eye on the frontier officer corps, Juan enlisted as an unsalaried cadet. He cheered Gabriel Antonio's appointment as captain at Fronteras in 1754. A year later, just shy of his nineteenth birthday, Juan Bautista de Anza the younger assumed duties as lieutenant at the presidio where he was born.

Unlike his peninsular Spanish father, who had to learn the ways of the frontier upon arrival, son Juan was raised on them, a cultural heir of Sonora's Basque-Jesuit establishment. Born in America, a *criollo,* he sought continually to prove himself in the eyes of Spaniards from the old country, who always considered themselves superior. Day to day on the frontier, however, as officer and *patrón,* the younger Anza dealt naturally with peers whom the community considered *españoles,* with Indians at his side and those he fought, and with mixed bloods of European, Indian, and African extraction who served on campaigns under him or as mine workers or vaqueros on his ranches.

Back in the spring of 1752, the chastened leader of an uprising among mission Indians of the Pimería Alta had turned himself in to soldiers camped at a place called Tubac, twenty miles north of today's Nogales, Arizona. Cadet Anza, with Captain Vildósola, had tracked the offending Pimas, evidently the young man's earliest military experience. In 1753, while the governor of Sonora blamed the Jesuits for the recent rebellion and they blamed him, laborers had laid up at Tubac enough adobes to form the province's newest presidio, hardly a fortress. When Tubac's first captain, the Basque Juan Tomás de Beldarráin, died in September 1759 from wounds sustained on campaign against Seris in the south, the vacant post went to twenty-three-year-old Juan Bautista de Anza. Purchasing the captain's house from Beldarráin's heirs early in 1760, he moved his mother in with him.

Hispanic Sonora's two-front war, with Apaches across the north and Seris and other resisters to the south and west, added campaign after campaign to Anza's service record and luster to his reputation as a brave and sure leader. His personal life filled the spaces between. In October 1760, he grieved the loss of his mother, doña María Rosa. The following spring, the young captain petitioned his superiors for permission to marry. With license in hand, on the feast day of his name saint, June 24, 1761, in the church at Arizpe, Juan Bautista de Anza wed Ana María Pérez Serrano, daughter of a Basque business associate of his father. Jesuit Carlos de Rojas, the priest who had baptized the groom, officiated.

Talk of horses, drought, and Apaches occupied locals even while the imperial bounds of North America shifted. By the European treaty of 1763, French sovereignty no longer overlay midcontinent. Louisiana west of the Mississippi, including New Orleans, had passed to Spain. Great Britain's colonial sphere now extended west as far as the river. Spanish imperial strategists wanted to know how much of interior North America could be defended against Englishmen and the various non-Christian Indian nations already disputing expansion northward. It had been forty years since New Spain's far north had undergone gulf-to-gulf, on-site scrutiny. A new inspection, carried out between 1766 and 1768, fell to the high-ranking Marqués de Rubí.

Ever since the concurrent founding in 1718 of French New Orleans and Spanish San Antonio, families of Spaniards had ventured deep into forested and humid east Texas to people a log presidio and capital at Los Adaes right up against the territory of France. With Louisiana's transfer to Spain, the Marqués de Rubí would recommend the painful withdrawal of established settlers from east to central Texas. The provincial capital would follow them to semiarid San Antonio, a tight cluster of presidio, town, and five missions. La Bahía, another presidial community, lay about ninety miles southeast down the San Antonio River in watered and open brush country. Laredo, too, had attracted a growing population after a Spanish empresario colonized the lower Rio Grande Valley. Spanish Texas, sparsely settled and widely spaced, favored cattle over people. While the colony no longer served as outer barrier to a European rival, it remained an endless open range to Hispanic *tejanos* and their Indian trade partners and foes.

The Marqués de Rubí, his staff, and caravan crowded Tubac at Christmastime in 1766. In disbelief, having reprimanded a string of presidial commanders who gouged their men at the company store, Rubí noted that Captain Anza was selling supplies at discount. The garrison appeared well equipped and trained. Although Anza complained repeatedly of unmet government payrolls, he had access to loans through his Mexico City supplier's circle of fellow Basque financiers. Because he owned nearby ranches, people considered Captain Anza a local patrón. So many neighboring families, especially from properties to the south, had moved to Tubac for fear of Apaches that Rubí reckoned they could defend themselves. Hence he proposed that Anza's company be relocated farther north, a project undertaken at Tucson a decade later.

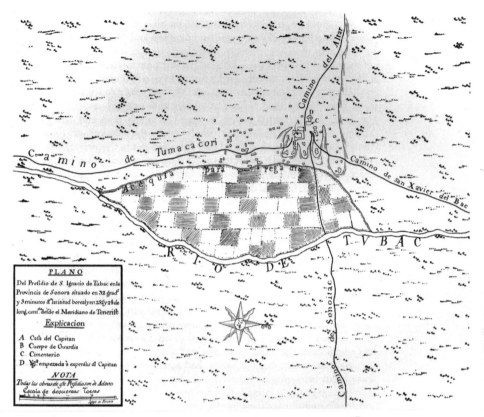

Figure 2.2: Lieutenant José de Urrutia's 1766 plan of the presidio at Tubac. British Museum, London. From John L. Kessell, *Mission of Sorrows; Jesuit Guevavi and the Pimas, 1691–1767* (Tucson: University of Arizona Press, 1970).

One of the few gripes of the soldiers at Tubac had to do with herding and guarding horses that did not belong to them. Anza, it seemed, had made a deal with the Jesuit priest at nearby Guevavi, a mission that supplied his presidio with beef and where his mother and Captain Beldarráin lay buried. The captain had offered to range the horses from Guevavi and two other missions with the presidial herd. The marqués decreed that the practice cease. Not long after the inspector departed, however, raiders made off with Guevavi's mares. Anza brought the rest of the mission horses back and put on a couple of Indian herders to care for them. Regulations be damned; neighbors came to understandings.

Like his father, Captain Anza recognized how intensely some of his acquaintances despised the Society of Jesus. Highly efficient, privileged, sometimes arrogant, Jesuits wielded disproportionate economic, political, and social power, especially in places like Sonora, where they were so concentrated. Earlier, in 1759 and 1764, the governments of Portugal and France, Spain's nearest neighbors, had banished all Jesuits from their dominions. But the Society was Spanish in origin. Surely Carlos III would resist his reforming ministers who wanted to expel the Jesuits on the grounds of their first loyalty to the pope and their abiding support of the old aristocracy.

An inscription across the sealed packet from Governor Juan Claudio de Pineda of Sonora read simply "Do not open until July 23." The secretive operation, begun with the king "locking away in his royal breast the reasons for his decision" and spread to the far corners of the empire in mid-1767 with near-infallible bureaucratic precision, now drew in Juan Bautista de Anza. The governor, availing himself of the Anza family's close ties to Sonora's Jesuits, ordered the captain of Tubac to Arizpe to arrest the father superior. Whether it eased or made more difficult their encounter, Father Carlos de Rojas had baptized and married don Juan. The captain's excuses made little sense as he escorted Father Rojas from mission to mission, collecting Jesuits en route south to Mátape, the designated detention center. There a royal official waited to read to them formally the king's decree of expulsion. A number would die in confinement, during a merciless voyage down the gulf, or on their forced march across New Spain to Veracruz for deportation. Shaken, Anza was back at his presidio by September 1.

He still owed money to the exiled priest of Guevavi. Since the government meant to seize all Jesuit assets, who precisely was he supposed to pay? The temporary agent placed in charge at the mission so mishandled its slim resources that Anza demanded the keys. All over Sonora, similar scenes unfolded. The disruption caused by crushing at one blow the province's most diverse and thriving corporation persisted for years. As for conventional, government-subsidized, semiautonomous Indian missions, the reformers thought they had a better idea, something like collective farms. Franciscan replacements would be granted a spiritual ministry only, while civilian overseers managed material affairs and discipline. Reaching Sonora in 1768, the first Franciscans let circumstances dictate. Ill provided and sparsely populated, most frontier missions simply could not support two masters, nor did mission Indians understand who to obey. Consequently, within months, the surrogate missionaries had regained full management, and reformers called for further study.

Juan Bautista de Anza responded. One of a number of officials required in 1772 to comment on proposed reform of mission administration, Anza apologized for any lack of understanding. Then, based on twenty years of close observation, he damned the missions of the Pimería Alta. Assuming Hispanic assimilation of Native peoples as the goal, he had seen little progress. Worse, whereas mission Indians once had numbered in the thousands, only hundreds survived. He laid most of the blame on excessive work demanded in the missions of formerly seminomadic peoples. In contrast, nonmission Indians seemed to be increasing in numbers. Anza had nothing to say about measles or small-pox, infant mortality, punishment in the stocks, or psychological trauma, nor did he mention the more reliable food supply, appeal of Spanish Catholic ritual, or protection afforded by the missionaries. If the missions were to attract heathen peoples in the future, argued the captain, they must undergo radical change.

Settling Spaniards within mission pueblos, establishing schools to teach the children Spanish, allowing mission Indians off the reservation to trade and seek outside employment, allotting to them private prop-erty, and consolidating small mission villages in formal towns of eighty to a hundred families—by all these means, Anza suggested, mission Indians would emerge from their backwardness. Sharing in the benefits of Hispanic civilization, they would also abandon thoughts of rebellion. Whatever humanitarian concerns may have motivated Anza, his response was also self-serving. He and his associates had long wanted freer access to mission Indians as consumers and workers. At the same time, the captain of Tubac wrote what he sensed the new viceroy's lead counsel wished to hear. Two months earlier, that same official, a member of Anza's Basque support group in Mexico City, had endorsed his pro-posal to lead an expedition overland to California.

Another more powerful government agent, archreformer José de Gálvez, the king's special envoy to New Spain, already had his eye on the far northwest. Gálvez had enjoyed expelling the Jesuits. Next he threw himself into the revitalization of Sonora and California, more suc-cessfully on paper than in the field. Taking up temporary residence in Baja California, he busily mapped out Spanish occupation of Alta California, something the Jesuits had failed to realize. Russian sea otter hunters coasting down from Alaska and English seamen seeking a northwest passage had lent the required urgency. Gálvez loved logis-tics. By sea, he ordered two ships to beat against contrary winds and cur-rents and put in first at San Diego and then Monterey. Simultaneously, a land party would mark the harsh six-hundred-mile track up the peninsula for Governor Gaspar de Portolá, fray Junípero Serra, and their train to follow. When at last scurvy-racked survivors embraced on the shore of San Diego Bay, it was July 1769. Within six weeks, Captain Anza at Tubac knew that coastal Indians in California had seen Spaniards with long muskets.

Much as he wanted to investigate in person, Anza had his orders to take part in Gálvez's grand but ultimately unsuccessful offensive against the Seris. While the captain campaigned, a potentially troublesome Franciscan explored. The friar could have got himself killed. Earthy but shrewd, fray Francisco Garcés had taken over at San Xavier del Bac, the northernmost mission formerly administered by Jesuits. On several occasions, the missionary ventured all but alone to the banks of the Gila, then downriver to its junction with the Colorado, and finally beyond far enough to make out distant blue mountains. Natives by signs relayed further intelligence of Spaniards to the west. Brave or foolhardy, Garcés, it appeared, could take care of himself. When Anza petitioned the viceroy from Tubac in May 1772 to lead half his garrison by land to California, he asked that Father Garcés be allowed to join them.

Officials who deliberated at Mexico City and Madrid remembered the similar proposal of Anza's father and made it part of the record. Now, with the precarious Spanish beginnings at San Diego and Monterey in jeopardy for lack of supplies, the time seemed right. Of greatest concern, even more than funding, was that Anza's passing not harm Native peoples along the route. No new settlement was planned, only a reconnaissance. Again thanks to his Basque connections in Mexico City, don Juan secured the necessary loans. The expedition's forty men, broken into smaller units as circumstances demanded, were gone from Tubac the first four and a half months of 1774. At the strategic Colorado River crossing, Anza presented Yuma Indian headman Salvador Palma a medal stamped with the likeness of Carlos III. Garcés, a nonswimmer and unwilling to trust his horse, let Yumas carry him across. Matching every challenge of dry camps, rocky ravines, and curious Indians, the captain of Tubac covered more than five hundred miles in ten weeks to the mission at San Gabriel, within today's greater Los Angeles.

The feat earned Anza a gala hero's welcome in Mexico City and promotion to lieutenant colonel from the hand of the viceroy. Although Father Garcés convinced a new governor of Sonora that a better trail could be found by ascending the Colorado River north of the Yumas to the latitude of Monterey, momentum lay with Anza. He now set about recruiting colonist families in Sinaloa and Sonora, outfitting the lot, and plotting their way to southern California and then up along the coast range to people San Francisco Bay. This commission too he carried off with élan. Taking leave of Tubac in October 1775, Anza led an exodus of some three hundred men, women, and children, among them a soldier escort, wranglers, scouts, camp hands, and cooks, to San Gabriel in about the same time as his previous trip. Although his second in command subsequently conveyed the colonists to San Francisco in 1776, Juan Bautista de Anza had personally chosen the site and unknowingly immortalized himself as the city's founder.

That same year, 1776, José de Gálvez, elevated to minister of the Indies upon his return to Spain, observed with pleasure royal implementation of a long-considered defense project he had made his own.

Figure 2.3: Juan Bautista de Anza's second California expedition sets out from Tubac, October 1775. Painting by Cal N. Peters. Courtesy of Tumacacori National Historical Park.

Recognizing that New Spain's far north lacked the wealth to support a full viceregal government, Gálvez urged a unified administrative and military jurisdiction to be known as the *Comandancia General de las Provincias Internas,* the General Command of the Internal Provinces. The governors of the six northernmost colonies—California, Sonora, Nueva Vizcaya, New Mexico, Coahuila, and Texas—would henceforth report not to the viceroy but to a commandant general. The new official would also assume overall command of the cordon of fifteen presidios set out roughly along the thirtieth parallel between the Gulf of California and the Gulf of Mexico. The presidial line, an expedient of the Marqués de Rubí, had been codified in the military regulations, or *Reglamento,* of 1772. Trouble was, virtually no roads going east or west bound the far north. Anza had made a start, joining Sonora and California. Yet he lived to see that linkage break and others come to nothing.

At a lavish reception in the viceroy's palace in early November 1776, powdered and bejeweled guests clustered around an odd attraction. Twice the hero, Juan Bautista de Anza had brought with him to Mexico City the Yuma headman Salvador Palma, his brother, and two other Natives. Palma had been decked out at royal expense in a uniform of shiny blue cloth with gold-trimmed scarlet vest. Three months later, after religious instruction, the four Indians processed for baptism into Mexico's City's cavernous cathedral, illuminated by thousands of candles.

The service might have been mistaken for a meeting of the Royal Basque Society. The celebrant and all four godfathers were Basque. Lieutenant Colonel Anza and his own godfather, seventy-eight-year-old Pedro Felipe de Anza, bound themselves ritually to Palma and his brother. En route home, the Native foursome appeared again at the center of an ornate ceremonial during their confirmation in the cathedral of Durango. Meanwhile, Carlos III had appointed Juan Bautista de Anza governor of New Mexico.

He had been warned. In high summer 1778, at a meeting in Chihuahua hosted by Teodoro de Croix, first commandant general of the Provincias Internas, Anza listened to a litany of woes from New Mexico's outgoing governor. He noted the facts. Including El Paso and its district, where the lieutenant governor resided, the province, with roughly twenty-five thousand souls dwelling in a recognizably Hispanic way, counted more than ten times the settled population of Texas, the Pimería Alta, or California. Increase in the eighteenth century had been natural for the most part, with little immigration. Collectively, New Mexicans, despite considerable racial mixing and blurring of class, saw themselves in two broad categories—españoles and Indians, the latter mainly inhabitants of twenty Pueblo Indian communities. New Mexico was poor. No mines or cash crops attracted outsiders or made rotations of Indian laborers a valuable commodity. Hence españoles and Indians lived and let live, each allowing the cultural identity of the other. Far removed from centers of power, exempt from sales tax, and battered by neighboring nonsedentary peoples, New Mexicans were a proud, self-dependent, and stubborn lot.

The new executive's caravan clogged the plaza in front of Santa Fe's mud-built palace of the governors in December 1778. Townspeople turned out to stare as this train of Sonoran Basques moved in. Although don Juan and doña Ana María had no children of their own after seventeen years of marriage, a source of abiding sadness, his older brother Francisco Antonio, married to Ana María's sister, had brought their two young girls. The governor doted on his nieces. Other relatives, retainers, and servants swelled the household. Never before had New Mexicans been governed by a native of the far north, rarely by a criollo. A few years earlier, no one would have imagined such a thing. The Bourbon policy of merit over lineage, which had benefited even José de Gálvez, favored the rapid rise of the second Anza. His reputation as military hero and pathfinder had preceded him. Nevertheless, New Mexicans withheld judgment.

Of his new subjects, none proved a greater source of information than retired captain, tradesman, cartographer, painter, and carver Bernardo

Figure 2.4: A portrait said to be Juan Bautista de Anza the
   younger, late nineteenth or early twentieth century.
   Courtesy of the Museum of New Mexico,
   neg. no. 50828.

de Miera y Pacheco. A peninsular Spaniard who had shown up at El
Paso in 1743 and subsequently moved to Santa Fe, Miera had served a
succession of governors. Better than anyone, he knew the difficult terrain southwest of New Mexico toward Sonora, through which Anza
intended to open a more direct trade route between Santa Fe and Arizpe.
Miera had also ridden with the little party of Fathers Francisco Atanasio
Domínguez and Silvestre Vélez de Escalante in 1776, hoping to find a
northern way to Monterey. It still angered him that they had turned
back. The new governor set Miera to work drawing a map of the colony,
finished in 1779.

Miera's map of upriver New Mexico told the tale. Its legend listed
by symbol not only chartered municipalities (Santa Fe, Santa Cruz, and
Albuquerque), dispersed settlements of españoles, pueblos of Christian
Indians, long-ruined pueblos, springs, and heathen villages, but also

settlements destroyed by enemies. A lengthy headnote described how the Spaniards' haphazardly scattered houses invited death and destruction at the hands of Comanche and Apache raiders. To illustrate the point, Miera retold a storied 1760 Comanche assault on colonists in the Taos Valley. The defenders put up a good fight, killing dozens of their assailants, yet all fourteen died and sixty-four of their dependents, young and old, were carried into captivity.

Although Anza had never met a Comanche, he been thoroughly informed about them. First mentioned in the documentary record of New Mexico in 1706, they had since become peerless horsemen and masters of the teeming buffalo herds of the south plains. From the beginning, Comanches had raided and traded in New Mexico, depending on their needs. During the 1760s, a respectful New Mexico governor had achieved a balance of commerce and peace with various elements of the Comanche nation, but his successor failed to maintain it. Commandant General Croix had discussed with Anza the desirability of forming an alliance with Comanches against Apaches. Since then, however, Governor Anza had learned of an obstacle, the hardened Comanche war leader known to New Mexicans as Cuerno Verde, second of that name, for a green horn sticking out of his headdress. These circumstances called for a different approach.

Why not an offensive in force, during late summer, when farmers were assumed to be in their fields and most vulnerable? Anza took personal command of many more men than had ridden on any previous Comanche campaign—nearly eight hundred, a majority of them Pueblo, Ute, and Jicarilla Apache Indians with whom spoils were to be shared equally. They ventured north up the west side of today's San Luis Valley in southern Colorado, then passed through the mountains to the Front Range, where Comanches were not expecting them. Their success resounded. North of present-day Pueblo, on August 31, 1779, the New Mexican force surprised and overran a crowded, half-made Comanche camp. Soon after, an outmaneuvered Cuerno Verde put up a brazen defense and died fighting. Anza rode home with the headdress and cause for promotion to colonel.

Within months of the new governor's signal victory, New Mexicans were complaining about him to Commandant General Croix. In the name of defense, Anza was upsetting their very way of life. Dutifully on his 1779 map, Bernardo de Miera had paraphrased the governor's decree that dispersed colonists consolidate, "building their ample square plazas of at least twenty families each in the form of redoubts, the small ones with two bulwarks, and the large with four." Worse, Anza proposed to raze part of Santa Fe, displacing its residents, and to relocate the plaza with government buildings, presidio, and attached barracks. Croix listened to a large, socially mixed delegation of aggrieved New Mexicans at his new headquarters in Arizpe. Taking their petitions under advisement, he instructed Anza to suspend consolidation for the time being.

On another matter as well, the commandant general reined in his energetic New Mexico governor. Croix wanted the Hopi pueblos, which had broken away in 1680, returned to the Spanish Catholic fold. Aware that they had been weakened by two years of severe drought, Anza proposed to bring the Hopis down from their mesas by force. The king, Croix countered, would never consent. The governor's relief expedition found Hopi families in desperate straits. And some accepted his invitation to resettle in the Rio Grande Valley.

Next, Anza tried unsuccessfully to find that more direct passage from Santa Fe to Arizpe. Although his column got there, campaigning against Gila Apaches en route, the one-way trip took almost six weeks and traversed terrain not conducive to regular travel. Unhappily, the governor's return to New Mexico coincided with the worst outbreak of smallpox on record, locally manifesting a pandemic that overspread much of North America between 1779 and 1781. More than five thousand New Mexicans died.

So drastic a decline in the colony's population suggested to Governor Anza a measure of economy. Smaller church flocks needed fewer shepherds. Hence by attaching diminished congregations to larger ones, the number of 330-peso annual government stipends to New Mexico's Franciscan priests could be reduced proportionately from twenty-six to twenty. That, more than any other grievance the friars had with Anza, propelled their representatives to Arizpe in protest. But since cost cutting was regularly rewarded by Bourbon administrators, the plan appealed to Croix. His own budget had been frozen since 1779, when Spain had joined France in war against Great Britain. The additional funding he had requested for the Provincias Internas had gone instead to Spanish forces operating against British posts in the Mississippi Valley and on the Gulf of Mexico.

Wartime economics also ruptured Anza's road to California. Like other projects, the fully garrisoned presidio, missions, and gifts promised to Salvador Palma's Yuma Indians at the strategic Colorado River crossing had to be scaled back. During the winter of 1780–1781, a grumbling contingent of Spanish settlers and their ravenous animals, along with the disapproving Father Garcés and three other Franciscans, had taken up uneasy residence among some three thousand Yumas. Abuses accrued. When the exasperated Indians rose in the heat of July 1781, killing the missionaries and more than a hundred colonists, government officials blamed Anza and the deceased Garcés for misrepresenting the Yumas' goodwill. The vision of a land bridge to California had once again faded.

Scarcely a month before the Yumas retaliated, forty soldier-colonists and their families en route to settle the pueblo of Los Angeles and a presidio at Santa Barbara had crossed successfully. They were the last. Alta California now depended on the sea. All the same, during the isolated colony's dozen years of trial since 1769, a temperate coastal environment and fertile soils blessed it. Surviving a violent rising of Ipai Indians at San Diego in 1775, Father Serra's mission regime prospered. Substantial stone and adobe walls replaced initial wooden palisades. As producers of surplus foodstuffs, the California missions supplied presidios and towns. Members of Indian families, however, enticed or coerced from their villages into the artificial compounds, lived an average of only twelve years. Outside, the several hundred culturally Hispanic *californios,* taking advantage of an unusually low infant mortality rate, multiplied steadily. The government's later plans to force convict and orphan relocation to California by sea proved disappointing.

In more populous New Mexico, Governor Anza's efforts to enforce laws customarily ignored struck at people's livelihood, especially those drawn to the colony's outer edges. Unlicensed trafficking in sheep, horses, hides and meat, variety goods, and captives with the so-called wild Indians encircling New Mexico—Utes, Navajos, Apaches, and Comanches—had become a lifestyle, upon which Anza meant to impose Bourbon order. Other mandates, for the citizens' own good, simply rankled. Adults who did not possess a firearm were required by the governor's order in 1782 to provide themselves with a bow and twenty-five arrows or face two months in the Santa Fe jail. So as not to discourage travel, Anza directed that families dismantle roadside shrines to victims of Indian attack. When the righteous governor tried to hold Franciscans to strict observance of the ban on personal Indian labor in the missions, friars joined the outcry. Soon enough, disgruntled New Mexicans found a willing ear.

Croix's replacement as commandant general, peninsular Spaniard Felipe de Neve, detested the decorated, American-born Colonel Juan Bautista de Anza. After meeting in Arizpe with another delegation from New Mexico, he wrote early in 1784 to José de Gálvez, accusing Anza of incompetence and recommending his dismissal. Furthermore, Neve demanded that Anza expunge from his service record that he had opened the overland road to California and had defeated Cuerno Verde. Since the next governor appointed in due course never reached New Mexico, Anza, who had requested reassignment, continued in office reluctantly. After Neve's death later in 1784, a succeeding commandant general set the record straight.

Anza's most enduring achievement was yet to come—a treaty of peace and commerce with the Comanche nation. Cuerno Verde's death

John L. Kessell

had begun the process. Drought, smallpox, and worrisome intercourse between Anglo Americans and Plains Indian rivals heightened Comanche initiative. Assassination of an heir to Cuerno Verde and the insistence of New Mexico's governor in the summer of 1785 that he treat ultimately with a representative of the entire nation led to a huge Comanche rendezvous on the Arkansas River that fall. Widely hailed, Ecueracapa, by the authority of his people, would talk as an equal with Anza about formal commerce.

Neither lost face. The ritual solemnity of this midwinter summit eased now and again into spontaneous shows of emotion. With military personnel, the Santa Fe town council, and leading citizens arrayed in the cold, Ecueracapa dismounted in front of the governor's palace and greeted Anza for more than ten minutes. The tense business inside of reconciling Comanche and Ute leaders ended auspiciously in a ritual exchange of garments. Later, the concourse wended its way eastward, surely through snow, to the symbolic site agreed upon earlier by emissaries. The gateway pueblo of Pecos, long a target of Comanche raids, in February 1786 looked out upon a scene of fervent peacemaking. A crowd of Comanches, estimated at over two hundred, mobbed the Spanish governor with such intimate expressions of affection that his staff thought them unbefitting. Anza did not object.

Terms of the treaty called for cessation of hostilities and a new and lasting peace. Comanches were allowed to move closer to New Mexico. They would enjoy safe passage through Pecos to Santa Fe, which implied a regular distribution of gifts and free trade at Pecos. In turn, Comanches pledged to join Spaniards as allies in the war against common Apache enemies. And finally, Anza agreed to bestow on Ecueracapa symbols of authority to certify the peace to Comanches not present. Next day, an inaugural trade fair went off splendidly. As surety, late that spring, the Comanche chief sent his twenty-year-old third son to Anza for a Spanish education. Before the governor left New Mexico, he evidently arranged for the young man's schooling in Mexico City. More remarkable, long after the passing of Anza and Ecueracapa, the Comanche peace of 1786 endured.

Although the governor's subsequent treaty legalizing commerce with Navajos and engaging them against Gila Apaches did not last, Anza could credit a sharp decline in violent deaths to the colony's four allied tribes: Comanches, Jicarilla Apaches, Utes, and Navajos. A new viceroy, with earlier experience in the far north, codified in 1786 instructions for peace by purchase, reminiscent of the waning years of the Chichimeca War two centuries before. Again, accounts for Indian affairs listed piles and crates of raw sugar cones, hard trade bread, ribbons, blankets, hats, and metal tools in government warehouses at Santa

Figure 2.5: Comanche war leader. Painting by Roy Andersen.
Courtesy of the artist and Pecos National Historical Park.

Fe and elsewhere. From Texas to California, the last decade of the eighteenth century and the first of the nineteenth were years of relative prosperity as populations recovered, flocks and herds swelled, small industries like weaving started up, and trade of all kinds flourished.

The talk of making him governor of Texas or transferring him to Spain as colonel came to nothing. When finally, in November 1787, Anza knocked the dust of Santa Fe off his boots, he was leaving behind his older brother Francisco Antonio, who had died two years earlier.

John L. Kessell

With the rest of his Basque household, don Juan made for Sonora, where he returned to active duty as commander of the presidio at Tucson and chief of military operations. Late the following year in Arizpe, anticipating a move to the presidio of San Miguel de Horcasitas in central Sonora, he sent doña Ana María, her widowed sister, and his two favorite nieces, now teenagers, ahead with an escort. He promised to follow in a few days. It was the last time they saw him. At midnight on December 19, 1788, Juan Bautista de Anza the younger, age fifty-two, died. The next day, while riders went to bring back his family, he was buried in the church at Arizpe.

News lagged. In November 1784, Governor Anza had reported to the commandant general that he had collected from New Mexicans 3,677 pesos in contributions to the war effort against Great Britain, unaware that diplomats in Paris had ended hostilities in due form more than a year earlier. By treaty, Great Britain had recognized the independence of its former colonies south of Canada, now the United States of America. Although Anza had been warned early in his governorship to watch for unauthorized Europeans on New Mexico's borders, he cannot have foreseen the shadow these erstwhile British colonials would cast across the far north. A mere decade after Anza's death, however, in 1798, the governor of Spanish Louisiana did. Apropos of these Anglo Americans, Manuel Gayoso de Lemos had a vision:

> First, they become acquainted with the Indians, trade with them, and afterwards engage in contraband trade with the natives of Mexico. Some stay in the territories. . . . They are settled in sufficient numbers so that they will establish their customs, laws, and religion. They will form independent states, aggregating themselves to the Federal Union, which will not refuse to receive them, and progressively they will go as far as the Pacific Ocean.

Indeed they would, little appreciating that everything they sought others had sought before them.

Essay on Sources

Late in the twentieth century and early in the twenty-first, Juan Bautista de Anza, father and son, have a new champion who, like them, is of Basque ancestry. National Park Service historian Donald T. Garate is writing their biographies in two volumes of the University of Nevada Press Basque Series. Don generously provided me with a copy of his manuscript for the first volume, *Juan Bautista de Anza: Basque*

Explorer in the New World, upon which I relied heavily. The book appeared subsequently in 2003. The author is at present working on the second volume. Garate's previous pertinent publications include "Who Named Arizona? The Basque Connection," *Journal of Arizona History* 40 (spring 1999): 53–82, and "Basque Ethnic Connections and the Expeditions of Juan Bautista de Anza," *Colonial Latin American Historical Review* 4 (winter 1995): 71–91. Seeking at the same time to introduce other scholars and enthusiasts of the Anzas to the culture of Sonora, Garate has been the moving force behind a series of World Anza Conferences held annually since 1996, most often in and around Arizpe, where the second Anza lies buried.

An older study, treating the elder Anza's special relationship with the Jesuits of Sonora, is Peter M. Dunne, "Captain Anza and the Case of Father Campos," *Mid-America* 23 (1941): 45–60. On military matters, the captain speaks for himself in "Juan Bautista de Anza Discusses Apache and Seri Depredations and the Need for a Presidio at Terrenate (1729–1735)," in *The Presidio and Militia on the Northern Frontier of New Spain: A Documentary History,* ed. Charles W. Polzer and Thomas E. Sheridan, vol. 2, part 1, *The Californias and Sinaloa-Sonora, 1700–1765* (Tucson: University of Arizona Press, 1997), 303–12.

Until we have Garate's inclusive biography of the second Anza, he will remain divided between Sonora, California, and New Mexico. While based in Sonora, he plays a prominent role in John L. Kessell, *Friars, Soldiers, and Reformers: Hispanic Arizona and the Sonora Mission Frontier, 1767–1856* (Tucson: University of Arizona Press, 1976). And from his post at Tubac, he takes a dim view in Kessell, ed., "Anza Damns the Missions: A Spanish Soldier's Criticism of Indian Policy, 1772," *Journal of Arizona History* 13 (spring 1972): 53–63.

Still at the head of the California list is Herbert Eugene Bolton's breezy *Outpost of Empire: The Story of the Founding of San Francisco* (New York: Knopf, 1931), supplemented by the diaries and other primary sources published in Bolton, ed., *Anza's California Expeditions,* 5 vols. (Berkeley: University of California, 1930). A library of popular retellings, authorization by Congress in 1990 of the Juan Bautista de Anza National Historic Trail (with its own newsletter, *Noticias de Anza*), and the launching in 1998 and recent development of the Web de Anza (http://anza.uoregon.edu/) have made Anza's two-phase overland passage to California by far the best-known episode in the Spanish colonial history of the American Southwest.

Serving as New Mexico's governor for a tumultuous decade was notably hard on Anza. Alfred Barnaby Thomas, ed., *Forgotten Frontiers: A Study of the Spanish Indian Policy of Don Juan Bautista de Anza, Governor of New Mexico, 1777–1787* (Norman: University of

Oklahoma Press, 1932), offers historical background and translated documents about Anza's dealings with Indian groups surrounding the colony. Rick Hendricks, "Church-State Relations in Anza's New Mexico, 1777–1787," *Catholic Southwest* 9 (1998): 24–42, explains how the governor offended New Mexico's Franciscan missionaries. The intended impact of administrative, judicial, military, and social reforms on all New Mexicans during the reign of Carlos III is examined in considerable detail by Carlos R. Herrera, "The King's Governor: Juan Bautista de Anza and Bourbon New Mexico in the Era of Imperial Reform, 1778–1788" (Ph.D. dissertation, University of New Mexico, 2000). Why the Bourbons' best-laid plans had so little effect, particularly on the colony's fringe populations, is evident in James F. Brooks, *Captives and Cousins: Slavery, Kinship, and Community in the Southwest Borderlands* (Chapel Hill: University of North Carolina Press, 2002).

Finally, to place the active careers of Juan Bautista de Anza, father and son, in the wider world of Spain's three-century-long colonial presence in North America, readers may wish to consult the text, notes, and bibliographies of David J. Weber, *The Spanish Frontier in North America* (New Haven, Conn.: Yale University Press, 1992), and John L. Kessell, *Spain in the Southwest: A Narrative History of Colonial New Mexico, Arizona, Texas, and California* (Norman: University of Oklahoma Press, 2002).

CHAPTER 3

Stephen F. Austin and Doña Tules

A Land Agent and a Gambler in the Mexican Borderlands

CHERYL J. FOOTE

Stephen F. Austin arrived in San Antonio de Bexar, the heart of Spanish Texas, in August 1821 to find the citizenry celebrating the news of Mexican independence. In Texas, as in New Mexico, Alta California, and the small outpost at Tucson, Spanish colonial rule had come to an end. Mexico's bloody conflict for independence lasted more than a decade before Spain reluctantly agreed to the Treaty of Cordoba, recognizing Mexico as an independent nation. Responses to the news varied widely on the northern frontier. Some *paisanos* (countrymen) were excited, but others hedged their bets until they saw whether Mexico could create a stable government. And still others may have wondered whether, or how, these faraway political changes would affect their lives. As Stephen Austin watched the revelry in San Antonio, he could not have known that twenty years hence, Texas no longer would be part of Mexico and that its new capital would be named in his honor. In New Mexico, doña María Gertrudis Barceló, a young woman in a small town along the Rio Grande, may have been more concerned about finding a husband than about the creation of a new nation. She hardly could have imagined that within two decades, she would be recognized as "a great lady and rich monte dealer of Santa Fe," the most famous woman in the territory.

Austin and Tules, as she was best known, prospered during the years (1821–1848) of Mexican rule in the borderlands despite differences in their backgrounds, methods, and accomplishments. Acquiring wealth, social status, and fame because of personal characteristics and drive, they also benefited from particular circumstances that emerged in Texas and New Mexico as a result of Mexican independence. Residents of the Mexican borderlands saw the beginnings of representative government, the opening of free trade, and an increasing foreign presence in the region, which ultimately led to Mexico's loss of about one half of its territory to the United States. In the process, most Hispanic residents of the region remained poor, while Native Americans found their nomadic lifestyles increasingly at odds with expanding settlements and finally were confined to reservations or disappeared altogether. Still, the Mexican period yielded greater individual opportunity for those, like Austin and Tules, daring or lucky enough to seize opportunities for self-advancement that also affected the fate of an entire region.

With independence, Mexico faced serious challenges. Spain or another European power might attempt to regain the territory. Mexico's economy was severely depressed because wealthy Spaniards had fled the country, and the war for independence had disrupted mining, ranching, agriculture, and trade. Internal disputes about the form and function of government also divided Mexican political leaders. Liberals, influenced by ideas of the Enlightenment, advocated individual freedoms and a decentralized government that would provide greater local autonomy, a broad-based electorate, and a reduction or abolition of special privileges for the wealthy, the Roman Catholic Church, and the military. Conservatives, in contrast, argued for a strong central government that protected these traditional institutions. Complicating the debate was Mexico's low literacy rate (barely 5 percent of its population could read and write) and lack of experience with representative government. As a result, political stability did not follow independence. Within three years, Mexico had abandoned a constitutional monarchy in favor of a republic, but conflict continued. Between 1833 and 1855, as historians Michael Meyer and William Sherman have noted, the "presidency [of Mexico] changed hands thirty-six times," keeping much of the country convulsed in civil unrest.

Mexico struggled to create a unified nation out of a vast territory that lacked good routes for internal communication and trade. Correspondence took months to reach the north, so that laws had been reversed or abolished before they reached the desks of the officials who were supposed to implement them. Foreign influence on the northern frontier was another pressing concern. Along the Pacific coast north of San Francisco the British and the Russians had established fur trading outposts, and Americans too clamored for territory and trading rights. East of the scattered missions of Alta California stretched the unsettled reaches of today's Arizona, Nevada, Utah, and Colorado. The largest population of Hispanic settlers in the northern borderlands lived in New Mexico, threatened by sporadic but deadly warfare with the Navajos, Apaches, Comanches, and Utes. And Texas, the easternmost of the borderlands since the United States purchased Louisiana in 1803 and Spain ceded Florida to the United States in 1819, now formed the bulwark against the Americans in the Mississippi valley.

Cheryl J. Foote

In contrast to Mexico, the young United States boasted an emerging market economy, a stable government, a propensity for territorial expansion, and a booming population. In 1800 the U.S. population was 5.3 million; twenty years later, it had climbed to 9.6 million. Mexico meanwhile lost 10 percent of its inhabitants during the war for independence, resulting in a population of 6 million people in 1820. Most *mexicanos* lived in the center of the country, leaving the frontier sparsely settled and vulnerable to foreign conquest. Unlike Americans, who saw opportunity in the new lands of the West, residents of Mexico saw little to be gained from living on the periphery. Settlers there engaged in subsistence farming and stock raising, and only a few garnered enough wealth to merit the designation *rico*. The Spanish mercantile system had prohibited trade with foreigners, and paisanos legally traded only with Mexico and with nomadic Indians, whose raids further discouraged settlement.

Now the Mexican government determined that the nation's economic recovery and internal security depended on the settlement and economic advancement of the northern frontier. Abandoning the mercantile policy of Spain, Mexico opened trade with foreign nations and developed a series of duties and taxes on trade to finance the government. Mexico also retained policies developed in Spain's last years as a colonial power to attract settlers to Texas, designed to create a buffer between nomadic Indians and the more heavily populated Mexican heartland as well as to obstruct American intrusion into the area.

When Stephen Austin first came to Texas in 1821, 2,500 Hispanics resided in the province, nearly all of them at San Antonio de Bexar and at La Bahia (now Goliad). Nacogdoches, three hundred miles away and the easternmost settlement in the province, was almost a ghost town. Comanches, Karankawas, Tonkawas, Wacos, and Tawakonis also lived in Texas, but as nomadic peoples they were considered outside of Spanish or Mexican jurisdiction. One positive development, from Mexico's perspective, was that in 1819 the United States signed the Transcontinental Treaty with Spain, abandoning its claims that Texas was part of the Louisiana Purchase and setting the southwestern boundary of the United States at the Sabine River. But would Americans, hungry for land, respect the boundary? If not, could Mexico protect its border? Clearly central and eastern Texas must be settled—and if not by Mexicans, then by foreigners—even Americans, who, in exchange for generous grants of land, would serve the needs of Mexico by preventing *unsanctioned* American entrance to the region.

On the eve of Mexican independence, Moses Austin was one American who had his eye on land in Texas. He had concluded an agreement with Spanish authorities that permitted him to bring three hundred American families to colonize Texas, but he died before he

Figure 3.1: Stephen F. Austin, early Texas leader and land agent,
engraving. Courtesy of the Texas State Library and
Archives Commission.

could do so. His son Stephen had not been receptive to his father's latest
venture; still, his strong sense of responsibility for his family's well-
being convinced him to see for himself what prospects the plan offered.

In 1821, Stephen Fuller Austin had behind him more than a decade
of business, military, and political experience on the Missouri frontier. His
father, Moses, was a Connecticut Yankee who had married Mary (Maria)
Brown in Philadelphia before settling in Richmond, Virginia, where he
owned a mercantile company. Soon Moses expanded his business interests into a lead mine in southwestern Virginia, and on November 3, 1793,
his son Stephen was born nearby. Three years later, Moses Austin had
borrowed heavily for his businesses and was deep in debt. Perhaps he
could move west and start over, as so many Americans did. Hearing of
unexploited lead deposits in Spanish Upper Louisiana (now Missouri),

he applied to the Spanish government for a land grant and moved his family there in 1798. He started another lead mine and traded with the Indians of the area. Within a decade he had amassed a fortune.

The frontier of eastern Missouri in the early nineteenth century brought young Stephen Austin into regular contact with French settlers as well as Spaniards, Native Americans, and African American slaves. From this experience with people of different cultures, Austin developed attitudes of tolerance that served him well later in life and set him apart from many other Americans of his day. He was also well educated, having attended school in Connecticut and Transylvania University in Kentucky. By 1810, though, his father was again in financial trouble. Stephen left college, and for the next ten years he operated the mines for his father and tried to make them pay while his father ventured into banking and commerce. During the War of 1812, Stephen joined the Missouri militia, organized primarily to quell Indian uprisings, and at the end of the war he entered politics, serving five terms in the Missouri territorial legislature between 1815 and 1820. As a legislator, he displayed the enlightened self-interest that Alexander Hamilton had advocated, marrying his own business interests to what he deemed the best interests of his constituents. Both Stephen and his father became well-regarded members of their community, but the family fortunes continued to decline. Eventually Moses Austin's mines and other properties were sold at public auction.

Determined to restore the family to solvency, Stephen Austin moved to Arkansas, speculated in land, and gained appointment as a circuit court judge. But these efforts provided no immediate solution to the family's precarious financial state. While Moses Austin cast his gaze on Texas, Stephen sought employment in New Orleans. Then his father died, and twenty-seven-year-old Stephen Austin felt the full weight of family responsibility on his shoulders. His widowed mother, his sister and her husband, and his brother all looked to him to carry out his father's plans. So did Joseph Hawkins, a business partner of Moses and a mentor to Stephen. Thus in the spring of 1821, Stephen Austin traveled to Texas to assess for himself the potential of his father's plans.

There officials assured him that his father's contract would be honored even with the change in government resulting from Mexican independence. Now Austin hastened to explore the unsettled lands east of San Antonio. He grew excited as he saw the agricultural potential of the area. Fertile soil, numerous rivers, and proximity to the coast made the region well suited for stock raising as well as raising cotton and food crops for export to the rest of Mexico and the United States. The area between the Brazos and the Colorado formed the center of this first colony and included Galveston and Matagorda bays, where

Austin hoped to open ports to facilitate trade. Any hesitation he had felt vanished once he realized the potential that Texas offered. Immediately he began to advertise in newspapers along the American frontier for families who could furnish proof of good character to come to Texas. Even though he had to borrow more money to launch the project, he was confident Texas would pay off.

Austin's optimism continued as his first colonists arrived in Texas, but he soon learned that authorities in Mexico questioned the validity and terms of his contract. On the advice of sympathetic local officials, Austin headed for Mexico City to petition the new government in person. From March 1822 to June 1823 this unusual frontiersman advanced his cause. Physically he was not an imposing man. His nephew described him as "slender, sinewy, of graceful figure . . . [with] dark hair . . . [and] large hazel eyes, fair skin when not sun-burned, about five feet eight or nine inches in height." He dressed well, rather than in frontier garb, and displayed good manners and a quiet demeanor as well as a sharp mind. Above all, he possessed considerable diplomatic skills, preferring conciliation over confrontation. During his stay in Mexico, Austin spent his time wisely. He greatly improved his skills in Spanish, applied for Mexican citizenship, and cultivated political figures of all persuasions, making friends and useful contacts all along the political spectrum. His patience brought results, for despite another change in government in Mexico, Austin returned to his colony in June 1823 with his papers in order and a more clearly articulated position as the head of the colony. He was the only empresario (land agent) to receive a contract at that time.

Austin's contract permitted him to recruit settlers, distribute land, and act as intermediary between the colonists and the Mexican government. In his colony, he was required to provide local government and justice and to serve as head of the militia. In return, Austin could collect a fee of one *real* (twelve and one-half cents) per acre from the colonists as well as receive land of his own from the government of Mexico. For their part, colonists pledged loyalty to Mexico and risked settling on the Texas frontier in return for an average of 4,428 acres of land, a seven-year exemption from customs duties, and a dispensation from other taxes for a decade. Many Americans in the southern states saw Texas as a chance for a new start, even with the fees they would owe Austin. In the United States, rapid speculation in western lands following the War of 1812, coupled with growing pains in the country's incipient industrial development, had brought about the Panic of 1819, a depression that resulted in the collapse of western state banks and foreclosure on those who had borrowed money to buy land. In 1820, to curb land speculation, the U.S. government set the price of

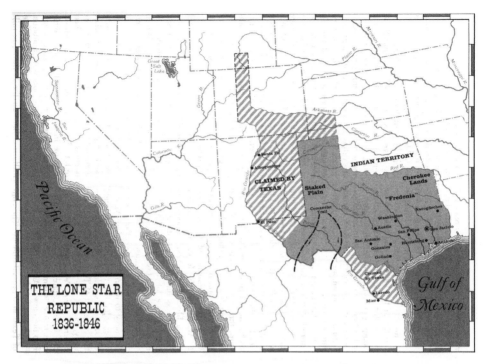

Map 3.1: The Lone Star Republic, 1836–1846. From Lynn I. Perrigo, *The American Southwest* (Albuquerque: University of New Mexico Press, 1975), 125. Courtesy of University of New Mexico Press.

public land at $1.25 an acre, raised the minimum purchase to eighty acres, and demanded payment in cash. Thus many Americans ruined in the Panic could not buy land on credit and start over, at least in the United States. But like Stephen Austin, they could leave their obligations behind, start a new life in Texas, and hope to prosper.

Still, immediate gain eluded both the empresario and his colonists. When Austin returned from Mexico in 1823, he found settlers contending with drought-induced crop failures and increasing problems with Indians. Many planned to abandon the venture, but Austin convinced most to stay. Next some settlers balked at paying Austin his fee, so Mexican officials removed this condition of settlement, leaving Austin to pay for surveys and land titles without recompense. Others complained that he showed favoritism toward certain colonists, including his brother, and provided them with larger amounts of land. Responding to these charges, Austin avoided inflammatory rhetoric and worked toward conciliation, deflecting most of the criticism and ensuring that his colony would endure.

Still, by the time he had fulfilled his first contract in 1824, Austin had nothing to show for his work other than twenty-two and a half leagues of land that he received from the Mexican government. In later years, this would be valuable property; then, he was no closer to solving his family's financial problems than when he first arrived in Texas. His faith in the potential of the venture remained unbounded, though, and he applied for a second grant to locate five hundred families. Eventually he received a total of five grants attracting an estimated five thousand American settlers, and his colony became the most successful one in Texas.

Several factors made this so. First, the land itself was some of the best agricultural land in Texas. Second, Austin's colony had few problems with the Indians since he preferred to deal with them through diplomacy rather than force. Also, in his colony Austin established representative government to provide settlers a voice in local affairs as well as a justice system that introduced some American features within the strictures of Mexican law. Finally, Austin's facility with Spanish, his preference for negotiation rather than confrontation, his relative freedom from prejudice toward Mexican settlers and leaders, and his comprehension of the realities of Mexican law and politics uniquely suited him to thrive where others failed.

For Austin, peopling Texas with industrious American settlers promised economic and permanent social development on this Mexican frontier. Although his initial interest was to rescue his family from financial troubles, Texas increasingly assumed a new significance for Austin. He had never married, remarking to relatives that he needed first to establish financial stability and see his colony secure before he would consider such a step. Then, following his father's death in 1821, Austin lost his brother-in-law, his mother, and his mentor, Joseph Hawkins, in the next three years. His widowed sister, Emily, whom Austin hoped to bring to Texas, chose instead to remarry and remain in Missouri. (She and her second husband finally moved to Texas in 1831.) And then his younger brother, Brown, who had accompanied him to Texas and been his closest confidant, died suddenly in 1829. Deprived of his dearest family members and friends, Stephen Austin channeled his emotional energies into the survival of another family, his colony in Texas.

By 1828, Austin and his colony were prospering. Under the provisions of his second and third contracts, settlers paid him fees directly, and he began to surmount his debts. Some contemporaries charged that he profited at the expense of his colonists or that his devious dealings with Mexican officials deprived other entrepreneurs of similar opportunities. Later historians, particularly those of Mexico, also charge him with duplicity, arguing that his loyalty to Mexico was fraudulent and self-serving. In reality, it appears that Austin often acted generously

Cheryl J. Foote

with other empresarios and aided many settlers who came to Texas even if they were not his colonists. He was also loyal to Mexico until events convinced him that the interests of Mexico and those of Texas no longer coincided.

Austin and his colonists were not the only Americans to recognize potential in Texas. Eventually twenty-five empresario grants were approved, though only a handful were successfully developed and none prospered as did Austin's. Many Americans also began to move to Texas independently, squatting on whatever unoccupied land they came to. Conflict over land titles loomed on the horizon. One empresario, Haden Edwards, lacked Austin's generous and conciliatory nature and his loyalty to Mexico. In 1826, dissatisfied with the terms of his contract and with the difficulty of settling land titles within his grant, Edwards launched a rebellion against the Mexican government. He called for the creation of the Republic of Fredonia and tried to enlist Austin and his colonists in the plan. But Austin would have none of it. Instead his militia joined with the Mexican army in putting down the revolt, demonstrating Austin's and his colonists' loyalty to Mexico. Next Austin convinced Mexican authorities to treat leniently the captured insurgents, which won him approval from other Americans in Texas, who feared that Mexican reprisals might be directed against them as well as those in Edwards's camp.

The Fredonian Revolt refocused the attention of Mexican leaders on the issue of American colonization in Texas at the same time that the American government was turning its gaze there. Already the United States had begun to press for an adjustment of the boundaries set under the Transcontinental Treaty of 1819. Then in 1827 the United States made its intentions even clearer by offering to buy Texas. The colonization of Texas was succeeding, to be sure, but Mexican politicians now questioned the wisdom of allowing further emigration from the very country seeking to acquire Texas. As Edwards's rebellion indicated, not all emigrants would retain the loyalty to Mexico that they once had professed.

Mexican politicians unanimously determined to hold on to Texas and the rest of the northern borderlands, but by 1828 their disagreements over other issues initiated a chaotic period in Mexican politics. Liberals advocated a federal system, with most of the power residing with local governments. Centralists, like the Federalists in the early American republic, desired a strong central government with minimal power assigned to local institutions and drew strong support from the elites in Mexican society as well as the Church and the military. In 1824, liberals had gained the upper hand and drafted the Constitution of 1824, establishing a federal system of states and territories that promised greater local control. Under that document, Texas became part of the state of Coahuila y Texas. Stephen Austin approved of the constitution because it resembled a proposal he had written during his stay in Mexico in 1823 and perhaps discussed with Mexican political leaders. In fact, Austin hinted that his plan was the basis for the federal system adopted, but historians have suggested that Mexican leaders independently came to conclusions similar to his. In any event, under the Constitution of 1824 most of the regulation of colonization and the disposition of public lands had fallen to the states, and Austin had benefited under the system. Still, like others in Texas, he looked forward to the time when Texas could attain statehood independent of Coahuila and enjoy greater self-government.

In 1829, a revolt in Mexico placed a centralist in the presidential chair, and the Mexican congress moved to centralize control of the borderlands. The national colonization law of April 6, 1830, forbade further emigration into Texas from the United States, prohibited the future importation of slaves, and encouraged Europeans and Mexicans to colonize and secure the borderlands. Austin, in the process of bringing new settlers to Texas under his latest contract, quickly sought an exemption from the new legislation. Once again, he brought his considerable skills to bear on the issue. Mexican officials permitted him to complete his contract and even though Mexico had abolished slavery nationally in 1829 allowed his colonists to bring slaves to Texas. But for how long? Austin knew that although most Americans had not brought slaves to Texas, those who had or those who might be contemplating moving to Texas would oppose any future interference in their right to slave property. Austin himself had owned slaves, and though not a strong proponent for slavery, neither did he seek to end it. He believed that the right to bring slaves to Texas must be guaranteed because cotton—dependent on slave labor—offered the greatest potential for an exportable crop for his colony.

In spite of the new colonization law, the rush of American emigrants to Texas continued unabated. Historians estimate that perhaps 10,000 Americans had moved to Texas by 1830; four years later, more than 20,000 Americans resided in Texas, compared to perhaps 3,000 Hispanic *tejanos*. These Americans, most of whom came to Texas illegally, lived in central and eastern Texas, away from the Mexican communities of San Antonio de Bexar and Goliad, and had little interest in assimilating to Mexican culture. Instead they wanted greater autonomy to regulate their own institutions, particularly the right to own slaves, and they could best do that through statehood. There were other issues at stake as well. In 1832, Americans in east Texas led another rebellion against customs officials, and again Stephen Austin threw his support behind the Mexican government in subduing the revolt. As

Cheryl J. Foote

these divisions among the settlers in Texas deepened, some recent arrivals favored open defiance of the centrist government in an effort to gain statehood. Austin, on the other hand, wished to avoid military action and advocated more conciliatory means to achieve statehood within the Mexican republic. A minority in Texas had begun to agitate for separation from Mexico, either to create an independent Texas or to seek annexation to the United States.

Meanwhile, in Mexico in 1833, Antonio López de Santa Anna led a revolt against the centrist president, declared himself a federalist, and restored a liberal presidency. The following year he switched sides, took control of the government, renounced liberalism, and directed a new congress to enact a centralist constitution to take effect in late 1835. As Santa Anna was moving the country away from local control, American residents in Texas had called an extralegal convention to advocate for immediate statehood. The convention sent Stephen Austin to Mexico City to present their petition and to argue for repeal of the colonization law of 1830. Once again, in April 1833, Austin headed south in the service of his adopted homeland.

This time Austin's luck ran out. In Mexico City, he lobbied Mexican officials without result and fell victim to the terrible cholera epidemic that claimed thousands of lives. Austin survived, but he was weak and despondent. The political turmoil in Mexico, as well as the growing sentiment in Texas for separation from Mexico, had ominous implications for his quest. In a letter to associates in Texas that fell into the hands of Mexican officials, Austin suggested that if Texas were to remain a part of Mexico, Texans must take the initiative to create a state government on their own instead of waiting for permission from the central government in Mexico City. Mexican officials considered this seditious and arrested Austin in January 1834. For the next eleven months, he was held without charges and without trial before he was released on bail. Another seven months elapsed before he was permitted to return to Texas.

During his absence, Texans had watched the centralist shift of the Mexican government resentfully. Many favored rebellion against Santa Anna's government in hopes of restoring federalism and with it statehood for Texas. A minority, particularly recent arrivals from the United States, muttered about independence from Mexico. Austin, of course, had always intended that Texas agitate for statehood within the Mexican nation, but during his incarceration he had become disillusioned with the conflicts in Mexico. Now he was convinced that the best course for Texas lay with independence, though he was not yet prepared to make such a declaration publicly.

While Austin made ready to leave Mexico, a revolt against Santa Anna broke out in Zacatecas; others threatened to erupt across the frontier, especially in Texas, where Santa Anna dispatched Mexican troops under the command of General Martín Perfecto de Cos to Texas to maintain peace. As Santa Anna later learned, threatening to use military might against the colonists in Texas was a mistake. Hearing that an army of occupation was on its way, they united, resolved to keep Cos and his army out of Texas. In October 1835, a small party of Texans fired on Mexican troops at Goliad, and even Austin agreed that the time had come to take up arms in self-defense. Still, he and others believed that declaring independence was too risky unless thousands of Americans flooded into Texas in the next several months to strengthen Texan forces. Austin hoped they would.

Thus the provisional government, still professing loyalty to the federalist system and the Constitution of 1824, issued a call to arms. Stephen Austin, in poor health from his months in Mexico, took command of the militia and marched toward the enemy. He found Cos occupying a fortified position in the Alamo, an abandoned mission in San Antonio de Bexar. Austin and his officers disagreed about their next step. Austin preferred to negotiate with Cos to effect his withdrawal from Texas; others favored an assault on the Mexican forces. And then word arrived that the provisional government, though delaying an outright announcement of independence, had chosen Stephen Austin as one of three commissioners to seek money and support for the Texas cause in the United States. Austin turned over his command of the militia and departed for the States.

Although Austin clearly was a better diplomat than a military leader, his mission met with limited success. The commissioners secured some loans, but much of their work was hampered because they did not know if, or when, Texas had declared independence. Without that announcement, the United States was reluctant to provide any official aid to the rebels. Also, Austin's absence from Texas during the next crucial months later led to criticism that he was enjoying a comfortable life in the United States while his fellow Texans bled and died at home.

In fact, after Austin left, military leaders attacked Cos's troops and forced him to surrender the Alamo in early December 1835. Elated with this good news, many Texans concluded that the struggle was over and went home. But Santa Anna would not allow this affront to Mexican honor to go unavenged. Taking command of some 6,000 troops, the president of Mexico arrived in San Antonio in late February 1836 to face the small force of Texans occupying the Alamo. Santa Anna's advance caught Texas leaders by surprise; they were not prepared, and their disorganization cost some Texans dearly. Although many American frontiersmen had flocked to Texas during the winter months, as Austin had hoped, most of them were not in the Alamo. And none arrived to reinforce the garrison in San Antonio before March 6, 1836, when Santa Anna's troops attacked. Suffering heavy casualties, the Mexican force overran the Alamo and took no prisoners. More than 180 men fighting for Texas died.

The defenders of the Alamo died in the cause of Texas independence, although neither they nor Stephen Austin had heard that on March 2, 1836, the provisional government had proclaimed the independence of Texas. When the news reached Santa Anna, it strengthened his resolve. Fresh from victory in San Antonio, Santa Anna's army marched unopposed farther east into Texas as colonists fled their homes in terror. Finally, on April 21, 1836, the Texan army under the command of Sam Houston defeated Santa Anna at the Battle of San Jacinto. Texans captured Santa Anna, who agreed to sign the Treaty of Velasco, recognizing Texas independence and agreeing that Mexican troops would retreat beyond the Rio Grande.

Two months later, Stephen Austin returned home. Although his own affairs had been badly neglected and required his attention, he was vitally interested in the future of Texas. He met with the captive Santa Anna and urged that he be returned to Mexico. In July Austin agreed to run for the presidency of Texas, promising to direct his efforts toward annexation to the United States. Certainly he had been the best-known and most widely respected figure in Texas, and he likely expected to win the presidency as a reward for his many efforts and sacrifices for the country he had so influenced. But now old grievances surfaced. Critics charged that Austin had engaged in unscrupulous business dealings, that he had abandoned Texas during the battle for independence, and that he was urging the release, not the execution, of Santa Anna. Even so, Austin might have carried the day. However, two weeks before the election, the hero of San Jacinto announced his candidacy. Sam Houston easily won the presidency, with more than ten times the votes that Austin garnered, and Austin retired from public service.

In the next several months, Austin devoted his time to his personal business and his nieces and nephews. In the fall Houston appointed him secretary of state for the Republic of Texas, and although Austin was very ill, he took the responsibility seriously and began correspondence with the United States. Then in early December, he caught a cold that lingered, and on December 27, 1836, Stephen Austin died at the age of forty-three.

He left behind grieving friends and family members and an estate valued at more than $500,000. He had gone to Texas to provide financial security for his family, and this he had accomplished. He had also been the person most responsible for populating Texas and for guiding its growth for more than a dozen years. His loyalty to Mexico endured until he came to believe that Mexico's internal conflicts retarded Texas's development. Then he supported Texas independence. Faithful to his own family, dedicated to the success of Texas, Austin was one who prospered on the Mexican frontier and shaped the history of a region as few others have.

The independence of Texas, and the area's eventual annexation to the United States in 1845, confirmed Mexico's worst fears while the country's chaotic political disputes drained energy and focus from the problems on the frontier. As Texas separated from Mexico, the same forces—expanding trade with foreign nations, efforts to populate remote regions as a buffer against foreign intervention, and political turmoil in Mexico—also affected Mexico's remaining borderlands, though to varying degrees. The least inhabited of these was today's Arizona. Under Mexico's Constitution of 1824, this was the northern tip of the Mexican state of Sonora; no settlements lay north of Tucson, and only a thousand or so Hispanic settlers lived between Tucson and the present U.S.-Mexican border. Tubac and Tucson were military outposts, with the two missions of San Xavier del Bac and San José de Tumacacori serving several hundred Pima Indians. Nearby, Hispanic settlers farmed, ranched, and mined for gold, silver, and copper, mindful of the Western Apaches, who often had been a serious deterrent to settlement.

Because Sonora lacked the agricultural potential of Texas and did not share a border with the United States, Mexico did not initiate colonization programs for the region. Moreover, foreign interest in northern Sonora was limited. In 1825, American trapper James O. Pattie came to trap beaver along the Gila River, and in later years more American trappers followed his lead. New Mexico traders also passed through present-day Arizona, trading sheep for horses in California, but they traveled across the northern reaches of the present state. Neither New Mexicans nor Americans stayed to establish permanent settlements. Although Sonora revolted against Santa Anna's centralist regime, no movement to separate from Mexico emerged. Instead of considering independence, settlers near Tucson and Tubac fought for their very existence against the renewed raids of the Western Apaches. Many retreated to the south, and the settlements were nearly abandoned.

In contrast, Alta California's Hispanic population more than doubled during the Mexican period, from about 3,200 to 7,000, and more than 21,000 Indians lived under the supervision of the Franciscan friars in the twenty-one missions near the coast between San Diego and Sonoma. Perhaps another 100,000 Natives lived in the central valleys of California, outside of Spanish or Mexican jurisdiction. Accessible only by sea, California was the most remote of Mexico's possessions, sparsely

Cheryl J. Foote

populated, vulnerable to foreign intervention, and desperately in need of economic development. Yet Mexico did not adopt the empresario system for California as it did in Texas, largely because most of the coastal lands remained under the mission system. Franciscan friars strongly resisted the move to secularize the missions, whereby some of the mission lands would be given to the Indians and the rest opened for private development. When this happened, the friars' oversight of the Indians would come to an end. Some in California feared that freed of missionary control, the Indians would revert to a life of paganism or, worse, turn to violence. Only after 1834, when the missions were secularized, did large land grants become available along the coast and gradually inland. Instead, after 1830, Mexican officials sent convicts and their families to increase California's population, a move that *californios* resented. Thus in California, land was not the magnet that initially attracted foreigners as it was in Texas. Instead the new policy permitting trade with foreigners opened the door to California.

So foreigners came to California, first in ships that plied the coastal waters for sea otter and later to trade in California ports for cowhides and tallow. In 1826 Jedediah Smith became the first American fur trapper to arrive in California from the Great Basin to the east. Soon others followed, as well as New Mexicans seeking markets for their sheep in exchange for mules and horses. In 1829, Antonio Armijo led the first party over the Old Spanish Trail from Santa Fe to the San Gabriel mission in California. Many New Mexicans were already familiar with much of the route, for they had traded into Utah for Indian slaves and furs since the Spanish colonial period. Some New Mexican families even relocated permanently to the San Bernardino area of southern California, citing their desire to avoid Indian warfare in their homeland. In general, though, fewer emigrants came to California than to Texas, and those who came more readily assimilated into the population of Mexican California than formed separate enclaves. Still, their presence reduced California's isolation and served to orient California's economic development toward the United States. This, coupled with disillusionment with the Mexican government, weakened California's ties to Mexico.

Under the Constitution of 1824, California became a territory, placing it under the direct jurisdiction of the government in Mexico City. Californios, particularly the elite families, instead desired statehood since that promised greater local autonomy and they resented Mexican policies on tariffs, the use of convicts as colonists, and the appointment of outsiders to key political posts. In 1828, 1829, and 1831 locals led revolts in California against officials they disliked and demanded greater local power. Mexican authorities, caught up in the continuing struggles in Mexico and contending with Texas, failed to respond vigorously to California's malcontents.

When Santa Anna's government sent a new centrist governor to California in 1836, californios removed him from office. The California legislature demanded the restoration of the federal system and threatened that if centralism prevailed, California, like Texas, would become independent. Perhaps if Santa Anna had led an army to California as he responded to similar threats from Texas, the citizenry would have taken up arms and made independence a reality. Instead Mexican officials and insurgent leader Juan Bautista Alvarado reached an accommodation that placed Alvarado in the governor's chair from 1836 to 1842. Greater local control, rather than independence, was the outcome in California for a time. In 1842, another governor was sent from outside the province, and again resistance built until he resigned and fled south in 1845. Ties between California and Mexico were badly frayed, but internal disagreements between northern and southern californios prevented a declaration of independence. Instead civil war threatened California on the eve of the U.S.-Mexican war.

Even as these events transpired, opportunity beckoned in California. Although the fur trade had declined, coastal trade remained vigorous. By the 1840s, land also had become a lure to California as larger grants became available and foreigners eagerly sought them. Mexico hoped that such men as John Sutter, a Swiss emigrant who had created an agricultural empire, would use their grants to form a buffer against American immigration, but Sutter's grant proved a magnet to more Americans dazzled by his success.

In New Mexico, too, some individuals seized opportunities to gain positions of wealth and prominence. One was doña María Gertrudis Barceló, better known as doña Tules, who gambled her way from obscurity to wealth and an exalted position in New Mexican society. Little is known about Tules's early life other than that she was born in Sonora in 1800. In 1820, the Barceló family, which included Tules's widowed mother, her older brother, and her two younger sisters, came to New Mexico, the oldest and most heavily populated region on the northern frontier of Mexico. By 1821 the province was home to more than thirty thousand Hispanos and more than nine thousand Pueblo Indians. (These figures do not include the villa of El Paso, which became part of the Mexican state of Chihuahua in 1824.)

Still, New Mexico shared the same problems of geographical isolation and poor economic development that plagued Texas, California, and northern Sonora. Most paisanos depended on subsistence agriculture and stock raising to support their families; those few New Mexican *ricos* had become so by raising sheep that they sold down the Camino

Cheryl J. Foote

Real to Chihuahua. Because Spain's mercantile policy had prohibited trade with foreign countries, *nuevomexicanos* had traded legally only with the so-called *indios bárbaros,* the nomadic Apaches, Navajos, Utes, Comanches, and Kiowas who brought buffalo hides, jerked meat, and captives to exchange for foodstuffs, woven goods, and livestock. During the war for Mexican independence, the treaties and trade alliances between Spanish authorities and these tribesmen broke down, and they turned toward American traders in the Mississippi valley, who willingly traded guns and ammunition. Often better armed than the nuevomexicanos, the Natives increased their raids against New Mexican villages while the government in Mexico failed to respond to settlers' pleas for additional manpower and weapons for adequate defense.

When Mexico opened her borders to foreign trade, Americans on the Missouri frontier wasted no time in seeking new markets. Two trading parties arrived in Santa Fe in late 1821, and more headed to New Mexico in the spring of 1822. As the Santa Fe trade developed, New Mexicans delighted in the bright-colored finely woven cottons, silk shawls, ribbons, buttons, mirrors, housewares, tools, jewelry, medicines, furniture, window glass, and other items manufactured in the United States or imported into the United States from Europe and shipped across the plains. For their part, American traders were even more pleased with the silver coin, gold and silver bullion, mules, and furs that they received in payment. The trade began hard on the heels of the Panic of 1819, when the Missouri frontier was almost devoid of hard currency, and the influx of Mexican silver strengthened the western economy as well as initiated New Mexico's transformation from a barter to a cash economy.

Within a few years the New Mexico market no longer could absorb more goods, so traders extended the scope of their operations down to Chihuahua, Durango, and Sonora, where some New Mexico ricos had traded sheep for years. In addition, many New Mexicans of differing social classes entered the trade, sending not only sheep but *efectos del país,* coarse woolens, stockings, hides and furs, to markets in the south. Other, wealthier New Mexicans purchased foreign products to resell in Mexico's interior, some of them traveling east along the Santa Fe Trail to Missouri and beyond to conduct their business. The Santa Fe trade also depended heavily on New Mexican and Mexican muleteers and packers, just as the trade required a wide array of service personnel on the American frontier. By 1843, heavy freight wagons lumbered across the prairies with merchandise valued at nearly half a million dollars. Mercantile capitalism had come to the borderlands.

As early as 1825, the U.S. government took an interest in the growing commercial significance of the Santa Fe trade and sent a party to survey the trail as far as the boundary with Mexico. Based on the Transcontinental Treaty of 1819, the boundary between the two countries ran north from the Red River along the 100th meridian to the Arkansas, which then served as the boundary west to the Rocky Mountains. From western Missouri the Santa Fe Trail struck the Arkansas and followed the river to western Kansas; there some parties headed southwest across the present-day Oklahoma panhandle on the Cimarron cutoff. Although a shorter route, the cutoff also offered two distinct drawbacks: the lack of reliable water sources and the threat of Indian attack. The mountain branch of the trail followed the Arkansas into eastern Colorado, ensuring a regular water supply and, after 1833, the opportunity to stop at Bent's Fort, a fur trade outpost established by William and Charles Bent. The mountain branch presented its own challenge in Raton Pass, a steep mountain passage into New Mexico.

The Santa Fe trade proved advantageous to trappers exploiting the fur resources of the southern Rockies. Many of them headed south to Santa Fe or Taos to trade their pelts and eventually married or cohabited with Hispanic women. Sometimes they sought official permission to engage in the fur trade, while others trapped illegally from southern Colorado through Utah, Arizona, and into California. The trade also may have stimulated the search for mineral wealth in New Mexico, for by 1825 nuevomexicanos panned for gold southeast of Santa Fe.

Other New Mexicans pursued additional avenues toward prosperity. In 1825, records in the rough mining camps of the Ortiz Mountains began to mention doña Tules Barceló, who was fined numerous times for dealing monte, a popular card game. What brought Tules to the placers? What led her to become a professional gambler? These and many other questions are impossible to answer because so few records for the period mention her at all. Apparently Tules never wrote a diary nor many letters that might provide insight into her history, her motivations, and her character. Still, some sources provide a framework for examining her life. For example, church records indicate that three years after her family arrived in New Mexico, doña Gertrudis Barceló married don Manuel Antonio Sisneros in Valencia in June 1823. Four months later, she gave birth to a son, who lived only a few weeks. Her second child, also a boy, was born in 1825, but he too died in infancy. Did such tragedies send the grieving parents in search of a fresh start? That question cannot be answered, but important information about Tules can be gleaned from these details. First, Gertrudis Barceló was entitled to use "doña" before her name, just as her husband employed the honorific "don." Once a designation of noble status, in nineteenth-century New Mexico these titles signaled that individuals were of high birth and worthy of respect. Tules, her sister, and her widowed mother

LADY TULES.

Figure 3.2: Doña Tules, saloon operator and gambler of Mexican
  New Mexico. Courtesy of the Museum of New Mexico,
  neg. no. 1854.

also married into the Sisneros, Sánchez, and Pino families, long-established and respected families in New Mexico. So despite what later
detractors claimed, Tules came from a family of good social standing.
Even more significant, Tules was able to read and write, which set her
apart from nearly every other woman of any social station in Mexican
New Mexico.

By 1826, Tules apparently had left the mines. Her name does not
reappear in official documents until 1835, and her whereabouts in the
intervening years remain a mystery, though she may have moved to
Taos, where her brother lived. Likely her close ties to her family and
economic incentives eventually led her to Santa Fe, where she took a
house next door to her mother. Her husband may have farmed, and
Tules resumed her place at the gaming table.

To the surprise of Anglo American traders who won and lost at
Tules's games, laws and social customs for women in New Mexico

differed significantly from those in the United States. For example, women not only kept their own surnames when they married but their property and control of it as well. Although Mexican law denied women political participation, it provided women with access to the legal system, where they could sue and be sued without male representatives. Women in New Mexico smoked cigarillos, gambled freely, and openly cohabited with men to whom they were not married. They earned money in businesses based on domestic tasks, such as cooking, sewing, and furnishing room and board, as well as the more public activities of mining, tending sheep, and selling goods from foodstuffs to whiskey.

To be sure, many women in the United States worked, despite the prevailing ideology of domesticity that required them to be pure, pious, and submissive housewives. Poor women took jobs in factories or as domestic servants, single women taught school, and wives and widows ran boardinghouses or taverns. But textile operatives or women who ran gambling houses had no place in polite society. In contrast, high-born New Mexican women did not forfeit their social standing because of their business ventures. As she garnered profits from dealing monte, Tules also rose to prominence in Santa Fe society.

From time to time, however, allegations surfaced that her behavior violated other community norms. New Mexican society was tolerant of sexual alliances outside of marriage, but adultery was condemned, no matter what the person's social status. In 1835, Tules responded vigorously to a neighbor's charges that she had adulterous relations with an American boarder and later defended herself against other insults from women envious of her independent behavior and financial success. Local rumors about her romantic liaisons persisted throughout her life and well beyond her death, but she also won recognition as a skillful businesswoman. And no one ever accused her of cheating at cards.

Tules and her husband lived a short distance north of Santa Fe's main plaza, where exchanges of all kinds took place. Heavy freight wagons disgorged their wares in the dusty streets and nuevomexicanos sold produce, local woolens, and liquor. There Tules dealt monte, one of the games of chance that attracted men, women, and children from all social classes and occupations, including the clergy. Visitors marveled at the popularity of gambling, calling it the national pastime. Spain and Mexico had attempted to abolish the practice but to no avail. Instead authorities imposed fines that went into municipal coffers. In this open, convivial atmosphere Americans and nuevomexicanos mingled in frequent casual encounters, and Tules came to know American traders as they won and lost at cards.

From the point of view of the Mexican government, the Santa Fe trade was a mixed blessing. Clearly it stimulated economic development in the region. Even New Mexico officials became successful traders. Yet these same officials knew that New Mexico's economic orientation was shifting toward the United States, and they were uncomfortable with the growing influence of Americans in the territory. Americans bitterly resented the high customs duties, though these revenues funded the government's necessary expenses, including defense, and Americans tried to circumvent Mexican laws (though often with the complicity of local officials). And many Americans were contemptuous of the nuevomexicanos, displaying the same ethnocentric and racist attitudes of many Americans in Texas.

At the same time, many New Mexicans increasingly found the government in Mexico unresponsive to their needs. Under the Mexican Constitution of 1824, New Mexico, like California, was organized as a territory under the direct administration of the national government in Mexico City. This decision was unpopular with New Mexican elites, who favored statehood as a means to greater political autonomy. Still, most men who served as governor between 1824 and 1835 were native to the territory and understood New Mexico's problems, particularly conflict with the Indians. The alliances that Spain had negotiated had broken down, and the tribes had resumed raiding. Navajos drove off thousands of head of stock and menaced settlements, while Apaches threatened the Santa Fe–Chihuahua trade route, Comanches were a danger on the Santa Fe Trail, and Utes troubled northwestern New Mexico. The government in Mexico City, beset with many problems, responded slowly, if at all, to New Mexican pleas for more money and manpower to fight the Indians. Instead nuevomexicanos provided for their own defense, despite inadequate weapons and a territorial government that had no funds with which to buy more.

In 1835, as Tules dealt monte in Santa Fe and New Mexicans petitioned the government in Mexico City for aid in defense, Albino Pérez assumed the governorship of New Mexico. Appointed by Santa Anna's centralist regime that had sparked rebellion across the borderlands, Pérez quickly proved unpopular with nuevomexicanos. Elites resented him because he was an outsider, liberals because he brought the news of tighter centralist control and less chance for autonomy in New Mexico itself. Poorer New Mexicans were dismayed at rumors of new exorbitant taxes. In August 1837 residents of Chimayó gathered to protest certain of the governor's actions. Soon the protest grew into a revolt that inspired many New Mexicans, including Pueblo Indians, to take up arms against the centralist government and its representative, Pérez. Threatening independence if the liberal Constitution of 1824 were not restored, rebel forces decapitated the governor and killed more than a dozen of his supporters.

Residents of Santa Fe cowered inside their houses, not knowing where the insurgents might next direct their anger. American traders feared for their lives and worried that the uprising would be bad for business. William Donoho, a trader from Missouri, and his wife, Mary, likely the first Anglo American woman to come to New Mexico, had made Santa Fe their home since 1833. Now they packed up and left, taking with them two American women recently rescued from the Comanches. Sarah Harris, Sarah Horn, and other members of their families were fleeing Santa Anna's invasion of Texas in March 1836 when they encountered a party of Comanches, who killed their husbands and made captives of the women. Two months later, in another raid in Texas, Comanches captured Rachael Plummer and her cousin, Cynthia Ann Parker. Santa Fe traders, learning of the women's plight, raised funds to ransom Mrs. Harris, Mrs. Horn, and Mrs. Plummer. Horn and Plummer returned to Missouri with the Donohos, while Mrs. Harris later made her way with another party. But Cynthia Ann Parker grew to adulthood among the Comanches and gave birth to Quanah Parker, who in 1875 became the last Comanche chief to surrender to the U.S. government.

Tules likely heard these terrifying stories, as she learned of the murder of Governor Pérez and witnessed Manuel Armijo's suppression of the rebellion. A rico from the Albuquerque area, former governor and Santa Fe trader Armijo raised more than a thousand men to put an end to the Chimayó Revolt. He then persuaded the central government in Mexico City that his leadership could prevent another border province from pursuing the path of independence. In response, Mexico appointed Armijo governor of New Mexico from 1837 to 1844 and again briefly in 1846.

Armijo remains a controversial figure in New Mexico history, for there is little doubt that he profited from his position as governor and rewarded those who supported him. He lacked sympathy for poorer New Mexicans and distrusted American traders. But Armijo was also a pragmatist, and his most pressing concern was to raise money for defense. Accordingly, he tried to retain some of the wealth that the Santa Fe trade brought into New Mexico through relaxing restrictions on gambling and collecting licensing fees rather than fines. Likely it was early in his administration that Tules and her family became part of the governor's circle, for in 1838 Manuel Sisneros loaned money to the government. Could it have come from Tules's games of chance? Perhaps grateful for the loan from Manuel Sisneros, Armijo may have provided protection and sanction when Tules opened the first gambling parlor

Cheryl J. Foote

in New Mexico in 1839. Soon he became a frequent visitor to the establishment, which eventually occupied an entire block on Burro Alley west of the plaza between San Francisco Street and Palace Avenue. He may have been a business partner of Tules, and contemporaries and later writers also have speculated that Tules was his mistress. At the very least, they were close friends, and Armijo served as godfather to the child of Tules's adopted daughter.

With or without the backing of Armijo, Tules's business boomed. The gaming parlor served as the epicenter of Santa Fe entertainment, just as her home, several blocks away, became the social center. As for herself, she was recognized as "the supreme queen of refinement and fashion in the republican city of Santa Fe. . . . The highest court her favor, and the lowest look at her with wonder." So wrote Matt Field, an Irish-born journalist in 1839. Field's admiring descriptions of doña Tules contrast markedly with those of other American observers, particularly Josiah Gregg, who disapproved of Tules and implied that she had been a prostitute, though he conceded that she was "received in the first circles of society." Gregg's *Commerce of the Prairies* was widely read and influenced many other Americans, including Susan Magoffin, the only woman to write about Tules. These writers concurred that it was not Tules's beauty that was responsible for her success. Field noted that she was "not handsome" though "her figure was neat . . . and not ungraceful," whereas Magoffin, writing seven years later, alluded to her as "a stately dame of a certain age" and an "old woman with false hair and teeth." That same year, Richard Smith Elliott considered Tules as "a little *passe,*" noting that "she had been, in youth, very beautiful and very much admired." The only likeness of Tules, sketched when she was nearly fifty, is not flattering.

Beauty fades. More importantly, Tules had other assets that brought her wealth and the appellation "the Princess of Santa Fe." She impressed those she met with her charm, sense of humor, self-possession, and a "shrewd intelligence." A literate woman, she had the considerable advantage of being able to manage her earnings and defend her business interests in court. Observers also admired her competence with the game, for she dealt cards "with skilful [*sic*] precision" and "unchanging serenity." She also possessed a flair for the theatrical. Away from the monte parlor, Tules arrayed herself in silks and satins and sported necklaces, rings, and other jewelry that bespoke her wealth; at the gaming table, she wore a plain loose frock that emphasized her equality with her opponent. She could win, or she could lose. It was up to the cards.

As Tules acquired fame and fortune, her family grew. Her household included an adopted daughter, Rafaela, as well as Rafaela's daughter, Rallitos Washington, whose father was probably American trader Luis Washington. Tules adopted another young girl, Carmel, and gave her the surname of Barceló, while a young boy with the surname of Sisneros also lived with the family for a time. After 1841, no further mention of Manuel Sisneros appears in existing records; whether her husband died or left, Tules became the head of the family, and the money from the games supported her extended family.

In 1842 Tules closed her gambling parlor and moved to Chihuahua for about a year. Perhaps, with her larger family, she needed more money; perhaps she and her husband had parted company, and she was looking for a change of scene. The journey of nearly eight hundred miles was dangerous as well as arduous, for Apache raids on the southern part of the trail were notorious. Surely Tules remembered the women who had been captured by the Comanches and ransomed in Santa Fe and worried about a similar fate for herself and her adopted daughter. But she enjoyed the diversions of the bigger city, and her gambling there brought good returns.

Although Tules prospered, New Mexico's problems did not abate. Governor Armijo had raised more money for defense against the Indians and had negotiated a series of treaties with the Navajos that brought temporary relief. But by the mid-1840s, the Navajos and Utes were again raiding New Mexican settlements. Armijo worried too about foreign influence, not only from the American traders who came across the plains but from Texas. As a countermeasure, he tried to create a buffer between Texas and New Mexico through numerous large land grants in northeastern New Mexico made to nuevomexicanos and to Americans. Meanwhile New Mexico still received scant aid from Mexico, where strong opposition to the centralist government continued.

A rebellion in the northern states of Nuevo León, Coahuila, and Tamaulipas brought Mexican forces north to quash the revolt, and some rebels took refuge in Texas, whose independence Mexico had never recognized despite Santa Anna's promises in 1836. Now it appeared that Texas would be a haven for dissidents who stirred up trouble in Mexico as well as a catalyst for further conflict between Indians and Mexicans and an example to those in California and New Mexico who might favor separation from Mexico. In addition, Texas had sought annexation to the United States. Even though the United States denied the request in 1836, primarily because Texas would join the Union as another slave state, expansionist sentiment was growing in the United States by the early 1840s. To make matters worse, Texas claimed boundaries of the Rio Grande in the south and the west. If Texas acted to make good on that claim, Mexico would lose more than one-half of New Mexico. Finally, Texas enviously eyed the lucrative Santa Fe trade. Small wonder then that Manuel Armijo warned, "Poor New Mexico. So far from heaven and so close to Texas."

Nor were his concerns misplaced. In 1840 Texas president Mirabeau B. Lamar recruited more than three hundred men to travel to New Mexico, ostensibly to open a trade route between Santa Fe and the new Texas capital, named in honor of Stephen Austin. Lamar also believed that New Mexicans would gladly separate from Mexico to become part of Texas, and his Texan–Santa Fe expedition intended to effect the annexation of New Mexico to the Lone Star Republic. The plan collapsed, however, when the Texans got lost on the plains and straggled into New Mexican villages. Word of a Texas invasion reached Armijo, who arrested the Texans and dispatched them to prisons in Mexico City. George Wilkins Kendall, the owner of the *New Orleans Picayune,* who had accompanied the Texans as an observer, suffered with the other prisoners until their release in 1842. In 1844 Kendall published his *Narrative of the Texan Santa Fé Expedition,* detailing the brutal treatment the men received from Armijo and his subordinate. Armijo's reputation, already poor with many American traders, fell even farther. An epidemic of anti-Mexican sentiment spread across Texas and the western frontier of the United States, areas already inflamed when Santa Anna sent Mexican troops into Texas in 1842 to counter the republic's effort to annex New Mexico.

On the other hand, New Mexicans hailed Armijo as a hero who had saved New Mexico from the Texans. Disillusioned though they were with Mexico, nuevomexicanos were in no mood to become part of Texas. Soon they had even more reason to distrust and resent the motives of the Texas Republic, for in 1843 Texas commissioned two parties to overthrow the governments of California and New Mexico and annex these areas to Texas. These expeditions first intended to attack the Santa Fe trade, which led in April 1843 to the murder of Antonio José Chávez, a young trader from a prominent New Mexican family. His murder shocked Americans as well as New Mexicans, and his killers were found swiftly, tried, and executed in Missouri.

Even with this ominous news, 1843 was a boom year in the Santa Fe trade, with more than $450,000 worth of goods traded. Tules, back in Santa Fe, invested $10,000 in the trade, and it appears that she made good profits, for in 1844 she bought a large house and 160 acres of land next door to her home. She may also have invested in the trade again, for that year her neighbor Santiago Flores conveyed a shipment of merchandise to Chihuahua for an unspecified party. In her will, Tules left a house to Flores's daughter, so perhaps she was the unnamed owner of the cargo.

By 1846, Tules was at the peak of her career. Wealthy by New Mexican standards, well respected by local citizens, she was also appreciated by Santa Fe traders for her influence on Santa Fe fashions. Allegedly when she adopted the American style of dress, other women in Santa Fe quickly followed, boosting textile sales and leading many women in Santa Fe to become seamstresses to meet the demand. Nuevomexicanos and American traders interacted freely in her monte parlor, and Tules entertained Americans in her home. Still, she may have felt some grief and dismay in August 1846, when an American army marched toward New Mexico and Governor Armijo fled south to Mexico.

Whatever her misgivings, she quickly acted to ensure the survival of her family and her business under the new regime. On August 18, when the Army of the West occupied Santa Fe, doña Gertrudis Barceló invited General Stephen Watts Kearny and his staff to dinner at her home. As American forces occupied the capital, business flourished at her gaming house, and she furnished lodging to some American troops. In the months that followed, Tules provided more valuable aid to the Americans. When funds from the United States were delayed, Colonel Alexander Doniphan was not able to march toward northern Mexico as ordered. He tried to borrow money but found no lenders until an officer in his command agreed to escort doña Tules to a play. She then furnished the $1,000 that Doniphan needed. Perhaps Tules demanded such a public display because she felt that her position in Santa Fe was in peril. Even though American officers dined at her table and gambled in Burro Alley, they were judgmental about her occupation and distrustful of her character. Still, two months later, Tules again rendered valuable service to the United States. According to some sources, she learned of a New Mexican plot to overthrow Charles Bent, the American governor of New Mexico, and exposed the plan to American authorities, who quickly suppressed it. Unfortunately for Governor Bent, she had no counterpart in Taos, where a revolt erupted in January 1847 and Bent was killed.

Tules continued to operate her gaming parlor at least until 1849, but thereafter her health declined. Perhaps she closed her business at the time she made her will in 1850. Few records of her last years survived, although she apparently enjoyed the companionship of Augustus de Marle, a Prussian emigrant to Santa Fe. She died in January 1852 in Santa Fe, where her funeral drew crowds of local residents as well as unfavorable comments from American onlookers about the money lavished on the ceremony.

Tules could well afford this final indulgence. She was a wealthy woman who had earned the money and managed it with skill. More

Cheryl J. Foote

than that, she maintained a strong sense of duty and devotion to her family, which is evident in the disposition of her property. Bequests included houses to her sister, to her adopted granddaughter, and to Delfinea Flores, daughter of Santiago Flores, as well as personal effects including jewelry, clothing, and a carriage to family members and money to support her adopted granddaughter and daughter.

Stephen Austin and Gertrudis Barceló, then, were emblematic figures during the Mexican period of western history. They acquired money, position, and fame on Mexico's northern frontier. Acting under Mexican law, Stephen Austin brought Americans to settle in Texas. Mexican law and custom also permitted doña Tules to gain wealth and social standing through her own efforts. Beyond their personal accomplishments, Austin and Tules took part in the sweeping changes that propelled the northern Mexican frontier into the American sphere. Colonization grants in Texas and the Santa Fe trade in New Mexico, designed to strengthen Mexico's ties to the area, instead opened the door to American acquisition of the Mexican borderlands.

Essay on Sources

Any study of the Mexican period must begin with David Weber's excellent *The Mexican Frontier 1821–1846: The American Southwest Under Mexico* (Albuquerque: University of New Mexico Press, 1982). I have drawn heavily on this work for the present essay. Also useful are Hubert Howe Bancroft, *History of Arizona and New Mexico 1530–1888* (1889; Albuquerque: Horn & Wallace, 1962), and Hubert Howe Bancroft, *History of California*, vols. 2–3 (San Francisco: A. L. Bancroft & Company, 1885). For reactions to independence in New Mexico, see David J. Weber, "An Unforgettable Day: Facundo Melgares on Independence," *New Mexico Historical Review* 48 (January 1973): 27–44.

The history of Texas is well told in T. R. Fehrenbach, *Lone Star: A History of Texas and the Texans* (New York: Macmillan, 1968). The first biography of Stephen Austin is Eugene C. Barker, *The Life of Stephen F. Austin, Founder of Texas, 1793–1836* (1926; Austin: University of Texas Press, 1969), which provides much useful information though it presents Austin in a most heroic light. A recent and more balanced treatment is Gregg Cantrell, *Stephen F. Austin: Empresario of Texas* (New Haven, Conn.: Yale University Press, 1999), a superb volume that I have relied on throughout this study. Quotes about Austin are taken from this source. The story of the Alamo is recounted in Walter Lord's highly readable though dated *A Time to Stand* (1961; Lincoln: University of Nebraska Press, 1978). An alternative view is offered by one of Santa Anna's officers in José Enrique de la Peña, *With Santa Anna in Texas: A Personal Narrative of the Revolution,* ed. and trans. Carmen Perry (College Station: Texas

A&M University, 1975). Other recent works that discuss the tejano experience are Arnoldo De León, *Mexican Americans in Texas: A Brief History* (Arlington Heights, Ill.: H. Davidson, 1993), and Emilio Zamora, Cynthia Orozco, and Rodolfo Rocha, eds., *Mexican Americans in Texas History: Selected Essays* (Austin: Texas State Historical Association, 2000). Native Americans in Texas are treated in W. W. Newcomb, *The Indians of Texas from Prehistoric to Modern Times* (Austin: University of Texas Press, 1961), which provides ethnographic information about the tribes Austin encountered in Texas.

California history during the Mexican period is concisely presented in Weber, *The Mexican Frontier,* and in greater detail in Bancroft, *History of California.* Richard Henry Dana's *Two Years before the Mast* (1841; New York: Signet Books, 1964) discusses the hide and tallow trade from a sailor's point of view. California Indians are the subject of Albert L. Hurtado's *Indian Survival on the California Frontier* (New Haven, Conn.: Yale University Press, 1988). The final chapter of Joseph P. Sanchez's *Explorers, Traders, and Slavers: Forging the Old Spanish Trail 1678–1850* (Salt Lake City: University of Utah Press, 1997) deals with the Mexican period. Still recommended is Eleanor Lawrence, "Mexican Trade Between Santa Fé and Los Angeles, 1830–1848," *California Historical Society Quarterly* 10 (March 1931): 27–39.

No book-length study about doña Tules is available, but I am deeply indebted to the two fine articles by Janet Lecompte, "La Tules and the Americans," *Arizona and the West* 20 (autumn 1978): 215–30, and Janet Lecompte, "La Tules: The Ultimate New Mexican Woman," in *By Grit and by Grace: Eleven Women Who Shaped the American West,* ed. Glenda Riley and Richard W. Etulain (Golden, Colo.: Fulcrum, 1997), 1–21, which provided much of the information for the section about her. Deena González examines Tules from the perspective of gender in "La Tules of Image and Reality: Euro-American Attitudes and Legend Formation on a Spanish-Mexican Frontier," in *Building with Our Hands: New Directions in Chicana Studies,* ed. Adela de la Torre and Beatríz M. Pesquera (Berkeley: University of California Press, 1993). Fray Angélico Chávez first defended Tules's reputation in "Doña Tules: Her Fame and Her Funeral," *El Palacio* 57 (August 1950): 227–34; a more popular treatment is Walter Briggs, "Venal or Virtuous? The Lady They Called La Tules," *New Mexico Magazine* 49 (March/April 1971): 8–16. For a discussion of Tules's loan of $1,000 to U.S. forces, see Mary Jean Cook, "Pizarro and Doña Tules at the Palace," *Compadres* 3 (July–Sept. 1994): 4–8, and Richard Smith Elliott, *The Mexican War Correspondence of Richard Smith Elliott,* ed. Mark L. Gardner and Marc Simmons (Norman: University of Oklahoma Press, 1997). A more general discussion about women in New Mexico is found in Janet Lecompte, "The

Cheryl J. Foote

Independent Women of Hispanic New Mexico, 1821–1846," in *New Mexico Women: Intercultural Perspectives,* ed. Joan M. Jensen and Darlis A. Miller (Albuquerque: University of New Mexico Press, 1986), 71–94. Rebecca M. Craver, *The Impact of Intimacy: Mexican-Anglo Intermarriage in New Mexico, 1821–1846* (El Paso: Texas Western Press, 1982), discusses the unions between Hispanas and American trappers. Also see Deena González, *Refusing the Favor: The Spanish-Mexican Women of Santa Fe, 1820–1880* (New York: Oxford University Press, 1999).

The literature about the Santa Fe Trail is voluminous. A good place to begin is Jack D. Rittenhouse, *The Santa Fe Trail: A Historical Bibliography* (Albuquerque: University of New Mexico Press, 1971). Stephen G. Hyslop, *Bound for Santa Fe: The Road to New Mexico and the American Conquest, 1806–1848* (Norman: University of Oklahoma Press, 2002), is an excellent treatment that incorporates much useful information about Native Americans into a single volume. Essential for examining the role of Hispanos in the trade is Susan Calafate Boyle, *Los Capitalistas: Hispano Merchants and the Santa Fe Trade* (Albuquerque: University of New Mexico Press, 1997). Josiah Gregg, *Commerce of the Prairies,* ed. Max L. Moorhead (1844; Norman: University of Oklahoma Press, 1954), remains the classic account of the Santa Fe trade. For a woman's perspective, see Susan Shelby Magoffin, *Down the Santa Fe Trail and into Mexico,* ed. Stella M. Drumm (1926; New Haven, Conn.: Yale University Press, 1962). Also see John E. Sunder, *Matt Field on the Santa Fe Trail* (Norman: University of Oklahoma Press, 1960).

Information about Manuel Armijo is available in Janet Lecompte, "Manuel Armijo's Family History," *New Mexico Historical Review* 48 (July 1973): 251–58, and in Daniel Tyler, "Mexican Indian Policy in New Mexico," *New Mexico Historical Review* 55 (April 1980): 101–20. The Chimayo Revolt is treated in Weber, *The Mexican Frontier,* and in Janet Lecompte, *Rebellion in Rio Arriba 1837* (Albuquerque: University of New Mexico Press, 1985). The story of the Donohos and the women rescued from the Comanches is told in Marian Meyer, *Mary Donoho: New First Lady of the Santa Fe Trail* (Santa Fe, N.Mex.: Ancient City Press, 1991); Cynthia Ann Parker's tragic tale may be found in Margaret Schmidt Hacker, *Cynthia Ann Parker: The Life and the Legend* (El Paso: University of Texas at El Paso, 1990).

George Wilkins Kendall, *Narrative of the Texan Santa Fé Expedition,* 2 vols. (1844; Austin: Steck Company, 1935), is a detailed account by a participant in the ill-fated expedition. Noel M. Loomis, *The Texan–Santa Fe Pioneers* (Norman: University of Oklahoma Press, 1958), contends that the expedition intended only to open a trade route between Texas and New Mexico. Marc Simmons, *Murder on the Santa Fe Trail: An International Incident, 1843* (El Paso: University of Texas at El Paso,

1987), places the murder of Antonio José Chávez in the context of the interest of Texas in acquiring New Mexico.

CHAPTER 4

George Vancouver, Lewis and Clark, and David Thompson
Exploring the Pacific Northwest by Tide and Trail

WILLIAM L. LANG

In early February 1778, Captain James Cook sailed HMS *Resolution* east from Hawai`i to the Northwest Coast of North America, setting in motion a series of events that would forever change the region. Cook was on his third voyage of discovery in the Pacific, one that took him up the maritime edge of the continent and into the Arctic Ocean before he sailed back to Hawai`i for refitting. The consequences of his voyage were harbingers of four decades of exploration in the Pacific Northwest. Cook's exploration resulted in the first published maps and scientific descriptions of the region, the discovery of commercial wealth in sea otter furs gathered from Natives and traded to merchants in China, and a British challenge to Spain's presumed hegemony over the area. In ways profound and mundane, the region would never be the same.

The grand purposes behind Cook's explorations were part of what historian William Goetzmann calls the Second Great Age of Discovery, a Euroamerican effort that unleashed Enlightenment science and international commerce on distant and unknown maritime and continental regions. It initiated a new era in world history, the second modern globalization effort, which in many ways has continued ever since. Cook and those who followed brought new technologies, new economics, and a different set of ideas about the prerogatives of individuals in society to the northwest corner of North America. Within five decades, a relatively few progenitors of Euroamerican imperialism—no more than a few thousand—would radically alter the content and texture of life that had sustained millions of Native people for thousands of generations. These were events and actors that changed history.

Cook's exploration of the Northwest Coast had two specific goals that were symptomatic of the era and also specific to the region. The first focused on a theoretical geography that posited the existence of a water passage through the continent from Atlantic to Pacific oceans—a Northwest Passage. In 1771, Samuel Hearne had all but eliminated the possibility of a middle latitude passageway on the Atlantic side as a result of explorations north of Hudson's Bay to about the 65th parallel, leaving few likely alternatives. That left the North Pacific as the location for the western end of the fabled passage, which led Britain to send Cook there and charge him "very carefully to search for, and to explore, such rivers or inlets as may appear to be of a considerable extent, and pointing towards Hudson's or Baffin's Bay." If that purpose tended toward commercial benefit, then the second tilted toward British imperialism.

In the mid-1770s, geographical knowledge of the North Pacific came from spotty information gleaned from Russian explorations in the Arctic Ocean and Aleutian Islands and from secretive Spanish explorations, which had been rendered as maps by cartographers Gerhard Muller and Thomas Jefferys. For three decades before Cook's voyage, Russians had felt their way along the extreme edge of Alaska as they extended a fitful fur-trading enterprise to North America. Believing that they had legitimate claim to the region, Spain fretted over the Russian activity and in the early 1770s sent clandestine reconnaissance expeditions north of the 50th parallel. Both nations tried to keep their discoveries to themselves, hoping to dominate whatever advantages the region might deliver to a maritime power. Nonetheless, maps included enough information to suggest a coastline above 45 degrees. Britain also hoped for gain from the unknown area, although what place it might take in imperial visions was unclear. In that context, the Admiralty instructed Cook to identify resources in the North Pacific and "to take possession, in the name of the King of Great Britain" of any prospective location that might bolster Britain's wealth or strategic position in the region. Among all British mariners, Cook was the only choice for this duty. A new member of the Royal Society and a national hero, he stood at the acme of his fame, easily the greatest explorer of his day, a master sailor and cartographer who had ended speculation about a predicted great continent in the South Pacific in two previous voyages and had also strengthened the British navy by introducing a shipboard diet that prevented scurvy.

As American colonists fought through their first year of conflict against their imperial master and declared to the world their plans for independence, James Cook took the 462-ton *Resolution* out of Plymouth harbor with scientists and artists on board, along with the latest technology and advanced instruments, including Larcum Kendall's newest maritime chronometer. Days later, the *Resolution*'s sister ship, the 268-ton

Map 4.1: Significant maritime and land exploration routes in the Pacific Northwest, 1792–1811. Map © 2003 by Herbert K. Beals; used by permission.

Discovery, followed under the captaincy of Charles Clerke. In late January 1778, eighteen months into the voyage and sailing across the Pacific from a respite in Tahiti, Cook and Clerke bumped into an unknown group of islands. Settled by Polynesians in the eighth century, Hawaiʻi offered the perfect refitting station for European exploration and trading voyages in the Pacific, a role the islands would play for decades to come. By early February, Cook had sailed east toward North America. He struck the present-day Oregon coastline in early March at about 44 degrees latitude, near a promontory Cook named Cape Foulweather. Following orders to gain the 65th parallel and begin his survey, he hastily coasted north but somehow missed the mouth of the Columbia River and the Strait of Juan de Fuca; storms had pushed him off the coast for much of the distance. At the end of March, the *Resolution* and *Discovery* dropped their anchors in an appealing harbor on the west coast of Vancouver Island, a place Cook named King George's Sound—soon changed to Nootka Sound.

Cook spent a month at Nootka refitting his vessels for the survey in search of the Northwest Passage and conducting relations with the first group of Natives Cook encountered on the North Pacific coast. Sailing north from Nootka into the Gulf of Alaska, Cook probed every estuary along the coastline for the Northwest Passage. He filled his charts with notations about conditions on a rugged coast, but he found no water corridor, no Northwest Passage save a broad estuary near present-day Anchorage—Cook Inlet, or Turnagain Arm. He failed to confirm its length, leaving it suggestively on his map as a large opening that might lead to a substantial river. Nonetheless, his explorations had nearly eliminated the possibility of a Northwest Passage.

After Cook's tragic death in Hawaiʻi at the hands of Natives in early 1779, Charles Clerke and James King returned to complete the survey and led the voyage home. It was on the return that Cook's expedition made a discovery equal to its cartographic successes. In Canton, China, sailors who had traded a shilling's worth of iron at Nootka or some beads at Cook Inlet for sea otter skins sold the skins for $120 apiece, turning a nearly 300 percent profit. It is arguable which news was more important when the *Resolution* and *Discovery* returned to Plymouth, Cook's documentation of the North Pacific or the fabulous profits to be had in trading sea otter skins to Asia.

The great bonanza in sea otter furs in the North Pacific generated nearly thirty years of competition among Russian, British, and American entrepreneurs. What had begun with Cook's voyage of discovery for science quickly devolved into an international race for command of the region, its natural wealth, and a trading relationship with its Natives. Three contests developed. One put empires at odds, initially Britain and Spain but soon also Russia and the upstart United States. A second developed between British and Russian imperially backed merchant companies and American private entrepreneurs. A third competition mixed fur trading and empire building in the inland Pacific Northwest between British and American interests. These competitions brought several results, but in common they hastened a profound transformation of Native cultures, a process that began with Cook at Nootka and extended until after the establishment of American hegemony by the Oregon Treaty of 1846.

The first imperial conflict occurred at Nootka Sound in 1789. The publication of Cook's maps and exploration narrative in 1784 made public what Spain had long known was likely: that Britain meant to pursue commercial and state interests in the North Pacific. The government in Madrid would not abandon its interest without protest. It had established outposts at Monterey and San Francisco and had sent daring explorers north as early as the seventeenth century. More recently Juan Pérez had sailed to the Queen Charlotte Islands from Mexico in 1774, and the following year Bruno de Hezeta and Bodega y Quadra cruised the Oregon and Washington coastlines. Both explorations returned detailed charts, including Hezeta's notation of a broad estuary at about 45 degrees, which he called "Assumption Bay" but which turned out to be the Columbia River.

In the immediate post-Cook years, John Meares, James Hanna, and other British maritime fur traders had made claims on Nootka Sound as a prime North Coast entrepôt, American traders had rushed in, and some believed even the Russians planned to make a move on the harbor. Meares had brought Chinese workers with him from Macao in spring 1788 to establish a fur post and shipbuilding facility at Nootka. He negotiated with Chief Maquinna of the Nootkas for a plot on the sound, where he built a rough post. Early the next year, Spain responded by sending Estéban Martínez on the *Princesa* and López de Haro on the *San Carlos* to enforce its claim to the region. In spring 1789, Martínez built a solid fort at Nootka Sound, equipped with cannon, and ceremoniously claimed the place for Spain. When James Colnett, a British fur trader and partner of John Meares, arrived in the *Argonaut* from Macao to set up a British trading fort, Martínez acted in presumed defense of Spain's interests and captured him, his crew, the *Argonaut,* and the *Princess Royal,* an additional British trading vessel, refusing to let them infringe on Spain's claim and requiring that they be taken to San Blas, the Spanish port in Baja California. The events created a furor in London, where the government decided to use its navy to avenge Spain's actions at Nootka. As Britain mobilized its war fleet, Spain tried to recruit allies for its side of the dispute. By October 1790, Britain had issued an ultimatum that threatened war if Spain did not relent from its claims to Nootka. They avoided war by signing the Nootka Convention on October 28, which restored British property, opened the Pacific to trade and fishing, and established places of commerce for both nations.

Settling the Nootka crisis had repercussions beyond the near use of the war frigates both nations had put to sea. In April 1791, Britain sent Captain George Vancouver in the *Discovery*, a 330-ton refitted merchant sloop, and Lieutenant William Broughton in the *Chatham*, a 131-ton tender, to Nootka to work out details of the convention with Spanish counterparts. That mission—Vancouver's voyage—would gather more information, much more, about the Pacific Northwest than Cook had recorded and would conclusively close out any hope for a Northwest Passage. Vancouver's survey of Puget Sound, the Strait of Juan de Fuca, and Vancouver Island created what geographer Daniel Clayton calls a "calculable geography," one that defined the region in commercial, scientific, and political terms through meticulous cartography and rendered control over place by applying names and drawing maps that represented British claims. It is no exaggeration to say that Vancouver and his men executed the first Euroamerican creation of the Pacific Northwest. There would be other historic iterations, but Vancouver's had enormous impact and staying power. Some of his maps had utility into the twentieth century.

The British Admiralty had good reasons to choose Vancouver. He had served on Cook's second and third voyages as a midshipman, so he knew the challenges of sailing in the Pacific. He had recently returned from four years—1784–1789—on the *Europa* in the West Indies, where he had completed important harbor and coastline surveys. Promoted twice during his service in the Caribbean, Vancouver was thirty-one years old when he became captain of the *Discovery* in 1790. The Admiralty ordered him to conclude the Nootka business by confirming Spanish compliance with the international agreement and to carry out an extensive survey of the North Pacific region. The second purpose turned out to be far more important than the first for British interests and the fortunes of Native people in the Pacific Northwest.

George Vancouver was the sixth and last child born to John and Bridget Vancouver on June 22, 1757, in the port city of King's Lynn on England's east coast. King's Lynn lay along the river Ouse, where it emptied into The Wash. The town dated from the twelfth century, when it was a salt-producing area and market town that served the Fen Country, a lowland agricultural region that was among England's most productive. With access to the North and Baltic seas, King's Lynn teemed with ships and boasted a rich customs district. George's father held the deputy collector of customs position for twenty-two years,

Figure 4.1: Captain George Vancouver, a veteran of James Cook's voyages of discovery, led the most thorough exploration of the maritime Northwest in the early 1790s. Courtesy of the Washington Historical Society.

which gave him considerable political influence and likely explains how his son landed a spot on Cook's second voyage. Why George inclined toward a seafaring life is unclear, but as the youngest child his opportunities may have been circumscribed. From whatever motive, he happily enlisted in the Royal Navy in 1771 at age fourteen and through political influence took his spot on the *Resolution,* one of the few selected among many applicants.

Nothing Vancouver did on Cook's voyages merited mention in the captain's journals or in published accounts. Nonetheless, as a midshipman he learned seamanship under a captain who ran a most orderly vessel, took care of his sailors' health, and modeled effective, if not stern, captaincy. Vancouver also gained an important apprenticeship at the hands of William Wales, the astronomer assigned to the *Resolution* by the Board of Longitude. Wales had instructions to teach any officer or mate on ship how to use instruments, such as the astrolabe and sextant, to calculate longitude through lunar sightings. Vancouver used the knowledge he gained from Wales during his surveys on the *Europa,* and many years later he paid tribute to Wales as the man who taught him how "to traverse and delineate these lonely regions." Vancouver had also participated in trading with Natives at Nootka, and he had witnessed the conflict in Hawai`i that ended James Cook's life.

In 1791, Vancouver prepared for his voyage by selecting men who he trusted could help him fulfill his instructions, which boiled down to two: carry out the Nootka Convention and investigate the Strait of Juan de Fuca and Cook's River to determine if a waterway to the interior existed—the pursuit of the Northwest Passage yet again. He looked no further than his fellow officers from his years on the *Europa* to aid him, including Peter Puget, Zacariah Mudge, Joseph Baker, and Joseph Whidbey. Vancouver did not choose Broughton, nor did he request a surgeon, Archibald Menzies, as the expedition's official naturalist. Menzies owed his presence to Sir Joseph Banks, president of the Royal Society and a veteran of Cook's first voyage. Banks and his fellow scientists wanted Vancouver's voyage to collect information for science, including the collection of plants destined for Kew Gardens. That purpose prompted Menzies to secure a greenhouse on the *Discovery*'s quarterdeck, an installation that nettled Vancouver and added friction to his relationship with the surgeon/naturalist. Menzies knew a good deal about Native trading habits and desires, for he had been at Nootka with fur trader James Colnett two years earlier. His list of trading goods for transport on the voyage and his opinions on trading procedures added to his conflict with Vancouver. The trading goods cargo included iron, woolens, copper, nails, vermilion, and beads, totaling more than £10,000. Banks had drawn up a list of instructions for Menzies that requested information on subjects ranging from soil types and flora species to Native languages and details of Native manufacturing techniques. In addition, Vancouver had three talented artists along—John Sykes, Thomas Heddington, and Henry Humphrys—who sketched landscapes, coastal elevations, Native villages, and scenes of crew members surveying the coastline.

The *Discovery* and the *Chatham* left Falmouth harbor in early April 1791 and would not return until October 1795, after sailing seventy-four thousand miles, about 15 percent farther than Cook. By April 1792, Vancouver intersected the continent north of San Francisco and proceeded north to Nootka Sound. Although he coasted close to shore, he completely missed the mouth of the Columbia River, a mistake that British diplomats later rued when discussions about claims to the Pacific Northwest became politically charged. Vancouver focused on his instructions to explore the Strait of Juan de Fuca. When he met up with American maritime trader Robert Gray on April 28, he quizzed him about the strait and whether, as John Meares had reported, Gray had sailed around Nootka's landmass to prove it an island. To Vancouver's relief, Gray called Meares's report erroneous. He had more interest in the appearance of a river mouth at about the 46th parallel. Vancouver discounted that idea, but Gray held fast to his interest and decided to investigate as he traded for furs along the Washington coast.

On May 11, Gray poised his ship, the 212-ton *Columbia Rediviva*, off a line of breakers at the mouth of a large estuary. A Boston-based trader, Gray had become the first American mariner to sail around the world in 1788, which had taken him to Nootka. Gray returned to the region in 1791–1792 on another fur-trading voyage, but this time he traded south of Nootka at Clayoquot Sound, where he wintered and built a small sloop, the *Adventure*. A no-nonsense trader, Gray had little patience with Native trading practices and often overreacted to perceived threats. Two months before his meeting with Vancouver, Gray had destroyed the village of Opitsat at Clayoquot to avenge trading slights, and in May at anchor in Gray's Harbor he blasted a large canoe of Indians with a nine-pound cannon for pestering the *Columbia*.

Three days after the incident at Gray's Harbor, Gray sent a tender across the breakers into the Columbia River, following at a distance in the larger *Columbia*. A sixteen-year-old mate on the *Columbia,* John Boit, recorded the ship's entrance into the river:

> We directed our course up this noble river in search of a Village. The beach was lin'd with Natives, who ran along shore following the Ship. Soon after above 20 Canoes came off, and brought a good lot of Furs and Salmon, which last they sold two for a board Nail. . . . We lay in this place till the 20th May, during which time we put the Ship in good order and fill'd up all the water casks along side itt being very good. . . . This River in my opinion, wou'd be a fine place for to sett up a Factory.

Gray drew a chart of the estuary and ocean headlands, naming the river Columbia's River after his ship and sailing north to collect more furs. In late June, the *Columbia* struck a rock and laid up in Nootka for repairs at the pleasure of the Spanish. Perhaps in repayment for their hospitality, Gray passed along his chart of the Columbia River to the Spanish. When Vancouver finally arrived at Nootka in late August for consultations with Juan Francisco de la Bodega y Quadra, the Spanish captain handed him Gray's chart. The two commanders, who had become friends through sharing meals and comparing details of their voyages, decided to let their governments sort out details of the Nootka Convention. Two years later, Britain and Spain concluded the issue in Madrid by demilitarizing the North Pacific and pledging an open trading policy, especially at Nootka.

Vancouver acquired Gray's chart at the end of a busy three months of charting the inland waters of Puget Sound, Hood Canal, Admiralty Inlet, and the Strait of Georgia, a survey that established the dimensions of Vancouver Island and the breadth of the Strait of Juan de Fuca and that laid down place names still in use today. Mapping the inlets, bays, and punctuated coastline required time, the use of small boats, and surveying skill. Using several coordinated methods, regular lunar observations, and two advanced chronometers to establish longitude, the surveyors drew accurate maps that included depth-sounding data, coastal elevations, and their survey tracks. During part of the survey, Vancouver joined Antonio Galiano, Spanish commander of the *Sutil*, to cooperatively chart many of the inlets and straits. When he reached the mouth of the Columbia in October, Vancouver realized the *Discovery* could not safely pass the bar, so he directed Lieutenant William Broughton in the *Chatham* to enter the river.

Broughton eased the *Chatham* across the Columbia's bar on October 19, 1792. In the words of Edward Bell, ship's clerk,

> I must here acknowledge that in going into this place, I never felt more alarmed & frightened in my life, never having been before in a situation where I conceived there was so much danger. The Channel was narrow, the water very Shoal, and the Tide running against the Wind at the rate of 4 Knots an hour, raised a Surf that broke entirely around us, and I am confident that in going in, we were not twice the Ship's length from Breakers, that had we struck on, we must inevitably have gone to pieces. . . .

A quick survey of conditions in the estuary and reference to Gray's chart convinced Broughton that they must use cutter boats to conduct a survey of the river. He anchored the *Chatham* in Baker's Bay on the north bank of the river and proceeded upriver in two boats propelled by oars and sails. For ten days, Broughton's men rowed against the current until they reached a point near present-day Washougal, Washington, a location he called Point Vancouver. Broughton rendered the Columbia in considerable detail on the chart he produced, but his calculations about the river's

Figure 4.2: The *Discovery* and the *Chatham* in Salmon Cove, where Vancouver's crew established an observatory camp to take celestial readings and survey measurements. Courtesy of the Washington Historical Society.

volume, its current, and especially its origin misrepresented its true character because they conducted the survey in the fall, when the Columbia's seasonal flow dwindled. If Broughton or Gray had gone upriver in May or June, they would have seen triple the river volume, hundreds of Native people fishing, and the result of the annual spring freshet that brought silt and debris in a flood down the river. Broughton mistakenly guessed the Columbia's source as near Mount Hood (he named it for Lord Samuel Hood of the British Admiralty), which could not have been more than 40 miles from the end of his upriver paddle. (The river's actual source—Columbia Lake in southeastern British Columbia—is more than 1,200 miles from the Pacific.) Broughton also mistook the extent of the Columbia because he perceived the river from a mariner's viewpoint and in fact disagreed with Vancouver about the location of the river's mouth. Vancouver argued for the opening to the Pacific, but Broughton believed that the river's great estuary effectively made the mouth about 30 miles upriver, near present-day Skamokawa. The difference is important. Vancouver's interpretation gave Gray legitimate claim to discovery because he had traveled only 15 miles upriver, or about half the distance to Skamokawa. Gray and the Americans claimed the river, its name, and its significance in subsequent property disputes.

Broughton's survey of the lower Columbia included notations on encounters with Indians, which suggests a larger theme—the impact of Euroamerican exploration on Native people. Near Sauvie Island on

October 28, 1792, Broughton fired a musket ball into the water when twenty-five canoes and nearly 150 Indians surrounded his boats. He need not have flexed his armaments, for he soon discovered that the Indians hoped for trade, not conflict. From the first contact between Russian fur traders in the Gulf of Alaska to the invasion of large fur-trading companies in the Pacific Northwest, the relationships between Native peoples and the imperialists balanced on a fine edge. In place after place, maritime explorers and traders attempted to create profitable relations with Indian groups, usually by identifying a specific Native leader to represent constituent people and to strike a mutually beneficial exchange. Sometimes these relationships went terribly wrong and violence resulted. In all situations, however, the Euroamericans pursued agreements that favored them over Indian traders and also gave them a competitive advantage over other Euroamerican traders. For the British and Spanish mariners, Nootka Sound and Clayoquot Sound were flash points, while the American and British competed on the lower Columbia. It was endemically an imperialistic game.

Trade had been prevalent among Northwest people for generations before the Euroamericans came, but the method and purpose of the new trade brought destabilizing forces to the region that changed the landscape in four basic ways. First, the new traders represented a global economy that operated on the basis of market exchange values, not on the basis of utility, barter, or intertribal politics. Second, new technologies, especially firearms, made trade more efficient and dangerous, which produced environmental damage and more deadly conflicts. Third, the Euroamerican organization of trade favored some Indian groups and families over others and created new political and social relationships. Fourth, and most devastating, the trade brought new pathogens to the region, creating rampant epidemics that raced through the densely inhabited villages along the coast and major rivers. These "virgin soil epidemics," as historian Alfred Crosby has called them, killed perhaps 80 percent of the coastal people during the first century after contact with Europeans.

There is no greater consequence of the exploration of the Northwest Coast of North America than the decimation of the Native population. Vancouver's journals include numerous notations about the ravages of smallpox. "This deplorable disease," the journal entry in Hood's Canal related,

> is not only common, but it is greatly to be apprehended and is very fatal among them, as its indelible marks were seen on many; and several had lost the sight of one eye . . . owing most likely to the virulent effects of this baneful disorder.

Impact of disease

Not only did disease render many groups defenseless against the invaders, but it also killed off people in waves of infection that included malaria and other crowd diseases besides smallpox. The disease episodes extended throughout the early nineteenth century and blasted Indian cultures by profoundly disrupting political and social leadership. In addition, according to anthropologist Robert Boyd, the epidemics affected birth rates, further depressing the Native population. As a result, it was far easier for nineteenth-century traders and later settlers to dominate the region, especially in the Columbia and Willamette river valleys, where disease held sway for the longest period.

Broughton's survey in 1792 produced the first detailed map of the lower one hundred miles of the Columbia River. Included in Vancouver's *A Voyage of Discovery* in 1798, the map advertised a river of great commercial potential. After Broughton's trip up the Columbia, *Vancouver* Vancouver sailed another two years before returning to England in October 1795. He had completed the greatest maritime survey in British history, thoroughly charted the Northwest Coast, and confirmed the nonexistence of the Northwest Passage. Still, his fame never approached Cook's. Calumny and conflict dominated the three years he lived after his return, mostly the result of a crew member's enmity toward him for discipline that Vancouver had meted out during the voyage. The dispute became public and Vancouver suffered in popular opinion, dying before his *A Voyage of Discovery* came off the presses. Nonetheless, the work put an exact shape on a distant corner of North America even if it drew mixed reviews. By 1801, a new edition created more interest, and the following year Spain published maps drawn by Antonio Galiano in 1792. At the turn of the century, accurate maps existed to lead a new rush to the Northwest Coast, especially in the region dominated by the Columbia River.

Thomas Jefferson, the young nation's third president, burned with curiosity about the world. He stacked his library with natural histories, maps, travel accounts, scientific surveys, and reports about nature and its contents, including Cook's *A Voyage to the Pacific Ocean,* Vancouver's *A Voyage of Discovery,* and Alexander Mackenzie's *Voyages from Montreal.* A child of Linnaean science, Jefferson corresponded with Enlightenment scientists in America and Europe and eagerly participated in finding order in nature and discovering its beatitudes and mysteries. He also understood geopolitics. From his vantage point in the recently designated capital city of Washington, he looked west to the "Stony Mountains" and wondered about not only what was there but also which political power would control it. Even before his tenure in the White House, Jefferson had coveted the landscape west of the

T.J

Mississippi Valley, and he had tried on several occasions to send observers to document that terra incognita. Among his chief interests was a compelling vision that lay at the heart of the Northwest Passage idea—a commercial and political route to Asia.

Jefferson's great opportunity came in early 1803. Anticipating the purchase of France's North American holdings between the Mississippi River and the Rocky Mountains, Jefferson sent a secret message to Congress, requesting support for a military reconnaissance

> to explore this the only line of easy communication across the continent, and so directly traversing our own part of it. The interests of commerce place the principal object within the constitutional powers and care of Congress, and that it should incidentally advance the geographical knowledge of our own continent can not but be an additional gratification.

To lead the expedition, Jefferson chose Meriwether Lewis, a twenty-nine-year-old army veteran who had served on the frontier, understood army procedure, and had been the president's personal secretary since 1801. A native of Albermarle County, Virginia, Lewis was the son of a Revolutionary War veteran who died when Meriwether was five years old. His mother remarried and took her family to Georgia, where Meriwether first became enamored of natural history. By his early teens, he had moved back to Albermarle County and came under the tutelage of several prominent teachers, from whom he learned geography, history, literature, and mathematics. In 1792, at age eighteen, he had charge of the family farm. Two years later, he joined the local militia to put down the Whiskey Rebellion in Pennsylvania, and from that engagement he threw himself into the soldiering life.

When Jefferson called him to be his private secretary in 1801, Lewis had been on the frontier engaged in battles against recalcitrant Indians in the Ohio River Valley for several years, including service with George Rogers Clark, William Clark's older brother. Lewis's western experience played an important role in his selection, for the president planned to involve him as an aide-de-camp in the western expedition preparations. By late 1802, Lewis had served Jefferson at the White House, taken in the president's learning and enthusiasm for the great expedition, helped him gather materials, and become the president's choice to lead the Corps of Discovery. To ensure the success of the mission, Jefferson suggested that Lewis pick a co-leader. By July 1803, Lewis had named William Clark as his partner. He had also received lengthy instructions from Jefferson that set out an impossibly ambitious agenda for the exploration of the Missouri and Columbia rivers, with special attention to the potential for an all-water transportation route across the continent, the establishment of commerce with Native peoples, the careful mapping of the route and strategic locations, and a full catalog of natural phenomena, flora, and fauna encountered on the journey. A measure of the importance Jefferson placed on the mission is an open letter of credit on the U.S. Treasury that the president drafted for the captains, if by chance they needed assistance and encountered officials of other nations, principally Britain, Spain, and France.

Lewis's choice to share leadership of the expedition came easily, for he had served with William Clark on the frontier. Four years older than Lewis, Clark was a native of Caroline County, Virginia. By his teenage years, his family had moved to Kentucky, and William gained what education he acquired through instruction from his older brother, George, mostly in natural history, geography, and practical arts, with a thorough grounding in Enlightenment sciences. Clark served in the army on the frontier between 1789 and 1796, where he mastered engineering tasks, cartography, and intelligence work, including diplomatic missions for General Anthony Wayne on the Mississippi River. He left the army to pursue a mercantile career in the western territories. At the time Lewis tapped him for duty, Clark had inherited much of the family's holdings, including twenty-four slaves (York, his personal servant, would accompany him on the great expedition), a mill, and thousands of acres of Kentucky land, but he had not established his desired trading business. In reply to Lewis's recruitment letter in July 1803, Clark wrote:

> As my situation in life will admit of my absence the length of time necessary to accomplish such an undertaking I will cheerfully join you . . . and partake of the dangers, difficulties, and fatigues, and I anticipate the honors & rewards of the result of such an enterprise, should we be successful in accomplishing it.

Clark proved to be an exceptional complement to Lewis, although the refusal of the War Department and Congress to grant him equal military status with Lewis—to identify both as captains—threatened to destabilize the operation from the outset. Lewis remained true to his promise, however, and accorded Clark equity in command throughout the expedition. Historians have traditionally cast Lewis as more contemplative and literate than Clark, with Clark the master of practical arts, frontiersmanship, and cartography, but it is clear that both men embraced the Enlightenment's pursuit of "useful knowledge," as historian James Ronda has argued. That meant an empirical examination, ordering, and rational rendering of the experienced world.

Lewis and Clark recorded the majority of their experience in copious journals, maps, field notes, ethnographies, and botanical and celestial observations. The two captains and several Corps members—Charles Floyd, Patrick Gass, John Ordway, and Joseph Whitehouse—kept journals that documented expedition activities. They were "the writingest explorers of their time," as historian Donald Jackson characterized them, and embedded in this thorough and first catalog of the northern West is the fundamental characteristic of their accomplishment—the description of a new territory on the ground and along the trail. The expedition took twenty-eight months, and they traversed some seven thousand miles from the lower Missouri, up the great river to the Continental Divide, down the Columbia to the Pacific, and back along the Yellowstone and Missouri rivers to their starting place—St. Louis, Missouri.

No less purposeful than Cook and Vancouver, Lewis and Clark sought practical knowledge for imperial and commercial reasons. Their achievement meant a great deal to the young republic, and it has become iconographic in the nation's westward expansion. By nearly any measure, the exploration is heroic in accomplishments, but it is also heavy in historic consequences, which are more important to remember and understand. The expedition's most profound legacies veer directly from its experience, propelling generations of demographic, economic, and social changes across the northern West. The plotline for America's future in the region began with the Corps' principal findings: that no easy water passage across the continent existed, that the American West was more expansive than geographers had conceived, that Native people showed great interest in trade but meant to defend their territories, that the vast region they traversed contained resources of great magnitude and value, and that the nation could establish a line of commercial development to the Pacific.

In sending the captains west, Jefferson had consciously joined imperial and commercial purposes. That symbiosis suggests most of the consequences that trailed on in the half century after the expedition, and it is also reflected in the equipage and cargoes that the Corps carried with them up the Missouri in May 1804: twenty bags of goods for trading with Indian groups, including cloth, iron implements, kettles, needles, colored beads, buttons, and other manufactures packed on board with fifteen short-barreled .54-caliber rifles, several .44-caliber long rifles, and three mounted swivel guns. If the captains did nothing else in their relations with Native people, they worked to attach them to an American warehouse of desirable goods. Residing not too faintly behind this diplomatic purpose was a deft, yet poised visage of power. When the captains encountered Indians, they proffered peace and goodwill, but their proclamations and statements as emissaries of the

William L. Lang

Great Father in Washington laid down claims of sovereignty, spiced with gifts and the benefits of official relations with a much larger and more powerful nation to the east.

The presence of a woman and child in the expedition entourage advertised the explorers' peaceful purpose and likely reduced the potential for conflict. Lewis and Clark met Sacagawea some 1,500 miles upriver from St. Louis at the Mandan and Hidatsa villages, where the expedition spent the 1804–1805 winter. A teenage mother and wife of Touissant Charbonneau, whom the captains hired as an interpreter for the westward trek from Mandan, Sacagawea had been in the villages since Hidatsa bison hunters had captured her from her Shoshoni family on the upper Missouri in 1800. Although some historians have exaggerated her role as a guide, claiming that she pointed the way west, she did play an important supportive role at a crucial time in the expedition. On the eastern slope of the Continental Divide, she spotted Beaverhead Rock, near present-day Dillon, Montana, which confirmed the correctness of their route. Two weeks later, after Lewis had made contact with the Shoshoni in mid-August 1805, she may have aided in securing horses and guidance from her people, for her brother was Cameahwait, chief of the tribe.

How much Sacagawea aided Lewis and Clark is a speculative question, but the centrality of Indian aid to the expedition's success is beyond question. Time and again, the Corps found themselves in desperate need of cordial reception, crucial material aid, geographical information, and even direct support. It is a testament to their skill as politicians that they secured aid and generally avoided friction, but it is also confirmation that Native people met the explorers with goodwill and often perceived Lewis and Clark as potential bearers of new wealth. This point is especially important for tribes that needed more access to guns and metal manufactures, such as the Shoshoni and Nez Perce, to defend themselves against armed adversaries. The captains emphasized trade and the benefits of gaining the friendship of the Great Father in Washington. They selected the headmen who professed peace, and they distributed gifts and peace medals to signify their goodwill. Nonetheless, their messages to the chiefs were often direct and proscriptive, as Clark told assembled Crow people on the Yellowstone in 1806:

> Children, Your Great father the Chief of all the white people has derected me to inform his red children to be at peace with each other, and with the white people who may come into your country under the protection of the Flag of your great father. . . .

Their promises of protection, aid, and other benefits came with an acceptance of American friendship over rival international powers. The Great Father in Washington, the captains assured tribal leaders, would reward faithful relationships with guns, ammunition, and goods.

In the Columbia River Basin, the Corps had mixed results in their encounters with Native people. The Shoshoni and Flathead tribes aided their crossing of the Continental Divide and Bitterroot Mountains by trading horses and providing a guide. The passage took its toll on the explorers, however, especially the trek across the game-poor Bitterroots. The members of the expedition were famished and sick when they finally reached Nez Perce camps on the Clearwater River, a tributary of the Snake River in present-day Idaho. Lewis and Clark welcomed the aid rendered by the Nez Perce, who freely offered sustenance for the weakened men and helped make dugout canoes for the explorers' descent of the Snake and Columbia rivers. More important, the Nez Perce sketched out the geography of the region, including the location of a great trading area on the Columbia—Celilo Falls—where they regularly traded for goods, including European manufactures. One of their chiefs agreed to guide the Corps down the Columbia. Lewis and Clark's two-week respite in the Nez Perce camps established friendly relations, which they reinforced on the return trek in 1806, when the Corps spent a month with the Nez Perce waiting for mountain snow to melt. In council with the explorers in mid-May, the Nez Perce agreed with Lewis and Clark's admonishment to maintain peace with their neighbors and to cement their friendship with whites. Lewis recorded a Nez Perce chief's promise in his journal on May 12, 1806:

> That when we had established forts on the Missouri as we had promised, they would come over and trade for arms Amunition &c. and live about us. that it would give them much pleasure to be at peace with these nations [Blackfeet and Shoshoni] altho' they had shed much of their blood. He said that the whitemen might assured of their warmest attachment and that they would alwas give them every assistance in their power; that they were poor but their hearts were good.

On the lower Columbia, where the Corps spent the winter of 1805–1806, relationships with local tribes produced different results. The Clatsop and Chinook people of the lower Columbia were experienced traders who had long been key players in the indigenous trade networks that connected interior with coastal tribes. Since the arrival of maritime traders on the coast a generation earlier, they had also become familiar with Euroamerican trading practices and had become expert salvagers of wrecked vessels. Living in dense communities, these trading and fishing tribes lived in prosperous, stratified societies quite unlike the ones Lewis and Clark had encountered in the Rockies.

The Corps arrived on the Columbia late in the year. They had endured several months of rough river travel through an unexpected and sere landscape, where they navigated rapid after rapid on the lower Snake River, then through the Cascade Mountains in a deep gorge on the Columbia, and finally to the damp environment of the estuary. Drenching rains, strong winds, and difficult navigation on the lower river delayed their progress, and then they faced the necessity of wintering over on a cold and forbidding coast. The captains argued against going back upriver to a drier location near Celilo Falls on the east side of the Cascade Mountains, a remarkable place where they had passed Indians taking salmon in impressive numbers. Staying near the coast held out the possibility that a trading vessel might arrive in the spring and offer the Corps material aid.

Anticipating trade, the Clatsop people welcomed the captains to camp on the south side of the Columbia. The captains remarked on the Indians' hard trading, calling them "higlers," but relations were positive until the Corps erected Fort Clatsop, a stockaded log structure meant to control Indian visits. Relations soon soured. For one thing, Lewis and Clark were nearly bereft of attractive trade items, and the Clatsop and Chinook people had grown accustomed to valuable items from maritime traders. Worse, the explorers became suspicious of Indian motives. The suspicions hit their high-water mark in a rant Lewis included in his journal on February 20, 1806:

> We never Suffer parties of Such numbers [Indian visitors] to remain within the Fort all night; for not withstanding their apparent friendly disposition, their great averis and hope of plunder might induce them to be treacherous. At all events we are determined always to be on our guard, as much as the nature of our Situation will permit us, and never place our selves at the mercy of any Savages. We well know, that the treachery of the Aborigene of America and the too great confidence of our country men in their friendship and fadility has caused the destruction of many hundreds of us.

Historian James Ronda labels Lewis's diatribe a "dangerous flirtation with paranoia," but it is also characteristic of their broader evaluation of the Indian people they had encountered since leaving Fort Mandan in spring 1804. In general, the captains favored equestrian tribes, the nomadic bison hunters, over the river tribes, people who made their way by fishing and trading. The Columbia tribes' trading practices caused the captains no end of anxiety, and the pilfering of equipment at camp locations set the captains on edge. At Celilo Falls in October 1805, Clark noted in his journal that the Corps selected a camp location near upper Chinook people "on an ellegable Situation for the protection of our Stores from Thieft, which we were more fearfull of, than their arrows." At Fort Clatsop, they rationalized their own theft of a Clatsop canoe, which they wanted for the upriver return journey, as repayment for Clatsops pilfering some of the Corps' elk meat. By the time they left the coast in March 1806, Lewis and Clark had categorized the Indians of western America as good or bad. A familiar pattern from earlier trading frontiers had lodged itself on the continent's far shore.

In the interests of empire, Lewis and Clark had answered many of President Jefferson's queries about the Indian nations and their interest in trade. They had also taken the measure of the landscape. Their geographical and environmental descriptions may well have been the most immediately important consequences of the expedition. The expedition's maps dispelled a myth about the North American continent, that a singular "height of land" made it likely that a very short distance separate the headwaters of the Missouri and Columbia river systems. Although their maps would not be published for more than a century after their return to St. Louis, Lewis and Clark brought back detailed information on the rivers, mountains, and landscapes that had only been imagined. The great outline of western America appeared in Clark's 1810 map, which Nicholas Biddle published in 1814. The map, which geographer John Allen calls "an item of superlative craftsmanship and analysis," made it clear that development of the region would require significant effort. Clark compiled his map using additional sources from fur traders and subsequent explorations. The expedition's catalog of the resources available in the West stimulated business interests in St. Louis, New York, and Montreal to mount commercial ventures. Even before the Corps reached St. Louis in September 1806, John Colter had left the expedition to guide a fur party into the Yellowstone country. After the return, another expedition member, George Drouillard, became a partner with Manuel Lisa in upper Missouri fur trading.

Meriwether Lewis and William Clark, as President Jefferson told Congress in December 1806, "had all the success which could have been expected," Congress showed their pleasure by paying the captains $1,228 for their service and granting them each 1,600 acres of land. Jefferson appointed Lewis governor of Louisiana Territory and Clark territorial superintendent of Indian affairs. Governing the region had devolved on the two government men who knew it best. For Clark, the post suited his interests and abilities, but Lewis faced a series of difficulties, including political conflict in the new territory and a failed mission to return Mandan chief Sheheke home to his village after his visit to Washington in 1808. In 1809, some politicians questioned Lewis's handling of territorial accounts. To clear his reputation, Lewis left St. Louis for Washington in late September 1809. In a wayside house on Natchez Trace, a despondent Lewis took his life on October 11, 1809.

As governor, Lewis had given Clark responsibility for establishing a militia and for rationalizing American trading policies with Indians. Clark also took on himself an additional responsibility—raising Sacagawea's son, Jean Baptiste. Writing to Charbonneau in August 1806, Clark offered to "take and raise him as my own child. I once more tell you if you will bring your son Baptiest to me I will educate him and treat him as my own child." He fulfilled his promise and provided an education for Baptiste, who later traveled to Europe and participated in the fur trade in the West, dying in Oregon in 1866. Clark also invested in a major fur-trading company and served as governor of the newly named territory of Missouri from 1813 to 1820 and as superintendent for Indian affairs on the Missouri River until his death in 1838. Clark was in St. Louis in 1831, when members of tribes he had encountered on the expedition came with a request for Christians to visit their people, the call that prompted Protestant and Catholic clergy to establish missions in the Northwest during the 1830s and 1840s.

The arrival of missionaries in the Northwest began a new era in Indian-white relations, but significant changes came much earlier as a consequence of the Corps of Discovery. Accurate geographical knowledge had changed ideas about fur-trading strategies in the Far West. Rather than funnel furs from the Pacific Northwest back to St. Louis, fur trade investors saw an opportunity to use the maritime trade's shuttling of furs to Asia and focused on establishing an embarcadero at the mouth of the Columbia River. Foremost proponent of this scheme was John Jacob Astor, a wealthy New York merchant, who hatched his idea for a private and monopolistic trading venture that would bring furs to the Pacific coast from a series of posts strung out along Lewis and Clark's route. By spring 1810, Astor had formed the Pacific Fur Company and decided to send two parties to the mouth of the Columbia to establish Fort Astor. One group went by sea in the *Tonquin*, commanded by the stern Captain Jonathan Thorn, and the second by wagon train, led by Wilson Price Hunt, a merchant who had yearned to engage in the western trade and had met with Lewis in St. Louis not long after the explorer's return.

The *Tonquin* arrived at the mouth of the Columbia in March 1811, bringing the first Americans to the Pacific coast who planned to build a settlement. Passing over the dangerous bar posed a challenge that Captain Thorn met by sending pilot boats to find a channel, which consigned eight men to their deaths before the *Tonquin* anchored in Baker Bay, where Chinook traders canoed out to the ship. The overland party also faced dangers on their trek to Astoria. Beginning their westward journey in October 1810 from St. Louis, where they met with Governor Clark, Hunt's group went up the Missouri to the Arikara Villages, struck west to the Big Horn River, and then trekked along the Snake River to the Columbia. Trouble in finding the route, bad weather, and sparse supplies slowed Hunt's progress. Dividing his party into two groups in Idaho, one column under Donald Mackenzie made it to Astoria by January 1812 while Hunt and the larger segment arrived in February.

By the time the overland party reached Astoria, the *Tonquin*'s contingent had constructed several buildings, including a trading house, a dwelling, shops, and storage areas on a point of land well inside the estuary. Astor's plan required a substantial entrepôt at the Columbia's mouth to collect, store, and ship furs from inland points. The fort opened its gates to local traders—unlike Lewis and Clark—but the Astorians also complained about thievery, especially pilfering of tools and metal items. The promise of the trade, however, directed Astorians' eyes to the interior, and they outfitted a party in July 1811 to scout up the river for good trading locations and to see if there was any competition from the Montreal traders, the Northwest Company. They need not have worried about the Montrealers, for as they prepared to leave, a canoe skidded up on the shore carrying David Thompson, a partner in the Northwest Company. As far as Thompson knew, the Astorians were business associates, since he had been out of communication and did not know that the agreement with Astor had not materialized. To keep all options open, the Astorians feigned knowledge of the deal, and within days Thompson's canoe joined the Astorians, led by David Stuart and Alexander Ross, heading back up the Columbia. In his journal, Thompson tersely noted:

> July 22 [1811] Monday. A Fine day. Arranged for setting off for the Interiour in company with Mr David Stuart & 8 of his Men in 3 Canoes. I pray kind Providence to send us a good Journey to my Family & Friends.

Praying for the benevolence of providence was Thompson's refrain in journals he kept throughout his long and amazing career as a trader in the Canadian-American West. Born in Westminster, England, in 1770, Thompson had been bound out by his single-parent mother to the Hudson's Bay Company at age fourteen. He had attended Grey Coat

William L. Lang

Figure 4.3: Henry Warre's 1845 sketch of Columbia Lake, source of the Columbia River, where David Thompson camped with local Indians in 1807. Courtesy of the Washington Historical Society.

School, an institution for children of poor families, and had gained a good knowledge of mathematics, geography, and navigation. The company ship sailed in 1784, and Thompson stepped onto the wharf at Churchill on Hudson Bay in time to settle in for the winter and his first year as an HBC clerk.

Thompson became one of the great early cartographers of North America, but he did not develop his expertise quickly. His first mentor was Samuel Hearne, the man who had made a heroic overland trek to the mouth of the Coppermine River on the Arctic Ocean in 1770 and wrote an influential account of his travels. His second mentor was Philip Turnor, the HBC's "surveyor and astronomer," who instructed Thompson in 1789–1790 in the arts of land navigation and chart making. By that time, Thompson had been posted out on the plains, where he had traveled as far as the Saskatchewan River. As he went about the business of fur trading and traveling more than nine thousand miles across Canada, Thompson became more and more practiced and interested in navigation and mapmaking, so much so that in 1797 he jumped from HBC to the rival Northwest Company, in part because they promised to support his nearly compulsive cartographic hobby.

Thompson worked as a surveyor and trader for the Northwest Company in the plains and the Rockies. His surveying methods nearly took over his days, which reading his journals readily discloses, for they are peppered with astronomical observation data, distance calculations, and geometric measurements. Unlike mariners, who carried accurate clocks to determine longitude, Thompson could not haul such a fragile instrument, so he had to calculate his position by making numerous astronomical observations and mathematical plottings.

By 1806, Thompson had charted much of the eastern slope of the Continental Divide, and the company sent him west in the Columbia River country. Pushing over Howse Pass, he found the source of the Columbia River in two lakes at the western base of the divide. There he built Kootenae House, near present-day Lake Windermere in southeastern British Columbia. The river flowed north for nearly two hundred miles before turning sharply south and running through two long kolk lakes and crossing into the United States. The Kootenay River, which rose in the Canadian Rockies, flowed very near the Columbia, which led many early explorers, including Thompson, to be confused about the river courses. It took Thompson some time to sort out the fractured drainages on the west side of the divide, which he did by surveying the region south of Kootenae House and establishing posts on Pend d'Oreille Lake and the Clark Fork River near present-day Thompson Falls, Montana. In 1810, he pioneered a northern route over the divide through Athabaska Pass and established a winter camp at the mouth of Canoe River, where the Columbia makes its sharp turn south. The next year, Thompson descended the Columbia to Astoria, surveying as he went and establishing relationships with Indians who might become trading partners with the Northwest Company.

Thompson traveled up the Columbia faster than the lumbering Astorians. By the time Alexander Ross and David Stuart reached the mouth of the Snake River, Thompson had arrived at Spokane House, far to the interior. At an Indian camp near the Snake, Ross discovered a British flag "planted there," as he later recounted, "by Mr. Thompson, as he passed, with a written paper, laying claim to the country north of the forks, as British territory." Ross was wrong about when Thompson had planted the flag—he had jammed it into the ground on his descent of the Columbia on July 9, when he had promised guns and goods to the principal chief, a leader who also held a peace medal from Lewis and Clark—but Ross was not wrong about the Nor'wester's motive. Thompson's flagpole meant a claim, and Ross set about to undo the effort by promising more American goods for the Indians' allegiance.

Despite the possibility that company principals had agreed to a cooperative enterprise in the Northwest, traders pursued a competitive policy on the ground, for no one knew how the territory west of the divide might be split up. With that in mind, the Pacific Fur Company established interior posts at Spokane and on the Willamette, Clearwater, Okanagan, and Thompson rivers, each positioned to compete with

Nor'wester's. The tit-for-tat scramble for trading position in the Northwest in 1811–1813 was a reflection of a larger commercial and diplomatic conflict between the United States and Great Britain. The war some called the "second war of revolution" erupted in spring 1812, pitting forces in battles from New England to New Orleans. Although the main battlefields were far from the mouth of the Columbia, the conflict washed up to the fort's dock. Realizing that they could not defend the fort, Astor's men in the Northwest decided to abandon the location. At the end of November 1813, the HMS *Racoon* arrived, "having on board, Mr. John McDonald (of the N.W. Co.) with 3 Canadians and a Small Supply of Dry Goods," as the scribe noted in the Pacific Fur Company log. The occupiers renamed the place Fort George, hoisted a new flag, and stocked the shelves with trade goods, ending Astor's dream and with it proprietary claim to the Northwest.

Planting a fort at the mouth of the Columbia in 1811 had been a bold move by an aggressive merchant in a young nation. Added to the accomplishments of Robert Gray in 1792 and Lewis and Clark in 1805–1806, the effort bolstered an American claim to the area. At the conclusion of the War of 1812, all properties seized during the war were to revert to their previous owners, but in the case of Astoria an agreement between the United States and Britain in 1818 put a broader policy in place. Both nations had twenty years to occupy the region in common and to develop commerce and settlements. The British had the advantage because the Nor'westers had established more than a dozen fur posts. But the potential for an overland supply line to the Northwest, part of the uninterrupted American dream for a commercial passage to India, received a boost when the Astorians returning to St. Louis in 1813 discovered South Pass in the Rockies, a gentle wagon-friendly crossing. Not until 1846 did American and British negotiators find common ground over what nation held sway in the Northwest. By that time, Americans had inundated the Willamette Valley and camped out in numbers in south Puget Sound, even though the Hudson's Bay Company had dominated trade and economic activity for more than twenty-five years. Britain finally relinquished their claim to land south of the 49th parallel in a diplomatic agreement that avoided war and closed out a chapter in imperial competition in North America.

During the deliberations over the Oregon Question, as many called the two nations' dispute over the region, David Thompson sent British negotiators a highly detailed and comprehensive map of the region. The negotiators did not use his map, but his work made its way into the discussions from other cartographers who freely purloined it. After leaving the Columbia in 1813, Thompson continued surveying and took on the job of plotting the boundary line between British North

America and the United States between 1815 and 1826. He did not enjoy fame for his work because his employers funneled all of his work to London, where maps of North America never credited Thompson.

By the time Thompson died in Montreal in 1857, the North American fur business had long passed its heyday. The world he knew had given way in the Northwest to agricultural settlement and the exploitation of natural resources. Fort George on the Columbia had struggled for several years after the end of the War of 1812, and by 1821 it was part of a larger Hudson's Bay Company. The Hudson's Bay Company inherited all of the Nor'wester's posts, including those Thompson built, and a new business model dictated from London came to the Northwest.

During the following twenty-five years, the new company's post factors developed extensive operations throughout present-day Oregon, Washington, British Columbia, Idaho, and Montana. From a headquarters sited not too far from Broughton's Point Vancouver, Chief Factor John McLoughlin managed a trading enterprise that extended from the southern Gulf of Alaska to the 42nd parallel and east to the Continental Divide. The furs from this vast region funneled to Fort Vancouver on the Columbia. The posts, their employees, the agricultural operations required for supply, and the intense trading relationships with Indian tribes completed what James Cook, George Vancouver, and Lewis and Clark had helped engineer—an imperialistic reordering of power relations on the Northwest Coast of North America. The explorers had come by tide and by trail, and they had taken the measure of the land and its inhabitants. What began in part as a search for the Northwest Passage became a four-decade juggernaut that remade the region forever.

Essays on Sources

The best overview of the era of exploration that includes the first cartographic renderings of the Pacific Northwest is William Goetzmann's *New Lands, New Men: The Second Great Age of Exploration* (New York: Viking, 1986). There is also a sizable bibliography on explorations by European maritime nations in the North Pacific. Among the most important are Warren L. Cook, *Flood Tide of Empire: Spain and the Pacific Northwest, 1543–1819* (New Haven, Conn.: Yale University Press, 1973); Derek Pethick, *First Approaches to the Northwest Coast* (Seattle: University of Washington Press, 1979); Donald C. Cutter, *Malaspina and Galiano: Spanish Voyages to the Northwest Coast, 1791 and 1792* (Vancouver: University of British Columbia Press, 1991); and Derek Hayes, *Historical Atlas of the Pacific Northwest: Maps of Exploration and Discovery* (Seattle: Sasquatch Press, 1999).

Recent scholarship on the encounters between maritime explorers and Native people has opened new areas for research and has yielded important reinterpretations of the events between *1778* and *1825*. Geographers, linguists, ethnohistorians, and other specialists have expanded our understanding of this pivotal era in Northwest history. Some use postmodern analysis, especially with regard to European and American perceptions of Native peoples and their cultures. Among the best are John L. Allen, *Passage Through the Garden: Lewis and Clark and the Image of the American Northwest* (Urbana: University of Illinois Press, 1975); Daniel B. Botkin, *Our Natural History: The Lessons of Lewis and Clark* (New York: Putnam, 1995); Paul Carter, *The Road to Botany Bay: An Essay in Spatial History* (London: Farber and Farber, 1987); Daniel Clayton, *Islands of Truth: The Imperial Fashioning of Vancouver Island* (Vancouver: University of British Columbia Press, 2000); Robin Fisher and Hugh Johnson, eds., *From Maps to Metaphors: The Pacific World of George Vancouver* (Vancouver: University of British Columbia Press, 1993); James R. Gibson, *Otter Skins, Boston Ships, and China Goods: The Maritime Fur Trade of the Northwest Coast, 1785–1841* (Seattle: University of Washington Press, 1992); Cole Harris, *The Resettlement of British Columbia: Essays on Colonials and Geographical Change* (Vancouver: University of British Columbia Press, 1997); Richard Mackie, *Trading Beyond the Mountains: The British Fur Trade in the Pacific Northwest, 1793–1843* (Vancouver: University of British Columbia Press, 1997); Gananath Obeyesekere, *The Apotheosis of Captain Cook: European Mythmaking in the Pacific* (Princeton: Princeton University Press, 1992); James P. Ronda, *Lewis and Clark Among the Indians* (Lincoln: University of Nebraska Press, 1984); Ronda, *Finding the West: Explorations with Lewis and Clark* (Albuquerque: University of New Mexico Press, 2001), and *Astoria and Empire* (Lincoln: University of Nebraska Press, 1990); Albert Furtwangler, *Acts of Discovery: Visions of America in the Lewis and Clark Journals* (Urbana: University of Illinois Press, 1993); Elizabeth Vibert, *Trader's Tales: Narratives of Cultural Encounter in the Columbia Plateau, 1807–1846* (Norman: University of Oklahoma Press, 1997); and Thomas P. Slaughter, *Exploring Lewis and Clark* (New York: Random House, 2003). On the decimation of coastal Indian groups by disease, the most complete source is Robert Boyd, *The Spirit of the Coming Pestilence: Introduced Infectious Diseases and Population Decline among Northwest Coast Indians, 1774–1874* (Seattle: University of Washington Press, 1999).

The original exploration narratives written by George Vancouver, Lewis and Clark, and David Thompson have modern reprints and compilations that include scholarly commentaries. On George Vancouver, consult W. Kaye Lamb, ed., *George Vancouver: A Voyage of Discovery to the North Pacific Ocean and Round the World 1791–1795,* 4 vols. (London:

Hakluyt Society, 1984). The new edition of the Lewis and Clark journals has advanced scholarship considerably. See Gary Moulton, ed., *The Journals of the Lewis and Clark Expedition,* 13 vols. (Lincoln: University of Nebraska Press, 1983–2000). On David Thompson see J. B. Tyrell, ed., *David Thompson: Narrative of his Explorations in Western North America, 1784–1812* (Toronto: Champlain Society, 1916), for the traditional interpretation and Richard Glover, ed., *David Thompson's Narrative, 1784–1812* (Toronto: Champlain Society, 1962), for one that is more critical of Thompson.

Numerous studies have been done, from several distinct viewpoints, on each of the featured explorers in this chapter. Older studies tend to emphasize the triumphalist interpretation of Euroamerican exploration and conquest, while recent studies include additional perspectives, especially ones that take cultural and environmental consequences into account. The best biographies of George Vancouver are Bern Anderson, *Surveyor of the Sea: the Life and Voyages of George Vancouver* (Seattle: University of Washington Press, 1960), and Alison Gifford, *Captain Vancouver: A Portrait of His Life* (King's Lynn, England: St. James Press, 1986). A recent discussion of Vancouver's voyage to the Northwest is Robin Fisher, *Vancouver's Voyage: Charting the Northwest Coast, 1791–1795* (Seattle: University of Washington Press, 1992), which emphasizes Vancouver's understanding of geography and his difficulties with Native peoples. Biographers have tended to write adulatory biographies of Meriwether Lewis and William Clark. The best are Stephen Ambrose, *Undaunted Courage: Meriwether Lewis, Thomas Jefferson, and the Opening of the American West* (New York: Simon & Schuster, 1996), which treats the expedition as a triumphal and patriotic military experience. Jerome O. Steffen, *William Clark: Jeffersonian Man on the Frontier* (Norman: University of Oklahoma Press, 1977), interprets Clark as an Enlightenment figure, not a backwoodsman. There is no modern biography of David Thompson, but four studies cover his surveying in the Pacific Northwest: M. Catherine White, ed., *David Thompson Journals Relating to Montana and Adjacent Regions, 1808–1812* (Missoula: University of Montana Press, 1950); Barbara Belyea, ed., *Columbia Journals: David Thompson* (Montreal: McGill-Queens University Press, 1994); Victor Hopwood, ed., *David Thompson: Travels in Western North America, 1784–1812* (Toronto: Macmillan, 1971); and Jack Nisbet, *Sources of the River: Tracking David Thompson Across Western America* (Seattle: Sasquatch Books, 1994).

CHAPTER 5

Jedediah S. Smith and Marcus and Narcissa Whitman
Mountain Men and Missionaries in the Far West

BARTON H. BARBOUR

Dateline: The Cimarron River near the Kansas–New Mexico border, May 1831

A lone horseman, his sun-bronzed face ravaged by deep scars, is seeking desperately needed water for parched men and live-stock. His suffering companions lag a few miles behind him, in a traders' caravan crawling across the "water scrape" toward Santa Fe under a mercilessly hot and brazen sky. Halting at a water hole close by the Cimarron River, the rider suddenly realizes that he is not alone. Several Comanche warriors have appeared out of nowhere. This man, having already survived a perilous decade as a mountain man, senses that he is done for, but he is ready, as the contemporary phrase went, to "sell his life dearly." As nervous horses snort and shuffle, a Comanche shoots him in the chest. The white man fires his rifle, killing one of the leaders. He grasps for his pistols, but other Comanches fire their guns and he tumbles from his horse. The Indians gather up a few of the dead man's belongings and hit the trail. Some *comancheros*—Hispanic men who trade with Comanches—later bring some of the man's belongings and a few details of the encounter to Santa Fe. The man's body is never recovered. That brief, bloody moment snuffed out the spectacular career of a trapper and explorer named Jedediah Strong Smith. Few men roamed—and none mapped—more of the early West than Smith.

Dateline: Waiilatpu Mission Station on the Walla Walla River, Oregon Territory, November 30, 1847

A rambling adobe house in a picturesque valley occupies the center of a productive-looking farm showing signs of a recent harvest. It ought to be a scene of peaceful contentment, but it is far from being so. Instead, the smell of death lingers on the rainy, chill autumn breeze. Here and there sprawl mutilated corpses, two of them with heads sawn in half. They are mostly men, but one woman lies facedown in a mud puddle beside a bloodied settee next to the broken door of the ransacked mission head-quarters. She was called Narcissa, the wife of Dr. Marcus Whitman, an "assistant missionary" to the Cayuse Indians. They and two other couples journeyed from New York State to "Old Oregon" in 1836 to serve the American Board of Commissioners for Foreign Missions (ABCFM), the missionary arm of the united Congregational and Presbyterian churches. Twelve years after their arrival at Waiilatpu, though, things went terribly wrong. Cayuse Indians killed the Whitmans and twelve others among seventy-five inhabitants of the isolated mission station. Survivors—some had been captives of the Cayuse—described a terrifying sequence of events that has ever since been remembered as the "Whitman Massacre." The story they told assured Marcus Whitman of a martyr's place in the nation's mythic memory. Whitman's crusade to "civilize" and Christianize Indians and his support of emigrating Americans, it is said, "saved" the Oregon country from British domination and guaranteed U.S. acquisition of the Pacific Northwest.

Although separated by sixteen years and a thousand miles, these glimpses of death involve people whose destiny led them to the Pacific Northwest before the United States owned it. Mountain men and missionaries played important roles in early western history, when fur trading was the dominant economic enterprise and Indians still owned the land. Jedediah Smith and Marcus and Narcissa Whitman were just such people, and their stories help explain how a few hundred American men and a handful of women shaped the course of far western history in the 1830s. An evaluation of their "meaning" also highlights important differences between historical myth and historical reality.

Neither Jedediah S. Smith nor Marcus Whitman was cut from everyday cloth. The two men exhibited extraordinary talents and drive, and both lived alongside Indians for years. Contemporaries deemed them capable and experienced "leaders," yet both died in violent confrontations with Indians. Not least, each became a larger-than-life character in western mythology. Fortunately, the documentary record on Smith and the Whitmans is rich. Their journals and letters and other contemporary documents describe their activities, reveal their temperaments, and help us understand the important roles they played in early western American history.

　　　　　Barton H. Barbour

For the purposes of this chapter, the history of the trans-Mississippi West may be said to begin with Thomas Jefferson's winning the presidency in 1800. That presidential campaign was so vigorously contested that Jefferson's election was called the "Revolution of 1800." Despite Federalists' dire predictions that the infant republic would plunge into anarchy and chaos, the nation survived the election and went about its business. Relations with Great Britain were dangerously tense, and Jefferson focused his attention mainly on preventing a second war with Britain. The Louisiana Purchase, today considered his greatest presidential achievement, was by no means uniformly celebrated in 1803. Some Americans thought it was money wasted; others complained there was no constitutional warrant for such acquisitions. Jefferson sent Lewis and Clark's expedition to inventory Louisiana, but their return in 1806 generated about as much ridicule as applause, and Jefferson's political opponents lost no opportunity to poke fun at the expedition.

Most Americans were only dimly aware of events taking place outside their narrowly constructed worlds formed by hamlets, farms, cities, and towns. A small but growing number of them, however, had fallen under the thrall of a siren song emanating from the Far West. That song whispered of a remote, almost fabulous land called "the Oregon." A few prescient Americans foresaw, like Jefferson, that Oregon was destined to be a keystone in the future continental empire they envisioned. Contemporary geographers hoped, as geographers had since the days of Columbus, that the long-sought Northwest Passage—a water route "to India" through North America sometimes called the Northern Mystery or the Strait of Anián—might yet be hidden in "the Oregon."

American desire for the Pacific Northwest, first kindled around 1800, grew so heated after 1820 that it could have ignited a war against Great Britain. During the 1844 presidential campaign, Democrat James K. Polk capitalized on the "54° 40' or fight!" slogan of bellicose expansionists and won office. Polk redeemed his promise to make the United States a continental nation and confirm its "manifest destiny." Annexing Texas in 1845 precipitated a costly war with Mexico, resulting in the U.S. seizure of New Mexico and California, but in 1846 the "Oregon Question" was decided without bloodshed.

Fur traders' business took them to North America's farthest reaches, and governments sometimes found the trade a convenient tool for securing national geopolitical objectives. Robert Gray's 1792 voyage allowed the United States to claim the Columbia River and adjacent territory by "right of discovery." In 1804–1806, Lewis and Clark's Corps of Discovery (which included several trappers) buttressed the U.S. claim to the Pacific Northwest, examined the assets of the Louisiana Purchase,

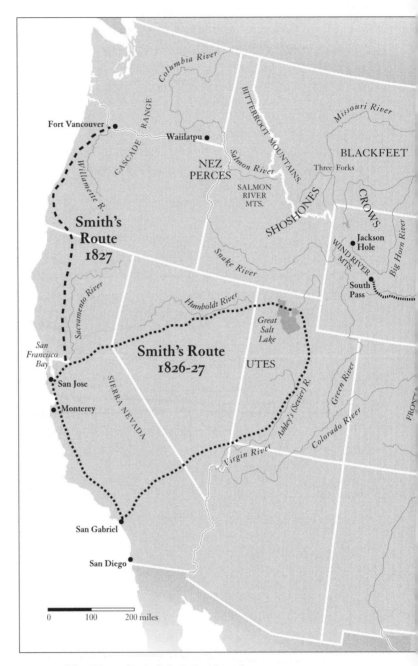

Map 5.1: The West of Jedediah S. Smith and
Marcus and Narcissa Whitman.

Barton H. Barbour

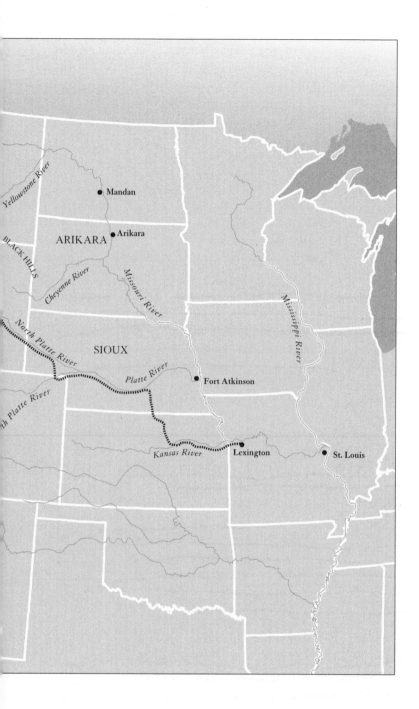

Mandan

ARIKARA •Arikara

Yellowstone River

BLACK HILLS

Cheyenne River

Missouri River

North Platte River

SIOUX

Platte River •Fort Atkinson

h Platte River

Kansas River •Lexington •St. Louis

Mississippi River

and proved that the Northwest Passage existed only in men's imaginations. The most immediate economic opportunities lay in the fur trade, and that stimulus inspired some Americans to look toward Oregon. They were not alone, however, for the United States was but one of four contenders for the fur-rich "Oregon Country."

Spain and Russia had longstanding interests in the Pacific Northwest. In 1819, however, a faltering Spain signed the Adams-Onís treaty with the United States. In exchange for defining the disputed Louisiana Purchase boundary, Spain yielded its claim to Oregon. Russian exploration of the Northwest commenced in 1728, and by 1812 fur traders with the Russian-American Company (founded in 1799) established Fort Ross on the Russian River in California, some sixty miles north of San Francisco. In 1824 Russia promised the United States it would keep its traders above north latitude 54° 40'.

Great Britain likewise claimed "the Oregon," asserting that activities of North West Company and Hudson's Bay Company (HBC) fur traders gave it ownership of the Columbia River's interior drainage. Despite Spanish and Russian pretensions, it was clear soon after 1800 that the United States and Great Britain were the real contenders for the Pacific Northwest. With neither nation willing to go to war over Oregon or the disputed U.S.-Canada boundary line, in 1818 the two nations negotiated an open-ended treaty establishing "joint occupancy" of the region. Renewed in ten years, the agreement extended joint occupation until 1848, thus deferring settlement of the "Oregon Question."

After decades of competition, the HBC and the North West Company merged under the HBC banner in 1821. Company officials probably believed their supremacy in the Pacific Northwest would continue unchallenged, for American fur traders stayed out of Oregon from 1812 until 1825. Then, to discourage competition from Yankee fur traders at its posts along the Columbia, the HBC decided to strip the Snake River country of beavers. From 1825 to 1830 the "Snake River brigades," led by Peter Skene Ogden, Alexander Ross, and John Work, attempted to create an insulating "fur desert." Despite HBC policy, after 1829 American interest in Oregon's fur trade declined, while its zeal for "settling" farmers there grew lustier. This was in large part because of the enthusiastic boosterism of men such as Senator Thomas Hart Benton, Representative John Floyd, and a New Englander named Hall Jackson Kelly, from whose fevered pen flowed several exaggerated promotional screeds touting the richness of Oregonian soils and the ease with which bumper crops might be harvested.

Kelly created most of his propaganda before he ever saw the country. When Kelly finally did arrive in Oregon in 1834, he got there by trekking north from Mexican California with an American trapper named Ewing Young. Kelly's strange and belligerent behavior soon set him at loggerheads with Dr. John McLoughlin, the HBC's chief factor at Fort Vancouver (1825–1846), across the Columbia River from modern Portland, Oregon. Within a few months McLoughlin (Kelly labeled him a "prosecuting monster") had grown weary of Kelly's harping and sent the troublemaker home via the Sandwich Islands (Hawai`i), courtesy of the HBC. Kelly's call for settlers was premature, but American fur hunters had already been in Oregon for a decade.

American trappers and traders came to the Columbia in 1811, when John Jacob Astor launched his own drive to the Pacific. A New York capitalist who tried to monopolize the American fur trade, Astor organized the Pacific Fur Company in 1808. He sent seaborne and overland expeditions to the Columbia to establish Astoria, a trading post and depot that would furnish a commercial connection to China, where sea otter skins fetched amazingly high prices. By 1811 Astoria was operational, but a few months into the War of 1812 Astor's own traders sold out to the North West Company. In December 1813 a Royal Navy sloop, the *Racoon,* officially seized Astoria and renamed it Fort George. Astoria was a financial disaster, but it bolstered the U.S. claim to Oregon. The 1814 Treaty of Ghent restored the trading post to the United States, but by then Astor's interests lay elsewhere. A key player in North America's fur trade, Astor reaped sensational success, becoming America's first millionaire and an influential man in government circles.

At about the same time, fur traders based in St. Louis, Missouri, began moving up the Missouri River. Founded by French fur traders just before New France fell to Britain in 1763, St. Louis and the rest of Louisiana were ceded by King Louis XIV to his Spanish cousins in order to keep it out of British hands. Although perfectly sited to become a western fur trade emporium, St. Louis languished under Spanish dominion. Over several decades, Spanish colonial administrators' feeble efforts to probe the Missouri River yielded no substantial economic results. In 1800 Spain retroceded Louisiana to France; three years later it was sold to the United States, and Americans began moving to St. Louis. Lewis and Clark's return heralded an expansion of the fur trade into the Upper Missouri region and the Rocky Mountains. Even so, the St. Louis–based fur trade stagnated after the War of 1812, although it would be resuscitated around 1820.

The colorful era of the mountain men began in 1825 and lasted until roughly 1840. Jim Bridger, Thomas Fitzpatrick, John Colter, Joseph Meek, and, not least, "Jed" Smith loom large in western legendry, but in reality the mountain man period constituted only a brief chapter in North American fur trade history. At its height during the

1830s, however, several hundred "Rocky Mountain men" annually scoured the watercourses of western North America. Their primary target was the beaver, whose fur provided raw material for fine felt hats made in Europe and America. In the 1830s beaver skin prices soared to a high of six dollars a pound, making the animals highly prized by hunters.

"Free trappers" and "mountain men" included all sorts of Euroamerican and mixed-blood men—learned and ignorant, peaceable and murderous, Bostonians and backwoodsmen—who hoped they would master their craft, avoid being killed, and leave the mountains with money. For some fur trappers and Indian traders, sheer thirst for adventure was a sufficient inducement to choose their vocation. Most, however, were motivated by economic necessity, whether that meant bailing out a mortgaged backcountry farm or amassing capital to fund other commercial or political ventures. Some fur companies hired men on a yearly salary basis; others paid hunters according to the amounts of fur they harvested. As they trapped and traded through the West, fur hunters acquired much knowledge about western land and the peoples who lived there. Little wonder, then, that missionaries—like emigrants traveling on the Oregon-California Trail during its early years—found fur traders' aid indispensable to success in crossing the continent.

To early-nineteenth-century Americans, the "fur trade" meant fur hunting as well as trade with Indians. Often considered a frontier enterprise, the trade actually operated on a global scale. Indians exchanged furs for goods made in Europe, North America, and Asia. Furs were marketed in New York, Montreal, London, Leipzig, and China. The fur trade nurtured international capitalism and banking practices and gave rise to the modern corporation. It also was the first industry subjected to federal regulatory oversight, and it directly affected the evolution of U.S. Indian policy. Federal laws prohibited hunters from taking any game on Indian land, but fur hunters ignored the regulations. The government lacked the wherewithal to enforce fur trade laws until about 1865, which left the "Indian Country"—a vast region between the Mississippi River and the Pacific Ocean—wide open for traders eager to maximize opportunities for profits. North America's earliest big business, the fur trade deeply influenced U.S. and Canadian history.

New York State is almost as far from Oregon as any place in the United States can be, but it produced many notable nineteenth-century westerners. Mormon leaders Joseph Smith and Brigham Young and abolitionist John Brown spent years in New York. John Wesley Powell attended college near Albany. Patrick Gass, a sergeant with Lewis and Clark's expedition, resided in the Finger Lakes region, as did John Chapman, the legendary "Johnny Appleseed." Jedediah S.

Smith (1799–1831) and Marcus Whitman (1802–1848), as well as his bride, Narcissa (1808–1848), and other missionaries, also grew up in western New York.

Still a raw, dangerous frontier during the Revolutionary War, western New York had long been a "dark and bloody ground." French and British soldiers, fur traders, and settlers during the colonial era vied for the allegiance and trade of the Iroquois Confederacy, the area's dominant military power. Following American independence, Anglo-American settlers infiltrated the region, a process that rapidly accelerated between the end of the War of 1812 and the completion of the Erie Canal in 1825. Thousands of western "Empire State" residents hailed from New England. In time some of them, like Jed Smith's family, moved westward to Pennsylvania and Ohio.

An overpopulated region with notoriously poor farmland, New England brimmed with folk who had never entirely shucked the Calvinist theology or the social consciousness of John Winthrop, who led the Puritan exodus of 1630 from England to found Massachusetts Bay Colony. The "New Eden" that Puritans envisioned for North America proved vaporous, but modified secular and religious vestiges of Winthrop's ideology still stirred in the minds of transplanted New Englanders. This legacy helps explain the social-religious ferment called the Second Great Awakening, a revivalist frenzy that swept across western New York during the 1820s with such vigor that the region was dubbed the "Burned Over District."

Out of that multifarious hubbub arose Shakers, Transcendentalists, Latter-day Saints, Free Love communitarians, Millerites, and other "seekers" whose hopes, fears, and proselytizing helped determine the region's society and culture. Abundant documentation suggests that religious revivalism shaped Marcus and Narcissa Whitman's decision to become missionaries. Likewise, Jedediah Smith's journals and letters reveal an introspective young man, entangled, in his words, "altogether too much in the things of time." Tormented by doubts of his own spiritual rectitude, he feared he was an unworthy prodigal son of honored parents.

In 1821, when twenty-two-year-old Jedediah set out from his family's home in Ohio to find a career, the nation lay in the grip of an economic depression spawned by the Panic of 1819. Working his way across Illinois and down the Mississippi River, he arrived at St. Louis early in 1822. Like many young men on the move seeking opportunity, Smith thought the fur trade offered a way out of hard times, and St. Louis was the best place to find such work.

A bustling river town of around five thousand residents, St. Louis was poised to become the West's leading city. Mexican independence

Figure 5.1: Jedediah Strong Smith. The only extant portrait of Smith with any claim to authenticity, it was drawn by an unknown artist sometime after Smith was killed on the Santa Fe Trail in 1831. Close examination of the image shows that the artist sketched in some of the scars on Smith's face that resulted from his 1823 encounter with a grizzly bear. Photograph courtesy of the Utah State Historical Society.

in 1821 legalized the Santa Fe trade and helped solidify St. Louis's role as a commercial center. Wagon makers, blacksmiths, gunsmiths, and numerous merchants stood ready to supply the Santa Fe trade as well as the burgeoning Missouri River fur and Indian trades. In February 1822 "General" William H. Ashley and "Major" Andrew Henry placed an advertisement in the *Missouri Gazette and Public Advertiser* soliciting "100 enterprising young men" to sign up for two or three years as Rocky Mountain trappers. Jedediah Smith applied for the job and was hired as an "Ashley man."

An accomplished woodsman, Jed Smith was also literate and could "cipher," unlike many among the rough lot with whom he associated. During his first year in the mountains with Ashley, Smith proved himself as a hunter and a prudent, trustworthy individual. Recognizing Smith's leadership ability, Ashley rewarded the "confidential young man" with the command of a portion of his trappers.

Smith's second year with Ashley found him heading up the Missouri in May 1823. Ashley paused for a few days to trade for horses at the Arikara villages in South Dakota. For reasons unknown, a white man was killed one night, and the next morning a firefight erupted. Smith's shore party, stranded on a sandbar, took cover behind dead horses while the Arikaras poured in a withering fusillade from their stockaded village. With no other way out, the trappers swam for Ashley's keelboat, anchored in the Missouri. Thirteen of them died in the bloody affray, and several were wounded, but Smith emerged unscathed.

A few months later, Jed Smith led his first "brigade" west from Fort Kiowa toward the South Dakota badlands. During a hot day's march through dense underbrush, a grizzly bear burst from a thicket and seized Smith, breaking several of his ribs. Then the grizzly's fangs raked Smith's head, laying bare the top of his skull and leaving a mutilated ear dangling beside the torn scalp. After the attack, the still-conscious Smith beseeched his comrade James Clyman to find a needle and thread and sew up his face; then he mounted his horse and rode to camp. Smith soon recovered, but he was badly disfigured. Supposedly he took to wearing his hair long to conceal his mangled ear and facial scars. In quaint prose James Clyman wrote, "This gave us a lisson on the charcter of the grissly Baare which we did not forget."

Over the next seven years, Jedediah Smith logged some ten thousand miles of travel across plains, mountains, and deserts. In February 1824, seeking a route from the Sweetwater River to the Green River, he led his trappers through an unprepossessing declivity of major significance. Smith called it "the South Pass." Offering the easiest wagon passage through the Rockies, it determined the future route of the California–Oregon Trail. Others before him had seen the pass, but Jedediah is credited with its "effective discovery." As Dale L. Morgan noted, "To this wide depression along the continent's spine, missionaries followed the mountain men, settlers and gold seekers coming in their turn, thousands on thousands pursuing the vision or driven by the need."

William Ashley named Smith his "resident partner in the mountains" late in 1825. After the 1826 rendezvous at Cache Valley, Utah, Ashley and Henry retired from the mountain trade, selling out to Smith and two other mountain men, David Jackson and William

Sublette. During four years in business, Smith, Jackson & Sublette kept trappers in the mountains and secured the partners' financial independence. In 1830 the firm was dissolved and Jedediah decided to try his luck in the Santa Fe trade, thought to be safer than the mountain trade. Ironically, Smith may have been the least successful of the partners in economic terms, mainly because of circumstances beyond his control. Still, Smith, Jackson & Sublette's four years netted a profit of nearly $90,000.

In August 1826, Smith wrote, the partners "came to the conclusion that in order to Prosecute our Business advantageously it was necessary that our company Should be divided." One contingent would trap the Snake River, another would work the Three Forks of the Missouri region, and Smith's brigade was to "go to the South." Smith worked hard at making money, but he was as irresistibly drawn to exploration as a moth is to a candle.

"In taking the charge of our S[outh] western Expedition," he wrote, "I followed the bent of my strong inclination to visit the unexplored country and unfold those hidden resources of wealth and bring to light those wonders which I readily imagined a country so extensive might contain. . . . I wanted to be the first to view a country on which the eyes of white man had never gazed and to follow the course of rivers that run through a new land." With about fifteen men Smith headed southwest from Soda Springs in Idaho toward the "Spanish Missions" of Mexican California. No man until then, it is thought, had ever attempted to traverse the harsh deserts and unmapped mountain ranges that lay between the Great Salt Lake and southern California.

After a punishing dose of hunger, thirst, and fatigue, Smith and his worn-out men arrived at Mission San Gabriel in mid-November. They wintered in California, exchanging pleasantries and information with Catholic priests and government officers, some of whom nursed suspicions that Smith was an American spy. In spring 1827 Smith left most of his trappers in California and with two other men crossed the Sierra Nevada, the first white men of record to do so. Arriving at the rendezvous near Bear Lake, Utah, Smith recruited another party of eighteen trappers to return to California.

In mid-August 1827, Jed Smith encountered the Mojave nation for the second time at a Colorado River crossing on the California-Arizona border. This year, however, there was trouble, for another trapping party had killed some Mojaves during a fight in the autumn of 1826. While Smith and several men rafted gear across the broad river after three days of peaceable trade the Mojaves attacked, killing ten trappers and capturing livestock, guns, and provisions. Having lost more than half his men, Smith and his fellow survivors trekked onward, reaching Mission San Gabriel a few weeks later.

Seeing Jed Smith again did nothing to quell Mexican officials' worries about his motives for being there. Smith's biographers generally argue that he was no spy and that he was unnecessarily detained in Monterey, the victim of inept local authorities who dared not take action on his case without orders from above. Recent discoveries in Mexican archives by historian David J. Weber throw this interpretation into question. As Weber observed, Smith "was more devious in dealing with Mexican officials than has been supposed and . . . they had good reason for hostility toward him." After several frustrating months among the *californios,* Smith struck a bargain with the officials. Thanks to American merchants at Monterey willing to guarantee his good behavior, Jed Smith was permitted to depart and rescue the men he left behind a year earlier.

Smith led some twenty men away from California, having promised to go east. Instead he turned north, trapping along his way toward Oregon. While struggling through dense coastal rainforests he and his men had several ominous encounters with Indians but avoided serious violence. In July 1828 Smith's trappers made camp near the Oregon coast among the Kelawatsets on the Umpqua River and spent several days trading for skins and foodstuffs. On the morning of July 14, as Smith and two men canoed across the river seeking a northward path, Kelawatset warriors attacked the trappers' camp, killing all save the canoe party and one other man, who escaped in a different direction.

The destitute survivors trudged 150 miles up the coast and inland, reaching Fort Vancouver on August 10. The "White Headed Eagle," John McLoughlin, took them in and dispatched some men to try to recover their property. Hudson's Bay Company policy discouraged commerce or communication with Americans, but McLoughlin always offered assistance to needy travelers. Like Smith and the Whitmans, John McLoughlin played a hand in the geopolitical poker game that led to a settlement of the "Oregon Question." His unstinting aid to Americans in the 1840s embroiled him with HBC superiors who demanded that he repay thousands of dollars in unpaid debts and led him to resign from the HBC in 1846 and petition for U.S. citizenship. Ironically, after the Willamette Valley became U.S. soil, a few political enemies cheated him out of much valuable property. No man lost more money, or found fewer friends, than did John McLoughlin when the chips were down in the Oregon game's final hand.

An important element in Jedediah Smith's story is the assertion of some biographers that he brought Christianity to the western Indians. A few monuments celebrating Smith's achievements suggest that he was a missionary to Indians. One marker near Mobridge, South Dakota, claims Smith was not only a "trapper," "trader," and "explorer," but was also "truly a missionary by example." The text on another commemorative monument in Davis County, Utah, states—inaccurately— that Smith was "trained for the ministry in New York," adding that he "carried a Bible in one hand & his rifle in the other" and provided a "spiritual touch to the mountain men."

A careful analysis suggests that Smith's reputation as a missionary rests on shaky historical foundations. In 1831, the year that Smith was killed on the Santa Fe Trail, four "Flat-Head" Indians—Salishan speakers from the Salmon River near the Idaho-Montana border—journeyed to St. Louis seeking instruction about the white man's God. Out of that appeal, some say, came the mission program that "saved" Oregon for the United States. The story furnishes an important link connecting Smith with the Whitmans, for both Jedediah Smith and Marcus Whitman have been credited with setting that process in motion.

In actuality, the delegation consisted of three Nez Perces and one Flathead-Nez Perce. The Nez Perce tribe was well known to fur hunters, who reckoned them above the average intellectual and moral capacities of Indians, possibly because they tolerated American trappers. Around 1834 Captain Benjamin Bonneville, a soldier-turned-fur-trader who wrote about his western experiences, described the Nez Perces as "more like a nation of saints than a horde of savages." Bonneville's editor, Washington Irving of *Sleepy Hollow* fame, noted that the "antibelligerent" Nez Perces had "imbibed some notions of the Christian faith from Catholic missionaries and traders who had been among them."

To be sure, Smith's journals and letters confirm his piety, but they offer no evidence that he "preached" to any Indians. He did spend part of the winter of 1824–1825 among the Flatheads, but there is no hint that he discussed religion with them, nor is it certain that he possessed a Bible at the time. On the other hand, reliable evidence points to a probable source for motivating the Nez Perce delegation that went to St. Louis.

In 1825 HBC governor Sir George Simpson persuaded two Indian lads named Spokane Garry and Kootenay Pelly to attend the Red River Mission school at today's Winnipeg, Manitoba. The youths learned to read and write English, and they learned about Anglican Christianity too. Baptized in 1827, they returned to Oregon in 1829, having acquired "an education that would serve as a linguistic key to open the door for the entrance of Christianity among their tribes." Their mastery of English would also serve the HBC, for the company needed able translators from the Oregon tribes. Spokane Garry probably inspired the Flathead delegation's trip to St. Louis. In 1839 ABCFM missionary Asa B. Smith wrote that when Garry returned from the Red River school, he "communicated what he had heard to his people. Soon after wh[ich] six individuals set out for the States, in search . . . of Christian teachers."

Aspects of Jed Smith's personality buttressed the missionary myth that grew up around him. A quiet man, he rarely joked or drank liquor and seldom smoked tobacco. He never married and left no hint of a romantic attachment to a "girl back home." Unlike many mountain men, Smith apparently made no liaison, lustful or otherwise, with an Indian woman. Like most Protestant Americans he looked askance at Catholics, though he and his clerk, a Calvinist named Harrison Rogers, appreciated the generosity and kindliness of Catholic priests they encountered in California.

Smith exhibited many admirable traits, but it should be recalled that he lived in a dangerous kill-or-be-killed world. Indians and fur trappers alike adopted the principle of retributive justice, which required that acts of bloodshed must be repaid in kind. Preemptive killings of Indians, too, were not unknown. Smith was not by nature violent, but he did not hesitate to employ force against Indians whom he believed threatened his life or property. On the other hand, Smith was no mere racist, and he always sought amicable relations with Indians. Like his fellow trappers, Smith's responses to Indians ran the gamut from admiration to loathing. Fur traders' primary loyalty was to one another, but the trapping fraternity was multilingual and multiethnic, and on the whole they were less bigoted than most Americans. Jed Smith's own brigades mustered Americans, Hispanos, French Canadians, Indians, mix bloods, and at least one African American.

Smith's character reflects both altruism and egoism. He wished to be, and be seen as, a "worthy son" of beloved parents. Smith's letters often allude to his familial responsibilities, and on several occasions he sent money to parents and siblings. He also provided for his childhood teacher, Dr. Titus Vespasian Simons, whom he held in the highest regard. Smith drove himself to "make good" financially; that is why he became a fur trader. By the time Smith, Jackson & Sublette folded, Jedediah Smith had amassed about $30,000. Unlike many traders, apparently, he made money without making enemies. The only extant documents critical of Smith are those penned by Mexican officials in California.

Smith self-consciously modeled his role as an explorer on the example of Lewis and Clark, whom he admired. He often made ethnographic notes in his journal and several times mentioned Lewis and Clark's expedition. On July 12, 1827, in what must have been a particularly gratifying meeting, Smith spoke with William Clark and presented him a Paiute stone pipe he obtained while en route to California a year earlier. He also sent Clark a sample of salt he collected near the Virgin River in Utah.

A researcher recently unearthed a remarkable letter that Smith sent to the secretary of war in March 1831, a month before his fateful departure on the Santa Fe Trail. The letter contains Smith's offer to lead a Lewis-and-Clark-style expedition "to the Rocky Mountains." Jedediah was willing to share leadership with a military officer, though he insisted that ultimate command must be his, for he wrote, "I cannot consent to take a subordinate part in a business that several years experience has qualified me for." A hint of pride emerges as well in his statement that he had "for several years hazarded all that a man can hazard and acquired more than the Government would be disposed to give any man for his services." Jed Smith soon died on the road to New Mexico, but several cohorts, such as James Clyman, Ewing Young, Robert Newell, and the flamboyant Joseph Meek, wound up in Oregon, successfully transforming themselves from mountain men into American settlers.

Marcus Whitman, neither trapper nor explorer, left a durable imprint on early western history as a missionary. Even more than Jed Smith's biographers, however, hagiographic writers have cloaked Marcus Whitman with a significance that overreaches the facts known about him. Whitman's vocation in the Far West is historically significant, but the claim that he "saved" Oregon is an exaggeration.

Marcus Whitman's decision to go west was rooted in the centuries-long North American missionary tradition. Ever since their arrival in North America, European newcomers felt obligated to "civilize" and "Christianize" the "heathen" Native Americans, who had inhabited North America for about twelve thousand years. Members of Christian churches generally believed that "inferior" Native cultures lacked worthwhile attributes, but they also thought that it was their duty to save Indians' souls through conversion. The seventeenth century saw energetic Catholic missionary campaigns in New Spain and New France and Puritan conversion programs in New England. Disruptive "Indian Wars" from roughly 1620 through the 1760s—usually caused by white trespassers who appropriated Indian land and abused or enslaved Indians—terminated several North American colonial missionary adventures. Relative success, from a Eurocentric perspective, crowned the Jesuit and Franciscan Catholic missionary activities in Canada, New Spain, New Mexico, and California.

By 1800, Indian-white wars had ceased in the northeastern United States, and American missionary interest was mostly focused on Asia, Africa, and the South Pacific. Scant attention was paid to potential conversion prospects among Indians in western North America. In 1810 a group of Massachusetts Congregationalists founded the ABCFM, and

Figure 5.2: Marcus Whitman. This image was painted for the National Park Service's Whitman Mission National Historic Site in about 1970 by Drury V. Haight after a likeness of Marcus Whitman drawn from life by the Canadian artist Paul Kane in 1846. Identified by historian Clifford Drury, Kane's drawing is the only known authentic portrait of Marcus Whitman. Photograph courtesy of the National Park Service, Whitman Mission National Historic Site.

Presbyterians joined forces with them in 1812. One congregational minister who shared the ABCFM's goals, Samuel Parker, would help turn the board's attention to Oregon and the Far West.

Born and trained for the ministry in Massachusetts, Parker moved to the western New York town of Danby, near Ithaca, to serve a congregation in 1812. Resigning his position in 1826, he drifted for the next few years from church to church. Parker returned to western Massachusetts in 1832 as pastor of the Middlefield Congregational Church. In March 1833, an article in the *Christian Advocate and Journal and Zion's Herald* arrested his attention. The piece told of some "Flat-Head Indians" who came to St. Louis late in 1831 to see William Clark, the western superintendent of Indian affairs. (This was the same Nez

Perce delegation that supposedly resulted from Jed Smith's apocryphal "preaching.") These "Wise Men from the West," as Parker called them, had been told that their religion was "displeasing" to the "supreme Being" and that the white men possessed "a book containing directions how to conduct themselves in order to enjoy his favor." Deeply impressed, Parker decided his destiny was to convert Indians who were "perishing without the gospel."

Parker was fifty-four years old in 1833 when he petitioned the ABCFM to send him to Oregon as a missionary. Considering his age, and his wife and three children, the board dismissed Parker's application. The next year Parker successfully appealed the board's decision, and it authorized him to conduct a preliminary "exploring tour" to investigate prospects for an Oregon mission. While fundraising in western New York in November 1834, Parker spoke before a congregation at Wheeler. Among his listeners was the thirty-two-year-old Dr. Marcus Whitman. Parker soon informed the board that he had "found some missionaries. Dr. Whitman of Wheeler, Steuben County, New York, has agreed to offer himself to the Board to go beyond the mountains. He has no family. Two ladies offer themselves, one a daughter of Judge Prentiss of Amity. . . ." That "daughter" was Narcissa Prentiss, and it is likely that Parker urged Whitman to consider courting Narcissa because the board preferred married couples. Soon the two were engaged to be wed.

Months earlier, Whitman had submitted an application to the board, but they turned it down because he had long suffered chronic, sometimes debilitating pain in his left side, and he was not an ordained minister. As a young man in the 1820s, Whitman strongly considered a ministerial career, but financial exigencies forced him to choose medicine as an alternative. After attending an excellent medical school at Fairfield in western New York, Whitman practiced medicine for a few years in New York and Upper Canada. Yielding in 1830 to his first vocational love, at age twenty-eight Whitman entered a theological seminary, but his ill health (he attributed it to "an inflammation of the spleen") soon forced the abandonment of religious studies and a resumption of his medical practice.

Although aware that few missionary candidates were willing to work among Indians, the board informed Whitman that "it seems doubtful whether your health is such as to justify your going on a mission at all." Whitman persisted, and in February 1835, thanks to his medical expertise, apparently robust physique (he claimed his health was fully restored), and useful mechanical skills, he secured an appointment as a volunteer "assistant missionary" slated for service in Oregon.

But first, Marcus Whitman was ordered to accompany Parker on his western tour. Making his way from Amity, New York, to St. Louis, Missouri, early in 1835, Whitman joined Parker on April 1. As the two made final preparations for their trip, tensions arose. Parker seemed parsimonious in authorizing the purchase of necessary supplies, livestock, and gear. (Historian Clifford Drury characterized him as "tactless, fussy, and dogmatic" and "more suited for the study than for the rough life of western travel.") The two men had only a pair of horses and a mule to carry themselves and their barely adequate trail equipage.

Parker generally refused to assist in the day-to-day camp routine, did not get along well with Lucien Fontenelle's mountain men in the caravan with which the two missionaries traveled, and complained that the fur men threw rotten eggs at Whitman. Both Whitman and Parker nursed fears that the fur hunters meant to kill them. Parker claimed that the fur men "plotted our death & intended on the first convenient occasion to put this purpose into execution." As well, the greenhorn New Yorkers' refusal to travel on the sabbath delayed the arrival of trade goods and men at the rendezvous site in Wyoming.

Fortunately, two events occurred that raised the missionaries' standing among the mountain men and may have salvaged their mission program. When deadly cholera broke out in the traders' caravan, Whitman attended to the sick and probably saved lives. Later, he extracted an iron arrowhead that had been embedded in Jim Bridger's back for three years and performed similar operations on two other men, to the delight of the "mountaineers."

Soon after Fontenelle's caravan arrived at the Green River rendezvous, Whitman turned back to the States to wed Narcissa Prentiss and prepare for his missionary venture. Parker wandered on to the Columbia River, then returned by sea via the Hawaiian Islands to Connecticut, where he wrote a book describing his two-and-a-half-year trip. Marcus Whitman took the trail with two young Nez Perce lads, reached western New York in December 1835, and was married to Narcissa Prentiss in February 1836. By that time, Whitman had persuaded another couple to go to Oregon, but it was a tortuous association from the start.

Henry H. Spalding and his wife, Eliza, planned to missionize among the Osage nation on western Missouri's frontier before agreeing to accompany the Whitmans. Back in 1828, however, Spalding had courted Narcissa Prentiss, but she refused to marry him. An embittered Spalding said shortly before departing for Oregon, "I do not want to go into the same mission with Narcissa Prentiss as I question her judgement." Relations between the two couples would often be strained and sometimes turned downright nasty. But with no one else willing to go to Oregon, the bargain was struck.

The Whitman-Spalding party set out early in 1836, making their way to St. Louis, then on to the plains with a fur traders' caravan. By autumn they reached Oregon and after visiting the HBC's Fort Vancouver to purchase supplies decided to establish two "mission stations." The Whitmans chose a site on the Walla Walla River called Waiilatpu, in Cayuse land, while the Spaldings selected a tributary of the Clearwater River in present Idaho called Lapwai Creek, among the Nez Perce nation.

The missionaries built a few rude lean-tos and managed to survive the first winter. By the spring of 1838 an adobe house stood nearly completed at Waiilatpu, but floodwaters from the Walla Walla irreparably damaged it. On higher ground, a larger house made of adobes and lumber from Whitman's nearby sawmill took shape by the close of 1838. Over the next few years the Whitmans completed their house; planted fruit trees, grapevines, and several acres of grain and vegetables; and began breeding hogs, sheep, horses, and cattle.

Samuel Parker and the Whitman-Spalding party were not the first missionaries in the Far West. That distinction belongs to Jason Lee and four other Methodists who traveled to Oregon in 1834 in company with Nathaniel Wyeth, a Bostonian who tried, and failed, to reprise John Astor's Pacific coast fur-trading scheme. Like the ABCFM, the Methodists knew of the "Flat-Head mission" to the States, and they sent Lee to minister to them. Instead he established a station at French Prairie, on the Willamette River, about sixty miles from its confluence with the Columbia. Jason Lee's motives are not easily pinned down, but he spent more time building an American colony in Oregon than redeeming Indians' souls. In 1838 Lee journeyed to New York to solicit reinforcements and more money for his Willamette mission, and in 1840 he returned to Oregon, shepherding about fifty American settlers.

In the same year the first Catholic missionaries, Fathers François Blanchet and Modeste Demers, arrived in Oregon. They received financial and logistical support from HBC officers who believed the priests might help them achieve a twofold objective: to offset the growing American ecclesiastical and civil influence and to administer to the spiritual needs of a small community of retired French Canadian employees at the Cowlitz River Portage, about a hundred miles north of present-day Portland, Oregon. After reading much acerbic criticism of Jason Lee in letters from Dr. Elijah White and other Methodists, in 1843 the Methodist mission board at New York recalled Lee and canceled his mission, claiming that it had become secularized. Lee went east and persuaded the board he was innocent of wrongdoing, but he

Figure 5.3: Narcissa Whitman. This image was
painted for the National Park Service's
Whitman Mission National Historic Site in
about 1970 by Drury V. Haight after a likeness of Narcissa Whitman drawn from life
by the Canadian artist Paul Kane in 1846.
Identified by historian Clifford Drury,
Kane's drawing is the only known authentic
portrait of Narcissa Whitman. Photograph
courtesy of the National Park Service,
Whitman Mission National Historic Site.

was worn out and sickly. In August 1844 he returned to his former
home at Stanstead, Québec, in an effort to restore his health, but tuberculosis claimed him in May 1845.

Lee's replacement, Dr. George Gary, closed all the Methodist missions in Oregon, selling some to other denominations. The decade-long
effort had involved the energies of roughly seventy people and
allegedly cost about $250,000, but it produced meager results. One sym-
pathetic historian admitted that "the missions exerted but little
influence on the Indians," adding that if the proselytizers "could not
convert the red man they could prepare him for the day when the

why should they be?

whites would dominate the land." Such a thing may have been possible, but it was never an official objective of the Methodist missionary board in New York. Few today would argue that Indians were adequately "prepared" when white Americans took their lands.

The place of Indians within U.S. law and society remained unclear as of 1840, but grim indications of their future were evident. In 1830 Congress passed the controversial Indian Removal Act. The Cherokees were forced west of the Mississippi in 1838, and dozens of tribes would follow. According to federal laws and the Supreme Court, Indians were no longer sovereign; instead they were government "wards," subject to federal oversight and federal orders. But most of the western tribes, including the Cayuse, made no treaties with the United States before 1850. Their first exposure to Americans came with the mountain men and missionaries.

Pragmatic architects of the mission programs in "Old Oregon" aimed to transform Indians into property-owning "American" farmers. The change was supposed to induce Indians to renounce their "savage" lifestyle in favor of a "civilized" one founded upon simplified Christian ideological and moral principles. Some missionaries thought that Indians would be metamorphosed into "Americans" merely by learning the English language. Given the self-confidence, indeed the arrogance, of such notions, it is not surprising that few missionaries acquired facility in Indian languages, and they rarely identified positive aspects of Native cultures.

Like almost all Americans, missionaries believed that Indians' days were numbered and that whites ought to take their land. In 1842 a Methodist missionary named Gustavus Hines wrote that he was "under the impression that the doom of extinction is suspended over this wretched race, and that the hand of Providence is removing them to give place to a people more worthy of this beautiful and fertile country." Missionaries' concern for Indians' souls was too often trumped by their contempt for Indians as people. Ironically, the sense of cultural and racial superiority that these attitudes reflected would help guarantee failure for the Oregon missions.

Marcus Whitman was not a gifted linguist. By the time he learned enough of the Cayuse language to instruct them, they were fast losing interest in his message, which included repetitious Calvinistic warnings that they were hell-bound. Narcissa wrote that "husband tells them that none of them are Christians," and in response, the Cayuse "threaten to whip him and destroy our crops. . . . Their cattle were turned into our potato field every night to see if they could not compel him to change his course of instruction to them." Increasingly, Marcus spent his days attending to sick patients and superintending Waiilatpu's expanding farm and ranch operations. Henry Spalding, it turned out, was an adept linguist, and his wife, Eliza, enjoyed greater popularity among Indians than did Narcissa Whitman. According to Clifford Drury, "Whitman never enjoyed such wholehearted cooperation from the natives at Waiilatpu as Spalding received at Lapwai."

Convincing Indians to cast off their old religion was scarcely the only problem facing the Whitmans. Their tiny missionary settlement was riven by dissent and discord, and life at Waiilatpu exacted a grievous psychological toll from its inhabitants. The Congregational-Presbyterians feared and distrusted Catholics, but they fell into harsh criticism of Methodists and of each other, too. Especially corrosive was the petty bickering between the Whitmans and the Spaldings, for it divided the mission community.

Among the most seriously affected was Narcissa Whitman. She had already reached the brink of nervous collapse by March 1839 because of cramped conditions in a house full of people who antagonized one another. In a letter to her sister, Narcissa complained, "Now how do you think I have lived with such folks right in my kitchen for the whole winter?" A few months later, her beloved two-year-old daughter, Alice, drowned in the Walla Walla. Thereafter, Narcissa suffered frequent bouts of sobbing, she missed meals, she seemed always short-tempered; obviously, she was anxiety-ridden and deeply depressed. Her patience with Indians was exhausted, too. "They are," she wrote, "exceedingly proud, haughty and insolent people." Oddly, after she was killed, some Indians used identical words to describe Narcissa Whitman.

Several indigent "independent" missionaries, authorized and funded by no organization, arrived at Waiilatpu in 1839. Among them were Asahel and Eliza Munger, "religious zealots" (in Clifford Drury's words) from Oberlin, Ohio, whose "abysmal ignorance of conditions in Old Oregon" deluded them into believing they could create a self-supporting mission. Things did not go as they had planned. Early in 1841 Asahel Munger went insane at Waiilatpu, and he committed suicide later that year. According to Narcissa, "after driving two nails in his left hand," Munger "drew out a bed of hot coals and burnt it to a crisp, and died four days later." Munger's case is a standout, but even well-adjusted people found life as an Oregon missionary exceedingly hard.

In 1840 Marcus Whitman became so distressed by the community squabbling that he considered leaving Oregon and going home. After 1841 the ABCFM sent no more missionaries to the Far West. By early 1842, high maintenance costs, discouraging assessments of evangelical success, and complaints concerning the missionaries' behavior persuaded the board to recall several of its people in Oregon, close Waiilatpu and Lapwai, and order the Whitmans to live at Tshimakain mission, northwest of today's Spokane, Washington. The recall notice prompted Whitman to hasten east in the fall of 1842 to make his case for preserving the mission.

Risking a winter journey under brutal weather conditions, Whitman traveled south to the Santa Fe Trail, paused briefly at Bent's Fort on the Arkansas River, and continued on, reaching Washington, D.C., in late March 1843. There he spoke with President John Tyler and Secretary of State Daniel Webster about the "Oregon Question," though he had no influence on U.S.-British treaty negotiations then under way, as some have asserted. Whitman went on to Boston and persuaded the board not to close down Waiilatpu, thus—according to the myth—"saving" Oregon. Whitman carried the board's consent to maintain his mission back to Waiilatpu. About a thousand emigrants also took the trail to Oregon that summer, and Whitman was paid to guide some of them through the Snake River plains past the HBC's Fort Boise and on to the Columbia River.

Two years earlier, in 1841, the Oregon-California Trail had burst into life when the Bidwell-Bartleson party, comprising about 70 persons, crossed the continent under the guidance of mountain man Thomas Fitzpatrick. Stretching westward from St. Joseph, Westport, and Independence, Missouri, and Council Bluffs, Iowa, some two thousand miles to Sutter's Fort, near Sacramento, or to The Dalles in Oregon (and later to Oregon City), the Oregon-California Trail was an extension of the earlier fur traders' path to the Great Salt Lake via South Pass. The old-time fur trade era was fast disappearing; after 1841 trail traffic swelled as mounting numbers of settlers, many of them from Midwestern states, ventured west. The trip typically required four to six months of hard traveling in loosely organized "companies." Almost 20,000 emigrants crossed the continent before gold was discovered in California in 1848. In 1852 about 60,000 people went to California, and roughly 10,000 Latter-day Saints emigrated to Utah. By 1860 nearly 300,000 Americans had traversed the California-Oregon Trail.

In the early years emigrants often wisely hired mountain men as guides. Several "boosters" published trail guidebooks, some with dangerously inaccurate information and maps. In 1843–1846 the "Pathfinder," Lieutenant John C. Frémont, an army topographer, produced the first reliable "road atlases" for overlanders, but by 1849 the trail was so littered with abandoned household goods, wagons, and dead livestock that maps and guides became practically superfluous. Tragedies such as befell the unfortunate Donner Party of 1846 notwithstanding, most overlanders survived the trip, though in some years cholera, scurvy, and mountain fever claimed many lives. Indeed, disease accounted for nine out of ten deaths on the trail, while mortality from Indian attacks was numerically negligible. In 1850–1852 California and Oregon established several relief stations to succor undersupplied or ill travelers. Meanwhile the government established army posts such as Fort Laramie and sent soldiers and Indian agents to protect emigrants and Indians from each other, but the effort failed, and the mid-1850s marked the beginning of three decades of Indian-white wars for domination of the plains. Most of the Oregon-California Trail fell into disuse with the completion of the transcontinental railroad in 1869, but by then it was permanently enshrined in the mythic ethos of the "Old West."

After 1843, the Waiilatpu mission's principal role was providing food and other relief to the growing number of Americans on the Oregon Trail. Cognizant of that fact, the Boston board noted that the "southern branch of the Oregon mission" must remain open to serve the "wave of white population which is rolling westward." But the board also warned Whitman, "Your mission, like that of the Methodists, will get the name and credit of a trading or money-making establishment." The Oregon Trail saw practically no eastbound traffic in the early 1840s; everyone seemed to be going west. As traffic surged, the Cayuse and other tribes grew more and more disenchanted with the missionaries. By 1846 Waiilatpu's mission program had been jettisoned. Dealing with hungry, exhausted emigrants and their broken-down gear and livestock and planting crops to feed the next season's emigrants consumed the residents' time and energies.

The violence that terminated the Waiilatpu mission in 1847 was not without warning or precursors. Friction between missionaries and Indians had been on the rise for several years. In September 1841 Marcus Whitman experienced three ominous confrontations with a Cayuse chief named Tiloukaikt and some of the other men who later killed him. The Cayuses punched Marcus several times and threatened him and Narcissa with a hammer, an ax, a club, and a gun. The assaults prompted the pacifist Whitman to write: "We had showed the example of our non-resistance as long as it was called for & as we went to bed, we put ourselves in a state of defense." Indians also let their cattle eat the Whitmans' garden crops, broke down fences, and flatly ordered the missionaries to depart several times. Ironically, it was the HBC's factor at Fort Walla Walla, Archibald McKinlay, who defused the 1841 situation by threatening reprisals against the Cayuse should they harm the missionaries.

The rising tide of American emigration dismayed and angered Indians throughout the West, and Oregon was no exception. Emigrants killed and scattered game, but worse, they spread diseases such as measles, cholera, and dysentery. These ailments killed white people, but they wrought far greater mortality among Indians, whose immune systems could not outmaneuver the exotic killers. In summer 1847 a measles epidemic erupted at Waiilatpu, afflicting many mission residents, especially children, and a number of HBC men at their fort. The Cayuse nation, already sapped by decades of epidemics, numbered only a few hundred souls. By October, dysentery and measles had killed dozens of tribal members. Because so few Americans succumbed, the Indians suspected that Whitman was poisoning them in order to take their horses, cattle, and land.

Cayuse fears were not as irrational as they may seem. In 1841 a mission resident named William H. Gray had "injected a strong emetic into watermelons to discourage Indians from stealing them," and stories circulated among the Cayuse that Whitman regularly poisoned wolves with arsenic. Moreover, Whitman's medical practice made him a *te-wat,* a "medicine man" or "shaman." Among many tribes, a patient's death might lawfully be blamed on the would-be healer, so a te-wat was sometimes liable to be killed by aggrieved relatives of the dead person.

Hudson's Bay Company governor George Simpson—a cynical man who mistrusted Americans—took a dim view of the missionaries' work. Convinced that Indians adopted Christianity to attain material rewards, he declared that the missionaries "could gain converts only by buying them" and that the Cayuse expected missionaries to "procure guns and blankets for them from the Great Spirit, merely by their prayers." Simpson's final assessment was that "the Indians, discovering that the new religion did not render them independent of the traders, any more than their old one, regarded the missionaries as mere failures, as nothing better than imposters."

Simpson's comment, callous though it may be, underscores an important point. The cosmologies of Indians and whites in Oregon had little in common. Native religion, like Native life, manifested itself in ways that perplexed and irritated Christians. Most missionaries dismissed Native religion as mere "savage superstition," and their own certitude of cultural and intellectual superiority sometimes betrayed bigotry. When Gustavus Hines visited the Willamette Falls in 1842, he encountered Indians whom he dubbed "the most filthy and degraded looking beings in human shape, that our eyes ever beheld," adding, "It will require the labor of many years to elevate these Indians from the depths of their pollution into a civilized and christian people."

In reality the American missionary episode in the Far West was short-lived, and no missionary campaign truly succeeded, whether Catholic or Protestant. Few Indians proved willing to repudiate their ancestral traditions, religion, and languages. Out of several hundred Cayuse tribal members, Waiilatpu's Native congregation numbered only twenty-two persons in 1844. It did not help that the Oregon Catholics and Protestants disparaged each other and attempted to discredit their ecclesiastical rivals among the Indians. Robert Newell, a mountain man turned Indian agent, wrote in 1849, "No protestant missionaries are doing anything at present in the way of teaching and instructing Indians in the territory," adding that "many of them have no influence at all." After the missionaries departed, the vulnerable tribes were overrun by thousands of emigrants who flooded into "Old Oregon" in the 1840s and 1850s. Tribal life was thoroughly, often violently, disrupted.

And so at length we turn again to the historical significance of Jedediah Smith and Marcus and Narcissa Whitman. Unquestionably, Jed Smith's fame today rests securely upon his achievements as an explorer. The recovery of numerous Smith documents and a printed John C. Frémont map bearing penciled notations lifted around 1850 from Smith's own lost manuscript map have validated his place among the "greats" in North American exploration. Smith was the "discoverer" of South Pass, and his knowledge of western geography was unsurpassed. He led the first overland expedition from U.S. territory to California and the first that trekked through the Great Basin. He guided the first white men across the Sierra Nevada, and he led the first party up the Pacific coast from California to Oregon. Jedediah Strong Smith stands tall enough. It is needless to impute to him more than the facts will bear, for that would do him an injustice.

The known facts do not sustain the contention that Smith was a protomissionary or that he inspired the Nez Perces' request for Christian instruction. Neither is it arguable that Marcus Whitman's 1843 trip to the States "saved" Oregon for the United States. The Whitman myth was energetically promoted after 1850 by Henry Spalding and other Oregon mission veterans who published numerous books and pamphlets featuring what Clifford Drury termed "apocryphal stories and legends" based on "erroneous, biased, or distorted" evidence. Spalding's anti-Catholic bias also led him unfairly to blame Catholic priests in Oregon for inciting the Cayuse to murder the Whitmans.

Missionaries were not evil men and women bent on the cultural or physical destruction of the Indians they served. To the contrary, highminded and well-intentioned idealism motivated them. They believed that they offered Indians a better life, that they could perhaps shield Indians from the uglier aspects of white culture. Certain that the Christian faith could, and would, work spiritual wonders among the Natives, missionaries seemed unaware that the new faith undermined tribal society and bred disruptive factionalism. In the case of the Cayuse tribe, that factionalism foretold the destruction of the Whitman mission.

Few events are truly inevitable, but the U.S. acquisition of Oregon was, in essence, simply a matter of time. Fur traders pointed the way to Oregon, missionaries brought it to the public's attention, but 2,000 or 3,000 emigrant settlers tipped the balance in favor of American sovereignty. Powerless to alter circumstances, by 1846 the HBC withdrew to develop "New Caledonia," now British Columbia. A mere handful of Canada's roughly 1 million inhabitants emigrated west, so Oregon fell to the restless, acquisitive Americans, who numbered about 20 million in 1845. The Oregon Indian missions, Protestant and Catholic alike, failed to achieve their putative goals and in the end converted relatively few Indians. President James Polk, by contrast, made good his vow to settle favorably the "Oregon Question" in 1846. Indeed, the "Whitman Massacre" occurred in U.S. territory. By the 1850s Oregon's Indians, like Indians everywhere in North America, endured warfare with the newcomers, then suffered the loss of their lands, their wealth, and their sovereignty. To a good many Americans, the missionary era and subsequent U.S. acquisition of "Old Oregon" seems a noble and righteous chapter in our history. For the Oregon Indians, it was anything but triumphal.

Essay on Sources

The literature on fur traders and missionaries is vast; only items of direct relevance to this article are here listed. Good background on the Rocky Mountain fur trade can be found in Don Berry, *A Majority of Scoundrels: An Informal History of the Rocky Mountain Fur Company* (New York: Harper Brothers, 1961); Hiram M. Chittenden, *The American Fur Trade of the Far West,* 2 vols. (New York: Francis P. Harper, 1902); and a recent summary, Robert M. Utley, *A Life Wild and Perilous: Mountain Men and the Paths to the Pacific* (New York: Henry Holt, 1997). LeRoy R. Hafen's ten-volume series, *The Mountain Men and the Fur Trade of the Far West* (Glendale, Calif.: Arthur H. Clark, 1965–72), offers almost three hundred fur traders' biographies and many references for further reading.

For Spain's presence in Oregon, see Warren L. Cook, *Flood Tide of Empire: Spain and the Pacific Northwest, 1534–1819* (New Haven, Conn.: Yale University Press, 1973). Additional background on early Oregon is in Oscar Osborn Winther, *The Old Oregon Country: A History of Frontier Trade, Transportation, and Travel* (Bloomington: Indiana University Press, 1949).

Sources on Jedediah Smith include Maurice L. Sullivan, *The Travels of Jedediah Smith: A Documentary Outline* (Santa Ana, Calif.: Fine Arts Press, 1934), and *Jedediah Smith: Trader and Trailbreaker* (New York: Press of the Pioneers, 1936). Dale L. Morgan's biography, *Jedediah Smith and the Opening of the West* (1953; Lincoln: University of

Nebraska Press, 1964), and his *The West of William H. Ashley* (Denver: Old West Publishing Company, 1964), are excellent. Many articles on Smith and his family appeared in a journal, *The Pacific Historian* (Stockton, Calif.: University of the Pacific). An outstanding recent item is David J. Weber, ed., *The Californios versus Jedediah Smith: A New Cache of Documents* (Spokane, Wash.: Arthur H. Clark, 1990). For Smith as a cartographer, see Dale L. Morgan and Carl I. Wheat, *Jedediah Smith and His Maps of the American West* (San Francisco: California Historical Society, 1954). For Smith as a "missionary," see Don M. Chase, *He Opened the West and Led the First White Explorers Through Northwest California, May–June 1828* (Crescent City, Calif.: Del Norte County Historical Society, 1958), and Esther L. Vogt's children's book *God's Mountain Man: The Story of Jedediah Strong Smith* (Springfield, Mo.: Gospel House Publishing, 1991).

The most complete historical work on the Whitmans and their contemporaries—and on the Whitman myth—is Clifford M. Drury, *Marcus and Narcissa Whitman and the Opening of Old Oregon,* 2 vols. (Glendale, Calif.: Arthur H. Clark, 1973). Firsthand accounts of life at Waiilatpu and the "Whitman Massacre" are found in Narcissa Whitman, *The Letters of Narcissa Whitman* (Fairfield, Wash.: Ye Galleon Press, 1996), and Catherine, Elizabeth, and Matilda Sager, *The Whitman Massacre of 1847* (Fairfield, Wash.: Ye Galleon Press, 1981). Good narrative histories include Nard M. Jones, *The Great Command: The Story of Marcus and Narcissa Whitman and the Early Oregon Pioneers* (Boston: Little, Brown, 1959); Cecil P. Dryden, *Give All to Oregon! Missionary Pioneers of the Far West* (New York: Hastings House, 1968); and Julie Roy Jeffrey, *Converting the West: A Biography of Narcissa Whitman* (Norman: University of Oklahoma Press, 1991). Primary sources for missionaries' attitudes and experiences include Samuel Parker, *Journal of an Exploring Tour Beyond the Rocky Mountains* (1838; Minneapolis: Ross & Haines, 1967), and Gustavus Hines, *Life on the Plains and the Pacific: Oregon, Its History, Condition and Prospects* (Buffalo, N.Y.: Geo. H. Derby and Company, 1850). For Henry Spalding's point of view, see *Letter from the Secretary of the Interior Communicating . . . the Early Labors of the Missionaries of the American Board of Commissioners for Foreign Missions in Oregon, Commencing in 1836* (1903; Fairfield, Wash.: Ye Galleon Press, 1988).

CHAPTER 6

Sam Brannan and Elizabeth Byers
Mormons and Miners at Midcentury

ANNE F. HYDE

Mormons and miners stand at the center of how we imagine the American West at the formative moment of the mid-nineteenth century. They reflect the divergent impulses that drew people to the region. One group came to sequester themselves from the American economy and culture and to create a kingdom on earth by making the Utah desert bloom, while the other came to grasp the ultimate brass ring in American culture, instant wealth, and then intended to hightail it home to live in comfort. However, as is often true in western American history, such intentions had ironic consequences. The two sets of people couldn't avoid each other, and their stories became deeply entwined. Miners went home with their pockets turned inside out or begrudgingly became the small farmers and business owners who built western communities, looking a lot like the Mormons who got rich but lost many of their communal impulses. Both groups gambled by traveling into the largely unknown western interior, reflecting the mobile and risk-taking culture from which they came. And both groups built towns and cities in the mountain West that instantly changed the texture of life in the region and integrated it into the American nation. Finally, the very presence of Mormons and miners had unintended effects on Native people and other folks who considered the region theirs.

This essay uses two less-well-known figures, a much-maligned Mormon named Samuel Brannan and Elizabeth Byers, a Colorado socialite who never picked up a pan, pick, or drill, to examine these stories. Their lives illustrate the broad significance of Mormons and miners to the American West by highlighting the complex intentions and outcomes for each group and for the people they displaced and conquered. The mining booms that occurred with striking regularity in the period between 1848 and 1898 in all parts of the West, from California to Alaska, from the San Juans to the Coeur d'Alenes, certainly drew huge numbers of people west and poured billions of dollars into the global economy. However, mining offered a poor platform for a permanent conquest of the region. Miners mostly came and went, leaving ghost towns, piles of tailings, and environmental and human ruin in their wake. The puzzle for westerners became how to achieve permanence in a boomtown world. Mormons, on the other hand, started as an insular religious sect that simply wanted to get away from the rest of the United States. They hoped to set down deep roots in a place where they could protect themselves from the corrosive forces of American individualism. In this effort to create a safe place, ironically, they brought tens of thousands of converts who took risks and became successful entrepreneurs—the living image of the American dream.

Someone looking at Salt Lake City and Denver in the 1890s could see many similarities in these two cities that had emerged out of blank spaces on the Anglo American map. Their presence as successful metropolises indicated the conquest of the United States over the Indian, Mexican, Russian, and British peoples in the region, a process that required wealth and power, much of it created by Mormons and miners. In 1846 no one would have considered the possibility of places like Salt Lake City or Denver. Even though Mormon cooperation built one city and mining fortunes the other, the histories of these two cities and their inhabitants are intimately connected. They both required visionaries, entrepreneurs, and mavericks along with the hard work of thousands of people who simply wanted a new life and a chance in the Far West.

One such maverick was Samuel Brannan, a man who eventually became a notoriously bad Mormon but began his career as a protégé of Joseph Smith and a leader of the Church of Jesus Christ of Latter-day Saints. In 1846 he landed in San Francisco Bay as a respected church elder, looking for a spot to plant a Mormon empire. Like many Americans, Brannan got distracted by golden opportunity, but unlike most Mormons, he gave in to it entirely. He became one of those astounding characters that, like the Mormons in general, appeared at every important moment in western American history. After inciting the 1849 Gold Rush, making and losing a fortune several times, being excommunicated from the Mormon Church, and having a career in extralegal politics and business, Brannan died in 1889, dreaming of another mining empire in Mexico. His life and career mirrored much of the story of Mormon success in creating an empire around Salt Lake City. Mormons, having little choice at the start, experimented with cooperative farming, stock-raising, and industrial enterprises. Like Brannan, Mormon leaders and businesspeople were inventive about practices and products, and they didn't take failure, arrest, or outright attack as signs they should give up. But again mirroring Brannan, they

Anne F. Hyde

finally did have to blend with the mainstream to succeed, giving up on polygamy and theocracy (at least in their most obvious forms) in order to survive and flourish.

Elizabeth Byers, who arrived in Denver during the first summer of the Colorado gold rush in 1859, never panned for gold and never owned a mining claim. Yet in the most important ways, she was a fifty-niner and a true city founder. The mining rush brought her to Denver, its wealth created a city around her, and its hard realities created a set of social problems for her to solve. Elizabeth Byers's life, made comfortable by her husband's creation of the *Rocky Mountain News* and her own investment in Denver real estate, reflected the reality that most people who got rich in mining rushes did it away from the mines. Her career as a philanthropist and social visionary demonstrated her desire to build a real city and highlighted the social costs and human challenges created by western mining booms. Impoverished miners and their unfortunate families, far more common than those who struck it rich, rarely appeared in the sights of entrepreneurs or city boosters. But Elizabeth Byers saw them clearly. When Byers looked back on her efforts in 1900, she saw a legacy of social and cultural organizations that provided a safety net for poor people and a place that had changed from a collection of tents into a regional capital. She had helped Denver meet the ultimate challenge of western mining booms: it had evolved from a "flash in the pan" to "Queen City of the Plains."

Mining and Mormons began their ironic relationship in 1848. Just as gold was discovered at Sutter's Mill along the American River in the western foothills of the Sierra Nevada, California had become part of the United States as a piece of the spoils of the Mexican War. The workers at John Sutter's mill, many of them refugees from the Mormon battalion that had marched with General Stephen Watts Kearny into California, didn't know they were part of a new nation when they saw gold glinting in the water. Similarly, the negotiators at the Treaty of Guadalupe Hidalgo had no idea they were either giving up or gaining a mother lode of gold that would create hundreds of millions of dollars in new wealth. And, Brigham Young's first Mormons were spending their first miserable winter in what they thought would be permanent isolation from both the U.S. and Mexican governments. Military conquest and its final result on paper would change and link these groups' separate worlds.

The Mormons who settled in the Great Basin in the middle of the century, like many utopian communities who headed west, hoped to avoid and perhaps to chastise by example mainstream Americans for their profit-minded and practical bent. However, the Mormons received far more attention and persecution than most other groups.

Their insistence on divine revelation, theocracy, and polygamy brought them into direct conflict with American culture and government. In the end, though, their strong communalism and obedience to the church also made them excellent farmers and businesspeople, preparing them to succeed in the mainstream at the very moment they were most actively trying to avoid being contaminated by these values. By the close of the nineteenth century, Mormon communities had spread from Canada to Mexico along the western slope of the Continental Divide, but they had both failed and succeeded in their aims. Sam Brannan and his infamous career well illustrate the challenges presented to the Saints as American society surrounded and enticed them.

Generalizing about Mormons is particularly hazardous. Notorious for their practice of polygamy as well as for their financial successes, Mormons changed in fundamental ways from the group who arrived in the Great Basin in 1847 to become the wealthy and powerful group who hosted the 2002 Olympics. The Mormons can be held out as useful examples of people who resisted the centrifugal forces of the frontier and who built successful and prosperous communities that used land, water, and labor wisely. Mormons, of course, have also been described as a clannish and dangerous threat to frontier development, as an anti-American aberration festering in the Great Basin.

The Mormons are neither as good nor as bad as these two sets of images portray them. From the beginning they were far more mainstream than their detractors understood them to be, and at the same time, they were far more radical than their present-day supporters would have them be. Mormonism evolved out of the tumult of American religion that burned most fiercely across the northern United States in the 1820s and 1830s. Joseph Smith's dissatisfaction with the acquisitive, individualistic culture he found himself surrounded by was not at all uncommon in that time and place, and neither was his revelation about building a new religion. Concern over market pressures and the culture it created drove many people to question the basic precepts of American culture and to experiment with new forms of community and religion. Smith and his Latter-day Saints, as directed by the angel Moroni and the Book of Mormon, did differ in the number of converts they attracted, the range of social mores they challenged, and the reaction they got from the people who lived around them, but many of these sects shared their critique of America. Like many of those who led communitarian experiments, the Shakers or the communities at Oneida or Amana, Smith wanted to build an egalitarian society that actively made its members equal before God. The new social and economic order, codified in 1831 as "the Law of Consecration and Stewardship," emerged as central to Mormon doctrine. It required

Anne F. Hyde

giving up material possessions, status, and worldly attachments and developing a truly cooperative style that ensured sustenance but not comfort for all. The Mormons never quite lived up to this egalitarian ideal, but it remained central to their behavior.

Joseph Smith's preaching about an egalitarian kingdom on earth appealed to young Samuel Brannan, a sixteen-year-old printer's apprentice living near Kirtland, Ohio. Young Brannan's prospects in Kirtland, where Smith had begun to gather his converts in the 1830s, seemed pretty grim. His drunken father had no way to set him up in business, his first efforts at founding a paper with his brother ended in the loss of the press and his brother's death, and the great panic of 1837 swept away his hopes for employment. The Mormon Church offered a different path that allowed Brannan to escape his loneliness and economic misery. He became an elder in the church and part of a prosperous, tightly knit, and passionate group. After serving for a couple of years as a traveling missionary in New England, in 1843 Brannan was "called" to New York City to practice his printing skills and to set up a newspaper for the eastern Mormons.

Meanwhile, the thriving Mormon communities in the Mississippi River valley found themselves under attack, largely because of their success. Active persecution, with the final catastrophe of Joseph Smith's murder in 1844, drove them from Nauvoo, Illinois. The new leaders of the church, which now numbered 20,000 people, concluded that they must all leave the borders of the United States. Led by youthful and charismatic Brigham Young, the Mormon faithful gathered near Omaha, Nebraska, in temporary winter quarters to decide where to go next. Suddenly twenty-five-year-old Samuel Brannan was given the task of evacuating the eastern Saints. He proposed taking them by ship to California, unaware that what seemed a safe and distant haven in 1845 was now territory being eyed by American imperialists. Brannan managed to raise funds, find a ship, outfit it, and load 238 Saints. They left New York Harbor on February 4, 1846, the very same day Brigham Young crossed the Mississippi River with the first contingent of overland Saints. The two groups shared zeal and desperation but fared differently.

Young's evacuees, after spending a miserable year camped on the western side of the Mississippi in Iowa, intended to migrate west into what was Mexican territory to build a new Zion. As he gathered the Saints and planned the mass exodus from his "Winter Quarters" along the western banks of the Missouri River, Young didn't know whether he would settle in coastal California or Oregon or someplace farther east; he simply wanted an isolated and fertile spot far from the gaze of government. He sent Brannan and his small contingent of Saints ahead

Fig. 6.1: Samuel Brannan, Mormon entrepreneur.
Courtesy of the California Historical Society,
DeYoung Collection, FN-4312.

by ship to scout out possibilities along the Pacific coast, but by the time
the main group of Mormons was ready to leave, the Mexican War had
broken out, and California no longer looked like an attractive spot.
Brannan didn't know it, but Young had decided that the great interior
of the West offered more protection for Mormon settlement.
Demonstrating the organizational skill and the cooperative ethos that
would come to characterize Mormon communities, in the spring of
1847 Young led his advance team of Saints to an isolated mountain
valley on the western slope of the Wasatch Mountains. In short order
the Saints built a fort and laid out a city, began farming using crude
irrigation, and organized another mass migration. And they did this

not as individuals, but as a group that agreed to put their "mites together for that which is the best for every man, woman, and child."

The Saints who traveled with Samuel Brannan to California via Cape Horn and the Sandwich Islands (present day Hawai'i) demonstrated a similar preparedness and unity of purpose. One member of the group noted proudly that the ship was "loaded with Agricultural and Mechanical tools enough for eight hundred men . . . a printing press and type, paper, stationery, school books consisting of spelling books, sequels, history, arithmetic, astronomy, grammar, Morse's Atlas and Geography, Hebrew Grammar and Lexicon, slates. Also Dry Goods, twine, brass, copper, iron, tin . . . two new milch cows, forty or fifty pigs, and fowls." With this impressive load intact, they sailed through the Golden Gate on July 21, 1846, only two weeks after the United States had seized California from the Mexican government. Although Brannan hadn't expected this turn of events, he gamely went about the business of turning Yerba Buena (which would become San Francisco) into a Mormon community. The group surveyed the situation and decided to move farther inland, forming a cooperative community in the San Joaquin Valley called New Hope. There they started a logging business to bring in cash and began clearing land and planting crops in preparation for the main body of overland Mormons that Brannan still assumed was on its way.

Samuel Brannan's vision of Mormon California never came to pass. The New Hope community squabbled over organization and leadership from the beginning. Brannan, ambitious and overbearing, demanded complete obedience from his flock. In one of his earliest reports from California, Brannan admitted that he had been forced to excommunicate twenty men on the sea voyage and three more in California for what he labeled apostasy and sedition. Chafing under Brannan's rule and frustrated by a series of crop failures and floods, the California Saints began to abandon New Hope for better individual opportunities. Brannan, meanwhile, was branching out from his duties as a Mormon elder. In short order he started a newspaper, built himself an elegant house, and became a leading citizen of the new American California. For Brannan and his fellow Mormons, California offered too many possibilities and temptations. Still, Brannan wanted to live up to his promise to Brigham Young and the church as a whole. In early 1847, impatient with the lack of news from the overland Saints and frustrated by the failure of his California experiment, Brannan headed east to find his fellow Mormons and lead them to California.

Brannan met up with Brigham Young along the banks of the Green River as the Mormon contingent straggled into what would become their new home. Brannan attempted to talk Young out of settling in

Utah, which he saw as a foolhardy gamble in a dry and arid climate. He insisted that California offered more fertile land, a gentler climate, and more opportunities for a Mormon kingdom. Young ignored Brannan's advice, claiming that God had commanded him to choose the desert. Young hoped that because of its isolation and forbidding landscape, no other Americans would covet the Great Basin, leaving the Mormons free to create their vision of heaven on earth. Crushed by this rebuff from his leader, Samuel Brannan turned his back on the new Zion and returned to California.

Brigham Young turned out to be right, but only for a while. In the isolation of Utah, Mormondon used its distinctive qualities to great advantage. From the beginning, the Utah Saints developed cooperative practices and laws to divide up land, water, and labor. With specific instructions from the Council of Twelve that formed church leadership, Mormon pioneers plowed, fenced, and irrigated one "Big Field," devised a system of building houses on evenly spaced city blocks, and gave out farm lots with the idea that they would be "equal according to circumstances, wants, and needs." Some of this cooperative effort came out of necessity in the first desperate need to feed and shelter a large group of people in an unfamiliar environment. But the community's success and continuity came out of religious conviction and the desire to live up to Joseph Smith's vision of an egalitarian kingdom on earth. Because of their early experiences in the Midwest and their deeply held belief in communal effort, the Mormons succeeded where other groups could not.

The Mormons practiced real cooperation, especially during the long and important years of Brigham Young's presidency. Their earlier persecution in Ohio, Missouri, Illinois, and Iowa had only increased their determination to succeed in Utah. In the decades after they arrived in Utah, the Mormon faithful signaled their difference from mainstream American culture by attempting to farm, merchandise, and manufacture with commonly owned and worked lands, products, and cash. Everything from railroad building, banking, stock grazing, sugar production, and lumbering was undertaken with two related goals: to make the Mormons entirely self-sufficient so that they could cease all contact with the unfriendly United States and so that they could create the Kingdom of God on earth where all people shared according to their abilities and needs in work, profits, and grace.

These two goals, and the fact that few Mormons had much cash, made many of these early cooperative experiments successful. Some of this success had practical reasons. Because no one had enough capital to start manufacturing enterprises or to build irrigation systems, people had to pool resources. Several theological practices made this easier.

Anne F. Hyde

Mormons believed that they all served as stewards of the church's wealth and that basically everything, in the end, belonged not to individual Mormons, but to the church as a whole. Even though the law of stewardship was not always fully lived, every Mormon understood that the practice of tithing took its place and observed it very seriously. At least a tenth of every person's product and labor went directly to the church. Many people spent every tenth day working on communal building projects such as forts, meetinghouses, roads, and other public works. The produce and stock donated to the church required that each community and ward set up a tithing house to store, sort, grow, and redistribute this increasingly significant source of wealth.

If hard work and cooperation had been the only Mormon practices in Utah, the Mormon story would be fairly unremarkable. But in 1852, the church announced publicly that one of its fundamental beliefs was "plural marriage." Even though few Mormons ever practiced polygamy, the concept of polygamous marriage had been part of church doctrine since Joseph Smith introduced it. Brigham Young's celebrated twenty-seven wives and fifty-six children alone were enough to ignite a storm of protest against the Mormons. Although a few Mormons had practiced polygamy in the 1830s, only in the heated atmosphere of the national politics of 1850s, when political parties were looking for any excuse to avoid talking about sectional politics and slavery, did the Mormons become an easy target. And had the new Zion of Salt Lake City remained a backwater, no one would have cared much what the Mormons did. However, the Treaty of Guadalupe Hidalgo made the Mormon kingdom part of the American nation, and the California Gold Rush placed the Mormons at the center of a national traffic jam.

Ironically enough, it would be Sam Brannan who brought the Gold Rush to national attention and who put the Mormons on center stage. As the Mormons planted their first crop of winter wheat in the winter of 1848, Brannan had again taken up residence in San Francisco and was making another go at making a personal fortune. He had not given up on Mormonism entirely and continued to hope that the Saints or their leaders would see California as a viable part of the Mormon future. Meanwhile, he worked at his newspaper business and opened a new store in Sacramento to supply new American settlements like Sutter's Mill along the American River. In the early spring of 1848, while Brannan was visiting his store, he heard reports that gold had been discovered along the river. He took a vial of gold dust back to San Francisco to have it assayed, announced the news to local San Franciscans, and published a special edition of his *California Star Express,* which he sent east immediately. By May, San Francisco had become a ghost town and hundreds of thousands of Americans itched to get to the diggings as newspapers in the eastern United States fanned gold rush fever into the forty-niner exodus the following spring.

The cycle begun by the discovery of placer gold in the streams in the western foothills of the Sierra Nevada was followed by the rush of eager men to get to the diggings and the instant wealth of a few and the disappointment of the many. The cycle continued with the maturing of the mining industry and a more permanent economy and society built around it and would be repeated many times in the next several decades. And each time the booms and busts occurred, they changed the lives of huge numbers of people, with ripple effects ringing out in unexpected ways. The California mother lode, first tapped by the men at Sutter's Fort, first announced by Samuel Brannan, and finally confirmed in President James K. Polk's State of the Union address in 1849, represented a hope and gamble for people everywhere. Most of those willing to take the gamble were young men, with time and little traveling money on their hands. White farmers, laborers, and mechanics from New England and the Ohio River valley, from the old South and the new cotton country along the Mississippi delta, were joined by Cherokees and Choctaws from Indian Territory along the old emigrant trails. Immigrants from all around the world poured into California from Europe, Asia, and South America, hoping to find fortune in this newest American wonder.

Few did. Gold is hard to get out of the ground, and the hundreds of thousands who arrived expecting simply to pick it up off the ground were disappointed. Only a small percentage of gold reaches the surface of the earth, a few tiny flakes eroded out of the main lode lying deep beneath the ground safely encased in hard rock. Only those miners who arrived in California early enough to claim a spot on a likely stream, who were allowed to keep their claims, and who were willing to do the hard work of standing in a cold stream digging up its bed to find the eroded bits could make any money this way. The Mormons working for John Sutter were in this category, but the huge percentage of the three hundred thousand people who arrived in California were not. Most had experiences like William Swain, a young man from western New York, who left his farm and family in the care of his brother, joined a company of men who planned their trip extremely carefully, and headed west in the spring of 1849. He expected to stay in California for a while, gathering the "gold fellows" in his pockets until he had amassed a nice nest egg for his family. But Swain found, like many others, that life didn't go according to plan. He arrived too late in the fall of 1849 to get a good spot on a promising riverbank. He discovered that the work was extremely hard and the cost of living extremely high, and after a year

Anne F. Hyde

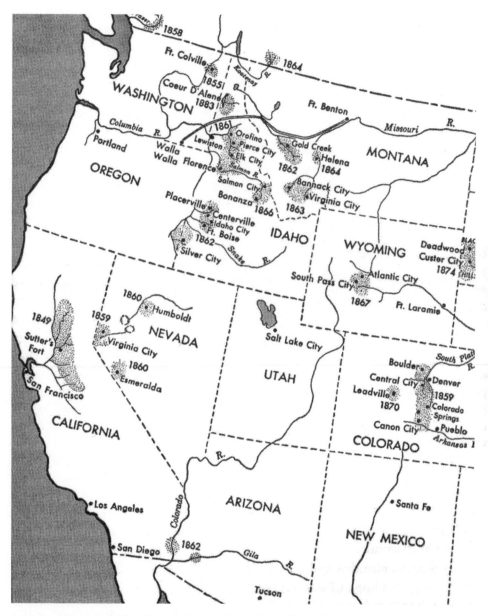

Map 6.1: The miners' frontier, 1858–1875. From Ray Allen Billington and Martin Ridge, *Westward Expansion: A History of the American Frontier,* 6th ed. (Albuquerque: University of New Mexico Press, 2001), 263.

and a half of standing in cold streams, he headed home with less money but more experience than he had when he started.

Only after the initial placer excitement had faded and when those with skill and capital could follow the veins of the lode deep into the earth did mining produce huge fortunes. More people made their "piles" by supplying miners, like two entrepreneurs named Levi and Strauss who discovered that miners needed special pants, durable ones made out of denim and metal rivets. Storekeepers, like Leland Stanford, who set up shop in San Francisco or Sacramento and who then avoided investing in the mining excitement but instead put their money in railroads and land, made enormous fortunes. Mining did change the face of California forever. Many of the American and immigrant gold seekers never made enough money to go home. They stayed and built San Francisco, Sacramento, San Jose, and Los Angeles, making the United States a truly continental nation. Although mining turned out to be a rich man's game, it continued to have the aura of possibility and excitement. As news of each successive mining strike flashed through the press, the hope of easy wealth burst out anew. But as the glitter of each strike faded, only the reality of hard work created the places where people stayed and lived.

This pattern took shape vividly in Colorado in 1858, when a new surge of mining excitement reached a nation deep in depression. Rumors about promising "color" in the Rocky Mountains had circulated for years. Earlier, several parties of forty-niners headed to California noticed promising streams along the Arkansas and South Platte rivers but chose to hurry along to more certain wealth in California. Two men from Georgia, William Green Russell, who had grown up near the only gold strike east of the Mississippi in Georgia, and John Beck, a Cherokee who had lived in this Georgia gold region until his removal to Indian Territory, did a little panning on some tributaries of the South Platte on their return from California in 1850. They both found some gold, but not enough to convince either one to look further. Mining rushes uncover veins and lodes that have lain untapped for centuries, but they require a certain cultural context to be discovered.

The Colorado gold rush emerged in the context of the Panic of 1857. In the summer of 1857, a railroad stock scandal in Cincinnati initiated a wave of bank failures. An economy already bloated by huge amounts of new money in circulation as a consequence of California gold couldn't easily absorb these failures. Because many people, from railroad tycoons to Missouri farmers, had taken out loans for new lands, equipment, and investments, no one had any cash as banks began to fail. With stunning immediacy, as one New York financier put it, "the American monetary system now lies before us a magnificent and melancholy ruin." This ruin had its most extreme impact on the Mississippi and Missouri River valleys, where growth had been most spectacular and more people had taken chances with mortgages, stock investments, and credit. By the end of 1857, thousands of people were out of work, off their land, or out of business.

In this new situation, a trip to the Rockies to look for gold seemed perfectly reasonable. William Green Russell contacted John Beck, now living on a Cherokee reservation in Indian Territory, and together they planned a prospecting trip for the spring of 1858. When they finally arrived at the confluence of Cherry Creek and the South Platte at the end of May, more than a hundred men accompanied them, all hoping to find a quick way out of debt. But even after finding some pay dirt, after a couple of weeks of averaging less than a dollar a day, most of the men decided to head home. Digging and hauling mud and water all day for less than the price of a meal seemed hardly worth it. The Russell brothers and ten other men stayed on, and during the first days of July 1858 they found "good diggings" at the mouth of Dry Creek. They panned out several hundred dollars' worth, and from this meager showing the great Pikes Peak gold rush developed.

The news hit the Missouri River towns in the fall of 1858 and spread eastward like a flood in the desert. In the depths of a depression stories about gold for the taking that would require only a quick six-hundred-mile trip from the Missouri River swept away any caution or judgment. However, because the mining season had passed, most people could only plan a trip for the next spring, hoping to get themselves to the "jumping-off point," outfitted, and out to the Pikes Peak diggings as early in the spring as possible. A huge wave of eager would-be miners, with little cash in their pockets and gold in their eyes, arrived in Independence, St. Joseph, or Kansas City, Missouri, or farther north in Council Bluffs, Iowa, or Omaha, Nebraska. Another group, equally quick to take advantage of the news from Pikes Peak, were merchants and shop-keepers in towns along the Missouri River. Times were difficult for them; maybe their salvation had appeared in the guise of gold news because they could make mints outfitting gullible gold seekers.

This was the world of William and Elizabeth Byers, newlyweds living in Omaha, Nebraska. William Newton Byers, born in 1831, and Elizabeth Sumner Byers, born in 1834, were both born in Ohio and raised in Iowa. Both received some formal education at the same time they learned skills suitable for life on a frontier. William became a surveyor in 1850 but, like many young men, wanted to experience something beyond his hometown. He signed on with a party heading west to Oregon in May 1852 and became a federal surveyor in Oregon and Washington. News of the goldfields in California continued to be enticing, so he headed for

San Francisco in late 1853. William explored the city and the gold country around Sacramento for a month, found it disappointing, and sailed home. He arrived in Iowa early in 1854 and began courting Elizabeth Sumner that summer. Seeing his future lying in the West, William started his own surveying business in Omaha and returned home to marry Elizabeth on November 16, 1854. The two left for their new life in Omaha the same day.

Solidly middle class and typically ambitious, the young couple became active in politics and civic affairs in their new community. As William's surveying business boomed in frontier Nebraska, he became an alderman in 1857. Elizabeth busied herself with keeping the books for William and raising two children. When the crash came in 1857, businesses like the Byers's that depended on land sales, rapid growth, and easy credit were the first to be hit. Omaha, like its residents, sank into a deep depression. When the news of the gold strike in Colorado hit town in the fall of 1858, many people, including the Byerses, saw a way out of their bad situation. William Byers, having seen the elephant in California, knew just what to do when he heard the news because he knew that riches were in servicing the rush, not in panning for gold.

William, drawing on his earlier experiences on the Oregon Trail, immediately got into the business of writing guidebooks. Scores of guidebooks, based on no research or reality, flooded the country. They announced that gold was as common in the Pikes Peak region as the waters of mountain streams or the sands along their banks. Byers's book, to give him credit, did warn would-be miners of the hard work and dangers that mining involved, but it also included a map that made Denver look considerably closer than it was. Still, no one seemed to care much whether these books were full of nonsense, and in the early spring of 1859, more than one hundred thousand people surged out of the Missouri border towns, more people than in any single year of the California Gold Rush. The trails teemed with "Pikes Peak or Bust" travelers, mounted and in wagons, buggies, and stagecoaches or on foot, pushing wheelbarrows. Few seemed prepared for what their futures might entail, setting off on the trail with little but a slab of bacon, some cornmeal, and blankets, along with the ever-present guidebook.

William Byers joined those other young men. He and Elizabeth had decided that Omaha and surveying were no longer a good gamble. The new communities developing along the front range of the Rockies looked far more promising. Elizabeth Byers thought that the region would need a newspaper and that William had the skill to edit one. With a large loan from Elizabeth's father, Colonel Horatio N. Sumner, William bought up a used printing press and several huge wagons. Elizabeth's father also provided two teams of horses to help draw the

Anne F. Hyde

press wagons and sent along four of his sons to help the Byers family move. One brother, Charles, stayed in Omaha to help Elizabeth, but the other three accompanied William. The trip across the plains took six weeks, and they struggled with the heavy wagons in the spring mud. William arrived in Denver on April 20, 1859, and published the first edition of the *Rocky Mountain News* two days later.

Instantly Byers and his paper became prime boosters for gold mining and for the future of Denver. But the situation he faced in the first months of publishing the *News* made his position challenging. Although the Pikes Peak rush was real, gold wasn't lying around on the ground for the taking. Few of the tens of thousands of eager would-be miners who arrived in the spring of 1859 had any conception of how to mine, and they were quickly frustrated. Many headed home as early as April, and cries of "humbug" echoed in the ears of those just reaching the goldfield. Byers, as the author of a guidebook, heard rumors that he was being hanged in effigy by disappointed men now back trailing home with empty pockets. His sources reported a popular couplet among the humbuggers:

Hang Byers and D. C. Oakes [another guidebook author]
For starting this damned Pikes Peak hoax.

William responded to these accusations early and quickly. In his second edition of the paper, April 23, 1859, he warned his readers that "all of this has been brought about by the action of a few restless spirits who are no advantage to any country. They arrive in the vicinity of the mining region, stop a few hours or a day or two, perhaps prospect a little in the places the most unlikely in the world for finding gold, and, because they cannot shovel out nuggets like they have been accustomed to dig potatoes, they raise the cry that it is all a humbug, there is no gold in the country." Byers went on to advise lower expectations but noted that he himself had found a little gold in his first two panfuls.

However, Byers was speaking out against a nearly universal conviction of humbug and made little impression either with ridicule or with pleas for common sense. By early May, Denver had lost two thirds of its population, and Byers admitted the region's future looked grim. But rich placer mines began to produce impressive amounts of good "color" just north and west of Denver. When happy prospectors displayed their wealth in Denver, many miners felt reassured. Now the task was to salvage the region's reputation in the rest of the nation. Byers and other influential men implored three leading journalists, Henry Villard of the Cincinnati *Commercial,* Albert D. Richardson of the *Boston Journal,* and Horace Greeley of the *New York Tribune,* to see for themselves and to provide disinterested testimony. They went to Gregory Gulch and signed a joint dispatch that reported that a single sluice might yield anywhere from $21 to $494 per day. Published as an extra in Byers's *Rocky Mountain News* on June 11, 1859, the report was widely copied in eastern papers, with Greeley's name giving it the necessary weight. Although the last third of the "Greeley Report" was an extended admonition against extravagant hopes, the next month saw the recurrence of Pikes Peak mania.

Having averted disaster for his new town, William rushed back to Omaha to get Elizabeth and the two children, Frank and Mollie. By now, the trails teemed with eager fifty-niners, huge wagons carrying supplies to the gold country, government soldiers and mail services, and, most significantly, Wells Fargo couriers carrying gold dust and gold bars. Such sights must have reassured William and Elizabeth that their gamble would pay out. The entire family moved into a "hotel" with no furniture or beds in early August 1859. The community that greeted Elizabeth Byers was much different from an orderly and friendly Mormon town. Another woman who arrived that summer noted with evident disgust that Denver was "an exceedingly primitive town consisting of numerous tents and numbers of rude and illy constructed cabins with nearly as many rum shops as cabins." "No wonder," she concluded, "that so many coming into this dismal village, chafed and irritated . . . were disheartened and discouraged and turned their faces homeward."

In that first summer, Denver looked as if a giant toddler had arranged houses, wagons, streets, and people along a dusty creek bed and then kicked them into broken disorder in a tantrum. Elizabeth felt lucky to be able to move into a cabin attached to the print shop of the newspaper. Although it had dirt floors and a single window, it offered privacy that few Denverites enjoyed. Unlike the Byerses, most people had no intention of staying in Denver or Colorado. They planned to mine some gold, have some excitement, and move on or return to their homes and families. Miners were willing to endure discomfort and to live in cold and wet tents, to eat poor-quality and monotonous food, and to weather illness alone in the short term. This transient attitude meant that no one cared where they built temporary shacks, where sewage would flow, if dirt streets turned to mud in the summer rains, or if there were no churches, schools, hospitals, or libraries. Miners wanted saloons, boardinghouses, banks, stores, and, most of all, the easy wealth they felt was their due.

As the chaotic and heady days of the first summer turned into fall and the weather turned too cold to mine in the mountains, thousands of men poured into Denver. Most had used up all of their cash and were

Anne F. Hyde

Figure 6.2: Elizabeth (Mrs. William N.) Byers, mining town pioneer. Courtesy of the Denver Public Library, Western History Collection, Z-2323.

now stuck in Denver, a raw community with few resources to provide for this destitute and angry population. Many of them actively blamed William Byers for their situation, and Elizabeth remembered that she waited anxiously for William to arrive as he sneaked home each evening to avoid being accosted in the streets. As winter approached, the situation grew more dangerous. The combination of single restless men, women and children who had been abandoned by their husbands and fathers in the rush for gold, and destitute Indians whose winter camping grounds had been destroyed by the flood of fifty-niners created a toxic human brew. By December, more than ten thousand people crowded into the tattered tents or scrap lumber shacks that made up Denver. Prices for staple goods had always been high, but the increased demand and the shortages created by winter weather made costs for food, fuel, and clothing skyrocket. Many people were literally starving, many were sick, and the *Rocky Mountain News* warned of the danger of epidemic disease.

The "state" was in no position to respond. Like most mining booms, the rush to Pikes Peak had occurred in a part of the United States that was largely unorganized and unknown. The federal government considered the region to be an outer county of Kansas, but in the context of the bitter territorial debates that had plagued the West in the context of the Kansas-Nebraska Act of 1854 and the impending Civil War, few politicians wanted to deal with creating a new territory or state. William Byers and a few other enthusiasts had attempted to set up a new state of Jefferson but had been completely ignored. Leaders in Denver had managed to appoint a city council to oversee property transactions, but these people had little experience in managing urban problems. Byers did convince the fledgling city government to provide a stipend for the poor, but a city council in a new territorial government had little to offer and the tiny fund was exhausted immediately.

Elizabeth thought she could do more. She invited the women she knew to her home, and they agreed to form an organization called the Ladies Union Aid Society. The sixteen charter members decided to keep the group nondenominational so it would serve everyone equally and that it would simply "give aid and comfort to those in need." Because there was so much need, Elizabeth Byers and the Ladies Union Aid Society were creative and aggressive in raising money. They solicited contributions from business owners, organized dances to raise money, set up food banks, and sewed underwear and nightshirts to keep people warm. They passed out packages of food, organized soup kitchens, and provided nursing care for the sick. These activities reflected the reality of a boomtown in winter: no one could mine or even prospect in the deep mountain snows, so no cash came in and people were cold and hungry and needed charity to survive until spring.

But spring came and with it hopes for renewed mining riches. The Byers family celebrated the anniversary of the *Rocky Mountain News* by making the paper into a daily and by moving into a new frame house, complete with windows, muslin-lined walls, and finished floors. And with spring came hordes of new and eager gold seekers. Elizabeth Byers intended to present these newcomers with a community that would convince more of them to stay. She worked to found the first school, library, and Methodist Church in Denver. The problem of destitute women and orphaned children continued to worry her, and she eventually founded the Women's Relief Home and the Byers Home for boys. During the next few winters, Denver had more services in place to help people because, as Elizabeth recalled later, "people were generous" and "gold was more plentiful in those days."

But the Colorado gold rush and the future of Denver were far from assured. Fires were common in mining towns because of the cheap construction and lack of people and equipment to fight them. Nearly every boomtown in the West suffered a series of fires until buildings were made of brick and communities supported fire departments. San

Anne F. Hyde

Francisco and Sacramento burned to the ground several times, and Samuel Brannan responded by forming volunteer fire departments in both places. Denver had its share of disasters as well. The Byers family house burned to the ground in October 1860, and Elizabeth barely saved her new infant. In 1863 a major fire destroyed most of downtown, while citizens looked on helplessly because the carts and fire buckets ordered for the new fire brigade had not yet arrived. Just over a year later, when the city had barely recovered from the fire, Cherry Creek overflowed its bed during torrential spring rains. All of downtown was flooded, and the *Rocky Mountain News* building lay under five feet of mud. The Byerses, occupying a new house on the outskirts of town, found themselves marooned on their roof while floodwaters swirled around them. The entire family waited for nearly a day until soldiers rescued them with a boat made from an old wagon. The family lost everything, including William's newspaper and Elizabeth's "pretty things that made home life possible." And like the rest of Denver, they rebuilt and went on.

Buildings could be rebuilt, but the mining industry faced more intractable problems. By 1862, people began leaving the Pikes Peak region in droves because the gold boom was waning, at least in terms of gold that was easy to mine. As in every mining boom, the placers played out, and only those who had the time, skill, and capital to sink deep shafts continued to mine. However, the geology of the Colorado lode presented distinctive challenges. Even skilled lode miners were having trouble with their gold veins as shaft holes deepened. Near the surface the veins gave up their gold because the rock enclosing them had been softened by erosion. Lower in the shaft the gold resisted separation by any known process. Everyone knew the ore had gold in it, but they didn't know how to get it out. Dozens of the camps that had boomed in 1860 were almost ghost towns by 1865, and only a few hangers-on believed that their luck would turn, maybe tomorrow.

As the population dwindled in Denver and the boom lost some of its golden glow, disappointed men got mean. It is in this context that the tragedy of the Sand Creek Massacre took place. Indians and Anglos had coexisted uneasily in Colorado, but the huge numbers of people that flooded the plains put new pressures on the already stressed Native people. Epidemic disease, rapidly declining buffalo numbers, and increasing limitations on hunting areas had devastated Plains Indian society. As gold rush traffic swelled on the roads leading to Colorado, the Indians reacted by attacking travelers and stealing horses, cattle, guns, ammunition, and food. The government built forts and Indian agencies and demanded that Indians come to reservations, but they didn't provide enough food to keep the Indians who did come in from starving or enough military power to contain the plains warriors who refused to stop fighting.

In the summer and fall of 1864, Indian raids essentially shut down the roads into Denver, panicking citizens and making prices even higher. The army, occupied farther east with the Civil War, provided little help. William Byers and his *Rocky Mountain News* fanned the flames, demanding in angry headlines and editorials that the government had to act, to kill the "hostiles," or the besieged citizens would. Finally Governor John Evans deputized a group of volunteers, largely frustrated miners with time on their hands, to become an emergency militia unit under the command of Colonel John Chivington. Byers reported on this action with evident delight, and the newly minted Colorado Third Regiment marched around Denver, shot their new guns, and drank in preparation for a fight.

On the morning of November 29, 1864, Chivington and his seven hundred men marched into an encampment of Cheyenne gathered on the banks of Sand Creek in southern Colorado. The Indians, led by a chief named Black Kettle, had turned themselves in to a nearby fort and thought they were being protected by the army. Even when they saw the troops coming, the Cheyenne assumed they were some kind of military escort. Chivington, however, had made no mistake. As he had told his men, he had "come to kill Indians" and "it is right and honorable to use many means under God's heaven to kill Indians." In an absolute massacre, the Colorado Third did kill Indians. In moments, hundreds of Cheyenne lay dead, two thirds of them women and children. And just killing the Indians wasn't enough for the volunteers from Denver: they mutilated bodies and took souvenirs of women's genitalia and children's hair. Proudly they marched back into Denver to be feted by their fellow citizens. Byers wrote in the News that "Colorado soldiers have again covered themselves in glory" and that the fight was "among the brilliant feats of arms in Indian warfare."

This "brilliant feat" backfired. The massacre ignited open warfare with the Plains Indians that would take years to subdue. And even in the context of the Civil War, the reports of the massacre horrified white Americans living in the East. Their outrage, combined with the complaints of military officers who had disapproved of Chivington's volunteers from the start, sparked a congressional investigation that revealed a shocking disregard for human life. Governor Evans was forced to resign, Chivington was censured, and William Byers's triumphant crowing in the *News* was subdued. Both William and Elizabeth had been close friends of Colonel Chivington and never understood the national outrage at the Sand Creek Massacre. They remained angry that the government seemed not to understand the seriousness of the "Indian problem" in Colorado. The region did have an Indian problem in that the Pikes Peak rush had ended a way of life for the Plains Indians and the new society emerging there offered no place for them.

The year 1864, with its poor mining output, the flood that cost Denver nearly a million dollars, and the national disgrace of the Sand Creek Massacre, represented a low point. The city, with William Byers as its chief booster, struggled to attract new residents and new businesses. Elizabeth continued to build institutions and organizations, like the YWCA and the Colorado Seminary, that would improve life in Denver. It was a slow process. The permanent population of the city grew by only ten residents between 1860 and 1870, though there were much higher populations at many points between those dates. Mining got a reprieve when a chemist named Nathaniel P. Hill from Brown University became interested in new smelting processes. He knew that mines in Gregory Gulch and other places could be profitable if someone could figure out how to process the ore. He took samples of Colorado ore to the great smelter experts in South Wales. He got advice about smelting techniques and in 1866 imported a group of Cornish experts to build a smelter in Black Hawk. Hill's Boston and Colorado smelter began treating ore in December 1867. The plant was a success almost from the start. Its very presence stopped a stampede of Denver businessmen north to the coming rail metropolis of Cheyenne, Wyoming, a rival to Denver created by the building of the Union Pacific Railroad. The new Hill smelters stimulated the dormant gold production and the infant silver industry near Denver and set the stage for the spread of Colorado mining three hundred miles along the Continental Divide. This industrial maturity also made a strong case for railroad builders, the men with the Midas touch in the 1860s, to look at Denver more seriously.

With an enormous lobbying, fundraising, and outright bribing effort, William Byers and his influential friends managed to keep Denver as the logical spot to become a transportation and industrial center in Colorado. The first trains arrived in Denver in 1870, officially ensuring its future. The mines and new smelters were now producing millions in gold and silver ore and finished bullion each year. The arrival of the railroad, announced in four-inch headlines on the front page of Byers's *News,* also signaled the end of the heady boom days of prospectors and gold strikes. The mines now employed thousands of men, but most of them earned a three-dollar-a-day wage, and increasingly they were immigrants from northern Europe or Ireland. William Byers's newspaper reflected the new maturity by boosting farming, ranching, and industrial enterprises. The population of Denver grew nearly tenfold in the 1870s, and Elizabeth's work now involved solving long-term urban problems. The Ladies Union Aid Society, founded in the winter of 1860, evolved into the Ladies Relief Society. The group organized itself into districts representing different parts of the city and the different needs of children, women, men, and immigrants. The rush to Colorado had created a prosperous city, but not without social costs. Not everyone got rich, and those who did depended on the cheap labor of others for their profits. An entire Indian culture had been uprooted to allow this economic transformation of the West, and the few remaining Indians living in the squalor of the "Bottoms" by Cherry Creek reflected the great loss these people had endured.

By the 1870s, Elizabeth Byers could assure herself that Denver would survive and that its roughest boom days were over. Her efforts had made the community a more livable place and created a safety net for those who grabbed for the golden ring and missed. Denver looked like a substantial city with broad streets, elegant houses, a transportation system, effective city government, and a wide range of public and private support services—entirely different from the disordered collection of shacks that had made up the city a decade earlier. Salt Lake City and the Mormon kingdom had undergone enormous changes as well. Because the various gold rushes and the resulting transcontinental railroad had brought maturity and success to both cities, Salt Lake City and Denver looked remarkably similar. However, their moral compasses remained quite different.

When Sam Brannan turned his back on the Salt Lake City Mormons and marched back to California in the summer of 1848, neither he nor Brigham Young could have envisioned the changes that loomed. The discovery of gold offered both worldly profits and spiritual dangers. Brannan, as first elder of the California Mormons, advised his flock to make the most of their opportunity. He made a fortune selling merchandise to eager miners, and other Mormons found real wealth in the diggings. Brannan, faithful Mormon that he was, collected a healthy tithe from all of them. The truth of what happened to this considerable sum of money collected in the name of the Mormon Church will be forever unclear, but little of it ended up in Utah. Brigham Young instantly recognized the spiritual dangers of gold mining and recalled all Mormons, including Elder Brannan, to Utah. Brannan, embarked on a lucrative career as a store owner, hotel keeper, and investor in the China trade, had little interest in heading to the Utah desert. Young, sensing he was losing Brannan and the money he had collected, sent a group of Mormon elders to demand that Brannan pay up. Brannan resented being accused of theft and greed and simply refused. This stubborn action led to Brannan's public excommunication from the Mormon

Anne F. Hyde

Church. Brigham Young denounced him as an apostate and admonished other Mormons to consider him as spiritually dead and never to speak of him again. Brannan, deeply wounded, intended never to think of the Mormons again.

But he and the Mormons seemed forever joined by their ambitions and frustrations. As Brannan's business holdings broadened, so too did the aspirations of the Mormons. In 1851, Brigham Young ordered a group of Utah Mormons to travel overland to southern California so that the Utah kingdom would have a path to the sea. Their trip across the Mojave Desert into San Bernadino left the colonists without supplies or the cash to buy them. In desperation, the leaders of the new colony traveled to San Francisco to ask Sam Brannan for a large sum of cash. He refused personally but gave a large sum of money through his mother-in-law, saving face for all concerned. The San Bernadino colony grew and prospered, representing the zenith of the spread of Mormondon. Like Samuel Brannan's fortune, this expansive version of Zion didn't last long.

The Mormons, with their success and their importance on the map of the western United States, began to look threatening to other Americans. Had the federal government allowed a strange and immoral theocracy to take control in the heart of this rich new region? By the winter of 1856, newspapers and politicians, eager to find an issue that did not involve debate between North and South, raised opposition to the Mormons to a positive frenzy. In July 1857, President James Buchanan demanded that Brigham Young give up his position as territorial governor and appointed some non-Mormons as the official leaders of Utah. Then he sent in the army to enforce his order. Young, having endured persecution in other places, instantly prepared for Zion's defense. He called in all of the outlying colonists, including those in southern Colorado, Las Vegas, and San Bernadino. He then prepared Salt Lake City for war and ordered his militia to be on the lookout for spies, advance cavalry, and the troops themselves. As the U.S. Army approached, ready to make war on its own citizens, Young evacuated Salt Lake City and prepared to burn it to the ground.

This situation, not unlike the one festering in Denver in November 1864, furnished the tensions that created the Mountain Meadows Massacre. As the Mormons waited for signs of the impending attack, everyone and everything seemed threatening. The Saints, tensely gathered in forts and fortified towns, had no idea who their friends or enemies might be. In a horrifying moment of fear and anger, a group of Mormons in southern Utah attacked a wagon train and killed most of its passengers and then attempted to place the entire blame on local Indians. In fact, Indians and Mormons had joined together in the atrocity. The Indians believed these people had poisoned some of their wells, killing off their cattle. The isolated Mormons believed the group was an advance reconnoitering party for the U.S. Army. Various sources also reported that the emigrant train had carried travelers from Missouri who boasted of having been involved in atrocities against the Mormons. Perhaps these charges were true, but they hardly seem a reason to kill 120 men and women.

This event, from the perspective of Brigham Young, could not have happened at a worse moment. How could the people of the United States interpret such an attack as anything but more evidence of the heinous behavior of the Mormons? A set of government emissaries provided a set of face-saving deals for both sides in hopes of averting any further disasters. Young, realizing the futility of finding a haven from the United States or of taking on the U.S. Army, worked out a compromise with the federal government. The Mormons would no longer practice polygamy openly, and they agreed to non-Mormon leadership in the territorial government, but Utah remained a Mormon enclave. Americans first tolerated and then celebrated Mormon success as it became a testament to American enterprise.

Samuel Brannan would have recognized the necessity of Young's compromise. He became for a time the richest man in California, with a well-established bank, huge investments in the Napa Valley, and a fleet of China clippers, but he overextended himself as well. He lost a fortune in mining speculation but even more when his wife, Eliza, divorced him after years of enduring his very public affairs with actresses, singers, and other beautiful young women. Just as Brigham Young had predicted, Sam Brannan had traded his spiritual core for ephemeral wealth. However, the Mormons in Utah seemed to be doing much the same thing. Salt Lake City became a major entrepôt on the overland train and on the transcontinental railroad. Eager travelers bought Mormon produce and shopped at Mormon stores for the goods they needed. Wealth from church-owned enterprises and from tithes and donations poured into the coffers of the Mormon Church. Unlike the individual fortune that Brannan had amassed, this wealth was, initially, created and held collectively. Mormon leadership invested in a variety of enterprises from a church-owned telegraph company, to iron mills, newspapers, sugar-beet-processing companies, and finally to the Zion Cooperative Mercantile Institution, which became a vast merchandising cooperative with branches in every community and a set of major department stores by the end of the century.

Two examples indicate the significance of this cooperation to Mormon culture and economic success: the Perpetual Emigrating Fund and the practice of irrigated agriculture. Serious about, as Brigham

Anne F. Hyde

Young put it, their "one great work—the building up of the Kingdom of God of Earth," the Mormons faced disadvantages in terms of their location. Getting new converts, who tended to be the poor and dispossessed of the new commercial industrial world of eastern America and Western Europe, to the isolated Great Basin Kingdom cost a lot of money. Few emigrants could pay their own passage from Europe, much less the cost of emigrating across the Great Plains, and even fewer had the means to set themselves up in business or as farmers in such a forbidding setting as Utah. To solve this problem, Young and the Council of Twelve came up with the concept of the Perpetual Emigrating Fund in 1849. It would operate out of voluntary contributions of church members, repayments by those assisted by the fund, and interest accrued on loans given, and it would exist purely to fund the emigration of poor Mormons to Utah. As soon as Young announced the plan, Utah Mormons raised $5,000. They sent it east with an agent instructed to make the money stretch as far as he could by providing only minimal supplies and homemade wagons for any potential converts. This maximized the numbers of new converts while tempering their faith with hardship on the trail.

Upon arrival in Utah, new Saints received land or employment through the new Office of Public Works created out of the wealth accumulating in tithing houses. Throughout the 1850s, hundreds of men worked as blacksmiths, carpenters, painters, adobe makers, and stone cutters building the infrastructure of Salt Lake City. With their wages or their farm produce, some emigrants managed to pay back the Perpetual Emigrating Fund, but most of the money to support it came from more established Mormons. In fact, most beneficiaries of the fund never paid it back, and by 1880 owed it nearly $2 million. As a nod to the fiftieth-year jubilee of the Church, its leaders decided to forgive the debts in 1880 and cleared the books, declaring the experiment a grand success. The fund eventually brought more than ten thousand Saints to Utah.

Irrigation represented another success for Mormon communities. The combination of practical need and theocratic principle made irrigation work. The Mormons recognized that water was Utah's most precious commodity and that only communal effort and ownership would protect this resource. Within a few years, Mormons had figured out the organizational and agronomic skills necessary for irrigated agriculture. Canals, ditches, gates, and the equitable apportionment of water became part of the Mormon social fabric. Water doled out equally by fractions of stream flow so that no one could use water at someone else's expense reflected Mormon ideals of fairness and cooperation. Such practices stood in opposition to the system that developed in much of the rest of the West, which rewarded early comers and allowed single owners to use all the water in a stream. The unique Mormon system, codified into the Utah Irrigation District Act of 1865, defied all traditions of both riparian water law and Colorado water law. It encouraged the development of small farms, gathered around tightly knit villages, where the work on canals and gates could be easily supervised and organized. And irrigation enthusiasts like John Wesley Powell and Elwood Mead singled out the Mormons as examples of how it should be done.

Although by many measures the Mormons succeeded, they did not create an egalitarian kingdom, something deeply important to Brigham Young and many early leaders in the church. The tight community with its protective impulse that had attracted young men like Sam Brannan was eroded by success. Young's goal and its ultimate failure were showcased in the story of the United Order of Enoch. As the Mormon state grew and prospered and as American culture in the form of the Gold Rush, political leadership, and the transcontinental railroad enriched the coffers of the kingdom, they also threatened the spiritual core of the church. Even as the church as a whole and many individual Mormons amassed considerable wealth, Brigham Young continued to see Joseph Smith's Law of Consecration and Stewardship as an ideal. Every cooperative experiment could be seen as a step toward the goal of a society of cooperating Saints, all united in the single purpose of sharing wealth to create God's kingdom on earth. Tithing, cooperative sugar mills and department stores, communal farming practices, water rights, cattle herds, and road-building teams were only steps to a purely communitarian society.

In the early 1870s, Young decided that the Saints were ready for the final stage. He announced a new structure, the United Order of Enoch, that would take over all private property in Mormon communities, and initiated a great religious revival. The preamble to the articles of the United Order, which contained specific instructions on how to manage community land, bees, tools, stock, and profit, also indicates the kinds of pressures Young felt to create "a closer union and combination of our labor for the promotion of our common welfare." He implored his followers to take up simple habits, to give up extravagance, and to have energetic and faithful dealings. He began in St. George, in southern Utah, and worked his way north, demanding that all good Mormons surrender their private property and combat the "feeling of Mine," thus avoiding the dangers of "grasping individualism" that Young feared had taken over the hearts of many Saints. In Young's vision, each community would be entirely self-sufficient and entirely without private enterprise, with the ultimate belief that "to be friends of God we must become friends and helpers of each other."

Anne F. Hyde

The revival ended in a grand fizzle. Like Sam Brannan, Brigham Young had imagined too grandly. Although many communities initially responded to Young's pleas with enthusiasm, only a very few could live up to his standards. By 1880 only the town of Orderville, formed out of a nucleus of families who left failed United Order communities to band together, remained to practice Young's principles. The economic success of the Mormons, their central location on the railroad, and their importance in the growing mountain west region made cooperation obsolete. Brigham Young was right—the Mormon community had succeeded too well. Most Mormons, much like Sam Brannan, had intended to sequester themselves from the grasping and profane culture of the United States but instead had come to share mainstream economic values. With the death of Brigham Young in 1877 and the continued legal attack on polygamy, new Mormons leaders chose to compromise. Utah outlawed polygamy and became a state, reflecting the ways the Mormons had lost much of their distinctive critique of American society. When Mormon entrepreneurs in the twentieth century decided to invest in Las Vegas, the ghost of Sam Brannan would have cheered them on.

Brannan, as he became famous in California and infamous all over the West for his wealth and his various political ambitions, became a sort of antihero for both Mormons and miners. He represented what they could all so easily become. When Brannan lay dying in San Diego in the late 1880s, he was visited by Mormon elders looking for land to buy for new colonies in Mexico, where Brannan himself had schemed to make his last fortune. But even then, they could not forgive him or consider buying his land. When Brannan made one last visit to San Francisco, the city he had been so instrumental in building, his few remaining acquaintances shunned him because of his poverty. Far too many of the gold rushers in 1849 or 1859 had lost fortunes. Brannan was an uncomfortably effective reminder of how easily this fall from grace could occur.

Elizabeth Byers, on the other hand, found herself memorialized as a glorious pioneer long before she was ready. Decades before her death, she was asked to prepare her memoirs and to have her picture made in stained glass in the new capitol rotunda in Denver. She refused to do both. She insisted that the work she had done was a group effort, something that women in Denver had done together. She wanted to honor the cooperative effort of Denver's ladies, who had persevered, much like the Mormons, in making everyone's lives better. She shared a vision that Mormons would have recognized of a society that cared for its weakest members.

Both Elizabeth Byers and Samuel Brannan were gamblers. They believed the American West would provide happiness and fortune for their families and communities, and they took great personal risks to ensure this vision. But both were also iconoclasts: Brannan for seeking personal fortune at the expense of his Mormon faith and Elizabeth Byers for looking for safety and stability rather than instant wealth. Although Byers never picked up a mining pan and Brannan was excommunicated from the Mormon Church, both of these individuals represent the larger stories well. The significance of mining in the Far West was fundamentally not about a few lucky prospectors, but more about the slow development of communities and cities built by a combination of mining wealth and the work of people like Elizabeth Byers. And the story of the Mormons is not just about an isolated, strange religious experiment, but about the power of American culture to incorporate a distinctive sect and give it the power to build a kingdom in the desert with the wits and wealth of people like Sam Brannan.

Essay on Sources

Given their contentious history, the members of the Church of Jesus Christ of Latter-day Saints, or Mormons, have written or have had written about them much history with an agenda to make them out as sinners or as saints. These images are as old as the Mormons. Newspapers in the 1830s are as divided about how to understand the Mormons as they are in the 1850s, the 1890s, or the present. Most textbooks tend to point out the clannish behavior and violent episodes that made the U.S. government attempt to control and undermine Mormon leadership. Historians range in similar ways, depending on their connection to the church, knowledge of the subject, and so on. Wallace Stegner, who grew up in Salt Lake City as a non-Mormon, depicts the history of the Mormons very favorably. See, for example, *The Gathering of Zion: The Story of the Mormon Trail* (New York: McGraw-Hill, 1964) and more recently several of the essays in *Marking the Sparrow's Fall: Wallace Stegner's American West,* ed. Page Stegner (New York: Henry Holt, 1998). Many non-Mormons have written with careful objectivity about the religious practices of the Mormons. For helpful descriptions of the context of early Mormonism and its combination of conservatism and radicalism, see Klaus J. Hansen, *Mormonism and the American Experience* (Chicago: University of Chicago Press, 1981), and Jan Shipps, *Mormonism: The Story of a New Religious Tradition* (Urbana: University of Illinois Press, 1985).

Because historians who are practicing Mormons have access to church records that non-Mormons often do not, they have written much of what we rely on for understanding the Mormons. Leonard Arrington, the embattled librarian of the Mormon Church, spent a career writing excellent history. See, for example, *Great Basin Kingdom; An Economic History of the Latter-day Saints, 1830–1900* (Cambridge,

Mass.: Harvard University Press, 1958); and *Brigham Young: American Moses* (New York: Knopf, 1985); and, with Feramorz Y. Fox and Dean L. May, *Building the City of God: Community and Cooperation Among the Mormons* (Urbana and Chicago: University of Illinois Press, 1992). Eugene Campbell, *Establishing Zion: The Mormon Church in the American West, 1847–1869* (Salt Lake City: Signature Books, 1988), and Nels Anderson, *Desert Saints: The Mormon Frontier in Utah* (Chicago: University of Chicago Press, 1942), are also very helpful on the early years of the Mormon kingdom. See also D. Michael Quinn, *The New Mormon History: Revisionist Essays on the Past* (Salt Lake City: Signature Books, 1992), and *Early Mormonism and the Magic World View* (Salt Lake City: Signature Books, 1998). On Mormon irrigation and cooperatives, see William Smythe, *The Conquest of Arid America* (New York: Macmillan, 1905); Richard W. Sadler and Richard C. Roberts, *The Weber River Basin: Grass Roots Democracy and Water Development* (Logan: Utah State University Press, 1994); and Leonard J. Arrington and Dean May, "A Different Mode of Life: Irrigation and Society in Nineteenth Century Utah," *Agricultural History* 49 (1975): 1–23.

Samuel Brannan appears incidentally in many accounts of Mormon history and is often held up as a disciple of the devil. Several accounts centering on Brannan tell a more complex story. Paul Bailey, *Sam Brannan and the California Mormons* (Los Angeles: Westernlore Press, 1953), and Will Bagley, *Scoundrel's Tale: The Samuel Brannan Papers* (Logan: Utah State University Press, 1999), seem most complete.

Mining in the western United States has an industrial-strength literature as well. The California Gold Rush has thousands of books, and each succeeding mining rush produced its own bonanza. Most useful and recent on California are Malcolm Rohrbough, *Days of Gold: The California Gold Rush and the American Nation* (Berkeley: University of California Press, 1997), and Susan Lee Johnson, *Roaring Camp: The Social World of the California Gold Rush* (New York: Norton, 2000). Still essential are Rodman Paul, *Mining Frontiers of the Far West, 1848–1880* (New York: Holt, Rinehart, 1963); Richard E. Lingenfelter, *The Hardrock Miners: A History of the Mining Labor Movement in the American West, 1863–1893* (Berkeley: University of California Press, 1974); and Ralph Mann, *After the Gold Rush: Society in Grass Valley and Nevada City, California, 1849–1870* (Stanford: Stanford University Press, 1982). As an account of a single miner's experience, J. S. Holliday's compilation of letters, diaries, and drawings about William Swain and his family, *The World Rushed In: The California Gold Rush Experience* (New York: Simon & Schuster, 1981), is spectacular.

On the Pikes Peak Rush and Colorado mining, Elliott West's *The Contested Plains: Indians, Goldseekers, and the Rush to Colorado* (Lawrence:

University Press of Kansas, 1998) adds context and powerful analysis to the story. Several broad texts, including Carl Ubbelohde, Maxine Benson, and Duane A. Smith, *A Colorado History,* 7th ed. (Boulder, Colo.: Pruett Publishing, 1995), and Carl Abbott, Stephen Leonard, and David McComb, *Colorado: A History of the Centennial State,* rev. ed. (Niwot: University of Colorado Press, 1982), tell the basic story well. Duane A. Smith, *Rocky Mountain West: Colorado, Wyoming, and Montana, 1859–1915* (Albuquerque: University of New Mexico Press, 1992), puts the history of mining in the intermountain West into a useful context. The work of Leroy and Ann Hafen, which includes several excellent monographs as well as a mountain of edited documentary sources, is essential for Colorado history. Thomas Noel, *The City and the Saloon: Denver,* 1858–1916 (Lincoln: University of Nebraska Press, 1982), and Lyle Dorsett, *The Queen City: A History of Denver* (Boulder, Colo.: Pruett Publishing Co., 1976), provide useful and colorful histories of Denver. The *Rocky Mountain News* offers much detail about Denver and the Byers family during their early years in the city.

Elizabeth Byers has no biography, but the William Byers Papers at the Denver Public Library include her personal letters and memorabilia, as well as a brief set of reminiscences. Robert L. Perkin, *The First Hundred Years: An Informal History of Denver and the Rocky Mountain News* (New York: Doubleday, 1959), provides a mostly reliable history of the paper and its colorful editor but rarely mentions Elizabeth. To tell her story, I relied on Anne Cameron Robb, "Raising a City: Women and Urban Development in Denver, 1859–1900" (honors thesis, Colorado College, 2002), and Elizabeth Byers, "The Experiences of One Pioneer Woman," William Byers Papers, Box 2, Denver Public Library, as well as several older histories that included accounts of Denver's founders, such as Wilbur Fiske Stone, *History of Colorado,* vol. 1 (Chicago: S. J. Clarke Publishing Co., 1918). Several important works in women's history gave Elizabeth Byers's life a richer context, including Peggy Pascoe, *Relations of Rescue: The Search for Female Moral Authority in the American West, 1874–1939* (New York: Oxford University Press, 1990); Elizabeth Jameson, *All That Glitters: Class, Conflict and Community in Cripple Creek* (Urbana: University of Illinois Press, 1998); and Paula Petrik, *No Step Backward: Women and Family on the Rocky Mountain Mining Frontier, Helena, Montana, 1865–1900* (Helena: Montana Historical Society Press, 1987).

CHAPTER 7

Mariano Vallejo and María Amparo Ruiz de Burton

Cultural Conflicts and Compromises in the Late-Nineteenth-Century West

RICHARD GRISWOLD DEL CASTILLO

In the last half of the century stretching from the 1840s to the 1890s, the American Southwest experienced dramatic changes that led to notable cultural conflicts and compromises. Among these were the U.S.-Mexican War, the destruction of the Mexican landholding class, movements of rebellion and resistance by both Mexicans and Indians against the Americans, and the economic transformations wrought by the California Gold Rush, railroad construction, and mass western migrations. These events changed the lives of thousands of Mexicans and Indians who lived in the Southwest. The lives of two notable southwesterners, Mariano Vallejo and María Amparo Ruiz de Burton, are revealing illustrations of the shaping power of several of these transformations.

Mariano Guadalupe Vallejo was born on July 4, 1807, in the Spanish town of Monterey, Alta California. His life spanned the transition years between the Mexican and American eras of the American Southwest. As a person with confidence in the future, Mariano Vallejo had faith in the improvement of mankind through education, industry, and good faith. This optimism continued despite his enlarging impoverishment because of the American takeover of his beloved land. Vallejo believed in compromising and adapting to the new order, and in his lifetime he saw many changes as California went from a half-forgotten pastoral Spanish colony to a prosperous metropolitan American state. As a result his life touched on many of the important themes during this era: Manifest Destiny and war, commercial expansion, immigration, and state building.

A close friend and confidant of Mariano Vallejo was María Amparo Ruiz, the Mexican-born wife of Henry S. Burton, an officer in the U.S.

Army. María was born into a prominent political family in Loreto, Baja California, on July 3, 1831. When only sixteen, because of the U.S.-Mexican War, she and her family had to flee their home and migrate to Alta California. She soon met, fell in love with, and married Captain Henry Burton. María was a remarkably intelligent and forceful woman who taught herself English and became intimate friends with wealthy and powerful Americans in California as well as in Washington, D.C. After the American Civil War, María wrote in English and published her first novel, *Who Would Have Thought It?* (1872), a romance that critically commented on contemporary society. When her husband died in 1869, María returned to California and San Diego, where she wrote her second novel, *The Squatter and the Don* (1885), which criticized American treatment of *californio* landholders. María also discussed the major problems of the nineteenth century in a voluminous correspondence with Vallejo and other important individuals. Her commentary provides another point of view about the American conquest and colonization of the Southwest. Like Vallejo, Ruiz de Burton believed in compromising with the new world that the Americans were creating in the Southwest. Also like Vallejo, she had many discouraging encounters, but she persisted and fought to retain her culture and dignity.

Both Mariano Vallejo and María Amparo Ruiz de Burton were unwillingly caught up in the war that erupted between the United States and Mexico in May 1846. The war caused them to change their political loyalties even while retaining a cultural bond with their homeland. As with thousands of their compatriots, they had little idea of what the future brought.

The war between the United States and Mexico resulted primarily from American expansionism, illustrated in the policies of President James K. Polk and Texas insistence on the Rio Grande as a southern boundary with Mexico. The term "Manifest Destiny" captured the American mood, a body of ideas and sentiments that claimed to justify the territorial expansion of English-speaking Americans into territories held, occupied, or claimed by Mexicans and Indians. Disparate groups, from rustic backwoodsmen to sophisticated New England poets, from northern abolitionists to southern slaveholders, fervently believed that God had ordained that Americans had a Manifest Destiny to populate and govern a vast expanse of land west of the Mississippi River.

A precipitating cause of the war was the U.S. annexation of Texas in 1845 and the dispute over the southern boundary of that province with Mexico. In this disputed area in south Texas, the war began. The Mexican army believed that their country had been invaded and thus attacked Zachary Taylor's troops, sent there by presidential orders. Like most wars, the war between Mexico and the United States grew

Richard Griswold del Castillo

Figure 7.1: General Mariano Vallejo with his wife and children on the front porch of their home. Courtesy of the California Historical Society, FN-30504.

out of conflicting interpretations of history. With the annexation of Texas accomplished, and now with a declaration of war, a prime objective for the United States was to occupy California and link it to Texas by marching into New Mexico.

In the early morning hours of June 14, 1846, Mariano Vallejo was at home in Sonoma, California, when thirty-three rough and dirty men forced their way into his parlor, demanding the surrender of his command of the Mexican military forces in the region. Ironically, Vallejo had been one of the leading californios who had, for years, argued in favor of union with the United States. He believed that American democracy and economic progress would ensure the best future for his beloved homeland. That morning was the beginning of the Bear Flag Rebellion, which preceded by a few days the news that the United States had declared war on Mexico. The Bear Flaggers imprisoned Vallejo, a forlorn ally, at Sutter's Fort for more than two months while the American forces commanded by John C. Frémont and Commodore Robert Stockton occupied the major towns of Monterey, Los Angeles, and San Diego.

The bulk of the fighting in the conquest of California took place in the south. In the summer of 1846, General Mariano Castro and Governor Pío Pico joined forces in Los Angeles to await the American advance but soon concluded that they were hopelessly outnumbered and outgunned. Both leaders departed for Mexico to seek reinforcements. Meanwhile Commodore Stockton and Frémont marched south and occupied Los Angeles and San Diego. In August 1846 the conquest of California seemed complete, and Stockton issued a proclamation stating that California was now officially part of the United States. He promised that the Americans would respect Mexican political institutions and laws.

A wave of californio resistance against the American invaders soon erupted. In Los Angeles, resentments over the occupying army grew until finally, on September 22, 1846, a revolt occurred in Los Angeles, led by José María Flores and Serbulo Varela. The californios surrounded the American fortified position and issued *El Plan de Los Angeles,* calling on all Mexicans to fight against the Americans who were threatening to reduce them to "a condition worse than that of slaves." The officer in charge of the American troops, Lieutenant Archibald Gillespie, soon saw that his situation was hopeless. So on September 29, he signed Articles of Capitulation, marched his men to San Pedro, and sailed away. Flores and Varela were soon joined by other prominent californios. They declared California in a state of siege, secured loans to pay for a war, and began to recruit more troops.

During all this time Mariano Vallejo was a prisoner in Sutter's Fort in Sacramento. News of these rebellions did not reach him until the next spring. During the last four months of 1846 Los Angeles remained in californio hands; their military forces also reoccupied San Diego, Santa Bárbara, Santa Inés, and San Luis Obispo. The californios used guerrilla tactics to effectively win several victories at Chico Rancho (September 26–27, 1846), Domínguez Rancho (October 8), and Natividad (November 29). The Battle of San Pascual (December 8) pitted General Andrés Pico against General Stephen W. Kearny and was the high-water mark of the californio resistance during the war. It was the bloodiest battle in California and both a victory for the partisan forces and evidence of the californios' determination to resist the American conquest. Despite the californios' valiant though somewhat hopeless resistance against the invaders, the American forces eventually recaptured all of southern California by winter 1847. Following the defeat of the last californio army near Los Angeles, Andrés Pico signed a surrender agreement at Cahuenga Pass on January 13, 1847.

In 1847, the U.S.-Mexican War forced María Amparo Ruiz and her family to flee their home in Baja California. When the American forces, led by Lieutenant Colonel Henry S. Burton, occupied La Paz, Baja California, in early 1847, many of the local families welcomed the U.S. troops. They hoped that the invaders would bring new prosperity to the struggling town. María's family was among many that cooperated with the American commander. Soon, however, fighting broke out between Mexican partisans and the U.S. troops. After the end of the war, those siding with the Americans received free transportation north to California along with a small stipend to help them in settling in a new land. María and her family arrived in Monterey, California, in September 1848.

As Maria's parents wrestled with the problems of loyalty in Baja California, similar dramas of conquest and resistance took place in New Mexico. In August 1846, General Kearny and his men occupied the territorial capital of Santa Fe. As they had in California the Americans issued a proclamation promising to respect the people's rights and stating that the area was now a permanent possession of the United States. Colonel Alexander Doniphan marched south to complete the conquest of the territory, defeating a New Mexican force at Brazitos near Las Cruces.

Although the conquest of New Mexico seemed complete, signs of discontent soon erupted into rebellion. In early January 1847, the Taos Indians, led by Tomasito Romero, in alliance with some of the local Hispanos, headed by Pablo Montoya, rebelled against the American occupiers. They killed the American military governor, Charles Bent, and recaptured several towns in northern New Mexico. On January 24, 1847, a Hispano-Indian army of 1,500 met the Americans at La Cañada near Santa Fe but were defeated. The American army commanded by Colonel Sterling Price descended on the town of Mora and destroyed it, then marched north to surround Taos pueblo, where almost 4,500 Hispanos and Pueblo Indians had entrenched themselves. In the days that followed, the Americans killed more than 150 defenders and captured the leaders. In a display of mock justice, Colonel Price tried and executed 15 of the rebels for conspiracy, murder, and treason. Later in Santa Fe 30 more prisoners were hanged for their part in the rebellion against the U.S. forces. These events marked the end of armed resistance in the New Mexico and the Southwest.

Meanwhile, in northern and central Mexico the fight against the American invaders killed tens of thousands of soldiers and civilians in massive clashes of armies, at first in the north, near Monterrey, Mexico, and then in the Valley of Mexico. By January 1847, the U.S. Army, commanded by General Winfield Scott, occupied Mexico City and waited to hear results of peace negotiations.

The Mexican government felt more and more pressure to end the war and sign a treaty. Pressed by European creditors, lacking money to pay their own troops, racked by internal rebellion, and facing the occupation of their principal cities, the Mexican government finally signed a treaty of peace, giving in to the Americans' territorial demands in exchange for the removal of troops from their homeland. The negotiators signed the Treaty of Guadalupe Hidalgo, ending the war on February 2, 1848. The treaty would be proclaimed official by

President Polk on July 4, 1848. The provisions in the treaty specified that a new boundary between the new nations would start "one marine league due south of the southernmost point of the Port of San Diego" and run east to the Colorado River, then farther east, following the Gila River and an as yet undefined latitude line to the Rio Grande. The Mexican provinces of California and New Mexico were now part of the United States. Articles 8 and 9 gave assurances in regard to the property and citizenship rights of the Mexicans in the newly conquered territories. Article 8 specifically promised to protect the rights of absentee Mexican landholders and to give U.S. citizenship for all Mexicans who wanted it. Article 9 said that Congress would give citizenship "at the proper time" and that the Mexicans "in the mean time shall be maintained and protected in the free enjoyment of their liberty and property, and secured in the free exercise of their religion without restriction." Finally, the treaty transferred more than five hundred thousand square miles of Mexican territory to the United States.

The war against Mexico awakened new nationalist impulses in the 1850s within Mexico and eventually produced a reform movement led by Benito Juárez. In the United States, the Mexican cession provoked a new and heated debate over slavery in the newly acquired territories. That debate played a major role in the outbreak of the U.S. Civil War in 1861, the bloodiest conflict in American history.

In the conquered territories Native people far outnumbered the Mexican settlers and the Anglo Americans. They had not been consulted about the treaty, and the majority had never really been conquered by the Spanish or the Mexicans. Most tribes, with the exception of the Taoseños and scattered bands in California, remained unaffected during the war, particularly those living on their traditional homelands away from the Euroamerican settlements. Some Indians joined the U.S. Army as scouts and guides, and a few capitalized on the war to settle old grievances against the Mexicans. By 1848, those Native peoples who had become Hispanicized and had worked on the ranchos and in the pueblos now found themselves with more aggressive masters, the Americans. Still, Indian laborers were the backbone of the agricultural and ranching industries in California and influential in New Mexico and Arizona. The Americans inherited a dependence on this labor force as well as the job of subduing fierce and independent nations such as the Navajo and the Apache.

Few Mexicans or Indians could foresee the impact of the loss of their lands and the erosion of their culture. They could not dream of being victims of rampant, and sometimes violent, anti-Mexican and anti-Indian sentiments. Mariano Vallejo and María Amparo Ruiz de Burton (who married Lieutenant Colonel Burton on July 9, 1849) represented an influential minority willing to compromise and accommodate themselves to the new political system and culture, hoping that it would produce a better future.

By complete coincidence, a few weeks before the signing of the Treaty of Guadalupe Hidalgo, John Marshall discovered gold in the American River at Coloma, near Sutter's Fort in California. Several months elapsed before news of this discovery was verified and many more months for the first immigrants to begin travel north or west. The California Gold Rush was one of the most significant events in the history of the American West. It rapidly changed California society and gave the West a sudden economic importance in national and world affairs. Later backwash migration of former California gold miners populated remote corners throughout the West. In the fall of 1848, about six thousand miners, many of them Sonorans, entered California and set up mining camps along the American River. The first American miners to arrive knew nothing about gold mining and learned their mining techniques from the Mexicans. Soon news of the gold strike in California rapidly spread, first to Hawai`i, Oregon, and Utah and then to South America, Australia, China, the eastern seaboard, and Europe. In 1849 thousands of immigrants from around the world, but especially from the eastern United States, flooded into northern California. Overnight San Francisco was transformed into an international city, an entrepôt for miners and mining supplies. The pastoral life of the californios in the north changed rapidly while the rancheros of the south enjoyed a brief flare of prosperity. Their cattle had increased in value in the demand for food from the mining camps and growing population of the North. By 1850 fully one quarter of California's population was foreign born, many of them Latin Americans or Mexicans.

From his home in Sonoma, Mariano Vallejo saw the newcomers as they rushed east from San Francisco toward the Sierra Nevada in search of easy riches. The most dangerous immigrants, in his opinion, were the lawyers. "No sooner had they arrived than they assumed title of attorney and began to seek means of depriving the Californians of their farms and other properties. . . . These legal thieves . . . enthroned themselves in our homes like so many powerful kings. For them no law existed but their own will and their caprice."

During the first chaotic years of the Gold Rush the American military governed California, but the American residents protested this situation and held mass meetings to demand that a civil government be organized. Beginning in the fall of 1849 forty-eight elected delegates met in Monterey to construct a state constitution. Eight were native californios, including Mariano Vallejo. For his part, Vallejo had hopes that the californio delegation would help shape the future of the state. Following the biases of their age, the framers of the state constitution sought wording that would exclude African Americans and Indians while including Mexicans. Eventually, the first section of the state constitution limited the suffrage to "every white, male citizen of Mexico who shall have elected to become a citizen of the United States." The state constitution did leave open the question of Indian citizenship when it stated that "nothing herein contained, shall be construed to prevent the Legislature, by a two-thirds concurrent vote, from admitting to the right of suffrage, Indians or the descendants of Indians."

Under the provisions of the Treaty of Guadalupe Hidalgo, those who did not want to become citizens of the United States had a year to declare this intention; they were also free to go to Mexico. How many from California returned to Mexico is uncertain, but during the early 1850s several colonization expeditions consisting of californios went south, settling in Sonora and Baja California. Of course the main issue in California was possession of the land. In this regard the proposed constitution was silent, and the former Mexican citizens had to trust their fate to the courts. The new state constitution required that all laws had to be published in both Spanish and English in recognition of the Mexican minority. Following Mexican custom, California adopted the concept of community property: that a married woman had joint ownership of property along with her husband. Mariano Vallejo, one of the californio delegates, protested that the state flag and seal should not show a grizzly bear, a reminder of the Bear Flag Rebellion and his own personal humiliation, but his objections did not win a sympathetic hearing.

As in California, the people of New Mexico were anxious to rid themselves of military rule. Accordingly, in May 1850 delegates assembled in Santa Fe to draft a constitution for a state government. After ten days they drafted a document that outlawed slavery but excluded Indians from citizenship. In a short time a legislature was formed, a new governor elected, and congressional delegates chosen. These acts were done under protest by the U.S. military commander, who declared the elections illegal. When the New Mexico delegate arrived in Washington, D.C., to present the petition for statehood, he found that Congress had already passed a series of laws that embodied the Compromise of 1850, giving New Mexico a territorial form of government. But the territory lacked the requisite population to become a state.

The Compromise of 1850 settled the boundary dispute festering between New Mexico and Texas about the Rio Grande. New Mexico Territory included the present-day area of the state as well as Arizona (not a separate territory until 1863), and the federal government gave Texas $10 million to relinquish its claims to New Mexican lands. The Compromise of 1850 also admitted California as a free state but allowed the new territories of Utah and New Mexico to determine whether to allow slavery. To get California admitted as a free state, northerners agreed to pass the Fugitive Slave Law. This law, establishing a federal program to capture runaway slaves, caused much moral anguish among abolitionists, intensifying the controversies eventually resulting in the Civil War.

New Mexico did not experience massive numbers of immigrants like California. The native Hispanic and Indian populations were the overwhelming majority, with the upper-class Hispanos enjoying a significant voice in the territorial government. Nevertheless, they were unable to stop the aggrandizement of speculators, railroad companies, and mining and timber companies who used Anglo American control of the courts to acquire millions of acres of land formerly the grazing and agricultural lands of Hispano *pobladores*.

In 1853 Captain Burton and María Amparo bought Rancho Jamul, east of San Diego. At the same time Mariano Vallejo was mortgaging his lands to develop a new town of Vallejo, which he hoped would become the capital of the new state. Eventually both María's rancho and the lands of Vallejo fell victim to speculators, squatters, lawyers, and bankers who used the courts to take over the holdings. Their story was that of hundreds of Mexican landholders in California.

María and her husband left San Diego in 1859 when the military posted Captain Burton to Washington, D.C. They left behind their rancho, which, after Captain Burton's death, had to be mortgaged to help paying living costs for María and her family. Until 1891, María engaged in lengthy legal battles but finally lost Rancho Jamul to her creditors. During that struggle, María wrote her second novel, *The Squatter and the Don,* in which she offered a critical view of the injustices the californios suffered. One of the main characters in the book is don Mariano Alamar, patterned after Maria's friend don Mariano Vallejo. She has don Alamar comment on the unfair laws that violated the Treaty of Guadalupe Hidalgo:

> The treaty said that our rights would be the same as those enjoyed by all other American citizens. But, you see, Congress takes very good care not to enact retroactive laws for Americans; laws to take away from American citizens the property which they hold now, already with a recognized legal title. No, indeed. But they do so quickly enough with us—with us, the Spano-Americans, who were to enjoy equal

rights, mind you, according to the treaty of peace. This is what seems to me a breach of faith.

Mariano Vallejo also lost his vast rancho lands following decades of legal battles and even a trip to Washington, D.C., to lobby the government. Unfortunately, Vallejo trusted his son-in-law Levi Frisbie to manage his financial affairs; the result was disastrous. By the end of his life Vallejo was reduced to a small home in Sonoma and survived on the charity of his friends and family.

Hundreds of californio landholders shared María and Mariano's fate. Thousands of gold rush migrants had encroached on the californio land grants and demanded that something be done to "liberate" the land. The result was the Land Act of 1851, which established the Board of Land Claims to adjudicate the validity of Mexican land grants in California. Every grantee was required to present evidence supporting title within two years. Those failing to do so would lose their property to public domain.

The Board of Land Claims in California examined 813 claims and eventually confirmed 604, involving approximately 9 million acres. These claims did not mean, however, that a majority of Mexican landholders retained their lands. On the contrary, most californio landholders lost their lands because of the tremendous expense of litigation and legal fees. To pay for the legal defense of their lands, californios were forced to mortgage their ranchos. Falling cattle prices and usurious rates of interest also conspired to wipe out the californios as a landholding class. Even after some landholders fulfilled the terms of the 1851 land law, they soon encountered tremendous pressure from Anglo American squatters to vacate their rights. Others who were able to survive economically lost their holdings because they had not fulfilled the terms of the 1851 land law. A number of court cases in this regard involving Mexican and Spanish grants took place, but the most famous one pertaining to the Treaty of Guadalupe Hidalgo was *Botiller et al. v. Dominguez* (1883). In that case the court held that the sovereign laws of the United States took precedence over international treaties. This important precedent guided the court in its future interpretation of conflicts between treaty obligations and domestic laws.

These occurrences meant that a generation of Mexicans grew up alienated from the land once theirs. The social dislocation of the gold rush and loss of rancho lands created a caste of dispossessed youths, some of whom became social bandits, outlaws to American authorities but folk heroes to the Spanish speaking. Perhaps the most famous of these was Joaquín Murrieta, a Sonoran miner who came to California in 1849 with his wife and brother. In May 1850, in Murphy's Camp in northern California, Joaquín's brother was lynched, accused of stealing a mule. A few days later, a group of Americans attacked Joaquín at his gold claim. Believing him dead, the invaders raped and then killed his wife. These dramatic events set the stage for Joaquín's war of revenge against the *americanos.*

Nearly a hundred *mexicanos* and californios joined Joaquín's band. They stole horses, robbed miners, and killed more than twenty-four people, mostly Chinese immigrants and Anglo Americans. To combat this threat, the state of California created the California Rangers, a special mounted police force modeled on the Texas Rangers, whose purpose was to apprehend Joaquín, dead or alive. The state government placed a price of $1,000 on his head. In 1851, the rangers, headed by Captain Harry Love, killed several Mexicans in a shoot-out and, to claim their reward, chopped off Murrieta's head and brought it back for identification. Even though Love gathered a number of testimonials certifying that the head was indeed Joaquín's, some doubted that Murrieta had been killed. To this day, many believe that Joaquín escaped and returned to his home in Sonora, Mexico.

Joaquín Murrieta became one of California's first legendary figures. Other lesser-known but even more verifiable social bandits were Tiburcio Vásquez, Reyes Durate, Ramón Amador, Chico Lugo, and Pedro Vallejo, many of them landless sons of former land grant owners. The military conquest of California had taken six months, but the violence accompanying the economic conquest lasted for many decades.

In New Mexico, a similar pattern of dispossession and violent reaction occurred. Since New Mexico was a territory and not a state, federally appointed officials were in charge. This meant that these officials had to have Congress approve their decisions—a lengthy and often politicized process. In 1848 private and communal land grants in New Mexico covered about 15 million square miles. To determine the federal domain, Congress established the office of surveyor general, who was given broad powers to "issue notices, summon witnesses, administer oaths," and to report to the secretary of interior and, ultimately, to Congress on the status of New Mexico land grants. Until Congress acted to confirm the findings of the surveyor general, all lands were to be withheld from sale.

In August 1854 Congress appointed William Pelham to the office. By 1863 Congress had confirmed only 25 town and private claims and 17 Pueblo Indian grants. By 1880, the surveyor general had filed 1,000 claims, but the federal government had acted on only 150. As the number of unconfirmed grants in litigation piled up before the surveyor general and the Congress, so too did the legal expenses of the Hispano pueblos and ranchers. Financial opportunities for lawyers and speculators spun out of control. In this dangerous vacuum, Stephen Benson Elkins and Thomas Benton Catron formed the nucleus of a group of speculators called the Santa Fe Ring. This confederation of opportunists used the long legal battles over land grants to acquire empires extending to millions of acres. The most famous example of the land-grabbing activities of the ring was the creation of the Maxwell Land Grant, a Spanish claim of 97,000 acres that became inflated through the actions of the ring to a final patent of 1,714,074 acres.

The native Hispanos victimized by the legalized theft of their communal lands took up arms. The most notable movement in New Mexico was that of Las Gorras Blancas (White Caps). It was a secret society of Hispanos who attacked the homesteaders taking over the traditional village commons lands and fencing them in to prevent Hispano livestock from getting water and food. The night riders cut fences, burned barns, and otherwise intimidated the new settlers, reminding them that the land they were encroaching on was contested. Among the leaders of Las Gorras Blancas were Juan José Herrera and his brothers in San Miguel County. Herrera and other members of the Gorras Blancas were also members of the Knights of Labor and the core of the political party El Partido del Pueblo Unido. On the political front this populist movement confronted large corporations, political corruption in Santa Fe, and loss of village lands to speculators. The Gorras supported candidates in local elections who were anti–land grabber, anti-railroad, and anti-monopolist. They were successful in electing slates of candidates in some of the northern New Mexican counties, but the land issue remained a festering wound well into the next century.

Violence among Hispano villagers, farmers, and ranchers and the new owners of the land erupted in Maxwell County. Armed shoot-outs and killings characterized the 1880s. To the south a range war simmered for several years between Texan immigrants and Hispano ranchers, resulting in the Lincoln County War of 1878. This conflict led to Billy the Kid's joining with the Hispano faction and many people losing their lives.

Finally in the 1890s, after years of skirmishes and social banditry, Congress established the Court of Private Land Claims to "finalize" the land problem in New Mexico. The decisions of this court resulted in the rejection of two thirds of the claims. Ultimately, only eighty-two grants received congressional confirmation. This number represented only 6 percent of the total area land claimants sought. In essence, the New Mexican Court of Private Land Claims had enlarged the U.S. government's national domain at the expense of hundreds of Hispano villages, leaving a bitter legacy for the next century.

In Texas, land transfer was more complicated. There most of the lands had been part of the United States before the outbreak of the U.S.-Mexican War in 1846. Unlike New Mexico or California, Texas had been admitted to the Union with full control over its public lands. Instead of federal laws guiding the settlement of land disputes, state laws and courts played the dominant role. Two Texas historians, Arnoldo De León and Kenneth Stewart, conclude that most *tejanos* lost part or all of their patrimony through "a combination of methods including litigation, chicanery, robbery, fraud, and threat." As early as 1847 the citizens of Laredo, Texas, fearing how they would fare under the Texas administration, requested assurances from the state government that their property rights would be protected. Receiving no reply, they petitioned to be allowed to remain part of Mexico. Many violent episodes marked the struggle between tejano and Anglo Texans for control of the land. The Cortina Rebellion in the Brownsville-Matamoros area in the 1850s and 1860s and the El Paso Salt War in the 1870s pitted entire communities against the Texas Rangers in a struggle for the land. Hundreds of lesser struggles that resulted in lynchings, beatings, and riots also had their origin in conflicts over land. Obviously, tejanos had good reason to distrust the Texas government in its implementation of laws. Over the decades tejano landholders lost their lands because of fraud, confiscation, and disastrous market competition. For example, a large part of the sprawling King Ranch in south Texas was pieced together from the forced sale of tejano ranches during frequent recessions in the cattle market.

In the first half century after the end of the U.S.-Mexican War, hundreds of state, territorial, and federal legal bodies produced a complex tapestry of conflicting opinions and decisions on land. The property holdings of former Mexican citizens in California, New Mexico, and Texas proved to be fragile until new immigrants into the Southwest took over their lands. As a result, within a generation, new U.S. citizens like Mariano Vallejo and María Ruiz de Burton became a marginal, disenfranchised, and poverty-stricken minority.

Conflicts over land tenure were also evident in international affairs as the United States and Mexico continued their struggle over the demarcation of the southern boundary. The two countries established a joint boundary commission charged with surveying and marking the new international border, and representatives of each country met in San Diego in July 1849 to begin the task. A year later they finished tracing and marking the line between the two Californias. When the commissioners met in El Paso to begin surveying the boundary between the New Mexico territory and Chihuahua and Sonora, they discovered serious geographical errors in the original map the negotiators of the treaty used. The map cited in the treaty, an edition of Disturnell's map of North America, located the town of El Paso del Norte (Ciudad Juárez) about thirty miles northeast of its true location. If the map were to be followed literally, the rich Mesilla Valley and Santa Rita de Cobre mines would remain in Mexican territory. This conclusion proved unacceptable to the expansionist Democrats in Congress, who wanted the minerals and a suitable transcontinental railroad route through the region. The American member of the commission, John Russell Bartlett, and the Mexican member, General Pedro García-Conde, argued the issue. Eventually both agreed that the defective map should be used to set only the southern boundary of New Mexico. There were enough discrepancies in the map favoring the U.S. position to disregard the map altogether, but the Mexican commissioner agreed to a compromise. This line gave the Americans a railroad route and the Mexicans possession of the mining district. The U.S. Congress, however, refused to ratify this compromise agreement.

The situation in the Mesilla strip became more explosive as Mexican repatriates and Anglo Texan and New Mexican cattle ranchers moved into the area. The governor of Chihuahua claimed jurisdiction, and the governor of New Mexico threatened to occupy the area with force.

This volatile situation, along with the desires of key members of the American Congress for rights of transit across the Isthmus of Tehuantapec and a release from the obligations of the Treaty of Guadalupe Hidalgo's Article 11, led in 1853 to the dispatch of a new American minister to Mexico, James Gadsden. After meetings with President Santa Anna and threats of military force by the United States, Mexico signed the Gadsden Treaty or Tratado de Mesilla. As eventually modified by the American Congress, the treaty stipulated that the United States agreed to pay $10 million for Mexican cession of the territory the Americans wanted for a railroad. It also allowed the United States to abrogate Article 11 of the 1848 treaty and granted the rights of transit across the Isthmus of Tehuantapec. This new boundary separating Sonora from Arizona forced some Mexicans to move again from ranches and towns that had formerly been part of Mexico.

A year after María Burton and her husband arrived in San Diego, William Walker, a doctor from Tennessee, invaded Baja California, intending to establish a separate republic there. María indignantly read the reports in the local newspaper of how Walker was called the savior of the "indolent and half civilized" Baja Californios. María's mother and extended family lived in La Paz, and by force, Walker's men took over her cousin's house for their headquarters. Filibustering expeditions like that of Walker's introduced María to the American idea of Manifest Destiny, for which she developed a deep dislike.

Richard Griswold del Castillo

In 1853 Walker and an army of adventurers captured La Paz and then Cabo San Lucas and Enseñada, but they were unable to hold these towns because of a lack of supplies. Nonetheless, Walker proclaimed himself president of the Republic of Sonora and pronounced the annexation of Baja California and Sonora. Then he invaded Sonora by marching overland from Enseñada. This tactic failed because his troops deserted. After a brief skirmish with Mexican troops near San Diego, Walker and the remnant band surrendered to Captain Burton's U.S. Army troops as they crossed the border. Eventually, Walker invaded Nicaragua with another filibustering expedition, but there he was killed.

Walker's filibustering was only one of many attempts by adventurers who recruited U.S. citizens into armies that invaded Mexico during the unsettled period between the end of the U.S.-Mexican War and the U.S. Civil War. Usually they had as their purpose trying to get rich at the expense of the Mexican frontier settlers. Two years before Walker's expedition, Joseph C. Morehead had invaded and annexed Baja California, but his expedition disappeared before it reached La Paz. And in 1852 Charles de Pindray, a Frenchman from San Francisco, led a group of colonists and adventurers to Guaymas, Sonora, and then to Cocospora to found an agricultural colony with the support of the Sonoran government. The suspicions by Mexican officials about the motives for the colony led to the group's dispersal and the death of Pindray.

In 1852 Count Gaston Raousset-Boulbon, a Frenchman from San Francisco who dreamed of being the sultan of Sonora, led an all-French expedition to Sonora, where he fought local troops to secure supplies for his expedition. His small army defeated the Mexican state militia at Hermosillo but eventually abandoned Sonora after the count was incapacitated with dysentery. Two years later he returned with an army and occupied Guaymas. After his forces fought three battles with the Mexican army, Raousset-Boulbon was captured and shot. His army disbanded.

Still another attempt to invade Sonora was that of Henry Alexander Crabb, also a Californian. In January 1857, he crossed into Mexico near Yuma with one hundred men, but his army encountered a Mexican force near Caborca, Sonora, which defeated the invaders and shot Crab.

In Texas the most notable attempt at filibustering was that of José María Carvajal, born and raised in San Antonio. In 1851, with the support of wealthy merchants in Brownsville and south Texas, he raised an army to conquer Tamaulipas and set up the Republic of Sierra Madre. Commercial interests in the United States supported this because possible new markets could be opened. Carvajal briefly invaded and occupied Mexican territory in 1852, 1853, and 1855. The Republic of Sierra Madre, however, remained an illusive dream.

The U.S. Army sent Captain Henry Burton and his family to the East Coast in 1859. The next year María and her children rented a home in Georgetown near Washington, D.C. As an officer's wife María attended many official social functions, including both of Lincoln's inaugurations. She became a friend of Mary Todd Lincoln, and, in person, María asked the president for a promotion for her husband. She was also friend and correspondent with Matias Romero, the Mexican ambassador to the United States, and came to know the Mexican expatriate community in the nation's capital. María felt a sympathy for the defeated southerners, thinking them closer in temperament and condition to her own people, the mexicanos and californios.

Mariano Vallejo probably met María Burton when he traveled to Washington, D.C., in 1865 to get a reversal of the Supreme Court's rejection of his ownership of Rancho Soscol. Mariano's wife, Francisca, was a cousin to María, and for years they had maintained a correspondence. In the East, Vallejo visited all the historic sites in Boston, New York, and Washington, but he too felt uncomfortable in these eastern urban places. Residents there appeared "money mad . . . ; the madness they have is a desperate madness," he wrote. After the Civil War, Mariano and María continued their lengthy correspondence discussing politics, history, religion, society, and especially their persisting feelings of alienation within this new culture.

The Civil War increased the level of disorder and violence in the American Southwest, especially in New Mexico. The conflict also provided an impetus for the construction of new railroads, which would have a profound effect on future economic and social development of the region.

During the Civil War, Texas joined the Confederacy and raised an army under General Henry H. Sibley to invade New Mexico Territory. The Confederates quickly occupied Albuquerque and Santa Fe after defeating a Union detachment of Hispanos and Anglo New Mexicans near Valverde in southern New Mexico in early 1862. For a time the capital of the new Confederate territory was at La Mesilla, near Las Cruces, New Mexico. The invasion of New Mexico lasted briefly, owing to the scorched-earth policies of the native New Mexicans, who burned their crops rather than give them to Texans, and to a successful counterattack by Union troops from Colorado. At the battle of Glorieta Pass (north of Santa Fe) in March 1862, Major John Chivington and four hundred volunteers from New Mexico and Colorado defeated the Confederate forces. The Texans were forced on a long retreat back to San Antonio.

Concurrently another group of rebels invaded Arizona under Captain Sherod Hunter. They occupied Tucson briefly and then retreated when

Richard Griswold del Castillo

confronted by a superior Union force from California led by Colonel James Carleton. During the Civil War, approximately seventeen thousand Californians served the Union as U.S. volunteers. Their job was to fight Indians and to prevent the Confederates from threatening U.S. Army posts in the West.

When Texas entered the Confederacy, hundreds of Mexican Americans fled the forced army draft by crossing the Rio Grande. They left behind farm and stock lands that fell into Texan hands. A number of Mexicans on both sides of the river fought a guerilla war against the Confederates in south Texas, since they considered the Southerners their traditional enemies.

Among those fighting was Juan N. Cortina. A wealthy tejano rancher, he led a localized rebellion against the Anglo Texans in the Brownsville region when the Civil War broke out. Cortina's rebellion grew out of the many oppressions Mexicans suffered on the American side of the Rio Grande. In 1859 Cortina's army occupied Brownsville and defeated the Texas Rangers. The U.S. Army, led by Lieutenant Colonel Robert E. Lee, forced him to cross the river in 1861, where he eventually became a general in the Mexican army, governor of Tamaulipas, and a supporter of Juárez's government. Cortina fought both the French (who invaded Mexico in 1862) and Confederate armies in northeastern Mexico and along the Rio Grande. His army, composed of Mexican Americans and Mexican nationals, helped Union forces recapture Brownsville in 1865. Later Cortina lived in northern Mexico until 1875, when Mexican officials arrested him under pressure from the U.S. government. He died in Mexico City in 1894.

At the end of the Civil War, the U.S. government gained a new appreciation for the strategic importance of the American Southwest and for that reason began a concerted effort to link it with the East Coast. Undoubtedly the most far-reaching economic and social changes in the Southwest came as a result of a new railroad network connecting the American Southwest with metropolitan markets and population centers to the east. One of the consequences of the Civil War was a great realization of the need for a transcontinental railroad linking the gold- and silver-mining regions of California with the industrializing eastern seaboard. To encourage private enterprise in this endeavor, the U.S. federal government gave subsidies of land and loans to various companies. The first transcontinental line, the Central and Union Pacific Railroad, completed in 1869, spurred the formation of competing lines in the northern West and through the southwestern deserts and mountains. Soon the Atchison, Topeka and Santa Fe and the Southern Pacific railroads were built, along with feeder lines, joining most of the important population centers in the border region.

The railroads increased the value of the region's natural resources by uniting them with new labor supplies in Mexico, processing plant distribution centers, and urban markets. Mines in southern Arizona and northern Sonora and Chihuahua were now able to ship ores to smelters in El Paso. Timber stands in the mountains of northern New Mexico and Arizona also became lumber for the new homes in southern California and west Texas. In addition railroads helped open new agricultural lands for settlement and exploitation. The Winter Garden area of south Texas, the Salt River Valley in central Arizona, and the Imperial Valley in southern California became important agricultural regions because of new irrigation technology, railroad connections to markets, and cheap labor.

The prosperity of the American Southwest and the border region was determined, in large part, by the availability of a large cheap labor force, mostly Mexican Americans, Mexican nationals, and Asians. Mexicans, immigrant and native born, constituted the majority of laborers. They were miners, section hands, and fieldworkers who developed the U.S. border region.

Economic integration through railroad construction also meant an end to the isolation of the region from distant metropolitan centers. Towns like Tucson, El Paso, San Antonio, and Los Angeles increased in population as a result. El Paso, for example, grew from a sleepy border town in the 1860s to a major city by 1900, largely because of the influence of the railroad, which brought thousands of Mexican and Anglo immigrants. Less-spectacular but nevertheless impressive population growth took place in other border towns, with the exception of those along the border of the two Californias. Their demographic growth would be mostly in the twentieth century.

Both Vallejo and Ruiz de Burton invested their fortunes in the new economy. Vallejo mortgaged his ranchos to raise $370,000, which he gave to the state of California to build public buildings for a new capital on land that he donated. Although his motives were largely philanthropic, he nonetheless hoped that the result would be a new urban, cultural, and commercial center. Unfortunately this venture failed when the legislature moved the capital to Sacramento in 1855. Vallejo was somewhat more successful in his association with Agoston Haraszthy, a wealthy Hungarian who built the first winery in Sonoma (Buena Vista) and imported European vines. In other ventures Vallejo organized the Sonoma Water Works to provide water for the local community, managed small truck-gardening plots, and engaged in various projects of manual labor, attempting to make ends meet.

In 1869 María Amparo Ruiz de Burton's husband died. She then returned to San Diego to use her talents to survive economically. She

Figure 7.2: Lime kilns on Jamul Rancho in 1891. This building was constructed by María Amparo Ruiz de Burton and her son as part of the Jamul Portland Cement Company. The two unidentified women in the foreground could be María Amparo Ruiz de Burton and her daughter. Courtesy of the San Diego Historical Society Photography Collection, neg. 13031.

held an interest in a Mexican land grant near Enseñada, but court battles with Mexican heirs cost her more and more money. In the 1870s her patent to the Rancho Jamul was approved, but this decision was followed by years of costly legal challenges. María also planned to develop a water company, Jamul Waterworks, but this venture did not materialize. For a time she cultivated castor beans as a cash crop on her rancho. She and her son eventually formed the Jamul Portland Cement Company, and together they invested in developing this business. The business unfortunately failed, unable to compete with other cement works.

The business difficulties of Mariano Vallejo and María Amparo Ruiz de Burton were indicative of the difficulties that mexicanos faced in the transition to the new order. They were willing to cast their lot with the bankers, lawyers, and speculators, hoping to prosper, as was the American promise. They also learned how to manage their lives with a new language and legal and economic systems. Despite these compromises most mexicanos of Vallejo and Burton's generation were unable to find their way within the bounds and limits of this new order.

Mariano Vallejo died on January 18, 1890. He was eighty-three and had witnessed many changes in his beloved homeland: the end of Spanish empire, the Mexican regime, the U.S.-Mexican War, the California Gold Rush, the coming of railroads, and the expansion of commerce and agriculture. Vallejo's optimistic faith in progress and democracy persisted despite his own personal fall from power. Tragically, when he died, all that remained of his once-extensive ranchos was 228 acres surrounding his home, one cow, and two horses. His brother-in-law had to pay Vallejo's funeral expenses. During Vallejo's middle years, Hubert Howe Bancroft, the noted California historian, asked Vallejo to compile his notes for a history of California. Eventually this project became a five-volume work written in longhand. It has never been published, a revealing testimony to the ways his own history and culture have been ignored.

María Amparo Ruiz de Burton died five years after her friend Mariano Vallejo, on August 12, 1895. She spent the last years of her life fighting legal battles trying to retain title to the lands she had inherited in Enseñada, Baja California. To accomplish this, she moved to Mexico City for two years but failed to get redress from the Mexican government. While traveling to Washington, D.C., to lobby the U.S. government on the same issue, she died in Chicago, Illinois. Eventually, forty years later, her land title in Mexico was confirmed as part of an international claims arbitration.

Ultimately the blend of cultures and peoples represented in the lives of Mariano Vallejo and María Amparo Ruiz de Burton illustrate the dynamic energies that were at work to create a new kind of southwestern society, one that, in the twentieth century, would have worldwide influence. The conflicts and compromises that they experienced gave shape to a new American Southwest, one that would have roots deep in a multicultural soil.

Essay on Sources

Only a few surveys of the history of the American Southwest cover the period from 1848 to 1880. Generally after the Americans came, the history of this region is absorbed into the history of the American West. Older texts by W. Eugene Hollon, *The Southwest: Old and New* (New York: Knopf, 1961), and Lynn Perrigo, *The American Southwest: Its Peoples and Cultures* (New York: Holt, Rinehart, 1971), do not incorporate the newer social and cultural history of the region but still serve as good introductions to the history of this period. For an overview of revisionist perspectives, read Patricia Nelson Limerick, *The Legacy of Conquest: The Unbroken Past of the American West* (New York: Norton, 1987). A modern retelling of the histories of New Mexico and Arizona in this period appears in Howard Lamar, *The Far Southwest, 1846–1912: A Territorial History,* rev. ed. (Albuquerque: University of New Mexico Press, 2000).

Richard Griswold del Castillo

In the past thirty years the most important development in south-western history has been the rapid rise of Chicano historical writing, which takes 1848 as the starting point and the historic Spanish border-lands as locale. This rich and exciting field has produced hundreds of monographs and essays telling the story of working-class communities in the American Southwest. The most influential overview text of the history of this period, from a Chicano point of view, is Rudolfo Acuña, *Occupied America: A History of Chicanos,* 4th ed. (New York: Longman, 2000). The first six chapters of this book give a detailed critical view of how the American conquest affected Mexicans in the Southwest.

The two protagonists of this chapter have their biographers. Mariano Vallejo's life is well told in Alan Rosenus, *General M. G. Vallejo and the Advent of the Americans: A Biography* (Albuquerque: University of New Mexico Press, 1995). María Amparo Ruiz de Burton's life has been sur-veyed in the introduction to María's second novel, *The Squatter and the Don,* edited by Rosaura Sánchez and Beatrice Pita (Houston: Arte Público Press, 1997). An even more detailed account of her life and times appears in the commentary on María's letters, many of them to Mariano Vallejo, published as *Conflicts of Interest: The Letters of María Amparo Ruiz de Burton,* ed. Rosaura Sánchez and Beatrice Pita (Houston: Arte Público Press, 2001). Together these books provide an important record of the ways Mexican Americans reacted to the American conquest as well as an exposition of the themes of conflict and compromise.

For a discussion of how the Treaty of Guadalupe Hidalgo affected land tenure and ethnic relations in the Southwest, read Richard Griswold del Castillo, *The Treaty of Guadalupe Hidalgo: A Legacy of Conflict* (Norman: University of Oklahoma Press, 1990). A helpful nar-rative about the adventurers who sought to annex Mexico in the years immediately after the treaty is Joseph Allen Stout, Jr., *The Liberators: Filibustering Expeditions into Mexico, 1848–1862, and the Last Thrust of Manifest Destiny* (Los Angeles: Westernlore Press, 1973).

A number of highly regarded regional histories flesh out the themes of conflict and compromise for the four U.S.-Mexican border states. For California, Leonard Pitt, *Decline of the Californios: A Social History of the Spanish Speaking Californians, 1854–1890* (Berkeley: University of California Press, 1998), is a classic. For New Mexico, Roxanne Dunbar Ortiz, *Roots of Resistance: Land Tenure in New Mexico, 1680–1980* (Los Angeles: UCLA Chicano Studies Research Center, 1980), and Robert Rosenbaum, *Mexicano Resistance in the Southwest: "The Sacred Right of Self Preservation"* (Austin: University of Texas Press, 1980), are excel-lent for exploring the complex issues of the struggle for land. For Texas, Arnoldo De León, *The Tejano Community, 1836–1900* (Albuquerque: University of New Mexico Press, 1982), is a masterpiece of social and cultural reconstruction. Arizona's best study is Thomas E. Sheridan, *Los Tucsonenses: The Mexican Community in Tucson, 1854–1941* (Tucson: University of Arizona Press, 1986).

The commercial and agricultural economic development of the Southwest in this period is well told in the classic western history by Ray Allen Billington and Martin Ridge, *Westward Expansion: A History of the American Frontier,* 6th ed. (Albuquerque: University of New Mexico Press, 2001). Regional histories have sections that discuss the economic changes and their impact on the land and people. For California, Kevin Starr, *Americans and the California Dream, 1850–1915* (New York: Oxford University Press, 1973), examines the Golden State's economic and demographic transitions. New Mexico and Arizona's development is well told in Howard Lamar's previously cited book. The impact of economic changes on Texas's peoples is analyzed in the award-winning work by David Montejano, *Anglos and Mexicans in the Making of Texas, 1836–1986* (Austin: University of Texas Press, 1987). Railroads in the Southwest, so important to economic change, have their historian in Ira Clark, *Then Came the Railroads: The Century from Steam to Diesel in the Southwest* (Norman: University of Oklahoma Press, 1958).

On the Internet, computer users will find literally thousands of sites that give instant details about many subjects in this brief essay. For articles, readers should utilize Web sites that have full text resources. An up-to-date listing of online historical journals is maintained by Tennessee Technology University at www2.tntech.edu/history/journals.html. The national historical associations have their most recent journals online as well. See the *American Historical Review* at http://www.jstor.org/ journals/00028762.html and the *Journal of American History* at www.historycooperative.org/jahindex.html. Local historical journals with full text online include the *Journal of San Diego History,* www.sandiegohistory.org/journal/journal.htm, and *Aztlan: International Journal of Chicano Studies Research,* at www.sscnet.ucla.edu/csrc/library/aztoc.html.

CHAPTER 8

Sarah Winnemucca, Chief Joseph, and Native America's Dilemma

ELLIOTT WEST

good

To the public eye, the Indians lost the West on the battlefield. The story of Indian-white relations after the Civil War seems to unfold from one conflict to the next—the roundup of the Navajos and fighting with central plains tribes in the 1860s; in the 1870s the Buffalo War with the Comanches, the supremely famous conflict with the Sioux on the northern plains, and the poignant running chase with the Nez Perce; in the 1880s the on-again, off-again engagements with the Apaches in the southwestern deserts. Sprinkled throughout are other wars with the Modocs, Bannocks, and Paiutes. Watching and reading the numberless movies and pulp novels about these events, it is easy to think that Indians and whites came together primarily in violence.

Yet for all their drama, the Indian wars represent only a small aspect of the interaction between Indians and those who poured into Native lands during the nineteenth century, and the military threat was far from the greatest of the troubles stirred up by that invasion. Western Indians were not up against an army. They were threatened by a way of life. Euroamericans brought into the West a culture that began to change Native peoples from the first moment of contact. Some of those changes Indian peoples eagerly encouraged; some they bitterly resented and resisted; many were subtle and largely unnoticed until well advanced. The invasive cultures also began a transformation of the western environment that continues today. The cumulative impact was to undercut the foundations of Native cultures as they had been lived out before the waves of outsiders washed into the West. Military confrontations were part of this interaction among peoples. Typically, however, they came late in the erosion of Indian independence. Often they were a final blow that ended any illusions of resistance except within the framework of white political control. That gives events like the Great Sioux War and Captain Jack's stand in the lava beds an enormously poignant appeal, an appeal perhaps all the stronger in this generation that places great value on "closure" in every situation of contention and crisis. But always these violent episodes must be understood as only part of a much broader process and a much more convoluted interrelationship.

It is a tangled story, one sometimes best told through individual lives. The Northern Paiute Sarah Winnemucca and Chief Joseph (Hin-mah-too-yah-lat-kekht), a Nez Perce, illustrate many of the trends and forces at work among and against Indian peoples of the Far West after the Civil War. Both felt the impact of war. Joseph, in fact, would emerge as the best-known figure of one of the last and most famous conflicts of the century. Both, however, tell us most about the more fundamental challenges faced by Indian peoples, the conflicts they generated within Native cultures, and the remarkable efforts by figures like these two to forge paths of compromise and to devise some means to protect and preserve what they could of their people's ways of life. Like the histories of Indian peoples generally, their lives were full of tragedy and loss, but ultimately they remind us that the Native American story is about survival and persistence as well as defeat.

People of all cultures have one thing in common: everybody has to eat. Every society has an economic base, the material means of satisfying demands and needs fundamental to all human life. When people have reasonably secure command over what provides for those basic needs, they can act independently as a group. Should they lose that command, their independence goes with it. Historians often undervalue this obvious and commonsensical point when explaining the conquest of Indian America. In discussions of western history we usually refer to the "defeat" of Indian peoples by whites. The word is useful shorthand, but because we associate defeat with a battlefield, it tempts us into simpler, falsely dramatic military explanations. It is more accurate to say that Euroamericans took control of the West's elemental resources so they could set them to their own uses, and by doing that they denied to Indians the resources *they* had to have if they hoped to live as they chose. This denial, far more than any military campaign, spelled disaster for Native interests.

Some far western tribes practiced agriculture, notably southwestern groups who irrigated their fields and others on the eastern edges of the Great Plains who farmed along the rivers, but the majority of Indians in the West lived by variations of a hunting-and-gathering economy. They relied heavily on wild game and plant life for food and materials for clothing, shelter, and other essentials. All groups also traded for what they needed or wanted but could not provide for themselves, again relying on what they hunted and gathered for their side of the bargaining. Such an economy was especially vulnerable on two counts. First, hunters and gatherers required a large area to support themselves. Even in country rich in resources, like the homeland of the Nez Perces, they needed plenty of room to find enough animals and a sufficient range of plants, and in harsher environments, like the Great Basin of Winnemucca's Paiutes, the area necessary for survival was enormous. The loss of even a small part of a home territory is troubling, and anything beyond that can be disastrous. Second, use of this large area was exceptionally intricate and thus easily disrupted. Even if hunters and gatherers kept control of the area they needed, that area still might feel the shock of change from events nearby or even farther afield. If animal migrations were disrupted, streams fouled, or trade upset by some development twenty-five or a hundred miles distant, the impact on a home territory could be as hurtful as losing part of the territory itself.

Changes after the Civil War seem almost calculated to play on this twin vulnerability. Ranching and farming fundamentally altered ecosystems. The scattered nature of new western settlements demanded long lines of supply that in turn could have consequences far beyond the immediate surroundings of a town or army post. Of all developments, mining rushes arguably were the most threatening to Indian economies. *Mining* Few enterprises did so much damage so quickly to the environment. Hillsides were stripped of timber, nearby game quickly hunted out, and the steams polluted by erosion and diverted in the search for gold. Because most mining booms began in isolated regions, they also stimulated intense local development to supply the needs of each new camp, adding the disruptions of agriculture and stock raising to those of mining. Virtually every far-western Indian war had its origins in a gold- *see* or silver-mining rush—a convincing reminder that military defeats were typically codas to a more profound defeat, the Indians' loss of control over their means of living.

Sarah Winnemucca's people, the Paiutes, had survived in one of the harshest settings in North America through a deep understanding of their homeland, its limits and possibilities. The largest game the Paiutes could count on were rabbits, which supplied food and clothing. They also hunted smaller desert animals, including a variety of reptiles, insects, and invertebrates dug from the ground, and gathered a wide range of vegetation. Crucial to their diet were the highly nutritious seeds harvested from grasses growing along the streams. The subsistence base of the Paiutes was suggested by the names of their bands: the Ground Squirrel Eaters, the Cattail Eaters, the Jackrabbit Eaters, the Cui-cui Eaters (referring to a black sucker fish). Each band moved frequently, for the Great Basin could not provide its people enough in any one place for more than temporary habitation.

The Paiutes' life was an extreme example of how western peoples could squeeze the most from limited possibilities. Sadly, this left them supremely susceptible to change. Extended and entwined in the basin's fragile environment, they would feel the jolt of the slightest alterations in the environment. Changes in the middle of the nineteenth century, however, were anything but slight. Discovery of California gold brought floods of emigrants across the basin, then strikes of gold and silver around Virginia City, Nevada, pulled a backwash of settlement onto the eastern slopes of the Sierra Nevada. These mining rushes had the usual effects. Trees were cut for timbering the mines and smaller growth taken for fuel, stripping the hills of their vital produce of piñon nuts. Streams were vigorously fished. Herds of cattle were loosed on the grasslands. Effects were just as profound along the emigrant trails that followed the Humboldt and Truckee rivers across the desert. Tens of thousands of oxen devoured the river grasses and the seeds that had fed Sarah's people; then ranchers took up permanent residence along the streams. Settlement and overland travel brought a more direct and devastating threat—diseases that struck more viciously at Native peoples with little resistance to illnesses they had never known. In the wake of the 1849 rush many Paiutes died—tradition says up to half, although probably the toll was less—from an epidemic that was likely Asiatic cholera, which raged that year along the emigrant trails and in the California camps. Such devastating losses naturally crippled further the Paiutes' ability to reap what they needed from the world they had known—a world rapidly coming apart.

These calamitous changes left the Paiutes, and all Indian peoples who faced similar crises, with basically two options. One was to strike out at those responsible. Some of Sarah's people blamed the epidemic on the whites' poisoning of the Humboldt River, a charge that might have been indirectly true, since the disease could have been spread through unintentional contamination of the water. They called for retaliation. Some raided ranches and settlements for livestock and supplies, in essence a shift in hunting and gathering away from the old sources of game and plants to the new occupants that had replaced them. The other option was to search for a place within the economy that was rapidly pushing aside their own. Paiutes found work in various capacities, but always at the most menial jobs and at the lowest pay. Many were ultimately reduced to begging and living as best they could on the edges of the new order. Many whites, wholly unaware of the Paiutes' subtle uses of the desert and their rich religious life, in turn dismissed them as filthy primitives of disgusting habits (the derogatory epithet "digger Indian" referred to the practice of rooting for grubs, lizards, and other foods). Nonetheless, prominent leaders counseled that accommodation with whites was the only practicable approach to the revolutionary changes that had come to the Great Basin.

Sarah Winnemucca's lineage naturally inclined her in that direction. In 1844, probably the year she was born, her grandfather, given the name Truckee by whites, had guided the first party to cross the Sierra Nevada with wagons. Two years later he traveled with John Charles Frémont during the seizure of California. In visits to California, Truckee was impressed by the size of the white population and its range of power, and partly out of genuine affection and partly as practical diplomacy he consistently counseled peace with the whites and adoption of at least some of their ways. (He taught those in his band "The Star Spangled Banner" and the army roll call.) He died in 1860, despondent over deepening tensions and the Paiutes' degenerating situation. Sarah's father, Chief Winnemucca, continued the search for common ground and peaceful solutions to conflict, again in part from understanding the ultimate futility of resistance. Until his death in 1882 he worked as a cultural and political liaison with white authorities. Thus Sarah's lifelong efforts to forge a relationship that nonetheless protected her people and maintained some cultural integrity was the third generation of family tradition.

Chief Joseph's life was another variation of Native America's search for a viable middle ground between militant resistance and cultural capitulation. He was born in about 1840 and grew up in the Wallowa valley of eastern Oregon. This beautiful area was part of a region where today Oregon, Washington, and Idaho come together. Here, in the watersheds of the Salmon and Snake rivers, lived the Nee-Me-Poo (the Real People), called by whites the Nez Perces (Pierced Noses). Joseph's Nez Perce name translated as Thunder Rising to Loftier Mountain Heights. Like Sarah Winnemucca, his family tradition was one of accommodation, although in his case with a different wrinkle. The Nez Perces had a history of friendship with whites since their first contact in 1805, when they fed the starving party of Lewis and Clark as the famous explorers were stumbling along the final part of their passage to the Pacific. By then the Nez Perces had acquired horses and become perhaps the most accomplished horse breeders on the continent. In country much richer in resources than the Great Basin, they hunted a variety of game, including bison during forays over the northern Rocky Mountains and onto the plains, and gathered from the array of useful plants, especially the nutritious black-skinned bulb of the camas lily. The Nez Perces lived well, but like the Paiutes and all hunter-gatherers, they required free access to a vast area to sustain themselves.

Geography and luck kept the Nez Perces mostly free of the convulsive changes that struck the Paiutes and other tribes in the 1840s and 1850s, but early in the next decade discoveries of gold and silver brought the rush of prospectors and the disruptions that had so unsettled much of the West during the previous generation. Soon the pressure was mounting to open much of the Nez Perce homeland to white settlement. At this point one force of change had already been at work. In 1836 the Presbyterian missionary Henry Spalding arrived, began a vigorous program of conversion, built a school, and set out to transform the Nez Perces into settled farmers. Hot tempered and sometimes violent, Spalding met limited success, but among his early converts was a band leader, Tu-ke-kas, whom whites took to calling Old Joseph. Spalding's work helped create a deep rift between converts, who clustered near the mission and took up farming, and those who lived by traditional ways. This division deepened in the wake of gold discoveries when leaders close to Spalding signed a treaty in 1863 surrendering 90 percent of what the government had recognized as Nez Perce land eight years earlier. Many leaders, however, refused to recognize this treaty. One was Old Joseph, who reportedly showed his anger by ripping to shreds a copy of the Gospel of Matthew given him by Spalding.

The religious nature of Old Joseph's dramatic gesture was not accidental. Christianity properly could be seen as a nexus of white cultural values; to reject that faith was to turn from a way of life. By the same terms Old Joseph and others would turn toward an alternative cultural allegiance by embracing a Native religion emerging during these years. Its prophet was the stooped and wizened Smohalla of the Wallolas, who lived in the Columbia River basin. Proclaiming revelations gathered during a visit to heaven, he promised his followers that if they remained faithful to traditional lifeways, God would soon bring back to life their honored dead and would sweep away the whites who had brought such mischief to the Pacific Northwest. Smohalla opposed most fiercely the very heart of the whites' economic culture, agriculture. Missionaries like Spalding and government agents alike insisted that Indians take up the plow if they were to have any place in the new order. To Smohalla, however, farming and mining were assaults on the source of life itself:

> You ask me to plough the ground! Shall I take a knife and tear my mother's bosom? Then when I die she will not take me to her bosom to rest. You ask me to dig for stone. Shall I dig under her skin for her bones? Then when I die I cannot enter her

body and be born again. You ask me to cut grass and make hay and sell it, and be rich like white men, but how dare I cut off my mother's hair?

As for hunting wild game and harvesting wild plants, he said, "We simply take the gifts that are freely offered. We no more harm the earth than would an infant's fingers harm his mother's breast." Religious, cultural, and economic confrontations were of a piece. White newcomers brought with them particular means of working and relating to the environment, which in turn were inextricably bound up with particular social structures and perceptions of man's proper relation to his world and to God. Smohalla's followers were taking a stand against all of it.

Converts to Smohalla's teachings were called Dreamers. Their religion was one of many that had appeared among North America's Native peoples in response to the expanding colonial empires. Most of these movements produced a messiah figure, like Smohalla, who presented a new teaching and usually called for a return to traditions and a rejection of white culture while also infusing their religions with Christian themes, especially a faith in an apocalyptic end time when the wicked would be destroyed and the faithful uplifted. Some messiahs counseled against physical resistance, but even so, the energy and inspired opposition of these movements flashed into violence more often than not. The bloody war of resistance centering around the Ottawa leader Pontiac (1762–1764) began partly with the spiritual movement of the Delaware prophet Neolin; the famous Shawnee Tecumseh's campaign to lead tribes east of the Mississippi against the encroaching United States was equally an effort at religious revival led by his brother, Tenskwatawa. In the late 1880s another such movement would arise among Sarah Winnemucca's people. Led by the prophet Wovoka (called Jack Wilson by whites), this Ghost Dance religion would spread from the Paiutes to tribes throughout the West, eventually to the western Sioux. The tensions around this revival led to the killing of Sitting Bull and the massacre at Wounded Knee in 1890, often cited as the last spasm of resistance among western Indian peoples.

Wovoka and Smohalla, Paiute Ghost Dancers and Nez Perce Dreamers, are critical to understanding the dynamics of Indian-white interaction in the Far West during these years. They tell us that the conflict was as much one of worldviews and cosmologies as of anything else; behind disagreements over seemingly worldly issues like land policy, dress, and length of hair, and certainly behind the more dramatic military confrontations, were clashes that ultimately involved the divine and visions of the universe. These movements are also necessary simply to understand the flow of events. Indian peoples, like whites, did what they did partly out of spiritual considerations. In the case of the Nez Perces, when Old Joseph rejected the treaty of 1863 and renounced Christianity, he and others outraged by the treaty apparently turned to the Dreamer religion. His beliefs were taken up by his son, called Young Joseph by whites and later simply Chief Joseph, who assumed leadership of his band on his father's death. Joseph, his brother Ollokot, and other Dreamers wore their hair in a distinctive upsweeping pompadour as a sign of their religious identity. Their convictions would guide them as their differences with white authorities came to a head in the late 1870s.

For Indian peoples striving to retain some independence—religious, cultural, economic, political, or any other sort—life in the years after the Civil War must have felt like a steadily tightening noose. Their sovereignty had eroded considerably before the 1860s, but during the quarter century after 1865 the federal government extended its control over Native tribes more rapidly and aggressively than in any other comparable period in American history. Partly this change reflected national developments. The Civil War strengthened the authority of the federal government generally and set in motion developments of various sorts meant to consolidate the nation and integrate its regional parts into a whole. In the West transcontinental rail lines and telegraph systems effectively shrank what had been debilitating distances. Except for the Southwest and Oklahoma, the region was organized into states and brought fully into the federal political system by 1900. Mining rushes, the rise of the cattle industry, and agricultural expansion integrated the West into a national (and international) market economy. As the West was pulled more fully into the nation, pressure increased to open Indian lands to white settlement.

That prospect in turn forced consideration of a more fundamental question: How would Indian peoples fit into national life? Always there had been a paradox at the heart of the government's official stance on this issue. On the one hand, tribes held something close to a sovereign status. Chief Justice John Marshall in 1832 called them "domestic dependent nations," which in practice meant Washington recognized tribal governments and negotiated treaties with them much as they would other foreign nations while also exercising practical authority in some matters, since tribes lived physically within the boundaries of the United States and ultimately were dependent on the nation's blessing. On the other hand, the federal policy presumed that eventually these sovereign peoples would be absorbed into the society and culture that increasingly outnumbered them. The government encouraged assimilation through its agents and encouraged missionaries to live among the tribes and convert them not only to Christianity but to a full embrace of the Euroamerican way of life. Indian tribes, that is, were dependently independent: they were distinct peoples destined to be no different from the rest. In the past the contradictions involved in the government's stance could be avoided through the simple fact of the physical size of the nation. When a supposedly sovereign tribe felt irresistible pressure from encroaching white settlement, it could be sent farther into the continent, "removed" to where the paradox of dependent independence could be sustained a bit longer. Native peoples of areas like the Great Plains, Great Basin, Columbia Plateau, and Southwest could be assigned to large fuzzily defined regions, "Indian country," because those areas, although officially part of the nation, were well away from centers of white development.

Then came the Civil War, the rapid changes in the West, and the vigorous efforts to integrate all regions more cohesively into a consolidated United States. Mining booms brought swift development to previously isolated places and forced the building of long lines of communication and transportation that had their own transforming effects. The agricultural frontier crept westward onto the plains and leapt into appropriate areas close to new urban centers. Cattle ranching intruded into grasslands and desert as yet unable to support farming. Military outposts attracted supporting industries and stimulated settlements wherever they appeared. Before, the continental interior had offered room to escape the implications of official policy's contradictions. By the 1870s it was obvious that there was no place else to run.

The government's response began with the reservation system. In this more formalized arrangement tribes were assigned clearly delineated areas, usually carved out of what had been recognized as Native homelands. Reservations, each with its government agent, were grouped into larger administrative units ultimately under the Department of the Interior. Under encouragement of the Peace Commission, which toured the West in 1867, the government pressed tribes to accept reservations as the most likely way to avoid conflict with whites and with each other. In one sense reservations were merely an extension of earlier approaches by which the government had recognized tribal lands and had designated its representatives among particular tribes. Yet in another sense this policy was different. It acknowledged that reservations were to be temporary. Their purpose, besides providing a buffer, was the transformation of their inhabitants so they might enter the mainstream of national life. Indians would learn the skills to farm in the traditional European way. They would be given the educational basics, starting with the English language. They would be converted to Christianity and taught the

Figure 8.1: Chief Joseph (Thunder Rising to Loftier Mountain
    Heights) with the Dreamers' distinctive hairstyle.
    Courtesy of the Haynes Foundation Collection, Montana
    Historical Society, H-51.

social fundamentals of white society. In short, on reservations Indians
would be cultural and economic interns, citizens in training.

Reservations implied a significantly more authoritative role of the
government and its agents. That implication became steadily more real
during the 1870s and 1880s. In 1871 the system of negotiating treaties
ceased when Congress simply declared that in the future relations with
tribes would be set through congressional fiat. Government agents
assumed the authority to replace balky tribal leaders with ones of their
own choosing. Under a system of Indian police, cooperative tribal members became an enforcement arm of the agent. In 1883 Congress created Courts of Indian Offenses, also staffed by amenable Native leaders,

with the power to suppress indigenous culture, notably polygamy and religious ceremonies dismissed as "heathenish practices." Two years later the Major Crimes Act made reservation residents subject to the criminal courts of their surrounding states and territories. Meanwhile the government and missionary groups established schools, both "day schools" on reservations and boarding schools where children lived for long periods apart from their families. By 1900 more than twenty thousand students attended 225 day schools and 148 boarding schools. Agents pressured parents to enroll their children, threatening to withhold supplies and even jailing recalcitrant fathers and mothers. Some children were simply seized in raids to fill classroom quotas.

So on reservations the federal government tightened greatly its controls over Indian peoples in the name of an accelerated program of assimilation. The goal was to be the abolition of reservations themselves—a process officially set in motion by the Dawes Severalty Act of 1887. By this law Indians living on reservations first would be identified and listed on tribal rolls. Tribal lands next would be surveyed and divided, then families and individuals would be allotted homesteads. Collective ownership by the tribe thus would end. What land remained after allotment would be opened to settlement by outsiders. The land parceled out would initially be held in trust by the government, ostensibly to guard against exploitation of newly landed Indians. Thus Indian peoples would at last be brought into American society as equal members, working the land as family farmers, engaging fully in cultural and political life, and enjoying the fruits of a prospering nation.

Or so the theory went. The reality, however, was nothing like that. Almost invariably the government created reservations on the least desirable land incapable of supporting the tribes. Many Indians were understandably reluctant to give up their cultures, and those who made the effort often found that both whites and their more traditional kinsmen treated them with equal contempt. Then there were the agents. Some genuinely tried to make the system work and treated their charges fairly, but others were petty tyrants, and many were corrupt political appointees who milked the already inadequate budgets for personal profit. To combat corruption, President Ulysses Grant appointed missionaries as most agents, which improved the situation somewhat, but in 1877 the spoils system returned, and so did the old level of graft. Indians bitterly resented pressures to suppress their religious life and especially the disruption of families through forced education of their children. In contrast to the high-blown expectations, reservation life more often than not was one of anger, starvation, disease, and despair.

One of the most consistent—and potentially destructive—results of the reservation system was a deep split within tribes between those who

Figure 8.2: A comely Sarah Winnemucca in costume for her
performance. This item is reproduced by permission of
The Huntington Library, San Marino, California.

tended toward accommodation and those who resisted. As among the
Nez Perces, this split was religious and fell along lines of bands, clans,
and families. Especially as the government relied more on Indians themselves to enforce policies, through the Indian police and judges of the
Courts of Indian Offenses, tensions over these divisions could reach an
extraordinary pitch. Not infrequently they turned violent. It is in the
context of those divisions and the conditions behind them that the lives
of Sarah Winnemucca and Chief Joseph are best appreciated. In their
troubled lives each illustrated the effort to promote a peaceful way
through the increasingly angry conflicts, both between Indians and
whites and among their own peoples. Each sought to preserve some
measure of cultural independence and integrity for Native Americans.

The particulars of their lives differed. Joseph, as will be seen, kept his base firmly within his tribe and found his greatest notoriety in one of the last wars fought with white America. Sarah chose to work much more within white society, to cultivate the persona of a champion of peace, and to manipulate brilliantly popular perceptions of Indian peoples.

Begin with her looks. Like most Paiutes, Sarah was stocky. (A creation myth told of the tribes of the region being carried down from the north in a jug. The more slender peoples escaped into the Pacific Northwest through the jug's narrow neck, while the Paiutes couldn't pass through and so were dumped farther south in the Great Basin.) She also shared her people's broad face and rather flattened features, but her voluptuous figure, long black hair, and jet black eyes gave her a striking appearance that outsiders, especially males, found appealing. Throughout her adult life she would use her looks for public effect. She learned early about the public's interest and how to play to it. At twenty she and her father staged a series of performances in Virginia City, Nevada, and in San Francisco to raise money to supplement the pitiful rations on their reservation. The act showed a considerably sophisticated understanding of what her audiences wanted to see. Rather than dressing in their usual dress of rabbit skins, daughter and father were in buckskins, matching the generic popular view of Indians everywhere. They offered several tableau vivants, frozen scenes representing dramatic moments with such titles as "The War Council" and "Taking a Scalp." In San Francisco they added a brief drama based on the most mythic Native American female, Pocahontas, and her saving of John Smith. Sarah was fluent in English, and the performances included a lecture on Indians and an appeal for donations. Audiences were enthusiastic.

These performances presaged a career that brought Sarah something like what would today be called celebrity. She would lecture widely and successfully, but equally intriguing as her fame and abilities were the motive and strategy behind them. In 1879 she was one of many Paiutes sent to the Yakama reservation far to the north on the Columbia River, where they suffered under grim conditions and a religiously driven agent. When efforts to obtain permission to return home went nowhere, Sarah turned to the tactic taken by her father years earlier, a public appeal through a stage performance, this time not to raise money but to create public pressure. She chose as her venue San Francisco. Her strategy required a subtle understanding of her audience as well as a sense of showmanship. She would appeal to public sympathy and conscience, yet that public had no doubt about the rightness of white domination of Indians. Sarah proved up to the challenge, however. She developed a remarkable stage presence. Her performances sometimes included others—kinsmen performed a Paiute chant and gave short speeches—but she was the centerpiece. Sometimes she wore a buckskin dress, sometimes one of black velvet, but always her bearing and self-confidence won the interest and affection of the audience. She spoke extemporaneously, with passion and what some called true eloquence. Her program included stories from her own life, Paiute folk tales, and history. Her goal was her people's return to a reservation on Paiute homeland and decent treatment there, and she leveled withering sarcasm against her nemesis, the agent William Rinehart. Her lecture's high point was a vigorous assault on treatment of her people and other Indians. Some was outright scolding:

> Oh, for shame! You who are educated by a Christian government in the art of war . . . you who have knelt upon Plymouth Rock, covenanting with God to make this land the home of the free and the brave. Ah, then you rise from your bended knees and seizing the welcoming hands of those who are the owners of this land, which you are not, . . . and your so-called civilization sweeps inland from the ocean wave; but oh, my God! Leaving its pathway marked by crimson lines of blood. . . .

This censure was combined, however, with artful pleas for compassion and her assurance of common ground:

> Where can we poor Indians go if the government will not help us? If your people will help us, and you have good hearts, and can if you will, I will promise to educate my people and make them law-abiding citizens of the United States. [Loud applause.] It can be done—it can be done. [Cheers.] . . . We want you to try us for four years, and if at the end of that time we don't learn, or don't work, or don't become good citizens, then you can do what you please. [Cheers.]

The San Francisco lectures, delivered to packed halls, generated much publicity, and Sarah followed up with a trip to Washington, D.C., several months later. She charmed high social circles there, got more attention from the press (the *Washington Post* referred to her as "Dashing Sarah"), met with President Rutherford B. Hayes, and won from Secretary of the Interior Carl Schurz a promise that her band would be allowed to leave the hated Yakama reservation. The government reneged on that pledge, but eventually a more sympathetic agent simply stopped trying to keep Sarah's band there. By the end of 1884 all had left and headed south toward their homeland. The toll there

Elliott West

had been terrible. More than five hundred had been transferred to Yakama; even with births during the years since then, barely half that number were left. Meanwhile Sarah had traveled to the East on her most ambitious effort yet to raise public awareness about reservation conditions and corruption of reservation agents. Between the spring of 1883 and midsummer of 1884 she lectured more than three hundred times in Boston, Philadelphia, New York, Baltimore, and Washington. In her deerskin dress and red leggings, her black hair hanging long down her back, Sarah performed to full houses, leveling diatribes against missionaries and corrupt officials. She called for educational opportunities and financial help for her people. She suggested appointing women as agents.

Simultaneously with this tour, in 1883, Sarah published *Life Among the Paiutes: Their Wrongs and Claims*. The book might be seen as an expansion of her lectures, combining in nearly three hundred pages a history of her tribe, some of its lore and much of her own life and impressions of the general state of affairs for Native peoples. She wrote it in Boston at the home of and with the encouragement and help of two sisters from the uppermost crust of the city's elite, Elizabeth Peabody and Mary Mann. It was taken at the time in the same spirit as her lectures and surely meant (both by Sarah and her benefactresses) as an extended version of her appeals for support. As a document of insights into Indian life—and into the life of this remarkable woman—*Life Among the Paiutes* is considerably more complicated. Certainly plenty is left out of Paiute history. Sarah's own story is similarly cut back and elaborated. The book does contain much that fits what we do know, however, and so it illuminates the inner history of the Paiutes during these years. It is also the first book published by a Native American woman and the first by an Indian from the Far West. It caused quite a stir.

All this makes *Life Among the Paiutes* doubly revealing. Not only is it a personal narrative of a critical juncture in Paiute history, but its tone and its reception also say something about American cultural politics and evolving popular portrayals of Indians. From the start, Europeans in America and their descendants held divided and contradictory views of Indians, a perspective that revealed less about what they saw than about their own projected values, desires, anxieties, and fantasies. They portrayed Indians as a mix of savagery and childlike innocence. Especially when a particular people occupied land the newcomers wanted, the savage side of the image dominated, whereas the innocent side inspired calls to "save" these children of the wild by schooling them in religion and the ways of civilization. Once a tribe was defeated or neutralized as a threat, the public was prone to express nostalgia about a "vanishing" people (who were more dispossessed than vanished) and even to recall them as an American nobility—courageous and blessed with an inherent dignity. Warrior leaders like the Shawnee Tecumseh, a generation or so after public excoriation as the scourge of the Ohio Valley, rose resurrected after death into legendary models of virtue. The man most responsible for overseeing the crushing of Indian resistance in the Far West was the Ohioan William T. Sherman. His middle initial stood for Tecumseh. By the 1870s, with virtually all Indians subdued and the others able to inflict only occasional blows in grotesquely lopsided struggles, the appeal of the romantic image of defeated nobility was considerable, especially in the East, where any real threat from Indians had receded farthest in time and space.

One result was the rise of philanthropic and missionary organizations. The more activist among those sympathetic with defeated Native peoples, the self-proclaimed "Friends of the Indian," called for a war on corruption and intensified efforts to Christianize and educate Indian peoples and to introduce them to the tasks of agriculture as practiced by white farmers. They pushed many of the programs adopted by the government during these years—land allotment, heightened missionary work, and cultural conversion. Another result was a spate of Indian lecturers who appealed to a much broader, diffuse public half intoxicated with romantic notions and twinging with some feelings of guilt. Sarah Winnemucca was one of the most successful examples of the latter; her performances reached thousands of people whose cheers surely reached the ears of officials. *Life Among the Paiutes* was an expression of both consequences. The book's Boston midwives, Elizabeth Peabody and Mary Mann, were prominent among the "Friends of the Indian," who used its descriptions and charges in their campaigns. Sarah's books also fanned the feelings of that larger, less-involved population and reached thousands more beyond her live appearances.

Unfortunately Sarah's lectures and book showed as well the limits of appeals like hers. Tours and performances to full houses might produce spikes of sympathy, but any resulting pressure on the federal bureaucracy was temporary and easily absorbed. Lectures like Sarah's were entertainment, and the applause in most cases not much more than a catharsis for an audience feeling some remorse but unwilling to pursue any real remedies. In fact, by the mid-1880s the public interest in Indian lecturers generally was fading fast. Much the same could be said for *Life Among the Paiutes*. Whatever effect it had on the public at large was certainly fleeting. The book may have made a more lasting impression with activists, but here another problem arose. Sarah's views were not always compatible with those of the Indians' "Friends." At one point she advocated a return to full military control over reservations—a proposal reformers found outrageous. Sarah's suggestion was born of her relatively good experience with army commanders and her nearly universally wretched history with civilian agents. She saved her most withering sarcasm and vitriol for missionaries, whom she described as thieving bullies and hypocrites. The "Friends," however, considered Christianization and reliance on missionaries as agents as fundamental to their vision. Besides particular conflicts of opinion, Sarah's strategy was likely to bear fruit only if her tours generated significant funds for direct relief to reservations or financing of long-term support. Such funds, however, were committed to reform and philanthropic groups—ones that were dominated by the religious enthusiasts at odds with her.

In the end, then, Sarah's remarkable public career had less impact than might be thought from her considerable (albeit brief) celebrity. Her hundreds of lectures and *Life Among the Paiutes* tell us something about the realities of Native life in the West. But they tell us more, or at least as much, about the cultural crosscurrents of Gilded Age America and about the rigid constraints around what even the most articulate Native American might accomplish through public appeals.

Chief Joseph lived out a different approach to the search for a peaceful alternative to conflicts with white America and among the Nez Perces themselves. Both conflicts were aggravated greatly by events of the mid-1870s. The mining rushes of the 1860s quickened the flow of whites into the Nez Perce homeland and heightened the pressure to open fully to settlement the beloved valleys and pasturelands of Joseph's and other bands committed to a traditional way of life. As more outsiders moved in, friction and clashes inevitably followed, and the Nez Perces charged whites not only with occupying land that wasn't theirs but also with various abuses of individuals, including theft, physical assault, murder, and rape. The government's official position was that all Nez Perces had agreed to move within the vastly reduced confines of the reservation, there to take up farming and the Christian life. This claim rested on the argument, used many times in the past, that the leaders who had signed the treaty in 1863 did so on behalf of all tribal members. In fact, the tribal structure allowed something close to full autonomy for each band. Traditionalists like Joseph's band felt no obligation to live by the decisions of those choosing religious conversion and the reservation. Neither did they necessarily feel hostility toward those who chose differently, except if reservation leaders (the most prominent had the intriguing name of Lawyer) accepted the government's reading of the treaty. The government itself, although formally claiming that all Nez Perces were obliged to move onto the reservation, did not press the point for years after the treaty of 1863. Although tensions gradually increased, the situation remained in a kind of stasis.

Then came the dramatic events of 1876. On the other side of the Rockies, on the northern plains, the western (Lakota) Sioux had their legendary confrontation with the government and its army. This crisis too had its origins in a mining rush—the discovery of gold in the Black Hills in 1874—and it was triggered by the familiar insistence that all Sioux and their allies, the Northern Cheyennes, move onto reservations and surrender the roaming life. To enforce the demand, Washington ordered a three-pronged expedition into Montana in June 1876. A reconnaissance of one of the groups, commanded by George A. Custer, was crushed when it attacked a huge village on the Little Big Horn (Greasy Grass) River. This, the most famous Indian battle of its era, perhaps of all Indian wars, was followed, however, with the relentless pursuit of the scattering Sioux and Cheyennes, the smothering of resistance by early 1877, the surrender of most of the bands, and the retreat of some, led by Sitting Bull, across the border into Canada. The famous defeat of June, that is, tends to obscure the army's total victory within eight months afterward.

Custer's defeat and the government's follow-up victory had an enormous impact on national sensibilities and a considerable influence on official policy. Stung and humiliated, yet victorious over the most powerful Native group in the West, Washington was primed to force its will on others still resisting its demands, and the public was in a supportive mood. That was the context of an escalation of efforts to force a resolution with the Nez Perces in the spring of 1877. Its architect was the commander of the Department of the Columbia, General Oliver O. Howard, ardent abolitionist, one-armed Civil War veteran, former head of the Freedman's Bureau and a founder of Howard University, and the officer who had persuaded Cochise and Arizona's Chiricahua Apaches to surrender in 1872. Howard represented a mix between the military and civilian approaches to Indian policy—a military commander who was an impassioned Christian determined to apply his religious convictions to the "Indian problem." In practice, this translated as humane treatment (as Howard defined it) combined with an insistence on cultural transformation and a hostility to Native religion. Interestingly, after an officer filed a report extremely sympathetic to the traditionalist bands, Howard initially recommended basically leaving them alone, but after another clash and under the influence of the missionary agent, John Monteith, he reversed his position. What proved to be a climactic council was called for early May 1877 in Lapwai, Idaho.

At this meeting and in earlier exchanges, Joseph stood as the leading spokesman for the bands. Consequently, histories often have portrayed him as the tribe's acknowledged leader in all things, including in the war soon to come. That portrayal is wrong, and the reasons reveal another fundamental misconception bedeviling Indian-white relations from the start. The Nez Perces, like most groups, relied on different leaders for different functions. Some, like Joseph, sometimes called "peace chiefs," took the lead in diplomacy because of their special skills in oratory and negotiation. Others took over in situations when other abilities were called for. Some took charge during hunts, others when it was time to move, others when diplomacy gave way to war. Leadership, that is, was fluid and shifting and conditional. Whites, however, tended to project onto a tribe their own structure of leadership, with power flowing downward from an individual (president, king, governor, commander). This basic misunderstanding contributed to three hundred years of mischief. Without a grasp of who was in charge, the most well-meaning negotiations were usually doomed. Peace chiefs like Joseph, furthermore, kept what authority they had only by accurately reflecting their people's sentiment. They were not so much leaders as high-status spokesmen. Forcing one of them into an agreement clearly out of line with popular sentiment was self-defeating in the sense that it would simply be repudiated. Violence might or might not follow, but certainly there would be mutual frustration and ill feeling.

The crucial May council illustrated this problem. Joseph took the lead for the Nez Perces, and he genuinely sought some middle ground, but with him were others adamantly opposed to surrendering their way of life. Joseph seems to have been taken off guard by Howard's iron insistence that all bands submit, and with no room to maneuver, those taking a harder line spoke up, especially the gravelly voiced Toohoolhoolzote, a war leader who flung Howard's tough language back at him. What must have been more galling, he did so in the language of Smohalla and the Dreamers:

> You white people get together, measure the earth, and then divide it. . . . The earth is part of my body, and I never gave up the earth. . . . So long as the earth keeps me, I want to be left alone. You are trifling with the law of the earth!

The militant Christian Howard finally lost his temper and ordered Toohoolhoolzote seized and locked in a guardhouse—a major error. A stunned Joseph made a conciliatory statement, and the meeting ended. The delegation left Lapwai under the understanding that all bands would report to the reservation within a month. What seemed a full victory for Howard, however, was far from that. The Nez Perces would comply only to the degree that Joseph and like-minded leaders could convince them, something Howard's impetuous action had made even harder. As the deadline neared, the bands began to move toward Lapwai in a mood of despairing surliness. The arrangement for peaceful resolution was exceptionally brittle.

On June 14 it snapped. Three young men, resentful over both the current situation and a festering memory of abuse by some nearby settlers, left the encampment and killed four whites. Word of their attack set other Nez Perce warriors off on a rampage of killing, rape, and destruction. Joseph and other leaders, appalled at the implications, gathered everyone at the camp of White Bird's band to consider options. There at dawn on June 17 a mixed force of army regulars and local militia launched a bungled attack that was quickly reversed by the rapid maneuvers and marksmanship of the Nez Perces. At the end of the rout thirty-four whites were dead and only two Nez Perces slightly wounded.

Whether Joseph and other peace chiefs could now convince their people to accept reservation life was moot. After the raids and the stinging defeat, military and civil leaders would demand punishment. Matters were not helped when Howard arrived and directed another attack, only to be held at bay while the Nez Perces withdrew. At this point band leaders plotted an uncommon course. Rather than choose between the horns of the usual dilemma—surrendering or standing and fighting where they could not win—they opted to run for it. They would follow their old route over the Rockies to the plains, this time not to hunt bison but hopefully to find refuge among their traditional allies, the Crows. Such a strategy would be chancy under any conditions. That this extended military retreat was taken with women, children, the elderly, a core of the bands' possessions, and an estimated two thousand horses was astonishing.

The next months witnessed an episode both remarkable in the history of Indian wars and legendary in public memory. In the first case the Nez Perces' running withdrawal over 1,500 miles of mountains and plains was a strategic masterpiece. The conflict's background hopefully teaches the reader that war, when it did come, merely placed the final seal on a fate determined by forces that went far beyond any military pressure. This is not to say, of course, that Indian wars were not historically revealing; certainly they were dramatic demonstrations of courage and sacrifice as well as the worst in human nature. The Nez Perce War had ample helpings of all that. As popular legend, the conflict also has plenty to say. The perception of events and of Joseph, like the response to Sarah Winnemucca as a public personality, reflected the conflicted mass emotions of white America at a turning point in its history and that of Native America.

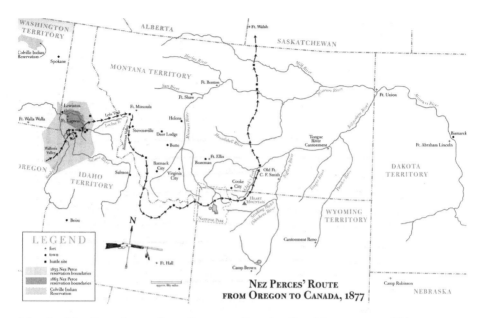

Map 8.1: Nez Perces' route from Oregon to Canada, 1877. Map courtesy of Montana Historical Society Press.

The shift from diplomacy to war changed Joseph's role. He would help direct his band's march, but overall strategy shifted to those respected as war leaders—Joseph's brother Ollokot, Toohoolhoolzote, Yellow Wolf, and others. They led their people eastward over Lolo Pass, where Lewis and Clark had approached from the opposite direction seventy-two years earlier, simply bypassed a hastily constructed military position (derisively nicknamed "Fort Fizzle" by locals), entered the valley of the Bitterroot River, secured provisions in the nervous town of Stevensville, and proceeded southward. Howard's pursuit lagged far behind, but General John Gibbon meanwhile had joined the chase, and with regular troops and Montana volunteers he hit the Nez Perces as they rested and grazed their herds along the Big Hole River. The bands suffered heavy losses, including many women and children killed in or near their lodges, but the warriors rallied, counterattacked, and pinned down Gibbon's command on a wooded hillside for more than two days while the survivors withdrew. Again the retreating Nez Perces outdistanced their pursuers as they passed across the high desert of southern Idaho, then pushed up into the newly created Yellowstone National Park. There they paused. Since the Big Hole their mood had soured—they killed five men in Idaho and another in the park—but they also released a hostage and generally avoided confrontations. As Howard slowly made his way into the high country from the west, yet another column under Colonel Samuel Sturgis approached from the eastern side of the park to catch the bands as they emerged onto the plains, but in a stunning maneuver the Nez Perces feinted that command out of position and began moving rapidly northward into the Yellowstone River valley. When Sturgis caught up, he became the latest to be embarrassed when warriors repulsed his advance and again held off the attackers until noncombatants could escape the valley and start northward onto the open plains.

At this point the Nez Perces faced the especially grim realization that their old allies, the Crows, not only would not help; they were serving as army scouts. The war leaders' answer now was typically audacious—they would head for Canada and refuge among the Sioux led there by Sitting Bull the year before. As the exhausted Indians broke for the border, however, the army finally found the right combination of leadership and luck. Colonel Nelson Miles led the Seventh Cavalry, Custer's unit now remanned, from his post on the Tongue River and with the help of Cheyenne scouts caught the bands as they rested at the base of an isolated mountain cluster called the Bear's Paw. In the furious first assault both sides took heavy losses. The Nez Perces protected their camp, dug in, and held off Miles. But the end was near. Many of the bands' best warriors had been lost, including Toohoolhoolzote and Ollokot, and children, women, and the elderly were suffering terribly from cold and hunger. Worst of all, most of their horses had been captured or dispersed, leaving no chance of escape. Now the time had come again for diplomacy, and Joseph came to the fore. Howard finally had caught up. On the morning of October 5, after negotiations through Christianized Nez Perces accompanying Howard, Joseph rode slowly to the army's lines and handed over his rifle, symbolically ending his people's extraordinary effort. In the final hours of the siege at least 150 had slipped through the lines and made their way across the Canadian border only forty miles away.

As military history, the Nez Perce War was recognized at the time as something remarkable. Miles called the warriors the best Indian marksmen he had ever encountered, and Sherman, hardly known for his sympathies for Native peoples, praised their campaign for its defensive brilliance. Over and over the Nez Perces displayed coolness when attacked, a shrewd sense of battlefield tactics and use of terrain, and above all courage and persistence when facing what, after all, must have seemed long odds from the start. Indian combatants typically fought more individualistically than white troops—a warrior "goes into battle on his own guidance," as one put it—yet at the battles of White Bird canyon, the Big Hole, and the Bear's Paw the Nez Perces worked in concert, flanking and manipulating their opponents with impressive counterthrusts and choice of position. Perhaps this achievement is part of the reason behind the praise: these Indians fought like whites.

see

Elliott West

The 1,500-mile running fight reveals plenty as well about our cultural history. It stands as one of the best known of the Indian wars, partly because of the military performance just described but also because of a unique appeal. There was, first, its timing. Coming on the heels of the Great Sioux War of 1876 and the Custer debacle, it caught the public eye more than it might have a few years earlier or later. And even though the Sioux, Cheyennes, and Nez Perces all fought whites only when attacked, the first two of those tribes seemed paragons of wild raiders, whereas the public perceived the Nez Perce campaign as more in essence defensive. After the first assaults that set off the war, the Nez Perce bands only occasionally lashed out at white noncombatants. With the long trains of families, guarded by mounted warriors, the Indians' military effort had a domestic feel the public could more easily picture as a brave response of victims protecting their own. The episode unfolded with the pattern of a great tragedy. Moments of high drama and courage led to heartbreaking defeat just short of sanctuary. Finally there is Joseph himself, in particular his part at the end of the conflict. Soon after the surrender, accounts in Montana newspapers included Joseph's words of submission:

> Tell General Howard I know his heart. . . . I am tired of fighting. Our chiefs are killed. . . . The old men are all dead. . . . He who leads the young men [Ollokot, Joseph's brother] is dead. It is cold and we have no blankets. The little children are freezing to death. My people, some of them, have run away into the hills and have no blankets, no food; no one knows where they are— perhaps freezing to death. I want time to look for my children and see how many of them I can find. May be I shall find them among the dead. Hear me, my chiefs; I am tired. My heart is sick and sad. From where the sun now stands I will fight no more forever.

It has become one of the most famous short speeches in American history. Its vivid images, the poignant pain of an honorable leader and loving father, the simple formality, and the pervasive pathos—all this spoke powerfully to the public's notion of the American Indian's doomed nobility. The "I will fight no more forever" speech can be seen and heard as a companion piece to Sarah Winnemucca's public presentations. Spoken not from a stage but a battlefield, it is a male warrior's stoic equivalent of Sarah's eloquent appeals for justice. Like her lectures, it piqued white America's emotional blend of romance and guilt directed toward Indians.

Problem is, Joseph might never have said those words. Certainly he never said them literally—he spoke no English, so whatever he said was translated—and even in his own language he never said them directly to Howard, as is often portrayed. Research, furthermore, strongly suggests that the speech was embellished or even invented by Howard's aide-de-camp, Charles Erskine Scott Wood. Wood became a prolific writer and poet, freethinker, and ardent critic of Indian policy, and even at the time he apparently had considerable sympathy for the people he was helping run to ground. The speech seems to have been inserted in the official report by someone else after Howard wrote his first draft, and there is the nagging feeling that the oratory is *too* good by standards of what would be its reading public—that it conforms too perfectly to how readers expected Indians to speak. Did Wood concoct the words from the whole cloth? Did he revise some spare comments of Joseph into something more literary? Or did he pass on faithfully a speech that has moved those who read it for a century and a quarter? Probably it is too late now to answer with certainty. The larger point is that these words, whatever their provenance, have continued to speak with such appeal. In the response to "I will fight no more . . ." we see the instant creation of myth from history, the transformation of factual moment into a reflection of public feeling and need.

Sarah had her own brush with war. In 1878 the Bannocks of southern Idaho lashed out from the same sorts of frustrations that had triggered the Nez Perce conflict the year before, including in this case packs of settlers' hogs rooting and eating the camas roots that were a staple for the Bannocks as well as the Nez Perces. Sarah's first concern was for her father's band, and once they were out of harm's way, she worked with the same Oliver Howard who had chased down Joseph. She scouted for him, reported on the Bannocks' movements, provided other essential intelligence and advice, and on one of those Paul Revere rides that sprinkle through American legend, she alerted a vulnerable army post about a possible attack. Howard admired her greatly, but predictably she also earned the suspicion and censure of some whites, who thought her guilty of collusion, and of some Indians, who dismissed her for betrayal.

Divisions within her own people would always add distress to her life, as was the case with Joseph, yet like the Nez Perce leader, she persevered. When her lecturing career ended, she shifted her attention to another approach to mediating between Indian and white culture—education. In Lovelock, Nevada, she founded a school for Paiute children. Its curriculum alone might suggest that Sarah's intent was little different from those of educators in government schools. Her pupils learned to speak and write English. They worked at mathematics, sang hymns, and learned what at the time were called "industrial skills," such as sewing for the girls. Government schools, however, had as a prime goal the eradication of Native cultures. As a speaker at the most famous of these schools in Carlisle, Pennsylvania, told the students: "You cannot become truly American citizens, industrious, intelligent, cultured, civilized until the INDIAN in you is DEAD." Carlisle was one of many boarding schools where children were kept, sometimes for years, without contact with their families, while at agency schools boys and girls attended daily or for weeks. In all cases, however, students faced enormous pressure to jettison the lifeways of their parents. Not surprisingly, families resisted, and in some cases sons and daughters were physically seized in raids and packed off to boarding schools. Sarah believed that the Paiutes' future required that their children learn English and the educational basics of white culture, but she saw these as essential tools for advancing in what was now the dominant culture. She was equally committed to maintaining the fundamentals of Paiute culture and rejecting the most destructive elements of the whites' way of life. Sarah's dream was for her students to use their education to become teachers who would help usher their people into a new life while respecting and preserving their Paiute identity. Her school, in short, was an expression of her life. This remarkable effort, however, failed to secure government funding or much support from private donors. Within a few years it closed. Sarah's beloved brother Natches meanwhile failed at his own experiment in adaptation, a ranch (where her school was) developed and run entirely by Paiutes.

In 1887 Sarah's estranged husband died—one more loss in what had always been a turbulent personal life that included other failed marriages and relationships and bouts of heavy drinking. Her enemies always had portrayed her as a debauchee and even, preposterously, a prostitute, and though the charges were mostly a mix of lies and exaggerations, she was unquestionably a passionate, hot-tempered woman whose impulses could get away from her. On the evening of October 16, 1891, she was struck by sudden, intense stomach cramps and died. Of the various opinions of the cause—tuberculosis, suicide, poisoning, witchcraft, or the doctor's diagnosis, "too much chokecherry wine"— none is conclusive. Sarah was buried in an unmarked grave, its location now uncertain too. She was forty-seven.

Joseph's life after the Bear's Paw was longer but at least as troubled. The war and its terrible losses were followed by an even more bitter blow. At the surrender Nez Perce leaders believed the army had promised they could return to Idaho, but the government instead ordered their exile to Indian Territory (later Oklahoma). There the Real People languished, crowded into a bleak corner about as different from their homeland as it was possible to be, their numbers dropping. After protest and pleading and supported by public petitions, they were allowed to return to the Pacific Northwest in 1885. Nearly half, however, including Joseph, were sent not back to Idaho but to the Colville reservation in northern Washington, in part apparently because they refused to convert to Christianity. Through these years and afterward Joseph continued to play mediator and advocate for his people. His public image, burnished by the famous speech he may or may not have made, gave him minimal political clout, which he used to get slightly better treatment for his people in captivity and later for some advantages on the reservations. He maintained friendships among his former adversaries, including Howard and Wood, his possible ghostwriter, whose young son spent his summers with Joseph. He traveled back east a couple of times to ask for a reservation in the Wallowas. In 1897 he attended the opening of Grant's tomb and in 1903 dined on buffalo steaks with President Theodore Roosevelt. His requests were not granted, however. In September 1904 he died in his tepee, apparently of a heart attack. He was buried at Colville, three hundred miles from his father's grave in the Wallowas.

Chief Joseph and Sarah Winnemucca remind us that behind the famous Indian wars were other stories and other leaders working to find some middle way between bloodshed and submission. Indian peoples persevered, and the lives of this man and woman can teach us about the remarkable durability of these original Americans and their cultures. Their most troubling lesson, however, is how little they were able to cushion their people from the terrible impact of conquest and change. Joseph worked mostly from outside white society, brokering first for preservation of a traditional life and then for a peaceful transition to a new one. He failed in both efforts, although his fame gave him some limited leverage to mitigate his tribe's suffering in the years that followed. Sarah worked mostly from inside white culture. She was able to blunt somewhat the harshest treatment of the Paiutes by calling on her linguistic talents, dramatic sense, and intuitive manipulation of what her public expected and wanted to hear, but it would be hard to argue that if she had not done what she did, the broad outlines of government action toward her people would have been significantly different.

The federal government during these years, on many levels and through many programs, was using the authority and power it gained from the Civil War to consolidate what had been a fractured nation sprawling over huge distances and checkered by dozens of largely independent cultures. Out West, that meant pulling Indian peoples toward economic and cultural lifeways the government determined as the norm. However bungling in any particular execution, it was relentless in pursuing those goals. Paiutes and Nez Perces and many other Native peoples, furthermore, lived on land deep in resources that the new economic order would put to its own uses. Indian claims to that land, and their attachment to their own way of living on it, were always considered negotiable and ultimately inferior to goals of development done in the name of national progress. These were the overriding realities of Indian policy in the generation after 1865, and it is in their context that the famous episodes of the Indians wars—the Little Big Horns and Sand Creeks—should be understood, as well as the campaigns for peace of Sarah Winnemucca and Chief Joseph and others who chose their approach. The government's disposition toward Indians finally was about power. Warriors like Toohoolhoolzote and Yellow Wolf *See* (and Crazy Horse and Geronimo) could not resist it for long. Neither could Joseph and Sarah and others who pursued compromise soften by much how power was exercised on the tens of thousands of Native Americans who, like most of us, had no grander strategy than getting by day by day. — *And stay alive + protect children + old.*

Essay on Sources

Curious readers might begin with what the two principal characters in this essay had to say: Sarah Winnemucca Hopkins, *Life Among the Paiutes: Their Wrongs and Claims* (Boston: Cupples, Upham and Co.; New York: G. P. Putnam's Sons, 1883), and Joseph's own version of the Nez Perce War, dictated and translated as "An Indian's View of Indian Affairs," *North American Review* 128 (April 1879): 412–33. There are two biographies of Winnemucca, Sally Zanjani's excellent recent work, *Sarah Winnemucca* (Lincoln: University of Nebraska, 2001), and the earlier Gae Whitney Canfield, *Sarah Winnemucca of the Northern Paiutes* (Norman: University of Oklahoma Press, 1983). For a recent spirited analysis of Winnemucca in comparison with two other intriguing figures, see Siobhan Senier, *Voices of American Indian Assimilation and Resistance: Helen Hunt Jackson, Sarah Winnemucca, and Victoria Howard* (Norman: University of Oklahoma Press, 2001). The best biographical treatments of Joseph are embedded in books on his people. Begin with Alvin M. Josephy's masterpiece, *The Nez Perce Indians and the Opening of the Northwest* (New Haven, Conn.: Yale University Press, 1965), and add to it Francis D. Haines, *The Nez Perces* (Norman: University of Oklahoma Press, 1955).

This essay has stressed the importance of factors other than warfare in determining the fate of Indian peoples. Historians nonetheless have paid considerable attention to Indian wars, and the Nez Perce conflict has attracted more than its share. Among the best works are Bruce Hampton, *Children of Grace: The Nez Perce War of 1877* (New York: Henry Holt, 1994); David Lavender, *Let Me Be Free* (New York:

HarperCollins, 1992); and Mark H. Brown, *The Flight of the Nez Perce* (New York: Putnam, 1967). Oliver O. Howard has left his memories and opinions in *Nez Perce Joseph* (Boston: Lee and Shepard; New York: Charles T. Dillingham, 1881). We also have an invaluable perspective of a Nez Perce participant as recorded by Lucullus McWhorter, *Yellow Wolf: His Own Story* (Caldwell, Idaho: Caxton, 1948). On the two major conflicts in the life of Sarah Winnemucca, see William C. Miller, "The Pyramid Lake Indian War of 1860," *Nevada Historical Society Quarterly* 1 (September and November 1957): 35–53, 99–113, and George F. Brimlow, *The Bannock Indian War of 1878* (Caldwell, Idaho: Caxton, 1938). The best overviews of these conflicts are by Robert M. Utley, *The Indian Frontier of the American West, 1846–1890* (Albuquerque: University of New Mexico Press, 1984); *Frontiersmen in Blue: The United States Army and the Indian, 1848–1865* (New York: Macmillan, 1967), and *Frontier Regulars: The United States Army and the Indian, 1865–1891* (New York: Macmillan, 1973).

Historians have long recognized that the period following the Civil War was a crucial transition in national policy toward Indian peoples. The starting place for an understanding of Indian policy generally is Francis Paul Prucha's monumental *The Great Father: The United States Government and the American Indians,* 2 vols. (Lincoln: University of Nebraska Press, 1984). An earlier, more specialized work from Prucha is also exceptionally insightful: *American Indian Policy in Crisis: Christian Reformers and the Indian, 1865–1900* (Norman: University of Oklahoma Press, 1976). Whatever changes occurred during these years, the goal from the beginning of the republic had been assimilation of Native Americans. In the late nineteenth century that goal was to be accomplished through the twin programs of education and allotment in severalty. The two leading works on those programs are David Wallace Adams, *Education for Extinction: American Indians and the Boarding School Experience, 1875–1928* (Lawrence: University Press of Kansas, 1995), and Loring Benson Priest, *Uncle Sam's Stepchildren: The Reformation of United States Indian Policy, 1865–1887* (New Brunswick: Rutgers University Press, 1942). For broader perspectives on assimilation, see Frederick E. Hoxie, *A Final Promise: The Campaign to Assimilate the Indians, 1880–1920* (Lincoln: University of Nebraska Press, 1984), and Robert Winston Mardock, *The Reformers and the American Indian* (Columbia: University of Missouri Press, 1971). On the background of the reservation system is Robert A. Trennert, *Alternative to Extinction: Federal Indian Policy and the Beginnings of the Reservation System, 1846–51* (Philadelphia: Temple University Press, 1995). All these works note that during the years right after the Civil War, Indian policy was shaped in part through competition and tension between two powerful postwar sets of interests, the military and religious institutions. On these, see Robert Wooster, *The Military and United States Indian Policy, 1865–1903* (New Haven, Conn.: Yale University Press, 1988), and Robert H. Keller, *American Protestantism and United States Indian Policy, 1869–82* (Lincoln: University of Nebraska Press, 1983).

Apart from official policy, Native Americans faced the formidable pressures of disease and the undermining of their economies through environmental changes set loose by the advance of white society. For an overview of the impact of diseases, see Russell Thornton, *American Indian Holocaust and Survival: A Population History Since 1492* (Norman: University of Oklahoma Press, 1987), and for a recent critical analysis of those claims, consult David Henige, *Numbers from Nowhere: The American Indian Contact Population Debate* (Norman: University of Oklahoma, 1998). The impact of environmental change has emerged as a useful theme in the writing of Indian-white relations. See for examples Brigham D. Madsen, *The Shoshoni Frontier and the Bear River Massacre* (Salt Lake City: University of Utah Press, 1985), and Elliott West, *The Contested Plains: Indians, Goldseekers and the Rush to Colorado* (Lawrence: University Press of Kansas, 1998). Another broader cultural factor, one so significant and basic it is sometimes overlooked, was the perception of non-Indians toward Native peoples. Among several fine books on this topic, two are especially worth noting: Robert F. Berkhofer's overview, *The White Man's Indian: Images of the American Indian from Columbus to the Present* (New York: Knopf, 1978), and for the time covered in this essay, Brian Dippie's superb *The Vanishing American: White Attitudes and U.S. Indian Policy* (Middletown, Conn.: Wesleyan University Press, 1982). Indian persistence, like the forces undermining Indian independence, has taken many forms. None has been more powerful in its effects than religious revival movements. The Indian peoples who are at the center of this essay found strength in two of those movements. On the Dreamer religion of Smohalla, see Robert H. Ruby and John A. Brown, *The Dreamer-Prophets of the Columbia Plateau: Smohalla and Skolaskin* (Norman: University of Oklahoma Press, 1989), and on the ghost dance religion originating in the Great Basin, see Russell Thornton, *We Shall Live Again: The 1870 and 1890 Ghost Dance Movements as Demographic Revitalization* (New York: Cambridge University Press, 1986). And for a global perspective on such movements, consult Vittorio Lanternari, *The Religions of the Oppressed: A Study of Modern Messianic Cults* (New York: Knopf, 1963).

CHAPTER 9

Miller and Lux, Rachael Calof, Nannie Alderson, and the Settlement of the Agricultural Frontier

R. Douglas Hurt

L and, which meant opportunity, lured most settlers to the trans-Mississippi West during the last half of the nineteenth century. Beginning in 1841, the burning desire of "Oregon Fever" became a siren song as powerful as any in Greek mythology. Many who followed its nearly irresistible call found the promised land of the American West the fulfillment of their dreams. Letters home from settlers on the agricultural frontier beckoned family and friends to join them. In 1856, Jane Carruth, who migrated to Kansas with her husband and children from New York State, wrote home, saying: "How I wish that thousands of our poor but worthy people could be transferred here; what homes they would have."

By 1860, settlers had developed a host of farms in the Pacific Northwest, in California's Central Valley, near the Great Salt Lake, and on the fringe of the Great Plains. Between 1862 and 1890, nearly half of the homesteaders in Kansas gained title to their claims. In Colorado and Wyoming women filed approximately 18 percent of the homesteads and received title at a higher rate than men. In 1882, one observer noted that the Dakota Territory was "alive with emigrants." More followed after the Dawes Act of 1887 opened Indian lands in the Dakotas for lease and sale to white settlers, and the Sioux Act of 1889 transferred more than 9 million acres in South Dakota to public domain. The Santa Fe, Union Pacific, Northern Pacific, and Great Northern railroads, among others, aided settlement by aggressively recruiting settlers from the East as well as abroad. The transcontinental lines sent agents and promotional literature to Europe and drew tens of thousands of immigrants to the West. Many settlers, however, found only hardship and disappointment.

In most cases the patriarchal customs of the day and the gendered expectations that women would keep their families together at all costs determined the agricultural settlement of the American West. Indeed, the agricultural settlement of the frontier West was a family matter, which, in turn, meant a rough sex and age balance. In 1860, men constituted half of Utah's settlers. Twenty years later, males totaled 50 percent of the agricultural population in Kansas and, by 1890, 58 percent of the farm population in Oregon. The Great Plains of Kansas, Nebraska, and the Dakota Territory would be a country for young men and women and children for a decade or more after most of the land had been claimed. Half of the population in those areas ranged between fifteen and forty-five years in age from 1860 to 1890. Although cholera made the early trail along the Platte River from St. Joseph to Fort Laramie a graveyard, later settlers on the plains were healthy young men and women, and with the exception of children, death rates were low, which along with high birth rates contributed to the rapid population growth of the region.

Economic betterment based on the acquisition of free land proved motivation strong enough for settlers to risk their lives to achieve it. Indeed, the men and women who trekked west over the Oregon Trail and other routes literally bet their lives for the sake of acquiring land in the West. Although many young women contributed to the agricultural settlement of the frontier West and although many migrated and settled willingly, others often came reluctantly. The West did not appear as a "land of promise" for everyone. Migration meant leaving family and friends, whom most would never see again. Certainly many married women moved west because their husbands decided to go and they could keep their families together only by migrating. A sense of obligation, expectation, and duty rather than the lure of free land and the promise of a better life drove them. One woman remembered leaving for the West: "Agreeable to the wish of my husband, I left all my relatives in Ohio . . . & started on the long & . . . perilous journey. . . . It proved a hard task to leave them but still harder to leave my children buried in . . . graveyards." Like most women as well as men, she knew that she would never return. This westward migration and settlement differed from previous family moves because distance and time were far greater than in the past. These settlers would forsake familiar surroundings and embark on a venture with both hope and despair.

No matter how they came, the men, women, and children who settled on the agricultural frontier between the 1840s and 1900 were bound by the common bond of a shared experience, whether they migrated by wagon, train, or ship. For them, migration for the purpose of agricultural settlement was the most important event of their lives. It was a decision that no one made lightly, and they usually made it only after considerable soul-searching and anguish. As a result, migration

Figure 9.1: Women not only helped settle the West with their husbands and families, but many also filed for homesteads in their own names as provided by the Homestead Act of 1862. In 1886, the Chrisman sisters filed adjacent claims in Custer County, Nebraska. Courtesy of the Nebraska State Historical Society Photograph Collections.

and settlement in the American West became a personal and family demarcation that separated the past from the future. Once the trip had been made and their new homes taken up on the land, their lives would be forever changed, whether for better or worse, only time would tell.

Without question the westward movement between 1840 and 1900 marks one of the great migrations in history. The men and women who were part of that settlement experience knew that they were taking part in the expansion of the United States and the American empire to the Pacific Coast. Most of these settlers had been farmers and possessed the skills needed to settle on the western frontier. They also understood the value of land for personal betterment, particularly if it was free for the taking and improvement with their own hands, either for purposes of sale and capital gains or for family prosperity and security. Yet none of them knew what awaited them between the jumping-off places, such as Independence and St. Joseph, Missouri, or Council Bluffs, Iowa, and their destination of "free land" in the West. But their experiences as well as the experiences of those who followed proved so profound and life changing that many could not help but record them. Their voices and experiences from the past give a fuller understanding to the reality of settlement on the western agricultural frontier during the late nineteenth century.

In the Willamette Valley of Oregon, the early settlers claimed land that drew them to this frontier by preemption or use. The independent provisional government, organized in 1843, limited land claims in the Organic Code to a generous 640 acres per man (changed in 1844 to include widows) who intended to occupy and improve it. Settlers could hold only one claim at a time, and they had the responsibility to survey, mark, and record their property lines. By the mid-1840s, the open-range cattle industry thrived in the Willamette Valley, but as more settlers arrived, they quickly occupied the grasslands. Soon wheat, potatoes, and fruit trees grew where cattle once grazed. In 1850, Congress passed the Oregon Donation Act, which validated previous land titles and reaffirmed the right of settlers to claim 640 acres through 1855, after which individuals could claim only 160 and families 320 acres, still more than any farmer could cultivate given the technology, labor, and markets available. Even so, this legislation continued to make Oregon attractive to settlers, and it encouraged intruders who trespassed and settled on lands claimed by others until evicted by the legal process or violence. By the early 1860s, settlers in southeastern Washington produced cattle, grain, and fruit for the mining camps in Idaho and Montana. Most of the sixty-four thousand settlers in present-day Washington and Oregon lived west of the Cascades in the Willamette Valley, with a few settlers between the Columbia River and Puget Sound, while the dry lands east of the mountains attracted few settlers. By 1870, Willamette Valley farmland brought as much as $50 per acre, which gave considerable capital gains to speculators and early settlers who owned land and chose to sell. Portland had become an important shipping point for wheat and flour, particularly to San Francisco.

By 1875 settlers were establishing farms in the Palouse country between the Snake River and Spokane Falls north of Walla Walla, which some promoters called "the best poor man's country in the world." There they found the dry plateau of eastern Washington ideal for grain production. During the 1880s, they rapidly plowed that country for wheat. Settlers acquired land under the Homestead, Timber Culture, and Preemption acts and created an "Inland Empire." In 1883, one observer wrote that the Palouse country looked like a great wheat field. "We gaze for miles and see nothing but fields of grain, stretching away in one continuous succession of farms until they blend with the distance. Such another view cannot be seen on the continent." By the late 1880s, settlers plowed the Big Bend country west of Spokane for wheat, and the railroads, particularly the Northern Pacific (completed in 1883), enabled farmers to reach markets in Portland and St. Paul, transporting plows, binders, threshing machines, and other implements into the region to enable still greater agricultural expansion.

Settlers occupied the entire Willamette Valley by 1880, and farms spread south of Portland while the immigration bureaus of Washington and Oregon worked hard to recruit German and Scandinavian settlers. Soon more than 2 million acres in the Columbia Valley and southeastern Washington had been plowed, sheep grazed on the arid lands, and agricultural settlers moved into the Snake River Valley of Idaho. Still, distance and difficulty prevented a great rush to settle the Pacific Northwest until the completion of the Oregon and California Railroad between San Francisco and Portland in December 1887, and settlers found the Pacific Northwest isolated and hard to reach.

To the south, Mormon settlers began moving into Utah during the late 1840s, where they developed extensive church- or publicly controlled irrigation systems along the Wasatch Front. By digging extensive irrigation systems more efficiently than other immigrants without government aid, the Mormons became the first Anglo American settlers to establish productive farms in the arid West. Among the Mormon settlers, strong supervision and distribution of the land and water by church officials superseded the individualism characteristic of the other settlers in the West. The church used the Preemption, Homestead, Timber Culture, and Desert Land acts to acquire land and, although illegal, distribute it in smaller allotments to Mormon settlers. The distribution of land by the church and the development of publicly controlled irrigation, along with early marriage (usually before the women reached twenty years of age) and a high birth rate, made extensive agricultural settlement possible and enabled the Mormon settlers to endure a host of environmental trials and foster an economic democracy in the American West. By 1890, the Mormons had settled isolated farms across the Great Basin in Utah, Nevada, and southeastern Idaho, where they practiced their religion and kept to themselves.

Although the shared experience of migration was the most important bond of settlers, the second most common characteristic was their poverty or at best their middling economic circumstances. The settlers who reached the Oregon country during the mid-1840s had the least wealth because they left behind economic hard times fostered by the Panic of 1837. A rough trail and nearly insurmountable mountains forced them to abandon most of their few remaining possessions in the form of furniture, implements, and personal memorabilia. Many of their livestock fell to overwork or the necessity of the butcher's knife, and wagons littered the trail. Even the homesteaders on the Great Plains who arrived by train during the late nineteenth century and who had heeded the advice of those who went before them, taking approximately $1,000 to pay for expenses and the early costs of starting a farm, often found that drought, grasshoppers, and low agricultural prices ruined hopes of economic success and a better life built on the land.

Although the migrants who moved west on the overland trails often typify the determined, hardy, and stoic settlers bound for the Pacific Northwest and California, the cowboys and cattlemen characterize a different type of settler in the frontier West. Many cowboys were rootless, landless men who worked for large-scale ranchers or cattle companies. Later they personified in the public memory carefree, independent men who loved sun and saddle and helped bring civilization to the grasslands, whereas the ranchers epitomized powerful westerners who marshaled considerable capital and skillfully used federal land policy to expand their holdings. The truth about these settlers in the American West, of course, differs considerably from the myth of cowboy life, as the experiences of Charlie Siringo, Henry Miller, and Charles Lux clearly testify.

Born near the Gulf Coast of Texas a decade before the Civil War, Siringo, at the age of sixteen, was hired to work for a large-scale rancher. Without a wife, children, or land, he became a man who drifted from one ranching job to another as fate or fancy determined. Like other cowboys, he had a propensity to spend his hard-earned monthly wages on necessities such as a saddle or a night in town, and he could be satisfied with both expenditures. Siringo and the cowboys who trailed cattle to Abilene, Wichita, and Dodge City or the grasslands of Montana were young, single men. Between the opening of the Chisholm Trail in 1867 and the collapse of the range cattle industry twenty years later, approximately thirty-five thousand cowboys, five thousand of whom were African American, made their way to the plains and worked the long drives north from Texas. Some eventually acquired land on the plains, while others remained ranch hands. Like the range cattle industry that retreated west before the push of settlers claiming land, Siringo drifted with it into the panhandle of Texas and the eastern plains of New Mexico, driven in part by a restlessness and independence that prevented him from putting down roots. Settlement for Siringo meant peopling the Great Plains with a few ranchers and cowboys who would keep much of the West for themselves while they used the public domain free of charge for their own purposes. They were men whose independence served them best in positions of routine with minimal supervision, that is, as cowboys. They saw farmers as a threat to their chosen way of life.

Although the West was not entirely free, much of it could be acquired for the taking when Siringo began working as a cowboy in 1871. At that time, his employer grazed cattle on 250,000 acres in Wheaton County, Texas. Even though this ranch soon passed into the possession of Allen, Pool & Company, it remained an operation too large for anyone to miss a few cattle. Quickly Siringo had learned the advantage of registering a brand in his own name and putting it on unmarked cattle that belonged to someone else. By branding these "maverick" cattle, he began building a herd of his own. Siringo recalled, "I always carried a piece or iron tied to my saddle so in case I got off on the prairie by myself I could brand a few mavericks for myself." The branding of mavericks made him "feel like a young cattle king." For Siringo, the law, like art, was in the eye of the beholder. Soon Siringo worked for another rancher, who operated a slaughterhouse for taking only hides and tallow, and he drove cattle, seldom those of his employer, to it.

In 1874, Siringo made his first trip up the Chisholm Trail to Abilene, Kansas. He drew wages of $35 per month, food, and railroad fare back to Texas. "Everything went smoothly," he reported, "except a stampede now and then." Without a monetary interest in the ranches that employed him, Siringo did not worry about the weather or much else beyond his immediate control. When blizzards struck from the north and cattle died, he took advantage of the opportunity to earn extra money by skinning the carcasses and selling the hides. By so doing, Siringo plied this trade alongside the buffalo hunters, whom he called "mostly Indians and Mexicans." Soon he reported that the range, once "black with buffalos, is now stocked with seventy-five thousand blooded cattle, and all fenced in." Siringo played a role in stocking cattle on the southern Great Plains, and he enjoyed driving livestock north to shipping points in Kansas "over a wild strip of country where there was no tracts nor scarcely any ranches . . . until reaching the southern line of Kansas." Often he spent months on the trail. By the mid-1880s, Siringo had married and attempted to settle down, but the life of a businessman proved too boring, although he gave up life on the range. By the turn of the twentieth century, Siringo worked for the Pinkerton Detective Agency, pursuing various lawbreakers and troublemakers throughout the West, and he more than most settlers recognized that "time makes changes, even out here in the 'western wilds.'"

Where Charlie Siringo typified the cowboys on the open range, many cattlemen, more skilled at manipulating capital than a lariat and more at home in a leather-covered office chair than a saddle, also made important contributions to the settlement of the frontier West. Two German immigrants, Charles Lux and Heinrich Alfred Kreiser, which he changed to Henry Miller, immigrated to the United States in 1839 and 1847 respectively. Both looked forward to "freedom and opportunity" as well as to owning land. Both worked as butchers in New York City before making their way via ship to San Francisco, where they continued their

Figure 9.2: Ranchers usually branded their newborn calves in the spring and used the fall roundup to catch those they had missed. Some cowboys, such as Charlie Siringo, registered their own brands and put them on "mavericks," creating herds of their own by taking cattle that belonged to others. Courtesy of the Western History Collections, University of Oklahoma Libraries.

trade and quickly became independent businessmen who owned their own butcher shops. Miller and Lux soon acquired enough capital to invest in the wholesale cattle trade and to purchase land. With capital to invest, Miller and Lux saw vast potential in the grass-covered San Joaquin Valley. Although drought often parched the grass and flooding frequently drove cattle to the high ground, Miller and Lux believed that large-scale land purchases in the valley would give them sufficient ecological and environmental flexibility to raise the cattle needed for the San Francisco market. As early as 1853, Lux acquired a half interest in 1,700 acres south of San Francisco. About the same time, Miller began purchasing small herds of Mexican cattle and grazed them on rented land until ready for slaughter and sale in his butcher shops. Miller reflected, "They varied in price, sometimes they were high and sometimes they were cheap. I took advantage of the number in the market and when cattle were scarce, I got a good price for them."

During the 1850s, Miller and Lux formed a partnership, married into the same prominent family, and entered the elite world of San Francisco's high society. After joining as partners Miller and Lux aggressively purchased land and cattle for the company. They also bought cattle cheap when the market collapsed during the early 1860s because of drought and the need of cattlemen to sell livestock that they could no longer feed. One contemporary observed, "While hundreds of stockmen were going broke Miller was making a killing. . . . Cattle

R. Douglas Hurt

could be bought for two to six dollars a head. Miller bought cattle right and left and filled the Santa Rita swamp grass fields to capacity. . . . It was commonly agreed among valley stockmen that by 1866 Miller had cleared $250,000 from the resale of these cattle."

Miller and Lux also made large purchases of land in the San Joaquin Valley, where Mexican and American owners confronted unpayable debts and taxes when cattle ranching proved unprofitable because of flooding and drought. By the late 1860s, Miller and Lux had acquired more than 300,000 acres, on which they raised their own cattle. Miller and Lux also purchased considerable acreage in the Mexican land grants and used their wealth and the legal process to confirm their titles. They particularly capitalized on the Land Law of 1851, which required owners of Mexican land grants to prove their titles before the California Land Claims Commission in order to keep their lands. By the mid-1870s, Miller and Lux owned more than 520,000 acres, primarily in the San Joaquin Valley. Twenty years later they controlled approximately 1.2 million acres in California, Nevada, and Oregon. Consequently, they significantly restricted the settlement of the San Joaquin Valley and other locations in the West. Other large-scale landowners were also absentee landlords, which prompted one observer to remark, "There is by far too much of a disposition to farm in the San Joaquin Valley and live in San Francisco."

Miller and Lux hired agents to help them locate and claim government land. They used land, college, and military scrip or warrants, which they purchased from speculators at reduced prices to pay for their acquisitions. In addition, they arranged to pay their land taxes in Fresno County with land scrip rather than cash, thereby reducing their costs in real money while protecting their monetary capital. They used their ownership of the San Joaquin and King's River Canal and Irrigation Company to deliver the votes of their employees to elect a friendly tax assessor who would value their property lower than warranted.

Completion of the Southern Pacific Railroad in the late 1860s linked the ranch lands of Miller and Lux to their slaughterhouses and butcher shops in San Francisco. By the early 1870s, however, at a time when the long cattle drives characterized the open-range cattle industry on the southern Great Plains, the Southern Pacific Railroad enabled Miller and Lux to end their practice of driving cattle to market. Moreover, in contrast to many cattle ranchers on the Great Plains, Miller and Lux owned their land, and they fenced their cattle in and settlers out who might squat and claim preemption rights on their lands. During the late 1860s Miller and Lux targeted land purchases to consolidate, that is, block in, their holdings as well as to fence their lands, which by 1870 extended for forty-five miles, with more yet to build. A contemporary observed that "Miller's fence" was as yet "the biggest construction undertaking ever attempted in the San Joaquin valley."

Miller and Lux understood that control of water for irrigation in the San Joaquin Valley would not only provide protection against periodic drought but also determine their profit from investments in land and cattle. In 1871, when Miller and Lux bought a major interest in the San Joaquin and King's River Canal and Irrigation Company, they granted it a right-of-way across their lands, provided that it furnished irrigation water to them during the year even though their 200,000 acres of alfalfa and wheat might take all of the water that flowed through the canal. The other investors in the canal company, however, wanted to use the water to irrigate 5 million acres in the valley and promote rapid immigration and settlement, which would increase land values and company profits from the lands that it owned as well as from the sale of water. Miller and Lux and the canal company had vastly different views about the settlement of the San Joaquin Valley.

Indeed, the *San Francisco Chronicle* reported that "Miller & Lux, having their lands assessed at a very low rate, and having waters free for the use of their cattle, have not cared to go to the trouble and expense involved in irrigating and dividing into farms the lands that could be watered by . . . canals. They have all the pasturage they require for their present profitable business, and prefer to go slow in the matter of improving and settling their lands." In reality, Miller and Lux had no intention of selling their lands to settlers in the San Joaquin Valley. They attempted to purchase as much land as possible for themselves. By late 1878, they gained control of the canal company and easily fended calls for them to sell their land to small-scale farmers. In many respects, Miller and Lux were both land and water barons, even "industrial cowboys."

Although Miller and Lux and other large-scale landowners blocked the settlement of small-scale farmers throughout the Central Valley, they contributed to the rapid influx of migrant laborers into the region. Between 1870 and 1900, the Miller and Lux workforce increased from 200 to more than 1,200 men. The division of labor among these immigrants contributed to the great diversity of landless workers in the San Joaquin Valley; Mexicans served as cowboys for herd management, while Chinese worked as cooks, Italians labored in the fields and maintained irrigation ditches, and northern Europeans held management positions. Racial and ethnic prejudice determined the division of labor and provided the basis for the organization and control of the workforce. The monthly turnover rate sometimes reached 50 percent. As many workers drew less than a dollar per day in wages and moved on after a few days or weeks, others took their place. Miller and Lux eventually paid approximately $1 million annually in labor costs. By so doing, they played a major role in the economic development of the West based on land, cattle, and agriculture, but they did so by excluding or preventing the settlement of thousands of families instead of dividing their land into small-scale farms and selling it rather than cattle for a profit.

Ultimately uncertain Mexican land titles and large estates during the 1860s and economic hard times in the 1870s prevented California from becoming a homesteader's paradise. Consequently, settlers in search of free or cheap lands looked to the foothills bordering the Central Valley, where relatively inexpensive lands prevailed. Periodic drought south of Stockton, however, made farming risky until irrigation systems provided water that few new settlers could afford. By 1880, the best land had been occupied by large-scale, capital-intensive, heavily mechanized farmers who raised specialty crops, particularly wheat on a commercial scale. In general, then, through the late nineteenth century, California remained a land of "haves" and "have-nots" in regard to agricultural settlement.

As a result of great landholdings, such as those by Miller and Lux, California did not experience agricultural settlement similar to that of the Great Plains and the Pacific Northwest, and it never became a land of homesteaders. Settlers who succeeded in establishing small-scale farms usually purchased their land from the railroads or the state, to which the federal government granted 20.4 million acres of public domain to finance railroad construction and state affairs. Homesteaders, however, claimed more than 2.5 million acres in California by the late 1870s, but many were fraudulent or dummy claims intended for merger with or acquisition by large-scale landowners, whereas other settlers purchased some 7 million acres in small tracts. By 1900 many homesteaders and small-scale farmers in California had failed, while approximately 5,000 farms averaged 4,000 acres, and farms 1,000 acres or larger constituted nearly two thirds of the state's 28 million acres of agricultural land. Clearly, agricultural settlers in California confronted a far different situation than the settlers on the Great Plains, where 160-acre farms often prevailed. The large-scale landowners in California marshaled land, labor, and capital on an industrial scale that made agricultural settlement, particularly in the Central Valley, far different from that of the Great Plains or Pacific Northwest.

Passage of the Homestead Act in 1862, the building of transcontinental railroads, and the removal of the Indians to reservations by 1890 opened the Great Plains to rapid settlement. The Homestead Act granted 160 acres free, except for small filing and patenting fees, to any head of a household, including women or immigrants, if they were citizens or had applied for citizenship and agreed to make improvements and live on the land for five years. Moreover, with the railroads selling

Figure 9.3: On the Great Plains settlers used sod in the absence of trees to build
their houses. In 1892, this family in Custer County, Nebraska, made
their home in a dugout, which they built by digging into a hillside and
laying up sod walls. Courtesy of the Nebraska State Historical Society
Photograph Collections.

lands, granted by the federal government, at prices ranging from $2 to
$10 per acre to finance construction, millions of acres became available
for settlement relatively cheap. Although a severe drought during the
late 1880s and early 1890s slowed settlement in Kansas and Nebraska,
railroad promotion in the Dakotas continued to lure settlers, who
boosted the population from 540,000 to 721,000 by 1900.

Settlers also pressured the federal government to open Indian
Territory for homesteading. In 1889, Congress responded by providing some 2 million acres for settlement. The federal government also
made available several million additional acres during the early 1890s,
including some 6 million acres in 1893 along the Oklahoma-Kansas
border, an area known as the Cherokee Outlet. Government land
officials believed forty thousand 160-acre homesteads could be claimed
in that area. For many who participated, the land run in 1893 that
officially opened much of this area to settlement was "a godsend . . . a
place to escape from big mortgages and bad memories."

At the same time, New Mexico, Colorado, Wyoming, and Montana
also increased in agricultural settlers, particularly in ranching areas of
Wyoming near Casper and Sheridan, while cultivated lands tripled

R. Douglas Hurt

among the Mormons in Utah from 1.3 to 4.1 million acres during the 1890s. Governor John A. Martin observed, "To populate a country thirty miles square within six months . . . may seem like fiction, but they have been realities in Kansas." With the Indians removed and land free, settlers claimed homesteads or purchased railroad or state lands with astonishing speed. In less than thirty years after 1860, agricultural settlers claimed an area more than four hundred miles wide between the Missouri River and the Kansas-Colorado line. Nebraska and the Dakota Territory expanded with similar speed. Together Kansas, Nebraska, and the Dakota Territory increased from a population of 136,000 in 1860 to 3 million by 1890. During that same time, Texas grew in population from 604,000 to 2.2 million, while the population in the Lone Star State west of the 100th meridian nearly doubled to 108,000 by 1900. Generous land grants from the Texas legislature, not the federal government, stimulated much of that settlement because Texas retained its public lands after gaining statehood.

Overall, the Homestead Act proved well suited for lands east of the 100th meridian, but 160 acres of unirrigated land to the west was insufficient to provide a living. Congress erred after 1880 by not expanding the acreage that could be claimed under the Homestead Act. Even so, many settlers took advantage of this legislation. Yet even larger claims would not have ensured economic success if settlers could not afford the technology required to farm more acres, and the Desert Land Act of 1877, which provided 640 acres for $1.25 per acre to settlers who promised to irrigate it, also proved unrealistic. Although some homesteaders failed, many stayed. Others sold their lands for capital gains and moved on. Despite the weakness of the Homestead Act, however, it gave thousands of men and women the opportunity to own land and settle in the West. For them, homesteading paid.

The life of Rachel Calof, a Jewish immigrant from Russia, epitomizes the settlement experience of many women who homesteaded on the Great Plains. Calof was born in 1876, the second of four children. Her mother died when she was about seven years old, and Rachael's father remarried. The marriage soon disintegrated, and Calof's father sent Rachael to live with her paternal grandfather. When Calof was about fourteen, she moved to a city and began work as a maid for an aunt. In 1894 a great-uncle arranged to send her to the United States to marry a recent Jewish immigrant who wanted a wife. In time, her future twenty-two-year-old husband, Abraham, sent Rachael money for steerage passage to the United States. Her relatives were glad to see her go because she was an unmarried young woman who worked as a servant. They helped her reach Hamburg, Germany, by giving her food and a little money.

Figure 9.4: Rachael Calof epitomizes women homesteaders in the West. Although she settled on the
Great Plains of North Dakota late in the nineteenth century, her struggle to create a home,
raise a family, and achieve prosperity proved
daunting and little different from that of many
other women who settled earlier. Success came
only after more than a decade of hardship.
Courtesy of J. Sanford Rikoon.

After twenty-three days at sea, Calof's ship arrived in New York
Harbor and the passengers disembarked at Ellis Island, where apprehension overcame all lingering feelings of seasickness in an "enormous
room with bars across the windows." Calof wrote: "In short order the
various examinations began which for each immigrant would determine
his or her fitness to enter 'Heaven.'" The fear that Calof and the other
immigrants experienced was overwhelming. Ellis Island created great
anxiety for most immigrants because they knew that an arbitrary word

or gesture from an official could deny them entry to the United States and force their return. In time, her name was called, and she passed through the gate ultimately leading to a homestead in North Dakota.

Calof's husband-to-be met her at Ellis Island. After some conversation they agreed that the risk had been worth it, and they left New York for North Dakota, where Abraham's parents, two brothers, a sister-in-law, and two children waited for their arrival. Calof reflected: "Abraham was convinced that our best chance of making something of ourselves was to avail ourselves of the offer of the free land. With our mutual effort we would build and prosper." Then she added, "I had to agree. It seemed a godsend to penniless people who could not hope to buy land." Like many foreign-born immigrants, Calof neither knew the location of North Dakota nor the incredible hardship that waited. "And so," she wrote, "two weeks after setting foot on the golden *medina* (land) of America, I was on my way to becoming a pioneer woman and to help build my new country. My life in Russia already seemed remote."

Rachael and Abraham arrived in Devils Lake, North Dakota, by train. A twenty-five-mile wagon ride across the prairie awaited them. The sight of her new family and home thoroughly depressed her. A "miserable shack," a single bed, a table made from boards, two benches, a stove, a pile of cow dung or chips for fuel, and a dirt floor attested to the hardscrabble poverty that accompanied most homesteaders during their early years on the Great Plains. "This was the first sight of what awaited me as a pioneer woman," she wrote. She would never forget the feeling of overwhelming despair. Calof's keen powers of observation and remembrance let her reflect that "I may have only sensed it at the moment, but what I was seeing was probably the greatest hardship of pioneer life, the terrible crowding of so many people into a small space." Lack of money and building materials as well as insufficient fuel in the forms of wood or coal meant that settlers lived in cramped sod houses, dugouts, or shacks until they could afford to purchase lumber, the delivery of which depended on the construction of a railroad. When Rachael learned that her own house was even smaller, she lost nearly all of her remaining optimism. She recalled, "Of all the privations I knew as a homesteader, the lack of privacy was the hardest to bear," and for many years she and her husband could only find privacy for making love on the open prairie. Little did she realize that her life as a homesteader would get worse.

Calof did not know at the time that she and her husband were squatters. Her husband thought that he had situated his twelve-by-fourteen-foot shack on public land that he intended to claim for a homestead. Since Rachael had not yet married Abraham, the law permitted her to claim 160 acres as well, and they intended to have both homesteads join into one farm of 320 acres, an undreamed of acreage for new, landless immigrants. Six weeks before their marriage, they traveled to Devils Lake to file their homestead claims. Despite the harsh conditions of living on the prairie the opportunity to claim 160 acres in her own name gave her a pride of ownership. Land Office officials, however, informed them that they had mistakenly settled on state land, but open public domain was available farther away, and they took it. The need to select new land proved little more than a minor setback, and they worked hard, believing that "we were at last creating our own future and we were inspired with a new stimulation and purpose."

Rachael's life now became one of hardship and want. She mixed plaster from clay to help insulate her clapboard cabin and provide smooth and more appealing walls, trekked numerous times to the well, prepared meals primarily from bread and cheese, the latter of which she made from the milk of their cow, and gave birth to her first child, a daughter. After Abraham cut the umbilical cord, she rested for several hours and contemplated the life before them. She did not rest long, but postpartum depression, isolation, and a superstitious mother-in-law drove her to the edge of a nervous breakdown before a niece of her husband visited for a few days.

When the second winter arrived, Abraham's father, mother, and brother moved into Rachael's shanty to help save fuel and pool their meager food supplies. She remembered the winter as incredibly severe with extreme cold and heavy snows. The nearness of her relatives had its drawbacks in a situation where "moving around was impossible without rubbing and bumping against each other. Sanitation, bad to start with, deteriorated steadily as did our composure, and as the bitter winter wore on our physical and mental state worsened." Her nerves frayed, and she argued with her husband, during which times she "stood face to face with him and gave as good as I received." Ultimately, spring came, her in-laws moved back to their cabin, and she was relieved and thankful once again to be mistress of her humble home. Then she went to work whitewashing the inside of her cabin and making curtains from flour sacks. The future looked bright until her daughter became deathly ill. With a doctor two or three days away who charged a dollar per mile plus a $15 visitation fee, the trip would cost $75, which they could not afford. Calof prepared for death, but her daughter improved, and the danger passed. A second child delivered on a "straw-covered table" that she found "prickly and cold" soon added to her daily burdens.

With ten acres plowed, primarily for wheat and by cutting prairie hay for their own use and sale, Abraham and Rachael earned enough to build a barn, and she raised potatoes, milked the cow, churned butter, and tended a flock of chickens. She sold some of the butter and eggs thirty miles away in Devils Lake. A failed wheat crop helped ensure that the coming winter would be "particularly vicious and long-lasting." Soon pregnant again with her third child, Calof reflected, "I must say that personally the most dependable state of affairs I knew during the many years I lived on the prairie was pregnancy."

By the late 1890s, Calof remembered that despite hardship, they slowly made the land productive for crops and livestock and their farm increasingly profitable. Although the extended family worked together stacking hay, shocking grain, and engaging in other mutual tasks, they no longer shared their income. Abraham and Rachael now enjoyed the fruits of the own labor. She worked in the field with her husband, raking hay and binding sheaves of wheat. They bought additional land and planned to acquire even more, all the while knowing the environmental risks of farming on the Great Plains.

Rachael's apprehension was justified. In the summer of 1900, just as she and Abraham prepared to reap their largest wheat crop, a hailstorm knocked it to the ground. Although the storm passed quickly, their wheat and hay crops lay in ruin, their windows broken, and their horses dead. She and her husband now realized that they were defeated. Amidst the mud, wind, and destitution, she knew that they had every reason to give up farming and leave their homestead. But they did not. Instead, they rebuilt their home and began again, with still another newborn child. Fortunately, the beginning of the twentieth century brought bountiful wheat crops, and their lives improved. Rachael and Abraham now began to feel a bond with the land and a sense of place, that is, a feeling of belonging and home.

If the West ultimately became the promised land for many immigrants and agricultural settlers, it was so only for those who had the initiative and strength to endure, which often was their only success. At the age of sixty, Calof reflected: "I stood shoulder-to-shoulder with my husband and proved capable of meeting the challenges which so many settlers failed to survive. I took life as it was presented to me and then did my best to improve it." If North Dakota proved less than Canaan, homesteading for Calof and women like her provided freedom and opportunity and in the end enabled her to say, "We tamed the land."

As a Jew, Rachael Calof was a minority among women homesteaders, but beyond the practice of her religion and customs shared with other Jewish neighbors, her life differed little from that of other women who settled on the Great Plains. They all experienced cramped, uncomfortable, even dirty living conditions, unending work, and often worry caring for family and farm. Privation and want were familiar feelings for most

Figure 9.5: In 1883, Nannie Alderson settled on a ranch near Miles City, Montana. Alderson experienced the boom years of the open-range cattle industry, and she knew disappointment as well as the tenuous balance between economic success and failure as a rancher. She reflected on her life as a rancher's wife with a sense of accomplishment and inner peace. Courtesy of Montana Historical Society, Helena.

women settlers, and Calof's life epitomizes the resilience, tenacity, and stoicism that characterized their lives, all of which make a lie of anyone's romantic visions of their experiences settling the agricultural frontier.

Not all women homesteaders had as grueling an experience as Rachael Calof or moved west unwillingly. Nannie Tiffany, for example, left West Virginia at the age of seventeen to live with an aunt in Atchison, Kansas, where she met her future husband, Walter Alderson. In 1883, at the age of twenty-three, she moved west to a ranch near Miles City, Montana. There, she recalled, "everyone, it seemed was making fabulous sums of money or was about to make them; no one thought of losses; and for the next year my husband and I were to breathe that air of optimism and share all those rose-colored expectations." During the course of the Aldersons' lives together they would move several times after their fortunes faded. "In all the years of my marriage," she wrote, "I never had trees over my head; they could have been planted, but we never lived long enough in one place for them to grow." Even so, a boundless spirit of optimism characterized this settler on the western frontier. "We didn't mind the hard things because we didn't expect them to last," she observed. "Our little dirt-roofed shack didn't matter because our other house was building. And even the new house was to be only a stepping stone to something better. We didn't expect to live on a ranch all our lives."

Like many who moved west to settle on the land, raise cattle and crops, and prosper, Nannie Alderson remembered, "It all looked so easy. The cows would have calves; and two years from now their calves would have calves, and we could figure it all out with pencil and paper, how in no time we'd be cattle kings." Drought that began during the summer of 1884, however, stunted the grass, and the inordinately severe winter of 1886–1887 killed many of their cattle and ruined her dreams of wealth and luxury from settling on Montana's grasslands.

Despite the loss of their cattle and near bankruptcy, Nannie and her husband began anew, living and working with the hired hands in a spirit of equality that proved extraordinary even in the West. "Few families living in Montana had their cowboys live with them as we did," she remembered. "Nobody then thought of them as romantic. They were regarded as a wild and undesirable lot of citizens, but I always thought there was much injustice in this. Nice people in Miles City would as soon have thought of inviting a rattle snake into their homes as a cowboy." Certainly a sense of class divided the early settlers in Montana, and Alderson recalled, "The *only* places that made them [cowboys] welcome were the house of prostitution and the saloon. The wonder is that despite all that they kept their finer qualities intact," particularly good manners, cleanliness, and "pride of appearance." She did allow, however, that when the cowboys went to town, "their first idea was to get drunk and make a lot of noise; their next was to squander their money."

Although drought, hard winters, and the boom and bust years of cattle ranching in the West brought periodic economic setbacks, Alderson remained optimistic. When her years of ranch life ended in 1893, after she and her husband moved to Miles City so that their ten-year-old daughter could attend school, she looked back on her decision to settle in the West. "I always felt that I personally had a great deal to be thankful for," she wrote. "I was healthier than the average woman." Although she admitted that she had led a "hard life," she did not regret her decision to make a life in the West.

Even though many settlers, like the Aldersons, particularly those on the Great Plains, migrated along roughly parallel lines of latitude from Ohio, Indiana, Illinois, and Missouri, many foreign-born immigrants, like Rachael Calof, also considered settlement in the trans-Mississippi West the best solution for their own private economic problems and personal aspirations, with Germans, Canadians, British, Scandinavians, German-Russians, and Bohemians or Czechs providing most of the cultural and ethnic mix of the settlement population. Lured by family and friends, railroad literature, and agents and a generous federal land policy, foreign-born immigrants, most of whom were farmers, particularly considered the Great Plains an inviting region for settlement. Like native-born settlers, most European immigrants who settled in the West migrated as families. They were pulled by the possibility of land ownership and pushed by poverty, land enclosure for grazing, and overpopulation that decreased employment opportunities at home. Some, like the Germans and German Russians, fled military service, whereas others, like the Jews, escaped persecution, but all sought economic opportunity, and landownership was an overpowering and empowering attraction that offered security, independence, and prestige.

In addition to the letters home that spurred chain migration, a host of colonization societies, like the Irish Catholic Colonization Society, Hebrew Union Agricultural Society, and the Swedish Agricultural Society, served as philanthropic organizations to aid the settlement of various ethnoreligious groups on the Great Plains. Leaders in these organizations believed such settlers would not only improve their own economic fortunes but also preserve their religion, language, and culture by settling together. The immigration societies worked closely with the railroads and government officials to help the immigrants acquire railroad, state, or federal lands. The churches also provided important support for settlers on the Great Plains. Lutherans, Catholics, and Mennonites, for example, urged immigrants to settle where congregations of their own faith already existed. The church would provide security, identity, and unity while helping newcomers adapt to life on the plains. By so doing, the church became the most important institution of the immigrant settlers and the only one to survive their transition to English-speaking society.

The Germans and German-Russians were the most numerous immigrants to settle on the Great Plains, particularly in Nebraska, Kansas, and the Dakota Territory. Although most were farmers, they divided themselves in Lutheran, Catholic, and Mennonite communities, but they did not associate with each other or outsiders. Immigrants from the British Isles constituted the second-largest group of foreign-born settlers on the Great Plains, whereas the Norwegians made up the largest group of Scandinavians, half of whom settled in North Dakota, followed by the Swedes, who, like the Czechs, took a particular liking to Nebraska, where they formed strong rural communities.

The speed of assimilation of foreign-born groups depended on the frequency of interaction with American-born settlers, the size of the ethnic community, wealth, mobility, education, and the ability to learn English. Among the various immigrant groups, the English, Scots, Irish, and Welsh assimilated the most rapidly because of cultural similarities with their American-born neighbors, whereas the Scandinavians assimilated the quickest of the non-English-speaking settlers because they learned English rapidly and their social, cultural, and political customs easily integrated with those of their American counterparts on the frontier. The German Russians were the slowest foreign-born ethnic group to assimilate.

The German Russians who settled in Kansas, Nebraska, and the Dakota Territory during the 1870s and 1880s lived in or near agricultural villages, either Catholic or Protestant, and they commonly moved from one colonized area to another. The German Russian networks of migration and social communication were well established for themselves but closed to outsiders socially and culturally, though not economically. The German Russian communities in the Dakota Territory as well as Kansas and Nebraska became grain-shipping points along the railroads, open to all farmers in the area. The German Russians were accustomed to a harsh climate and prairie lands, and they easily adapted to their new environment while maintaining their language and cultural practices.

The Norwegians and Swedes who settled in North Dakota, Kansas, and Nebraska developed important links to their home countries by sending a considerable volume of letters to family and friends, urging them to settle on the Great Plains. Communications between those who had gone and those who remained via letters and newspaper articles provided assurances and reduced the uncertainty of migration and settlement in the West. The agricultural settlement of foreign born in the West also involved more than the mere population of rich grasslands and river valleys and the development of small-scale farms. The immigrants from abroad transferred their culture and social habits, and small enclaves of ethnic homogeneity prevailed until acculturation and assimilation into English-speaking American society began to occur, usually with the second generation, that is, the sons and daughters of the immigrant settlers.

In general, American-born settlers expected foreign-born settlers to accept American cultural and social standards, and they had little appreciation for their problems born of psychological and cultural stress because of emigration and settlement in a strange, new land. Simply put, American-born settlers welcomed foreign-born immigrants provided they conformed to American social standards. In 1870 foreign-born settlers constituted 39 percent of the population in Wyoming and Montana, 34 percent in the Dakota Territory, 25 percent in Nebraska, and 13 percent in Kansas. At the turn of the twentieth century, foreign-born immigrants and their native-born children constituted 78 percent of North Dakota's and 47 percent of Nebraska's population. Consequently, distinctive cultural differences prevailed among the settlers.

Hispanics, particularly near Santa Fe, also moved onto the southern Great Plains. By 1870, Hispanic settlers claimed considerable land along the headwaters of the Pecos and Canadian rivers as well as on the plains east of the Sangre de Cristo Mountains northward to the upper reaches of the Arkansas River. Hispanic settlers also moved into the San Luis Valley and located along the streams flowing into the Rio Grande as well as the headwaters of the San Juan and Little Colorado rivers. By the early 1870s, Texas cattlemen and Mormon farmers competed for the lands of these Hispanic settlers, who usually lost title to their claims in court. The desert Southwest, however, had little appeal to settlers who found the rich lands and climate of the Pacific Northwest and Great Plains more desirable. Moreover, the Southern Pacific Railroad was not completed through the area until 1882, and periodic Indian problems until the surrender of Geronimo in 1886 also discouraged many settlers. In addition, the lack of irrigation slowed, if not prevented, agricultural settlement of the Southwest. Self-interest, however, superseded individualism, and some residents turned to the federal government for aid to develop irrigation systems that would permit and enhance the agricultural settlement of the region. In 1879, John C. Frémont, territorial governor of Arizona, correctly contended that without irrigation water, "this country cannot be used for what it is worth." But the federal development and financing that he and others sought would not come until the twentieth century.

Although African American settlers reached the Great Plains before the Civil War, primarily as slaves for the Cherokees and Creeks and as bonded servants for army officers, after 1865 black settlers worked as cowboys and cooks for railroad construction crews. In 1877, however, large groups of African Americans began settling in the West. Known as Exodusters, they fled persecution and poverty in the South. They established the largest black colony, called Nicodemus, in Kansas, because African American settlers considered it the epitome of a free state. In Kansas, John Brown had made an important stand for their freedom, and the Republican-ruled government offered economic opportunity based on land ownership uncolored by racial prejudice.

R. Douglas Hurt

The Oklahoma Territory also attracted black settlers during the late 1880s. Drought and economic hard times prevented most African American settlers from remaining on the land, and the majority soon sought employment in the towns and cities, usually as menial workers. Texas did not permit homesteading by African Americans.

Speed and adaptation, then, characterized the agricultural settlement of the frontier West. By 1900 settlers had occupied the best lands from the Great Plains to California and the Pacific Northwest. Until the twentieth century mostly native-born men, women, and children from the Northeast and Midwest primarily settled the western agricultural frontier, except for the predominant settlement of Texas and Oklahoma by southerners. No matter where the settlers originated, they claimed and exploited the land on an unprecedented scale.

Despite drought and economic depression in the Great Plains during the late nineteenth century and large-scale, highly capitalized industrial agriculture in California, the West continued to lure agricultural settlers who sought the American dream of independence and prosperity that they believed could be best gained through the ownership of land and an agricultural life. Foreign-born settlers tended to remain on their lands, but American-born settlers frequently considered land an investment for future sale, given the right price. For them, land equaled capital more than security.

Every agricultural settler in the frontier West had his or her own story wrought on the anvil of individual experience and usually tempered by hardship. Most settlers accepted their problems and difficulties as facts of life, and only a comparative few returned to the East. At the same time settlement was fluid and the people in frequent motion—moving, visiting, and traveling. Isolation lasted only a few years, and it frequently resulted more from inadequate transportation than the absence of neighbors within a reasonable distance no matter the season. With the exception of a few ethnic groups, like the German Russians, or religious groups, like the Mennonites, many settlers moved again after their original trek into the West. Complexity, variation, and mobility, then, characterized the agricultural settlement of the West. Although the Pacific Northwest and Great Plains drew settlers anxious to acquire land and improve their fortunes, California never served as a promised land for poor agricultural settlers.

By the turn of the twentieth century, success and failure as well as hope and despair characterized the agricultural settlement of the frontier West. Time of settlement, location, and the environment as well as ethnicity, capital, transportation, perseverance, community support, and government policy were responsible for lasting settlements, with the absence of any one bringing possible failure. Settlers always hoped life would improve during the next year. Hope and options permitted adjustments, that is, the adaptation necessary for settlement in the frontier West. As a result, approximately 1.1 million farms and 130.7 million acres of cropland were created in the western states and territories between 1860 and 1900. By 1900 western farmers and ranchers raised 50 percent of the cattle, 56 percent of the sheep, 25 percent of the hogs, and 58 percent of the wheat in the nation.

If the frontier West, however, proved disappointing for many agricultural settlers between 1840 and 1900, it continued to lure immigrants. Tens of thousands of private, personal decisions determined the settlement of the frontier West during the last half of the nineteenth century. Most settlers from within the United States and abroad, however, chose migration and settlement far from their homes because the West promised a better life. Beyond this generalization any analysis of settlement is fraught with difficulty, and it reveals a complexity best likened to a puzzle with a multiplicity of pieces shaped by economics, culture, and government policy and colored by ethnicity, race, class, and gender, the dimensions of which were determined by the environment, chance, and circumstance. Still, they came. Indeed, more homesteaders would claim 160 acres during the early twentieth century than before, particularly in North and South Dakota, although these lands were marginal and the failure rate proved high. Moreover, without the promise of free or cheap lands on which to build a better life, the agricultural settlement of the frontier West would have developed far differently, largely determined by the boom and bust of the mining camps scattered across the region and by the cities that developed for commerce, particularly along the coast. No matter whether the agricultural settlers stayed on the land or sold out and moved to claim other lands, the West proved the promise of American life a reality. No matter what the economists would say later about the profitability and economic viability of settling on the agricultural frontier, most settlers thought the potential rewards worth the risks and land ownership in the West the equivalent of the promised land.

Essay on Sources

Broad introductions to the settlement of the American West can be found in Walter Nugent, *Into the West: The Story of Its People* (New York: Knopf, 1999), and Richard White, *"It's Your Misfortune and None of My Own": A History of the American West* (Norman: University of Oklahoma Press, 1991). Nugent emphasizes immigration and migration, whereas White focuses on the relationship of settlement to the environment. White also provides a good overview of federal land policy, with Nugent furnishing important statistical evidence of immigration and settlement rates.

R. Douglas Hurt

For an introduction to cowboys and cattlemen, see Charles Siringo, *A Texas Cowboy: Or, Fifteen Years on the Hurricane Deck of a Spanish Pony,* ed. Richard W. Etulain (New York: Penguin, 2000), and Robert R. Dykstra, *The Cattle Towns* (New York: Knopf, 1968). David Igler provides the most comprehensive assessment of the lives of Henry Miller and Charles Lux, particularly in regard to environmental change and settlement in the San Joaquin Valley. See his *Industrial Cowboys: Miller & Lux and the Transformation of the Far West, 1850–1920* (Berkeley: University of California Press, 2001), as well as Igler, "Industrial Cowboys: Corporate Ranching in Late Nineteenth-Century California," *Agricultural History* 69 (spring 1995): 201–15.

Western historians differ considerably about the migration and settlement experiences of women. Lillian Schlissel found women reluctant to leave home for settlement in the West and their decisions dependent on their husbands. She also argues that gendered work roles blended on the overland trails but that women assumed far more male duties and women ultimately found opportunity in the settlement experience. See Schlissel's *Women's Diaries of the Westward Journey* (New York: Schocken, 1982). John Mack Faragher contends that traditional divisions of labor according to gender as well as the domination of men typified relations on the overland trails in *Women and Men on the Overland Trail* (New Haven, Conn.: Yale University Press, 1979). Sandra Myers provides a more complex assessment of women settlers in *Western Women and the Frontier Experience, 1800–1915* (Albuquerque: University of New Mexico Press, 1982), whereas Julie Roy Jeffrey argues that women who migrated west worked to preserve their gendered roles and femininity, that is, their identity, within their domestic world. See Jeffrey, *Frontier Women: "Civilizing" the West? 1840–1880,* rev. ed. (New York: Hill and Wang, 1998), and Joanna L. Stratton, *Pioneer Women: Voices from the Kansas Frontier* (New York: Simon & Schuster, 1981). Glenda Riley provides a comparative study of the women who settled the prairie and plains in her *The Female Frontier: A Comparative View of Women on the Prairie and the Plains* (Lawrence: University Press of Kansas, 1988). See also Sarah Deutsch, *No Separate Refuge: Culture, Class, and Gender on an Anglo-Hispanic Frontier in the American Southwest, 1880–1940* (New York: Oxford University Press, 1987). For a brief survey with excellent photographs of women settlers, see Linda Peavy and Ursula Smith, *Pioneer Women: The Lives of Women on the Frontier* (Norman: University of Oklahoma Press, 1996). Two important recollections of settlement by women homesteaders are J. Sanford Rikoon, ed., *Rachael Calof's Story: Jewish Homesteader on the Northern Plains* (Bloomington: Indiana University Press, 1995), and Nannie T. Alderson and Helena Huntington Smith, *A Bride Goes West* (Lincoln: University of Nebraska Press, 1969).

William A. Bowen provides an excellent introduction to the early agricultural settlement of Oregon in his *The Willamette Valley: Migration and Settlement on the Oregon Frontier* (Seattle: University of Washington Press, 1978). William G. Robbins discusses the way settlers changed the ecology in Oregon in *Landscapes of Promise: The Oregon Story, 1800–1940* (Seattle: University of Washington Press, 1997). Alexander Campbell McGregor traces the settlement and development of the Columbia Plateau and Palouse country for sheep and cattle raising and its transformation to wheat raising in his *Counting Sheep: From Open Range to Agribusiness on the Columbia Plateau* (Seattle: University of Washington Press, 1982). See also John Fahey, *The Inland Empire: Unfolding Years, 1879–1929* (Seattle: University of Washington Press, 1986).

For land policy, see Paul W. Gates, *History of Public Land Law Development* (Washington, D.C.: Government Printing Office, 1968), and John Opie, *The Law of the Land: Two Hundred Years of American Farmland Policy* (Lincoln: University of Nebraska Press, 1987). The work of land agents is best studied in David M. Emmons, *Garden in the Grasslands: Boomer Literature of the Central Great Plains* (Lincoln: University of Nebraska Press, 1971), and Jan Blodgett, *Land of Bright Promise: Advertising the Texas Panhandle and South Plains, 1870–1917* (Austin: University of Texas Press, 1988).

Gilbert Fite offers an important, detailed study of the agricultural settlement of the trans-Mississippi West in *The Farmers' Frontier, 1865–1900* (New York: Holt, Rinehart, 1966), whereas James R. Shortridge emphasizes the migration and location of settlers in the central Great Plains in his *Peopling the Plains: Who Settled Where in Frontier Kansas* (Lawrence: University Press of Kansas, 1995). See also Shortridge, "The Heart of the Prairie: Culture Areas in the Central and Northern Great Plains," *Great Plains Quarterly* 8 (fall 1987): 206–21. For differences among ethnic groups that influenced settlement patterns as well as assimilation and acculturation, see D. Aiden McQuillan, *Prevailing Over Time: Ethnic Adjustment on the Kansas Prairies, 1875–1925* (Lincoln: University of Nebraska Press, 1990), and Frederick C. Luebke, "Ethnic Group Settlement on the Great Plains," *Western Historical Quarterly* 8 (October 1977): 405–30.

John Hudson has written extensively on the settlement of the West. See "The Study of Western Frontier Populations," in *The American West: New Perspectives, New Dimensions,* ed. Jerome O. Steffen (Norman: University of Oklahoma Press, 1979), 35–60; "Two Dakota Homestead Frontiers," *Annals of the Association of American Geographers* 63 (December 1973): 442–62; and "Migration to an American Frontier," *Annals of the Association of American Geographers* 66 (June 1979): 242–65.

Chapter 10

"Buffalo Bill" Cody and Annie Oakley
Romancing the West

Glenda Riley

On a dreary December day in 1884, William F. Cody, better known as Buffalo Bill, declined adding a woman sharpshooter to his fledgling Wild West troupe. Despite Cody's rejection, Phoebe Ann Moses, or Annie Oakley, did not give up hope. The following spring Oakley and her husband/manager, Frank Butler, learned that the famed shooter Doc Bogardus had left Cody's employ, so they approached Cody again, this time suggesting that Annie give three unpaid trial performances. After Cody hesitantly agreed, Oakley and Butler traveled to the Wild West location in Louisville, Kentucky, where Annie took advantage of seemingly deserted grounds to practice. As she finished, an elegantly dressed man approached, shouting, "Fine! Wonderful!" The man was Nate Salsbury, Cody's partner, who hired Annie on the spot, initiating a seventeen-year association between Cody and Oakley.

When Cody and Oakley joined forces, the American frontier had a well-established image in literature, art, and popular media. Cody and Oakley carried it to another level. Cody's genius lay in giving the romanticized western frontier shape and form in three dimensions. His epic figures were of flesh and blood who acted out the western saga in front of spectators' eyes. Noise and smell reinforced the aura of reality, and scenery transported the spectator to a western scene. Cody's West jumped from the page or picture frame, no longer flat words or one-dimensional art. Annie Oakley added the female element, much appreciated by the women and girls in Wild West audiences. Oakley portrayed a western woman adept with those important symbols of the West—guns and horses—yet retained her modesty and femininity, thus appealing to Victorian audiences as a true lady.

From the mid-1880s into the early twentieth century Cody and Oakley became wildly successful performers who helped artists and writers mythologize the American West. Yet they were far more than showpeople. In the highly effective format of a living West, Cody and Oakley exposed millions of adoring fans—primarily white—to their performance subtexts, or tropes, which had an incalculable impact on viewers' attitudes and beliefs. In addition to presenting a heroic western frontier, where men and women proved themselves strong, courageous, and determined, Cody and Oakley became leading interpreters of Manifest Destiny and of its casualties, American Indians. For largely white spectators in the United States and Europe, Cody and Oakley not only validated imperialistic principles, but stereotyped American Indians as primitive "others." Cody and Oakley also defined the nature of the western men and women who secured the West for the United States. By creating the cowboy and the cowgirl and imbuing them with ideals of white manhood and womanhood, Cody and Oakley entered the era's ongoing debate concerning proper gender roles for men and women, popularizing standards to which many Americans soon aspired. Unfortunately, along the way, Cody and Oakley also encouraged inaccurate and even careless ideas about western peoples and landscapes.

When on that important day in 1885 that Cody and Oakley decided to link their careers, they seemed an odd pair. Neither was a native westerner, an accomplished thespian, or an experienced producer. They came from the Midwest, where their childhoods had followed remarkably similar courses. Cody was born in 1846 just west of the Mississippi River in LeClaire, Iowa, the year this frontier territory achieved statehood. He spent his early years in Kansas, where his father was embroiled in abolitionist politics. When Cody was eleven, his father died, leaving the boy the economic mainstay of a family of six. A few years later, in 1860, Oakley was born east of the Mississippi in Darke County, Ohio, fifty-three years after Ohio had become a state. Annie Oakley's father died when she was six; like Cody, she learned to help support her mother and six siblings. When they were youngsters, Cody and Oakley became proficient at trapping and shooting small game, which left little time for formal schooling.

As young adults, however, Cody's and Oakley's life paths diverged. Cody became the prototype westerner, building a reputation as an intrepid rider for the short-lived Pony Express, a formidable buffalo hunter, an exceptional shooter and horseman, an expert guide for hunters, and a fearless Indian scout. In 1872, he received a Congressional Medal of Honor for his service as a scout and made his stage debut in *The Scouts of the Prairie; or Red Deviltry As It Is.* In the meantime, Cody had become a family man, albeit one more often absent than at home. In 1865 he had married Louisa Frederici. Because Louisa disliked the West and show business, Cody maintained a family home first in Leavenworth, Kansas; next, during his stage touring days,

Figure 10.1: Principals of the Wild West troupe in London in 1887. Buffalo Bill Cody is third from left in the first row, and Annie Oakley is third from right in the second row, holding a rifle. Courtesy of the Annie Oakley Foundation, Greenville, Ohio.

the Codys lived in Rochester, New York; and beginning in 1878, Cody built a home for Louisa in North Platte, Nebraska. Rather than hugging the land, Cody's North Platte house, an imposing Victorian design of Louisa's choosing, jutted against the windy Nebraska sky as defiant of frontier life as Louisa herself.

Annie Oakley followed a very different course. As a teenager in southwestern Ohio, she earned respect as a hunter of small game, which she shot cleanly through the head, preserving the meat for eating. Probably in 1876, she defeated stage shooter Frank Butler in a local shooting match, then later married him. The date of their marriage is disputed, being either in 1876 or 1882. During the early 1880s, the couple—billed as Butler and Oakley—established their reputation as team shooters on the vaudeville circuit and with the Sells Brothers Circus. By the mid-1880s, Frank and Annie were looking for a better venue, one that offered family entertainment, fair pay, and the opportunity to keep their act free of deception. In December 1884, Frank noticed an announcement in the *New Orleans Picayune* that Buffalo Bill Cody's recently formed Wild West Park would soon arrive on Canal Street, near the Sells Brothers' lot. Frank decided that Annie, who was often more popular with crowds than he, should apply for a position with the Wild West.

Figure 10.2: Buffalo Bill, Arta (daughter), and Louisa (wife) Cody, c. 1870. Courtesy of the Buffalo Bill Historical Center, Cody, Wyoming.

Show business brought Cody and Oakley together. Despite their differences, Cody and Oakley were a good match in many ways. Because of their impoverished childhoods, both understood the importance of earning a good income. They also adhered to such values as hard work, loyalty, honesty, and generosity to those in need. Soon Cody and Oakley came to like and admire each other; he called her "Missie," and she addressed him as "Colonel." On one occasion, he inscribed Oakley's autograph book to "the loveliest and truest little woman, both in heart and aim in all the world." Another time Oakley described Cody as "one of the nicest men in the world."

Moreover, Cody and Oakley were talented, attractive people who had a strong sense of the theatrical and were masters of guns and horses. Clearly, Cody knew far more about the West than Oakley, but both had a canny sense of audience appeal. Even though they were not natives of the Great Plains, which Americans increasingly considered the heart of the Wild West, Cody and Oakley became adept at presenting the West their viewers wanted to see. Both were highly attuned to audience response, even to the point of modifying bits of themselves for the good of the show. Cody, for example, had to forgo some of the historical points he hoped to make about Indian culture. Oakley, who was a sensational shot when standing on her head with her skirts strapped around her legs, refused to perform such an unladylike feat in public and taught shooter Johnny Baker to do the trick instead. Nor were Cody and Oakley satisfied with a static program. The pair changed with the times, sometimes in small ways and other times large. Cody, for example, developed new acts and in 1893 introduced his Congress of Rough Riders of the world, whereas Oakley added more difficult stunts and gradually shortened her skirts to harmonize with current fashions.

Cody and Oakley were also natural showpeople. Cody's drive for authenticity included convincing audiences they had been transported temporarily to the West. For a man of inventiveness, such as Cody, sounds and smells were easy. For example, the vignette known as "The Prairie" opened with Cody chasing real bison. In 1887, the Smithsonian ranked Cody's herd as fourth largest in the nation. Scenery was a bit more difficult. To re-create western vistas, Cody used every artifice, including elaborate painted backdrops set up in the arena to enhance the historical sketches played out in front of them. Some of the backdrops were remarkable in size and detail, depicting a rocky terrain with old-growth forests, yet showing every rut and every leaf.

Oakley, too, used props and elegant stage scenery when she appeared apart from Cody's Wild West. Because Oakley and Butler had to earn a living during the winter months, or the off-season of the Wild West, they produced a number of western plays starring Annie. Of course, sounds and smells were less attractive in theaters than in open-air arenas, so Oakley and Butler relied on scenery and lighting to re-create the frontier West. One of their productions was *Miss Rora,* a melodrama that played American and English theaters the winter of 1896–1897 and was billed as "illustrative of life on the frontier." The West of *Miss Rora* was a domesticated place where guns were used in play and horses were pets. On theater stages, Annie shot glass balls thrown in the air, as well as a variety of other objects. Oakley even rode her horse Gipsy onstage, although Gipsy's hooves sometimes broke through stage floors. Gipsy also went up and down with Annie in theater freight elevators.

A later production, *The Western Girl,* opened in November 1902. In addition to guns and horses, Oakley and Butler incorporated lavish spectacular scenery, painted on high-grade linen cloth, which advance publicity explained reproduced the "days of the wild and wooly West." One of the most spectacular scenes was the canyon of the Colorado River by moonlight, which, advertising noted, added a touch of realism to this "startling picture of the Wild West." Annie used her own horses onstage, especially Little Bess, whom she rode, and several others that pulled the old Leadville stagecoach, which looked much like Cody's much-vaunted historic Deadwood stage that appeared in virtually every Wild West performance. Oakley and Butler had learned well from Cody, yet they went one step farther. Their West, assembled on a theater stage, seemed even more accessible than Cody's arena West.

Even though Oakley's *Western Girl* was a hit of the 1902 season, Cody's Wild West was a hit from the mid-1880s to the early twentieth century. Cody's skill in combining entertainment and "fact" and Oakley's willingness to add a female frontier to the mix led to large audiences and many competitors. Because Cody's Wild West claimed to give a historically accurate picture of the development of the West, Cody, and later Oakley, had to address the prevailing philosophy of Manifest Destiny, which held that providence intended white settlers to sweep across the West, spreading "civilization" and "progress" in their wake. Because Cody and Oakley viewed the West as a frontier where white expansion fueled all action, their performance texts often reflected the wildly popular idea of white people struggling and eventually conquering the West, its earlier inhabitants, and its resources. Always with their eyes on the bottom line, they tried to present what their audiences wanted—successful white conquest of the frontier West.

Of course, the concept of conquest was well established by the time Cody and Oakley came along. The principles of what was eventually dubbed Manifest Destiny had numerous proponents, including a huge number of writers. One of the best-known and earliest examples was James Fenimore Cooper, whose 1826 novel, *The Last of the Mohicans,* clearly indicated that whites would always prevail over Native Americans, many of whom, male and female, were "barbarous" and "devilishly cruel." In later novels, fictionalized white explorers, traders and trappers, and pioneers became even more heroic and adventuresome. Cooper's *The Pathfinder* (1840) set the tone with his white hero prevailing over all difficulties, including Native American resistance.

Meanwhile, captivity narratives, a long-established genre in which women and men held by American Indians told their stories for profit, became widely available, courtesy of improved printing presses. For example, a captivity survivor named Abbie Gardner-Sharp wrote her version of Iowa's Spirit Lake Massacre of 1857 and sold her account in a souvenir shop that was formerly, she explained, the very cabin in which the "depredations" took place. Newspaper journalists also joined

Glenda Riley

the clamor. In 1866 (the year the less-than-enthusiastic Louisa Cody arrived in Leavenworth), the *Leavenworth Daily Times* reported on two female captives who had been held for ten weeks, during which time they "suffered all the cruelties that the fiend-like malignity and heart-lessness of their cowardly captors could invent."

By the 1860s, small pamphlets called dime novels further enhanced the image of white western heroes and eroded that of Indians by includ-ing outrageous tales about Indians who were supposedly "murderous" and "barbarous" foes of all whites. Dime novels, the first of which appeared in the United States in 1860, were small books, originally in bright orange wrappers, that sold for ten cents and contained highly patriotic, nationalistic stories. Some dime novelists specialized in west-ern tales, often showing white men saving damsels in distress. In one case, men placed "white maidens" in a grotto, then fought off approaching "savages." During the 1870s and 1880s, other writers scoured the West for real-life heroes—or for colorful personalities like Calamity Jane or Wild Bill Hickok—that they could transform into characters in their books. By the 1870s and 1880s, such authors as Prentiss Ingraham and Ned Buntline cranked out novel after novel. Beginning with the first installment of Ned Buntline's serial story *Buffalo Bill: The King of Border Men,* which appeared in the *New York Weekly,* Cody became a staple of western adventures. He received more coverage in dime novels than any other figure, starring in 557 original dime novels by twenty-two authors; adding reprints brought the total to 1,700 issues.

At the same time, artists and sculptors added their perspectives on the western frontier. One early artist was Seth Eastman, an army officer who painted homey scenes around his post, Fort Snelling in Minnesota. In 1848, for example, Eastman's *The Tanner* depicted a Native American woman preparing a skin for use or perhaps for trade. Meanwhile, more prolific and well-known artists like George Catlin and Karl Bodmer traveled alone or accompanied royal, scientific, or military expeditions that penetrated deeper into the West. These men recorded in sketch-books and on canvas their impressions of western landscapes, wildlife, and humanity. For example, Catlin and Bodmer characterized American Indians as stoic, unrefined, and a bit exotic. Other artists, notably John Mix Stanley, represented them as a "vanishing" people. In his 1857 painting, *Last of Their Race,* Stanley presented a touching por-trait of a handful of Indians who had been pushed, by white settlement, to the very edge of the Pacific Ocean.

When Cody became an impresario of outdoor performances during the early 1880s, he had two widely known and loved legends to draw on: one of the West, the other of Buffalo Bill. Yet he hoped to produce more than an amusing show. He envisioned himself as a purveyor of history. Even as the frontier West was fast disappearing, Cody was determined to bring the Wild West as he had known and lived it to viewers increasingly enmeshed in the turmoil of urban living, stratification of social classes, and an industrial revolution, replete with labor problems, including strikes and riots.

To achieve his ends, Cody had experimented with a number of productions. The first was the "Old Glory Blow Out" on July 4, 1882, in his hometown of North Platte, Nebraska. Cody hoped for at least a hundred participants; he was stunned when a thousand showed up. The following year, Cody joined with the stage shooter W. F. Carver to present the Hon. W. F. Cody and Dr. W. F. Carver's Rocky Mountain and Prairie Exhibition, which opened in Omaha, Nebraska, in May 1883. Cody later wrote that it "was my effort, in depicting the West, to depict it as it was." When the troupe played in Connecticut, the *Hartford Courant* pronounced the performance the "best-open air show ever seen." Although public interest in a Wild West exhibition clearly existed, Cody and Carver could not resolve their differences and parted with great bitterness.

Cody next turned to stage entrepreneur Nate Salsbury, convincing him to become a partner in "Buffalo Bill's Wild West—America's National Entertainment," to open during spring 1884. Salsbury insisted on tighter management, which he provided. He also asked Cody to fight less with his wife and avoid alcohol, both of which Cody repeatedly promised but found difficult to achieve. Salsbury also recommended stronger themes, but the content of these came largely from Cody, who pictured this new Wild West as "a true prescript of life on the frontier as I knew it to be, and which no fictitious pen can describe." Also, Cody now had more in mind than re-creating a genuine West. In this and succeeding seasons, he presented what he called an "object lesson" that would inform and "instruct" audiences on no less a topic than the "nation's progress," by which Cody meant white domination of the Great Plains and its Indian inhabitants.

Cody hoped his approach would attract viewers—male and female, native and immigrant, old and young—who had, or would soon develop, a patriotic allegiance to white expansionism in the West. After all, the nineteenth century was one of Manifest Destiny, a term first used in 1845 (the year before Cody's birth) by newspaper reporter John Louis O'Sullivan. Manifest Destiny meant that the movement of whites westward was not only a sign of progress, but was divinely inspired. Along with thousands of other Americans, Cody grew up listening to Manifest Destiny discourse and believing that white people held the key to the nation's future. By moving westward, "settling" the land, and removing Native inhabitants, whites not only fulfilled God's plan, but gave Americans elements of their national character, including such qualities as persistence, hard work, and dominance over "barbaric" peoples who opposed them.

Manifest Destiny also had its altruistic side, enjoining western settlers to help "civilize" Native Americans. Whether Native Americans agreed or not, migrants were to give white civilization in exchange for Indian land. Nationalistic rhetoric told white pioneers that it was their responsibility to teach their religion, technology, and white values to Native Americans. Moreover, given growing worry about ethics and integrity raised by industrialization, Americans who migrated westward to help others would also offset fears about the declining morals of Americans. These goals appeared so ethical, at least to whites, that critics usually kept their opinions to themselves. Today critics label Cody a racist. Other commentators see him as a man who reflected his times. It is unlikely that a nineteenth-century white man like Cody would reject his era's values and beliefs, replacing them with twenty-first-century attitudes. Still, current scholars of colonialism argue that a person's acceptance of the ideas of his era does not make his or her views moral or excuse the damage done.

Cody certainly wielded tremendous power over public opinion. As a skillful contributor to popular culture, he endorsed white dominance, hegemony, and policies. More specifically, by presenting Indians as a simple and inevitably doomed people, he in essence underwrote damaging policies. For example, missionaries who believed it was their responsibility to spread Christianity, along with American-style democracy, helped Indians in some ways but also drove a wedge between Indians and their cultures. Another case of harmful and wrongheaded thinking was the "Indian wars" that erupted on the plains after the Civil War to force Indians onto reservations, to keep them on reservations, or to exterminate them. In 1879 and in 1880, for instance, Mimbres Apache Chief Victorio and his people shuttled back and forth between New Mexico and Old Mexico to avoid going to a reservation where they had starved and seen others die because of broken promises and inadequate rations. Even though Cody the individual opposed such treatment of Native peoples, Cody the showman encouraged destructive actions by portraying Indians as a primitive and "vanishing" race.

In 1886, Cody and Salsbury adopted a new and enlarged format that made the themes of Manifest Destiny and declining Indian peoples even clearer. Called *The Drama of Civilization*, this Wild West performance contained five segments: "The Primeval Forest," "The Prairie," "The Cattle Ranch," "The Mining Camp," and "Custer's Last Stand." The succession of scenes led viewers from the days of wild Indians and wild animals to the arrival of white "civilization." Included were "The Attack on the Settlers' Cabin," "The Rescue of the Deadwood Stage," "The Pony Express," "The Buffalo Hunt," and later "The Battle at Summit Springs," in which Cody reenacted a real fight but transformed it from a skirmish into an impressive military engagement. Shooting acts were also included, notably one by Annie Oakley, who carried out the western theme in her costume, a buckskinlike dress (never trousers) and a cowboy-style hat with a star pinned to it.

Even though the program concluded with Custer's 1876 debacle at the Little Big Horn, the show avoided any suggestion of defeatism. It was made clear to the audience that sneaky Indians had mounted an ambush, not quite thought to be cricket in European-style warfare. In this scenario, Indians became unscrupulous assailants, whereas whites were innocent and unsuspecting prey who made the patriotic sacrifice of their lives. Then Cody himself appeared to wreak revenge by fighting Yellow Hair (also known as Yellow Hand) and his band of Cheyenne in the Battle of War Bonnet Creek in Nebraska in 1876.

Confident of success, Cody and Salsbury decided to give up one-night stands and to stage the new Wild West for an extended period at the recently constructed open-air arena and amphitheater at Erastina resort on Staten Island outside of New York City. The revised program proved so popular that the Wild West played at Erastina for a full six months. Within four weeks, the Wild West attracted fourteen thousand people a day to a twelve-thirty performance or a seven o'clock show under artificial lights. Such crowds not only meant profits for Cody and Salsbury but added up to millions of minds to absorb the Wild West's messages, including the idea that white settlement of the American West, with its attendant devastation of Native peoples, was a triumph for Americans and for democracy. In case viewers could not figure out the message for themselves, publicity agent "Arizona" John Burke guided their interpretations by means of a "Salutory" printed at the beginning of program booklets. After invoking Americans' patriotic and intense interest in "our rapidly extending frontier," Burke noted that the "pressure of the white man," especially in settlement and railroad building, worked with "the military power of the General Government" to destroy the "barriers behind which the Indian fought and defied the advance of civilization." Burke could not have given a more direct statement of American colonialism.

When Cody took his troupe to England in 1887, as well as on subsequent visits, he tapped into a slightly different phenomenon. Especially in London, Liverpool, and Manchester, the press, as well as people on the street, engaged in what one historian called "a momentous debate" about imperialism. Unlike in the United States, critics seemed to be everywhere. Yet in the face of growing criticism that imperialism and its "racial theory" were destructive for Native peoples, the English kept expanding their empire. Colonialist attitudes that drew on a common heritage of evangelical Christianity, Darwinian social theories, British patriotism, and whites' convictions of their own superiority were too strong to die. In practice, these ideas allowed the British to push into other people's countries, appropriating land and destroying native cultures. Cody's Wild West gave the English the assurance they needed that "settling" an empire—as Americans were doing in the West—was not only good at the time, but would prove right in the long term.

Cody also presented Native peoples in a way that allowed the English to see their own impositions of empire on peoples around the globe as somewhat positive. Although artist George Catlin had taken his collection of paintings of Indians and Indian artifacts to London as early as 1840 and Carl Hagenbeck, producer of ethnographic performances, took a number of Bella Coola Indians from Vancouver to London in 1885, two years before Cody arrived, both men met with far less than Cody's spectacular success. Cody not only whipped up interest in American Indians in extensive advertising, but had with him numerous living examples of Great Plains Indians, who were well known to Britons through dime novels. Also Plains Indians, in their buckskin, beadwork, and feather headdresses, were colorful and dramatic. Although Cody viewed the Indian parts of Wild West performances as educational, he presented Natives in a theatrical manner. Another crucial point was that Cody represented Indians as a barrier to "progress" and "civilization," so that their conquering was inevitable and ultimately for their own good.

Undoubtedly, Cody would have been nonplussed had he seen his beloved Wild West as supportive of what today would be called white greed and racialist attitudes. He might have pointed out that he was aware of cultural diversity, that he added differing types of people to the cast, ranging from Hispanic vaqueros to Argentinean gauchos, and even Russian Cossacks. Cody would have especially lamented any harm the Wild West caused Indians. Cody always insisted on recruiting genuine Indians, many from Sioux reservations in the Dakota territory. Eager to earn wages, having few other employment opportunities, and anxious to see something apart from their own villages, Native Americans signed on with enthusiasm. Most spoke of Cody with true regard, indicating that although they were glad to return to their way of life, Cody had treated them well. During performances, Cody introduced his slogan "An Enemy in '76, A Friend in '85," meaning that although Indians and whites had once been enemies, they could now learn to be friends. Cody characterized the Wild West troupe as a model, where whites and Indians, whom he referred to as "real Americans," worked together and lived near each other. Cody made a point of setting up a separate camp for Indians, where they could socialize and live in their own way. At the end of shows, Cody invited audience members to stroll around the village, where they viewed Indian life, talked with individual Indians, and perhaps wondered about the scalp locks hanging on wigwam walls.

Cody clearly had his favorites among the Indians. He once said that Sioux chief Iron Tail "is the finest man I know, bar none." He also liked Chief Sitting Bull. In 1890, Cody responded to a request from officials at Standing Rock to come reason with Sitting Bull, who had gotten more rancorous as the years passed. Although Cody went to Fort Yates near Standing Rock, he never met with Sitting Bull. After Cody departed, the Indian police tried to arrest the chief, but his supporters opened fire and the police fired back. Sitting Bull, seven Sioux men, and six police officers died. Reportedly, during the gunfire, the gray trick horse that Cody had given the chief sat down and raised its front leg to shake hands, just as it had been trained. Again reflecting his ambivalence, Cody the sympathetic individual grieved Sitting Bull's death, but Cody the entrepreneur retrieved the horse and in future seasons traded on the chief's reputation in Wild West advertising.

Like Cody, Annie Oakley and Frank Butler also thought of themselves as friends of American Indians. Their connection with Indians began in March 1884, when Sioux chief Sitting Bull saw Annie perform at the Olympic Theater in St. Paul, Minnesota. The next day he requested a meeting with her, during which he christened her "Waytana Cecilla," or "Little Sure Shot" and declared her his adopted daughter. Before Frank and Annie had even thought of seeking employment with Cody's Wild West, Sitting Bull had connected Annie to his West, the plains of Dakota Territory. In return, Annie sent Sitting Bull coins and a red silk handkerchief, but she did not see the chief again until they appeared together in the Wild West in 1885. During that season, Annie listened to Sitting Bull's complaints and seemed to be the only person who could bring him out of frequent depressions. Sitting Bull's laments related to his people at Standing Rock. Army troops, he told Annie through an interpreter, had trespassed on Sioux hay and timber lands. He feared that poverty would result. He also talked about cattle ranchers who counted twice each cow intended for Sioux consumption and agents who gave Indians "half-and-half instead of sugar—the other half being sand."

In October, Sitting Bull announced his intention to leave the Wild West and return to Standing Rock. He said goodbye to Annie and gave her several Indian artifacts. Annie promised to write. In 1887, she remembered that Sitting Bull had "made a great pet" of her. She added, "He is a dear, faithful, old friend, and I've great respect and affection for him." Again in 1890, after Sitting Bull's death, Annie defended him. "His disposition was neither aggressive nor cruel, nor would he have molested anyone if he had not been first molested." Years later, in 1926, Oakley was still upset at the way whites had treated Sitting Bull. "Had he been a white man," she declared, "someone would have been hung for his murder."

During their sixteen seasons with the Wild West, Annie and Frank befriended other Native Americans, giving advice and help. On one occasion, Pawnee Long John, who Annie said had been "shaking dice with a Mexican," gave her his money to hold so he could avoid gambling. Frank, too, spent time with the Wild West's Indians, even learning to speak a bit of Sioux. He told stories that placed American Indians in a favorable light and invented games for them to play in camp. Apparently Annie and Frank liked a number of the show's Indians. Had they been told they acted in paternalistic ways, they would probably have been hurt. Had they been accused of exploiting Sitting Bull by allowing mention of him in advertising, they might have responded that they did so with great pride and sympathy. Like Cody, they would have been stung by the thought that they demeaned Indians in any way.

Yet Cody, Oakley, and Butler could not have been unaware of a national debate about "Indian reform" that was taking shape. Many reformers—largely easterners and a number of former abolitionists—especially opposed the phenomenon of "show" Indians. In 1893, it became clear that other critics of Cody's Indian policy existed. The board of managers for the World's Columbian Exposition in Chicago, who, like Cody, called exhibits "object lessons," denied Cody permission to perform on the fairgrounds. Board members objected to what they thought of as Cody's popularized representation of the history and culture of American Indians. In response, Nate Salsbury leased a fourteen-acre area outside the entrance to the fairgrounds and had bleachers constructed that would hold eighteen thousand people. To the seventy-four Sioux Indians from the Pine Ridge reservation already in the cast, Cody added another hundred from Pine Ridge, Standing Rock, and Rosebud. He was well aware that the recent white-Indian conflicts in the West had whetted people's curiosity about Indians.

Cody's interpretation of the West was not the only view represented in Chicago in 1893. As historian Frederick Jackson Turner put forth near the fairgrounds his own view of the frontier as a democratizing force, Cody played just outside the fairground gates. Taking a scholarly approach, Turner suggested that the frontier experience had shaped America's institutions and national character. Turner emphasized an agriculture frontier settled by hardworking farmers; his ideas were later known as the Turner thesis and influenced students and scholars of the West into the twenty-first century. Cody told a more violent story, one of explorers and scouts warring with fierce buffalo and savage Indians to open the West for the coming of white settlers. Despite their differences, however, Turner and Cody agreed that the conquering of the West was fortuitous for Americans, at least white male Americans. As a matter of record, Cody was far more cognizant of women and peoples of color than was Turner, who virtually ignored these groups.

Capacity crowds at the Chicago site must have convinced Cody that Indian reformers and others who opposed the use of "show" Indians in Wild West performances were wrong. Many of these reformers argued that shows damaged the cause of Native Americans by presenting them as little more than savages at the same time that the Indian Bureau assured white people that Indians were productive and, according to white standards, "civilized." Reformers especially feared that audiences—who were probably less gullible than they thought—would believe Cody's assertions that his Wild West presented Indians in a realistic way when, in the arena, Cody's Indians were one-dimensional, cardboard characters who appeared to have lives only in relation to white settlers. Of course they never died; rather, they popped back up smiling and sold souvenir programs and memorabilia at the end of performances. Some said that Cody's establishment of an Indian village on every show lot and his invitations to audiences to stroll around them presented a false picture of Indian life, as well as acting as a living handbill for uninformed western tourism. During postshow meetings, Cody's Indians were friendly and their camp tame, which encouraged visitors to expect more of the same when they visited the West, where, indeed, Indians adapted to tourism by donning garish outfits and performing "war" and "rain" dances.

In addition, "Friends of the Indians" groups lobbied successfully against Cody displaying in store windows prior to a performance the scalp and feather headdress that he claimed to have taken from Yellow Hair. Reformers were further disturbed by endorsements of Cody's Wild West from such notables as General William Tecumseh Sherman and General George Armstrong Custer's widow, Elizabeth, that helped make Indian attacks on wagon trains, burning cabins, and scalping acceptable family entertainment. In 1895, when the *Boston Sunday Post* observed that "years of study could not teach what here may be learned in one night," it meant to extend a compliment, but Indian reformers despaired because they disliked what the Wild West taught people about Native Americans. In their view, such figures as Cody and Oakley were enemies of Indians rather than friends.

In the meantime, Cody and Oakley discovered that they also had to concoct personalities for white westerners. They soon found themselves immersed in a social issue of the era: proper gender roles and appropriate qualities of manhood and womanhood. Cody cast the answers to these dilemmas in the form of western characters. He invented a living, breathing cowboy who was both like and unlike those in dime novels and other print media. Cody transformed the cowboy from a rough manual worker who engaged in low-paid, seasonal labor into an American hero. Cody seemingly ignored the cowboy's unsavory reputation. In 1881, President Chester A. Arthur had requested Congress to suppress, along with Indians, those desperadoes and renegades known as cowboys. For Cody, however, the widely disparaged cowboy became a symbol of what American men could, and should, be. Unlike real cowboys, Cody's cowboys were winners. They dominated horses and cattle, used their guns to run off toughs, always triumphed over Indians, and won fair damsels. In an era when men, from office clerks to factory workers, wondered what had become of guns, horses, macho behavior, tough talk, and noble hearts, Cody offered a model of manhood—the American cowboy—to assuage men's fears and give them a historical image with which to identify.

Cody himself was the first of the Wild West cowboys, an example of American manhood at its finest. In the event that audiences failed to notice this quality in Cody, early program booklets pointed out that Cody was "young, sturdy, a remarkable specimen of manly beauty" and was in all ways "the exemplar of the strong and unique traits that characterize a true American frontiersman." Other programs noted that Cody was rugged but also sensitive, "a natural gentleman in his manners as well as in character." Cody even became well mannered enough to impress British royalty. Eventually Wild West rhetoric described the performance as "The Mirror of American Manhood," with Cody, of course, as the exemplar of all men; that is, of all white men.

Cody was not the only cowboy, however. He instructed others who then carried his ideals of manhood to additional circles of people. For example, Cody taught his foster son, Johnny Baker, the skills he needed to appear in the Wild West arena. Louisa remembered that Cody had trained young Johnny to shoot "in the days in which he played around our house." Later, calling himself "The Cowboy Kid," Baker thrilled audiences with his shooting ability. After his wife died, Baker exhibited another quality of a true man, compassion, by raising his two daughters on his own. Similarly, William Levi "Buck" Taylor learned to be a cowboy at Cody's ranch, Scout's Rest, in Nebraska. Again, according to Louisa, "there was never a time when guns were not booming" around Scout's Rest. Taylor performed with the Wild West

Figure 10.3: Buffalo Bill in showman dress, c. 1909. Courtesy of the
Buffalo Bill Historical Center, Cody, Wyoming.

beginning in the mid-1880s. Later Taylor, who stood six feet, five inches
tall and was dramatically good looking, became a matinee idol. Calling
himself "King of the Cow-boys" long before singing cowboys Gene
Autry and Roy Rogers used similar phrases, Taylor toured the country, teaching young boys that the cowboy's qualities included not only
good shooting and good riding, but honesty, sincerity, intelligence,
manners, and a forgiving nature. When a boy developed all of the latter,
he could call himself a man.

Cody especially favored the dashing manhood of Theodore
Roosevelt. After growing up a puny, spoiled lad, Roosevelt had gone
west to restore his health and vigor. When Roosevelt returned to the

East, he released his multivolume *The Winning of the West* (1885–1894), thus capturing Cody's attention and affection. Roosevelt built his political career on projecting the image that he was a specimen of vigorous western manhood who could accomplish anything from riding and shooting to running the country. After Roosevelt led the charge up Cuba's San Juan Hill in the Spanish-American War in 1898, Cody created a reenactment, "The Battle of San Juan Hill," which first appeared in 1899. To Buffalo Bill, Roosevelt's Rough Riders appeared to be cowboys, "playing out their destiny on a world stage." In the 1899 program book, Cody and Burke even pointed out that the Wild West had first used the term "Rough Riders" as early as 1893. Roosevelt said he had been unaware of the Wild West association of the term but supposedly admitted that frontiersmen "made up the bulk of the regiment and gave it its peculiar character." Although critics of American imperialism were now vocal, Cody continued to support American expansionism, not only in Cuba, but in Hawai'i and the Philippines. American expansionism was also a gender issue for Cody: in his view, it took a manly nation to help those in need, quell riots, and give the gift of democracy to lesser ("brown-skinned") beings who could not create democracy for themselves. One journalist agreed with Cody's approach. "Somehow," he wrote, "as they race about the tan-bark doing their stunts and waving their flags, you feel like getting up and throwing up your hat and giving three cheers for the red, white and blue!"

Cody, however, never gave up his place as premier cowboy. One young lad, John Roath of Maytown, Pennsylvania, who first saw Cody and the Wild West perform in Lancaster, said he took Cody as his "idol" and "legendary hero." Roath remembered that when he played cowboys, he "was Buffalo Bill riding the prairie in search of buffalo." Probably in 1913, Cody and his then partner Gordon W. "Pawnee Bill" Lillie returned to Lancaster, and Roath, by then a teenager, went to see him again. Roath decided he would satisfy his desire for "contact" with the great man by "sneaking up behind him and touching the long fringes on his deerskin jacket," but Cody turned around and shook the boy's hand. When Roath arrived home, he later said, "I went to bed— the most tired but the happiest boy in the world."

In the meantime, Cody, with Oakley's help, created the cowgirl. After all, if Cody wanted to attract female customers, he would have to include women in his Wild West. Because popular culture indicated that women in the West often fell prey, especially to Indians, Cody included female victims who screamed and wailed through "The Attack on the Settlers' Cabin." But this was not enough for late-nineteenth-century viewers, who saw assertive women everywhere they looked: in jobs, professions, politics, and reform activities. Even though

American women had not yet achieved the right to vote, many of them found ways to metamorphose into what were then called "New Women," who went where they wished and did what they pleased.

Cowgirls were also appealing because women in the West were enlarging customary female roles. Western women often rode horseback and handled firearms. By 1890, 13 percent of western women worked outside their homes, compared to 17 percent nationally, but a huge number of women produced income at home, ranging from selling butter and eggs to working in family fields at planting and harvesting time. During the 1890s, women went west as homesteaders; in Colorado they accounted for 11.9 percent of all homesteaders and in Wyoming numbered 18.2 percent. Some women ran ranches, wrangled cattle, and drove herds to market, whereas others worked in shops, for newspapers, and in factories. Also, 14 percent of western women were in the professions, whereas nationally only 8 percent of women were professionals. In 1889, for example, Ella L. Knowles passed the Montana bar examination with distinction, began practicing law in Helena, and actively campaigned for Populist goals and for woman suffrage.

Even as early the mid-1880s, Cody must have realized, as humorist Josh Billings later put it, that in the West "wimmin is everywhere." A male-dominated Wild West would not have the appeal or generate the profits Cody wanted. Hiring Annie Oakley in 1885 was a beginning. At the time, Cody introduced Oakley to his all-male white cast as the "first white woman" to work for the Wild West. Although Cody had worried about Annie's ability to lift heavy rifles and feared that male cast members might heckle and take advantage of her, his fears were needless. Annie was a strong, talented shooter who, rather than becoming a disreputable "show" girl, wanted to preserve her "ladyhood." Even without Frank's considerable assistance, the intrepid Annie would have maintained her ladylike comportment and reputation.

Cody, too, wanted to stress femininity. Although in 1899 he stated that women should have the right to hold paid employment and to vote, he did not believe they should wear what he called "bloomer pants" or ride bucking horses. He also wanted to avoid irritating early audiences needlessly. Thus he billed Annie and others he hired, like Emma Lake Hickok, Lillian Smith, and Della Farrell, as rancheras, prairie beauties, and natural flowers of the American West, at the same time explicitly denying that cowgirls were "New Women." Rather they were spirited, athletic young women with exceptional riding and shooting skills. Only a few rode their horses astride; program booklets explained that they did so to move quickly and safely. During the 1890s, a saddle with a padded center, padding across the front, and thick leather between the saddle and stirrup appeared, intended to protect women's reproductive

Glenda Riley

Figure 10.4: Annie Oakley, Frank Butler, and poodle George, 1884. Courtesy of the Annie Oakley Foundation, Greenville, Ohio.

systems. Annie Oakley never rode astride, which she declared a "horrid idea," but most of those who did preferred men's lighter roping saddles.

As the first female cowgirl in America, Annie had a large task before her. For women ranging from shopgirls to wealthy matrons, Annie wanted to model what she saw as the best and most enduring of female characteristics. Consequently, she often surprised people. In 1888, for example, a reporter who expected to meet a "strong, virile, masculine-like woman, of loud voice, tall of stature and of massive proportions," discovered that Annie stood five feet tall, weighed just over a hundred pounds, and spoke in a quiet, cultured voice. Annie cultivated her ladylike image by wearing her hair long and loose and by avoiding makeup, as well as jewelry and medals, which she put on only for publicity photographs. When other arena cowgirls adopted split skirts, bloomer outfits, and trousers, Annie wore her calf-length skirts, leggings, and sensible low-heeled shoes. Even when Oakley, who retired from Cody's Wild West in 1901 after the troupe experienced a disastrous train accident, later toured with Vernon Seaver's Young Buffalo Show between 1911 and 1913, she still wore her usual clothing, meaning no trousers or bloomers.

In all likelihood, Oakley's Midwestern and Quaker background encouraged her to think of herself as what Victorians called a "true woman." Certainly she saw no gain to be had in perpetuating her image as an uncultured, gingham-clad farm girl from Ohio. Instead she displayed the five characteristics that she associated with true women, who should be modest, married, domestic, benevolent, and a civilizing force. Despite her fame, Annie was successful at remaining modest; she preferred that Frank handle her publicity. Second, Annie and Frank developed what was then called a companionate marriage, based on equality and pliable roles. On the other hand, Cody unsuccessfully tried to divorce his wife, Louisa, in a messy divorce trial in 1904. In an era when the divorce rate had skyrocketed to about one out of thirteen marriages nationally ending in divorce—with the highest divorce rate in the western states—Annie and Frank remained happily married for their lifetimes. As to the third characteristic, Annie tried to be domestic. She hosted tea parties and informal receptions in her tent, which she furnished with a Brussels carpet, couches, a rocking chair, and satin pillows. Between shows, Annie often sat in a rocking chair doing fine embroidery. But when it came to full-scale housekeeping, first in a house in Nutley, New Jersey, and later one in Cambridge, Maryland, she admitted that her talents and interests lay elsewhere. Annie was far better at the fourth characteristic, benevolence, giving money and gifts to everyone from family members to orphans. Lastly, Annie was a civilizing force who refused to let even the roughest roustabouts or canvasmen get away with cursing, smoking, or drinking in her presence.

Obviously Annie Oakley set high standards for women of the late nineteenth and early twentieth century. She entered a male domain and competed with men on their own terms, yet remained ladylike in appearance and demeanor. She was an athlete who watched her diet and exercised daily; people referred to her as tiny, dainty, or girlish. These depictions pleased Annie, who did not want to be thought of as a "New Woman." Nor was she a supporter of woman suffrage because she feared that "not enough good women would vote." Perhaps her only regret was that she and Frank did not have children. As a good Victorian woman, Annie never talked about the topic,

Glenda Riley

but she loved children and lavished attention on them, from relatives to strangers.

As the nation's first cowgirl, Annie answered the questions that women of the era asked about femininity. She set a middle and just course, navigating between unusual achievements for a woman and all the trappings of what was then called a "woman's sphere." Oakley could shoot, ride, and perform a wide variety of authentic feats, yet she could also be traditionally feminine in appearance and conduct. As a result, she won respect from colleagues, friends, family members, and fans. She showed women how to capitalize on the opportunities opening to them during the late 1800s and early 1900s without totally deserting the world of women and becoming lost somewhere in between women and men. In other words, she subtly subverted customary gender expectations to serve her own ends but was so graceful about it that most people applauded rather than criticized her.

Oakley's image of athletic ladyhood appealed especially to women attending colleges and universities that encouraged their female students to take part in such athletic games as tennis, basketball, and competitive shooting. Also during the 1890s, the bicycle craze hit. Oakley was partly responsible in that she brought an unassembled bicycle from England to the States. She also designed a modest outfit, in which unseen garters held down the skirt, and was soon riding and shooting from bicycle-back in the arena. Baseball followed, not for Annie, but for thousands of young women who played in amateur, semiprofessional, and professional teams, like the Bloomer Girls of Texas.

Obviously western women also took to sports. They not only played on teams, but competed in shooting matches, hunted, climbed mountains, and engaged in other active games. One example is Louise Pound of Nebraska, who in 1900 earned a Ph.D. at the University of Heidelberg. During the 1890s and early 1900s, Pound gained repute as a player of lawn tennis and golf. When she became a professor at the University of Nebraska, she supported a women's basketball team as well as organized a female military company who drilled carrying 1880-model Springfield rifles. It was women like these who followed Oakley and thought she had just the right blend of athleticism and femininity. Women shooters especially formed gun clubs honoring her. In England as well women applauded her; as one journalist said in 1892, Oakley "won the hearts of the ladies" with her singular shooting and feminine appearance.

Perhaps Oakley's ladylike demeanor was the reason that dime novelists, who generally preferred racier characters as prototypes, virtually ignored her. The one exception was the Dauntless Dell series by Prentiss Ingraham. Dell, like Oakley, could ride and shoot, yet she never cursed, never drank or smoked, and dressed modestly in a blouse, knee-length skirt, tan leggings, and "small russet shoes, with silver spurs at the heels." In one novel, *Buffalo Bill's Girl Pard; or, Dauntless Dell's Daring* (1908), Dell rebuked two cowboys who had chased away two bandits whom Dell planned to capture. As she slapped her holsters, Dell told the men, "I try to be a lady, both at home on the ranch and when I'm abroad in the hills. But I don't think any the less of a lady because she's able to take care of herself." Subsequently Dell rescued a female friend, saved an Indian boy from harm, shot a rifle out of a villain's hand, and escaped from Fort Grant. Dell's daring so endeared her to Buffalo Bill that he declared her "Class A among Western girls" and accepted her as his "pard."

Although the adventures of Dauntless Dell now sound old-fashioned and melodramatic, they were an important part of the emerging cowgirl image. Dell idealized feminine virtues in a time of wrenching change, whether on the western frontier or the eastern urban frontier. Dell, alias Annie, modeled bravery, assertiveness, ladyhood, and loyalty. She never let down a friend, and she always triumphed over evil. Dell's creator, Prentiss Ingraham, wrote for a female audience. Even the name Dauntless Dell suggested that Dell was a laudable woman, one who was as courageous and capable of brave deeds as men. This was the way Cody and Oakley wanted western women, and their counterparts in the Northeast and South, to think of themselves.

Clearly by the early 1900s, Cody's and Oakley's Wild West was more fantasy than reality. The Wild West was now often referred to as the Old Wild West, indicating that its time had come and gone. At the turn of the twentieth century, the Old West was giving way to an increasingly urbanized and industrialized West. And because railroads and automobiles made western travel possible, settlers were replaced by tourists, who searched for remnants of the frontier that their predecessors had largely destroyed. Growing mobs of white tourists took magnificent sites lightly and treated them recklessly. For example, during the late 1880s and early 1890s, when deserted Indian villages still existed, tourists committed such atrocities as using wigwam poles for firewood and tore "souvenirs" of deer horn and strips of buffalo skin from Native burial platforms. In 1890, Yellowstone visitor Margaret Long decried the destruction she noted everywhere: "We find names, initials with dates, cut into the yielding rock, even visiting cards, and placed in spots one would consider inaccessible."

Can these ills be laid at least in part at Cody's and Oakley's feet? Perhaps. A number of early-twenty-first-century critics indict Cody's Wild West for having strong overtones of what are now considered sexism, racism, and ecological imperialism. Such tropes encouraged harmful circumstances, ranging from the widespread destruction of Native Americans to the plunder of western resources. In Cody's and Oakley's defense, they were hardly alone in capitalizing upon and enlarging the legend of the Old Wild West. From writers and journalists to artists and photographers, many people had a hand in romancing the frontier West. The West itself had changed radically, yet numerous interpreters continued to produce stock images. For example, in 1902, sculptor Frederic Remington created *The Cheyenne,* a mounted warrior in the heat of battle. Although Remington personally respected Indian warriors and their considerable skills, this piece represents its subject as wild and savage. Similarly, artist and sculptor Charles Russell, who especially favored Northern Plains Indians, in 1918 juxtaposed "wild" Indians against infringing and soon to become dominant white civilization. Other people expressed a pseudo-scientific interest in Native Americans. During the early years of the twentieth century, Chicago's Field Museum commissioned detailed paintings of Indians, like Apache chief Geronimo, one of the last holdouts against settlers and soldiers.

The Wild West was a social construction that fit its times. During the late nineteenth and early twentieth centuries, the romanticized Wild West appeared widely to be a carefree and promising region, an image that had many adherents and few critics. It was in that milieu that Cody and Oakley became historians of sorts, presenting their version of westward settlement and instructing white citizens, immigrants, and children in the American national ideology. They also reinforced in people's minds the erroneous image of a largely homogenized West, its harmony disrupted only by supposedly wild and disappearing Indians who gave way to cowboys and cowgirls, all with idealized attributes of manhood and womanhood. And they even encouraged nonchalant and harmful behavior toward western resources and landscapes.

As times and ideas changed, however, Cody and Oakley did what they could to adapt. In 1907, for example, Cody identified himself as an "advocate" for Americans Indians, saying he was "a bit ashamed" of his role in defeating them. In retirement, Oakley stayed away from such issues, devoting her time instead teaching women to shoot and raising money for such charitable causes as orphanages.

Still, these two natives of the Midwest who grew up in poverty and without much formal education were among the foremost interpreters of the West. The pair combined their talents with hard work so that primarily white Americans and Europeans viewed them as archetypal westerners. As performers and show-business entrepreneurs, Cody and Oakley dazzled their audiences with a visible, moving, and noisy West whose characters lived, fought, and died as audiences watched. After their deaths, Cody in 1917 and Oakley in 1926, their personal images, as well as those of the West presented to the public in arenas and onstage, did not fade. If anything, Cody and Oakley lived on through stage shows, films, statues, museums, grave sites, parades, and celebrations.

At the same time, Cody's and Oakley's performance texts became magnified and, thanks to theater, film, and television producers always on the lookout for popular and profitable themes, continued to be popular. Artists of all kinds have also restated Cody's and Oakley's take on the frontier West. During the early 1960s, for example, sculptor Henry Lion's *Lewis and Clark and Sacagawea* and, during the early 1970s, illustrator John Clymer's *Tribal Hunt* showed a frontier West of exploration, cultural contact, and plenty, as well as suggesting the eventual "disappearance" of Indian peoples. Obviously Cody's and Oakley's rendition of the West was not as "authentic" as Cody had hoped. It was, however, a highly usable West, especially meaningful to many Americans at the turn of the twentieth century and still meaningful to many at the turn of the twenty-first century.

Essay on Sources

A number of books analyze changing myths and images of the Old Wild West in the nineteenth and twentieth centuries, including Henry Nash Smith, *Virgin Land: The American West as Symbol and Myth* (Cambridge, Mass.: Harvard University Press, 1950); Kent L. Steckmesser, *The Western Hero in History and Legend* (Norman: University of Oklahoma Press, 1965); Richard Slotkin, *Regeneration through Violence: The Myth of the American Frontier, 1600–1860* (Middletown, Conn.: Wesleyan University Press, 1973); Daryl Jones, *The Dime Novel Western* (Bowling Green, Ohio: Bowling Green University Popular Press, 1978); Ray Allen Billington, *Land of Savagery/Land of Promise: The European Image of the American Frontier in the Nineteenth Century* (New York: Norton, 1981); William H. Goetzmann and William N. Goetzmann, *The West of the Imagination* (New York: Norton, 1986); Robert G. Athearn, *The Mythic West in Twentieth-Century America* (Lawrence: University Press of Kansas, 1986); Christine Bold, *Selling the Wild West: Popular Western Fiction, 1860–1960* (Bloomington: Indiana University Press, 1987); Richard W. Etulain, *Re-Imagining the Modern American West: A Century of Fiction, History, and Art* (Tucson: University of Arizona Press, 1996); Robert A. Hall, *Performing the American Frontier, 1870–1906* (Cambridge, UK: Cambridge University Press, 2001); and David M. Wrobel, *Promised Lands: Promotion, Memory, and the Creation of the American West* (Lawrence: University Press of Kansas, 2002).

Several relatively recent biographies of William F. "Buffalo Bill" Cody are John Burke, *Buffalo Bill: The Noblest Whiteskin* (New York:

Putnam, 1973); Nellie Snyder Yost, *Buffalo Bill: His Family, Friends, Fame, Failures, and Fortunes* (Chicago: Swallow Press, 1979); Henry Blackman Sell and Victor Weybright, *Buffalo Bill and the Wild West* (New York: Oxford University Press, 1955); Joseph G. Rosa and Robin May, *Buffalo Bill and His Wild West: A Pictorial Biography* (Lawrence: University Press of Kansas, 1989) and *Buffalo Bill and His Wild West* (Lawrence: University of Kansas Press, 1978); Eric V. Sorg, *Buffalo Bill: Myth and Reality* (Santa Fe, N.Mex.: Ancient City Press, 1998); and Robert A. Carter, *Buffalo Bill Cody: The Man Behind the Legend* (New York: Wiley, 2000).

Helpful interpretations of Cody and his Wild West include Joseph J. Arpad, *Buffalo Bill's Wild West* (Palmer Lake, Colo.: Fetter Press, 1971); Richard Slotkin, "The 'Wild West,'" in *Buffalo Bill and the Wild West* (Pittsburgh: Brooklyn Museum and University of Pittsburgh, 1981), 27–44, and *Gunfighter Nation: The Myth of the Frontier in Twentieth-Century America* (New York: Atheneum, 1992); Sarah J. Blackstone, *Buckskins, Bullets, and Business: A History of Buffalo Bill's Wild West* (Westport, Conn.: Greenwood, 1986); Anne M. Butler, "Selling the Popular Myth," *Oxford History of the American West* (New York: Oxford University Press, 1994), 771–801; Richard White, "Frederick Jackson Turner and Buffalo Bill," in *The Frontier in American Culture,* ed. James R. Grossman (Berkeley: University of California Press, 1994), 7–66, and "When Frederick Jackson Turner and Buffalo Bill Cody Both Played Chicago in 1893," in *Frontier and Region: Essays in Honor of Martin Ridge,* ed. Robert C. Ritchie and Paul Andrew Hutton (Albuquerque: University of New Mexico Press, 1997), 201–12; Gordon M. Wickstrom, "Buffalo Bill the Actor," *Journal of the West* (January 1995): 62–69; Jonathan D. Martin, "'The Grandest and Most Cosmopolitan Object Teacher': Buffalo Bill's Wild West and the Politics of American Identity, 1883–1899," *Radical History Review* 66 (fall 1996): 92–123; Thomas Antony Freeland, "The National Entertainment: Buffalo Bill's Wild West and the Pageant of American Empire" (Ph.D. diss., Stanford University, 1999); Joy S. Kasson, *Buffalo Bill's Wild West: Celebrity, Memory, and Popular History* (New York: Hill and Wang, 2000); Louis S. Warren, "Buffalo Bill Meets Dracula: William F. Cody, Bram Stoker, and the Frontiers of Racial Decay," *American Historical Review* 107 (October 2002): 1124–56; and Warren, "Cody's Last Stand: Masculine Anxiety, the Custer Myth, and the Frontier of Domesticity in Buffalo Bill's Wild West," *Western Historical Quarterly* 34 (spring 2003): 49–69.

For analysis of Wild West shows, see Paul Reddin, *Wild West Shows* (Urbana: University of Illinois Press, 1999), and Kristine Fredricksson, *American Rodeo: From Buffalo Bill to Big Business* (College Station: Texas A&M University Press, 1985). Specific aspects of Wild West shows are considered in Jay Kimmel, *Custer, Cody and the Last Indian Wars: A Pictorial History* (Portland, Oreg.: Corey/Stevens Publishing, 1994); John F. Sears, "Bierstadt, Buffalo Bill, and the Wild West in Europe," in *Cultural Transmissions and Receptions: American Mass Culture in Europe,* ed. R. Kroes, R. W. Rydell, and D. F. J. Bosscher (Amsterdam: VU University Press, 1993), 3–14; and Stephen Currie, *Life in a Wild West Show* (San Diego, Calif.: Lucent Books, 1999).

For coverage of Native Americans and Wild West shows, see Robert E. Bieder, "Marketing the American Indian in Europe: Context, Commodification, and Reception," in *Cultural Transmissions and Receptions: American Mass Culture in Europe,* 15–23; Cindy Fent and Raymond Wilson, "Indians Off Track: Cody's Wild West and the Melrose Park Train Wreck of 1904," *American Indian Culture and Research Journal* 18, no. 3 (1994): 235–69; and L. G. Moses, "Indians on the Midway: Wild West Shows and the Indian Bureau at World's Fairs, 1893–1904," *South Dakota History* 21 (fall 1991): 205–29, and *Wild West Shows and the Images of American Indians, 1883–1933* (Albuquerque: University of New Mexico Press, 1996). An Indian's viewpoint is Chauncey Yellow Robe, "The Menace of the Wild West Show," *Quarterly Journal of the Society of American Indians* 2 (July/September, 1914): 224–28.

Ideas of masculinity are discussed in Gail Bederman, *Manliness and Civilization: A Cultural History of Gender and Race in the United States, 1880–1917* (Chicago: University of Chicago Press, 1995); Geoffrey Canada, *Reaching Up for Manhood: Transforming the Lives of Boys in America* (Boston: Beacon Press, 1998); and Stephen M. Frank, *Life with Father: Parenthood and Masculinity in the Nineteenth-Century American North* (Baltimore: Johns Hopkins University Press, 1998).

One young man's memories of Cody is John R. Roath, "Me and Buffalo Bill," *Journal of the Lancaster County Historical Society* 97 (summer 1995): 66–71. Other personal accounts include Charles Eldridge Griffin, *Four Years in Europe with Buffalo Bill* (Albia, Iowa: Stage Publishing, 1908); M. I. McCreight, "Buffalo Bill as I Knew Him," *True West* 4 (July/August 1957): 25, 41–42; Milt Hinkle, "Memoirs of My Rodeo Days," *Real West* 11 (September 1968): 35–37, 65; and Tex Cooper, "I Knew Buffalo Bill," *Frontier Times* 33 (spring 1969): 19–21.

For other primary sources, consult Cody's autobiography, *Buffalo Bill's Life Story: An Autobiography* (New York: Rinehart, 1920). His letters are collected in *Letters from Buffalo Bill,* ed. Stella Adelyn Foote (El Segundo, Calif.: Upton and Sons, 1990). A massive collection of Cody's documents, artifacts, and ephemera is located at the Buffalo Bill Historical Center in Cody, Wyoming.

Works about Cody for young adults are William R. Sanford and Carl R. Green, *Buffalo Bill Cody: Showman of the Wild West* (Springfield, N.J.: Enslow Publishers, 1996); John Hamilton, *Heroes and Villains of the Wild West: Buffalo Bill Cody* (Minneapolis: Abdo and Daughters, 1996); and Charles J. Shields, *Famous Figures of the American Frontier* (Philadelphia: Chelsea House Publishers, 2002).

For Annie Oakley, the two most recent biographies are Shirl Kasper, *Annie Oakley* (Norman: University of Oklahoma Press, 1992), and Glenda Riley, *The Life and Legacy of Annie Oakley* (Norman: University of Oklahoma Press, 1994). Older and less reliable works are Courtney Ryley Cooper, *Annie Oakley: Woman at Arms* (New York: Duffield, 1927); Annie Fern Campbell Swartwout, *Missie: An Historical Biography of Annie Oakley* (Blanchester, Ohio: Brown Publishing, 1947); and Walter Havighurst, *Annie Oakley of the Wild West* (New York: Macmillan, 1954). A more thoroughly researched account is Isabelle S. Sayers, *The Rifle Queen: Annie Oakley* (Ostrander, Ohio: n.p., 1973).

Helpful analyses include Tracy C. Davis, "Annie Oakley and Her Ideal Husband of No Importance," in *Critical Theory and Performance,* ed. Janelle G. Reinelt and Joseph R. Roach (Ann Arbor: University of Michigan Press, 1992), 229–312, and "Shotgun Wedlock: Annie Oakley's Power Politics in the Wild West," in *Gender in Performance: The Presentation of Difference in the Performing Arts,* ed. Lawrence Senelick (Hanover, N.H.: University Press of New England, 1992), 141–57; Paul E. Ross, "Annie Oakley and the Hillbilly Jinx," *Appalachian Journal* 22 (winter 1995): 262–75; Glenn Charles Leader III, "Annie Oakley in Performance: The Evolution of an Image" (Ph.D. diss., Florida State University, 1997); Glenda Riley, "Annie Oakley: Creating the Cowgirl," in *Frontier and Region: Essays in Honor of Martin Ridge,* ed. Paul A. Hutton and Roy Ritchie (Albuquerque: University of New Mexico Press, 1997), and "Annie Oakley: The Peerless Lady Wing-Shot," in *By Grit and Grace: Eleven Women Who Shaped the American West,* ed. Glenda Riley and Richard W. Etulain (Golden, Colo.: Fulcrum Press, 1997); and David B. Broad, "Annie Oakley: Woman, Legend and Myth," *Journal of the West* 37 (January 1998): 11–18.

For show cowgirls, see Sarah Wood-Clark, *Beautiful Daring Western Girls: Women of the Wild West Shows,* 2d ed. (Cody, Wyo.: Buffalo Bill Historical Center 1991), and Kathryn Derry, "Corsets and Broncs: The Wild West Show Cowgirl, 1890–1920," *Colorado Heritage* (summer 1992): 2–16.

Archival evidence concerning Annie Oakley is slim, primarily scrapbooks of clippings and articles that are found, along with ephemera, vertical files, and artifacts, at the Buffalo Bill Historical Center in Cody, Wyoming. Oakley wrote one small book, *Powders I*

Have Used (Wilmington: Du Pont Powder Company, 1914), and an unpublished and undated autobiography, held by the Annie Oakley Foundation in Greenville, Ohio.

Despite the paucity of extensive source materials, books for general and especially for young readers abound, including Edmund Collier, *The Story of Annie Oakley* (New York: Grosset and Dunlap, 1956); Shannon Garst, *Annie Oakley* (New York: Julian Messner, 1958); Ellen Wildon, *Annie Oakley: Little Sure Shot* (Indianapolis: Bobbs-Merrill, 1958); Charles P. Graves, *Annie Oakley: The Shooting Star* (Champaign, Ill.: Garrard, 1961); Jan Gleiter and Kathleen Thompson, *Annie Oakley: Great Tales* (Nashville: Ideals Publishing, 1985); Robert Quakenbush, *Who's That Girl with the Gun? A Story of Annie Oakley* (New York: Prentice-Hall, 1988); Ellen Levine, *Ready, Aim, Fire! The Real Adventures of Annie Oakley* (New York: Scholastic, 1989); Jan Gleiter and Kathleen Thompson, *Annie Oakley* (Austin, Tex.: Raintree Steck-Vaughn, 1995); Judy Alter, *Wild West Shows: Rough Riders and Sure Shots* (New York: Franklin Watts, 1997); Debbie Dadey, *Shooting Star: Annie Oakley, the Legend* (New York: Walker, 1997); Jean Flynn, *Annie Oakley: Legendary Sharpshooter* (Springfield, N.J.: Enslow Publishers, 1998); Charles J. Shields, *Famous Figures of the American Frontier: Annie Oakley* (Philadelphia: Chelsea House, 2001); Stephen Krensky, *Shooting for the Moon: The Amazing Life and Times of Annie Oakley* (New York: Melanie Kroupa Books, 2001); Sue Macy, *A Photobiography of Annie Oakley* (Washington, D.C.: National Geographic Society, 2001); and Frances E. Ruffin, *Annie Oakley* (New York: PowerKids Press, 2002).

CHAPTER 11

James J. Hill, Jeannette Rankin, and John Muir
The American West in the Progressive Era, 1890 to 1920

MARK HARVEY

In December of 1889, John Stevens, a civil engineer with James J. Hill's Great Northern Railroad, set out from Fort Assiniboine near Havre, Montana, bound for the Rocky Mountains in search of a pass over which the railroad could build. Stevens was asked to locate a route over the mountains that would enable the Great Northern to haul heavy freight in both directions without taxing the engines over steep grades. Arriving in the mountains south of present-day Glacier National Park on December 11, Stevens located Marias Pass, where he spent a frigid night near the summit, stomping his feet to maintain circulation. Yet even with the temperature hovering around forty degrees below zero, Stevens was elated, knowing that he had located the lowest pass in the northern Rockies that would ably serve the Great Northern trains running between Puget Sound and the Twin Cities.

Hill fully appreciated what Stevens had found at Marias Pass. In the next four years Hill drove his construction crews to finish building the Great Northern line. Its completion in 1893 opened the last of the great transcontinental lines spanning the West and linking the region to the rest of the nation. Stevens had thought in terms of grades and mountain passes—and the challenges of coping with the West's physical geography—while Hill had his mind on what William Cronon has called the geography of capital, of the profitable connections that steel rails could forge between the mines, forests, and grasslands of the West with markets in the Midwest and East.

James J. Hill embodied the outlook of a generation of business leaders and investors who remade the West's landscape and incorporated the region into the national and international economy between 1890 and 1920. These decades witnessed a massive transformation of the region's economy that built on the industrial and agricultural expansion following the Civil War and brought new waves of urban and rural growth. The West possessed abundant wealth in minerals, forests, and grasslands, and these resources found growing markets in the latter part of the nineteenth and early twentieth centuries. Investment capitalists like Hill linked the West with the national and global economy more tightly than ever before. In the process, their enterprises affected the nature of work and labor-management relations and magnified the region's pattern of employment that placed people of Euroamerican descent at the top and Hispanics, Asians, and African Americans near the bottom. Such sweeping economic changes also caused massive environmental alterations in the West's forests, grasslands, mountains, and plains. All these economic and environmental changes convinced western residents that they must come to terms with the ways capital and industrial development shaped their lives. Here was the great challenge facing the West from 1890 to 1920.

Although he did not foresee all these changes, Hill had an intuitive sense of how the West would grow and of how he might cash in on that growth. From his youth, Hill had an eye for business. Born in 1838 in Wellington, Ontario, to parents of Scotch-Irish background, he went to work at age fourteen in a general store and quickly developed a taste for business. Ambitious to experience the larger world, Hill left home in 1856 and moved west to St. Paul, a bustling community dominated by old Fort Snelling, steamboats on the Mississippi, and a vibrant fur trade tied to Winnipeg. He soon found work as a shipping clerk for a steamboat firm, keeping its books and transferring freight from boats to wagons going north to Winnipeg and other communities. His work on the river taught him the fundamentals of freighting, shipping, and transportation and how to connect residents of northern Minnesota and Manitoba with goods and services in urban areas serving the frontier.

This ability to connect people with markets underlay Hill's career as a great railroad magnate. In 1879, he took over the Minnesota and Pacific line, the recipient of a 2.5-million-acre land grant from the state of Minnesota. Hill turned this line into the St. Paul, Minneapolis, and Manitoba anchored in the Twin Cities and capitalized on the Great Dakota boom in hard spring wheat to establish the Manitoba as the premier railroad in western Minnesota and Dakota Territory.

Despite his success, Hill looked anxiously in the 1880s as the Northern Pacific and Union Pacific captured passenger and freight traffic from the Far West. Fearing that his regional Manitoba line was vulnerable to a takeover by one of the giants, he drove his crews in 1886 to extend the railroad across Dakota Territory into the High Line country of northern Montana. Then, seeing the booming copper industry centered at Butte, Montana, as a major prize to be captured, he subsidized a branch line, the Montana Central Railroad, from Great Falls

Figure 11.1: James J. Hill at Williston, North Dakota,
September 29, 1909. Courtesy of the State Historical
Society of North Dakota, A3616.

to Helena and Butte and promised Butte's copper magnate, Marcus
Daly, cheap shipping rates. Hill's decision to tap the Butte copper boom
proved enormously successful. In the 1890s Butte was a hub of the
world's copper industry, serving the vast market for copper wiring
growing out of the electrical revolution.

Completion of the Great Northern to Seattle in 1893 enabled Hill
to cash in on the other great extractive industry in the Pacific
Northwest: timber. By the 1890s, the intensive logging of forests in
Michigan, Wisconsin, and Minnesota compelled lumber firms to log
the Douglas fir, spruce, pine, and cedar forests of the Pacific Northwest.
Centers of lumber production soon emerged on the Olympic peninsula
and around Puget Sound in Washington; at Coos Bay, Klamath Falls,

and Bend in Oregon; and near Potlatch and Lewiston, Idaho. Technological advances in cutting and transporting logs also fueled the Northwest timber industry, especially the steam "donkey," which proved more efficient than teams of oxen for pulling felled timber out of the woods. Taking advantage of these changes, Hill cashed in on the burgeoning lumber industry, outdueling his competitors by hauling lumber to Midwestern markets for 50 percent less.

His tactic of carrying a high volume of freight at low cost proved highly successful. In the first decade of the new century, Hill's net income rose steadily from $10,426,000 in 1900 to $17,517,000 in 1910 to more than $27,600,000 in 1916. Nor did he stop looking for ways to improve his service and enhance his accumulated capital. For Hill, the American West provided the physical setting for a grand game of "connect the dots," tying resource hinterlands to distant urban markets and linking customers to finished goods. He pursued this interest in the geography of capital with an intense single-mindedness.

While Hill and other like-minded capitalists integrated the West into the national and global economy, many residents within the region struggled over how to accommodate to the myriad ways that capital manifested itself in their daily lives. It was a difficult paradox. The West was rich in land and resources but poor in capital. The James J. Hills of the world provided the capital for cutting forests, extracting minerals, and raising crops, and the infrastructure built by railroads and businesses provided employment, income, and tax bases to build communities, schools, and local government services. Yet railroads and large business enterprises also wielded enormous power that dwarfed individual communities and states and held sway over entire regional economies. Mining dominated the economic and political sectors of Nevada, Arizona, Utah, and Montana, and both weighed heavily in Colorado and Idaho. The silver mines near Coeur d'Alene, Idaho, were owned by Andrew Mellon, Jay Gould, the Bank of England, and the Union Pacific Railroad. In Arizona, the Phelps-Dodge Corporation dominated copper mining at Bisbee, Clifton-Morenci, and Globe. John Rockefeller, Jr., held the purse strings of Colorado Fuel and Iron Company in Pueblo, Colorado, which operated smelters and iron and steel manufacturing enterprises. In Montana, a Wall Street–dominated firm, the Anaconda Copper Mining Company, exerted powerful control over Butte and Anaconda and by extension much of the state.

The West's reliance on eastern and European capital placed the region in a subservient position to the sources of that capital, to stockholders and governing boards of corporations headquartered in the Twin Cities, Chicago, and New York. Joseph Kinsey Howard, a writer from Great Falls, Montana, once wrote that the region was at "the end of the cracked whip," an apt phrase suggesting westerners' frustration with political and market forces beyond their control.

Still, the big enterprises in mining, logging, oil extraction, and the railroads brought a wage economy into the region, and wages were generally high because of the sudden growth of these industries and the strong demand for labor. Real wages (reflecting cost-of-living rates) were higher in the West than any other region of the United States, luring thousands of workers from other regions and abroad. In the Southwest, wage rates offered by railroads attracted growing numbers of migrants from Mexico after 1890. The Southern Pacific, Santa Fe, and Texas and Pacific railroads employed hundreds of Hispanics as laborers, machinists, repairmen, and bolt makers. Smelters and building trades also employed Mexicans, in part because they agreed to work for lower wages than Europeans and Anglo Americans. In this way, the dual labor system evident in the West's mining camps and on its railroads since the 1870s became more firmly entrenched. Hispanics, Asians, and African Americans were frequently employed in less-skilled and lower-paid positions.

Nonetheless, Mexicans had an even greater motive to enter the United States following the violent upheavals during the Mexican Revolution, which began in 1910. Thousands more now entered the country, encouraged by the U.S. government and many corporations and agribusinesses that viewed them as temporary residents who would work cheaply. The sugar beet industry in Colorado, cotton industry in California, and lettuce-, spinach-, and bean-growing areas in southern Texas and Arizona all relied heavily on Mexican laborers. From Texas to California, growers resorted to the racist argument that Mexican workers were eminently suited for hard, manual labor. In the Pacific Northwest, the Great Northern, Northern Pacific, and Milwaukee railroads began to hire Japanese, Bulgarians, and Greeks. Interjecting ethnic diversity into their workforce allowed railroad lines to undercut labor solidarity.

Still, racial and ethnic diversity in the mines, logging camps, railroads, and fields did not eliminate conflict between workers and employers. Layoffs, wage cuts, and dangerous working conditions shaped the daily lives of the region's wage workers. Industrial work in the West held a multitude of dangers. Railroad workers risked life and limb linking cars, while miners suffered or died from cave-ins, fires, heat exhaustion, and silicosis and other lung diseases. Logging carried high risks as well, especially after the advent of power saws. Many lumberjacks lost hands and fingers or were crushed beneath falling trees.

These difficulties contributed to the formation of unions and efforts to enact workers' compensation laws. The Butte Miner's Union counted

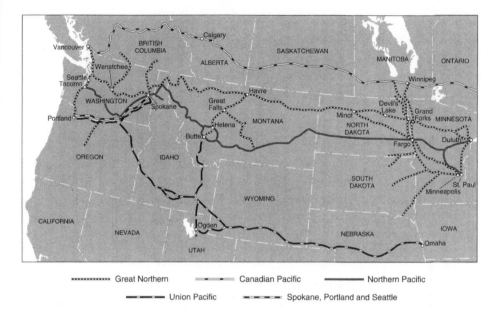

·············· Great Northern	═·═·═ Canadian Pacific	━━━━━ Northern Pacific
━·━·━ Union Pacific	━·━·━ Spokane, Portland and Seattle	

Map 11.1: The primary lines of the Great Northern Railway along with the trunk lines of
the Canadian Pacific, the Northern Pacific, and the Union Pacific railroads. From
Michael P. Malone, *James J. Hill, Empire Builder of the Northwest* (Norman:
University of Oklahoma Press), 118. © 1996 by the University of Oklahoma Press.
Reprinted by permission.

seven thousand members in 1900, nearly 80 percent of the city's miners.
The BMU had a reputation as a conservative labor organization, but the
national depression that began in 1893 contributed to the emergence of
a markedly more radical labor movement. In the depression, prices for
silver and copper fell dramatically, prompting mining companies at
Coeur d'Alene, Idaho, to cut wages. Miners there promptly went on
strike, and seven died in a gun battle when state and federal troops
arrived to break the strike. Soon after, labor delegates from across the
region met in Butte and organized the Western Federation of Miners
(WFM), hoping to attract all miners into one big union. The WFM perceived an irrepressible conflict between labor and capital, a notion that
appealed to migratory workers in the Northwest's lumber camps,
California grape fields, and Idaho silver mines. In the 1890s and early
1900s, the WFM and its radical successor, the Industrial Workers of the
World (Wobblies), staged strikes and campaigned to end capitalism.
Both proved unable to destroy the capitalist system, expending most of
their efforts on strikes and maintaining unity in the face of often bitter
resistance by employers. Although radicals failed in their principal aims,
they succeeded in making clear the dangers and risks of industrial labor
and the ruthless forces of capital that perpetuated these conditions.

Many of the West's farmers and ranchers also became militant in the 1890s, feeling oppressed by the geographies of capital. In small communities dotting the rural West, the railroad tracks stretched out of town and across to a distant horizon, ferrying cattle and wheat to urban markets, slaughterhouses, flour mills, and processing centers far away. Yet many plains residents deeply distrusted railroads and the web of merchants, grain traders, and elevator operators who seemed to dictate their fate. Farmers' anger against high shipping rates mounted during droughts in the early 1890s, when several plains states lost population. As producers of grain and beef, farmers and ranchers felt that the transportation and marketing system was rigged against them.

That belief gave birth to the Farmers' Alliances, rising out of Texas in the 1870s and spreading throughout the plains. In 1892, members of the alliances joined with the Knights of Labor to form the Populist Party. At its convention in Omaha, the new party chose Iowa's James Weaver as its presidential candidate and adopted a platform calling for a graduated income tax, an eight-hour workday, government ownership of railroads, and a subtreasury system to enable farmers to take out loans based on grain stored in federally operated warehouses. Populists also called for an expanded money supply by coining silver at a ratio of sixteen ounces of silver to one ounce of gold. The party made deep inroads on the plains, electing a number of governors and state and federal lawmakers. Populism showed strength in Colorado, Montana, and Nevada also, owing to the severity of the depression and the powerful appeal of "free silver" to western miners, who anticipated a revival of their industry with an expanded money supply. Even in Wyoming, where mining was negligible, Populists drew on the discontent of small ranchers with large cattle barons, who dominated the open range and legislature. The party also gained strength from women, who tied the need for political reform to the quality of their home life and children's well-being. The women's suffrage campaign thereby gained a boost in the Populist uprising. "Ours is a grand and holy mission," said Mary Lease, a Kansas Populist, "to place the mothers of this nation on an equality with the fathers."

The Populist crusade crested in the election of 1896. Many Populists were urged to vote for William Jennings Bryan of Nebraska, a Democrat who decried the monopolies and their gold standard for dominating the country and making the West and South colonies of the industrial Northeast. Bryan took up the free silver banner, although the Democrats rejected other planks of the Populist platform. Populists who "fused" with the Democrats did so in the hope that a Bryan victory would lead to an enlarged currency. When Bryan lost to the Republican candidate William McKinley after a memorable campaign, the Populists quickly faded from the national scene. Yet the grievances that gave rise to the party—and the West's struggle to come to terms with big business in particular—hardly disappeared, leaving to a new generation the task of making good on reform.

In the new century, the subregions of the West witnessed major population growth. The railroads opened a new phase of construction after 1900, building dozens of new branch lines on the plains and adding segments to their main trunks in mining and logging regions in the Southwest and Northwest. This expansion refined the rail network and integrated once-remote regions and resource areas into the regional and national economy. Railroad expansion fueled the growth of Denver, Salt Lake City, Sacramento, and Phoenix as well as smaller communities that benefited from resource development and market integration.

Los Angeles grew faster and larger than any city in the West because of the unusual blend of attractions it possessed. Besides a fast-growing oil industry, these included a sunny and warm climate that attracted residents from Indiana, Illinois, Iowa, and other midwestern states. Its favorable climate allowed for a relaxing lifestyle that people from colder states could not resist. Indeed, the West's first great tourist promoters and image makers plied their trade touting the supposed paradise of southern California and the greater Southwest. One promoter, Charles Lummis, touted the old missions, archaeological ruins, and scenery of the Southwest and built an image of a cultural wonderland that no respectable tourist should miss. In his 1911 book, *Some Strange Corners of Our Country,* Lummis sought to interest upper-class travelers in the Grand Canyon, Canyon de Chelly, and intriguing historic sites.

California, of course, was more than a home to transplanted Midwesterners. It also became a magnet for other peoples, including forty thousand Japanese laborers and farmers from Hawai'i and Japan who entered the state by 1910. California nativists who earlier decried the numbers of Chinese now spoke about a new "Asiatic peril." Other Japanese migrants settled in Oregon, Washington, and Idaho. Meanwhile, the African American population remained small in most western cities before 1920, with the largest black communities in Los Angeles, Dallas, Houston, and San Antonio. African Americans experienced segregation in schools and public facilities, and most worked in low-paying positions as servants or conductors on streetcars or railroads.

Another demographic revolution took place on the Great Plains. With railroads building new branch lines and offering cheap transportation, a second great wave of homesteaders poured into the region, encouraged by favorable weather and rising commodity prices. The government helped them as well by providing additional ways to obtain land with the Enlarged Homestead Act of 1909 and the Stock

Mark Harvey

Raising Homestead Act of 1916, which permitted the purchase of 640 acres. Not surprisingly, James J. Hill promoted homesteading and advocated dry farming and irrigation, wanting newcomers to thrive on the land. In Montana, the so-called honyockers poured into the eastern plains, and a similar influx began in Oklahoma and Texas just after 1900, creating new counties, farms, schools, churches, and fields of winter wheat and beef cattle. These newcomers were a diverse lot. Norwegians, German Russians, and Ukrainians settled in North Dakota and Montana; Germans, Danes, and Swedes in South Dakota and Nebraska; and a similar variety of ethnics in Oklahoma and Texas.

This growth in the rural and urban West contributed to the great wave of reform that emerged between 1900 and World War I. But growth alone cannot explain the rise of Progressivism in the West. While that movement took its cues from Progressives elsewhere in the country, it also drew on regional characteristics. Of these, the most crucial were a frontier tradition of democratic politics, a "stick-it-in-your-eye" attitude against entrenched corporate power, and a weaker allegiance to established parties than in the East. Nourished by a rising population of middle-class people with more refined cultural sensibilities, western Progressives took aim at business monopolies, corrupt political machines, and exploitation of labor. To remedy these problems, Progressives adopted a variety of "direct democracy" measures. These included the direct primary, by which voters could choose candidates for office; initiative and referendum laws; and measures enabling voters to recall elected officials whom they deemed incompetent or corrupt. In San Francisco, Progressives forced Mayor Abraham Ruef out of office for accepting bribes from brothels and other businesses. In Denver, they challenged a political machine built on ballot box manipulation and reformed the city government and mayor's office. In North Dakota, Progressives targeted the powerful railroad machine of Alexander McKenzie by adopting an antipass law (disallowing free passes or tickets to lawmakers) and creating a state commission to regulate rates. Across the West, reformers attempted to curb the power of the railroads with antipass laws and state railroad commissions with the authority to set maximum rates.

In urban areas, Progressives placed garbage disposal, water supply, and electrical power under municipal control to dispense with expensive or corrupt private contractors. Seattle, Portland, and other cities built parks and boulevards and adopted aspects of the "city beautiful" movement. Oregon played a leading role in the Progressive movement in the nation, rallying behind William S. U'Ren, a former Populist who served in the Oregon legislature. U'Ren helped engineer initiative and referendum amendments to the state constitution in 1902, a direct primary amendment (it carried in every Oregon county) in 1904, and recall of elected officials in 1908. Oregon also adopted pathbreaking reforms setting maximum working hours and minimum wages for women.

As the Oregon laws revealed, western Progressives exhibited a marked moral agenda. Besides measures limiting child labor and women's working hours, they created state boards of health to serve as watchdogs of diseases and help ensure sanitary conditions in businesses and public places. In some states they sought to end practices that many associated with an older West, when boomtowns offered gambling and prostitution. California adopted the Anti–Race Track Gambling Act in 1909 to prohibit wagering or bookmaking and a law banning "red light" districts in 1913. In 1901, Wyoming Progressives pushed through an antigambling act in the state legislature, no small feat considering the longstanding clout of Harry Hynds and his saloon in the capital of Cheyenne.

Yet Progressive reform had its dark side. Although the leadership did not come from the West, some reformers sought to compel Native Americans to assimilate into society by adopting Christianity, learning English, and owning property. The annual conferences of Christian reformers at Lake Mohonk, New York, spearheaded this broad effort. Through their influence, young Native Americans were sent to off reservation boarding schools, where they were forced to cut their hair, wear uniforms, and speak and write English while suppressing their native languages. Because reformers believed Indians must reject their own cultural practices, the Bureau of Indian Affairs made various religious ceremonies illegal on reservations, a step that compelled Indians to establish the Native American Church. In a major legislative action in 1887, Congress passed the Dawes Act to break up the reservations and allot lands in severalty to individuals. The law reduced the land base of many tribes and ultimately contributed to greater impoverishment of Native Americans.

Perhaps the most visible moral reform was the temperance movement, active in some states since the 1870s. Kansas adopted a prohibition amendment in its constitution in 1880, but in subsequent years saloons and the liquor industry in that state battled to overturn the law. These efforts spawned a vigorous temperance crusade in the 1890s and early 1900s, led by the indomitable Carry Nation, who entered saloons with her hatchet and smashed bottles, glasses, and other property. Nation was not entirely an anomaly: in 1890, Norwegian farm women in tiny Hatton, North Dakota, felt emboldened to enter drinking establishments and employ similar tactics. Such attempts to link temperance with individual behavior and sin proved less effective, however, than newer arguments tying prohibition to public health and economic productivity.

Reformers' desire to prohibit drinking and the sale of alcoholic beverages dovetailed with the women's suffrage campaign. That effort, like temperance, had been ongoing in some western states since the 1870s. In Oregon, Abigail Scott Duniway had been a tireless advocate of suffrage for women since the 1870s, publishing a newspaper, *The New Northwest*. Continuing her work into the new century, Duniway was gratified to see suffrage efforts led by Elizabeth Preston Anderson in North Dakota, Emma Smith DeVoe and Mary Arkwright Hutton in Washington and Idaho, and Katherine Edson in California. The influx of Germans, Germans from Russia, and other European migrants into the West after 1900, however, compelled suffragists to distance themselves from prohibitionists, for they found stiff resistance to women's suffrage from ethnic groups who resented efforts to deprive them of the right to drink. Germans, for instance, feared that granting women the vote might threaten male authority in the home and guarantee enactment of prohibition.

A major figure in the suffrage movement was Jeannette Rankin of Montana. Born on a ranch outside of Missoula in 1880, Rankin grew up in an upper-middle-class family as the oldest of seven children. After graduating from the University of Montana with a biology degree in 1902, she taught in country schools and worked as a seamstress in Missoula before taking charge of her younger siblings after their mother's death in 1904. Four years later, Rankin moved east and enrolled at the New York School of Philanthropy. Here she studied criminal sociology, labor relations, and the theory and practice of charity organization. She also learned from such renowned Progressives as Louis Brandeis, Florence Kelley, and Booker T. Washington, who helped her understand that an individual's behavior was shaped by environment and was not merely a result of inborn "character." One of Simon Patten's books, *The New Basis of Civilization,* persuaded her that social misery did not automatically result from a Darwinian social struggle and could be eliminated through reform.

From New York, Rankin returned west and enrolled at the University of Washington, becoming active in the suffrage campaign in that state. Back in Montana in 1911, she spoke to the legislature and urged lawmakers to enact a suffrage law. That year the statehouse defeated a suffrage bill thirty-three to thirty, but Rankin and her supporters found encouragement in the close vote and pressed ahead. In 1912, Rankin worked as a field secretary for the National American Woman Suffrage Association and campaigned in a number of states. Two years later, she opened an office of the Montana Equal Suffrage Association in Butte. From this base, she sent letters to labor unions, farmer organizations, and women's clubs. She and her staff mounted

Figure 11.2: Jeannette Rankin (right) and Carrie Chapman Catt (left) in Washington, D.C., ca. April 12, 1917. Courtesy of the Montana Historical Society, Helena.

door-to-door campaigns across Montana and invited national suffrage leaders to the state. Rankin believed that publicity held the key to success. She arranged for booths at county fairs, distributing literature at some of the most popular gatherings and leisure-time activities in dozens of small towns. She spoke at countless meetings and gatherings across Montana, logging six thousand miles by train, stage, and automobile in 1914.

In some western territories, such as Wyoming and Utah, women had already achieved the right to vote earlier in the nineteenth century. Together with her colleagues in other states, Rankin now battled to make women's suffrage a right in every western state and across the nation. But opposition continued. Her opponents feared that once empowered to vote, women would neglect their homes, become embroiled in unsavory political matters, and love men less. In addition, liquor interests and many opponents of prohibition stood fast against women's suffrage. In Montana, mining companies feared that voting women would help enact workmen's compensation laws.

Rankin and her colleagues employed several counterarguments. They insisted that without women's suffrage, the nation could not consider itself a true democracy. They maintained that women had special moral virtues that must have a voice in policy making lest families—the economic and social backbone of society—suffer. They emphasized

Mark Harvey

too that voting took a minuscule amount of time and would not curtail women's devotion to their families. Rankin believed that men and women in Montana and the West had a heritage of shared work on farms and ranches and therefore accepted gender equality more than other Americans.

In 1913, the Montana legislature finally agreed with Rankin and passed a resolution providing for a statewide vote on a suffrage amendment to the constitution. Rankin labored two more years before a statewide popular vote brought triumph to her cause. In 1914 Montanans approved of women's suffrage, with 41,302 in favor and 37,558 opposed. The newer homestead counties in eastern Montana helped carry the winning vote. There men who supported the amendment apparently believed that voting women would enable counties to reconfigure boundaries and establish new county seats, thereby drawing state funding for roads, bridges, and other improvements. Elsewhere, following similar campaigns, women's suffrage gained legislative approval in Washington in 1910; Arizona, Kansas, and Oregon in 1912; and Nevada in 1914.

Equally notable in western Progressivism during these years was the push for conservation of forests, waters, and wildlife. Conservation resonated with Progressives, who favored greater efficiency in government and ensuring economic opportunity. Natural resources such as forests and water must not be monopolized by big corporations or agricultural enterprises, Progressives believed, but managed for the broad public interest. This conservation impulse also arose from the perception that natural resources were scarce. On the plains and throughout the high valleys, basins, and deserts in the Far West, water obviously was in short supply. In the 1890s and early 1900s, irrigation "congresses" convened in several cities, where delegates called on the federal government to help reclaim semiarid lands. The high priest of reclamation, William Smythe, extolled the many benefits of reclamation in his book *The Conquest of Arid America,* evoking images of prosperous farms and ranches in western states once the rivers were captured and irrigation canals built. In 1902, the Reclamation Act authorized federal reclamation projects to be funded by the sale of public lands. Reclamation proved successful in many areas, enabling farmers to raise sugar beets on the dry plains adjacent to the Missouri River near Buford, North Dakota, establish fruit orchards near Grand Junction, Colorado, and grow other crops along the Truckee River in Nevada, in the Columbia basin of Washington, and in the Salt River Valley of Arizona.

Reclamation emerged from the sense of a scarcity of water, and a similar perception about depleted forests gave rise to another facet of conservation—the national forests. In the late nineteenth century, scientists warned of a timber famine that would devastate the national economy, and they added the alarming prospect of soil erosion and flooding induced by intensive timber harvesting. As a result of these concerns, Congress approved the Forest Reserve Act of 1891, the most important conservation measure of its time. The law empowered the president to set aside forest reserves by proclamation to protect watersheds and maintain a supply of timber through regulated management. Presidents Benjamin Harrison, Grover Cleveland, William McKinley, and Theodore Roosevelt created dozens of reserves totaling about 50 million acres in the West. In 1908, Congress repealed the president's authority to create reserves, but by then millions of acres had been set aside and the new Forest Service created to manage them. The Forest Service soon became a necessary (and at times irritating) presence to ranchers who grazed cattle and sheep as well as timber companies obliged to follow its regulations. Forest Service chief Gifford Pinchot, like Smythe, preached a gospel of bounty and prosperity by the careful use of resources. Like Smythe, Pinchot viewed the natural world in practical terms. Water and trees were commodities to be managed carefully to ensure long-term prosperity.

For John Muir, another seminal western thinker about the environment, the West's lands were valuable not for their bounty of resources but for their spectacular beauty. Muir believed that some lands should be off-limits to commodity interests, and he became a spearhead of the national park movement. Born in Scotland in 1838, Muir emigrated with his family to Wisconsin in 1849. There he labored long hours under his father's authoritarian hand, waking early in the morning so he had time to read and work on his many inventions. After attending the University of Wisconsin in Madison, Muir set out on pilgrimages that took him to Canada, Indiana, the Gulf Coast, and Yosemite Valley in 1868. In the following four decades he traveled to Alaska, Arizona, Wyoming, and Washington as well as to Europe and South America. But the Sierra Nevada in California was his primary home. In the 1870s he lived in the valley, herding sheep and working at a sawmill while spending his free time wandering in the high country and climbing the peaks.

Muir was at once a botanist, geologist, and naturalist who became enchanted by the sublime beauty of Yosemite Valley and the Sierra Nevada. In the early 1870s, he gathered information and wrote essays about the glacial origins of the Sierra and its dramatically beautiful valleys and sheer mountain faces. Later, at the urging of his friend Jeanne Carr, he wrote nature essays for *Scribner's Monthly, Overland Monthly,* and *Century Magazine.* His articles in *Century Magazine* made a vital

Figure 11.3: John Muir takes in the quiet solitude of the Sierra Nevada about 1900. Reproduced by permission of The Huntington Library, San Marino, California.

contribution to the campaign to create Yosemite and Sequoia national parks in 1890. His essays also lauded the magnificence of Mount Rainier, which Congress set aside as a national park in 1899. In 1892, joined by a number of professionals from Oakland, Stanford, and San Francisco, Muir founded the Sierra Club, which aimed "to explore, enjoy, and render accessible the mountain regions of the Pacific Coast." Two years later he assembled his essays and published *The Mountains of California,* followed by *Our National Parks* in 1903. That same year, Muir played host to President Roosevelt in Yosemite National Park. Earlier Muir had assumed that the new forest reserves would be protected and little used; when he later learned that Pinchot supported sheep grazing in them, he became an avowed opponent of the forester. Muir also came to believe that national parks must be protected permanently and managed for public enjoyment and recreation, unlike the national forests, which were open to grazing and logging.

As a writer, John Muir created powerful images of the wild nature he found in the Sierra and elsewhere. His rhythmic prose evoked the sounds and sights of foaming rivers, high waterfalls, pristine mountain lakes, and sentinel-like mountains. As nature literature scholar Thomas Lyon wrote, "His is one of the great efforts to make nature come alive on the page." For example, in *The Mountains of California,* Muir richly described glaciers, meadows, and forests and wrote lovingly of Douglas squirrels and water ouzels. He described the latter as "the mountain streams' own darling, the humming-bird of blooming waters [and] among all the mountain birds, none has cheered me so much in my mountain wanderings, none so unfailingly."

Some Muir scholars have maintained that Muir's worship of nature constituted a sharp break with the imposed and strict brand of Christianity he learned from his father. Other scholars argue that Muir did not reject Christianity and point out that his descriptions of wild nature are at times tinged with Christian terminology. Yet Muir clearly rejected the notion from Genesis that mankind must subdue the earth and put its resources to use. He blamed "Lord Man" for assuming a dominant posture over God's other creatures. Muir understood nature as part of a universal order designed by a benevolent God. Even during windstorms, torrential rains, and the occasional earthquake he perceived a harmony and a purpose in nature. He especially took pleasure in contemplating the once-vast glaciers that covered the Sierra and sculpted the deep valleys and rock faces of Half Dome, El Capitan, and other peaks. Of the glaciers he wrote that "few . . . of Nature's agents have left monuments so noble and enduring as they. The great granite domes a mile high, the cañons as deep, the noble peaks, the Yosemite valleys, these, and indeed nearly all other features of the Sierra scenery, are glacier monuments."

Muir's experiences of being captivated by nature's power were deeply personal. When climbing alone on lofty heights or precipitous cliffs, he found sudden strength at the moment of greatest peril, enabling him to surpass the dangerous spot. Such an event occurred when he scaled Mount Ritter in the 1870s. Thereafter Muir realized that nature offered more than beauty, more than a sense of God's design, but also empowerment of mind and spirit. He believed nature's power had great potential to lift weary spirits of the masses residing in cities and laboring in menial jobs. "Thousands of tired, nerve-shaken, over-civilized people," he wrote, "are beginning to find out that going to the mountains is going home; that wildness is a necessity; and that mountain parks and reservations are useful not only as fountains of timber and irrigating rivers, but as fountains of life."

Beginning in 1907, Muir focused much of his efforts on saving the Hetch Hetchy valley within Yosemite National Park from a proposed dam. After an earthquake and fire devastated San Francisco in 1906, city officials campaigned to construct a dam on the Tuolumne River, flowing out of the valley. Since the dam site lay within the national park, they had to secure permission to build the dam from Secretary of the Interior James Garfield and then from Congress. For the next seven years, conflict over Hetch Hetchy pitted Muir, the Sierra Club, and the Society for the Preservation of National Parks against mighty San

Francisco with its influential banking and business interests and its savvy consulting engineer, John Freeman. Thirsty and weary of putting up with the high water rates of the privately owned Spring Valley Water Company, the city lobbied Congress for the dam, arguing that the Tuolumne River offered the best long-term water supply. Muir, joined by J. Horace McFarland and the American Civic Association, warned that allowing the dam would create a precedent for invading other national parks with intrusive developments. Finally, following numerous hearings and public debate, both houses of Congress approved the dam in late 1913. Muir was crestfallen. One year later, on Christmas Eve, 1914, John Muir died.

Yet the movement that he led against the dam endured. In 1916, President Woodrow Wilson signed the National Park Service Act, establishing a new agency within the Department of the Interior that was obligated to conserve the parks and their wildlife for future generations. The national parks soon fell under the firm hand of the agency's first director, Stephen Mather, who brought his public relations skills to bear in promoting them to the American public. Mather worked closely with railroads and automobile clubs to do so. As a result, one of the West's great capitalist enterprises put its marketing and investment savvy to the task of luring tourists to national parks in the region. Railroads did so through lavish advertising and by constructing grand, rustic hotels such as Old Faithful Lodge in Yellowstone and the Prince of Wales hotel in Waterton Lakes. Louis Hill, who succeeded his father, James, as head of the Great Northern, heavily promoted Glacier National Park and adopted the slogan "See America First." By the 1910s, highway boosters also become prominent advertisers of the West. They conferred patriotic names on various roads, including the Lincoln Highway, National Old Trails Road, Theodore Roosevelt International Highway, and Victory Highway, and promised enhanced revenues to communities along the way from auto-based tourism.

The success of promoters and boosters of national parks and other tourist destinations capped a series of changes to the region's economy and culture induced by conservation policies and programs. Since the late nineteenth century, investors with their machines had had virtually a free hand in exploiting the region's resources, exhibiting little regard for future economic needs or other values people placed on the natural world. Reclamation, forestry, and the national park movement wove a new ethic into the West. Conservation was a crucial aspect of how the West and nation responded to the challenges of capitalist development, which at its heart involved exploitation of resources. Conservation in the largest sense manifested a belief that nature in America could not long survive the demands of a capitalist economy with a voracious appetite for natural resources. It was a recognition that while capital was welcome and necessary, that there should be limits on how far it could go and where it could operate.

Many of the dominant themes of the West in the Progressive era surfaced again during World War I. These proved to be boom years for most of the large industries in the region, especially mining, logging, and agriculture. Military action provided a strong market for copper and zinc, and mining communities from Montana to Arizona profited accordingly. Western farmers and ranchers profited during the war, meeting a powerful demand for food from America's allies and aided by government price supports of agricultural commodities. In the Northwest, shipping, fishing, and canning prospered as well. The war economy thereby strengthened the West's natural resource industries and its agricultural base.

For the most part, westerners supported American involvement in the war, but several important exceptions must be noted. Many Germans, whose memories of their homeland remained strong, sought either to remain neutral or opposed the entry of the United States into the war. In part because of their viewpoint, Jeannette Rankin took a courageous stand against the war in Congress during her term as a Republican in the House of Representatives from Montana from 1917 to 1919. Rankin thought that war was no solution to diplomatic disagreements, and she founded her lifelong work as a pacifist on that conviction. Interviewed in 1963, she said, "I can't settle a dispute with a young man by shooting him. And a nation can't settle a dispute with another nation by killing their young men. . . . War is a method, and you can be either for or against it and I'm against it because of its futility, its stupidity and its ultimate destruction of humanity—of civilization." In North Dakota and the northern plains, members of the Nonpartisan League and the IWW denounced what they called a war of capitalists and imperialists. To farmers who belonged to the league and to the Wobblies, the exploitative forces that crushed labor and producers of the land fought wars to gain national supremacy. But the federal government mounted an intensive public relations effort denouncing such views, and millions of Americans rallied behind the patriotic cause. The war years proved devastating to both the league and the IWW when radicalism was discredited in a burst of patriotism.

Nonetheless, the end of the war revealed that the West still had not resolved its longstanding dilemmas involving absentee business and the role of big capital in the regional economy. After the conflict a precipitous decline in commodity prices and a rapid shrinkage of demand for minerals introduced a new bust cycle in many industries, while farmers and ranchers endured extremely low commodity prices and drought. Conditions became so bad on the northern plains that thousands of farms were abandoned or sold and millions of acres taken out of production. Meanwhile, in Seattle a general strike resulted from the economic downturn, lasting for five days. All of this turmoil revealed only too clearly how the West, despite all of its growth since 1890, continued its colonial dilemmas, ever reliant on outside markets and capital investments and subject to the relentless cycles of boom and bust.

Essay on Sources

Several of the major texts on western history furnish important interpretations of the Progressive era, including Richard White, *"It's Your Misfortune and None of My Own": A New History of the American West* (Norman: University of Oklahoma Press, 1991); Michael P. Malone and Richard W. Etulain, *The American West: A Twentieth-Century History* (Lincoln: University of Nebraska Press, 1989); Walter Nugent, *Into the West: The Story of Its People* (New York: Knopf, 1999); and Clyde Milner II, Carol A. O'Connor, and Martha A. Sandweiss, eds., *The Oxford History of the American West* (New York: Oxford University Press, 1994).

For James J. Hill standard works are Michael P. Malone, *James J. Hill: Empire Builder of the Northwest* (Norman: University of Oklahoma Press, 1996); Albro Martin, *James J. Hill and the Opening of the Northwest* (New York: Oxford University Press, 1976); and Ralph W. Hidy, Muriel E. Hidy, and Roy V. Scott, *The Great Northern Railway: A History* (Boston: Harvard Business School Press, 1988). A new and revealing work is Claire Strom, *Profiting from the Plains: The Great Northern Railway and Corporate Development of the American West* (Seattle: University of Washington Press, 2003). See also Ralph W. Hidy and Muriel E. Hidy, "John Frank Stevens: Great Northern Engineer," *Minnesota History* 41 (winter 1969): 345–61.

Indispensable treatments of the western economy in this period include William G. Robbins's two books, *Colony and Empire: The Capitalist Transformation of the American West* (Lawrence: University Press of Kansas, 1994) and *Landscapes of Promise: The Oregon Story, 1800–1940* (Seattle: University of Washington Press, 1997); William Cronon, *Nature's Metropolis: Chicago and the Great West* (New York: Norton, 1991), is a superb analysis of railroads, cities, and the geography of capital. W. Thomas White treats labor issues in "Race, Ethnicity, and Gender in the Railroad Work Force: The Case of the Far Northwest," *Western Historical Quarterly* 16 (July 1985): 265–83, and "Railroad Labor Protests, 1894–1917," *Pacific Northwest Quarterly* 75 (January 1984): 13–21. See also Carlos Arnaldo Schwantes, *Hard Traveling: A Portrait of Work Life in the New Northwest* (Lincoln: University of Nebraska Press, 1994). William Deverell, *Railroad*

Crossing: Californians and the Railroad, 1850–1910 (Berkeley: University of California Press, 1994), is a penetrating work.

For Hispanics during this period see David G. Gutiérrez, *Walls and Mirrors: Mexican Americans, Mexican Immigrants, and the Politics of Ethnicity* (Berkeley: University of California Press, 1995); Mario T. García, *Desert Immigrants: The Mexicans of El Paso, 1880–1920* (New Haven, Conn.: Yale University Press, 1981); and Lawrence A. Cardoso, *Mexican Emigration to the United States, 1897–1931* (Tucson: University of Arizona Press, 1980). Quintard Taylor, *In Search of the Racial Frontier: African Americans in the American West, 1528–1990* (New York: Norton, 1998), is a standard work. European ethnic groups are covered in William C. Sherman and Playford Thorson, eds., *Plains Folk: North Dakota's Ethnic History* (Fargo: North Dakota Institute for Regional Studies, 1988); Frederick C. Luebke, *Ethnicity on the Great Plains* (Lincoln: University of Nebraska Press, 1980), and *European Immigrants in the West: Community Histories* (Albuquerque: University of New Mexico Press, 1998); and David M. Emmons, *The Butte Irish: Class and Ethnicity in an American Mining Town, 1875–1925* (Urbana: University of Illinois Press, 1989). For Native Americans, see Peter Iverson, *"We Are Still Here": American Indians in the Twentieth Century* (Wheeling, Ill.: Harlan Davidson, 1998).

For Populism, the best overviews are Robert C. McMath, Jr., *American Populism: A Social History 1877–1898* (New York: Hill and Wang, 1993); John D. Hicks, *The Populist Revolt: A History of the Farmer's Alliance and the People's Party* (Minneapolis: University of Minnesota Press, 1931); and Robert W. Larson, *Populism in the Mountain West* (Albuquerque: University of New Mexico Press, 1986). For the Progressive movement, histories of individual western states are an excellent source, along with William Deverell and Tom Sitton, eds., *California Progressivism Revisited* (Berkeley: University of California Press, 1994); Robert W. Cherny, *Populism, Progressivism, and the Transformation of Nebraska Politics, 1885–1915* (Lincoln: University of Nebraska Press, 1981); Robert Smith Bader, *Prohibition in Kansas: A History* (Lawrence: University Press of Kansas, 1986); Barbara Handy-Marchello, "Land, Liquor, and the Women of Hatton, North Dakota," *North Dakota History* 59 (fall 1992): 22–29; and William Howard Moore, "Progressivism and the Social Gospel in Wyoming: The Antigambling Act of 1901 as a Test Case," *Western Historical Quarterly* 15 (July 1984): 299–316. Paula Petrik, *No Step Backward: Women and Family on the Rocky Mountain Mining Frontier, Helena, Montana, 1865–1900* (Helena: Montana Historical Society Press, 1987), analyzes how Montanans voted for women's suffrage.

The newest biography of Jeannette Rankin is Norma Smith, *Jeannette Rankin, America's Conscience* (Helena: Montana Historical

Society Press, 2002). Older works include Hannah Josephson, *Jeannette Rankin: First Lady in Congress* (Indianapolis: Bobbs-Merrill, 1974); Kevin S. Giles, *Flight of the Dove: The Story of Jeannette Rankin* (Beaverton, Oreg.: Touchstone Press, 1980); and Joan Hoff Wilson, "Peace Is a Woman's Job: Jeannette Rankin and American Foreign Policy, the Origins of Her Pacifism," *Montana: The Magazine of Western History* 30 (winter 1980): 28–41.

William Cronon surveys the origins of conservation in "Landscapes of Abundance and Scarcity," *The Oxford History of the American West;* Donald J. Pisani's two books are indispensable on water policy and irrigation: *To Reclaim a Divided West: Water, Law, and Public Policy, 1848–1902* (Albuquerque: University of New Mexico Press, 1992), and *Water and American Government: The Reclamation Bureau, National Water Policy, and the West, 1902–1935* (Berkeley: University of California Press, 2002); see also Mark Fiege, *Irrigated Eden: The Making of an Agricultural Landscape in the American West* (Seattle: University of Washington Press, 1999). Forestry is covered in Thomas R. Cox, et al., *This Well Wooded Land: Americans and Their Forests from Colonial Times to the Present* (Lincoln: University of Nebraska Press, 1985); Nancy Langston, *Forest Dreams, Forest Nightmares: The Paradox of Old Growth in the Inland West* (Seattle: University of Washington Press, 1995); and Char Miller, *Gifford Pinchot and the Making of Modern Environmentalism* (Washington, D.C.: Island Press, 2001).

On national parks and tourism, see Alfred Runte's *National Parks: The American Experience,* 3rd ed. (Lincoln: University of Nebraska Press, 1997), and *Trains of Discovery: Western Railroads and the National Parks* (Flagstaff, Ariz.: Northland Press, 1984); Richard West Sellars, *Preserving Nature in the National Parks: A History* (New Haven, Conn.: Yale University Press, 1997); Mark David Spence, *Dispossessing the Wilderness: Indian Removal and the Making of the National Parks* (New York: Oxford University Press, 1999); Marguerite S. Shaffer, *See America First: Tourism and National Identity, 1880–1940* (Washington, D.C.: Smithsonian Institution Press, 2001); and Peter Blodgett, "Selling the Scenery: Advertising and the National Parks, 1916–1933," in *Seeing and Being Seen: Tourism in the American West,* ed. David M. Wrobel and Patrick T. Long (Lawrence: University Press of Kansas, 2001).

The classic study of John Muir is William Frederic Bade, *The Life and Letters of John Muir,* 2 vols. (Boston: Houghton Mifflin, 1924); Linnie Marsh Wolfe, *Son of the Wilderness: The Life of John Muir* (Madison: University of Wisconsin Press, 1978); and Stephen Fox, *John Muir and His Legacy: The American Conservation Movement* (1981; Madison: University of Wisconsin Press, 1985). For penetrating analyses of Muir's thought, see Michael P. Cohen, *The Pathless Way: John*

Muir and American Wilderness (Madison: University of Wisconsin Press, 1984); Sally M. Miller, ed., *John Muir: His Life and Work* (Albuquerque: University of New Mexico Press, 1993); Donald Worster, "John Muir and the Roots of American Environmentalism," in his book *The Wealth of Nature: Environmental History and the Ecological Imagination* (New York: Oxford University Press, 1993); and Dennis C. Williams, *God's Wilds: John Muir's Vision of Nature* (College Station: Texas A&M University Press, 2002).

A fine collection of Muir's writings is *John Muir: Nature Writings* (New York: Literary Classics of the United States, 1997); see also Richard F. Fleck, *Mountaineering Essays, John Muir* (Salt Lake City: University of Utah Press, 1997); Edwin Way Teale, ed., *The Wilderness World of John Muir* (Boston: Houghton Mifflin, 1976); and Linnie Marsh Wolfe, ed., *John of the Mountains: The Unpublished Journals of John Muir* (Madison: University of Wisconsin Press, 1979).

CHAPTER 12

Sister Aimee Semple McPherson and the Interwar West, 1920 to 1940

KATHERINE G. AIKEN

"**D**id you ever hear the story of Aimee McPherson? Aimee McPherson, that wonderful person," asks the popular folk song. During the 1920s, Aimee Semple McPherson was one of the best-known women in America (she often garnered front-page headlines in America's most influential newspapers three times a week), she founded a major Protestant church, and she was a pioneer in the use of radio. Aimee McPherson was a remarkable woman, a transitional figure illustrating the "true woman" but also epitomizing the changing gender roles of the so-called new woman.

Much of Sister Aimee's life also illustrates major trends in the history of the American West in the 1920s and 1930s. People moved west in substantial numbers during both decades but for different reasons. In the 1920s, success often allowed people to retire to the West, but during the 1930s people moved west to escape the devastating impact of the Dust Bowl and the Depression. Aimee Semple McPherson understood both motivations, and she appealed to both types of immigrants.

During the 1920s, western society and culture reflected many of the trends evident in the larger American society—the 1920s is the first truly modern decade in American history. Westerners shared the general uneasiness that Americans felt regarding the vast array of changes that confronted them. New technology (especially automobiles and radio), expanded populations, and cultural adjustments defined the decade, and westerners struggled to make sense of it all. During the 1930s, the Depression and Franklin D. Roosevelt's New Deal transformed the American West. Aimee Semple McPherson's career provides an avenue for exploring these trends.

Aimee Elizabeth Kennedy was born October 9, 1890, in a farmhouse near Ingersoll, Ontario. Her parents, James Morgan Kennedy and Mildred "Minnie" Pearce Kennedy, were an unusual couple. James

Kennedy (1836–1922) had operated a small farm with his wife, Elizabeth. When Elizabeth became ill, James hired orphaned Minnie Pearce to assist with the nursing chores. Following Elizabeth's death, Minnie stayed at the Kennedy farm, much to the chagrin of neighbors, who worried about the proprieties involved. On October 3, 1886, James and Minnie (he was fifty and she was fifteen years old) went across the border to Michigan and were married.

Minnie consecrated the couple's only child to service with the Salvation Army when Aimee Elizabeth was only a few weeks old; her childhood was punctuated with Bible stories and hymns. In December 1907, Aimee asked her father to take her to a Pentecostal meeting as a lark. One of the preachers was Robert Semple, a tall (estimates range from six-foot two to six-foot five) Irish immigrant with a lilting voice. Aimee remembered, "I had never heard such a sermon. Using his Bible as a sword, he cleft the whole world in two." He divided humanity into Christians and sinners, and Aimee feared that her life placed her in the latter category. While she worried over the state of her soul, Aimee also fell in love with Robert Semple.

Aimee had a conversion experience and soon became immersed in Pentecostal beliefs, especially the idea that all true Christians must undergo a religious experience called the Baptism of the Holy Spirit with speaking in tongues (glossolalia) as the outward sign of this baptism. Despite Minnie's strongly voiced concern, Aimee continued to be inextricably drawn to the meetings until she herself experienced the Baptism of the Holy Spirit.

Aimee Kennedy married Robert Semple on August 12, 1908. He became the single greatest human influence on Aimee's life. She wrote of him, "He was my theological seminary, my spiritual mentor, and my tender, patient, and unfailing lover." She was deeply enamored and committed her life to being his helpmate. Semple was ordained on January 2, 1909, with Aimee following him in ordination a year later. It soon became apparent that Aimee possessed the gift of interpretation of tongues, which gave her cultural authority within the Pentecostal group.

Missionary efforts were central to Pentecostals' worldview. When Robert Semple felt called and traveled as a missionary to China, Aimee's life underwent dramatic change. In the mission field, both Aimee and Robert contracted malaria, and Robert died in Hong Kong on August 17, 1910. Exactly one month later, Aimee gave birth to a daughter, Roberta Star—named for her father and, as Aimee recalled, "because she was my star of hope." Six weeks later Aimee and the baby sailed for home.

Meanwhile, Minnie Kennedy had taken a sabbatical from her marriage and was working with the Salvation Army in New York City. Aimee and Roberta joined her there, where Aimee met Harold

McPherson. They were married on February 28, 1912 (her marriage to an American citizen gave Aimee citizenship as well). Although she went by the name Aimee Semple McPherson for the remainder of her life, Aimee's marriage to Harold was always on shaky ground. The couple had a son, Rolf Kennedy McPherson, on March 23, 1913. By the spring of 1915, Aimee took her two children and returned to Canada. She began preaching at local Pentecostal meetings.

As Aimee herself recognized, "A woman preacher was a novelty. At the time when I began my ministry, women were well in the background of life in Canada and the United States." Although recognizing the barriers to success as a Pentecostal preacher, Aimee Semple McPherson believed God had called her to serve in that capacity. She was determined to prevail. Soon she was traveling from New England to Florida, holding meetings along the way. For a while Harold McPherson joined Aimee and Rolf. The family traveled in an automobile Aimee christened her Gospel Car. She decorated the vehicle with banners that read: "Jesus is Coming Soon" on one side and "Where will you spend eternity?" on the other. Harold McPherson, quickly tiring of this nomadic life, left the family in January 1918. After Aimee wired her mother, Minnie and Roberta joined Rolf and Aimee. Minnie managed the funds and schedules while Aimee preached. By 1923, she had traveled by train and car from coast to coast six times and preached in more than a hundred cities.

Aimee Semple McPherson's early career as an itinerant tent preacher featured two notable elements. One dealt with race, the other with healing. As was the custom, her Florida meetings included only whites. But when Aimee became convinced that African Americans had the same spiritual needs as whites, she organized meetings for them. These meetings generated so much excitement that soon white people began to attend in violation of southern law and custom. This change established a pattern for Aimee Semple McPherson's evangelical career. She extended her ministry to all people, regardless of color.

Aimee Semple McPherson's experiences with faith healing are equally controversial and noteworthy. Faith healing has always been of paramount importance to Pentecostals. Although Aimee had seen the power of prayer heal herself and her son, Rolf, her early preaching career did not feature this dimension. However, between 1921 and 1923, Aimee Semple McPherson's emphasis on healing became a major element of her appeal and drew people to her meetings.

A vision turned Aimee Semple McPherson's eyes west, and she determined to take her family to southern California. She purchased a new Oldsmobile touring car with seven seats and along with her mother and children started out toward the West Coast. She became perhaps the first woman to drive across the United States without the company of a man. The travelers covered between eighty and a hundred miles per day, with Aimee stopping along the way to preach and hold meetings.

Appropriately, Aimee Semple McPherson and her family arrived in California via automobile in 1918, when the state was exploding with newcomers. The population of California, less than 3 million in 1914, jumped to 5.7 million by 1930. Los Angeles was the fastest-growing city in the United States during the 1920s. The newcomers, mostly middle-aged or older, came largely from the rural Midwest. In journalist H. L. Mencken's words, they were "middle brow middlewesterners." Many of these immigrants were looking for new roots, so even though Los Angeles was a rapidly expanding urban area, it featured the trappings of a small town or, as writer Louis Adamic put it in 1925, "an enormous village."

Aimee Semple McPherson's rise to prominence came during the era journalist Frederick Lewis Allen described as America's "convalescence from World War I and the Red Scare." The new residents of Los Angeles and the surrounding area sought to return to what were, in their view, traditional values. According to author Huntington Wright, Los Angeles had "adopted Puritanism as its inflexible doctrine." Later, writer Carey McWilliams added that Los Angeles was becoming "a center of Comstockism [antivice] and Fundamentalism." Similar viewpoints were present in other western cities such as Portland, Seattle, Denver, Salt Lake City, and Albuquerque.

Religious fundamentalism was also under fire at the time, particularly following the Scopes trial in 1925. Western fundamentalists, like their counterparts in the remainder of the country, feared that they were destined for exile from the mainstream of American society and culture. Many of the West's new residents were looking for a way to reestablish their identity. California became a center for revivalism during the 1920s. According to the *New Republic,* Los Angeles was a "paradise of all religious fanatics of every fifty-seventh variety." The economic expansion that characterized the West in the 1920s served only to accentuate this tendency.

Aimee Semple McPherson met the needs of this new population on a number of levels. She shared their attitudes toward the apparent decline of moral standards during the 1920s by proclaiming, "I had rather see my children dead than in a public dancehall." Her opposition to Darwin's theories remained adamant. She was also an outspoken proponent of prohibition, which most westerners embraced.

Sister Aimee unabashedly recognized that her followers tended to be middle class and, according to the *New Republic,* naturally rather simple people. She said, "I bring spiritual consolation to the middle

Figure 12.1: Sister Aimee Semple McPherson at the height
of her brilliant career. Reproduced by permission of
The Huntington Library, San Marino, California.

class, leaving those above to themselves and those below to the Salvation
Army." According to a Carey McWilliams recollection, on one occasion McPherson walked into a meeting and asked the audience how
many of them had ever lived on a farm. Everyone stood up. She wanted
fundamentalists, often people from rural backgrounds, to stop viewing
themselves as marginalized and to lose their self-consciousness. When
they sang, "Give me that old-time religion. It's good enough for me,"
Sister Aimee's disciples were in fact reaffirming their own steadfast-
ness, and others throughout the West shared the sentiment.

People flocked to hear Aimee Semple McPherson preach because
her message resonated with them. She believed that everyone should

enjoy, even revel in, the beauty of Christianity, and her preaching reflected this conviction. Although some of her contemporaries emphasized the retribution sinners would face in hell and damnation, Sister Aimee preferred to stress the glory and happiness that awaited believers. She preached a cheerful gospel: "Who cares about old hell friends? Why, we *all* know what hell is. We've heard about it all our lives. A terrible place, where nobody wants to go. I think the *less* we hear about hell the better, don't you? Let's forget about hell. Lift up your hearts. What *we* are interested in, yes Lord, is *heaven* and how to get there!" Her message especially suited the West, where rising expectations were a notable attraction.

Many of the new California residents had come seeking a climate that physicians believed might mitigate symptoms of various diseases. Sister Aimee spoke to these people. Her initial prominence in California stemmed from a successful healing meeting in Balboa Park, San Diego—a city where, according to one estimate, 24 percent of the population (four times the national average) suffered from illness of one kind or another. Illness, in part, explains their motivation for moving west; they wanted a life similar to what they had in the Midwest but in a more beautiful place with a more moderate climate.

Sister Aimee built the foundation for her theology in California as well. She pronounced her Foursquare Gospel in its final form for the first time in Oakland in 1922. The four cornerstones were Regeneration, Baptism in the Spirit, Divine Healing, and the Second Coming. Not only was the symbolism easy to grasp, but it conveyed a strong notion of rightness, "squareness," that appealed to Aimee Semple McPherson's followers.

As Sister Aimee's fame grew and her crowds expanded, she determined to build a permanent temple in Los Angeles, Angelus Temple. Three major evangelistic campaigns raised seed money for the temple. They were all in the West: Denver in June 1921, San Jose in August of the same year, and a return trip to Denver in July 1922. Sister's experiences help to illustrate one of the most significant trends in the West during the 1920s—urbanization. Most easterners viewed the West as a land of vast, wide-open spaces, and their perception was certainly true. But cities punctuated the western landscape; as historian Carol A. O'Connor has noted, the West was a "region of cities." Urban areas were a focal point for both economic and cultural development.

As a counterpoint to Sister Aimee's successes, Harold McPherson was granted a divorce in 1921 that gave him partial custody of Rolf. The irony of this situation is not lost. Here was a woman on the threshold of establishing a major church who was now a divorcee—anathema to many of her potential supporters.

Figure 12.2: The famed Angelus Temple, built by Sister Aimee in the early 1920s, at 1100 Glendale Blvd., Los Angeles. Reproduced by permission of The Huntington Library, San Marino, California.

Angelus Temple was an extraordinary accomplishment. Sister Aimee purposely sought to avoid traditional church architecture, which tended, in her view, to be dark and cold. She wanted a place that was welcoming and so chose an unsupported dome, painted blue with clouds, to convey an open feeling. She hoped to "emphasize in it not the torments of hell but the deep abiding joy of salvation." The building resembled a movie theater, apropos in Los Angeles, and featured a marquee to announce the topics of Sister's sermons. A lighted cross that rotated on the top of the dome was visible from fifty miles away. The temple was also known as the Church of the Foursquare Gospel and could seat 5,300.

The temple was an immediate success, with a Hollywood influence evident from the beginning. In fact, Aimee Semple McPherson's sermons were so entertaining that seats in the temple for Sunday nights were at a premium. Throughout most of the 1920s, the city had to schedule extra trolleys and hire more police for traffic control before and after the meetings. According to one church member, "No tourist who came to California in the twenties felt his trip was a success unless he could boast of hearing one of Aimee's sermons." And there were plenty of opportunities since Sister usually preached every weekday and three times on Sunday, a schedule that Bruce Bliven noted in the *New Republic* was "enough to kill four robust men."

Pageantry and performance were as much a part of Angelus Temple and Aimee Semple McPherson's ministry as prayer and preaching. Sister Aimee, usually attired in white robes, always carried large floral arrangements, most often her trademark roses. The hymns tended toward the traditional and the upbeat—"Jesus, Savior, Pilot Me," "Stand Up, Stand Up for Jesus," and "Rock of Ages." Sister Aimee's sermons were not noteworthy for theological argument but for their emotional impact. Her charisma and her presence added to the spectacle, as did elaborate staging, lighting, and sets. One observer called it a "sensuous debauch served up in the name of religion," whereas another termed it "supernatural whoopee." But thousands found solace and a sense of community at Angelus Temple. The services were never dull.

During the 1920s many fundamentalist ministers embraced the Ku Klux Klan, but Aimee Semple McPherson was not among them. Westerners were especially susceptible to the KKK. The Klan enjoyed considerable support in Oregon, where the organization elected a governor and came close to controlling the state legislature. Significant Klan activity was present also in California and in Colorado, where the Denver Klan was an active force in both state and local politics. Although Aimee Semple McPherson and her followers shared many of the Klan's precepts—anti-Bolshevism, fundamentalism, support of prohibition, and unabashed Americanism—she was not comfortable with KKK intolerance. The Klan made overtures to Sister in Denver, and one evening in 1924, a group of white knights in full regalia entered the Angelus Temple. Caught unaware, members of the congregation quickly gave up their coveted seats and waited expectantly for Sister Aimee to respond. She did with an extemporized sermon that recounted the story of an elderly African American farmer who traveled to an "unnamed" city to see the sights. When he attempted to worship at a beautiful church, an usher grabbed him, escorted him out, and directed him to a "nice little Negro church on down the road." As the elderly man sat disconsolate on the steps, he was joined by another traveler, a stranger, who said to him, "I, too have been trying to get into that church for many, many years." Of course the African American man soon recognized the traveler as the Master himself. Sister Aimee admonished the Klansmen, "You men who pride yourselves on patriotism, you men who have pledged yourselves to make America free for white Christianity, listen to me! Ask yourselves how it is possible to pretend to worship one of the greatest Jews who ever lived, Jesus Christ, and then to despise all living Jews? I say unto you as our Master said, 'Judge not, that ye not be judged.'" Aimee Semple McPherson then stood quietly in an atmosphere simmering with expectation until one by one the Klansmen exited the temple.

Katherine G. Aiken

According to reports, white hoods and robes were left in several trash cans around the temple.

Aimee Semple McPherson also made use of the new technology of the 1920s. She once wrote, "To thrive in the present day, religion must utilize present day methods." Not surprisingly, she was a pioneer in the use of radio. In 1922, she became the first woman to preach a sermon over the radio, and she was the first woman to receive an FCC commercial license. On February 6, 1924, only a year and a half after the pioneering station in the country, Radio KFSG (Kall Four Square Gospel), came on the air, the initial hymn was "Give the Winds a Mighty Voice—Jesus Saves." The station enjoyed the second-largest radio audience in the Los Angeles area, with a transmitter so powerful it sometimes disrupted other broadcasts.

Sister Aimee's convictions regarding this new technology were prescient as radio transformed American society during the 1920s, like the Internet has impacted contemporary America. As historian Mary Murphy has argued, the radio replaced magazines and catalogs as the lifeline to the world, especially in the West, where distance worked against a sense of community. Aimee Semple McPherson's voice was every bit as compelling over the radio as in person, so her early morning show, "The Sunshine Hour," drew large audiences. She would encourage listeners to put their hands on the radio and pray with her as she denounced the "many vices of modern America" using the most modern technology available.

At Angelus Temple, Kenneth Ormiston, a married man, was the KFSG radio technician. He and Aimee spent much time together when she delivered her radio addresses and going over technical aspects of her sermon broadcasts. Aimee's mother warned her that appearances were everything in her profession, but Aimee ignored Minnie Kennedy's counsel that she sever ties with Ormiston. He resigned his temple job in December 1925, and soon his wife left him while hinting that Sister had been responsible for the breakup. The stage was set for an incredible episode.

Shortly after noon on May 18, 1926, Aimee Semple McPherson and her secretary went to the beach at Ocean Park, where Sister often composed her sermons. Just before 5 p.m. Minnie Kennedy was informed that Sister was lost. When word of the disappearance reached her followers, they launched a massive search effort. Fishermen dragged the ocean floor for her body, glass bottom boats from Catalina patrolled the area, airplanes searched from the sky, and thousands of people scoured the beach. Los Angeles newsboys hawked extra editions several times an hour to keep the city updated on the situation. Despite the offer of a $25,000 reward for Sister's safe return, few held out hope, so on June 20 Minnie

Kennedy presided over a twelve-hour memorial service that included six thousand mourners in the temple and another fourteen thousand in the streets, who heard the proceedings over loudspeakers. Then on June 23, Aimee Semple McPherson walked in from the desert at Agua Prieta Mexico. She was hospitalized in Douglas, Arizona, and from her bed she related the story of her kidnapping and desperate escape.

Estimates indicate that fifty thousand people were present for Aimee Semple McPherson's triumphant return to Los Angeles on June 26, but the story did not end there. Members of the Los Angeles Chamber of Commerce feared that Aimee's escapade would result in disparaging remarks and embarrassment. They were particularly leery of any scandal that might damage the city's reputation and jeopardize efforts to sponsor the 1932 Olympic Games. The chamber pressured District Attorney Asa Keyes to investigate the disappearance. People all across the country watched with fascination.

Sister preached a sermon from her pulpit titled "My Story Is True!" and agreed to testify before the grand jury, despite advice from her lawyer. On July 20, the grand jury found that there was insufficient evidence that a kidnapping had taken place. Two days later, newspapers carried the story of a "love nest" in Carmel where ostensibly Aimee Semple McPherson had spent time with Kenneth Ormiston. The district attorney issued warrants for Aimee, her mother, and Kenneth Ormiston, charging them with corruption of public morals, obstruction of justice, and conspiracy to manufacture evidence. A feeding frenzy of interest accompanied the scandal. The city of Los Angeles constructed grandstands in the municipal courtroom for the huge crowds, and ticket scalpers had a heyday selling reporters' passes. This circus lasted six weeks and generated 3,500 pages of transcript. Despite the long hearings and considerable embarrassment, despite committing considerable resources to do so (perhaps as much as $500,000), the county was never able to prove any liaison between Aimee Semple McPherson and Kenneth Ormiston. The criminal charges against her were dismissed on January 10, 1927.

Throughout the ordeal, Aimee's story never changed. However, her reaction once the trauma was over is telling. She embarked on a cross-country tour to deliver her lecture "The Story of My Life." She had her hair cut and curled, began wearing makeup, and updated her wardrobe. Cutting her hair was a symbolic act; bobbed hair made a decided statement of female rebellion during the 1920s.

By all accounts Sister began to shun old acquaintances and seek new advisers. These developments put a strain on Sister's relationship with her mother, and by July 22, 1927, Minnie resigned. This act precipitated yet another crisis since all of the holdings, including Angelus Temple, were in the names of Minnie Kennedy and Aimee Semple McPherson. Kennedy received about $100,000 in an eventual settlement.

Her new advisers encouraged Sister Aimee to sanction controversial business ventures, including a summer camp at Lake Tahoe where one could "Vacation with Aimee" and a cemetery where plot holders could "Go Up with Aimee." Both investments were abject business failures. These schemes, in conjunction with the kidnapping fiasco, contributed to questions about Sister Aimee's sincerity. However, Sister Aimee's personal appeal was undiminished; one journalist explained, "She had *It,* and plenty of it." *Sunset Magazine* noted that even after 1926, Aimee Semple McPherson was still "shepherdess of one of the world's great religious revivals."

Viewed in context, Aimee Semple McPherson's career emphasized important trends in the West during the 1920s. Her political conservatism and support for the Republican Party were echoed throughout the region. More and more immigrants to the area brought with them fundamentalism and conservatism. Politically, in 1920 every western state but Texas voted for Warren G. Harding for president, and the region remained staunchly Republican throughout the decade. Herbert Hoover, who spent boyhood years in Oregon and attended Stanford University, considered himself a westerner and carried all the western states in 1928. Western representatives to the U.S. Congress tended to be among the more conservative members, such as Senator Reed Smoot of Utah (1903–1933) and Nevada senator Key Pittman (1913–1940).

Sister Aimee Semple McPherson was a staunch opponent of the liquor traffic even before prohibition became a central question in the West and the entire United States. Westerners tended to be divided on the liquor question along the same lines as the rest of the country—urban versus rural, Protestant versus Catholic, immigrant against native-born Americans. Workers in urban areas such as San Francisco and Seattle stridently opposed prohibition, while traditional fundamentalist rural people were in favor. According to historian Earl Pomeroy, of the ten largest western cities only Salt Lake City voted in favor of prohibition. However, the West, with the exception of California, was dry before the Eighteenth Amendment went into effect in 1920.

Although Aimee Semple McPherson founded her work in a prosperous southern California during the 1920s, the economic situation in the rest of the West was more tenuous. The region's economy was based on extractive industries and the production of raw materials to such an extent that many historians referred to it as a colony of the East. Since there was little high-wage manufacturing, westerners found themselves at the mercy of eastern markets.

Other sections of the West were experiencing a decade much different from Sister Aimee's Los Angeles. For example, western agriculture underwent change during the period, with the 1920s representing a turning point for farmers. In this decade, America's farm population began to decline, with more westerners living in urban areas than on farms. An increasing number of farms were large corporate entities rather than family-owned operations. Depressed agricultural prices were the norm, as western farmers did not recuperate from the 1921 economic downturn that hit agriculture nationwide. For example, in Idaho potatoes sold for $1.51 a bushel in 1919 and were down to $.31 cents by 1922. Thousands of dryland farmers failed and left the region. Those who stayed found that they needed to acquire more land and mechanize their farms. Western agriculture began to take on its modern appearance, with fewer farmers and more technology and machinery. Chronic overproduction and low prices also plagued the industry. Ranching was likewise in decline. The marginal nature of farming and ranching created such a dire situation that both Montana and Idaho experienced shrinking populations.

Senator Charles L. McNary of Oregon was at the forefront of efforts to aid farmers, especially western farmers. He introduced the McNary-Haugen Bill in 1924, and debates on the future of American agriculture were among the most contentious congressional discussions of the 1920s. The bill, which provided for the dumping of surpluses into foreign markets, could not get past a presidential veto.

Sister Aimee's California was a notable exception to these trends and pioneered in others. It became the second-largest agricultural producer in the nation, and even the agricultural depression of 1921 had little impact. The state enjoyed other areas of growth, perhaps most notably the motion picture industry in Hollywood (it is no coincidence that Aimee Semple McPherson's career mirrored developments in movies). Moviemaking took on its now familiar trappings during the 1920s; it was first among all industries in California to employ one hundred thousand workers. The largest studios were major enterprises, and Hollywood came to be viewed as the great American dream factory.

In other areas, timber and mining experienced boom-and-bust cycles in the 1920s. Although both industries had successfully defeated the Industrial Workers of the World and other labor radicals during the World War I period, they continued to struggle to achieve economic stability. Only the generally pro-business climate of the 1920s allowed these bastions of the western economy to prosper.

The federal government impacted the West in the 1920s through the Colorado River Compact that Secretary of Commerce Herbert Hoover negotiated in 1922. The agreement involved a division of the

Colorado River waters among the western states, except Arizona. Congress authorized the construction of Boulder Dam in southern Nevada in 1926. The dam was to provide electricity to Los Angeles and other cities and also to irrigate southern California land.

As it did for Aimee Semple McPherson, the automobile came to greater significance during the 1920s. In fact, by the end of the decade 10 percent of the nation's 23 million automobiles and trucks were in California. The federal government worked to expand the highway system through the Highway Act of 1921, which provided funds for the construction of many roads in the West. Oregon was the first state to enact a tax on gasoline, and funds were used to improve roads. Other western states soon followed.

The automobile and highways facilitated tourism, which became a major economic force in the West. On one occasion Aimee Semple McPherson noted that she had chosen Los Angeles as the site of her temple because "it is where the tourists come and take back the message—where they come and forget to go home—where they come with a one-way ticket." The federal government fostered tourism as well, most notably with the expansion of the national parks system.

Between 1931 and 1944 Aimee Semple McPherson's ministry focused on the Foursquare Gospel and her position as the leader of a growing fundamentalist denomination. But even this chapter was not without controversy. On September 13, 1931, Aimee Semple McPherson eloped with David Hutton, a sometime performer ten years her junior. No sooner had the couple announced their marriage to temple members than Myrtle Hazel St. Pierre charged Hutton with breach of promise. Aimee found herself the focal point of another highly publicized court case. This controversy was awkward for church members because according to church dogma divorced people were not allowed to remarry so long as their former spouse was still alive. Harold McPherson was very much alive and living in Florida. Eventually another divorce was the result, with Aimee Semple McPherson recognizing her marriage to Hutton as the greatest mistake of her life.

Sister Aimee's personal problems paled in the face of the larger economic crisis that confronted her followers and the nation. The Great Depression following the stock market crash of 1929 had a devastating impact on the West, just as it did on the remainder of the country. Western extractive industries tended to depend on eastern investors for infusions of capital. Those infusions were no longer forthcoming. At the same time, eastern industries ceased to require raw materials from the West, since production was greatly curtailed. Tourism dropped to less than half of its precrash numbers. The West's image as a land of opportunity was tarnished.

Inclement weather exacerbated the economic downturn in the Midwest. Between 1929 and 1939 there were nine years in which rainfall was below average. This drought, combined with high winds and grasshoppers, had a devastating impact on Midwestern farms. A half-million people sought refuge from the Dust Bowl in the West, about half of whom came to California. As in the Joads' odyssey, described so vividly in John Steinbeck's *Grapes of Wrath* and in the epic film of the same name, these were a very different group of immigrants than those generally prosperous midwestern farmers who came west during the 1920s. Steinbeck's novel, Carey McWilliams's journalistic discussion in *Factories in the Fields,* and Dorothea Lange's photograph *Migrant Mother,* immortalized in 1936, present a vastly different picture of the Far West than Aimee Semple McPherson and her offspring arriving in their touring car in 1918.

The Dust Bowl refugees were a different class of people than the immigrants of the 1920s, and Californians did not welcome these newcomers of the 1930s. These immigrants arrived with few funds and competed for few jobs. California agriculturists, also suffering from the economic downturn, had neither the desire nor the capacity to provide living wages or adequate working conditions for these migrants. Many of these workers lived in migrant camps where the conditions were unspeakable. Few had running water, living accommodations were minimal, there were no educational facilities, and infant mortality rates soared. The resulting tensions contributed to more than 180 agricultural strikes in California between 1933 and 1939, with more than ninety thousand workers participating.

People of Mexican descent made up a disproportionate part of the California poor during the 1930s. About 250,000 came from Mexico searching for any kind of job. At the same time, farmers could hire Okies and other white migrant workers, forcing Mexicans to seek employment in cities, especially Los Angeles. In fact, the Hispanic population of most western states grew in the 1930s. Perhaps a half million went to Texas, with significant numbers of Hispanic workers also in Colorado sugar beet fields.

By 1932 considerable sentiment existed in the West for some form of direct relief. California instigated a small program, the Unemployed Citizens League in Washington worked for this goal, and in Colorado private relief agencies made concerted efforts but were not up to the task. Reactions set in. The Bonus Expeditionary Force began in Denver in the summer of 1932. The Farmers' Holiday movement had strong support in Colorado, New Mexico, and Texas. When President Herbert Hoover opposed federally funded direct relief, his opposition encouraged western support for Franklin D. Roosevelt's presidential candidacy. Roosevelt toured the West as part of his history-making 1932 presidential campaign. He personally viewed the dramatic impact of the Depression on the region, and he announced plans for programs that would address western concerns. In 1932 Franklin D. Roosevelt carried every western state.

One dispute, a walkout among West Coast dockworkers, represented an early challenge for President Roosevelt. Harry Bridges led the strike that eventually shut down ports from Seattle to San Diego for almost four months in 1934. Historian Carlos Schwantes calls it "the single most important labor disturbance on the West Coast during the 1930s," and the episode illustrates the nature of worker militancy during the decade. Bridges and the Longshoremen led a general strike movement in San Francisco during July that was a focal point for organized labor in the country.

Franklin D. Roosevelt's New Deal and its agencies designed to combat massive unemployment led westerners to look to the federal government for aid. The Civilian Conservation Corps was perhaps the most welcomed since it concentrated on resource management. To this day there are few areas of the West where one cannot view the results of CCC work on trails, bridges, and campsites and other improvements. CCC recruits labored on flood control projects as well. In Idaho alone, CCC camps housed twenty thousand young men. Their major task was to combat the blister rust epidemic that was destroying the state's legendary white pine forests, and workers treated 2 million acres for the fungus. In fact, the U.S. Forest Service spent more in Idaho during the Roosevelt years than in any other state.

Not surprisingly, since water is the West's most precious commodity, the New Deal also addressed that subject. Roosevelt's programs took a multiple-use approach that included basic water supplies, erosion control, irrigation, electrification, recreation, flood control, wildlife conservation, and forest development. In the early years of the Roosevelt administration, the Bureau of Reclamation poured money into western projects. Boulder Dam construction was accelerated with an infusion of New Deal funds; it was the first project to combine all of these interests. That dam eventually cost $114 million to construct and provided water and electricity to southern California and Arizona as well as irrigation water for about 1.5 million acres of land. In addition the dam construction employed thousands of workers (fifty died during dam construction). Water storage behind the dam began on February 1, 1935, with President Roosevelt dedicating the dam eight months later. It remains a testimony to New Deal activism.

Two large dam projects on the Columbia River enjoyed widespread name recognition during the 1930s, Bonneville and Grand Coulee. Work

Figure 12.3: CCC camp—Camp Harry Marsh, F-30. Co. 967. Prichard, Idaho, 1933.
Courtesy of the Historical Photograph Collection, 5-081-1b, University of Idaho
Library, Moscow.

at Bonneville, about forty miles east of Portland, Oregon, began on
September 30, 1933. Part of the Public Works Administration, as proj-
ect number 28, it was the first federal government construction on the
Columbia River. The dam became primarily a power project, with
President Roosevelt starting the two hydroelectric generators at
Bonneville on September 28, 1937. Grand Coulee Dam also remains a
significant New Deal symbol. It was called at the time "the biggest thing
on earth." Both projects were immortalized in Woody Guthrie's song
"Roll on Columbia."

New Deal legislation greatly impacted several other areas of the
western economy. In 1930, the greater part of the western two thirds
of the United States was used for grazing. The Taylor Grazing Act of
1934 gave the president power to transfer public lands in national
forests from the Department of Agriculture to the Department of
Interior to restrict land use and provide for federal management. The
act also gave cattle producers access to public lands, setting aside 80 million acres of the public domain for cattle and sheep grazing. In return
for low fees, producers could secure ten-year leases. By the end of the
New Deal there were nine grazing regions under the supervision of the
director of grazing, and more than 11 million head of sheep, cattle,
horses, and goats grazed on federal rangelands. Critics argued that the
act included no enforcement clauses and that it favored large operators. But western author Wallace Stegner points to the significant
change the act represented when he notes that upon its passage, "a historical process was complete; not only was the public domain virtually
closed to settlement, but the remaining public land was assumed to be

Katherine G. Aiken

continuing federal property, income producing property to be managed according to principles of wise use for the benefit of the nation." The act was among the most popular New Deal measures in the West.

During the 1930s, mining was definitely depressed as a result of the economic downturn. William Borah of Idaho, Burton K. Wheeler of Montana, and Key Pitman of Nevada provided powerful voices in the U.S. Senate on behalf of western mining interests. They worked for the remonetization of silver. Although they did not achieve this goal, they were able to gain passage of the Silver Purchase Act of 1934, under which the Treasury Department was instructed to buy silver and thus provided a market for western mine production. Over the next ten years, the U.S. Treasury purchased about $1 billion of silver. The Silver Purchase Act revitalized western mining.

The New Deal agencies also devoted attention to the oil and timber industries. When Roosevelt took office, oil producers in many areas could not obtain a price that even covered the cost of production. As was true with most western industries, overproduction was a key problem. Under the aegis of the National Industrial Recovery Act, the New Deal attempted to limit oil production and competition. Lumber in the Pacific Northwest was especially hard hit, with 1933 production at only about one third of the 1926 level. New Deal policies worked to limit production, and eventually the industry revived.

Clearly the New Deal transformed the West. The federal government replaced eastern capitalists as the primary economic force in the region. Per capita federal expenditures were greater in the West than any other region. The three leading states of all the forty-eight in New Deal dollars expended per capita were Nevada ($1,130), Montana ($710), and Wyoming ($626). In fact, the top-ten states were all western states.

At the same time, westerners were proactive insurgents during the Depression. In Washington, the Unemployed Citizens League of Seattle (1931), the Washington Commonwealth Federation (1935), and the Washington Pension Union (1937) worked to foster progressive policies. In California, socialist Upton Sinclair formed EPIC, End Poverty in California, based on his book *I, Governor of California, and How I Ended Poverty: A True Story of the Future* (1933); EPIC clubs organized. Sinclair ran for governor on the Democratic ticket and received nine hundred thousand votes but, failing to gain Franklin Roosevelt's support, lost. Many of Sinclair's supporters became followers of Dr. Francis Townsend, a retired California dentist who headed a movement to obtain old age pensions. The Townsend plan called for $200 monthly stipends to all Americans over the age of sixty, provided that the funds be spent within thirty days. A federal transactions tax would fund the program. By 1934, five hundred local Townsend Clubs boasted 5 million members. Franklin Roosevelt's Social Security Act of 1935 included old age pensions, partly as a response to Townsend's popularity.

One exception to the general economic gloom of the 1930s was Hollywood and the motion picture industry. Americans sought to escape from their everyday troubles, and the local theater was often their destination. Although attendance did fall from a high of some 110 million moviegoers each week in 1930, for most of the Depression, 60 million people purchased movie tickets each week.

In these years Aimee Semple McPherson was well aware of the economic tribulations that marked the 1930s and their impact on her neighbors. During the Great Depression, Sister Aimee and the Angelus Temple made an important contribution to social welfare in Los Angeles. The Foursquare commissary opened on September 1, 1927, and anyone could get a meal there. In the first two months, eighty thousand people were fed. Soon this work expanded to include a soup kitchen and a free clinic staffed by volunteer doctors and nurses. In another effort, the White Sewing Machine Company donated machines, and dozens of female temple members sewed baby clothes and children's attire. Following each Sunday service, piles of canned goods and clothing filled the temple lobby, with workers serving 1.5 million meals during the 1930s.

Sister's policy was "give first and investigate afterward." Her organization earned a reputation for meeting needs quickly without eligibility requirements. They fed people, according to Sister, "without respect to race, creed, or color." Actor Anthony Quinn has noted that the temple was indispensable to the Mexican American community since many of its members were illegal immigrants and therefore could not avail themselves of government programs. (Quinn translated McPherson's sermons into Spanish and was one of Sister Aimee's most committed followers.)

During the 1930s the International Church of the Foursquare Gospel became more institutionalized, with a greater emphasis on the worldwide impact of the church. In a sermon, "This Is My Task," preached at Angelus Temple in 1939, Aimee Semple McPherson pointed out the responsibility all shared to spread the Foursquare Gospel and to contribute funds to missionary students to that end. "What is my task? To get the Gospel around the world in the shortest possible time, that every man, woman and child may hear before Jesus comes."

During World War II, Aimee Semple McPherson and the Church of the Foursquare Gospel accentuated the patriotism that had long been a part of the operation. On June 21, 1942, Sister Aimee led the temple brass band and color guard to Pershing Square in downtown Los Angeles to sell a record $150,000 worth of war bonds in half an hour. Sister delivered sermons for the blood bank and others on patriotic themes, including "Foursquaredom and Uncle Sam" (1942), "Remember Pearl Harbor" (1942), and "Praise the Lord and Pass the Ammunition" (1943). She also attracted considerable publicity with the curses she placed on Tojo and Hitler. The *Los Angeles Times* claimed in 1942, "A world war is the only thing that could have reduced Aimee Semple McPherson to an inside page position."

Then on September 27, 1944, Aimee Semple McPherson died while on a preaching trip in Oakland. She was fifty-three years old. Even her death was not without controversy. There was speculation that she had committed suicide since investigators found a half-empty bottle of Seconal by her bed. The coroner ruled her death an accidental overdose.

The funeral was held on what would have been her birthday, October 9, and no doubt would have appealed to Aimee Semple McPherson's theatrical sense. Fantastic floral arrangements included a nine-foot chrysanthemum harp, a large flowered globe to symbolize the Foursquare Gospel around the world, and a life-size replica of Sister Aimee's chair at the Angelus Temple done in orchids and asters. Even though only 2,300 mourners were invited to the internment at Forest Lawn Cemetery, more than 10,000 others gathered on the hillside hours before the burial. Twenty-five ministers held American flags on one side of the "Lane of Sorrow" and another twenty-five displayed the Foursquare Gospel flag on the other. The marquee at Angelus Temple displayed the verse "To be absent from the body is to be present with the Lord." She left an estate valued at about $10,000.

More than sixty years after her death, Aimee Semple McPherson's legacy continues to grow. The International Church of the Foursquare Gospel now includes more than 1,834 churches in the United States and more than 29,973 worldwide, with 3.5 million members in 123 countries. Despite this accomplishment, few Americans recognize her as the founder of a global church, the author of almost two hundred hymns, and the spiritual inspiration for millions. She is most often associated with the show-business qualities of her preaching career and called "the P. T. Barnum of Religion" or "the Mary Pickford of Revivalism."

But Sister Aimee has a much larger significance. First of all, she helped southern California to become an incubator of national trends. She also became a cultural icon in California during the 1920s and 1930s by appealing to the needs of a burgeoning population seeking to establish new social ties. In addition, she epitomized the cultural and social milieu in Los Angeles with her combination of flamboyant theatrics and comforting, old-time religion. She voiced a message of tolerance and practiced what she preached. Revealingly, she succeeded in a profession generally reserved for men. She was an innovator in using radio for religious purposes, and she earned the loyalty of tens of thousands of Californians and Americans across the West and the rest of the country. Aimee Semple McPherson inspired people to unselfconsciously declare their faith and to proclaim the joyous aspects of Christianity. In many instances she was able to follow the instructions she often gave ushers at the Angelus Temple—"clear the one way street to Jesus!" In short, her story illustrates much of the changing nature of the American West and the greater prominence the region acquired during the 1920s and 1930s.

Essay on Sources

Any study of Aimee Semple McPherson must begin with her own extensive writings. Her book *This Is That* (Los Angeles: Bridal Call Publishing Co., 1919) includes sermons and was reissued by the Echo Park evangelistic association in 1958. Her autobiography, *In the Service of the King* (New York: Boni and Liveright, probably ghostwritten), appeared in 1927, followed by *Give Me My Own God* (New York: H. C. Kinsey, 1936). *The Story of My Life* (Hollywood: International Correspondents' Publication, 1951) is a posthumously published compilation of Sister's writings. In one article, "Foursquare," *Sunset Magazine* (February 1927): 14–16, Sister Aimee describes some of her work.

Contemporary accounts of Aimee Semple McPherson and her career clarify her tremendous popularity and influence. Most historians have ignored these subjects, preferring to concentrate on her kidnapping and downplaying her many contributions to American culture and religion. Popular magazines carried frequent reports of Sister Aimee's activities. Articles that are especially informative include Bruce Bliven, "Sister Aimee: Mrs. McPherson (Saint or Sinner?) and Her Flock," *New Republic* (November 3, 1926): 289–91; Sarah Comstock, "Aimee Semple McPherson, Prima Donna of Revivalism," *Harper's* (December 1927): 11–19; Julia N. Budlong, "Aimee Semple McPherson," *The Nation* (June 19, 1929): 737–39; Shelton Bissell, "Vaudeville at Angelus Temple," *Outlook* (May 23, 1928): 126–37, 58; and C. H. Bretherton, "A Prophetess at Large," *The Nation* (December 1928): 11–19. Upton Sinclair's poem "An Evangelist Drowns" appeared in the *New Republic* (June 30, 1926): 171. A five-page photographic essay describes Aimee Semple McPherson's funeral: *Life* (October 30, 1944): 85–89.

Although no completely satisfactory biography of Aimee Semple McPherson has been written, Lately Thomas (Robert V. P. Steele), *Storming Heaven: The Lives and Turmoils of Minnie Kennedy and Aimee Semple McPherson* (New York: Morrow, 1970), examines the complex relationship between Sister Aimee and her mother and includes useful information on the evangelist's career. Edith Blumhofer, *Aimee Semple*

McPherson: Everybody's Sister (Grand Rapids: William B. Eerdman's, 1993), and *Sister Aimee: The Life of Aimee Semple McPherson* (New York: Harcourt Brace Jovanovich, 1993), by Daniel Mark Epstein, a religious scholar and poet, are more recent works. Blumhofer includes an extensive bibliography. Carey McWilliams, "Aimee Semple McPherson: 'Sunlight in My Soul,'" in *The Aspirin Age,* ed. Isabel Leighton (New York: Simon & Schuster, 1949), 50–80, is a generally sympathetic account by a contemporary.

A few articles in scholarly journals assess various aspects of Aimee Semple McPherson's life and career. These include David L. Clark, "Miracles for a Dime: From Chautauqua Tent to Radio Station with Aimee Semple McPherson," *California History* 57 (winter 1978–1979): 354–63; Harry Ebeling, "Aimee S. McPherson: Evangelist of the City," *Western Speech* 21 (summer 1957): 153–59; Gloria Lothrup, "West of Eden: Pioneer Evangelist Aimee Semple McPherson in Los Angeles," *Journal of the West* 27 (April 1988): 50–59; William McLoughlin, "Aimee Semple McPherson: Your Sister in the King's Glad Service," *Journal of Popular Culture* 1 (winter 1968): 193–217; and Susan Setta, "Patriarchy and Feminism in Conflict: The Life and Thought of Aimee Semple McPherson," *Anima* 9 (spring 1983): 128–37.

More than 2,400 Web sites are dedicated to Aimee Semple McPherson, but their reliability is certainly mixed. The International Church of the Foursquare Gospel page (www.foursquare.org), however, includes samples of Sister's sermons, excellent photographs, and a good brief biography.

Frederick Lewis Allen, *Only Yesterday: An Informal History of the Nineteen-Twenties* (New York: Harper and Brothers, 1931), is a classic discussion of the 1920s. Other helpful works are Michael E. Parish, *Anxious Decades: America in Prosperity and Depression, 1920–1941* (New York: Norton, 1992); Geoffrey Perrett, *America in the Twenties: A History* (New York: Simon & Schuster, 1982); Lawrence W. Levine, *The Unpredictable Past: American Thought 1917–1930* (Chicago: Rand McNally, 1990); Paul Carter, *Another Part of the Twenties* (New York: Columbia University Press, 1977); and Dorothy Brown, *American Women in the 1920s: Setting a Course* (Boston: Twayne Publishers, 1987).

Some useful studies of the Depression era are T. H. Watkins, *The Hungry Years: A Narrative History of the Great Depression in America* (New York: Henry Holt, 1999); William Leuchtenberg, *Franklin D. Roosevelt and the New Deal* (New York: Harper & Row, 1963); Michael Parrish, *Anxious Decades: America in Prosperity and Depression, 1920–1941* (New York: Norton, 1992); Paul Conkin, *The New Deal* (New York: Crowell, 1967); Frank Friedel, *Franklin D. Roosevelt: A Rendezvous with Destiny* (New York: Little, Brown, 1990); and Brad D.

Lookingbill, *Dustbowl, USA: Depression America and the Ecological Imagination, 1929–1941* (Athens: Ohio University Press, 2001).

Works dealing with the West in the 1920s and 1930s include Clyde A. Milner II, Carol A. O'Connor, and Martha A. Sandweiss, eds., *The Oxford History of the American West* (New York: Oxford University Press, 1994); Gerald D. Nash, *The American West in the Twentieth Century: A Short History of an Urban Oasis* (Englewood Cliffs, N.J.: Prentice-Hall, 1973) and *The Federal Landscape: An Economic History of the Twentieth-Century West* (Tucson: University of Arizona Press, 1999); Michael P. Malone and Richard W. Etulain, *The American West: A Twentieth-Century History* (Lincoln: University of Nebraska Press, 1989); Earl Pomeroy, *The Pacific Slope: A History of California, Oregon, Washington, Idaho, Utah, and Nevada* (New York: Knopf, 1965); Richard Lowitt, *The New Deal and the West* (Bloomington: Indiana University Press, 1984); Kevin Starr, *Material Dreams: Southern California Through the 1920s* (New York: Oxford University Press, 1990); Stephen Schwartz, *From West to East: California and the Making of the American Mind* (New York: Free Press, 1998); Carlos Schwantes, *The Pacific Northwest: An Interpretive History* (Lincoln: University of Nebraska Press, 1989); William G. Robbins, *Colony and Empire: The Capitalist Transformation of the American West* (Lawrence: University Press of Kansas, 1994); and Mary Murphy, *Mining Cultures: Men, Women, and Leisure in Butte, 1914–41* (Urbana: University of Illinois Press, 1997).

CHAPTER 13

Rosie the Riveter, J. Robert Oppenheimer, and the American West Transformed

JON HUNNER

World War II transformed the American West as much as the California Gold Rush of 1849. The war brought new peoples, new industries and technologies, and new attitudes to the region that changed how westerners saw themselves and how Americans viewed the West. From the opening up of workplaces for women and minorities to the birth of the atomic age, in four short years the West changed radically. The United States tilted westward in population, economic standing, and political power fueled by the war industries and the people who worked in those factories. The West also served as a staging area for the Pacific theater of operations and a training ground for bomber squads, amphibious regiments, tank battalions, and new weapons. Over the course of the war, the West rose in national prominence and crammed several decades of economic and political development into a mere half decade. In addition to the phenomenal transformation of the region's tangible assets, many of its residents also looked at themselves differently by war's end. Most historic change is gradual; however, during World War II, the American West underwent a rapid and dramatic shift that propelled it into national prominence in industry, technology, and lifestyles. The war transformed the West into a pacesetter for the rest of the country and indeed the world.

The New Deal, as seen in the previous chapter, prepared the West for its rapid mobilization and industrialization by creating a solid infrastructure for the defense industries. Even before the official declaration of war in December 1941, people had moved to the West Coast to find work in the defense-related factories. After the attack on Pearl Harbor and the entry of the United States into World War II, people and federal contracts poured west. Eight million people crossed the Mississippi River heading west in the 1940s and almost half landed on the West Coast. California gained 3.5 million new residents and the Rocky

Mountain region increased in population by 15 percent and the Southwest by 40 percent. Most of these new arrivals went to urban areas. From 1941 to 1945, the Los Angeles area increased by half a million people, and San Diego's population gained 147 percent, rising from 202,000 to 510,000. Seattle added 150,000 new residents, and Denver grew by 20 percent with 100,000 newcomers. Portland almost doubled, Las Vegas almost tripled, and by 1945, Vallejo in the Bay Area had increased by 500 percent. This explosive population growth transformed the cities of the West and altered the region forever.

Federal contracts for war-related activities also flooded west. With one of the two major combat theaters of World War II waged in the Pacific Ocean, the West Coast gained equal footing with the East Coast in landing military bases and securing defense contracts. Even cities in the interior of the West received federal monies that dramatically reoriented their economies away from their agricultural, mining, and railroad heritages. The federal government needed facilities in the West to mount attacks against Japan but also to manufacture the enormous quantity of war materiel necessary for fighting the Axis powers. The proximity to natural resources like lumber and raw metals, the availability of hydroelectric power from dams like Hoover and Bonneville, and the abundant good weather that permitted year-round outdoor production all helped to tilt the manufacturing of the machines and munitions of war to the West. The federal government spent more than $70 billion in the West during the war, with California receiving approximately 10 percent of all federal expenditures nationwide. Washington obtained well above its share per capita, and Oregon, Nevada, Montana, and Colorado each secured defense contracts above the national average. To be sure, factories across the country contributed to making the United States the arsenal of democracy, but with large shares of the federal monies going west, the region played a vital role in winning the war. Airplanes were built in California, Washington, Texas, and Kansas. Aluminum was made in Nevada and steel in Utah and California. Shipyards in California and Washington built thousands of ships, and even Colorado assembled oceangoing vessels, which were shipped by railroad to the Pacific Ocean over the Rocky Mountains. The region also had ideal locations in New Mexico, Washington, and Utah for the top-secret laboratories, production facilities, and training grounds necessary for the creation of an atomic bomb.

The peopling of the West during the war reinforced a longstanding reality about the region: the West is historically a diverse region. Native Americans and Hispanic Americans have lived together in the West for hundreds of years. As seen in chapter 7 about the Mexican-American War of 1846–1848, the relationships among the peoples of the West changed and other Euroamericans came to dominate the region. But despite the white patina, minorities have called the region home for centuries. For some Hispanics and Native Americans, World War II reversed a long decline of fortunes. The voracious need for workers in the war factories that came when 16 million men left to join the armed forces opened up the factory doors to groups of people previously locked out of factory jobs. By working in the assembly lines, women and minorities entered the economic mainstream and, through popular culture images like Rosie the Riveter, the national consciousness as well. For many people, wartime salaries allowed them to buy a house for the first time and feel financially secure after a decade of economic hardship brought about by the Depression.

Often when diverse peoples meet and interact, they adopt each other's cultures. In the West, on the border between Native American, Hispanic, Anglo, and other cultures, cultural borrowing occurs. It is part of the yeasty concoction of the border, where people who enter an unknown region borrow from those who are already there to assist with the transition. For as long as differing cultures have met, such cultural borrowing has taken place and created new types of recombinant cultures.

Wartime immigrants who came west during World War II brought with them their old ideas about how to live but were also inspired by their new land. Once in the West, they borrowed from the cultures of those who had lived there for centuries. They invented new communities and new identities by combining cultures and thus created new ways of living.

To investigate how World War II invented new communities and identities and changed the millions of people who lived in the region, we will focus on two distinctive groups: the women who worked in the war factories, represented by the icon of Rosie the Riveter, and the people who created the atomic bomb at Los Alamos, New Mexico, represented by Dr. J. Robert Oppenheimer.

Women played important and at times transforming roles to help win the war. To replace the 16 million men in uniform on the assembly lines of the war plants, the factories turned to women and minorities to fill the labor shortages. In the frontier West, many women had worked at nontraditional jobs since their survival and that of their families depended on it. Frankie Cooper, a crane operator at American Steel during the war, explained how she took inspiration from her frontier predecessors:

Women have actually had nontraditional jobs since the first wagon train went across the country. When they arrived at the place where they wanted to settle, they helped cut logs, they helped put them together, they helped put the mud between the logs, and they made a home and had their babies inside. And every time a war comes along women take up nontraditional work again.

As the frontier West of the nineteenth century shifted into the industrialized twentieth century, western women worked in the more traditional roles as homemakers, teachers, nurses, secretaries, and telephone operators. The culture of domesticity, where married women's roles were narrowly prescribed by homemaking and child rearing, dominated the notions of feminine behavior in the first three decades of the twentieth century. The economic hardships of the Great Depression changed this culture as married women worked outside the home to supplement or even be the sole providers for themselves and their families. So by 1941, most of the 11.5 million employed women (25 percent of all workers) worked out of economic necessity. Of that total, only 15 percent were married. Some women found employment in the war plants even before the attack on Pearl Harbor as the country started filling defense orders for the Allies' Lend-Lease program and began stockpiling war materiel for the country's eventual entry into the war.

Once the United States entered the war, the departure of men to the military opened up many of the traditionally male jobs to women, and the barriers of sex, race, and age fell. People already in the West or immigrating to the new defense plants found new opportunities in higher-paying jobs. One of these newcomers, Juanita Loveless, moved to Los Angeles from Oklahoma in 1941 and went to work at Vega Aircraft in early 1942. Recruited from her job at a gas station in Hollywood, she described her motivation for working at Vega:

Actually what attracted me—it was not the money and it was not the job because I didn't even know how much money I was going to make. But the ads— . . . "Do Your Part," "Uncle Sam Needs You," "V for Victory." I got caught up in the patriotic "win the war," "help the boys." The patriotism was so strong in everyone then.

Other motivations also steered women toward war factory work. According to women's historian Karen Anderson, women worked during the war for patriotism, the excitement and challenge of war work, the need to cope with the loneliness and anxiety caused by having loved ones overseas, to get away from housework and attain more financial and social independence, and from the sense of purpose that accompanied factory work. Freda Philbrick, who worked at the Puget

Figure 13.1a: This Rosie the Riveter is working on an airplane at the Douglas Aircraft Company in Long Beach, California, in the fall of 1942. Courtesy of the Franklin Delano Roosevelt Library.

Sound Navy Yard in the Seattle area, observed that "somehow the kitchen lacks the glamour of a bustling shipyard." Whatever the reasons for working in defense plants, many women ventured into a new frontier with factory work.

The image of a young single white woman as Rosie the Riveter is not truly representative of female wartime workers. Older women, married mothers, and minority women all stepped in to provide the necessary workers. Riveting the aluminum skins to the airframes was a priority job for women but so was drilling, forging, welding, sawing, filing, making explosives, and turning out cartridges as well as secretarial work, bus driving, agricultural work, and many other duties. But the icon of Rosie the Riveter grabbed the nation's attention. Many images of Rosie were used to recruit women to factory jobs. One of the best-known graced the cover of the *Saturday Evening Post* in 1943 when Norman Rockwell's painting *Rosie the Riveter* showed a woman with heavily muscled biceps, a riveting gun on her lap, and a foot resting on a copy of *Mein Kampf*. She was eating a sandwich from a lunch box with the name Rosie scrawled on it, goggles pushed up on her head and a lace hanky sticking out of a pocket of her denim overalls. Such images of women factory

Figure 13.1b: The woman is riveting, the man bucking to attach the aluminum skin to this Douglas plane at the Long Beach plant. Courtesy of the Franklin Delano Roosevelt Library.

workers illustrate the cultural borrowing that women undertook to work in the war industries. They had to do hard physical labor previously relegated to men but still retain their femininity. This and other such popular images of women war workers sought to break down the prejudice that women belonged only at home and not on the factory floor.

When a woman stepped onto the factory floor, she often entered an alien world. Several accounts demonstrate what women faced. Helen Studer, forty-four years old with sons in the service when she started at Douglas Aircraft in 1942, had immigrated to California with her family soon after Pearl Harbor. She trained for almost a month and then went into the plant: "I was awed, really awed. It is so huge. Well, you can imagine how big it would be to have that big airplane.... And the noise was absolutely terrible. There were times that the noise was just so bad, you'd have to lay your tools down and walk outside." She was assigned to work on the wing section: "I was going to be a riveter or a bucker. The one that drove the rivets had to have a drill and a whole set of different-sized bits, 'cause you never knew what size you were going to use. I didn't do a whole lot of bucking because I wasn't that strong." Sybil Lewis, an African American woman who left Oklahoma for California, remembered the routine of riveting metal onto airplane frames when she worked for Lockheed:

The women worked in pairs. I was the riveter and this big strong white girl from a cotton farm in Arkansas worked as the bucker. The riveter used a gun to shoot rivets through the metal and fasten it together. The bucker used a bucking bar on the other side of the metal to smooth out the rivets. Bucking was harder than shooting rivets; it required more muscle. Riveting required more skill.

Those who thought such work too challenging for women soon found out that the Rosie the Riveters rose to the challenge.

With the great influx of women workers to the war plants, companies and the government sought ways to address the difficulties that women faced and help make the transition to factory work easier. Hired by the federal government in 1943 to examine the training and working conditions of women welders in shipyards, home economist Augusta Clawson underwent standard orientation and training and then helped weld on ships. She kept a diary of her experiences. After her first day working on the Liberty ships at a West Coast shipyard, she wrote: "When you first see it, when you look down Way after Way, when you see the thousands each going about his own business and seeming to know what to do, you're so bewildered you can't see anything or make sense out of it." To report on the problems that women faced in the war industries, Augusta learned to weld and went to work. She wrote in her diary:

> I went into a room about four feet by ten where two shipfitters, a shipfitter's helper, a chipper, and I all worked. I welded in the poop deck lying on the floor while another welder spattered sparks from the ceiling and chippers like giant woodpeckers shattered our eardrums. . . . Now a door in the poop deck of an oil tanker is hanging, four feet by six of solid steel, by my welds. Pretty exciting.

The frenzied pace and the loud noises shocked Augusta. She observed: "Sometimes the din will seem to swell and engulf you like a treacherous wave. . . . It makes you want to scream wildly. And then it struck me funny to realize that a scream couldn't even be heard! So I screamed, loud and lustily, and couldn't even hear myself." Clawson's writings provided insights into some of the difficulties that women faced.

The physical demands of factory work were only a part of the challenges for women. Women faced discrimination on the factory floor. They earned lower pay for equal work, faced resentment for supposedly taking jobs away from men, and suffered sexist attitudes and sexual harassment. At Douglas Aircraft, Helen Studer felt that the "men really resented the women very much, and in the beginning it was a little bit tough. . . . The men that you worked with, after a while realized that it was essential that the women were doing a pretty good job. So the resentment eased." Betty Jeanne Boggs's male production manager at the Douglas plant in Los Angeles disliked her being there. As she recalled: "He could not stand to think that there was a woman white collar worker, and he didn't like it one bit. He thought that I should be home, and he hassled me every way he possibly could. He hassled me right up until practically the day I quit." When Adele Erenberg first entered the machine shop that made parts for the B-17 airplanes, the men stopped their machines and turned and looked at her. She recalled: "It took, I think, two weeks before anyone even talked to me. The discrimination was indescribable. They wanted to kill me."

Pay disparity also reflected prevailing sexist attitudes. The salary for a woman working at a defense plant averaged $40 per week, whereas men earned approximately $65 per week. Still, it improved previous wages for women. Marye Stumph moved to Los Angeles from Ohio in 1940, and in July 1941, she found work at the Vultee Aircraft factory. At a mop factory in Ohio in 1936, Marye had earned seventeen cents an hour, but at Vultee, she started at sixty-two and a half cents an hour. She operated a lathe in the machine shop.

Sexual harassment also occurred on the factory floor. Shirley Hackett inspected ball bearings. Since the trays of ball bearings weighed a lot, women were not allowed to carry them, and because of male resentment, some men delayed bringing new trays to slow the women's pace down. Shirley also noted: "Another thing the men tried to do was take advantage of you sexually. As they reached over to give you a tray of ball bearings, they'd rub against you in any way they could, try to feel or touch you. If you didn't let them get smart with you, they'd let you sit there waiting for that tray." Shirley started to get her own trays, and some women who had been at the plant longer than she suggested that when she got her own trays, she should drop them a couple of times, and then "the big man will come down, and you know who's going to get it." After a couple of dropped trays, the deliverymen were reprimanded, and she started getting her trays promptly.

Away from the workplace, women encountered other challenges. In addition to their long hours on factory floors, most women managed their own households. One in three of the women who worked in the defense industries were also former full-time homemakers, and married women outnumbered single women in the workforce for the first time in the history of the United States. Thus World War II marked a historic change in women's employment. With husbands away, working mothers cared for children, secured rationed food and supplies, and procured housing and day care in times of severe shortages. Because of these problems, working women faced great difficulties in taking care of their households during the war. Juggling work and home affected working women, especially if mothers had to choose between factory work and taking care of their children.

To counter such conflicts, Kaiser shipyards on the West Coast provided day nurseries, charging fifty cents per day for these services. The federal government also instituted a day care program under the Lanham Act, passed in early 1942 to provide emergency assistance for communities hit hardest by industrial mobilization. Over the course of the war, the federal government spent $51,922,977 at 3,102 centers that served 600,000 children. As sizable as this program was (and it represented the largest effort to date by the U.S. government in public child care), many working mothers still faced tremendous problems in securing child care for their young children.

As a result of the difficulties of factory work, the overcrowding of war plant communities, and the severe problems of homemaking during the war, some women had trouble keeping their jobs. Even though Rosie the Riveter smashed barriers at the factory, women at home continued to carry the majority of the responsibilities of running a household. Grandparents, husbands, and older children did assist in caring for children and purchasing the often-scarce food, but the traditional role of homemaking remained with women, whether they were working full time or not. As a consequence, absenteeism and job turnover reached troubling levels during the war. In the Pacific Coast aircraft plants, 150,000 new employees found work in the first six months of 1943 and 138,000 quit. In the war plants of Vancouver and Portland, the job turnover rate in 1943 soared to 150 percent annually. Granted, not all of those who quit were women, but the conflict between work and family in a world of shortages, rationing, and overcrowding led to a constant struggle for women to balance work and home.

The voracious need for factory workers broke the barriers not just for women but for other people not usually seen on the factory floor. In 1940, African Americans living in the West totaled 171,000, less than 1 percent of the total population of the region. By 1945, their numbers had grown to almost 650,000. Blacks from the Midwest and the Deep South flocked to the West, attracted by the lucrative work found in the defense industries. In 1942, African Americans came to Los Angeles at a rate of 10,000 a month. Discrimination, both individually and institutionally, remained pervasive, at least until 1944, when the wartime conditions eroded some of the segregation practices in housing and employment.

Despite the increased importance of black workers in the factories, discrimination remained a way of life. Blacks were segregated in the plants, did more menial work at times, and faced prejudice on the factory floor. Sybil Lewis, who described the riveting process earlier in this chapter, worked with an Anglo woman as her bucker at Lockheed. One day, her boss switched them, and she never got the riveting job back. She said

> That was the first encounter I had with segregation in California, and it didn't sit too well with me. It brought back some of my experiences in [Oklahoma]—you're a Negro, so you do the hard work. I wasn't failing as a riveter—in fact, the other girl learned to rivet from me—but I felt they gave me the job of bucker because I was black.

Marie Baker, who assembled B-25 bombers at the North American airframe factory, commented:

> There was a girl from the South. I guess she had never been around Negroes and she didn't want to work near them. I told her I had four brothers out in the Pacific and they were all fighting at the same time, and why couldn't she stand in there and work next to someone no matter who they were?

Fanny Christina Hill, another African American, remembered her sister telling her: "You just come on out and go in the war plants and work and maybe you'll make enough money where you won't have to work in the hotels or motels." She and her sister started working at the North American factory in April, and by Thanksgiving, they were able to buy a home. As African Americans, Fanny and her sister stepped into jobs previously closed to them and enjoyed a level of prosperity they previously had not known. Fanny acknowledged this historical change when she commented: "We always say that Lincoln took the bale off of the Negroes. . . . Well, my sister always said, . . . 'Hitler was the one that got us out of the white folks' kitchen.'" Fanny continued to work at North American for forty years.

As war materiel production wound down in late 1944 and 1945 and the end of the war grew near, factory owners and governmental officials worried about where returning veterans would work and whether the men could return to their old jobs in the factories. Harold Ickes, President Franklin Roosevelt's secretary of interior, warned men during the war: "When the war is over, the going will be a lot tougher, because [men] will have to compete with women whose eyes have been opened to their greatest economic potentialities." To convince women that their jobs in the factories were over and that they should return to domestic bliss, the publicity that created Rosie the Riveter now turned to persuading women to return to homemaking because the veterans needed their jobs.

Hiring practices changed, and women and minorities no longer received as favorable reviews as they did during the peak years of war production. For example, in 1948, 20 percent of the women who were denied employment at Boeing had previous work experience there whereas only 3.8 percent of the men denied were similarly experienced. Despite the wartime evidence that women could do factory work and do it well, employers now claimed that such work was too physically demanding, too skilled, or too responsible for women workers to handle. They also criticized women's work during the war as sloppy with a high incidence of absenteeism, that women had bad work attitudes, and that the presence of women distracted men and lowered productivity. So even though women workers made temporary gains during the war, after the war factory employment reverted to prewar attitudes. The Rosie the Riveters had served as a cheap labor force for this period of national emergency but then were forced through hiring practices and influenced by a national media campaign to return to a culture of domesticity.

Needless to say, women were divided over their return to homemaking. The vast majority felt pride and accomplishment in what they had done. Without women's work in the defense factories, the Allies would not have had the machines and firepower to defeat the Axis countries. Helen Studer thought: "I was glad it was over. I wasn't working 'cause I wanted to. I was working 'cause I thought it was necessary." After the war, she thought: "I'm going to stay home and be a housewife. My husband never wanted me to work in the first place. But I felt I had accomplished quite a feat. . . . You have to be pleased with yourself and know you've done a good job." Charlcia Neuman voiced similar thoughts: "The women got out and worked because they wanted to work. And they worked knowing full well that this was for a short time. . . . But it was a very good experience for me because of the challenges of doing something like that, to prove to myself that I could do it." Although going back to homemaking was attractive for some women, others disliked the idea.

Marye Stumph was one of them. She wanted to remain in factory work: "I could have enjoyed an assembler job. I could have just gone on and made a career out of that. But I didn't think that there was anything like that available for women." At the end of the war, Vi Moses, a parts saleswoman for a Ford distributor in Tacoma, Washington, commented: "I want to hold onto my job as long as possible." And Peggy Wolf, a chauffeur at the navy yard, remarked about the loss of their jobs: "Many women in here are plenty unhappy, though. The taste of independence has spoiled 'em."

Even before the end of the war, author and columnist Max Lerner wrote in the New York newspaper *PM:* "When the classic work on the history of women is written, the biggest force for change in their lives will turn out to have been the war. Curiously, war produces more dislocations in the lives of women who stay at home than of men who go off to fight." As the United States demobilized and returned to a peacetime economy, many women did return to homemaking, but their experiences as wartime workers had changed their attitudes about themselves and their place in society.

The legacies of Rosie the Riveter are numerous and varied. As historian Sherna Gluck notes, war work meant different things to different people, depending on their age and life cycle. Betty Jane Boggs, who worked as a teenager building C-47 airplanes for Douglas Aircraft in Los Angeles, said:

> War work, I think, showed me that a woman could work in different jobs. . . . [She has] a brain just as much as a man and the man is not the only one who can think.

Beatrice Morales Clifton, married and raising four children, encountered resistance from her family when she decided to work during the war at the Lockheed plant making P-38s. As she recalled, her experience in the factory changed her life:

> My life, it changed from day to night. . . . Because after I quit the first time at Lockheed, I wasn't satisfied. I started looking for ways of getting out and going to work. See and before, I had never had that thought of going out.

Working at a war plant and doing men's work exposed Beatrice and her female colleagues to the opportunities that such work held. The women who returned to homemaking had an appreciation of their expanded abilities and talents. As with other societal and cultural changes, such a transition sometimes takes at least a generation to play out.

Summing up the legacy of her wartime experiences, Margarita Salazar McSweyn observed: "I think women have more opportunities than when we were young. There's so many other things that they can do now. . . . Girls say they haven't progressed, like my daughter-in-law, Cara. She feels that they're still being held back. I said: 'But you still have a lot more than we did.'" Empowered by their war work, many of these women did not forget what they did and encouraged their daughters not to be limited by the culture of domesticity. Susan Laughlin, a counselor for woman in the Lockheed personnel division and a keen observer of the effect of the war on women, said: "I wouldn't take anything for the years I had at Lockheed. I was terribly impressed with the stamina and intelligence and the common sense of the majority of women. I think women are fantastic. . . . And so much of it has been carried on. A lot of it began right then. Because it had to."

Despite the improved economic opportunities that women and minorities generally experienced in the West during World War II, one minority group was targeted and suffered a great abuse of its civil liberties and constitutional rights. Japanese and Japanese Americans in the United States bore the brunt of both personal and governmental animosity after the attack on Pearl Harbor. Pursuant to Executive Order 9066, signed by President Roosevelt on February 19, 1942, all peoples of Japanese descent living within fifty miles of the Pacific Coast were relocated to one of ten internment camps in sparsely populated areas of Arkansas, Arizona, California, Colorado, Idaho, and Wyoming. Many had only twenty-four hours to settle their affairs, sell their homes and businesses, and pack the one suitcase that they were allowed to take with them. By the end of 1942, nearly 120,000 Japanese Americans (two thirds of them native-born U.S. citizens) from the West Coast were detained in the camps. In general, the War Relocation Authority ran the camps humanely, with inmates living in family groups. But incarcerating Japanese Americans behind barbed wire because of their ethnicity has been called America's "worst wartime mistake." Despite the blatant racism behind the Japanese internment camps, more than 3,600 detainees from the camps were inducted into the armed services and distinguished themselves, especially in the fierce fighting in the mountain campaign in Italy.

The end of the war brought an end to the internment camps but left Japanese American lives in disarray. When the internees left the camps, they often returned to find their businesses and homes owned by someone else or in disrepair due to neglect. The U.S. government finally acknowledged its abuse of the Japanese Americans' constitutional rights by passing the Civil Liberties Act of 1988, signed by President Reagan. By 1999, the Office of Redress Administration had given more than eighty-two thousand people awards of $20,000 each to help compensate for the wrongs of the government.

For Native Americans in the West, the war also created many changes. Some twenty-five thousand Native men and women served in the armed forces in both the European and the Pacific theaters.

Approximately three hundred Navajos served a vital role as code talkers who went ashore in the first waves of the amphibious assaults in the Pacific. They communicated with other units and with the ships offshore in the Navajo language to coordinate the attacks. Although the Japanese tried to crack the code by interrogating Navajos captured in the Philippines, they failed. Another Native American marine, Ira Hayes, helped raise the U.S. flag over Iwo Jima, and numerous Native Americans received decorations and citations for their valorous service in combat. Their experiences around the world left them with new expectations once they returned to civilian life, expectations that were often thwarted by the segregation they encountered back home.

In addition to the tens of thousands of Native Americans who fought in the war, another forty thousand left their reservations between 1941 and 1945 to work in war plants, on farms, and in other businesses that supported the war effort. The annual income of Native Americans in 1940 was $400, which by 1945 increased to $1,200. Due to the overcrowding in Washington, D.C., the Bureau of Indian Affairs (BIA) moved its offices from the nation's capital to Chicago. The disruption of BIA services and the decrease in its budget led to a decrease in services as well. On the other hand, the war saw a revitalization of some traditional practices, such as religious ceremonies to bless departing servicemen, to pray for victory, and to purify returning veterans. From fighting overseas to working in war plants, many Native Americans helped win the war.

A series of racially motivated riots that occurred in California in 1943 also illustrate the racial tensions that flared up on the Pacific Coast. Throughout the late spring and early summer, clashes between mainly Hispanic zoot-suiters and military men culminated in a weeklong riot that began in Los Angeles and expanded to other cities in southern California. Young men wearing the distinctive baggy pants with narrow cuffs, loosely cut coats with padded shoulders, wide brimmed hats, and thick-soled shoes constituted the zoot-suit look. They wore such clothes as an element of Hispanic identity. But for the servicemen, the zoot suit represented a lack of patriotism.

On June 3, fifty sailors on leave fought with zoot-suiters in response to an altercation that had occurred several days earlier. The next night, 200 soldiers and sailors cruised Mexican American neighborhoods in taxis and provoked fights with zoot-suiters. On the following nights, servicemen from as far away as Las Vegas, Nevada, crowded into free taxicabs and beat not just zoot-suiters, but other Mexican Americans and African Americans. At its height, 5,000 civilians and members of the armed forces attacked neighborhoods in the greater Los Angeles area. On June 8, after downtown Los Angeles was declared off-limits to servicemen by senior military officials, the attacks diminished. In all, 150 people were injured, and police arrested and charged more than 500 youths for rioting or vagrancy, many of them victims of the military men. When diverse cultures meet, especially under the tensions of war, clash and conflict can result.

Rosie the Riveter, the Japanese internment camps, and the zoot-suit riots all held the nation's attention at times as an advancement or a hindrance to the war effort. But not all war activities were splashed across newspaper headlines. During war, some preparations are of necessity kept secret, like what units are training where, how many airplanes are being manufactured, that Navajos are talking code, and what new weapons are being developed. In the West, some of the most top secret facilities of the War Department worked behind security fences and heavily guarded perimeters to create not just a new and powerful weapon, but a new age as well. This new age created a fresh wave of immigrants and a new type of people coming to the West.

The most famous top secret facility was Los Alamos, New Mexico. Selected by General Leslie R. Groves in November 1942 as the primary research laboratory for the Manhattan Project's effort to create an atomic bomb, Los Alamos combined the austereness of a wartime army post with the vibrancy of a university town occupied by Nobel Prize winners. Indeed, some of the best scientific minds of the twentieth century worked at Los Alamos during the war. Riding herd over all of them was Dr. J. Robert Oppenheimer.

Born in New York City on April 22, 1904, Oppenheimer went to Manhattan's Ethical Culture School and then to Harvard. In his third year at Harvard (where he graduated summa cum laude), Oppenheimer enrolled in six courses and audited four more. The normal quota was five courses. He later reflected on those early years: "My feeling about myself was always one of extreme discontent. I had very little sensitiveness to human beings, very little humility before the realities of this world." After Harvard, Oppenheimer went to Cambridge in England and then in 1927 on to Göttingen University in Germany. At Göttingen, Oppenheimer received his Ph.D. at the age of twenty-four. His doctoral thesis was a brilliant paper on quantum mechanics. Returning to the United States, he received a dual appointment in 1929 as a professor of physics at the University of California in Berkeley and at the California Institute of Technology in Pasadena. By 1939, Oppenheimer had twenty-five graduate students working under him.

Even though Oppenheimer was a theoretical physicist, he had far-ranging interests. Attracted to Hindu religion at Berkeley, Oppenheimer taught himself Sanskrit (his eighth language) so he could translate its religious texts. He admitted that he was apolitical until 1936, when the Great

Depression and the Spanish Civil War awakened his social consciousness. In 1938, Oppenheimer donated money to the Spanish Republicans by way of the Communist Party and eventually married Katherine (Kitty) Harrison, a party member, whose first husband had died fighting with the Republicans in Spain. Oppenheimer recalled this period:

> I woke up to a recognition that politics was a part of life. I became a real left-winger, joined the Teachers Union, had lots of Communist friends. . . . Most of what I believed then now seems complete nonsense, but it was an essential part of becoming a whole man. If it hadn't been for this late but indispensable education, I couldn't have done the job at Los Alamos at all.

As refugee scientists from the Soviet Union brought news of the purges and oppression in Russia, Oppie grew disenchanted with the Communists.

Oppenheimer turned farther away from left-wing causes in the autumn of 1941 as he began participating in the early conferences and research on the atomic bomb. It totally engaged him. As Oppenheimer later recalled: "Almost everyone realized that this was a great undertaking . . . the culmination of three centuries of physics." Despite some concerns over this candidate's left-wing political activities, Groves chose Oppenheimer as the civilian director of the laboratory at Los Alamos. Directed by Oppenheimer (who had previously not even led a physics department), the staff at Los Alamos eventually grew to two thousand people and included many eminent physicists, scientists, mathematicians, and engineers. These people came from around the world, and even for those from the East Coast, New Mexico often was a foreign country.

Oppie wanted the lab in New Mexico. He had always wanted to combine the two loves of his life, physics and New Mexico, and here was such an opportunity. With the selection of Los Alamos as the top secret nuclear physics laboratory, Groves and Oppenheimer were merely the point men for a new wave of military and industrial influence and expenditure that transformed the West. By siting the laboratory on an isolated plateau in north-central New Mexico, the federal government established a technological outpost for a new industry that would change forever the military and economic systems of the country. The men and women who came to work at Los Alamos and the other civilian and military nuclear communities in the West transformed the landscapes, cultures, environments, politics, and economics of the region. The inventions, processes, and machines that they created to build an atomic bomb revolutionized our world far beyond

Figure 13.2: Dr. J. Robert Oppenheimer directed the atom bomb laboratory at Los Alamos, New Mexico, during World War II. Courtesy of the National Archives and Records Administration.

the considerable impact of nuclear weapons. Early computers, lasers, nuclear medicine, and high-speed photography are just a few of the technological advances spun out of wartime work in the laboratories of Los Alamos.

As the Los Alamos residents explored the scientific border between the known and the unknown world of nuclear physics, they also encountered Native American and Hispanic cultures that had deep roots in the land. The various groups at Los Alamos exchanged cultural components. Scientists from top-notch American and European colleges collected Indian pottery and wore blue jeans and cowboy boots. Native Americans from nearby pueblos, like Popovi Da, son of famed potter Maria Martínez of San Ildefonso, assisted in the operation of the particle accelerator in the laboratory. Hispanics from northern New Mexico who came from predominantly agricultural communities worked during the day in the laboratories at Los Alamos and returned to their traditional villages at night.

Like the defense plant workers, immigrants to Los Alamos also followed in the footsteps of previous pioneers. For some, the journey to Los Alamos evoked images of the nineteenth-century westward movement. Ruth Marshak, who accompanied her physicist husband to Los Alamos from Canada and then taught third grade and worked at the housing office during the war, was one of them:

> I felt akin to the pioneer women accompanying their husbands across the uncharted plains westward, alert to danger, resigned to the fact they journeyed, for weal or for woe, into the unknown.

Like earlier pioneers, the women of Los Alamos picked up their families and belongings and journeyed to an unknown destination, sometimes with little discussion or debate. The aura of going west struck a resonant chord with some of these modern-day pioneers and helped them grapple with the journey into the unknown and secret world of Los Alamos.

Into this alien landscape, the Manhattan Project brought two new varieties of communication. First, it brought the language of nuclear physics and technology, one that few in the world outside this elite field understood. Second, since General Groves and the army imposed a veil of codes and military secrecy over the whole community, the Manhattan Project tried to silence language itself. For example, the name Los Alamos was seldom uttered but was replaced by "the Hill," "Site Y," or "Box 1663" (its mailing address in Santa Fe). Site Y holds the distinction as the only community in the United States where all the mail that left there was read by censors.

Los Alamos grew quickly as it marshaled the nation's resources to build an atomic weapon. In the spring of 1942, Oppenheimer wrote: "What we should need is a total of three experienced men and perhaps an equal number of younger ones." This estimate quickly escalated to a projected staff of fifty scientists with fifty assistants. Groves tripled Oppenheimer's figure to three hundred as a basis for planning the laboratory and residential parts of this instant city. As the need for more and more experts in the fields of science, engineering, and weaponry expanded to solve the numerous problems of constructing an atomic

Jon Hunner

bomb, the town's population skyrocketed. By 1945, approximately five thousand men, women, and children lived at Los Alamos.

For a town that did not officially exist, Los Alamos attracted a wide assortment of people. Men and women arrived from universities in the United States and Europe. Renowned scientists from England, Denmark, and Eastern Europe and refugee scientists who had fled the fascist regimes of Germany and Italy contributed their essential knowledge of nuclear physics. Engineers and technicians, many from the land-grant colleges of the United States, used their technical knowledge to actualize the theories of the nuclear physicists. The army assigned many men and women to operate the post. And civilians from around the Southwest flocked to Los Alamos to seek employment as construction workers, maintenance personnel, truck and bus drivers, house cleaners, commissary workers, and all the other services needed for a town of five thousand.

To attract the necessary personnel to this isolated town, Oppenheimer won permission for lab personnel to remain civilians and for families to accompany the men. Groves feared that problems would arise with families living at the site, but Oppenheimer prevailed. Indeed, tensions existed between the civilians and the military for the duration of the war. In 1944, Groves convened a meeting of all the army officers stationed at Los Alamos with this statement: "At great expense we have gathered on this mesa the largest collection of crackpots ever seen." Later Groves attributed the discord to

> the fact that the two dominant sectors of the group were composed of people of almost directly opposite backgrounds: scientists with little experience outside the academic field; and uniformed members of the armed services . . . who were only interested in bringing the war to a quick and successful end.

To end the war, the Manhattan Project sought to harness the incredible amount of energy that came from splitting an atom and channel that energy into a powerful explosion. Nuclear physicists in Berlin had succeeded in splitting uranium atoms in the late 1930s, a process that they called fission, a term borrowed from biology. At the time, no one knew how to pronounce "fission" in the verb form, so some people referred to it as "fishing."

Oppenheimer, as head of the research laboratory at Los Alamos, directed his personnel to pursue two different methods to create an atomic weapon. The first method experimented with shooting a small mass of refined uranium into a larger mass of the same material to achieve an explosive chain reaction. This method was code-named the

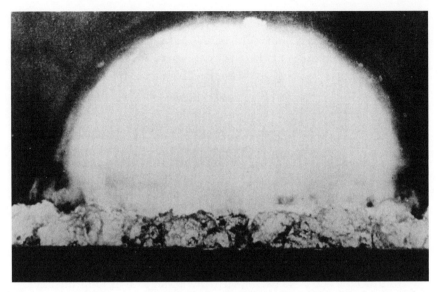

Figure 13.3: The first atomic explosion at the Trinity site in New Mexico opened up a new age, centered in the West. Courtesy of the National Archives and Records Administration.

Gun Assembly and later nicknamed Little Boy. The second method involved surrounding a core of plutonium with a sphere of conventional high explosives and, by imploding those conventional explosives, creating a shock wave that compressed the core until a chain reaction occurred. This became known as the Implosion Method and nicknamed Fat Man. In another example of secrecy and coding at Los Alamos, few people called what they were working on atomic bombs. Instead they called it the Gadget or the Gizmo.

After two years of feverish work, Oppenheimer arranged for a test of the Fat Man bomb for July 1945 at a place code-named Trinity in the desert two hundred miles southeast of Los Alamos. Early in the summer of 1945, Oppenheimer sent a veiled invitation to Dr. Arthur Compton, director of the Met Lab in Chicago and a key member of the Manhattan Project:

> Anytime after the 15th [of July] would be good for our fishing trip. Because we are not certain of the weather, we may be delayed several days. As we do not have enough sleeping bags to go around, we ask you please not to bring anyone with you.

Compton declined the invitation but replied: "Best luck to catch the big one." The atomic anglers from Los Alamos headed into the desert to go fishing.

At 5:29:45 a.m. on July 16, 1945, Fat Man imploded. The flash from the blast lit up the sky and was seen by people in three states and Mexico. After the flash, a shock wave rocked the surrounding area. Anyone standing was knocked to the ground, and a seismologist fifty miles away remarked that it felt like an earthquake. Eyewitnesses to the world's first atomic fireball struggled to describe what they saw. One of the better attempts came from Joan Hinton, a graduate student in physics from Wisconsin who worked on the nuclear reactor at Los Alamos. She observed the blast from a hill twenty-five miles to the south:

> It was like being at the bottom of an ocean of light. We were bathed in it from all directions. The light withdrew into the bomb as if the bomb sucked it up. . . . We were still talking in whispers when the cloud reached the level where it was struck by the rising sunlight so it cleared out the natural clouds. We saw a cloud that was dark and red at the bottom and daylight on the top. Then suddenly the sound reached us. It was very sharp and rumbled and all the mountains were rumbling with it.

Reactions from other eyewitnesses varied. Groves's assistant, Colonel Thomas Farrell, gasped: "Jesus Christ! The long hairs have let it get away from them." Fellow physicist Rudolf Peierls had mixed emotions—he was both awed and impressed by the violence of the blast. He was also relieved that the Gadget worked. Perhaps Oppenheimer was the most relieved of everyone. Around 6:30 a.m., he commented: "My faith in the human mind has been somewhat restored."

During that fateful event, Oppenheimer also recalled Hindu scripture from the *Bhagavad-Gita:* "I am become Death, the destroyer of worlds." In the Hindu religion, Shiva represents death and is eternally poised to destroy the earth. Fortunately for humans, Shiva has always relented because of an opportune benevolent action by one of his devotees. Oppenheimer knew the physics behind the explosion better than almost anyone, but he had to borrow from Hinduism to grasp the full implications of what they had unleashed in the desert that morning. Test director Kenneth Bainbridge searched out Oppenheimer to congratulate him by stating: "Well, now we're all sons of bitches." Victor Weisskopf summed it up for many at Trinity: "Our first feeling was one of elation, then we realized we were tired, and then we were worried." The people of Los Alamos had created an atomic bomb that three weeks later ended World War II.

The atomic bombs struck Japan with unprecedented destruction. On August 6, 1945, at 9:45 a.m. local time, a Little Boy device detonated above Hiroshima. Later estimates put the number of dead at

Hiroshima between 70,000 and 80,000, with an equal number of people injured out of a population of approximately 250,000. On August 9, a Fat Man bomb leveled the central part of Nagasaki, with somewhat smaller casualty figures. Little Boy and Fat Man ushered in a quantum leap in destructive capability. In Hiroshima, 4.7 square miles of the city were totally destroyed. In Nagasaki, the area of total devastation amounted to 1.8 square miles. The mortality rate per square mile in Hiroshima was 15,000. The most lethal attack previously was the firebomb raids against Tokyo on March 9, 1945, where the mortality rate per square mile amounted to 5,300. Thus the atomic bombs tripled the mortality rate of conventional bombs. In the Tokyo raids, 279 planes had dropped 1,667 tons of explosives. With Hiroshima and Nagasaki, two planes delivered one bomb each. Fat Man, the heavier of the two, weighed a mere five tons.

Back at Los Alamos, amidst the celebrations and somber reflections that heralded the end of the war and the start of the atomic age, people began to leave the Hill. Oppenheimer and his family were some of the first people to go. In a tribute to Oppie before he left, fellow scientists honored him at one of their assemblies by reading this testament:

> Let us thank him for the company we had, for the parties, and for the intellectual atmosphere. . . . He was our director. . . . It was his spirit of scientific dignity that made us feel we would be in the right place here. We drew much more satisfaction from our work than our consciences ought to have allowed us.

At a public ceremony honoring Oppenheimer before he departed in October, he accepted the Army-Navy "E" Award (a certificate of appreciation from the secretary of war) for Los Alamos. In his farewell address to the assembled residents of Los Alamos, Oppenheimer predicted:

> If atomic bombs are to be added as new weapons to the arsenals of a warring world . . . then the time will come when mankind will curse the name of Los Alamos and Hiroshima. The peoples of the world must unite, or they will perish. . . . By our works we are committed to a world united, before this common peril, in law, and in humanity.

Oppenheimer left the Hill soon thereafter, but he continued to participate actively in nuclear affairs. He served on committees for the Atomic Energy Commission (AEC) and advised Congress concerning atomic weapons until his security clearance was revoked in 1954 during McCarthyism.

Figure 13.4: Nagasaki, Japan, was leveled by an atomic bomb on August 9, 1945. The buildings in the foreground are the remains of a medical college. Courtesy of the National Archives and Records Administration.

On the day Oppenheimer accepted the Army-Navy E Award, Norris Bradbury replaced him as the new director of the laboratory. As Oppenheimer's replacement, Bradbury observed: "I feel that the bear which we have caught by the tail is so formidable that there is a strong obligation upon us to find out how to let go or hang on." Groves supported Bradbury: "The Los Alamos site must remain active for a considerable period." In his memoir, Groves addressed the transitory period for Los Alamos right after the war: "It was particularly important to continue the Los Alamos lab so that the nucleus of a staff for future weapon improvement would always be available." With both Groves and Bradbury committed to continuing the laboratory, and as people left Los Alamos to return to their lives at universities and colleges around the country, a new wave of immigrants arrived to work in the field of atoms that Los Alamos had pioneered.

The wide-open spaces that the nuclear weapons industry required to research, develop, manufacture, assemble, test, and store its products were ideally suited for western landscapes. In addition to Los Alamos, other laboratories were created in the postwar era at the Lawrence Livermore National Laboratory in northern California, at Sandia National Laboratories in Albuquerque, New Mexico, and at the Idaho Engineering National Laboratory, near Idaho Falls. Hanford, Washington, was expanded to process plutonium for atomic and then hydrogen bombs. Rocky Flats outside of Denver, Colorado, and Pantex near Amarillo, Texas, assembled the nuclear weapons. New bases were built or old ones enlarged to accommodate the new strategies for delivering nuclear weapons and the new policies for storing the warheads. In the 1950s, the AEC tested nuclear weapons in New Mexico, Colorado, Alaska, and especially at the Nevada Test Site north of Las Vegas. The aboveground (atmospheric) nuclear tests totaled over six hundred explosions between 1945 and 1961. At the North American Air Defense Command (NORAD) outside Colorado Springs, a mountain was hollowed out to create a military command center immune from most nuclear blasts. Other military establishments went underground to try to protect their facilities from attack. To dispose of military and non-military nuclear wastes, the Waste Isolation Pilot Project in southeast New Mexico and the proposed Yucca Mountain waste depository near the Nevada Test Site are dump sites that will hold radioactive toxins for tens of thousands of years. The environmental legacy of creating toxic materials that are hazardous for millennia remains unknown.

As the Cold War emerged from the rubble of World War II and a nuclear weapons arms race fueled a growing antagonism between the United States and the Soviet Union, Los Alamos played a pivotal role in this new war. To attract and retain nuclear workers, the atomic communities of the West reinvented themselves and became modern suburban towns. Inventing suburban communities in the West at Los Alamos and Hanford where none had existed before brought new cultures to such places. Granted, the postwar building boom at Los Alamos corrected a serious shortage in housing, but it also polished the image of Los Alamos for public scrutiny. As a worried public looked to the nuclear weapons laboratory for assurances of superiority in the atomic arms race, their gaze was blocked by the secrecy that surrounded the research facility. The American public saw instead the newly suburbanized residential community of Los Alamos, a shining city on the hill, as an example of the promise of the atomic future. The new suburbs also assisted some lab personnel in adjusting to making atomic weapons. By bringing suburbia to the Hill, the government normalized both housing issues and the residents' feelings about their community.

Along with the new peoples and industries that came west during World War II, new wealth also emerged. The war helped transfer wealth and influence from the eastern part of the United States to the western regions. This wealth partially came from the industries established during the war, but it also came from the West's new trading partners. As the gateway to Asia, western states such as California and Washington began reaping the economic benefits of the future postwar trade with Japan, South Korea, Malaysia, and eventually China. The wartime infrastructure development of the ports, transportation networks, and financial systems to handle the vast movement of men and machines all assisted the postwar development of Asian trade.

The American West has fascinated the public as one of the best places to realize the American dream. World War II transformed the West as defense contracts, military installations, atomic facilities, and westward migration all tilted the country westward. The war catapulted the region into the status of a major player in the nation's politics, economics, and culture and ended once and for all the dependency status of the West. In fact, the West began to rival the other regions of the United States because of the impact of World War II and established a shift that would eventually pit the Northeast and Midwest (as the Rust Belt) against the South and the West (as the Sun Belt).

Cultural borrowing between the diverse peoples assisted individuals in coping with the rapid changes brought about by World War II and also set the stage for the new society that would emerge after the war. The people of the West who helped win the war hailed from all over, but they lived in a region that has been historically diverse. Whites, African Americans, Hispanics, and Native Americans joined each other on the factory floors, at the secret installations, and in the military barracks to help win the war. Women also provided the extra workforce to produce the war materiel needed to fight the war. World War II showed women that they had alternatives to traditional feminine roles. The women who shifted to men's work shattered the barriers of the culture of domesticity and, even when they returned to homemaking after the war, often passed on this new appreciation of their abilities to their baby boom daughters. The atomic pioneers at Los Alamos and the other nuclear sites in the West reinvented their communities into model suburbs after the war to normalize their towns and to neutralize the public's fear of atomic energy. Both the Rosie the Riveters and the nuclear weapons workers adapted themselves to roles and identities that they had not had before the war. Their efforts helped win the war and also shifted society into new directions. Without all of these western peoples, the war might not have been won and certainly would not have ended in August 1945.

War brings about rapid change, both with individuals and with society in general. Many Westerners took pride in the way they helped win the war. Additionally, because of the role that the West played as a leader in war materiel production, as the staging ground for the combat in the Pacific theater, and as the center for atomic weapons research and development, the rest of the nation began to view the West differently. From the frontier image where the Wild West spirit predominated, the rest of the country now saw the West as a modern, vital, and even pacesetting region of the nation. As a result of its wartime experiences, the West secured its position as an equal partner with the other parts of the country. As a leader, the West also opened the door to the future, where a multicultural society would negotiate the shoals of atomic energy and learn how to conduct itself as a superpower with important trading interests in Asia as well as Europe.

By producing a large part of the war materiel and by creating a new atomic age in the West, the region escaped from the shadow of its frontier past and emerged as an important section of the country. A sea change occurred in the nation's perception of the West, no longer seen as a backward part of the country. Because of their dedicated efforts to help win the war, the people of the West helped propel the region into a new age of influence and prosperity.

Essay on Sources

People interested in the American West during World War II enjoy a wide variety of sources. From oral histories and community monographs to more regional overviews and comprehensive syntheses, many books and articles exist that explore the war's impact on the region.

In the 1970s, Gerald D. Nash began writing important syntheses about the West and World War II. His pathbreaking overview, *The American West in the Twentieth Century: A Short History of an Urban Oasis* (Albuquerque: University of New Mexico Press, 1973), 189—211, began to explore how the war affected the West. Nash argued that the war was one of the key events that transformed the West into a national pacesetter. He followed this book with several others that continued the focus on how World War II altered the West—*The American West Transformed: The Impact of the Second World War* (Bloomington: Indiana University Press, 1985), *World War II and the West: Reshaping the Economy* (Lincoln: University of Nebraska Press, 1990), and *The Federal Landscape: An Economic History of the Twentieth-Century West* (Tucson: University of Arizona Press, 1999). To be sure, these books are wide ranging in content, but Nash's in-depth examinations of the economic and political activities during World War II create a solid foundation for any discussion about the period. Nash collaborated with Richard Etulain as editors of *The Twentieth-Century West: Historical Interpretations* (Albuquerque: University of New Mexico Press, 1989), 71, 158–59, 353–54, in a diverse collection of essays about the West that includes insightful sections on World War II.

Focusing more narrowly on how the war transformed particular regions of the West, especially California, Roger W. Locthin authored *Fortress California, 1910–1961: From Warfare to Welfare* (New York: Oxford University Press, 1992) as well as edited *The Way We Really*

Jon Hunner

Were: The Golden State in the Second Great War (Urbana: University of Illinois Press, 2000). Marilynn S. Johnson's *The Second Gold Rush: Oakland and the East Bay in World War II* (Berkeley: University of California Press, 1993) also adds to the impressive scholarship about how the war changed the West, particularly California.

The role of women in winning the war has generated many interesting accounts. Sherna Berger Gluck's *Rosie the Riveter Revisited: Women, War, and Social Change* (Boston: Twayne Publishers, 1987) is a pivotal work that uses oral histories of women who worked in the war plants of California. Along similar lines, Mark J. Harris, Franklin D. Mitchell, and Steven J. Schechter's *The Homefront: America During World War II* (New York: Putnam, 1984), 115–40, also utilizes oral histories of people who worked in a variety of jobs around the country with some fascinating accounts from the West Coast. A collection of documents, first-person accounts, and governmental reports about women on the home front resides in *American Women in a World at War: Contemporary Accounts from World War II,* ed. Judy Barrett Litoof and David C. Smith (Wilmington, Del.: Scholarly Resources Books, 1997), 189–200. Karen Anderson wrote *Wartime Women: Sex Roles, Family Relations, and the Status of Women during World War II* (Westport, Conn.: Greenwood Press, 1981), 3–74, 122–82, to provide a synthesis of women's experiences throughout the nation as they helped to win the war. And Maria Diedrich and Dorothea Fischer-Hornung edited *Women and War: The Changing Status of Women from the 1930s to the 1950s* (New York: Berg Publishers, 1990), 21–35, which sets women's wartime experiences in a wider context.

Numerous sources exist about Oppenheimer and Los Alamos. Alice Kimball Smith (who knew Oppenheimer at Los Alamos) and Charles Weiner edited *Robert Oppenheimer: Letters and Recollections* (Cambridge, Mass.: Harvard University Press, 1980). Richard Rhodes's *The Making of the Atomic Bomb* (New York: Simon & Schuster, 1986) exhaustively recounts all aspects of the discovery and use of atomic weapons, including Oppenheimer and Los Alamos. On a more narrow focus, both Ferenc M. Szasz's *The Day the Sun Rose Twice: The Story of the Trinity Site Nuclear Explosion, July 16, 1945* (Albuquerque: University of New Mexico Press, 1984) and James Kunetka's *City of Fire: Los Alamos and the Atomic Age, 1943–1945* (Albuquerque: University of New Mexico Press, 1979) are good accounts of the wartime community and the feverish rush to invent an atomic bomb. Gregg Herken's new book, *Brotherhood of the Bomb: The Tangled Lives and Loyalties of Robert Oppenheimer, Ernest Lawrence, and Edward Teller* (New York: Henry Holt, 2002), presents some of the most recent scholarship on these distinctive men who created the atomic age.

For insights into the social history of Los Alamos, Bernice Brode's *Tales of Los Alamos: Life on the Mesa, 1943–1945* (Los Alamos: Los Alamos Historical Society, 1997), Ruth H. Howes and Caroline L. Herzenberg's *Their Day in the Sun: Women of the Manhattan Project* (Philadelphia: Temple University Press, 1999), Eleanor Jette's *Inside Box 1663* (Los Alamos: Los Alamos Historical Society, 1977), and Jane S. Wilson and Charlotte Serber's *Standing By and Making Do: Women of Wartime Los Alamos* (Los Alamos: Los Alamos Historical Society, 1988) present many first-person accounts of life on the Hill. Jon Hunner's *Inventing Los Alamos: The Growth of an Atomic Community* (Norman: University of Oklahoma Press, 2004) explores more fully many of the topics and themes in this chapter. Perhaps the best unclassified technical history of the creation of atomic weapons is in Lillian Hoddeson, Paul W. Henricksen, Roger A. Meade, and Catherine Westfall's *Critical Assembly: A Technical History of Los Alamos during the Oppenheimer Years, 1943–1945* (Cambridge, Mass.: Cambridge University Press, 1993). Since Oppenheimer was the civilian director at Los Alamos, he figures prominently in all of the above accounts.

Chapter 14

Walt Disney, César Chávez, Barbara Jordan, and the Evolution of the West's Identity, 1945 to 1980

Mark S. Foster

During World War II, millions of newcomers to the West were spurred by a sense of opportunity but also by intense patriotism and the stark realization that if they did not pull together, the existence of the republic was in peril. Many transplanted easterners from the mountains of Tennessee or the plains of Oklahoma, refugees of the Great Depression, filled high-paying jobs in the shipyards, aircraft plants, and hundreds of other facilities scattered along the coast. Others were war brides or girlfriends of servicemen, often seeking both employment and closer proximity to loved ones fighting in the Pacific. Many soldiers, sailors, and airmen who survived combat there mustered out in Los Angeles, San Francisco, or San Diego; millions considered these locations paradise. After the war, many servicemen decided to stay in the West; they were joined by millions of civilians in one of the great mass migrations in American history.

Some observers suggest that in the three decades following the war, the newcomers *made* the West. One claimed, "Newcomers could not be absorbed into the majority, for they were the majority." The postwar generation of migrants to the West was different from wartime arrivals. They felt little, if any, pressure to conform, and few possessed any sense of collective duty or patriotism. Most were exuberant optimists, their attention riveted on individual opportunities. Many ordinary Americans imagined the West as a dreamland, a fantasy world, where they would magically transform into rich and successful people. If they did not achieve fame and fortune, they could at least buy suburban tract homes with outdoor pools and maintain year-round tans.

To a far lesser extent than many newcomers realized, however, their expanded opportunities after the war had been shaped by strong individuals who preceded them west or were native to the region. Walt Disney, born and raised in the Midwest, moved to Hollywood in the

1920s. Disney helped shape Hollywood and the pervasive image of the West as a land of opportunity, a virtual fantasyland, where anything was possible. Hispanic visionary and labor leader César Chávez was born and raised in Arizona, and he helped a generation of marginalized and viciously exploited workers in the fields achieve visibility, human dignity, and a foothold on the lowest rung of the economic ladder. Barbara Jordan, a native of Houston, Texas, never forgot her roots. She demonstrated that a brilliant, driven African American woman from modest circumstances and segregated schools could become a major force in the highly competitive world of Washington politics. Jordan's strength, enormous savvy, and the respect she demanded provided Texas, and the West, with an even more powerful presence in the national political arena.

Walt Disney and Hollywood seemed made for each other. Long before World War II, the film industry nurtured fantasies, which were Disney's stock-in-trade. In some respects, Disney fit the Horatio Alger stereotype of a poor, ambitious, and hardworking young man who parlayed pluck and luck into fame and fortune. He was born in Chicago in 1901, the son of a "serially unsuccessful," peripatetic businessman. In 1910, the family moved to Kansas City, Missouri. For the next few years, while enrolled intermittently in school, Walt helped support the family by delivering newspapers. By most accounts he was an indifferent student, excelling only in art and drawing. Toward the end of World War I, Walt was old enough to join the Red Cross Ambulance Corps, and he served in France for a year. Returning to Kansas City in 1919, he and a partner produced moving cartoon figures in short advertising films. Dissatisfied with their early, crude efforts, Walt devoted most of his free time to animation experiments, and he gained thorough knowledge of film techniques. He set out for Hollywood in 1923 with $40 and a head full of ideas. Like tens of thousands of young people with similar ambitions, Walt hoped to make his fortune in the movie industry.

Walt's older brother helped him secure financial backing for a series of cartoons called *Alice's Wonderland*. The series enjoyed modest success, and Walt set up the Disney Studio near downtown Los Angeles. In 1926 the head of Universal Pictures suggested to Disney's distributor that he would like cartoons based on a rabbit, and Walt began work on a series called *Oswald the Lucky Rabbit*. Modest success led to another carton series based on a mouse, originally named Mortimer. His new wife, Lillian, disliked the name and suggested Mickey instead. Walt added sound (recently introduced into films) and synchronization of movement into the first Mickey Mouse shorts. Audience response was sensational, and Disney was on his way as distributors lined up.

Despite the success of Mickey Mouse and his growing reputation, money remained a constant worry for Disney, particularly after the onset of the Depression. Thanks to his innovations in Technicolor and numerous successful cartoon series, the Disney Studio was one of the few growth industries in the country. From a staff of 6 in 1928, Disney's organization mushroomed to 187 by 1934. During the decade, Disney's animated menagerie added Pluto, Goofy, and Donald Duck. Like most successful entrepreneurs, Disney was a gambler, never satisfied with playing it safe and taking small profits. In the late 1930s, Walt decided to introduce full-length animated feature films. Would adults actually sit through ninety or so minutes of an animated movie? Almost everyone who heard him discuss the idea thought he was crazy. But Walt forged ahead, and *Snow White and the Seven Dwarfs* opened on December 21, 1937. It was a smash hit, and money started rolling in. In short order, the studio released *Fantasia, Pinocchio,* and *Bambi.* Like other film producers in Hollywood, Disney Studios enlisted for the war effort. Walt spent most of the war years making war-related cartoons, but Disney Studios did not really profit from the war. A strike, plus four years of performing in essence uncreative work under government supervision, sapped the organization's strength and some of its spirit. Disney's animated cartoons had lost their creative edge over the competition. After winning eight consecutive Academy Awards for animated shorts, Disney had failed to win one since 1942. Walt sensed that the organization needed new direction.

The postwar years were marked by a shift to noncartoon shorts and feature-length movies. Both *Make Mine Music* and *Song of the South* included a lot of live action, in part to keep costs down. Disney hired a couple to spend a year in Alaska filming wildlife. The end product was *Sea Island,* a half-hour film featuring the antics of seals. At midcentury, Disney produced *Cinderella,* which greatly improved the studio's financial position. *Alice in Wonderland* received little critical acclaim, nor did it do well at the box office, but *Peter Pan* once again helped bail the company out of financial difficulties. The film *20,000 Leagues Under the Sea,* released in 1954, was also a major box office success. Disney Studios quickly adjusted to the new commercial medium of television. By mid-decade, ABC was running a weekly Disney-sponsored TV special called *Disneyland,* which helped promote his brand-new creation under that name in suburban Anaheim. The Davey Crockett series was also a smash hit. In the mid-1950s, it seemed that every other seven-year-old was wearing a coonskin cap.

In the early 1950s, when Disney had been a force in Hollywood for almost thirty years, he began the project that made him a household name to succeeding generations of Americans young and old: Disneyland. The idea had been brewing in his mind for years. When he took his young daughters to amusement parks, he was offended by the general seediness and grime, even vulgarity of the atmosphere surrounding most parks. Disney was very impressed with the cleanliness and general wholesomeness of Tivoli Gardens in Copenhagen, Denmark. He imagined creating a park that both children and adults could enjoy. He would charge admission, and the park would feature novel experiences rather than thrilling rides. Brother Roy was appalled by the idea, and bankers were unenthusiastic. But Walt plunged ahead. He originally considered building a small facility on eight undeveloped acres across the street from his studio, but he quickly sensed that land there was too expensive and space would be too limited. He set up an organization to design an extensive amusement park and then went to work securing property. He purchased 160 acres of orange and walnut groves in suburban Anaheim.

Despite countless glitches, Disneyland opened to great fanfare on July 17, 1955. Disney proved the prophets wrong. People *would* pay a hefty admission fee (which excluded most "undesirables") into a park that provided intense visual experiences, a clean and nonthreatening environment, and attractions appealing to all ages. By the early 1960s, Disneyland was drawing 5 million visitors each year. In 1970, patronage topped 10 million for the first time. On opening day, 1955, the park employed 1,280 people; fifteen years later, the figure reached 6,200. The growing profitability of Disney's enterprises coincided with the opening and expansion of Disneyland. In 1952, Disney earned just $500,000. In 1959 his operations earned $3.4 million, then $11 million in 1965. By the early 1970s, Disney's gross profits neared $150 million, and Disneyland, the "Anaheim Gold Mine," supplied half of the total. Wags called it "the people trap that a mouse built."

Walt's primary target was young people, and he hit on some ingenious marketing devices to attract them. He wanted something to compete with the popular *Howdy Doody* show. Less than three months after Disneyland opened, the *Mickey Mouse Club* premiered on ABC television. Within weeks, Annette Funicello, a pretty and lively twelve-year-old, and her two dozen sidekicks were national celebrities. Children by the millions clamored to become Mouseketeers, and sales of associated paraphernalia generated huge profits.

Although the majority of patrons lived in southern California, Disneyland quickly became a mecca for tourists in the West, particularly families with young children. It was, in the words of one observer, "a near religious shrine." One visitor noted that his children thought that Los Angeles was a suburb of Disneyland! As one prominent western historian noted, "Disneyland was western in more than its location. . . . It captured a popular West of romance, optimism, and fantasy in its scripted

Mark S. Foster

theme parks: Frontierland, Fantasyland, and Tomorrowland with its Autopia. . . . Disney created his clean, orderly park in opposition to what he regarded as chaotic, dirty eastern cities, and their Coney Islands."

Yet some aspects of Disneyland had a nonwestern feel. The West is typically associated with openness and spontaneity. Many attractions in Disneyland appeared whimsical, but they were all carefully planned. Every feature affecting the visitor's overall impression of the park was very tightly controlled. Prospective employees at the park (called "hosts") had to attend "Disney University" to learn the "dos and "don'ts" of grooming and conduct before they were allowed to interact with their "guests." Hosts were usually college age, and they were very "clean cut." Ride operators on such featured attractions as the Jungle Cruise memorized and recited canned spiel; original twists were frowned upon, and even the slightest off-color implication could get an employee fired. Such attention to detail paid off; questionnaires showed that visitors were generally satisfied with their Disneyland experiences.

Despite generous praise, Disneyland attracted considerable criticism. For some, everything about the experience was fake. Unpleasantness was shunted aside. Frontierland conveyed the message that the West was "won," but the Native American perspective was ignored. Disneyland's sugarcoated presentation of "history" omitted assassinations, urban squalor, and oppressive working conditions in factories and mines and virtually all conflict. Although critics panned Disneyland for "McDonaldization" of mass entertainment, most visitors loved it. When Disney died at age sixty-five in December 1966, the park was a western institution.

Whether one loved or hated Disneyland, it was a prime example of how entrepreneurs with big ideas could reshape entire regions. In 1950, Anaheim was a sleepy, conservative town of four square miles and less than 15,000 residents, surrounded by thousands of acres of citrus groves. Disneyland helped transform the area overnight. The 1960 census showed a sevenfold increase in population to 104,000; it doubled again by 1980. Civic leaders in Anaheim launched an aggressive annexation campaign, and fifteen years after the park opened, the town covered thirty-five square miles. One booster estimated that by 1970, Disneyland injected about $250 million worth of business annually into the local economy. In 1950 there were 87 hotel and motel rooms; by 1980, the total had mushroomed to 12,000. Numerous large hotels dotted the major boulevards adjacent to Disneyland, and the Anaheim Convention Center hosted many national conventions. By 1980, Orange County ranked second behind San Francisco as the West Coast's leading convention destination. Completion of a major-league stadium in 1966 brought the American League Anaheim Angels to the area.

The growth that Disneyland and ancillary tourist enterprises helped generate in southern California reflected the explosive overall population expansion in the American West following World War II, particularly in cities. Between 1940 and 1980, the urban population in the United States doubled from 57.7 million to 118.5 million. Total urban population in the West grew more than fourfold, from 11.8 to 50.9 million. Although many Americans think of the West as wide-open spaces, during these four decades the region became more urbanized than the nation as a whole. In 1940, 42.8 percent of all westerners lived in metropolitan areas, well below the figure of 55.2 percent for Americans in other regions; by 1980, the West had edged ahead of the nation's average, 77.5 to 73.7 percent.

Rapid population growth in the urban West was fueled by baby boomers, including millions of ex-GIs starting new families in new surroundings. Defense contractors who had turned out massive quantities of ships, airplanes, and other military hardware during the war had hardly retooled for peacetime production before the Cold War intensified. At midcentury they were once again producing weapons, just more modern ones. The nation's defense budget contracted between 1945 and 1948, but it edged up in 1949 and then surged after North Korea invaded South Korea in the summer of 1950. Western politicians successfully landed huge federal defense contracts. The three leading western states in defense contracting (California, Washington, and Texas) had received 14 percent of all federal defense work during World War II. That figure expanded to 20 percent during the Korean War, then shot up to 33 percent by 1960. In pushing for aircraft plants and missile development enterprises, western politicians capitalized on ideal testing conditions: wide-open spaces, generally blue skies, and warm weather. These advantages also attracted engineers and skilled workers to areas like Arizona and southern California. Although defense contractors might install aircraft engines built in eastern cities, the planes themselves were designed, assembled, and tested in the West. Regional economies in San Diego, Seattle, and Los Angeles centered around the establishment or expansion of military bases and defense contracting. The impact of defense spending on Los Angeles was immense. In 1950, the aircraft industry already employed 100,000 workers; seventeen years later, there were 350,000 aircraft workers in Los Angeles plus another 150,000 in surrounding counties. By the early 1960s, one estimate claimed that fully one third of the area's jobs were directly or indirectly dependent on military spending.

The economies of many western cities in the interior also profited enormously from the maturation of the military-industrial complex, including those of Houston, Denver, Salt Lake City, and Phoenix. Many

Figure 14.1: Bird's-eye view of Denver, Colorado, in the early 1950s. Note the omnipresent brown cloud of air pollution, one of the prices paid for rapid industrialization and unplanned urban growth in the postwar American West. Courtesy of the Western History Department, Denver Public Library.

smaller interior cities also expanded because of the defense boom; for example, Malmstrom Air Force base injected lifeblood into the economy in Great Falls, Montana. By the mid-1950s, Sandia Laboratories was the largest employer in Albuquerque, New Mexico. Without the Manhattan Project, Los Alamos, some sixty miles north of Albuquerque, would have had no reason to exist. By the late 1950s, research and engineering of nuclear weapons was big business, and the city's future appeared assured. Nowhere did the Cold War exert a stranger influence than in Las Vegas. The Nevada Test Site was just sixty-five miles north of the growing city. In the late 1950s and 1960s, ordinary Americans could actually witness nuclear weapons tests. The chamber of commerce even promoted weapons testing as a tourist attraction! In downtown Las Vegas, clocks provided countdowns to nuclear tests so that gamblers could briefly interrupt their activities to witness the spectacular formation of huge mushroom clouds. The chamber distributed road maps guiding curious visitors to the best vantage points. In a more "innocent" age, with the red scare in progress during the Eisenhower presidency or a recent memory during the Kennedy years, Americans generally accepted the assurances of federal officials that the responsible agencies knew what they were doing and that such experiments were perfectly safe.

Such trust was misplaced. In 1953, huge numbers of sheep in Utah died after grazing on vegetation covered with radioactive dust. Some ewes gave birth to deformed lambs. In several Utah and Nevada towns, significant numbers of citizens contracted cancer, apparently from prolonged exposure to the same source. Lawsuits would not be filed for many years; by then, the government had buried almost all embarrassing information. Although fears of contamination of the atmosphere led to the first constraints on nuclear testing in 1963, farmers and ranchers in Nevada and Utah who had been downwind from the testing would not receive reliable information from the government for decades about the devastating effects of long-term exposure to radiation. In the early 1950s, public officials in Denver were thrilled to attract the Rocky Flats Arsenal. This forbidding, top-secret facility, which converted plutonium into nuclear triggers, was situated on the outskirts of the city. Federal officials dismissed fears of contamination or that the presence of Rocky Flats made the city a prime target for the Russians. They claimed that a prudent, easy-to-implement civil defense plan would save tens of thousands of lives in the unlikely event of an attack. Perhaps state and local officials felt reassured by the development of the North American Air Defense Command (NORAD) post deep inside Cheyenne Mountain, plus the opening of the Air Force Academy, both near Colorado Springs.

There were many reasons for growth of western cities unconnected to defense. Numerous large corporations headquartered in the Northeast established important regional factories and branch offices in the West. There were a few resource-based corporations already centered in western cities, including Boise-Cascade, Kaiser Industries, and Morrison-Knudsen. In addition, by the mid-1950s, some corporate leaders sensed the competitive advantages that relocation to more attractive locations might create, and they moved entire companies west. After the development of air-conditioning ensured a viable year-round living environment in Phoenix, Greyhound moved there from Chicago. Similarly, Johns-Manville relocated from New York to Denver, and GTE transferred headquarters from Connecticut to Dallas. Western cities also began to become "major league" literally as well as figuratively with the arrival of top-level professional sports teams. The Cleveland Rams of the All American Football Conference was the first "major" league franchise to relocate to the West Coast, becoming the Los Angeles Rams in 1946. This move commenced a trend. The biggest splash involved baseball, when the Brooklyn Dodgers and the New York Giants moved to Los Angeles and San Francisco respectively before the 1958 season. More teams set up shop in other western cities. By 1980, nearly every major-league sport pursued almost nonstop (and

Mark S. Foster

sometimes reckless) growth, and sports fans in large western cities enjoyed menu choices rivaling those of their relatives back east.

Although few enterprises are indigenous to the postwar West, "high tech" comes close. The computer industry began in the 1930s, but until the 1960s, enormous, expensive, and often unreliable mainframe computers chiefly served the needs of large corporations and government entities. Perhaps nothing symbolized the rise of the New West more than the emergence of the personal computer. The Stanford Research Institute, created in 1946, was the brainchild of Frederick Terman, dean of the university's department of engineering. Terman had long been frustrated by the fact that although Stanford was able, by virtue of its location and reputation, to attract many of the nation's brightest students, few could settle nearby after graduation because there were insufficient jobs challenging their skills. If the nearby area could attract companies employing large numbers of highly skilled engineers, everyone could benefit.

Terman's vision was, in a nutshell, the origin of Silicon Valley. In 1951, the university established Stanford Industrial Park. In the mid-1950s, two of Terman's former students, William Hewlett and David Packard, set up computer research facilities in the area. Another key event was a commitment in 1955 to move Bell Laboratories to Palo Alto for work on commercial applications for the transistor. Fairchild Semiconductor arrived the same year. By then, research and development facilities for IBM, ITT, Xerox, Sylvania, and other companies creating major advances in communications technology were also sprouting up in the area. Although widespread adoptions of the personal computer (PC) by individual consumers would not occur until the 1980s, Silicon Valley had made a huge impact in Santa Clara County by 1980. In 1950, there were only 800 workers in manufacturing in the entire county, mostly in food processing. Thirty years later 3,000 electronics firms employed over 250,000 workers and boasted total annual sales of $40 billion. Although Silicon Valley contained the largest and highest concentration of high-tech development, similar cores were sprouting up elsewhere in the West, most notably around Seattle, Colorado Springs, Boulder, and Austin.

Almost everyone was thrilled with the emergence of "clean" industry. High tech exemplified profitable industries that beefed up local tax bases. They also drew in bright, educated citizens, who in turn built substantial homes and helped expand employment opportunities in burgeoning service industries. High-tech companies generated far less pollution than traditional smokestack industries; to most observers, there was virtually no downside to them. Yet not all observers wore rose-colored glasses. Critics noted that many of the jobs were entry level, either unskilled or only semiskilled assembly-line work, employing large numbers of low-paid Filipino, Vietnamese, and Mexican workers. As housing prices soared, these workers could not afford to live close to their work. Many of them added to freeway congestion in the Bay Area by virtue of forty-mile daily commutes from blue-collar homes in the East Bay or towns as far away as Morgan Hill, even Gilroy. Nevertheless, there were few critics of high-tech industry prior to the 1980s. The grotesque materialism of some of the less reflective dot.com millionaires and the yawning gulf between the super-rich "haves" and the poorly paid "have-nots" had not begun to grate on the public's consciousness. Nor had computer stocks yet experienced a significant reversal.

The emergence of high tech as a bellwether industry in the West between the 1950s and the 1980s reflected another basic truth about the maturation of the regional economy: it was going global. In fact, various western entrepreneurs had sensed at least since World War II that numerous countries in the Pacific Rim were ripe for economic development. As Japan rebuilt, American investors provided capital, and many of this nation's firms supplied engineering know-how. In World War II, Henry J. Kaiser had built numerous industrial plants in the West. After the war, largely under the direction of his son, Edgar, Kaiser Engineers helped the Japanese build modern steel plants, and the same company oversaw massive dams, pipelines, and other development projects in Africa, Australia, India, and elsewhere. Bechtel and Morrison-Knudsen were also major western international engineers. By the end of the 1970s, it was obvious that the Japanese, in particular, had absorbed lessons from America all too well; they had at least temporarily grasped the lead from their former mentors in several key industries: automobiles, electronic equipment, and cameras. In the decades after the war, however, numerous "low-tech" industries determined that huge profits could be made by establishing manufacturing plants in countries that had an excess of cheap, exploitable unskilled labor and little protection of rights of workers. By the 1950s, clothing and sports equipment manufacturers were setting up squalid plants from Singapore to Mexico. By the early 1980s, some six hundred "maquiladora" plants employing over one hundred thousand foreign workers supplied billions of dollars worth of cheap imports each year. Many of these plants were just across the Mexican border, in cities like Tijuana and Ciudad Juárez.

Well into the 1970s, almost every western politician and businessman, and the majority of citizens, accepted unquestionably the notion that perpetual economic expansion and constant population growth were good for the country, the region, and themselves. On rare occasions, when pro-growth coalitions became extremely arrogant or overly greedy or their decision-making process too remote from "outside" input, fellow citizens resisted. For example, when promoters attempted to foist the 1976 Winter Olympic Games on Colorado in almost total secrecy, the citizens rebelled. A petition drive in 1972 forced a statewide referendum, and voters humiliated the Establishment by soundly rejecting state funding for the games.

Two serious, persistent obstacles stood in the way of perpetual growth in the West: insufficient water and limits to the amount of energy that could be developed. Lack of adequate water had restricted areas of western settlement for thousands of years before the white man arrived, but Native Americans had learned to inflict minimal damage on the environment and to live within these limitations. This basic necessity had been evident from the first time white men loaded up wagons and attempted to traverse the enormous open spaces of the West. They quickly learned that it was prudent to stock up on water at every available riverbed. Far too many greenhorns died of thirst when anticipated sources of water ahead had dried up. Once large-scale white settlement came to the West, however, and the Indians were "pacified," the white man proved far more aggressive from the start in reshaping the landscape, including gaining access to water at almost any cost. By 1945, the West had a long-established tradition of conflict over water rights. In earlier years, fights over water had sometimes escalated to violence. After World War II, conflicts were usually confined to courtrooms, state legislatures, and Congress, but the stakes remained incredibly high. The battles were seldom between small groups of farmers and ranchers but usually between far larger entities: states and even countries.

The continuing battle over the contents of the Colorado River typified western water politics. The Hoover Dam, completed in 1935, helped control the flow of water and provided hydroelectric power. Almost every state in the water-starved Southwest had a stake in Colorado River water. If farmers in Colorado and Utah drew off too much water for their irrigation needs, the interests of various groups downriver would be adversely affected.

As cities in the West grew rapidly after World War II, water and power conflicts intensified. Arizona was a case in point. For decades, the state had been a minor player in the sweepstakes. As long as there was a small white population and little urban development, its voice in distribution of water and power was generally muted. With the development of air-conditioning, cities in the desert Southwest like Phoenix and Tucson mushroomed. Politicians in Arizona complained that California had hogged the lion's share of water and power in earlier agreements, and they demanded redistribution of Colorado River water. Receiving little satisfaction, they filed a suit that carried to the Supreme Court in 1952. The complex case dragged on for more than a decade. Arizona finally "won," but the settlement permitted California to "borrow" water from Arizona's share until the Bureau of Reclamation completed the Central Arizona Project (CAP), an expensive and complicated engineering achievement that would ultimately parcel out the state's share of water. Predictably, California politicians did everything they could to delay completion of the CAP. Meanwhile, various factions in California battled over available water resources within the Golden State. In the 1960s, Governor Pat Brown commenced what amounted to a massive transfer of water from northern to southern California. Although the California Water Project (CWP) marked an incredible engineering feat in pumping Feather River water over the Tehachapi Range into southern California, it delivered neither the volume of water nor power promised. Almost two decades later, Governor Jerry Brown (Pat's son) pushed for a far more expensive and complicated phase two of the CWP, but a complex combination of political activists beat back the proposal.

Other issues clouded the water situation throughout the West and affected U.S-Mexican relations. The Colorado River flows into the province of Sonora and then empties into the Gulf of California. Farmers in Mexico depended on steady flows of water from the river. As more politically connected interests north of the border siphoned off increasing amounts of water, Mexican farmers were left at the end of the line. Furthermore, damming the river also increased the salinity of what little water Mexico received. Mexican officials complained of unfair treatment by their "big brother" to the north, and the issue became increasingly sensitive. By the early 1980s, everyone was clamoring for water: businessmen opening up new plants, farmers in the few green valleys surrounded by desert, and suburbanites in Tucson and Phoenix who foolishly planted grass lawns. In Arizona, the demands of Indian tribes whose ancient burial sites were threatened by dams complicated the decision-making process. As explosive population growth in the urban West continued and interested parties had to dig even deeper and more expensive wells, the resolution of water issues appeared as elusive as ever.

Another emerging western concern was development of energy resources. For decades, petroleum companies had been extracting crude oil from Texas, Oklahoma, and California. Vast deposits of coal and natural gas also dotted the western landscape, and the region was a net exporter of energy resources to other parts of the United States, even to world markets. With the expansion of population in the region following World War II, however, the rising per capita use of energy, and the development of new energy-consuming industries, intelligent resource

Mark S. Foster

management became critical. There was a lot of coal in the region. Although industrial plants used some coal, its chief application was fueling plants that generated electricity. As demand for electricity grew at seemingly exponential rates, engineers responsible for long-range energy planning grew increasingly concerned over possible shortages.

By the early 1950s, nuclear power plants entered the picture. James Malloy of the Los Angeles Department of Water and Power presented a "Grand Plan" for the entire Southwest, in which coal-fueled plants would be built inland and nuclear power plants would dot the coastline of California. Ocean water could cool nuclear reactors. Massive transmission lines would direct energy where it was needed. By the mid-1960s, twenty-one large utilities in seven key southwestern states had formed a group called Western Energy Supply and Transmission (WEST) Associates. The compact continued to add members, and it became increasingly powerful. But its objective of establishing massive coal-powered plants on the upper Colorado River clashed with the Bureau of Reclamation's plans for water development in the same area.

In the late 1960s and early 1970s, increasingly outspoken environmentalists joined the debate. Energy suppliers were vulnerable from all sides. Backers of coal-fueled plants had a long and generally sordid history of taking advantage of Native American tribes in negotiating access to coal reserves. One of the worst recent examples of exploitation had been construction of the Navajo Power Plant near Page, Arizona, in the late 1960s. The plant produced electricity by burning coal supplied by the Peabody Coal Company, which gained access to the coal through a one-sided lease negotiated with the Navajos and Hopis. The lease permitted Peabody to mine the Black Mesa region and use Navajo water to transport the coal in a slurry pipeline. The exploitative arrangement provided the company coal at a fraction of market value, and it virtually gave away the precious Indian water. Ignoring their duty to protect Indian interests, Bureau of Indian Affairs (BIA) officials had colluded with the power companies in approving the contracts.

Private interests dominated the initial phase of the so-called Grand Plan for energy development, but they encountered considerably more trouble in pushing a vital second phase of the plan. It called for development of strip mining of coal and construction of a coal plant in the Kaiparowitz Plateau in Utah. The utility consortium hoped to develop forty-eight thousand acres of coal lands and build the largest single power plant in the world. The big California utilities would provide the lion's share of the financing and take more than half of the plant's output. Conversely, environmentalists argued that the plant would create massive air pollution. They observed that more than one fourth of the nation's national parks were within a 250-mile radius of the proposed operation, and pollution could cause irreparable damage to this price-less heritage. In the end, the environmentalists won the battle, and the Kaiparowitz project was scrapped in 1973, not so much because Nixon appointees to the Environmental Protection Agency (EPA) suddenly got religion, but because demand for energy experienced a temporary dip. In addition, the big utilities were by then fighting desperately to save two major nuclear power plants in California and Arizona.

Environmentalists won some battles, but they were hardly reas-sured by a federal official's declaration that "tomorrow the Colorado River will be utilized to the very last drop." Shortly after World War II, government officials had proposed 134 water projects, about 100 on the upper Colorado basin, the rest on the lower basin. Among other environmentalist concerns, construction of massive federal dams threatened to submerge some of the West's most beautiful canyons.

Exploitation of coal and hydroelectric power resources paralleled continued development of petroleum in the West. At the end of World War II, the United States was the world's biggest producer of petro-leum. Although the nation was also the world's greatest consumer of petroleum, until the late 1950s, the country was a net exporter of that vital resource. With increasingly gargantuan appetites for domestic consumption of gasoline and petrochemicals, the situation had changed dramatically by the early 1970s. The Arab oil embargo in 1973 caught the United States in a terribly vulnerable position. Federal officials and corporations cooperated in efforts to increase petroleum production and lessen the nation's growing dependence on foreign oil.

They met with mixed success. Although most of the easily accessi-ble domestic petroleum fields had either been largely depleted or were thoroughly developed, petroleum engineers and energy experts per-ceived a huge future in the development of oil shale. On the plus side, the West had large amounts of oil shale just waiting to be tapped. There were three problems. The development process was complicated and costly, and massive amounts of waste rock in turn caused air and water pollution. Second, the energy multinationals could wreak havoc in oil shale markets with relatively slight adjustments in the price per barrel of crude oil. Finally, federal regulations could adversely affect poten-tial profits. Given the relatively weak political leadership in Washington following the Watergate scandal, public policy analysts found it difficult to predict extended trends in decision making about national energy policy. Investment in oil shale was in essence a long-term proposition, and markets hate uncertainty. For all of these rea-sons, it was inherently risky.

Nevertheless, the 1970s and early 1980s marked the emergence of numerous oil shale boomtowns in the American West. One such pocket was northwestern Colorado and southwestern Wyoming. In Colorado, sleepy towns like Rangely became instant cities, reminiscent of the wild environments during the gold and silver booms a century earlier. Rock Springs, Wyoming, once a booming railroad town, relived its glory days. Saturday nights became bacchanalias as oil field workers flocked into downtown saloons and trailer park brothels in search of quick, intense pleasures. Oil and natural gas exploration companies also helped create a boomtown environment in Denver. By the end of the 1970s, Denver had twenty-seven new office buildings housing hundreds of energy-related companies. In Denver alone, four thousand geologists provided expertise to newly spawned energy companies, and smaller groups of geologists operated out of Albuquerque, Salt Lake City, and other western cities.

In the early 1970s President Nixon's energy czar, William Simon, talked of oil shale and synthetic fuels as the answer to the Arab oil embargo, but hard experience proved that rosy expectations were premature. President Ford was particularly sold on the long-term future of synthetic fuels, and he tried, unsuccessfully, to talk Congress into underwriting twenty privately owned synfuel production plants. The late 1970s ushered in a period when the nation's energy policy experienced frequent shifts and was inherently shaky. The Organization of Petroleum Exporting Countries (OPEC) vacillated between an apparent consensus that the West, particularly the United States, must be punished for supporting Israel and self-seeking efforts by some members to maximize their oil profits in the short term by undercutting prices established by OPEC leadership. Even sophisticated energy "experts" disagreed over whether the energy "crisis" was real or contrived. Cynical observers suggested that Big Oil in the United States was behind it, largely to force up retail prices and extract enormously advantageous tax breaks and promises of looser regulation by responsible federal agencies. According to one commentator, "The OPEC nations proved themselves the best friends Texas and Oklahoma oil producers had."

There were many potential sources of energy; each had advantages and disadvantages. Under President Eisenhower's Atoms for Peace initiative in the early 1950s, nuclear power had been touted as a cheap, efficient, and "clean" source of energy. Two decades later, it generated fear, even outrage and anger, among many consumers. A series of industrial accidents in the 1970s, including the widely publicized "meltdown" of a nuclear reactor at Three Mile Island in Pennsylvania in 1979, severely damaged its image as a clean, "safe" fuel. As noted, new dams for hydroelectric power threatened pristine natural canyons, and coal-burning plants promised massive air pollution. When Wyoming governor Stanley Hathaway envisioned turning his state into "the next Pennsylvania," thoughtful citizens stepped back. According to one prominent western historian, "Opponents of energy development feared that they could see the western future in the ravaged landscape and pervasive poverty of West Virginia, eastern Kentucky, and other Appalachian areas that depended on the strip mining of coal." Not surprisingly, as the 1970s ended, the notion of a viable national energy policy appeared to be an oxymoron.

Although visions of massive amounts of cheap energy fueled population growth in western cities, vast rural tracts in the Dakotas, Nebraska, Kansas, and Oklahoma looked little different in 1980 from how they had appeared in 1945: the only hint at modernity visible in 1980 would very likely be far more expensive and sophisticated farm equipment casual passersby saw in fields. Many rural counties experienced population declines, and some contained fewer than two people per square mile. Weather-beaten, dying small towns in eastern Colorado and the Oklahoma panhandle looked like movie sets for Larry McMurtry's novel *The Last Picture Show* (1966), set in the early 1950s.

There were other declining areas in the West after World War II. In particular, the lumber industry in Oregon and Washington suffered. To many tough old loggers in the Cascade Mountains, it had seemed inconceivable that their beloved industry could ever stagnate. For generations, timber seemingly grew back as fast as it was cut. In the immediate postwar years, the demand for housing brought flush times to even the more inefficient operators. Eventually the industry figuratively choked on its success. Modern harvesting techniques, including chain saws and more efficient mills, allowed big operators to satisfy demand and greatly deplete the huge stands of trees. Yet new environmental restrictions against burning wood chips and sawdust raised the costs of processing timber, helping push some marginal operators to the edge. Although lumber executives were fully aware of reforesting techniques, big operators like Weyerhaeuser and Georgia-Pacific abandoned sustained-yield harvesting. One reason was that by the 1970s, Canadian lumber was far cheaper, and operators in the Northwest could not compete with tree farms in Alabama and Georgia, where timber grew more quickly and could be harvested more economically. In the Pacific Northwest, the toll was largely human. As once-booming lumber towns like Coos Bay, Oregon, slowly declined, older loggers faced unemployment or years of eking out livings on pitifully small pensions.

Casual viewers might not realize when driving through farming regions that western agriculture also experienced significant changes after World War II. To most urban Americans, farmscapes looked timeless. In a nutshell, however, small, independent family farms were being swallowed up by huge, highly efficient "agribusiness" firms, often controlling many thousands of acres. In the San Joaquin and Coachella valleys in California, big farming outfits mushroomed and reaped millions growing cotton, grapes, lettuce, figs, dates, and other exotic fruits and vegetables. Farmers have always experienced boom-and-bust cycles, and the postwar period was no different. Whether they worked large or small amounts of land, farmers have always been gamblers, their fortunes subject to forces largely beyond their control: insects, weather patterns, crop diseases, inflation, fluctuating interest rates, and unpredictable foreign policy. Even farmers producing relatively hardy crops often found themselves in difficult straits very suddenly. For example, in the 1970s wheat farmers reaped bonanzas when the federal government purchased billions of bushels for foreign aid distribution to Third World countries and resale to the Soviet Union. When President Jimmy Carter abruptly cut off grain sales to the Soviets in 1980 in protest against that country's invasion of Afghanistan, many wheat farmers found themselves seriously overextended in loans used to purchase more land and expensive harvesting equipment.

In dusty towns like Chowchilla, California, and Wenatchee, Washington, big fruit growers producing perishable crops like grapes and apples relied on cheap labor, much of it from south of the border. For decades, Mexican workers had toiled in the white man's fields. Tens of thousands of Mexican nationals came north during harvest seasons and followed ripening crops from region to region, recrossing the border for the winter. The federal government alternately encouraged and discouraged the practice, depending on boom-and-bust cycles and relations with their southern neighbor. Historically, the presence of large numbers of dark-skinned foreigners had generated strong opinions among Americans. Advocates of migrant labor claimed that their willingness to work for paltry wages lowered the cost of producing foods, benefiting consumers. Since foreign workers had few if any rights, they seldom sent their children to public schools, and they made very few demands on public services. Conversely opponents blamed migrant workers for a host of social ills, including rising crime rates, declining public health, and for taking even the most minimal advantage of public services. Yet most fair-minded observers agreed that Mexican farmworkers received brutally low pay and had little choice but to live in squalid conditions.

Inspired by the hard-won progress African Americans were achieving in the civil rights movement, César Chávez was determined to improve the lives of migrant workers. He became a highly controversial figure in the 1960s and 1970s. As two biographers note, "Chávez ... lived and died shrouded in a veil of truths, lies, perceptions and myths." He was born in a small enclave of Hispanic families about twenty miles north of Yuma, Arizona, on March 31, 1927. His father ran a poolroom, grocery store, and auto repair shop, and he might have remained self-sufficient had he not borrowed money to buy a forty-acre parcel near the store. Unfortunately, during the Depression, César's father fell behind on payments for the land, and his fortunes gradually spiraled downward. When César was twelve, his family had to become migrant workers. Although they were American citizens, his mother spoke no English, and the children spoke very little. When they were on the road, public officials often assumed they were undocumented Mexican immigrants. During the early 1940s, the Chávez family followed the crops in California. They quickly discovered that it didn't matter if you were an American or Mexican citizen: if your skin was brown, you often experienced brutal exploitation by growers. Labor contractors might recruit too many workers for a certain harvest and then lower promised wages. Foremen short-weighted produce or short-counted boxes picked, pocketing the difference. Wages were docked for Social Security, which was not reported. Workers often had to bribe foremen for jobs, and women were regularly pressured to grant sexual favors.

Despite dreadful conditions in the field, the Chávez family had few alternatives but to work there. César quit school in the eighth grade to work full time. He recalled that the worst job was using a short-handled hoe to thin lettuce and sugar beets, which forced workers to bend over constantly. "There was a rhythm, it went very fast. . . . It's like being nailed to a cross. You have to walk twisted, as you're stooped over, facing the row, and walking perpendicularly to it. You are always trying to find the best position because you can't walk completely sideways, it's too difficult."

Young César had a rebellious streak. As a teenager, he refused to sit in the segregated section of a movie theater in Delano, California, and was arrested by police. He also dressed like and ran with the "zoot-suiters," attracting additional attention from the authorities. In 1944 he joined the navy, in part to get out of hard labor in the fields. César's two-year hitch did not expand his career possibilities. After mustering out in 1946, he married Helen Fabela and returned to the fields in California. Farm laborers had a long history of agitating for better work conditions, with little success. Through the efforts of several Catholic priests and social activists who saw leadership potential in him, César was initially drawn into helping Hispanics become active politically, then into union organizing in the early 1950s. The federal government had legalized seasonal migration of Mexican nationals (*braceros*) into the United States in order to harvest crops. Politicians sold consumers on the idea that the program would lower costs of fruits and vegetables.

Mark S. Foster

Figure 14.2: César Chávez in about 1962, during the early
years of his work in founding the Farm Workers
Association. Courtesy of the Western History
Department, Denver Public Library.

But many field hands were angry that braceros lowered wages for
American-born workers. Big growers cynically used the strategy of
divide and conquer. Chávez helped support boycotts of merchants who
supported the bracero program, then led sit-down strikes in the fields.

Although he helped achieve small victories in California's interior
valleys, Chávez realized by the early 1960s that until field workers
formed a strong union and negotiated formal contracts, they would
never possess adequate safeguards and workers' rights. While still toil-
ing in the fields, Chávez moonlighted after hours to organize the Farm
Workers Association (FWA) in the early 1960s. It was slow going at

first. Many workers were beaten down psychologically and financially by years of subservience and feelings of inferiority and powerlessness. They did not believe they could beat the mostly Anglo growers, whose economic power was reinforced by the legal and political system. In addition, paying union dues out of minuscule wages was a significant commitment. But Chávez's timing was excellent. With the civil rights movement and President Lyndon Johnson's Great Society programs, the mid-1960s marked the high tide of liberalism in the United States. It was the right time for minorities and the downtrodden to demand redress of longstanding grievances.

The event that gained national exposure for Chávez and the FWA was a strike against grape growers in Delano, California, beginning late in 1965. Chávez's face, along with views of marching picketers chanting, "*Huelga!*" (strike) and "*Viva la causa!*" began appearing on the nightly news. Although television cameramen seldom caught footage of growers employing their roughest tactics against picketers, nightly viewers heard union men describe them in graphic detail. Chávez organized a march from Delano to Sacramento to seek support from Governor Pat Brown, a liberal Democrat. Walter Reuther, the highly respected leader of the United Automobile Workers (UAW), provided financial assistance and spoke passionately on behalf of the march. It became almost literally a crusade, covering 250 miles in twenty-five days and ending in the state capital on Easter Sunday, 1966. Chávez was a superb communicator: soft-spoken and modest, yet firm in his convictions and passionate in his cause. He advocated Mahatma Gandhi's principles of nonviolence, and the public sensed his sincerity. Airing of an NBC special, *The Harvest of Shame,* which documented farmworkers' travails, also helped advance the cause. Consumers nationwide began honoring boycotts of produce harvested by what Chávez and his followers claimed were "unfair" labor practices.

The Delano strike and the march on Sacramento marked Chávez's emergence as a major figure in both the labor and civil rights movements and the United Farm Workers' (UFW, renamed from the FWA) emergence as a strong political and economic force. In subsequent years, the UFW signed contracts with some major growers, and working conditions gradually improved. As the union grew, however, discordant elements emerged, and workers occasionally retaliated violently against vicious tactics by the growers. Chávez implored his followers to maintain the principles of Gandhi, since even seemingly justified retaliation would severely compromise the union's "high road" position.

Chávez again placed his principles on public display in a strike against the nation's largest growers of table grapes by launching a widely publicized fast in Delano in the spring of 1968. He may have been as intent on shaming his followers into honoring nonviolence as he was on winning the strike. As his fast reached two, then three weeks, national media attention intensified daily. Chávez received letters and phone calls of support from congressmen and senators, even from Dr. Martin Luther King, Jr., and Robert Kennedy (both of whom would be assassinated within three months). With television cameras whirring and Kennedy at his side, Chávez finally ended his fast after twenty-five days.

Chávez and the UFW improved the lives of thousands of farmworkers, but they did not always win. After the dramatic, nationally publicized events of 1968, the UFW fought against the Teamsters Union for the right to represent workers. Egged on by the Nixon administration, the Teamsters appeared to have the upper hand in the early 1970s; at one point, membership in the UFW had declined by 90 percent from its peak, and union coffers were nearly empty. Fortunately for the UFW, the Teamsters were weakened by rampant corruption, the mysterious disappearance of their president, Jimmy Hoffa, and internal dissension. By the late 1970s, the UFW once again dominated the fields, but mechanization of many tasks and the rise of huge multinationals posed unprecedented threats to worker power and union solidarity. Chávez later lost some of his magic when he joined losing sides in other political battles in California.

As is almost inevitable with any strong leader, reaction to Chávez among Hispanics was mixed. Because he opposed the bracero program, some noncitizens of Mexican descent viewed him as a traitor to his race. Others thought he lacked "machismo" because he courted support from non-Hispanics and advocated nonviolence. Yet many others praised him for speaking out forcefully on human rights and insisting that workers of all races be treated with dignity and respect. Between the late 1950s and the end of the 1970s, other western Hispanic leaders promoted La Raza (the Race, a nationalistic slogan) as well. In Denver, Rodolfo "Corky" Gonzales forcefully headed a highly controversial and increasingly militant campaign called the Crusade for Justice. In New Mexico, Reies López Tijerina headed a movement in 1966 to regain lands "stolen" from Hispanics by whites under the notorious Treaty of Guadalupe Hidalgo in 1848. Tijerina's campaign ended violently in a shoot-out between his followers and law officers.

Across the West, Native Americans and African Americans also battled over civil rights. Throughout the nation, African Americans experienced widespread discrimination in war plants during the 1940s: they were the last hired and first fired, and only the most talented and determined advanced beyond unskilled jobs. Still, working and living conditions in the West were far better than many had experienced as disenfranchised sharecroppers in the South. In a reprise of the Great

Migration north during World War I, tens of thousands of African Americans moved west during and after World War II. Although a few found work on farms or in small factories in the interior, most moved to the West Coast: Seattle, Portland, San Francisco, and Los Angeles. Had they found the promised land? In the 1940s and 1950s, social commentators praised living conditions and general acceptance for African Americans in Los Angeles. They noted that high percentages of new arrivals purchased homes in Watts, a nearly all-black suburb southeast of downtown.

Unfortunately, appearances were deceiving. There were few employment opportunities in Watts. Since Los Angeles was so spread out, many African Americans lived miles from jobs, and challenges for job seekers were daunting. As the civil rights movement gained momentum nationwide, feelings of discontent among African Americans deepened. For most, progress was far too modest and much too slow. Many young people rejected the nonviolent tactics of Dr. Martin Luther King, Jr., labeling him an Uncle Tom, and they grew suspicious of support from liberal whites. The West was home to some of the most militant African American separatist movements, including the Black Panther party, organized by Huey Newton and Bobby Seale in Oakland.

Nevertheless, the nation was shocked at the outbreak of a race riot in Watts on August 11, 1965. The arrest of an allegedly drunk black motorist led to name-calling by onlookers, followed by rapidly escalating violence. Within hours, groups of young blacks were roaming the neighborhoods, indiscriminately smashing store windows, looting their contents, and often setting them on fire. Some adults, even the elderly, joined the pillage. "Burn baby burn" became the chant of choice. Snipers preyed on fire and police personnel sent in to restore order. The violence was hardly one-sided, as nervous police opened fire, not always on the most logical targets. Local authorities, including Mayor Sam Yorty and his racist police chief, Tom Parker, were unable to rein in the outbreak. When interviewed about the beginning of the riot, Parker fanned the flames by exclaiming, "One person threw a rock, then like monkeys in a zoo, others started throwing rocks." In a later investigation of the causes of the riot, Governor Ronald Reagan revealed his profound ignorance of underlying causes in labeling the rioters "mad dogs." It took the National Guard four days to restore order. All told, thirty-four persons died, and damage estimates exceeded $35 million.

Despite widespread discontent and militancy among African Americans in the West, many superb role models native to the region achieved amazing levels of success. They included Barbara Jordan, born in Houston on February 21, 1936. Her father was a Baptist minister, and both parents provided strict, uncompromising guidance.

Mark S. Foster

Although attending segregated schools, Jordan was a superb student; after high school, she entered segregated Texas Southern University, where she majored in government and history and graduated summa cum laude in 1956. Her greatest strengths were debate and oratory, and she won many competitions, often against white opponents. These triumphs bolstered her confidence. Jordan was accepted by Boston University School of Law; she struggled at first but received her degree in 1959. Although stimulated by the bracing intellectual climate and sophistication of Boston, Jordan sensed that there was more opportunity in the West, particularly in her booming hometown, Houston.

After a brief effort to launch a private legal practice, she embarked on a dazzling career in government, serving initially as administrative assistant to the judge of Harris County, Texas. Understanding the futility of challenging either the entrenched white establishment or a new generation of aggressive young capitalists, Jordan realized that she could best serve the interests of African Americans by working within the system. After two unsuccessful races for the state legislature, in 1966 Jordan was the first African American elected to the Texas senate since 1883. Although she received overt political support from only a few members of the white elite in downtown Houston, there was little opposition in that powerful quarter. Thanks in part to her ability to win over all but the most hidebound racists in the senate, she rose to the position of president pro tempore in 1972. When Texas added an eighteenth congressional seat later that year, many of the most powerful voices in Texas business and politics determined that Jordan deserved advancement. In the words of one biographer, Ben Barnes, her most powerful local backer "saw Barbara as part of the future, and she was necessary to his future, as well as to Texas and the nation." Houston Democrats nominated Jordan, and in winning the election, she became the first African American ever to represent Texas in Congress. According to Robert Strauss, the national head of the Democratic Party, "I thought we had a winner. . . . She had something I can't quite define."

Congresswoman Jordan was determined from the beginning to avoid the label "token" representative. As a single woman, she was not distracted by the needs of an immediate family. Her dominating yet beautiful voice and powerful physical presence made her immediately noticeable. Jordan's demonstrably brilliant mind, strong work ethic, and rock-solid integrity commanded the respect of her peers, and she quickly became a force in Congress. Thanks in part to the personal attention and behind-the-scenes maneuverings of a fellow Texan, former president Lyndon Johnson, Jordan gained important committee assignments. As a member of the House Judiciary Committee, she found herself in the national media limelight during the Watergate hearings. On nightly televised news, viewers across the nation frequently witnessed this imposing, brilliant woman speaking eloquently about issues ranging from fine points in the Constitution to personal morality. News commentators and talk show hosts invariably awarded Jordan high marks for her thorough research into complex issues, deeply penetrating analysis, discerning questions, and fairness. By the time of President Nixon's resignation in August 1974, she may have been the best-known African American woman in the nation, outside of entertainment and sports.

Although best known for her central role in the Watergate hearings, Jordan owed much of her success as a congresswoman to the fact that she never forgot her Texas roots or her constituents' interests. When important bills affecting oil, natural gas, or petrochemicals came up in Congress, she invariably lined up with her Texas colleagues. As one observer noted, "Just as she had not allowed herself to be taken for granted by her liberal colleagues in the Texas Senate, Jordan was not going to vote with her liberal colleagues in Congress on key energy issues that affected her district." Or her state. On occasion, she broke ranks with Black Caucus leaders in Congress. She supported many bread-and-butter social welfare issues, but she was no knee-jerk liberal.

Jordan was a very private person, yet she gained the affection and admiration of the vast majority of her countrymen. She gave one of the most moving and memorable keynote addresses in memory at the Democratic Convention in 1976. Jordan received honorary degrees from more than two dozen universities. Partly due to deteriorating health, she retired from Congress after only two terms and then taught at the Lyndon B. Johnson School of Public Affairs at the University of Texas for the remainder of her life. In 1992, she gave another keynote address at the Democratic convention. Two years later, President Clinton awarded her the Presidential Medal of Freedom, the highest award a civilian can achieve. Her life was cut short by leukemia and respiratory problems in January 1996 at age fifty-nine, but she had demonstrated to countless young people of all races that there were no limits to what ambitious African American women could achieve in the New West.

Like other minority groups, Native Americans also sought settlement of longstanding grievances in the postwar years. The most notable conflicts occurred in the West, where most Native Americans lived. Official government policy had for generations vacillated between those who wanted to "reassert Indian sovereignty and cultural autonomy" and others who pushed total assimilation and "termination" of the Indian's so-called special status. Although almost all observers saw that the BIA was, at best, a bumbling federal bureaucracy, there was virtually no consensus over what to do with the reservation system. Cynics claimed, with considerable justification, that many of those promoting termination simply used the rhetoric of "freeing" Native Americans to advance their real objectives of grabbing valuable lands and mineral rights for themselves. They cited the case of the Klamath tribe's agreement to terminate government protection and permit sale of their priceless Oregon timber. In a 1954 agreement, each member received $43,700 from division of the tribe's estate. Tragically, far too many Klamath families quickly squandered their windfalls; within a decade, most had descended into lives of poverty and hopelessness. Between 1954 and 1962, Congress passed a dozen "termination" bills, almost all involving tribes in the West.

In 1946, Congress had set up the Indian Claims Commission to settle disputes under long-forgotten treaties. Most were eventually settled quietly in the courts. By the 1970s, however, Native Americans' grievances could no longer be easily swept under the rug. In November 1969 the militant American Indian Movement (AIM) staged a highly publicized occupation of Alcatraz Island in San Francisco Bay, which lasted until the summer of 1971. The movement offered federal officials $24 worth of trinkets to pay for it (the amount the Dutch settlers had supposedly paid for Manhattan in 1626). In February 1973 armed resistance by militant groups of Sioux commenced at Wounded Knee, on the Pine Ridge reservation in South Dakota. In both locations, tribesmen, with guidance from AIM, "occupied" the disputed space and dared FBI and federal marshals to remove them. There was a ten-week standoff at Wounded Knee, with television providing nightly coverage. One army officer stated candidly that the government was dealing with "an embarrassment and not an insurrection." With public sentiment leaning overwhelmingly on the side of Native Americans, the government found itself under increasing pressure and in a no-win situation. Although a negotiated settlement ended the siege, later government efforts to send AIM leaders to prison backfired when the FBI was accused of tampering with witnesses.

Tragically, once public attention turned away, violent conflict among factions of Native Americans broke out at Wounded Knee. Numerous beatings, "accidents," and cold-blooded murders resulted in one hundred deaths. National attention returned to Wounded Knee when federal agents invaded the reservation in 1975. The American Indian Movement claimed that the government systematically murdered their members and sympathizers. Despite occasional setbacks, by the end of the 1970s groups and individuals representing Native American interests were learning how to hold their own against government authorities. In subsequent decades, Native Americans would make far greater strides in achieving tribal sovereignty.

By that time, however, most Native Americans no longer fit the stereotype of "reservation Indian." More than half chose to leave reservations and reside in urban areas. The harsh reality, particularly for young Native Americans, was that although it was easier to retain tribal customs and traditions on reservations, educational programs there were limited, and unemployment and substance abuse were rife. Many young persons agonized over these choices; some of those who successfully integrated into the larger society retained a gnawing sense that they had sold out their heritage.

In the 1960s and 1970s, the West became an increasingly powerful force in national politics. Between the annexation of Texas in 1845 and the end of World War II a century later, western politics was typically bumptious, confrontational, and largely local. For all of their vaunted independence and rugged individualism, many western politicians played up a sense of victimization, supposedly at the hands of malevolent eastern political and economic entities. These themes had been evident in the rhetoric of the Populists in the 1890s. A half century later, respected writers such as Bernard DeVoto still popularized an exaggerated image of the West as a "plundered province," whose priceless treasures were routinely expropriated by corrupt and calloused eastern decision makers.

There was an equally long tradition of radical politics in the West. Militant labor groups, including longshoremen, miners, lumbermen, and others under the umbrella of the Industrial Workers of the World (IWW), had shaped the agenda of radical labor demands in the early twentieth century. From the late 1950s forward, many of the most articulate critics of American society, from the Beats to the New Left, came from the West. The San Francisco area and the University of California at Berkeley campus became focal points of radical political debate and protest. No longer willing to be dismissed as the "silent generation," university students confronted the old political order, beginning in the early 1960s. The ineffectiveness of federal social welfare programs in creating a "just" society and ameliorating uneven distributions of wealth and the emergence of the Free Speech Movement at Berkeley helped raise the political consciousness among millions of students, not only in the West but across the nation, that something was amiss in the so-called Great Society of the 1960s.

The Vietnam War also served as the catalyst for explosive protest. Students at Berkeley and dozens of other campuses violently opposed university investments in corporations profiting from the war, and they occasionally took over administrators' offices. Sympathetic professors arranged teach-ins, condemning virtually every aspect of the war: non-stop lying by responsible officials, clandestine operations of the Central Intelligence Agency (CIA), defoliation of natural forests and threats to human health wrought by the mysterious substance Agent Orange, and "obscene" profits earned by companies like Dow Chemical, which produced the napalm that killed thousands of innocent women and children. Less politicized young people joined "hippies" and "flower children" trekking to San Francisco's Haight Ashbury district during the "Summer of Love" in 1967. In addition to wearing long hair and outlandish clothing, playing loud music, and mouthing platitudes rejecting their parents' "uptight" success ethic, their loose agendas included casual sex, lots of drugs, and almost anything else that would irritate adults.

The American Left lost its momentum in the late 1960s and the early 1970s, and many of the people effecting its demise were westerners. The assassinations of Dr. Martin Luther King, Jr., and Robert Kennedy in 1968 deprived the movement of two of its most inspirational symbols. Just two years after the overwhelming loss by right-wing Republican presidential nominee Arizona senator Barry Goldwater in 1964, Hollywood actor Ronald Reagan led a conservative comeback in being elected governor of California in a landslide over the incumbent liberal Democrat Edmund "Pat" Brown. In the presidential election of 1968, yet another westerner, Richard M. Nixon, narrowly defeated liberal Democrat Hubert H. Humphrey. The belief that Big Government could solve difficult social and economic problems through massive spending lost favor, even among many liberals. In addition, by the late 1970s, many environmentalists, feminists, abortion rights activists, persons promoting liberalization of drug laws, and a host of other causes had splintered into vocal but often ineffective single-interest groups. On the opposite end of the political spectrum, the Republican Party learned valuable lessons in the early 1960s. Barry Goldwater had suffered a humiliating defeat, thanks in part to frequent "shoot-from-the-hip" comments and support from the rough-edged, extremist John Birch Society. Spokespersons for conservative, even right-wing interest groups, many of which were centered in the West, modernized their appeals to voters and softened their harshest rhetoric.

The rapid emergence of a powerful New Right by the end of the 1970s astonished political pundits who had all but buried the Republican Party in the mid-1960s. California governor Ronald Reagan advanced his dazzlingly successful political career on his largest stage yet by dishing out simplistic homilies and large doses of anti–Big Government rhetoric. As two prominent social commentators noted, "Reagan won . . . because he had found the necessary enemies. Reagan made urban demonstrators, striking farm workers, black rioters, radical students, criminals, and wasteful bureaucrats from Johnson's War on Poverty his targets." Ironically, many westerners, historically the primary beneficiaries of Anglo conquest, still identified with politicians who portrayed them as victims. Western politicians articulating these views led what commentators labeled the Sagebrush Rebellion. Such self-styled "rebels" vowed to "get the government off the backs of the American taxpayer." In 1978, Howard Jarvis masterminded a successful initiative in California that drastically lowered property taxes and made it more difficult for legislators to fund existing state programs. Legislators seeking new approaches to burgeoning social problems in the nation's fastest-growing state found it nearly impossible to establish innovative new government programs. Federal programs, too, came under attack. Imposition of a national fifty-five-mile-per-hour speed limit during the Carter administration as an energy conservation measure was a universally hated measure, particularly in the wide-open spaces of the rural West, where drivers routinely cruised at eighty miles per hour. Even liberal western Democrats labeled the initiative bureaucratic meddling.

By 1980, the West had changed profoundly since the end of World War II. Decision makers faced many challenges, including explosive population growth, urban sprawl, and the rise of new technologies. In addition to giving the West added visibility in the national political arena, inspired leaders such as César Chávez and Barbara Jordan helped address increasingly intense demands for recognition by minorities, women, and other newly politicized interest groups. Perhaps the most daunting task for most westerners was learning to live with limited energy and other nonrenewable resources. Yet in some ways, the West appeared much as it had in 1945. In the mind of the nation's public, the American West still resembled a fantasyland, and Walt Disney vastly enhanced that image. Still, vast stretches of landscape between Lincoln, Nebraska, and Reno, Nevada, had changed little. Tens of thousands of farmers and ranchers were just hanging on; as had previous generations, ambitious young people still moved away in search of more opportunity. If there was a difference, the more ambitious youth in Limon, Colorado, and Wahoo, Nebraska, often sought their fortunes in Denver, Houston, and San Francisco rather than in the centers of civilization on the East Coast.

Essay on Sources

The best overviews of western development include Richard White, *"It's Your Misfortune and None of My Own": A New History of the American West* (Norman: University of Oklahoma Press, 1991); Patricia N. Limerick, *The Legacy of Conflict: The Unbroken Past of the American*

Mark S. Foster

West (New York: Norton, 1987); and Peter Wiley and Robert Gottlieb, *Empires in the Sun: The Rise of the New American West* (New York: Putnam, 1982). Carl Abbott, *The Metropolitan Frontier: Cities in the Modern American West* (Tucson: University of Arizona Press, 1993), provides an excellent overview of urbanization; Richard M. Bernard and Bradley Rice, eds., *Sunbelt Cities: Politics and Growth Since World War II* (Austin: University of Texas Press, 1983), furnishes additional insights into that topic. John M. Findlay, *Magic Lands: Western Cityscapes and American Culture After* 1940 (Berkeley: University of California Press, 1992), offers highly original and stimulating interpretations of landscapes. For economic development, consult Gerald D. Nash, *The American West in the Twentieth Century: A Short History of an Urban Oasis* (Englewood Cliffs, N.J.: Prentice-Hall, 1973). Other useful works include Hal K. Rothman, *Devil's Bargains: Tourism in the Twentieth Century American West* (Lawrence: Regents Press of Kansas, 1998); R. Douglas Hurt, ed., *The Rural West Since World War II* (Lawrence: University Press of Kansas, 1988); and Richard Lowitt, ed., *Politics in the Postwar American West* (Norman: University of Oklahoma Press, 1995). For works on western historiography, see Gerald D. Nash and Richard W. Etulain, eds., *The Twentieth Century West: Historical Interpretations* (Albuquerque: University of New Mexico Press, 1989), and Etulain, et al., eds., *The American West in the Twentieth Century: A Bibliography* (Norman: University of Oklahoma Press, 1994).

Numerous biographies of Walt Disney include Steven Watts, *The Magic Kingdom: Walt Disney and the American Way of Life* (Boston: Houghton Mifflin, 1997), and Richard Schickel, *The Disney Version: The Life, Times, Art and Commerce of Walt Disney* (New York: Simon & Schuster, 1968). For treatment of César Chávez, see Richard Griswold del Castillo and Richard A. Garcia, *César Chávez: A Triumph of Spirit* (Norman: University of Oklahoma Press, 1995); David Goodwin, *Cesar Chavez: Hope for the People* (New York: Fawcett Columbine, 1991); and Jacques E. Levy, *Cesar Chavez: Autobiography of La Causa* (New York: Norton, 1975). Works tracing the evolution of Chicano consciousness include Rodolfo F. Acuña, *Occupied America: A History of Chicanos* (New York: Harper & Row, 1988); Richard B. Craig, *The Bracero Program: Interest Groups and Foreign Policy* (Austin: University of Texas Press, 1971); and Richard Gardner, *Grito! Reies Tijerina and the New Mexico Land Grant War of 1967* (Indianapolis: Bobbs-Merrill, 1970). An excellent book on Barbara Jordan is Mary Beth Rogers, *Barbara Jordan: American Hero* (New York: Bantam, 1998); see also Ira B. Bryant, *Barbara Jordan: From the Ghetto to the Capitol* (Houston: D. Armstrong, 1977), and James Haskin, *Barbara Jordan* (New York: Dial Press, 1977).

The literature on the rising consciousness of Native Americans is massive. Start with Donald L. Fixico, *Termination and Relocation: Federal Indian Policy, 1945–1960* (Albuquerque: University of New Mexico Press, 1986); Stephen Cornell, *The Return of the Native: American Indian Political Resurgence* (New York: Oxford, 1988); and Alan R. Sorkin, *The Urban American Indian* (Lexington, Mass.: Lexington Books, 1978). For a caustic indictment of the white man's conduct under treaty obligations, see Vine Deloria, Jr., *Custer Died for Your Sins; An Indian Manifesto* (New York: Macmillan, 1969), and Edward Lazarus, *Black Hills! White Justice: The Sioux Nation Versus the United States, 1775 to the Present* (New York: HarperCollins, 1991).

Good works on environmental issues include Samuel P. Hays, *Beauty, Health and Permanence: Environmental Politics in the United States, 1955–1985* (New York: Cambridge University Press, 1987); Kirkpatrick Sale, *The Green Revolution: The Environmental Movement, 1962–1992* (New York: Hill and Wang, 1993); Donald Worster, *Rivers of Empire: Water, Aridity, and the Growth of the American West* (New York: Pantheon, 1986) and *Under Western Skies: Nature and History in the American West* (New York: Oxford, 1992); and Marc Reisner, *Cadillac Desert: The American West and Its Disappearing Water* (New York: Viking, 1986). Atomic weapons testing is treated in Howard Ball, *Justice Downwind: America's Atomic Testing Program in the 1950s* (New York: Oxford, 1986), and Tad Bartimus and Scott McCartney, *Trinity's Children: Living Along America's Nuclear Highway* (San Diego: Harcourt Brace Jovanovich, 1991).

CHAPTER 15

Paul Allen: High Technology and the High Country in a New West

CARL ABBOTT

At the opening of the twenty-first century, Seattle's Paul Allen was the third-richest person in the United States. His cofounder's stake in Microsoft and his other investments in communications and entertainment fluctuated between $20 and $30 billion—enough to equip every family from the Missouri River to Maui with a new laptop running Windows XP.

Allen's career has both created and expressed many of the forces that reshaped the American West in the last quarter of the twentieth century. The West that Allen helped to fashion is technologically sophisticated, economically complex, and globally connected. It is as much a platform as a place—a set of metropolitan nodes within global networks that originate and receive the pulsing information packets of the emerging age of communication. This networked region is the latest manifestation of the deep national belief that the American West is the leading edge, the pioneer region of the national future.

But Paul Allen is rooted as well as uplinked, tied by his own choices to a specific locality. With the ability to live anywhere and buy anything, he has chosen to remain in the rainy city where he was born in 1953 and grew up reading science fiction and fooling with computers. He invests in far-ranging high-tech business ventures, but he also buys regional sports franchises, contributes to regional causes, helps to build downtown Seattle, and constructs cultural institutions for his hometown, most notably the half-fantastic Experience Music Project, whose strange architecture seems to transform the home-wired electric guitar of his high school years as an interactive music museum.

Allen's loyalty to home raises the issue of regional distinctiveness as a counterbalance to global placelessness. Modern westerners may live modem-mediated lives, but they retain a strong penchant to view the West as a region apart. They also know that the nineteen states of the

Great Plains, Rocky Mountains, and Pacific coasts are not one place but many places—redwood forests and red rock canyons, prairie towns tucked in the shade of tall grain elevators and big city streets shadowed by towering office buildings. The West has a distinctive history, a peculiar mixture of peoples, and distinct and defining landscapes. It is a region of alternatives, of utopian visions, of places that bear the burden of optimistic policies and projected ideals. Around Paul Allen's career as inventor and civic entrepreneur we can array other western Americans who have tried to understand the singularities of western places. These are crafters of poetry and prose, not software. They are people like Ursula LeGuin, Sherman Alexie, or Kurt Cobain in Allen's own subregion, like California poet Gary Snyder or Utah essayist Terry Tempest Williams or north plains novelist Louise Erdrich.

The title for this chapter on the most recent history of the American West sums up these contrasts. Paul Allen's West is first and foremost a region of new technologies and new industries, a national and global center of economic and cultural change. But the high-tech West is embedded in the western "high country," the literal western mountains and high interior deserts and the imagined region of refuge and social possibilities. We can thus explore the recurring western tension between the headlong rush into the future and stubborn allegiances to the distinct identities and histories of western regions and places.

The City Kid and the Wired World

Paul Allen grew up a city kid. His home was in the Wedgwood neighborhood, part of the new northside Seattle that developed after World War II. Well within the city limits, Wedgwood nevertheless had a *Leave It to Beaver* feel with an eclectic mix of ranch houses, split levels, and two-story houses on tree-lined streets that run up and down Seattle's steep hills. There were low-rise commercial strips and the nation's first completely enclosed suburban shopping mall at Northgate a couple of miles to the north. With parents who were librarians at the University of Washington, Allen was well exposed to literature and science fiction, to movies, and to the world of provincial culture. Many of the favorite films that he lists on www.paulallen.com are from the exciting new wave of foreign cinema that reached U.S. audiences in the 1960s—*La Dolce Vita* (1960), *L'Avventurra* (1960)—or epics with undertones of western adventure stories like *Seven Samurai* (1954) and *Lawrence of Arabia* (1962).

Seattle was reinventing itself in the years that Paul Allen was passing through elementary school and high school. The city mounted the Century 21 exposition in 1962, with its futuristic monorail and iconic Space Needle. Tax dollars modernized port facilities to handle the new

Figure 15.1: Paul Allen grew up in a rapidly expanding, prosperous, and optimistic Seattle symbolized by the city's 1962 world's fair. Courtesy of the University of Washington Libraries, Manuscripts, Special Collections, University Archives, UW 397.

technology of containerized cargo, making Seattle a major player in trans-Pacific trade and "land-bridge" shipments from Japan to Europe via North America. Voters in 1968 also invested in the "Forward Thrust" initiative to clean up Lake Washington, acquire park lands, build roads, and otherwise keep up with growth. Just as importantly, the University of Washington was bootstrapping itself from an ordinary state university into a research powerhouse. Shrugging off bitter fights over Cold War loyalty oaths, the university went full tilt after post-Sputnik federal research grants in medicine and the sciences. A growing university helped to attract other research business, like a Battelle Institute think tank in 1965. By the late 1970s, just as Paul Allen's software company was arriving on the scene, Seattle ranked sixth among U.S. metropolitan areas in total federal research and development funds, far out of proportion to its population.

The 1960s were immensely confident years in Seattle (the infamous Boeing depression of 1970–1971 would not hit until Allen was preparing to leave for college). When Allen's high-powered private school installed a teletype connection to an off-campus mainframe computer in 1968, he got a jump on the emerging computer era. Thrown together at school, ninth grader Allen and seventh grader Bill Gates became the nerds-in-chief. They hung around the computer room in all their spare time and, as Paul Allen recalled, began to "take our little leather satchel briefcases and ride the bus downtown" to a computer center where they helped the professionals troubleshoot problems, and "we didn't have to pay for the time as long as we could find bugs in their system and report them." In the neighborhood Allen was considered smart, introverted, polite, and studious, burning his lights late at night. "He would be up there [in his room] with that Gates kid, working on computer stuff," one neighbor remembered.

The next few years were a hodgepodge of college and computer consulting. Allen went off to Washington State University in the fall of 1971. He and Gates also made use of Intel's new 8008 microprocessor chip to develop a computerized system for counting automobile traffic; they sold only a few versions of Traf-O-Data but started to learn about software marketing. In the summer of 1973, they worked for TRW in Vancouver, Washington, helping to computerize the management of the Northwest's vast system of hydroelectric dams. When Gates went east to Harvard in the fall of 1973, Allen took advantage of Richard Nixon's suspension of the military draft, dropping out of WSU and moving to a Boston-area programming job at Honeywell. In their spare time, Allen and Gates speculated about the spread of computers. Allen remembers that he first developed his idea of a "wired world" in a Vancouver pizza parlor, speculating that future consumers would receive their news and information via wires and computer screens.

It was the genius of Gates and Allen to realize just how much the development of a mass market for computers would depend on the software of complexly coded operating systems, word-processing programs, spreadsheet programs, file-reading programs, and games. Their own technological epiphany came with the January 1975 issue of *Popular Electronics,* which featured the new Altair 8800 personal computer being marketed by MITS of Albuquerque. Allen and Gates put together an Altair, wrote an operating system, and flew to New Mexico to pitch it to the company. They got the contract, incorporated as Micro-Soft, and began selling software to other manufacturers as well. They lived in the Sand and Sage Motel and worked out of a storefront adjacent to a vacuum cleaner shop. "I was probably the one always pushing a little bit in terms of new technology and new products, and Bill was more interested in doing negotiations and contracts and business deals," Allen recalled in a later interview for *Fortune* in 1995.

As MITS fell behind to newer computer makers, the partners decided to return to the Seattle area. On January 1, 1979, Micro-Soft of Albuquerque became Microsoft of Bellevue, Washington. The next year they struck their seminal deal with IBM, which wanted programming

Carl Abbott

Figure 15.2: Paul Allen as a twenty-first century investor.

languages for its closely guarded PC project. Allen bought partly finished operating software from another Seattle company, turned it into MS-DOS, licensed it to IBM, and worked closely with IBM engineers to craft the details of a new machine that would leapfrog over California-based competitors. As Microsoft grew rapidly in the early 1980s, Allen also made key contributions to Windows and Microsoft Word. He left active participation in 1983, when he learned that he had Hodgkin's disease and successfully underwent a two-year cycle of radiation therapy, but remained on the Microsoft board until 2000.

From the base that Allen and Gates constructed between 1975 and 1983, Microsoft became one of the nation's most powerful and successful companies. It was also the purported bully that vacuums up its rivals, with Gates as the tycoon whom people love to hate. Other software firms rose and fell with innovative and then outmoded programs. Microsoft parlayed its alliance with IBM into a dominant position that eventually triggered federal antitrust action at the end of the 1990s, from which it emerged intact but (perhaps) chastened. The obvious comparison is John D. Rockefeller and Standard Oil, which also combined technical

Figure 15.3: Albuquerque, New Mexico, was the starting place for Microsoft. Like many western cities, it lies open to view below a range of mountains. Courtesy of the Albuquerque Chamber of Commerce.

superiority with saturation marketing, careful neutralizing of competition, antitrust problems, and a founder with an image problem.

Microsoft changed the character of Seattle by attracting other information businesses to complement university research and development. After Boeing moved its corporate headquarters to Chicago in 2001, the most recognizable Seattle companies were the new-era companies Microsoft, Amazon, and Starbucks. The "Microsoft millionaires" who parlayed early participation in company stock plans into multi-million-dollar nest eggs and early retirement became a local cliché in the 1990s and a possible source of civic energy and philanthropy.

The takeoff of Microsoft was part of the second generation of the high-tech West. By 1980, the western states were the center of atomic research and production (still a rising industry after a decade of energy crises and reviving Cold War), aerospace companies, and companies that specialized in instrumentation and military control systems. Most important for the future, the invention of the microprocessor in 1971 had kicked the electronics industry into high gear. The farmlands of Santa Clara County, California, became a "silicon landscape" of neat one-story factories and research campuses. In 1950, the county had 800 factory workers. In 1980, it had 264,000 manufacturing workers and three thousand electronics firms.

Carl Abbott

The electronics boom at the end of the twentieth century was the offspring of extraordinary improvements in computing capacity. At the start of the microprocessor era, Intel cofounder Gordon Moore predicted that the number of transistors on a microchip would double every eighteen months, with consequent increases in performance and drops in price. "Moore's Law" worked at least to the opening of a new century as producers moved from chips with 5,000 transistors to ones with 50 million. The practical result was vastly increased computer capacities and transportability. The "portable" Osborne and Apple computers that came out of Santa Clara County in the early 1980s were suitcase-size packages with limited hard drives and tiny random access memories for running programs. Twenty years later, when students and business travelers pulled out their laptops at every opportunity, the first generation of personal computers were as outmoded as a Spanish galleon in an age of supertankers. "Portable computers" were found not only in business briefcases but in automobile diagnostic systems, cell phones, and handheld games.

Western high tech by the 1980s formed what regional development expert Peter Hall terms "innovative milieu." One industrial cluster centered on the San Francisco Bay Area around electronic data processing, another in southern California around aerospace. Both places had thick networks of suppliers, mobility of workers among competing firms, and relatively open marketplaces of ideas. There were certainly rivalries and trade secrets, but the West Coast style was more open and flexible than in rival East Coast centers like Boston. It was a remarkable manifestation of some of the common, self-satisfied assumptions about the superiority of the "western" style over the eastern.

In the 1980s and 1990s, branch hardware and microchip factories, spin-off companies, and software firms spread the information-processing industry throughout the West. The information business built on earlier foundations in Dallas, Portland, and Phoenix. It changed big cities like Denver and Salt Lake City and radically transformed Colorado Springs, Boise, and Austin. Local boosters in the 1980s talked up "silicon prairies," "silicon forests," "silicon deserts," and "silicon mountains" to complement California's original Silicon Valley.

The high-tech transformation also penetrated everyday life in the West. The most networked state in 2000 was Alaska, where computers helped to make up for vast distances and isolating winters. Close behind were Washington, Utah, Oregon, and New Hampshire. Through much of the West, high levels of Internet use marked dozens of small towns and cities where self-employed individuals could enjoy the amenities of the high country while interacting with the world. At the same time, larger western cities had taken the lead in the emergence of a networked society. The "Digital Economy Index" compiled in 2001 by the Progressive Policy Institute for the fifty largest metropolitan areas put thirteen western cities in the top third, led by San Francisco, San Diego, and Austin and closely followed by Denver, Dallas, and Seattle.

The Vital Metropolis

The high-tech explosion of the 1990s has been a drive wheel for the continued urbanization that marks the West as a leader in American social change. The West has long been a region of cities—from colonial-era San Antonio and Sitka to nineteenth-century towns like gold rush San Francisco, genteel Pasadena, and brawling Butte and then to twentieth-century boomtowns like Tulsa and Phoenix. At the beginning of the twenty-first century, civic leaders—including Paul Allen—are remaking western cities to meet the needs of an information economy.

The numbers sketch the outlines of the urban West. As early as 1900, more than half of all Californians lived in cities, as did more than a third of all Montanans, Coloradoans, and Washingtonians. A century later, the census reported that over five of every six westerners lived in metropolitan areas (large cities and the adjacent suburban counties). Las Vegas topped every other American boomtown with a metropolitan area increase of 83 percent for the 1990s. Among the nation's large metro areas (ones that counted over five hundred thousand people in 2000), thirteen of the twenty fastest growing were in the West.

The West is now a land of supercities scattered across sparsely settled countryside. The region's ten largest urban regions in 2000 had 49,568,434 people by official count—53 percent of the entire West. These urban complexes stretch seventy, eighty, or even a hundred miles. Many are squeezed into relatively narrow corridors by oceanfronts and mountains. Phoenix builds within the east-west ridges that frame the Salt River Valley. Seattle is pinched between Puget Sound and the Cascades, Salt Lake City between its lake and the Wasatch Mountains. Because the scarcity of water also makes compactness an imperative in much of the West, the densities of its cities are surprisingly high. They extend horizontally, but they don't necessarily "sprawl," if that means scattershot and leapfrog development. There were forty-nine metro areas in the United States with 1 million or more people in 2000. Ten of the twelve most densely settled were western—Las Vegas, Los Angeles, San Diego, San Francisco, Phoenix, Sacramento, Seattle, Portland, San Antonio, Salt Lake City.

Drive to the top of South Mountain on a clear day in southern Arizona. Look down on Phoenix, and very few vacant spaces will catch the eye. Greater Phoenix is built low but compact, and it is typical of southwestern and far western urban areas in that the density of

Carl Abbott

Metropolitan Growth in the West,
1990 - 2000

Large Metropolitan Areas (500,000+)
with 20% or more growth

Map 15.1: The West's fast-growing metropolitan areas are widely dispersed across
the region from Texas to Washington. Map by Cliff Hutchinson.

settlement has been holding steady even while total population has
boomed. Indeed, the entire "dry Sunbelt" of California, Arizona,
Nevada, Colorado, Utah, and New Mexico added new urbanized land
and urban population in roughly equal rates from 1982 to 1997,
according to the National Resource Inventory of the U.S. Department
of Agriculture, whereas the "wet Sunbelt" of southeastern states like

Alabama, Florida, Georgia, Tennessee, and the Carolinas added developed land at twice the pace of population growth.

The same view from South Mountain reveals that the Phoenix region has a very visible core: roughly six miles by ten miles, it is 4 percent of the built-up region and embraces state office complexes, downtown Phoenix, Central Avenue business towers, Sky Harbor airport, downtown Tempe and downtown Scottsdale, Arizona State University, and sports arenas. In short, this core is not a traditional downtown, but a set of districts that include and extend downtown with most of the regional institutions, high-end shopping, public offices, and sports venues. Similar cores cover about eight square miles in San Antonio, fifteen square miles in Salt Lake City, and twenty-five square miles in Denver.

Denver is a good representative of the revitalization of western cities. In the 1990s the city itself, exclusive of surrounding counties, recorded a population increase of 25 percent. The core is dotted with public university campuses, a new library, downtown housing, museums, riverbank amenities, and a downtown ballpark for the Colorado Rockies (Seattle and San Francisco also have new downtown ballparks, and San Diego opened another in 2004). A white-collar economy and young professionals and businesspeople have turned old immigrant districts on three sides of the core into trendy neighborhoods, while middle-class neighborhoods have held their value and attractions. Old Stapleton Airport and parts of Lowry Field are undergoing massive high-density development along "new urbanist" principles. Denver may be high and dry, but it is increasingly international. Latino newcomers account for much of the population growth. The new Denver International Airport is a claim on the future—a facility large enough to make the city the air hub of the continent in the vision of its boosters.

Paul Allen has been participating in the same sort of makeover of Seattle. His focus has been the historic core that reaches from the shores of Lake Union to the Port of Seattle container terminals on the Duwamish River flats. In what seems to be a classic Paul Allen story, he was buying laser discs at a Seattle neighborhood video store when he saw a petition to save the downtown Cinerama theater. He commiserated with the clerk about the great days of the theater (where he first saw *2001: A Space Odyssey*), signed the petition, and then bought and restored the building with comfy seats and updated sound and projection systems. He is helping to restore Seattle's Union Station and putting up an adjacent office building for his own operations. He gave money to the University of Washington for a new library wing named for his father and supports environmental and social service organizations in Oregon and Washington. He put up $21 million in the early 1990s for a "Seattle Commons" park and redevelopment project on the industrial and warehouse district north of downtown. When voters decided against the scheme, he ended up with eleven acres, to which he has been adding bits and pieces with an eye to transforming the area into a bustling district of high-tech and biotech offices, shops, and apartments—a sort of northern version of San Francisco's South of Market district that grew so rapidly in the 1990s.

In popular imagery, Paul Allen's city is a bit precious but eminently livable, the natural haunt of Microsoft yuppies and Starbucks lounge lizards. The notion is constructed from films like *Singles* (1992) and *Sleepless in Seattle* (1993), the popular television series *Frasier,* and a general impression of great views and clean streets. But writer Sherman Alexie, a member of the Spokane/Coeur d'Alene tribe, offers a darker vision of Seattle and the West in *Indian Killer* (1996). The novel is framed as a mystery about a serial killer who stalks the Seattle night, scalps the victims, and leaves feathers as symbols of Indian retribution, but the book's spiritual center is the struggle of John Smith to find his personal identity. Adopted out of his tribe and raised by middle-class whites in Bellevue, Smith wanders the nightside of Seattle as internalized rage turns him dysfunctional. In the process he encounters derelicts, racists, and enraged Indians, people who have been left out of the trendy town and the homogenized New West.

The biting lyrics of rock musician Kurt Cobain are yet another take on a different Seattle. A high school misfit who wanted to make music, Cobain grew up in Aberdeen on the Washington coast, a gray city too far from remaining trees to prosper as a timber town, too far from Puget Sound to transition into second-home tourism. Escaping to Olympia and then Seattle in the late 1980s, he became a key part of an intense Seattle music scene that journalists soon typed as a rock mecca with Nirvana (Cobain's group), Pearl Jam, and other "grunge" bands. Nirvana started with an alternative record label in Seattle but switched to a major company run by Paul Allen's later business partner David Geffen to record their breakout album *Nevermind* in 1991, only to be devastated by Cobain's suicide the next year. Cobain is not one of Allen's favorite musicians (we might guess that Cobain was too heavy into message and not dazzling enough as a virtuoso), but we can find some parallels in two obsessed northwestern teenagers who made names for themselves.

The same extremes of bright and somber mark our understanding of Los Angeles. Grunge bands in the 1990s drew on the Los Angeles punk rock of the previous decade, which played up the emptiness of southern California life in contrast to surfer songs. As featured player in scores of movies and backdrop in hundreds of others, Los Angeles takes much of its current identity from the film writers and directors who call it home. Critics who don't like what they see in Los Angeles "prove" their point with references to the dark dystopia of *Blade Runner* (1982), the violent alienation of *Falling Down* (1993) or *Pulp Fiction* (1994), and the old and new noir of *The Big Sleep* (1946), *Chinatown* (1974), and *L.A. Confidential* (1997). Those who are taken by the metropolis find the choice a bit more limited: *Earth Girls Are Easy* (1989) and *Clueless* (1995) as more appealing visions of everyday life, *Speed* (1994) as a parable of ethnic cooperation and social cohesion, *L.A. Story* (1991) with its upbeat view of the transforming capacity of the metropolis.

The American West in a Wider World

There was nothing upbeat about Seattle in the first days of December 1999, when the politics of a global economy came to Paul Allen's town with a hiss of tear gas. With their commitment to making Seattle a "world-class" city, its political and business leaders had worked hard for the opportunity to host a meeting of the World Trade Organization (WTO), the international organization that sets the terms for world trade. With finance ministers, foreign affairs ministers, and heads of government expected to attend, the meeting was supposed to gain invaluable worldwide publicity. Instead it gave the city a pounding headache. Organized with the help of Web sites and e-mail lists, fifty thousand labor unionists and environmental protestors converged on the meeting to publicize the loss of U.S. jobs to overseas producers and to call for stronger environmental and labor regulations on multinational corporations. Most demonstrators were peaceful, but several hundred started a rampage through downtown that triggered overreaction by unprepared police.

The WTO riots did indeed put Seattle in world company, for they followed similar demonstrations in Geneva, Switzerland, and preceded even nastier riots in Genoa, Italy. They also symbolized the extent to which the American West is enmeshed in a complex world economy that damages some of its traditional industries while promoting new enterprises. For example, western farmers worry about the competition of cheaper crops from Chile and China, but the global networking of the computer industry has helped to tilt the United States toward the nations and economies of the Pacific Rim.

Americans long dreamed of Asian markets and a Pacific destiny, trading sea otter furs to China, helping to open Japan and China to the industrializing West, cutting a trans-American canal across Panama, and fighting four Pacific wars in the seventy-five years after 1898. As national policy encouraged foreign trade and overseas economies boomed, the value of American imports and exports nearly tripled from 7 percent of the gross domestic product in 1965 to 20 percent in 2000. In 1982, the United States for the first time did more business with

Figure 15.4: Along with adjacent Long Beach, the Port of Los Angeles is one of the largest ocean ports in the world. The volume of trade through this complex reflects the importance of Pacific trade to the U.S. economy and the internationalization of the American West. Courtesy of the Port of Los Angeles.

Pacific nations than with Europe. A decade later, a bipartisan coalition passed the North American Free Trade Agreement (NAFTA). Negotiated by Republican George H. Bush and pushed through Congress in 1993 by Democrat Bill Clinton, NAFTA combined 25 million Canadians, 90 million Mexicans, and 250 million U.S. consumers in a single "common market."

NAFTA is part of the continuing economic integration of western North America along a north-south axis. In the later 1970s and early 1980s, a boom in energy development pumped U.S. capital and Texas expertise into the vast Rocky Mountain and high plains energy province, bringing boom times to Alberta, Canada, as well as Texas, Oklahoma, Colorado, Wyoming, and Montana. The Mexican government as early as the 1960s encouraged a "platform economy" by allowing companies on the Mexican side of the border to import components and inputs duty-free as long as 80 percent of the items were reexported and 90 percent of the workers were Mexicans. The intent is to encourage foreign corporations to locate assembly plants south of the border. Such factories can employ lower-wage workers and avoid strict antipollution laws (leading to serious threats to public health on both sides of the border). Maquiladora assembly plants, owned by U.S. and Asian corporations and employing roughly a million Mexican workers, transformed

Mexico's northern states and U.S.-Mexico border cities, especially San Diego–Tijuana (4.3 million people) and El Paso–Juárez (1.5 million). Northwestern economic boosters in the 1990s played with the idea of a transnational "Cascadia" that linked Vancouver, Seattle, and Portland along a superregional "main street."

Trans-Pacific trade and North American integration have accelerated an ethnic transformation of the West through Asian and Latino immigration. High-tech cities have been economic entry points for Asian investment and immigration. Capital for new plants came from Japan in the 1980s, Korea in the 1990s. Engineers and software writers immigrated from India, while U.S. companies built working relationships with subcontractors in the Indian city of Bangalore, center of that country's computer industry. Lower-paid immigrants filled the workforces of microchip plants. People in Silicon Valley knew the electronics company Hewlett-Packard as "Little Vietnam" in the mid-1980s and Advanced Micro Devices as "Little Manila."

The effects of the new immigration are most obvious in California. In 1960, a mere 1 percent of Los Angeles County's people were Asian Americans and 11 percent were Hispanic. By 2000, the figures were 12 percent Asian and 45 percent Hispanic. The sprawling neighborhoods of East Los Angeles make up the second-largest Mexican city in the world. The growth of Latino population in northern Orange County began to undermine the county's famous political hyperconservatism, especially in Loretta Sánchez's defeat of U.S. Representative Robert Dornan in 1996. New ethnic communities appeared in Los Angeles suburbs: Iranians in Beverly Hills, Chinese in Monterey Park, Japanese in Gardena, Thais in Hollywood, Samoans in Carson, Cambodians in Lakewood.

Ethnic mixing bowls were also racial cauldrons. The tensions that exploded in Los Angeles in April 1992 in the "Rodney King riots" seemed to many to substantiate pessimistic evaluations of L.A. as a disaster in the making. King was a black motorist who had been savagely clubbed and kicked by police officers while being arrested after a car chase on March 3, 1991. A nearby resident captured the beating on videotape from his apartment balcony. Within two days, the tape was playing and replaying on national television. The grainy pictures shocked the nation and confirmed the worst black fears about biased police behavior, as well as specific misgivings about the paramilitary approach that the Los Angeles police department favored for maintaining order.

Early the next year, the four officers stood trial for unjustified use of force before a suburban jury. The televised trial and the unexpected verdict of not guilty on April 29 stirred deep anger that escalated into four days of rioting. The disorder was far more complex than the Watts outbreak in South Central Los Angeles in 1965. African Americans from South Central participated, but so did Central American and Mexican immigrants in adjacent districts, who accounted for about one third of the twelve thousand arrests. The disorder spread south to Long Beach and north to singe the edge of Westwood and Beverly Hills. One contingent of rioters assaulted the downtown police headquarters, city hall, and the *Los Angeles Times* building. As in 1965, some of the targets were white passersby and symbols of white authority. But members of competing minority groups were also victims as Central American gang members battled each other and angry black people targeted Korean-owned and Vietnamese-owned shops as symbols of economic discrimination. The disorder left fifty-eight people dead, most of them African Americans and Latinos.

Demographic changes of the sort that fueled the Los Angeles riots have also had very clear effects on western politics. Proponents of cultural pluralism could take heart in two generations of black and Hispanic mayors in western cities. African Americans Tom Bradley in Los Angeles (1973–1993) and Lionel Wilson in Oakland (1977–1990) were pioneers, followed by Mexican Americans Henry Cisneros in San Antonio (1981–1989) and Federico Peña in Denver (1983–1990). Voters in the 1990s picked African Americans to lead Seattle (Norm Rice, 1990–1997), Denver (Wellington Webb, 1991–2003), and San Francisco (Willie Brown, 1996–2003). Hispanos have long been prominent in New Mexico state politics, while voters in Hawai'i in the last two decades have elected governors of Japanese American, native Hawai'ian, and Filipino heritage—George Ariyoshi (1974–1986), John Waihee III (1986–1994), and Benjamin Cayetano (1994–present). Washingtonians made Gary Locke (1997–2004) the first Chinese American governor.

But ethnic diversity has also meant political backlash. Partly because high immigration can strain local government budgets even if it benefits the nation as a whole, 60 percent of California voters approved Proposition 187 in 1994, cutting off access to state-funded public education and health care for illegal immigrants. In 1996, California approved a ballot measure to eliminate state-sponsored affirmative action; one effect was to prohibit state-funded colleges and universities from using race or ethnicity as a factor in deciding which applicants to admit. In the same year, the U.S. Supreme Court let stand a lower court ruling in *Hopwood v. Texas,* which had forbidden the University of Texas to consider race in admission decisions. The number of black freshmen in the university dropped by half in 1997 and the number of blacks and Hispanics among first-year law students by two thirds.

Language was another battlefield. Californians in 1998 adopted Proposition 227, banning bilingual public education, a system under which children whose first language is Spanish or another "immigrant" tongue are taught for several years in that language before shifting to English-language classrooms. Advocates of bilingual education claim that it eases the transition into American society, while opponents say that it blocks children from fully assimilating into American life. Arizonans followed in 2000 with a similar prohibition. Other states reacted to increasing immigration with English-only laws. Referendums or legislative action in Alaska (1996), Wyoming (1996), and Utah (2000) raised to twenty-six the number of states that declared English their official language. A similar Arizona law was on the books from 1988 until 1998, when the state supreme court struck it down.

The 2000 census reveals three "Wests" in demographic terms. First are fast-growing and ethnically diverse gateway states along the Mexican and Pacific borders. Non-Hispanic whites are now a minority in California, Hawai`i, and New Mexico. Hispanics are a rapidly growing presence in states that are otherwise as different as Texas and Washington. This is a "West" that is plunging headlong into a multiracial future. The second "West" is the Rocky Mountain states that are attracting both whites and nonwhites. White migrants leaving ethnically diverse California on the "white flight highway" (to borrow historian Mary Murphy's phrase) helped to make Nevada (66-percent growth), Arizona (40-percent), Colorado (31-percent), Utah (30-percent), and Idaho (29-percent) the fastest-growing states in the nation in the 1990s. However, so did millions of Latino service workers who washed dishes in Las Vegas casinos, staffed convenience stores in Colorado Springs, and cleaned motel rooms in Park City, Utah. Their presence is testimony to the way the development of a tourist economy looks both backward and forward, rooted in the regional resource of scenery but deeply entangled with the global economy. Slope County, North Dakota, epitomizes the third West. Situated in the cattle-ranching region of the cold plains, it was the whitest county in the nation: only 3 of its 767 people reported themselves as nonwhite. In turn, the Dakotas are part of a vast sparsely populated, slowly growing, heavily white, and economically troubled swathe of territory that also spans much of Nebraska and Kansas and the Great Plains counties of Colorado and Montana. Fixed in the ways of the settler generations of 1870–1920, it is drawn to a past that includes as many problems as success stories.

Paul Allen and the Age of Communication
Paul Allen's signature contribution to the Seattle scene is the curious Experience Music Project (EMP) that rears up in the afternoon shadow of the Space Needle. What started as a memorial to rock star Jimi Hendrix evolved into a museum of Pacific Northwest music and then

Table 1
States with Highest Proportions of Minority Residents in 2000

Hispanic	New Mexico (42 percent)
	California (32 percent)
	Texas (32 percent)
	Arizona (25 percent)
	Nevada (20 percent)
Asian	Hawai`i (51 percent)
	California (11 percent)
	Washington (6 percent)
	New Jersey (6 percent)
	New York (6 percent)
Black	Mississippi (36 percent)
	Louisiana (33 percent)
	South Carolina (30 percent)
	Georgia (29 percent)
	Maryland (28 percent)
American Indian	Alaska (16 percent)
	New Mexico (10 percent)
	South Dakota (8 percent)
	Oklahoma (8 percent)
	Montana (6 percent)

into a $240-million celebration of American popular music in all its styles and schools. The EMP leads us in two directions: toward entertainment and electronics and toward the content of the communications industry and its infrastructure.

EMP started with Allen's love of Hendrix, the Seattle-born guitarist who blazed through rock music for a few years in the 1960s before his death in 1970. For Allen, the distance between AM radio pop tunes and Hendrix was a revelation. "It was like hearing music from another planet," he has told *Rolling Stone*. As Allen was discovering computers as a high schooler, Hendrix's career connected Seattle to a global entertainment industry with its headquarters in Los Angeles (as Kurt Cobain would later do). Thirty years after Hendrix's death, the EMP drew on Los Angeles superstar architect Frank Gehry, who is noted for exploiting the possibilities of computer-assisted design in realizing his ideas. The building swoops and folds around the monorail like Hendrix's guitar sounds. Its glass, steel, and aluminum skin glitters in blue, red, gold, and purple—a sort of exploded memory of the brightly colored aluminum iced tea glasses that were popular in the 1950s.

What do we get inside? The EMP is a giant attic with eighty thousand artifacts, from the Fender Stratocaster guitar that Hendrix tormented at Woodstock in 1969 to concert posters and fan magazines. Exhibits are enhanced by commentary and sound tracks via a portable hard drive and touch screen. There are sophisticated interactive booths where visitors can play along with masters of rock and roll. Behind the scenes is an archive of manuscript materials (some of Hendrix's handwritten lyrics) and videotaped interviews with rap, punk, and rock performers. In 2003, Allen announced plans to supplement the EMP with the Science Fiction Experience, described as a hypermuseum of science fiction.

Allen is not just a fan but also a major investor in entertainment "content providers." He bought the Portland Trail Blazers of the National Basketball Association in 1988 because they are a well-established regional team, and Allen is a basketball nut. He used mostly his own money to build a new arena (officially it is the Rose Garden Arena, but I call it Paul's Blazerama). He bought the Seattle Seahawks of the National Football League in 1997 to keep the team in town and shared the cost of a new stadium with the public. Neither facility is perfect, but both are in the urban core, not the suburbs. He has a $500-million stake in the movie company DreamWorks SKG with Hollywood moguls Steven Spielberg, Jeffrey Katzenberg, and David Geffen. His Starwave company produced some of the early online news sites like ESPN Sportszone and Mr. Showbiz.

Paul Allen certainly enjoys his show business connections (many baby boomers would enjoy throwing parties where they could jam with Carlos Santana or Lou Reed), but his investments are a reminder of the importance of the larger media content/entertainment business for the western economy. The industry played a major role in the recovery of the southern California economy from recession brought about by the decline in defense spending after 1990. The same sorts of people in the 1990s also made other western cities both prosperous and intellectually innovative. Austin became a creative center for writers, popular musicians, and filmmakers. As software-writing skills also spawned a new world of multimedia entertainment, the dot.com and Internet boom of the 1990s completed the transformation of San Francisco into a informational city and even touched provincial cities like Portland.

Meanwhile Paul Allen remains an active investor pursuing the vision of a "wired world," a system of high-capacity data pipelines, home-based interfaces like TV screens and computers, and the organizational capacity to link them together. Allen has invested variously in America Online, Ticketmaster, cable television systems, and dozens of other companies, looking for synergy among information delivery systems and technologies. As he told Newsweek in 2000, entertainment and high tech "have traditionally been very different worlds, but these worlds are marrying as time goes on."

Allen's career has made him a practical prophet of an expected age of communication. A wired world has the potential to undercut the layers of organization and regulation that made the twentieth century an age of bureaucracy characterized by fascist police and Soviet commissars, by welfare bureaucrats in social democracies, and by organization men in U.S. corporations. Four years of devastating war from 1914 to 1918, socialist revolutions, the Great Depression, a second global war, and a forty-year Cold War all helped to transform the growing nationalisms of Europe and the Americas into rigid institutional barriers. Nations erected protectionist barriers to trade that have taken half a century to remove. The same governments created obstacles to international movement as they sought to hold their pool of workers and soldiers and to exclude dangerous influences. Control of borders was an important issue for the 1996 presidential campaign and again after the tragedy of September 11, 2001.

To its enthusiasts, a wired world promises an electronic reprise of the economic fluidity of the nineteenth century, when 50 million Europeans migrated across the Atlantic and millions of Asians crossed the Pacific to the Americas. As ideas move smoothly from one network node to another, individuals may be able to operate in many places at once without the challenges of physically relocating. Every location is potentially a platform for interaction—a hub airport of the mind. In turn, advocates envision that open exchange will make markets work more efficiently, build communities of interest, and undermine rigid institutions (for example, using the Internet to organize against the WTO). This said, Paul Allen's own spin on the age of communication is perhaps curiously conservative, emphasizing the importance of finding interesting content to ship through the information infrastructure—both specifically and metaphorically linking the Hollywood dream factory to the West's hardware makers and software writers.

Western Worlds

At first glance, Paul Allen and Ursula LeGuin are an unlikely pair. They are hard-driving, self-taught engineer and science-fiction writer, confident prophet of the future and writer of fiction about other places and times, successful man in a "man's business" and thoughtful feminist poet. But they share a sense of "westernness." Even in an age of communication, Allen has remained loyal to his place—to Mercer Island in Lake Washington, to the San Juan Islands of Puget Sound as a rural getaway, and to Seattle as a hometown and business base.

LeGuin grew up in northern California, has lived for several decades in Portland, and describes herself as a "western American."

The western land and its possibilities is a theme that pervades LeGuin's writing. *Always Coming Home* (1985) is about a northern California inhabited in ways never possible. In the imagined world of Earthsea, depicted in a series of young adult fables published from 1968 through 2001, some readers may see the islands of the Aegean. But I picture LeGuin at her keyboard in the green, misted hills of Portland as November storms pump off the Pacific. In Earthsea's high green islands I see the water-lapped margins of the Northwest coast—the fitfully sunny islands of Puget Sound and the cloud-racked coasts of British Columbia.

Allen and LeGuin both are confirmed environmentalists. Allen supports the protection of old-growth forests, whereas LeGuin has used forest as the metaphor for all natural systems in *The Word for World Is Forest* (1971). Allen envisions a single wired world and tries to speed its arrival. LeGuin explores a more complex dialectic of utopia and antiutopia in *The Dispossessed* (1974). *Always Coming Home* reimagines California as a nonindustrial ecotopia, conducting a thought experiment about the ways people might carefully interact with place.

This is the same landscape that poet Gary Snyder has made his own. In poetry and in essays collected as *The Practice of the Wild* (1990), Snyder explores the conflicts between resource development (logging, vacation homes) and the natural setting of the northern Sierra Nevada. He also combines a deeply emotional connection with nature and a scientific understanding of interconnections of ecological systems. He offers the possibility that westerners can make conscious choices for "rehabitation," living within sustainable limits.

In offering the West as a land of beginning again, the place where social experiments are conceivable and right choices are still possible, Snyder replays a long regional tradition. In the nineteenth and early twentieth centuries, utopian settlements sprang up in Colorado, California, the Pacific Northwest, and, most impressively, in Utah. In the 1960s and 1970s, isolation and a good climate for marijuana plants made New Mexico, Colorado, northern California, and Oregon into prime commune country. My own five acres near the West Fork of the Hood River on the north slope of Mount Hood still harbor hippie architecture from 1970—an octagonal cabin of unpeeled Douglas fir logs with scrounged, mismatched windows placed at peculiar and almost surely pot-inspired angles (although we had the junked cars and worn-out school bus hauled off for scrap).

As the people who created and abandoned their Hood River commune learned, breaking with the past is a tough task. A gifted writer like midwesterner Louise Erdrich writes about the tensions of continuity and change in the West. In *Love Medicine* (1984), *The Beet Queen* (1986), *The Bingo Palace* (1995), and other novels she follows interlocking families from the Turtle Mountain reservation on the far northern edge of North Dakota. Her characters struggle to reconcile traditional ways with Christianity, manufactured houses, and souped-up pickups. In *The Bingo Palace,* the New West of Nevada casinos is the modern equivalent of alcohol, grabbing and pulling down one of the characters as surely as whiskey. Characters move away (to Minneapolis in *The Antelope Wife,* 1998), but interlocking families and the strange appeal of the snow-swept plains pull them back.

For another writer, it is the recent past that is inescapable. Terry Tempest Williams's *Refuge: An Unnatural History of Family and Place* (1991) introduces the knotty issues of environmental politics. She interweaves descriptions of a bird sanctuary along Great Salt Lake with the story of her mother's death from cancer, probably triggered by downwind fallout from nuclear testing in Nevada, thus contrasting the "old" natural West to the "new" West of human actions that have been controlled by the imperatives of global politics. Primarily about personal journeys and interconnections with nature, the book is also a reminder of the importance of "big science" to the recent West—NASA facilities, Department of Energy laboratories, and astronomical complexes on Hawai'ian and southwestern mountaintops. The federal government has made the disposal of nuclear waste into one of the salient regional issues. New Mexico salt deposits now receive contaminated materials from Colorado's Rocky Flats and other military production facilities. The lightning rod has been plans for entombment of high-level nuclear waste that have focused since 1987 on Yucca Mountain, Nevada, ninety miles northwest of Las Vegas. In January 2001, the Bush administration reaffirmed the plans, raising the anger of Nevada politicians of all parties.

While the nuclear waste problem has been debated by politicians, scientists, and blue-ribbon commission, important changes in environmental policy emerged from grassroots organizing and activism. Passed in 1973, the Endangered Species Act became a key tool for environmentalists in the 1980s and 1990s. Activists made effective use of the act to block logging in the Northwest, halt expansion of the Kitt Peak Observatory in Arizona, and restrict urban development along streams used by migrating salmon. Grassroots activism by increasingly sophisticated environmental lobbying groups secured a variety of federal protections for the Santa Monica Mountains National Recreation Area (1978), the Columbia River Gorge National Scenic Area (1986), and new national monuments set aside by Bill Clinton in 2000.

What we might call the Old Growth religion took on timber corporations throughout the Pacific states and northern Rockies, battling clear-cutting and the comfortable ties between timber producers and the U.S. Forest Service. One of the biggest battles centered on the Tongass National Forest, which covers most of the islands and mainland of the Alaska panhandle. In the 1950s, the Forest Service inked contracts that guaranteed new pulp mills in Sitka and Ketchikan a fifty-year supply of trees; the contracts created a new industry by in essence giving away the resource to companies that wrecked watersheds and quashed labor unions. Organizations like the Southeast Alaska Conservation Council began to argue for balanced use rather than nineteenth-century exploitation, evolving from a handful of longhairs in Juneau to a powerful organization that could enlist the *New York Times*. Legislation in 1980 and 1990 protected substantial parts of the Tongass as national monuments and ended federal subsidies for the industry. Comparable issues of the proper balance between resource production and environmental preservation arose again in 2001 and 2002, when Americans debated whether to open the Arctic National Wildlife Refuge on Alaska's North Slope to petroleum exploration.

When unemployment hovers at 20 or 25 percent and young people pack up for better opportunities, western communities that have suffered from long-run declines in resource industries find little comfort in job-retraining programs and calls to shift to diversified, sustainable economies. Rural resentment helped to fuel the countermovement of property-rights activism. The so-called Sagebrush Rebellion began in 1979 in Nevada, a state 86-percent federally owned. Nevada demanded that federal lands be ceded to the states. The idea picked up local support within other mountain states with their own vast tracts of federal land, but it faded when the Reagan administration brought pro-development attitudes to federal land agencies. Nevertheless, distrust of federal agencies remained strong in the rural West. Ecoterrorism on behalf of a mysticized Nature has its counterparts in local officials who defiantly push roads into protected federal lands and angry individuals who take potshots at people in Forest Service uniforms and burn down ranger stations.

The property rights movement in its extreme form shows the dangers of isolation and self-indulgence. Wide-open spaces and high mountains can allow the illusion that people can escape the changing world. For example, white supremacists and survivalists have the northern Rockies as a prime location to build fortresses against an increasingly diverse America. The Aryan Nation brought unwanted publicity to Hayden Lake, Idaho, in the 1980s. Its presence sowed the seeds for a deadly, probably unjustified shoot-out between federal agents and the

Carl Abbott

white supremacist Weaver family at Ruby Ridge in 1992. Groups like the Posse Comitatus and the Freemen, who reject the authority of federal and state courts, find pockets of support across the northern plains—leading, for example, to a standoff and eventual surrender of eighteen Freemen on a ranch outside Jordan, Montana, in 1996.

What is the future for bypassed places like the northern plains of Jordan, Montana, and Turtle Mountain, North Dakota? Lacking the amenities of Jackson, Wyoming, or Aspen, Colorado, these are the sorts of western places that are never likely to face the "devil's bargain" of exploitive tourism or attract footloose information industries. Energy and mineral booms still crash into small communities like breaking surf, but little is left in the backwash a decade later. Some observers think that the century-long experiment with the ranching and dry-farming frontier should be written off, with the high plains of the western Dakotas and Nebraska returned to natural grasslands as a "buffalo commons"— not an idea that sits well with potentially displaced residents.

Certainly these parts of the West contrast with the powerhouses of Houston, Dallas–Fort Worth, southern California, and the San Francisco Bay region. These urban complexes have shaped and framed the economic opportunities for the new century. They are also models for the best and worst of American society—ethnic and racial mixing bowls that produce both conflict and cooperation. Their residents reach deeply into surrounding territories, claiming vast "weekendlands" for recreation and leisure, imposing environmental controls, and breaking down provincial isolation. McMurtry's novels about Thalia, Texas (a thinly disguised Archer City), reflect the thickening of connections between cities and hinterlands. In *The Last Picture Show* (1966), the 25 miles to Wichita Falls is a big trip. A generation later, the characters in *Texasville* (1987) readily drive 150 miles to Dallas for half-hour appointments or 200 miles to Oklahoma City for entertainment.

At the same time, even the emptiest West retains the capacity to inspire on its own terms. If the previous generation's hippies were looking for personal growth through contact with the wild, so are a contemporary generation of writers about nature and community. Gretel Ehrlich moved to Wyoming in 1976 to lose herself in the lonesome spaces. But as she tells in *The Solace of Open Spaces* (1985), the very emptiness of that very wide-open state became a "geography of possibility" where the challenges of the harsh climate and the ranching economy nurtured a deeper sense of self. Her experience contrasts with that of William Kittredge, who came slowly to realize the deep problems with the expectation of absolute ownership that American settlers brought to the rural West. His essays in *Owning It All* (1987) examine the missteps of the past and the need for ranchers and farmers "to find a new story to inhabit," a new way to understand their place and their place in the world.

Midwesterner William Least Heat-Moon in *PrairyErth* (1991) has also explored the links and discontinuities between the past and present. His focus is the interaction of nature and people in Chase County, in the Flint Hills of central Kansas. Here, a hundred miles or so from the city where he grew up, are the memories of previous generations frozen in the remnants of abandoned buildings and towns. Here also, amidst the remnants of the tall-grass prairies that nourished the bison, is the very spot where the East turns into the West: "On a clear day of summer the world changes in a few miles from green to blue, from shadows to nearly unbroken sunlight, from intermittent breezes to a wind blowing steadily as if out of the lungs of the universe."

So we find, coming full circle, that the networked West retains the spiritual power of western places. Westerners like Paul Allen have helped to construct the technologies that link the twenty-first-century world in previously unknown ways, but they remain deeply connected to the specific valleys, mountains, coasts, and deserts. I end with a passage by Oregon poet William Stafford, from "Camping at Lost Lake" (it's a real place, with postcard views, eight miles up the road from my Hood River acres):

> *Among these trees till morning comes*
> *we sleep, and dream thunders of fern*
> *alerting space by the way they wait,*
> *eloquent of the light's return.*

Essay on Sources

Paul Allen's Web site is www.paulallen.com. Laura Rich, *The Accidental Zillionaire: Demystifying Paul Allen* (New York: Wiley, 2002), draws on published information and interviews for a limited account. Business biographies of Bill Gates and Microsoft include James Wallace and Jim Erickson, *Hard Drive: Bill Gates and the Making of the Microsoft Empire* (New York: Wiley, 1993), and Stephen Manes and Paul Andrews, *Gates: How Microsoft's Mogul Reinvented an Industry—and Made Himself the Richest Man in America* (New York: Doubleday, 1994).

Carl Abbott, *The Metropolitan Frontier: Cities in the Modern American West* (Tucson: University of Arizona Press, 1993), gives an overview of urban growth from the 1940s to the 1990s, with examples drawn from cities of all sizes. By the same author, *Greater Portland: Urban Life and Landscape in the Pacific Northwest* (Philadelphia: University of Pennsylvania Press, 2001) defines a city's character in the context of history and region. Robert Kaplan, *Empire Wilderness:*

Travels to America's Frontiers (New York: Knopf, 1999), tries to take the pulse of the urbanized West.

A number of useful "urban biographies" bring the growth of individual western cities into the last quarter of the twentieth century. Some of the best are Stephen Leonard and Thomas Noel, *Denver: Mining Camp to Metropolis* (Niwot: University Press of Colorado, 1990); James Allen and Thomas Alexander, *Mormons and Gentiles: A History of Salt Lake City* (Boulder, Colo.: Pruett, 1984); and Anthony Orum, *Money, Power and the People: The Making of Modern Austin* (Austin: Texas Monthly Press, 1987).

Los Angeles is a special case—the supercity that simultaneously typifies and stands apart from the West. The Los Angeles city region elicits strong loyalties and excites deep antipathies. It is variously viewed as emblematic and exceptional, as a template for democratic city making and a city in the grip of a para-fascist power structure. The most vivid recent portrayals of the city are by Mike Davis, *City of Quartz: Excavating the Future in Los Angeles* (New York: Verso, 1990) and *The Ecology of Fear: Los Angeles and the Imagination of Disaster* (New York: Metropolitan Books, 1998), the latter to be taken with a grain of skepticism. On Los Angeles politics, see Raphael Sonenshein, *Politics in Black and White: Race and Power in Los Angeles* (Princeton, N.J.: Princeton University Press, 1994), which can be compared to Richard DeLeon, *Left Coast City: Progressive Politics in San Francisco, 1975–91* (Lawrence: University Press of Kansas, 1992). A number of scholars consider themselves to form a "Los Angeles School" of urban analysis that argues, in essence, that we have in the greater southern California metropolis a new urban form and dynamic that is postmodern. Its cityscape, economy, and social ecology are all seen as fragmented, flexible, and fluid. Thick sets of academic essays on the topic are found in Allen Scott and Edward Soja, eds., *The City: Los Angeles and Urban Theory at the End of the Twentieth Century* (Berkeley: University of California Press, 1996); Michael J. Dear, H. Eric Schockman, and Greg Hise, eds., *Rethinking Los Angeles* (Thousand Oaks, Calif.: Sage, 1996); and Michael J. Dear, ed., *From Chicago to L.A.: Making Sense of Urban Theory* (Thousand Oaks, Calif.: Sage, 2002).

Waiting in the wings is yet another boom city that may replace Los Angeles as the symbol of the western and regional future—Las Vegas, now with its encapsulated reconstructions of Paris and New York. See Eugene Moehring, *Resort City in the Sunbelt: Las Vegas, 1930–2000* (Reno: University of Nevada Press, 2002); Robert Venturi, Denise Scott Brown, and Steven Izenour, *Learning from Las Vegas: The Forgotten Symbolism of Architectural Form* (Cambridge, Mass.: MIT Press, 1977); Hal Rothman, *Neon Metropolis: How Las Vegas Started the Twenty-First*

Century (New York: Routledge, 2002); and Mark Gottdiener, Claudia C. Collins, and David R. Dickens, *Las Vegas: The Social Production of an All-American City* (New York: Blackwell, 1999).

An easy introduction to the western electronics industry is Everett Rogers and Judith K. Larsen, *Silicon Valley Fever: Growth of High-Technology Culture* (New York: Basic Books, 1984). There is more detail in Annalee Saxenian, *Regional Advantage: Culture and Competition in Silicon Valley and Route 128* (Cambridge, Mass.: Harvard University Press, 1994), and in Ann Markusen, Peter Hall, and Amy Glasmeier, *High Tech America: The What, How, Why and When of the Sunrise Industries* (Boston: Allen and Unwin, 1986). For the extent to which cities have engaged new economic trends, see the "New Economy Index" at www.neweconomyindex.org/metro/index.html.

The prolific Mike Davis looks at the Latinization of western cities in *Magical Urbanism: Latinos Reinvent the US City* (New York: Verso, 2000). Immigrant identity and experience in the Southwest are also the subject of Lawrence A. Herzog, *From Aztec to High Tech: Architecture and Landscape across the Mexico-United States Border* (Baltimore: Johns Hopkins University Press, 1999); Leland Saito, *Race and Politics: Asian Americans, Latinos, and Whites in a Los Angeles Suburb* (Urbana: University of Illinois Press, 1998); Oscar Martínez, *Mexican-Origin People in the United States: A Topical History* (Tucson: University of New Mexico Press, 1994); Nancy Abelman and John Lie, *Blue Dreams: Korean Americans and the Los Angeles Riots* (Cambridge, Mass.: Harvard University Press, 1995); and Roger Waldinger and Mehdi Bozorgmehr, eds., *Ethnic Los Angeles* (New York: Russell Sage Foundation, 1996).

An effort to explore the new regional patterns within the West is William Riebsame, James C. Robb, and Hannah Gosnell, *Atlas of the New West: Portrait of a Changing Region* (New York: Norton, 1997), which draws a cartographic portrait of a region in cultural change. Peter Calthorpe and William Fulton in *The Regional City: Planning for the End of Sprawl* (Washington, D.C.: Island Press, 2001) demonstrate that ideas about building more sustainable cities have taken stronger root in the West than elsewhere.

Issues of environmental politics and economic change are discussed in Norris Hundley, *The Great Thirst: Californians and Water* (Berkeley: University of California Press, 2001); Kathie Durbin, *Tongass: Pulp Politics and the Fight for the Alaska Rain Forest* (Corvallis: Oregon State University Press, 1999); Timothy Duane, *Shaping the Sierra: Nature, Culture, and Conflict in the Changing West* (Berkeley: University of California Press, 1999); Carl Abbott, Sy Adler, and Margery Post Abbott, *Planning a New West: The Columbia River Gorge National Scenic Area* (Corvallis: Oregon State University Press, 1996); Char Miller, ed., *On the*

Border: An Environmental History of San Antonio (Pittsburgh: University of Pittsburgh Press, 2002); Dan Flores, *Horizontal Yellow: Nature and History in the Near Southwest* (Albuquerque: University of New Mexico Press, 1999); and Mansel Blackford, *Fragile Paradise: The Impact of Tourism on Maui* (Lawrence: University Press of Kansas, 2001). William Robbins, *Hard Times in Paradise: Coos Bay, Oregon, 1850–1986* (Seattle: University of Washington Press, 1988), William Least Heat-Moon, *PrairyErth* (Boston: Houghton Mifflin, 1991), and Jonathan Raban, *Bad Land: An American Romance* (New York: Pantheon, 1996) examine the economic and cultural problems of economically bypassed communities.

Contemporary western culture invites explorations of a wide range of recent artists. Charles R. Cross, *Heavier Than Heaven: A Biography of Kurt Cobain* (Boston: Little, Brown, 2001), links Cobain's origins to his career. James McClintock, *Nature's Kindred Spirits: Aldo Leopold, Joseph Wood Krutch, Edward Abbey, Annie Dillard, Gary Snyder* (Madison: University of Wisconsin Press, 1994), puts recent nature writers in historical tradition. Krista Comer, *Landscapes of the New West: Gender and Geography in Western Writing* (Chapel Hill: University of North Carolina Press, 1999), places women at the focus of recent regional literature.

Chapter 16

The American West
A Bibliographical Essay

Richard W. Etulain

For well more than a century, scholars and other writers have published thousands of essays and books about the American West. This bibliographical essay samples these numerous sources on western history. The essay is divided into two parts: an opening section discussing reference works, general overviews, and topical works and a second section dealing with writings treating the major chronological periods of the western past.

Although most comments are summary in nature, I also venture a few evaluative comments on some books. I have tried, too, to include citations to works from dozens of authors rather than to limit comments to a short list of writings by well-known authors.

Bibliographies and Reference Works

No bibliography covers the full scope of western history, but several treat parts of this large subject. Dwight L. Smith's huge annotated bibliography, *The American and Canadian West: A Bibliography* (Santa Barbara, Calif.: ABC-Clio, 1979), now a bit dated, comments on hundreds of books and essays. Richard W. Etulain, et al., eds., *The American West in the Twentieth Century: A Bibliography* (Norman: University of Oklahoma Press, 1994), lists more than eight thousand items.

Scholars and students of western history will also want to peruse the bibliographical listings appearing in three journals, *Western Historical Quarterly, Journal of American History,* and the *American Historical Review.* In addition the Center for the American West (now the Center for the Southwest) at the University of New Mexico published, from 1990 to 2002, bibliographies listing five hundred or more items on several western topics. Some of these listings appear below. For those interested in the Southwest, there is Ellwyn R. Stoddard, et al., eds., *Borderlands Sourcebook: A Guide to the Literature on Northern Mexico and the American Southwest* (Norman: University of Oklahoma Press, 1983). Listings of numerous creative writers and critics are included in Geoff Sadler, ed., *Twentieth-Century Western Writers,* 2d ed. (Chicago: St. James Press, 1991), and Richard W. Etulain and N. Jill Howard, eds., *A Bibliographical Guide to the Study of Western American Literature,* 2d ed. (Albuquerque: University of New Mexico Press, 1995).

Howard R. Lamar's indispensable volume, *The New Encyclopedia of the American West,* rev. ed. (New Haven, Conn.: Yale University Press, 1998), is the outstanding reference work in the field. Also useful are two similar works: Charles Phillips and Alan Axelrod, et al., eds., *Encyclopedia of the American West,* 4 vols. (New York: Simon & Schuster–Macmillan, 1996), and Dan L. Thrapp, *Encyclopedia of Frontier Biography,* 4 vols. (Spokane, Wash.: Arthur H. Clark, 1988, 1994).

Clyde A. Milner II, et al., eds., *The Oxford History of the American West* (New York: Oxford University Press, 1994), which contains twenty-three topically and chronologically organized essays by leading western historians, is also a first-rate reference source. Among other such topical guides, Stephan Thernstrom, et al., eds., *Harvard Encyclopedia of American Ethnic Groups* (Cambridge, Mass.: Harvard University Press, Belknap Press, 1980), is particularly notable.

Those wishing geographical guides to the American West should begin with Warren Beck and Ynez D. Haase, *Historical Atlas of the American West* (Norman: University of Oklahoma Press, 1989). For a rather nontraditional atlas, one can consult William Riebsame, et al., eds., *Atlas of the New West: Portrait of a Changing Region* (New York: Norton, 1997).

Several volumes provide handy introductions to western historical writing. Two of these studies are collections of topical essays: Michael P. Malone, ed., *Historians and the American West* (Lincoln: University of Nebraska Press, 1983), and Roger Nichols, ed., *American Frontier and Western Issues: A Historiographical Review* (Westport, Conn.: Greenwood Press, 1986). A third and more extensive collection includes brief essays on dozens of well-known western historians: John Wunder, ed., *Historians of the American West: A Bio-Bibliographical Sourcebook* (New York: Greenwood Press, 1988). Still another collection gathers biographical essays on leading western historians: Richard W. Etulain, ed., *Writing Western History: Essays on Major Western Historians* (Albuquerque: University of New Mexico Press, 1991; Reno: University of Nevada Press, 2002). The only overview by a single author is Gerald D. Nash, *Creating the West: Historical Interpretations, 1890–1990* (Albuquerque: University of New Mexico Press, 1991).

General Overviews

The titan of western history, Frederick Jackson Turner, never completed his often-promised history of the American frontier, but several of his colleagues published such volumes. The most significant of these early overview syntheses was Frederic Logan Paxson's *History of the American Frontier, 1763–1893* (Boston: Houghton Mifflin, 1924), which won a Pulitzer Prize for its author. Paxson's volume remained the chief textbook for western historians until Ray Allen Billington's magisterial *Westward Expansion: A History of the American Frontier* (New York: Macmillan, 1949). Through its first five editions (an abbreviated sixth edition, coauthored by Martin Ridge, appeared in 2000) published between 1949 and 1983, Billington's long, thorough volume remained the most widely used book in western history courses.

Not surprisingly, changes in American historical writing led to new kinds of general overviews of the American West, including those by New Western historians. Richard White's mammoth synthesis, *"It's Your Misfortune and None of My Own": A New History of the American West* (Norman: University of Oklahoma Press, 1991), illustrated these historiographical transformations in its avoidance of Turner and the frontier and, conversely, in its stress on race, class, gender, and the environment. In the 1990s White's volume became the most widely cited textbook on the West. Patricia Nelson Limerick's lively and readable volume, *The Legacy of Conquest: The Unbroken Past of the American West* (New York: Norton, 1987), received large attention from other historians and general readers. The publication of Robert V. Hine and John Mack Faragher's *The American West: A New Interpretive History* (New Haven, Conn.: Yale University Press, 2000), a thoroughgoing revision of Hine's earlier volume, *The American West: An Interpretive History,* 2d ed. (Boston: Little, Brown, 1984), demonstrated that western historical writing might find a middle-of-the-road position between the Turnerians and the more recent New Western history.

The pioneering subregional history of the American West was that in Hubert Howe Bancroft's huge, multivolume series, *The Works of Hubert Howe Bancroft* (San Francisco: A. L. Bancroft and Company, 1882–1890). Bancroft's hefty volumes cover Central America, Mexico, and the American Far West. In the 1960s, Robert G. Athearn (*High Country Empire: The High Plains and Rockies* [New York: McGraw-Hill, 1960]), W. Eugene Hollon (*The Southwest: Old and New* [New York: Knopf, 1961]), and Earl Pomeroy (*The Pacific Slope: A History of California, Oregon, Washington, Idaho, Utah, and Nevada* [New York: Knopf, 1965]) provided valuable overviews of western subregions. Pomeroy's superb analytical and interpretive history has held up particularly well. Of the more recent subregional works, Carlos Schwantes's

The Pacific Northwest: An Interpretive History (Lincoln: University of Nebraska Press, 1989) merits continued attention.

A few western historians focus primarily on the twentieth century. The first volume devoted entirely to the twentieth-century West was Gerald D. Nash's *The American West in the Twentieth Century: A Short History of an Urban Oasis* (1973; Albuquerque: University of New Mexico Press, 1977). A more recent volume covering the same period but more of the West geographically is Michael P. Malone and Richard W. Etulain, *The American West: A Twentieth-Century History* (Lincoln: University of Nebraska Press, 1989). Also the earlier volumes by Athearn, Hollon, and Pomeroy contain extensive sections on the modern West.

Nearly every western state's history has been chronicled in at least one volume published since the 1960s. Useful models for future state histories are Michael P. Malone, et al., *Montana: A History of Two Centuries,* rev. ed. (Seattle: University of Washington Press, 1991), and Richard B. Rice, et al., *The Elusive Eden: A New History of California* (New York: Knopf, 1988). The most extensive of the state histories is Leonard J. Arrington, *History of Idaho,* 2 vols. (Moscow: University of Idaho Press, 1993).

A handful of volumes furnishing topical overviews of the West should also be mentioned. In his several geographical histories of the United States and American West, geographer Donald W. Meinig furnishes provocative perspectives on the environmental, economic, social, and cultural grids superimposed on western landscapes. One must see the three volumes published thus far in his four-volume geographical history of the United States, *The Shaping of America: Atlantic America 1492–1800* (1988), *Continental America, 1800–1867* (1993), and *Transcontinental America, 1850–1915* (1999), all published by Yale University Press.

Western Setting and Environment

Histories of the American West published in the first half of the twentieth century paid scant attention to the region's physical environment, except, perhaps, in an opening chapter to set the scene. These earlier writers often devoted more space to rivers, mountains, flora and fauna, and other landforms than to ecological relationships between humans and their natural environments. From 1970 forward, however, the trickle of essays and books in environmental history has turned into a flood of publications.

For full bibliographical listings of the early interpretations of the western setting and some of the later books and essays on conservation and environmental history, one should consult Ronald J. Fahl, *North American Forest and Conservation History: A Bibliography* (Santa Barbara,

Calif.: ABC-Clio Press, 1977); Lawrence B. Lee, *Reclaiming the Arid West: An Historiography and Guide* (Santa Barbara, Calif.: ABC-Clio, 1980); and Thomas Jaehn, comp., *The Environment in the Twentieth-Century West: A Bibliography* (Albuquerque: Center for the American West, University of New Mexico, 1990).

Pioneering environmental histories are available in the writings of historians Walter Prescott Webb, James C. Malin, and Roderick Nash. Webb's classic study, *The Great Plains* (Boston: Ginn, 1931), argued that the Great Plains environment clearly shaped the plant, animal, and human life of that region. Malin, a Kansan, wrote a series of essays and books that, before those of other scholars, demonstrated that knowledge of ecology broadened one's historical perspectives. See Malin's *Grassland Historical Studies* (Lawrence, Kans.: n.p., 1950), and Malin, *History and Ecology: Studies of the Grasslands,* ed. Robert P. Swierenga (Lincoln: University of Nebraska Press, 1984). In the 1960s Roderick Nash published a pathbreaking intellectual history of the American environment, *Wilderness and the American Mind* (New Haven, Conn.: Yale University Press, 1967), which has been reprinted (4th ed., 2001).

Noted western novelist Wallace Stegner wrote dozens of essays about western landscapes and early conservation efforts. Some of these notable articles have been collected in Stegner's *The Sound of Mountain Water* (1969; Lincoln: University of Nebraska Press, 1985); *When the Bluebird Sings to the Lemonade Springs* (New York: Random House, 1992); and *Marking the Sparrow's Fall: Wallace Stegner's American West,* ed. Page Stegner (New York: Henry Holt, 1998). See also Stegner's *The American West as Living Space* (Ann Arbor: University of Michigan Press, 1987).

In the past two decades several leading western historians have produced superb environmental histories. Of notable importance are Donald Worster, *The Dust Bowl: The Southern Plains in the 1930s* (New York: Oxford University Press, 1979), *Rivers of Empire: Water, Aridity, and the Growth of the American West* (New York: Pantheon, 1986), and *A River Running West: The Life of John Wesley Powell* (New York: Oxford University Press, 2001). Richard White has contributed first-rate environmental histories in his *Land Use, Environment, and Social Change: The Shaping of Island County, Washington* (Seattle: University of Washington Press, 1980), and *The Organic Machine: The Remaking of the Columbia River* (New York: Hill and Wang, 1995). One should also consult the numerous books and essays by William Cronon, Patricia Nelson Limerick, John Opie, Dan Flores, William deBuys, and Mark Harvey listed in the bibliographies noted above.

Other historians have focused on tourism as an important part of western cultural environmentalism. The classic volume in this area is

Earl Pomeroy, *In Search of the Golden West: The Tourist in Western America* (New York: Knopf, 1957). The most important of the recent studies dealing with tourism is Hal Rothman, *Devil's Bargains: Tourism in the Twentieth-Century American West* (Lawrence: University Press of Kansas, 1998).

Frederick Jackson Turner and the Frontier Thesis

Anyone who studies the American frontier and West must know about historian Frederick Jackson Turner and his "frontier" or "Turner" thesis. Presented first in 1893, Turner's argument that the American frontier, not European legacies, was the most important shaping factor in American history dominated historical writing about the United States in the first half of the twentieth century. Even though many western historians since the 1960s have downplayed or criticized Turner's impact on the field, his ideas remain the beginning place for understanding pioneering interpretations of the frontier and American West. In the 1920s, Turner advanced another valuable thesis about the significance of sections (regions) in the study of American history.

For an introduction to Turner's arguments about the frontier, readers should consult the collected essays in Turner's book *The Frontier in American History* (New York: Henry Holt, 1920). Another Turner volume, *The Significance of Sections in American History* (New York: Henry Holt, 1932), awarded a Pulitzer Prize, collects the author's salient essays on sectionalism/regionalism. The most recent brief collection of Turner's important essays is John Mack Faragher, ed., *Rereading Frederick Jackson Turner: The Significance of the Frontier in American History, and Other Essays* (New York: Henry Holt, 1994). Another new volume uses Turner's frontier thesis to raise questions about American exceptionalism: Richard W. Etulain, ed., *Does the Frontier Experience Make America Exceptional?* (Boston: Bedford Books, 1999).

Three books on Turner merit special mention. Ray Allen Billington mined the huge Turner manuscript collection at the Huntington Library in San Marino, California, to produce a magnificent biography, *Frederick Jackson Turner: Historian, Scholar, Teacher* (New York: Oxford University Press, 1973). Allan G. Bogue's *Frederick Jackson Turner: Strange Roads Going Down* (Norman: University of Oklahoma Press, 1998) is equally well researched, smoothly written, and more thorough than Billington on Turner's strengths and limitations. Wilbur Jacobs places Turner in historiographical perspective in his book *On Turner's Trail: One Hundred Years of Writing Western History* (Lawrence: University Press of Kansas, 1994). Also useful for understanding Turner as part of the American anxiousness over a closing frontier is David M. Wrobel, *The End of American Exceptionalism: Frontier Anxiety from the Old West to the New Deal* (Lawrence: University Press of Kansas, 1993). Some of the most penetrating commentary on Turner appears in key essays, including William Cronon, "Revisiting the Vanishing Frontier: The Legacy of Frederick Jackson Turner," *Western Historical Quarterly* 18 (April 1987): 157–76, and Michael Steiner, "The Significance of Turner's Sectional Thesis," *Western Historical Quarterly* 19 (October 1979): 437–66.

Indians

Although historians of the early twentieth century paid scant attention to Indians, except as barriers to westward-moving pioneers, Native Americans have become an increasingly popular topic since the 1960s. Indeed, more has been published about Indians than any other western group in the past two generations.

Extensive listings of early publications about Indians appear in Francis Paul Prucha, *A Bibliographical Guide to the History of Indian-White Relations in the United States* (Chicago: University of Chicago Press, 1977), and in subsequent additions by Prucha to that volume. See also Dwight L. Smith, ed., *Indians of the United States and Canada: A Bibliography* (Santa Barbara, Calif.: ABC-Clio, 1974), and the series of bibliographies on individual Indian groups jointly published by Indiana University Press and the Newberry Library's Center for the History of the American Indian. The multivolume series *The Handbook of North American Indians,* edited by William C. Sturtevant and published by the Smithsonian Institution, 1978–, is also a superb reference tool.

Students interested in Indian stories, tales, and creation myths should consult the anthology compiled by Richard Erdoes and Alfonso Ortiz, eds., *American Indian Myths and Legends* (New York: Pantheon, 1984). Early ethnographic studies still of use include John R. Swanton, *The Indian Tribes of North America* (Washington, D.C.: Smithsonian Institution, 1952); Clark Wissler, *Indians of the United States* (Garden City, N.Y.: Doubleday, 1946); and John Ewers, *The Blackfeet: Raiders on the Northwestern Plains* (Norman: University of Oklahoma Press, 1958).

Among the several one-volume overviews of Indians in the United States, one should begin with Robert M. Utley, *The Indian Frontier of the American West, 1846–1890* (Albuquerque: University of New Mexico Press, 1984). Also helpful are Angie Debo, *A History of the Indians of the United States* (Norman: University of Oklahoma Press, 1970); W. Thomas Hagan, *American Indians,* 3d ed. (Chicago: University of Chicago Press, 1993); and Roger Nichols, *American Indians in U.S. History* (Norman: University of Oklahoma Press, 2003).

Other writers have focused on non-Indian attitudes and ideas about Native Americans or Indian-white policies. Robert F. Berkhofer, Jr., *The White Man's Indian: Images of the American Indian from Columbus to the Present* (New York: Knopf, 1978), Brian W. Dippie, *The Vanishing American: White Attitudes and U.S. Indian Policy* (Middletown, Conn.: Wesleyan University Press, 1982), and Sherry L. Smith, *Reimagining Indians: Native Americans through Anglo Eyes, 1880–1940* (New York: Oxford University Press, 2000), are exemplary studies. Meanwhile Francis Paul Prucha's massive and authoritative *The Great Father: The United States Government and the American Indians,* 2 vols. (Lincoln: University of Nebraska Press, 1984) is the definitive account of Indian-white relations.

Still other scholars provide notable works on Indian cultural contacts with separate groups. Among these many studies, one should begin with Edward H. Spicer, *Cycles of Conquest: The Impact of Spain, Mexico, and the United States on the Indians of the Southwest, 1533–1960* (Tucson: University of Arizona Press, 1962); Elizabeth A. H. John, *Storms Brewed in Other Men's Worlds: The Confrontation of Indians, Spanish, and French in the Southwest, 1540–1795* (College Station: Texas A&M University Press, 1975); and the more controversial book by Ramón A. Gutiérrez, *When Jesus Came, the Corn Mothers Went Away: Marriage, Sexuality, and Power in New Mexico, 1500–1846* (Stanford, Calif.: Stanford University Press, 1991). The most recent volumes detailing such contacts are Gary Clayton Anderson, *The Indians of the Southwest, 1580–1830: Ethnogenesis and Reinvention* (Norman: University of Oklahoma Press, 1999), and R. Douglas Hurt, *The Indian Frontier, 1763–1846* (Albuquerque: University of New Mexico Press, 2002). A superb, well-written story of complexity appears in Albert L. Hurtado, *Indian Survival on the California Frontier* (New Haven, Conn.: Yale University Press, 1988). Glenda Riley deals with another important topic in her clearly written *Women and Indians on the Frontier, 1825–1915* (Albuquerque: University of New Mexico Press, 1984). For a useful comparative perspective, one should consult Roger L. Nichols, *Indians in the United States and Canada: A Comparative History* (Lincoln: University of Nebraska Press, 1998). The best study of the largest Indian tribe is Peter Iverson's authoritative *Diné: A History of the Navajos* (Albuquerque: University of New Mexico Press, 2002).

Several works written by American Indians are particularly noteworthy. Among these are Vine Deloria, Jr., *Custer Died for Your Sins: An Indian Manifesto* (New York: Macmillan, 1969); Donald Fixico, *The Urban Indian Experience in America* (Albuquerque: University of New Mexico Press, 2000); and Philip J. Deloria, *Playing Indian* (New Haven, Conn.: Yale University Press, 1998).

Richard W. Etulain

The Borderlands, the Spanish, and Chicanos

The beginning places for the early periods of these huge topics are David J. Weber's immensely thorough *The Spanish Frontier in North America* (New Haven, Conn.: Yale University Press, 1992) and John L. Kessell's invitingly written *Spain in the Southwest: A Narrative History of Colonial New Mexico, Arizona, Texas, and California* (Norman: University of Oklahoma Press, 2002). Another useful overview is Donald C. Cutter and Iris Wilson Engstrand, *Quest for Empire: Spanish Settlement in the Southwest* (Golden, Colo.: Fulcrum, 1996). These recent syntheses replace an earlier classic: Herbert Eugene Bolton, *The Spanish Borderlands: A Chronicle of Old Florida and the Southwest* (New Haven, Conn.: Yale University Press, 1921).

A number of other able volumes on the Spanish Borderlands merit notice. The previously mentioned volumes by Edward H. Spicer, Elizabeth A. H. John, and Ramón Gutiérrez provide thorough accounts of Spanish contact with varied groups. Marc Simmons, a major interpreter of early Spanish experiences in the Southwest, furnishes a brief, sprightly written biography in his *The Last Conquistador: Juan de Oñate and the Settling of the Far Southwest* (Norman: University of Oklahoma Press, 1991). For a helpful collection of excerpts and editorial commentary on the most important event of the seventeenth-century Southwest, one should examine David J. Weber, ed., *What Caused the Pueblo Revolt of 1680?* (Boston: Bedford Books, 1999).

Several rewarding histories of Mexican American/Chicano experiences have been published recently. For a particularly activist perspective, read Rodolfo F. Acuña, *Occupied America: A History of Chicanos,* 4th ed. (New York: Longmans, 2000). Other useful general accounts include Richard Griswold del Castillo and Arnoldo De León, *North to Aztlán: A History of Mexican Americans in the United States* (New York: Twayne, 1997), and Oscar Martínez, *Mexican-Origin People in the United States: A Topical History* (Tucson: University of Arizona Press, 2001).

A handful of model monographs illustrate the notable publications appearing recently on Mexican American/Chicano experiences in the American West. These include David Montejano, *Anglos and Mexicans in the Making of Texas, 1836–1986* (Austin: University of Texas Press, 1987); Sarah Deutsch, *No Separate Refuge: Culture, Class, and Gender on an Anglo-Hispanic Frontier in the American Southwest, 1880–1940* (New York: Oxford University Press, 1987); and George J. Sánchez, *Becoming Mexican American: Ethnicity, Culture and Identity in Chicano Los Angeles, 1900–1945* (New York: Oxford University Press, 1993).

Other topical studies should be mentioned. Vicki L. Ruiz provides a valuable examination of Mexican women's experiences in her *From Out of the Shadows: Mexican Women in Twentieth-Century America*

(New York: Oxford University Press, 1998). The best biography of the leading Chicano is Richard Griswold del Castillo and Richard Garcia, *César Chávez: A Triumph of Spirit* (Norman: University of Oklahoma Press, 1995). Among the several strong works by the senior Chicano historian Juan Gómez-Quiñones, see his *Chicano Politics: Reality and Promise, 1940–1990* (1990), *Mexican American Labor, 1790–1990* (1994), and *Roots of Chicano Politics, 1600–1940* (1994), all published by the University of New Mexico Press, Albuquerque.

Finally, Carey McWilliams's classic work, *North from Mexico: The Spanish-Speaking People of the United States* (Philadelphia: Lippincott, 1948), remains a valuable source. Likewise, Leonard Pitt's often-cited study, *The Decline of the Californios: A Social History of the Spanish-Speaking Californians, 1846–1890* (Berkeley: University of California Press, 1966), furnishes a helpful blueprint for those wishing to trace transformations in Hispanic experiences in the American West.

Other Ethnic Groups

Several important general works are available to researchers interested in examining ethnic and racial experiences of other westerners besides Native Americans and Hispanics. The volume by Stephan Thernstrom mentioned above in the reference section is an immensely useful guide. The most extensive bibliography on European groups is Florence R. J. Goulesque, comp., *Europeans in the American West Since 1800: A Bibliography* (Albuquerque: Center for the American West, University of New Mexico, 1995).

Walter Nugent's recent overview, *Into the West: The Story of Its People* (New York: Knopf, 1999), brilliantly traces immigration into and developing ethnic and racial complexities within the West from the earliest human inhabitants to the present. Written with more of an edge is Ronald Takaki's provocative volume, *A Different Mirror: A History of Multicultural America* (Boston: Little, Brown, 1993). Arnoldo De León shows what can be done in a cross-cultural study in his *Racial Frontiers: Africans, Chinese, and Mexicans in Western America, 1848–1890* (Albuquerque: University of New Mexico Press, 2002). Frederick C. Luebke has also published several important essays and books on immigrant and ethnic groups. See, first of all, his still very useful essay, "Ethnic Minority Groups in the American West," in *Historians and the American West,* ed. Michael P. Malone (Lincoln: University of Nebraska Press, 1983). Also consult Luebke, ed., *Ethnicity on the Great Plains* (Lincoln: University of Nebraska Press, 1980) and *European Immigrants in the American West: Community Histories* (Albuquerque: University of New Mexico Press, 1985). A recent thoughtful essay on these subjects is Elliott Robert Barkan, "Turning Turner on His Head? The

Significance of Immigration in Twentieth-Century American Western History," *New Mexico Historical Review* 77 (winter 2002): 57–88. See also Richard White, "Race Relations in the American West," *American Quarterly* 38 (Bibliography 1986): 396–416.

For studies of individual European groups, see Andrew Rolle, *The Immigrant Upraised: Italian Adventurers and Colonists in an Expanding America* (Norman: University of Oklahoma Press, 1968); William A Douglass and Jon Bilbao, *Amerikanuak: Basques in the New World* (Reno: University of Nevada Press, 1975); Moses Rischin and John Livingston, eds., *Jews of the American West* (Detroit: Wayne State University Press, 1991); Ferenc M. Szasz, *Scots in the North American West, 1790–1917* (Norman: University of Oklahoma Press, 2000); and the important study of one group in one town, David M. Emmons, *The Butte Irish: Class and Ethnicity in an American Mining Town, 1873–1925* (Urbana: University of Illinois Press, 1989).

For African Americans, one must begin with Quintard Taylor, *In Search of the Racial Frontier: African Americans in the American West, 1528–1990* (New York: Norton, 1998). See also Albert S. Broussard, *Black San Francisco: The Struggle for Racial Equality in the West, 1900–1954* (Lawrence: University Press of Kansas, 1993), and Nell Irvin Painter, *Exodusters: Black Migration to Kansas after Reconstruction* (1977; Lawrence: University Press of Kansas, 1986). The fullest bibliographical listings are those in Taylor's thorough volume and in Roger D. Hardaway, comp., *African Americans in the American West: A Selective Bibliography* (Albuquerque: Center for the American West, University of New Mexico, 1999).

On Asian Americans, one encounters a growing number of strong studies. Consult, for example, Shih-shan Henry Tsai, *The Chinese Experience in America* (Bloomington: Indiana University Press, 1986); Roger Daniels, *Asian America: Chinese and Japanese in the United States Since 1850* (Seattle: University of Washington Press, 1988); Ronald Takaki, *Strangers from a Different Shore: A History of Asian Americans* (Boston: Little, Brown, 1989); and Sucheng Chan, *Asian Americans: An Interpretive History* (Boston: G. K. Hall/Twayne, 1991). A recent revisionist monograph argues that Chinese had more opportunity in the American West than previous historians have thought: Liping Zhu, *A Chinaman's Chance: The Chinese on the Rocky Mountain Mining Frontier* (Niwot: University Press of Colorado, 1997). A full listing of books and essays on Asian Americans, including Chinese, Japanese, Koreans, and Southeast Asians, is available in N. Jill Howard and Jennifer Ann M. Clark, comps., *Asians in the American West: A Selective Bibliography* (Albuquerque: Center for the American West, University of New Mexico, 1996).

Families in the American West

Most of the earliest textbooks and monographs about the American West focused primarily on men's experiences, but publications in the past generation or so deal increasingly with women's experiences. Two collections of essays are beginning points for women's experiences in the West. They are Susan H. Armitage and Elizabeth A. Jameson, eds., *The Women's West* (Norman: University of Oklahoma Press, 1987), and Elizabeth A. Jameson and Susan H. Armitage, eds., *Writing the Range: Race, Class, and Culture in the Women's West* (Norman: University of Oklahoma Press, 1997). For the recent period, see Sandra K. Schackel, ed., *Western Women's Lives: Continuity and Change in the Twentieth Century* (Albuquerque: University of New Mexico Press, 2003).

Overviews of women in the West include Julie Roy Jeffrey, *Frontier Women: "Civilizing" the West? 1840–1880,* rev. ed. (New York: Hill and Wang, 1979, 1998); Sandra L. Myres, *Westering Women and the Frontier Experience, 1800–1915* (Albuquerque: University of New Mexico Press, 1982); and Glenda Riley, *The Female Frontier: A Comparative View of Women on the Prairie and the Plains* (Lawrence: University Press of Kansas, 1988). Three other volumes are helpful on women's experiences in western subregions: Cheryl J. Foote, *Women of the New Mexican Frontier, 1846–1912,* 2d ed. (Niwot: University Press of Colorado, 1990); Julia Kirk Blackwelder, *Women of the Depression: Caste and Culture in San Antonio, 1929–1939* (College Station: Texas A&M University Press, 1984); and Karen J. Blair, ed., *Women in the Pacific Northwest: An Anthology* (Seattle: University of Washington Press, 1988).

Other volumes provide illuminating models for analyzing the gender, class, or religious implications of western women's experiences. These include John Mack Faragher, *Women and Men on the Overland Trail* (New Haven, Conn.: Yale University Press, 1979); Peggy Pascoe, *Relations of Rescue: The Search for Female Moral Authority in the American West, 1874–1939* (New York: Oxford University Press, 1990); and the many essays and books of Joan M. Jensen, including a collection of her essays, *Promise to the Land: Essays on Rural Women* (Albuquerque: University of New Mexico Press, 1991).The most important book for understanding young westerners is Elliott West, *Growing Up with the Country: Childhood on the Far Western Frontier* (Albuquerque: University of New Mexico Press, 1989).

On families, one can begin with Richard Griswold del Castillo, *La Familia: Chicano Families in the Urban Southwest: 1848 to the Present* (Notre Dame, Ind.: University of Notre Dame Press, 1984); Scott G. McNall and Sally Allen McNall, *Plains Families: Exploring Sociology through Social History* (New York: St. Martin's Press, 1983); and a volume focusing on more recent families, Judith Stacey, *Brave New*

Families: Stories of Domestic Upheaval in the Late Twentieth-Century America (New York: Basic Books, 1990). One important subject is covered in Glenda Riley, *Building and Breaking Families in the American West* (Albuquerque: University of New Mexico Press, 1996).

No scholar has yet produced a full-scale study of masculinity in the American West. Until that book is published, readers should consult Robert L. Griswold, *Fatherhood in America: A History* (New York: Basic Books, 1993), and E. Anthony Rotundo, *American Manhood: Transformations in Masculinity from the Revolution to the Modern Era* (New York: Basic Books, 1993).

Although now a generation old, one pathbreaking article remains central to writing about women and families in the West. See Joan M. Jensen and Darlis A. Miller, "The Gentle Tamers Revisited: New Approaches to the History of Women in the American West," *Pacific Historical Review* 49 (May 1980): 173–213. A more recent helpful overview is Elizabeth A. Jameson, "Toward Multicultural History of Women in the Western United States," *Signs* 13 (summer 1988): 761–91.

Recent research on families in the modern American West is listed in Cindy Tyson, comp., *Families in the Twenty-Century American West: A Bibliography* (Albuquerque: Center for the American West, University of New Mexico, 2001). A similar listing for women is Suzanne Sermon, comp., *Women in the Twentieth-Century American West: A Bibliography* (Albuquerque: Center for the American West, University of New Mexico, 2000).

Religion

The preeminent authority on religion in the American West, Ferenc M. Szasz, argues that historians' biases and popular images of a Wild West have been barriers to numerous, wide-ranging studies of religion in the American West. As a corrective to this oversight Szasz's books are indispensable. His major study on the frontier period is *The Protestant Clergy in the Great Plains and Mountain West, 1865–1915* (Albuquerque: University of New Mexico Press, 1988; Lincoln: University of Nebraska Press, 2004). Even more expansive and pathbreaking is Szasz's overview of religion in the post-1900 West, *Religion in the Modern American West* (Tucson: University of Arizona Press, 2000).

Only the Mormons of the western religious groups have received extensive coverage. The first volume to examine the history of the Church of Jesus Christ of Latter-day Saints is Leonard J. Arrington and Davis Bitton, *The Mormon Experience: A History of the Latter-day Saints,* 2d ed. (1979; Urbana: University of Illinois Press, 1992). Jan Shipps, a non-Mormon, has produced a major study of the Saints in *Mormonism: The Story of a New Religious Tradition* (Urbana: University of Illinois

Press, 1985). The best work on the first significant Mormon leader in the West is Leonard J. Arrington, *Brigham Young: American Moses* (New York: Knopf, 1985). See also Thomas G. Alexander, *Mormonism in Transition: A History of the Latter-day Saints* (Urbana: University of Illinois Press, 1986).

Nearly all other religious groups lack a comprehensive history of their experiences in the American West. Until those volumes are available, readers will have to consult national or abbreviated regional histories. See, for example, Jay P. Dolan, ed., *The American Catholic Parish: A History from 1850 to the Present,* vol. 2., *Pacific States, Intermountain West, Midwest* (New York: Paulist Press, 1987); a popular history, Harriet Rochlin and Fred Rochlin, *Pioneer Jews: A New Life in the Far West* (Boston: Houghton Mifflin, 1984); and Carl Guarneri and David Alvarez, eds., *Religion and Society in the American West: Historical Essays* (Lanham, Md.: University Press of America, 1987).

Native American religious experiences have been subjects of an increasing numbers of books. See, for instance, Omar C. Stewart, *Peyote Religion: A History* (Norman: University of Oklahoma Press, 1987); Raymond J. DeMallie and Douglas R. Parks, eds., *Sioux Indian Religion: Tradition and Innovation* (Norman: University of Oklahoma Press, 1987); and for a more popular approach, Vine Deloria, Jr. *God Is Red: A Native View of Religion,* 2d ed. (1973; Golden, Colo.: Fulcrum, 1994).

Students may want to consult two reference guides for additional information and sources: Edwin S. Gaustad and Philip L. Barlow, with Richard W. Dishno, *New Historical Atlas of Religion in America,* rev. ed. (New York: Oxford University Press, 2001), and Richard W. Etulain, comp., *Religion in the Twentieth-Century American West: A Bibliography* (Albuquerque: Center for the American West, University of New Mexico, 1991).

Agricultural and Urban Wests

Historical writings about these two Wests illustrate transformations in western life and historiography. Most early writing, from Frederick Jackson Turner on, focused on the agricultural West. As the region became increasingly urban after World War II, historians turned to writing about the West's cities and suburbs.

On Native American agriculture, begin with R. Douglas Hurt, *Indian Agriculture in America: Prehistory to the Present* (Lawrence: University Press of Kansas, 1987). Still useful is Gilbert Fite's classic account, *The Agricultural Frontier, 1865–1900* (1966; Albuquerque: University of New Mexico Press, 1977); see also the same author's *American Farmers: The New Minority* (Bloomington: Indiana University Press, 1981). Another overview is John T. Schlebecker, *Whereby We*

Thrive: A History of American Farming, 1607–1972 (Ames: Iowa State University Press, 1975).

Other segments of the agricultural West are covered in John T. Schlebecker, *Cattle Raising on the Plains, 1900–1961* (Lincoln: University of Nebraska Press, 1963); J. Orin Oliphant, *On the Cattle Ranges of the Oregon Country* (Seattle: University of Washington Press, 1968); and Paula M. Nelson, *After the West Was Won: Homesteaders and Town-Builders in Western South Dakota, 1900–1917* (Iowa City: University of Iowa Press, 1986). See also R. Douglas Hurt, ed., *The Rural West Since World War II* (Lawrence: University Press of Kansas, 1998).

The best overview of the modern urban West is Carl Abbott, *The Metropolitan Frontier: Cities in the Modern American West* (Tucson: University of Arizona Press, 1993). Abbott has written dozens of other notable essays and books on western urban experiences. On the nineteenth-century urban frontier, see Lawrence H. Larsen, *The Urban West at the End of the Frontier* (Lawrence: University Press of Kansas, 1978). Earl Pomeroy's discussion of nineteenth- and twentieth-century urbanization in *The Pacific Slope: A History of California, Oregon, Washington, Idaho, Utah, and Nevada* (1965) still holds up very well.

Nearly every major western city has its biography. Among these are Eugene P. Moehring, *Resort City in the Sunbelt: Las Vegas 1930–2000*, 2d ed. (Reno: University of Nevada Press, 2000); Mike Davis, *City of Quartz: Excavating the Future in Los Angeles* (1990; New York: Random House, 1992); Roger W. Lotchin, *San Francisco, 1846–1856: From Hamlet to City* (1974; Lincoln: University of Nebraska Press, 1979); Bradford Luckingham, *The Urban Southwest: A Profile History of Albuquerque, El Paso, Phoenix, Tucson* (El Paso: Texas Western Press, 1982); and David G. McComb, *Houston: A History* (Austin: University of Texas Press, 1981). The most recent urban biography is Hal Rothman, *Neon Metropolis: How Las Vegas Started the Twenty-First Century* (New York: Routledge, 2003).

Other ingredients of western urbanization are discussed in John M. Findlay's valuable book, *Magic Lands: Western Cityscapes and American Culture After 1940* (Berkeley: University of California Press, 1992); Roger Lotchin, *Fortress California, 1910–1961: From Warfare to Welfare* (New York: Oxford University Press, 1992); and Kenneth T. Jackson, *Crabgrass Frontier: The Suburbanization of the United States* (New York: Oxford University Press, 1985).

For further information on the agricultural West, one should consult Edward L. Schapsmeier and Frederick H. Schapsmeier, *Encyclopedia of American Agricultural History* (Westport, Conn.: Greenwood Press, 1975), and Richard W. Etulain, ed., *Sheep and Sheepmen in the American West: A Bibliography* (Albuquerque: Center for the American West, University of New Mexico, 2001). On the urban West, see Carol A. O'Connor's essay "A Region of Cities," in *The Oxford History of the American West,* ed. Clyde A. Milner II, et al. (New York: Oxford University Press, 1994).

Cultural History

Western historians have been slow to till the gardens of cultural history, if one means by "culture" studies of literature, historiography, education, film, and popular culture. If "culture" is defined in its larger meaning as a society's total system of values and behavior, many recent western historians have moved into this fertile field in the last decade or two.

The most extensive overviews of western literature are Thomas J. Lyon, et al., eds., *A Literary History of the American West* (Fort Worth: Texas Christian University Press, 1987), and its sequel, Lyon, et al., eds., *Updating the Literary West* (Fort Worth: Texas Christian University Press, 1997). The classic study by Henry Nash Smith, *Virgin Land: The American West as Symbol and Myth* (Cambridge, Mass.: Harvard University Press, 1950), is still a must-read. Following in Smith's footsteps, Richard Slotkin has written three massive tomes on frontier and modern western myths: *Regeneration Through Violence; The Mythology of the American Frontier, 1600–1860* (Middletown, Conn.: Wesleyan University Press, 1973), *The Fatal Environment: The Myth of the Frontier in the Age of Industrialization, 1800–1890* (New York: Atheneum, 1985), and *Gunfighter Nation: The Myth of the Frontier in Twentieth-Century America* (New York: Atheneum, 1992). A critical reading of popular culture in the American West is Jane Tompkins, *West of Everything: The Inner Life of Westerns* (New York: Oxford University Press, 1992).

Solid studies of schools and schooling in the West are few in number. Among the most reliable of these are several essays by David B. Tyack in the bibliographies listed above; Guadalupe San Miguel, Jr.'s, *"Let All of Them Take Heed": Mexican Americans and the Campaign for Educational Equality in Texas, 1910–1981* (Austin: University of Texas Press, 1987); Margaret Connell-Szasz, *Education and the American Indian: The Road to Self-Determination Since 1928,* 3d ed. (Albuquerque: University of New Mexico Press, 1999); and Mary Hurlbut Cordier, *Schoolwomen of the Prairies and Plains: Personal Narratives from Iowa, Kansas, and Nebraska, 1860s–1920s* (Albuquerque: University of New Mexico Press, 1992).

The best one-volume history of Hollywood is Robert Sklar, *Movie-Made America: A Cultural History of American Movies* (1975; New York: Random House, 1994). For a model of probing cultural analysis, see Lary May, *Screening Out the Past: The Birth of Mass Culture and the Modern Picture Industry* (New York: Oxford University Press, 1980). More than eight hundred books and essays on the cinematic West are listed in the comprehensive finding guide by M. David Key and Angela Thomas, eds., *Hollywood and the American West* (Albuquerque: Center for the American West, University of New Mexico, 2001).

No one has done more to further the serious study of western American art than Canadian historian Brian Dippie. Among his dozens of essays and books are *Catlin and His Contemporaries: The Politics of Patronage* (Lincoln: University of Nebraska Press, 1990), and *Remington and Russell* (Austin: University of Texas Press, 1982). The best study of modern western art is Patricia Janis Broder, *The American West: The Modern Vision* (Boston: Little, Brown, 1984). The beginning place for the study of western photography is Martha A. Sandweiss, *Print the Legend: Photography and the American West* (New Haven, Conn.: Yale University Press, 2002). For an innovative examination of western cultural landscapes, see Anne Farrar Hyde, *An American Vision: Far Western Landscape and National Culture, 1820–1920* (New York: New York University Press, 1990).

Broad-based cultural histories of the American West are few in number, but several deserve mention. William H. Goetzmann and William N. Goetzmann, in *The West of the Imagination* (New York: Norton, 1986), survey artists, writers, films, and others forms of cultural history. Among the especially notable works of western cultural history are those of Kevin Starr, who has now produced a multivolume cultural history of California. One should start with the first book, *Americans and the California Dream, 1850–1915* (New York: Oxford University Press, 1973), but also sample later volumes in the series. Another cultural history of the recent West is Richard W. Etulain, *Reimagining the Modern American West: A Century of Fiction, History, and Art* (Tucson: University of Arizona Press, 1996).

Other authors focus on the popular culture of (or about) the American West. They include John Cawelti, *The Six-Gun Mystique* ([1971]; Bowling Green, Ohio: Bowling Green University Popular Culture Press, 1984); Daryl Jones, *The Dime Novel Western* (Bowling Green, Ohio: Bowling Green University Popular Press, 1978); Richard Aquila, ed., *Wanted Dead or Alive: The American West in Popular Culture* (Urbana: University of Illinois Press, 1996); and Paul Reddin, *Wild West Shows* (Urbana: University of Illinois Press, 1999). The most recent reference volume covering many of these topics is Richard W. Slatta, *The Mythical West: An Encyclopedia of Legend, Lore, and Popular Culture* (Santa Barbara, Calif.: ABC-Clio, 2001).

The American West, 1790s to 1850

The notable works of Bernard DeVoto remain essential reading for an understanding of this period. See his narrative-driven trilogy of remarkable histories: *Year of Decision: 1846* (Boston: Little, Brown, 1943), *Across the Wide Missouri* (Boston: Houghton Mifflin, 1947), and *The Course of Empire* (Boston: Houghton Mifflin, 1952). For the Southwest, one would do well to consult two new monographs: Ross Frank, *From Settler to Citizen: New Mexican Economic Development and the Creation of Vecino Society, 1750–1820* (Berkeley: University of California Press, 2000), and James F. Brooks, *Captives and Cousins: Slavery, Kinship, and Community in the Southwest Borderlands* (Chapel Hill: University of North Carolina Press, 2002). On the Mexican period of the Southwest (1821–1846), the superb overview is David J. Weber, *The Mexican Frontier, 1821–1846: The American Southwest under Mexico* (Albuquerque: University of New Mexico Press, 1982). For the nineteenth-century Southwest, see Howard Lamar's valuable volume *The Far Southwest, 1846–1912: A Territorial History* (1966; Albuquerque: University of New Mexico, 2000). The best work on the Santa Fe Trail is David Dary's *The Santa Fe Trail: Its History, Legends, and Lore* (New York: Knopf, 2000). For a recent monograph, consult Deena J. González, *Refusing the Favor: Spanish-Mexican Women of Santa Fe, 1820–1880* (New York: Oxford University Press, 2000).

On the Pacific Northwest, James P. Ronda has written numerous fine essays and several notable books. First of all, see two of his important books on Lewis and Clark: *Lewis and Clark among the Indians* (Lincoln: University of Nebraska Press, 1984) and *Finding the West: Explorations with Lewis and Clark* (Albuquerque: University of New Mexico Press, 2001). William Goetzmann's Pulitzer Prize–winning volume, *Exploration and Empire: The Explorer and the Scientist in the Winning of the American West* (New York: Knopf, 1966), brilliantly treats exploration in the early nineteenth century. On the Oregon and California trails, John D. Unruh's mammoth volume, *The Plains Across: The Overland Emigrants and the Trans-Mississippi West, 1840–1860* (Urbana: University of Illinois Press, 1979), remains the premier source.

In addition to the DeVoto volumes on the fur trade and mountain men, the classic earlier study is Dale L. Morgan, *Jedediah Smith and the Opening of the West* (Indianapolis: Bobbs-Merrill, 1953). Robert M. Utley's *A Life Wild and Perilous: Mountain Men and the Paths to the Pacific* (New York: Henry Holt, 1997) is a model of dramatic, readable narrative history. For a recent work by a historical geographer, see David J. Wishart, *The Fur Trade of the American West, 1807–1840: A Geographical Synthesis* (Lincoln: University of Nebraska Press, 1979). David J. Weber furnishes the most useful work on the Southwest in his *Taos Trappers: The Fur Trade in the Far Southwest, 1540–1846* (Norman: University of Oklahoma Press, 1971). A well-written new monograph is Barton H. Barbour, *Fort Union and the Upper Missouri Fur Trade* (Norman: University of Oklahoma Press, 2001).

The occupation of Texas leading to the Texas Revolution is treated in Gregg Cantrell, *Stephen F. Austin: Empresario of Texas* (New Haven, Conn.: Yale University Press, 1999). In a series of books, Frederick Merk explores the impact of Manifest Destiny and expansion on varied parts of the West. See his *Manifest Destiny and Mission in American History* (New York: Knopf, 1963). The ideas and events of the Mexican-American War receive coverage in John S. D. Eisenhower, *So Far from God: The U.S. War with Mexico 1846–1848* (New York: Random House, 1989).

The complexities of early California cultures, the Gold Rush, and other western mining booms are detailed in numerous volumes. Among these see Albert L. Hurtado, *Intimate Frontiers: Sex, Gender, and Culture in Old California* (Albuquerque: University of New Mexico Press, 1999). The best overview of the mining rushes is Rodman Wilson Paul (with Elliott West), *Mining Frontiers of the Far West, 1848–1880*, rev. exp. ed. (1963; Albuquerque: University of New Mexico Press, 2001). See also Malcolm J. Rohrbough, *Days of Gold: The California Gold Rush and the American Nation* (Berkeley: University of California Press, 1997). Susan Lee Johnson provides an innovative social history in *Roaring Camp: The Social World of the California Gold Rush* (New York: Norton, 2000).

A still useful and readable narrative history of much of this period is Ray Allen Billington, *The Far Western Frontier, 1830–1860* (1956; Albuquerque: University of New Mexico Press, 1995).

The American West, 1850 to 1900

For a helpful overview of this era with strong emphases on economic and social history, see Rodman W. Paul, *The Far West and the Great Plains in Transition, 1859–1900* (New York: Harper & Row, 1988). Gunther Barth tells the story of two of the most important urban places arising from mining rushes in his *Instant Cities: Urbanization and the Rise of San Francisco and Denver* (1975; Albuquerque: University of New Mexico Press, 1988). See also Duane A. Smith, *Rocky Mountain Mining Camps: The Urban Frontier* (1967; Lincoln: University of Nebraska Press, 1974) and *Mining America: The Industry and the Environment, 1800–1980* (Lawrence: University Press of Kansas, 1987). Michael P. Malone provides the interesting details of another mining extravaganza in *The Battle for Butte: Mining and Politics on the Northern Frontier, 1864–1906* (Seattle: University of Washington Press, 1981).

The events leading up to and through the Civil War in the West are covered in Alvin Josephy's smoothly written *The Civil War in the*

American West (New York: Knopf, 1991). Another part of the story is covered in Darlis Miller, *The California Column in New Mexico* (Albuquerque: University of New Mexico Press, 1982). Durwood Ball fills a large gap in western military history in his monograph *Army Regulars on the Western Frontier, 1848–1861* (Norman: University of Oklahoma Press, 2001).

The less-romantic story of western transportation in this period is covered in Oscar O. Winther, *The Transportation Frontier: Trans-Mississippi West 1865–1890* (New York: Henry Holt, 1964); W. Turrentine Jackson, *Wagon Roads West: A Study of Federal Road Surveys and Construction in the Trans-Mississippi West, 1846–1869* (Lincoln: University of Nebraska Press, 1980); and Carlos Schwantes, *Long Day's Journey: The Steamboat and the Stagecoach Era in the Northern West* (Seattle: University of Washington Press, 1999).

The conflicts between the U.S. military, incoming settlers, and Native Americans are surveyed in dozens of books. In addition to the afore-mentioned volumes by Robert Utley, one ought also to read his *Cavalier in Buckskin: George Armstrong Custer and the Western Military Frontier* (Norman: University of Oklahoma Press, 1988), the best brief biography of the most controversial frontier military leader. See also the stirring story told in Paul Andrew Hutton, *Phil Sheridan and His Army* (Lincoln: University of Nebraska Press, 1985). Of the more recent books on these complex issues, see Elliott West's superb, prizewinning work, *The Contested Plains: Indians, Goldseekers, and the Rush to Colorado* (Lawrence: University Press of Kansas, 1998), perhaps the best book on the American West in the last decade. The Indian side of the conflicts appears in Robert M. Utley, *The Lance and the Shield: The Life and Times of Sitting Bull* (New York: Henry Holt, 1993); Gregory F. Michno, *Lakota Moon: The Indian Narrative of Custer's Defeat* (Missoula, Mont.: Mountain Press, 1997); and Robert Larson, *Red Cloud: Warrior-Statesman of the Lakota Sioux* (Norman: University of Oklahoma Press, 1997).

Equally numerous are the books on the so-called Wild West. On the notorious Billy the Kid, two strong books are Frederick Nolan, *The Lincoln County War: A Documentary History* (Norman: University of Oklahoma Press, 1992), and Robert M. Utley, *Billy the Kid: A Short and Violent Life* (Lincoln: University of Nebraska Press, 1989). On two other famous characters, see Joseph G. Rosa, *They Called Him Wild Bill* (1964; Norman: University of Oklahoma Press, 1974), and Casey Tefertiller, *Wyatt Earp: The Life Behind the Legend* (New York: Wiley, 1997). The best studies of Buffalo Bill Cody, show Indians, and Annie Oakley are Don Russell, *The Lives and Legends of Buffalo Bill Cody* (Norman: University of Oklahoma Press, 1960); L. G. Moses, *Wild West Shows and the Images of American Indians, 1883–1933* (Albuquerque:

University of New Mexico Press, 1996); and Glenda Riley, *The Life and Legacy of Annie Oakley* (Norman: University of Oklahoma Press, 1994). A thorough study of legal conflict is available in Larry D. Ball, *The United States Marshals of New Mexico and Arizona Territories, 1846–1912* (Albuquerque: University of New Mexico Press, 1978). For a thoughtful commentary on violence on the frontier, see Richard Maxwell Brown, *No Duty to Retreat: Violence and Values in American History and Society* (New York: Oxford University Press, 1991). On prostitution in the late nineteenth century one should consult the best study of that subject, Anne M. Butler, *Daughters of Joy, Sisters of Misery: Prostitutes in the American West, 1865–90* (Urbana: University of Illinois Press, 1985).

The most useful book on Populism is Lawrence Goodwyn's *Democratic Promise: The Populist Movement in America* (New York: Oxford University Press, 1976). But two earlier studies of late-nineteenth-century western politics should not be overlooked: John D. Hicks, *The Populist Revolt: A History of the Farmers' Alliance and the People's Party* (1931; Lincoln: University of Nebraska Press, 1961), and Earl Pomeroy, *The Territories and the United States, 1861–1890: Studies in Colonial Administration* (1947; Seattle: University of Washington Press, 1970).

The American West, 1900 through World War II

Three books mentioned earlier provide general accounts of the twentieth-century West: Gerald D. Nash, *The American West in the Twentieth Century* (1973, 1977); Michael P. Malone and Richard W. Etulain, *The American West: A Twentieth-Century History* (1989); and Richard White, *"It's Your Misfortune and None of My Own"* (1991). Richard Lowitt focuses on the 1930s in his well-researched volume *The New Deal and the West* (Bloomington: Indiana University Press, 1984), and Gerald D. Nash furnishes the best book on the later period, *The American West Transformed: The Impact of the Second World War* (Bloomington: Indiana University Press, 1985).

The political history of the first decades of the twentieth century is covered in George Mowry's older but still helpful *California Progressives* (Berkeley: University of California Press, 1951). Also consult Robert W. Cherny, *Populism, Progressivism, and the Transformation of Nebraska Politics, 1885–1915* (Lincoln: University of Nebraska Press, 1981), and Danney Goble, *Progressive Oklahoma: The Making of a New Kind of State* (Norman: University of Oklahoma Press, 1980).

A number of valuable studies detail the social history of the period. The most useful overview on one important subject is Donald L. Parman, *Indians and the American West in the Twentieth Century* (Bloomington: Indiana University Press, 1994). For two particularly innovative and provocative studies, see James N. Gregory, *American Exodus: The Dust Bowl Migration and Okie Culture in California* (New York: Oxford University Press, 1989), and Neil Foley, *The White Scourge: Mexicans, Blacks, and Poor Whites in Texas Cotton Culture* (Berkeley: University of California Press, 1997). Labor historians have also produced several books furnishing valuable socioeconomic insights on this period. Consider, as an example, Carlos Schwantes, *Radical Heritage: Labor, Socialism, and Reform in Washington and British Columbia, 1885–1917* (Seattle: University of Washington Press, 1979). Pulitzer Prize–winner J. Anthony Lukas deals with a dramatic and violent incident in Idaho in his superbly written *Big Trouble: A Murder in a Small Western Town Sets Off a Struggle for the Soul of America* (New York: Simon & Schuster, 1997).

In the past two decades many historians have emphasized topics dealing with water, irrigation, reclamation, and other closely connected environmental subjects. Among the best of these books are Norris Hundley, jr., *The Great Thirst: California and Water, 1770s–1990s* (Berkeley: University of California Press, 1992); Donald Pisani, *From the Family Farm to Agribusiness: The Irrigation Crusade in California and the West, 1850–1931* (Berkeley: University of California Press, 1984); and the several previously mentioned books by Donald Worster. One model monograph is Mark W. T. Harvey, *A Symbol of Wilderness: Echo Park and the American Conservation Movement* (Albuquerque: University of New Mexico Press, 1994).

Books on cultural topics have been fewer in number. But readers must not overlook Kevin Starr's *Inventing the Dream: California Through the Progressive Era* (New York: Oxford University Press, 1985) and Starr, *Material Dreams: Southern California through the* 1920s (New York: Oxford University Press, 1990). Nancy Heller and Julia Williams furnish the best study of another subject: *The Regionalists: Painters of the American Scene* (New York: Watson-Guptill, 1976), which contains strong sections on western regionalists. Richard W. Etulain's *Telling Western Stories: From Buffalo Bill to Larry McMurtry* (Albuquerque: University of New Mexico Press, 1999) briefly discusses novels, films, and other forms of popular culture. No one should forget the appealing narrative Carey McWilliams spins in his still-useful *Southern California Country: An Island on the Mind* (New York: Duell, Sloan, and Pearce, 1946).

The American West, World War II to 2000

Historians are just beginning to produce well-researched books on the last half century of western history. Previously journalists and public figures provided insightful impressions and personal accounts. The

Richard W. Etulain

only abbreviated overview thus far is Gerald D. Nash, *A Brief History of the American West since 1945* (Fort Worth, Tex.: Harcourt Brace, 2000). Also useful is the edited collection by Kevin Fernlund, *The Cold War American West, 1945–1989* (Albuquerque: University of New Mexico Press, 1998). Journalist Timothy Egan, utilizing a hopscotch approach, surveys the recent West in his smoothly written *Lasso the Wind: Away to the New West* (New York: Knopf, 1998). Other journalists, including Neil Morgan, Jerry Hagstrom, and Peter Wiley and Robert Gottlieb, have written impressionistic accounts of the modern West and devoted large sections of their books to the 1960s, 1970s, and 1980s. Their books are listed in Gerald D. Nash and Richard W. Etulain, eds., *The Twentieth-Century West: Historical Interpretations* (Albuquerque: University of New Mexico Press, 1989), which also collects essays on most of the important western topics of the twentieth century. The most recent similar collection is Richard W. Etulain and Ferenc M. Szasz, eds., *The American West in 2000: Essays in Honor of Gerald D. Nash* (Albuquerque: University of New Mexico Press, 2003).

Those interested in economic history should begin with Gerald D. Nash, *The Federal Landscape: An Economic History of the Twentieth-Century West* (Tucson: University of Arizona Press, 1999). Marc Reisner provides a probing study of a controversial subject in his *Cadillac Desert: The American West and Its Disappearing Water* (New York: Viking Penguin, 1986). In *Henry J. Kaiser: Builder in the Modern American West* (Austin: University of Texas Press, 1989) Mark S. Foster deals with one of the giants of western history. Also helpful is Foster's overview of another interesting topic: *A Nation on Wheels: The Automobile Culture in America Since 1945* (Belmont, Calif.: Thomson/Wadsworth, 2003). William G. Robbins has written several books and numerous stimulating essays on various western economic and environmental topics. See especially his *Colony and Empire: The Capitalist Transformation of the American West* (Lawrence: University Press of Kansas, 1994). Arthur R. Gómez supplies an illuminating case study in *Quest for the Golden Circle: The Four Corners and the Metropolitan West, 1945–1970* (1994; Lawrence: University Press of Kansas, 2000).

Since most U.S. presidents after 1952 were reared west of the Mississippi, the political history of the American West has gained increasing attention. Dwight D. Eisenhower, Lyndon B. Johnson, Richard Nixon, Ronald Reagan, Bill Clinton, and George W. Bush have all been the subjects of at least one biography, some of several. Of these, Robert A. Caro's multivolume biography of Johnson and Stephen Ambrose's biographies of Eisenhower and Nixon are particularly noteworthy. Full citations to these and other journalistic overviews cited below are available in the previously mentioned volume, Richard W.

Etulain, et al., eds., *The American West in the Twentieth Century*. See also Garry Wills's *Reagan's America* (1987; New York: Penguin Books, 1988). The western career of another politician is available in Peter Iverson, *Barry Goldwater: Native Arizonan* (Norman: University of Oklahoma Press, 1997). A handy collection of essays on recent western politics is Richard Lowitt, ed., *Politics in the Postwar American West* (Norman: University of Oklahoma Press, 1995).

In addition to the earlier volumes mentioned under racial and ethnic groups, one should consult Alvin M. Josephy, *Now That the Buffalo's Gone: A Study of Today's Indians* (New York: Knopf, 1982), and James J. Rawls, *Chief Red Fox Is Dead: A History of Native Americans Since 1945* (Fort Worth, Tex.: Harcourt Brace, 1996).

Kevin Starr expands his study of California culture in *Embattled Dreams: California in War and Peace, 1940–1950* (New York: Oxford University Press, 2002), and Chris Wilson furnishes a model, illuminating case study in his *The Myth of Santa Fe: Creating a Modern Regional Tradition* (Albuquerque: University of New Mexico Press, 1997). Of the numerous urban studies appearing recently, one might begin with Carl Abbott, *Greater Portland: Urban Life and Landscape in the Pacific Northwest* (Philadelphia: University of Pennsylvania Press, 2001), and Hal Rothman, *Neon Metropolis: How Las Vegas Started the Twenty-First Century* (New York: Routledge, 2003).

Finally, on recent trends in western historical writing, consult Patricia Nelson Limerick, et al., eds., *Trails: Toward a New Western History* (Lawrence: University Press of Kansas, 1991), for a largely sympathetic view of New Western history. A balance of pro and con writings on New Western history is Gene M. Gressley, ed., *Old West/New West: Quo Vadis?* (1994; Norman: University of Oklahoma Press, 1997). Hundreds of possible research topics for writing about the twentieth-century West are discussed in Gerald D. Nash and Richard W. Etulain, eds., *Researching Western History: Topics in the Twentieth Century* (Albuquerque: University of New Mexico Press, 1997). Of the dozens of recent studies about western historical writing, two books are particularly provocative. See Gary Topping, *Utah Historians and the Reconstruction of Western History* (Norman: University of Oklahoma Press, 2003), and Kerwin Lee Klein, *Frontiers of Historical Imagination: Narrating the European Conquest of Native America, 1890–1990* (Berkeley: University of California Press, 1997).

Contributors

CARL ABBOTT is professor of urban studies and planning at Portland State University. He is the author of numerous books about urban growth and city and regional planning in the American West. His overview book, *Metropolitan Frontier: Cities in the Modern American West,* appeared in 1993. His most recent book is *Greater Portland: Urban Life and Landscape in the Pacific Northwest* (2001).

KATHERINE G. AIKEN is professor and chair of the Department of History at the University of Idaho, where she has been a faculty member since 1984. She is the author of *Harnessing the Power of Motherhood: The National Florence Crittenton Mission, 1883–1925* (1998), and articles in *Western Historical Quarterly, Journal of the West, Montana: The Magazine of Western History, Pacific Northwest Quarterly,* and the *Environmental History Review,* dealing with the city of Kellogg, Idaho's Bunker Hill Company, and Idaho congresswoman Gracie Pfost.

GARY CLAYTON ANDERSON is professor of history at the University of Oklahoma. He works in the fields of western and American Indian history and has published five books and numerous articles in these areas. His publications include *Kinsmen of Another Kind: Indian-White Relations in the Upper Mississippi River Valley, 1650–1862* (1984); *Little Crow, Spokesman for the Sioux* (1986); *Through Dakota Eyes: Narrative Accounts of the Minnesota War of 1862* (edited with Alan Woolworth, 1987); *Sitting Bull and the Paradox of Lakota Nationhood* (1996); and *The Indian Southwest, 1580–1830: Ethnogenesis and Reinvention* (1999). He has under contract and will soon publish a history of the American West titled *The Changing American West.*

BARTON H. BARBOUR is assistant professor of history at Boise State University and has worked as a museum curator, humanities lecturer, and national parks researcher. A specialist on the North American fur trade history, he authored *Fort Union and the Upper Missouri Fur Trade* (2001), a finalist for a Western Writers Spur Award in historical nonfiction. He is currently preparing a new biography of Jedediah Smith.

RICHARD W. ETULAIN is professor emeritus of history and former director of the Center for the American West at the University of New Mexico. A specialist in the history and literature of the American West, he is the author or editor of more than forty books. Among his recent volumes are *New Mexican Lives* (2002), *César Chávez: A Brief Biography* (2002), *Wild Women of the Old West* (with Glenda Riley, 2003), *The American West in 2000: Essays in Honor of Gerald D. Nash* (with Ferenc M. Szasz, 2003), and *Chiefs and Generals* (with Glenda Riley, 2004). He is at work on a general narrative history of the American West.

CHERYL J. FOOTE received her Ph.D. in history from the University of New Mexico. She has been a member of the history faculty at Albuquerque TVI Community College since 1990. She is the author of *Women of the New Mexico Frontier 1846–1912* (1990). Her current interests include the culinary history of New Mexico.

MARK S. FOSTER is professor of history at the University of Colorado at Denver. He is a specialist in early-twentieth-century American history and the history of transportation. His books include *Henry J. Kaiser: Builder in the Modern American West* (1989), *Castles in the Sand: The Life and Times of Carl G. Fisher* (2000), and *A Nation on Wheels: The Automobile in American Culture Since 1945* (2003). As a founder of the Colorado Vintage Baseball Association, he is also a historical reenactor of 1870s baseball.

RICHARD GRISWOLD DEL CASTILLO is professor and chair of the Chicana and Chicano Studies Department at San Diego State University. His published books include *The Los Angeles Barrio, 1850–1890: A Social History* (1980), *La Familia: Chicano Families in the Urban Southwest, 1848 to the Present* (1984), *The Treaty of Guadalupe Hidalgo: A Legacy of Conflict* (1990), *César Chávez: A Triumph of Spirit* (with Richard Garcia, 1995), and *North to Aztlán: Mexican Americans in United States History* (with Arnoldo De León, 1996).

MARK HARVEY is associate professor of history at North Dakota State University at Fargo. His research specialty is in the environmental history of the twentieth-century American West. He is the author of *Symbol of Wilderness: Echo Park and the American Conservation Movement* (1994) and numerous articles on wilderness and national park history and also water in the West. He is now completing a manuscript titled *Guarding the Wilderness: The Conservation Career of Howard C. Zahniser.*

JON HUNNER teaches history and directs the program in public history at New Mexico State University. His book *Inventing Los Alamos: The Growth of an Atomic Community* (2004) is a social history of Los Alamos. He has also coauthored two books of historic photographs: *Santa Fe: A*

Historic Walking Tour (2000) and *City of Crosses: Las Cruces, New Mexico* (2003). One of his current interests is how the public uses memory to construct history. In spring 2001, he was in Sweden as a Fulbright Fellow, assisting Växjö University in creating public history and American Studies programs.

R. DOUGLAS HURT is professor of history and chair of the history department at Purdue University. He is the author of *American Agriculture: A Brief History* (rev. ed., 2002) and *Problems of Plenty: The American Farmer in the Twentieth Century* (2002). He has also edited the *Rural West Since World War II* (1998), *The Rural South Since World War II* (1998), and *African Americans in the Rural South, 1900–1950* (2003). He has served as the editor of *Agricultural History,* the journal of record for the field, and he is past president of the Agricultural History Society.

ANNE F. HYDE is professor of history at Colorado College in Colorado Springs, Colorado. Her publications include *An American Vision: Far Western Landscape and National Culture, 1820–1920* (1990), and, with William Deverell, *The West in the History of the Nation,* 2 vols. (2000).

JOHN L. KESSELL is professor emeritus of history at the University of New Mexico and founding editor of the six-volume Vargas Series. His most recent book is *Spain in the Southwest: A Narrative History of Colonial New Mexico, Arizona, Texas, and California* (2002). He confesses a passion for blue corn, shredded beef enchiladas, half red, half green; telemarks down through a foot of new powder; and the 121st Psalm.

WILLIAM L. LANG is professor of history and former director of the Center for Columbia River History at Portland State University. He is the author of nearly a dozen articles on Columbia River history and coeditor of *Great River of the West: Essays on the Columbia River* (1999). His other publications include *Montana: A History of Two Centuries* (with Michael P. Malone and Richard B. Roeder) and *Confederacy of Ambition: William Winlock Miller and the Making of Washington Territory* (1996).

GLENDA RILEY is Alexander M. Bracken Professor Emeritus of History at Ball State University. She specializes in women's history and the American West. She has received many honors, including two Fulbright awards and the presidency of the Western History Association. Her most recent books are *Women and Nature: Saving the "Wild" West* (1999) and *Taking Land, Breaking Land: Women Colonizing the American West and Kenya, 1840–1940* (2003).

ELLIOTT WEST is distinguished professor of history at the University of Arkansas. He is a specialist in western social and environmental history and author of six books. Among these volumes are *Growing Up with the Country: Childhood on the Far Western Frontier* (1989) and *The Way to the West* (1995). His most recent book, *The Contested Plains: Indians, Goldseekers, and the Rush to Colorado* (1998), received the Francis Parkman, Caughey, and Billington prizes.

Index

maquiladora plants, 364, 397
Marqués de Rubí, 42, 43, 47
Marshall, John, 183, 206
McLoughlin, Dr. John, 114, 123, 129
McNary, Charles L., 316
McNary-Haugen Bill, 316
McPherson, Aimee Semple, 306–8,
    309, 310, 312–14, 317, 322–24;
    Angelus Temple and, 310, 311,
    312, 314, 322, 324
McPherson, Harold, 306–7, 310, 317
McPherson, Rolf Kennedy, 307, 310
McSweyn, Margarita Salazar,
    338–39
measles, 9, 45, 141
Mendoza, Juan Domínguez de,
    23–24
Menzies, Archibald, 96
Methodists, 136, 141
Mexican: -American War, 152, 328;
    Americans, 194, 340, 421;
    borderlands, 59–85, 178, 184,
    197, 398, 421–22; California,
    72–73, 128; colonization law of
    1830, 68–69; Constitution of
    1824, 70, 72–73, 79;
    government, 61, 64, 73, 79;
    independence, 59–61, 63, 125;
    nationals, 194, 372–73; period,
    85, 86; settlers, 66, 182
Mexicans (Mexicanos), 61, 182, 192,
    195; laborers, 287, 397–98 (see
    also braceros); migrants, 287,
    318, 371–73
Mexico, 6, 13, 23, 30, 32–33, 37, 39,
    43, 46, 61, 75, 79, 82, 287, 366;
    Austin, Stephen F. and, 66–69,
    72; California and, 72–74, 128;
    Chihuahua, 32, 48, 189–90;
    Constitution of 1824, 68; Gulf
    of, 32, 47, 51; maquiladora
    plants in, 364, 397; Sierra
    Madres, 37, 191; Sonora, 29,
    31, 34, 35–39, 40–41, 43–48,
    55–56, 72, 74–75, 189, 191;

Texas and, 66–67, 69, 178, 184;
    United States and, 67, 83
Microsoft, 385, 388–90. See also
    Allen, Paul; Gates, Bill
Miera y Pacheco Bernardo de, 48–50
migrant labor, 238, 287, 290, 318,
    371–73
migration, 248, 355
military-industrial complex, the,
    360, 390
Mille Lac Lake, 9, 15, 19
Miller, Henry (Heinrich Alfred
    Kreiser), 234–38
miners, 147–48, 183, 287–89
mining: booms, 147–48, 156–65,
    175, 431; frontier, **157**, 174, 175;
    impact on Native Americans
    of, 165–67, 201–204, 215–16;
    western development and,
    206–207, 252, 286–89, 300, 369
Minnesota, 9, 15, 19, 284;
    Minneapolis (St. Anthony's), 5,
    17–18
mission Indians, 12–13, 20, 33, 37,
    39, 41, 45
missionaries, 23, 32–33, 118, 124, 132,
    136, 139, 141, 144, 306; as
    government agents, 209,
    211–12, 216; Franciscan, 11–12,
    32–33, 51, 132; Jesuit, 35–37, 43,
    132; Native Americans and, 45,
    72, 133–34, 141–43, 204, 209,
    213–15, 263; Pacific Northwest,
    109, 125, 133–38, 142
missions, 13, 21, 29, 32–33, 44–45,
    52, 109, 128, 138; Californian,
    52, 72–73, 128, 132; Franciscan,
    11–12, 32–33, 51, 132; Jesuit,
    35–37, 43, 132; Native
    Americans and, 33, 37, 39, 41,
    45, 72–73; Oregon, 117–18,
    132–44
Mississippi: River, 5, 6, 9, 14, 15, 24,
    26, 27, 42, 102; Valley, 15,
    17–19, 34, 51, 60, 75